All Math Words Dictionary

3rd Dyslexic's Edition

By David E. McAdams

Version 2023

Copyright 2010-2023, Life is a Story Problem LLC. All rights reserved. No part of this publication may be copied, stored, transmitted, or otherwise disseminated without express written consent of Life is a Story Problem LLC, Colorado Springs, Co.

Other Books by David E. McAdams

Parrot Colors – An introduction to the concept of colors. For preschoolers. ISBN 9781632701671

Flower Colors – An introduction to the concept of colors. For preschoolers. ISBN 9781632701824.

Space Colors – An introduction to the concept of colors. For preschoolers. ISBN 9781632701855.

Shapes – An introduction to shapes. For preschoolers. ISBN 9781632701817.

Numbers – An introduction to the concept of numbers. For grades K-2. ISBN 9781632702616.

What is Bigger Than Anything? (Infinity) – An introduction to the concept of infinity. For grades 1-3. ISBN 9781632700551.

Swing sets (Sets) – An introduction to set theory. For grades 2-4. ISBN 9781632700186.

One Penny, Two – If Sig's penny doubles each day, how long until he can buy a dark green sports car? For grades 3-6. ISBN 9781632702005.

Learning With Money Activity Kit – Teach large numbers and counting with over $1,000,000 in play money. For grades 3-6. ISBN Color 9781632702319. ISBN Black and White 9781632702449.

My Favorite Fractals (volumes 1, 2 Barnes and Nobel exclusive) – Picture books of wondrous fractals presented as high resolution images. For all ages. ISBNs 9781632702463, 9781632702470.

Geometric Nets Project Book – 80 geometric nets to copy, cut out, and tape together into 3-dimensional polyhedra. For ages 9 and up. ISBN 9781632700346.

Geometric Nets Mega Project Book – 253 geometric nets to copy, cut out, and tape together into 3-dimensional polyhedra. For ages 9 and up. ISBN 9781632701770.

The First Million Digits of Pi – The first million digits of pi. For all ages. ISBN 9781632702272.

The First Million Digits of e – The first million digits of the Euler's constant e. For all ages. ISBN 9781632702296.

The Square Root of 2 to One Million Digits – The first million digits of the square root of 2. For all ages. ISBN 9781632702180.

Orders of Ten – A book that illustrates orders of ten with dots (1, 10, 100, ... dots). For ages 10-15. ISBN 9781632701732.

For an up-to-date list, see http://www.DEMcAdams.com.

Preface

All Math Words Dictionary is designed for students of pre-algebra, algebra, geometry, intermediate algebra, pre-calculus and calculus in middle school and high school. It is designed using the four 'C's of math writing:
- **Concise:** Definitions are compact, yet understandable.
- **Complete:** All words and phrases of interest to targeted students are included, plus a few just beyond the scope of the target classes. Tables of symbols and notations, formulas, and units of measurement, plus lists of properties of math objects gives the student all the information needed to weld their understanding of the concepts and decipher many problems.
- **Correct:** The definitions have been thoroughly reviewed for mathematical and literary correctness.
- **Comprehensible:** The definitions are written to be understood by targeted students. Abundant illustrations aid in understanding.

One of the difficulties many students experience in learning math skills has to do with the fact that an entire language, both spoken and written, has grown up around math. Students that acquire that language are successful in math studies. Students that do not acquire that language have serious problems with mathematics. This dictionary is designed to aid in the acquisition of the language of math.

This dictionary has:
- over 3600 entries,
- more than 200 notations defined,
- in excess of 1300 illustrations,
- IPA pronunciation guide,
- greater than 1400 formulas, equations, examples, identities and expressions.

While teaching high school math, the author, David E. McAdams, noted that some students did not understand even simple math statements, such as "This equation is determinate." Those students who had not acquired a basic math vocabulary were left behind, becoming frustrated and mentally dropping out of class.

Mr. McAdams quickly added vocabulary exercises to his classroom teaching, but found that there were no adequate resources for acquiring the needed vocabulary. All of the online math dictionaries and encyclopedias were either woefully incomplete, or written at a college graduate level.

The author began by creating a vocabulary resource for his students, using as a guide the vocabulary from the textbooks the students were using. The list of words swiftly grew, and the task of preparing these resources quickly grew beyond what a full-time teacher could accomplish with all the other activities important to teaching.

Mr. McAdams was amazed at the enormous size of the math vocabulary that students must gain to be fluent in math. He took the development of this important resource seriously, and after devoting more than nine work-years to its development, has created the 3rd edition of All Math Words Dictionary.

The list of words and phrases to be defined was collected from various textbooks in use in the United States and United Kingdom. Each of these words was carefully researched to find all of the ways the word was used in math classes for pre-algebra, algebra, geometry and calculus. The definitions were carefully crafted and critically evaluated to meet the goals of concise, complete, correct and comprehensible.

Usefulness of these definitions for non-native English speakers was also considered and pronunciation was developed using the International Phonetic Alphabet (IPA). Knowing that a picture is sometimes worth a thousand words, Mr. McAdams added abundant illustrations to assist students in placing words in a visual context.

The result of this extensive effort is *All Math Words Dictionary*, an important tool for math teachers and students. This book is available in four different editions:
- **Color Classroom edition** – typeset in 14-point Times New Roman font and with larger color illustrations. Best for any use, as the use of color guides the student through the illustrations. Available in paperback and hardback.
- **Home edition** – typeset in 10-point Times New Roman for home use. Available in color and black and white, both paperback.
- **Large Print edition** – typeset in 16 point Tiresias LP font for visually challenged students. Includes larger black and white illustrations. Available in paperback and hardback.
- **Dyslexic edition** – typeset in Open Dyslexic and Eulexia fonts with black and white illustrations. Available in paperback and hardback.

If budget allows, Mr. McAdams highly recommends either the Color Classroom edition, or the Color Home edition. These editions show the part of the diagram being defined in red, allowing the student to more quickly understand the words being defined.

Table of Contents

- How to Use this Dictionary ... 1
  - How Entries are Alphabetized ... 2
  - Conventional Plurals ... 2
  - IPA Pronunciation ... 3
- Notation ... 3
  - Numbers ... 3
  - Money ... 3
  - Arithmetic ... 3
  - Geometry ... 4
  - Logic ... 4
  - Set Theory ... 4
  - Sets of Numbers ... 5
  - Matrices ... 5
  - Vectors ... 5
  - Probability and Statistics ... 5
  - Calculus ... 5
- Numbers ... 6
  - A ... 6
  - B ... 15
  - C ... 18
  - D ... 33
  - E ... 42
  - F ... 48
  - G ... 52
  - H ... 55
  - I ... 58
  - J ... 65
  - K ... 66
  - L ... 66
  - M ... 71
  - N ... 77
  - O ... 81
  - P ... 85
  - Q ... 94
  - R ... 95
  - S ... 101
  - T ... 112
  - U ... 118
  - V ... 120
  - W ... 122
  - X ... 122
  - Y ... 122
  - Z ... 123
- Appendix ... 124
  - Algebra ... 124
    - Addition Facts ... 124
    - Multiplication Facts ... 124
    - Keywords ... 124
      - Keywords for Addition ... 124
      - Keywords for Subtraction ... 124
      - Keywords for Multiplication ... 124
      - Keywords for Division ... 124
      - Keywords for Equals ... 124
    - Properties of Real Numbers ... 125
      - Properties of Addition ... 125
      - Properties of Multiplication ... 125
      - Properties of Negation ... 126
      - Properties of Fractions ... 126
      - Properties of Exponents ... 127
      - Properties of Logarithms ... 128
      - Properties of Radicals ... 129
    - Factoring Formulas ... 129
    - Rules for Rounding ... 129
    - Inverse Algebraic Operations ... 129
    - Complex Numbers ... 129
      - Operations on Complex Numbers ... 129
      - Properties of Complex Conjugates ... 130
    - Properties of Vectors ... 130
    - Functions and Their Graphs ... 131
    - Graph Shifts ... 133
    - Properties of Determinants ... 134
    - Properties of a Limit ... 134
    - Roots of Integers ... 135
    - Divisibility Rules ... 135
    - Greek Letters ... 135
    - Algebraic Identities ... 136
    - Units of Measure of Area ... 136
  - Geometry ... 137
    - Figurate Numbers ... 137
    - Properties of a Circle ... 137
    - Equations for an Ellipse ... 138
    - Adjacent in Geometric Figures ... 139
    - Altitudes of Geometric Figures ... 139
    - Centers of Geometric Figures ... 140
    - Properties of a Line ... 140
    - Equations of a Line ... 141
    - Equations for a Parabola ... 141
    - Equations for a Hyperbola ... 142
    - Distance Formulas ... 142
  - Trigonometry ... 143
    - Trigonometry Definitions ... 143
    - Trigonometric Identities ... 143
      - Pythagorean Identities ... 143
      - Cofunction Identities ... 143
      - Even Odd Identities ... 143
      - Sum and Difference Identities ... 143
      - Double Angle Identities ... 143
      - Half Angle Identities ... 143
      - Power Reduction Identities ... 143
      - Sum to Product Identities ... 143
      - Product to Sum Identities ... 143
    - Rules for Converting to and From Polar Coordinates ... 143
    - Exact Values of Trigonometric Functions ... 144
  - Calculus ... 144
    - Differentiation Formulas ... 144
      - General Derivation Formulas ... 144
      - Derivatives of Exponential and Logarithmic Functions ... 145
      - Derivatives of Inverse Trigonometric Functions ... 145
- Measurement ... 145
  - International System of Units ... 145
    - Prefixes ... 145
    - SI Base Units ... 146
    - SI Defining Constants ... 146
    - SI Derived Units ... 146
  - Comparative Length ... 147
  - Comparative Mass ... 147
  - Comparative Time ... 147
  - Comparative Temperature ... 147
  - Comparative Angle ... 147
  - Comparative Speed ... 148
  - Comparative Acceleration ... 148

Help Your Child Learn Math..................148 | Illustration credits................................148

How to Use this Dictionary

This dictionary has alphabetized entries plus an appendix containing properties, formulas and identities. Most entries are laid out like this:

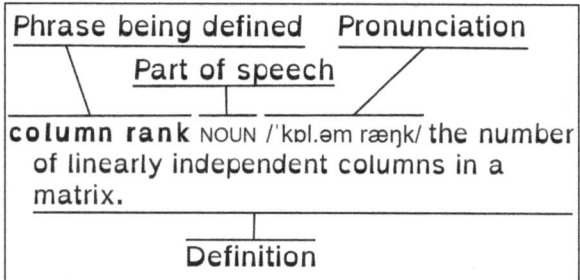

At the end of the entry, there may be additional notes such as synonyms and references to related words or to the subject index.

The pronunciation in this dictionary is given in International Phonetic Alphabet (IPA) style. A brief guide to the portion of IPA used in this book is found on page 3. For a more detailed explanation of IPA, see https://en.wikipedia.org/wiki/Help:IPA/English.

Some words and phrases have more than one distinct meaning. In this case, there will be several enumerated definitions:

> **odds** NOUN /ɒdz/
> 1) the likelihood of an event happening.
> 2) an estimate of the probability that an event will happen.

If parts of speech or pronunciations of a word with multiple definitions are different from each other, the part of speech or pronunciation will appear with each definition.

Multiple words (synonyms) with the same meaning are typically defined only once, with the less common usage referring to the main entry like this:

> **column graph** NOUN /ˈkɒl.əm græf/ see bar graph (p 20).
>
>   Main entry

Abbreviations and acronyms have their own entry, without a definition of the abbreviated word. An acronym is a set of letters that stand for a phrase, usually the first letter of each word in the phrase. You can look up the word once you know what the abbreviation or acronym stands for:

> **GMT** ACRONYM see Greenwich Mean Time (p 74).

Entries describing elements of computer languages related to math have COMPUTERS for the part of speech and

> **ln()** COMPUTERS the natural logarithmic function in most computer languages.

have no pronunciation, like this:

Entries for prefixes are similar to regular entries. Each prefix is followed by a hyphen. This tells the reader that the prefix is not a whole word, but is used to form other words:

> **macro-** PREFIX /ˈmæ.kroʊ/ very large scale.

If the plural of a word or phrase has an unusual spelling or pronunciation, that spelling and pronunciation appear at the end of the entry like this: Plural: *series* /ˈsɪər.iz/.

At the end of each definition there may be list of related words, examples and formulas. Related words can be synonym, antonyms, or variants of each word.

There is a section with common math notation starting on page 3. Since these symbols cannot be alphabetized, they are grouped by category. Within each category they appear in no particular order.

3rd Dyslexic's Edition

How Entries are Alphabetized

There are several things which influence the alphabetization scheme of this dictionary:
- This dictionary defines many phrases in addition to single words.
- Numeric digits are part of some entry headings.
- Hyphens and commas appear in some entry headings.
- Mathematical symbols are used in some entry headings.

Because of these issues, a special alphabetization scheme is used.

1) Capital letters are alphabetized the same as lower case letters. The following words are in the special alphabetical order.
   - abacus
   - Abelian group
   - abscissa
2) Spaces are ignored. The following words are in the special alphabetical order.
   - amplitude
   - analytical proof
   - analytic geometry
3) Numeric digits come before alphabetic letters and are in numeric order.
   - 1, property of multiplication by
   - 2-space
   - 3-space
4) Greek letters are alphabetized with their English equivalents. For example μ (mu) is alphabetized with words starting with m.
5) All punctuation such as commas and hyphens are ignored. The following entries are in alphabetical order.
   - half
   - half-angle
   - half life
   - half-line
6) Exception: In the case of a prefix, the entry with the dash comes after any entries with the same letters but no dash, but before any words using that prefix. The following entries are in the special alphabetical order:
   - a
   - A
   - a-
   - AAA

Conventional Plurals

The plurals (more than one) of nouns are shown at the end of an entry only if the spelling or pronunciation of the plural is unusual. The usual spellings and pronunciations of plurals are:

Conventional Plurals			
Ending	Spelling	Pronunciation	Example
'se' (silent e)	'ses'	səz	**inverse** – Plural: inverses /ɪnˈvɜr.səz/
's', 'x', or 'ch'	'ses', 'xes', 'ches'	səz	**class** – Plural: classes /klæ.səz/
'y'	'ies'	iz	**identity** – Plural: identities /aɪˈdɛn.tɪ.tiz/
All others	's'	s or z	**shift** – Plural: shifts /ʃɪftz/

IPA Pronunciation

Stress marks: /ˈ/ primary; /ˌ/ secondary. Syllable divider: /./.

Consonants

b	**b**ase, dou**b**le	ʃ	**sh**ow, addi**ti**on	ɛər	squ**are**, **are**a
d	**d**isk, an**d**	t	**t**rue, wri**t**e	eɪ	f**a**ce, r**a**te
ð	**th**e, fa**th**er	tʃ	**ch**eck, ca**tch**	ɪ	**i**n, l**i**d
dz	a**dds**	v	**v**alue, ha**v**e	ɪr	g**ir**l
dʒ	**g**eneral, pa**g**e	w	**w**ave, s**w**ap	ɪər	n**ear**, z**ero**
f	**f**rom, gra**ph**, **f**an	ʰw	**wh**y	ɔɪ	ch**oi**ce, b**oy**, p**oi**nt
g	**g**et, an**g**le	z	**z**ero, i**s**	ɔr	ch**or**d, c**or**ner
h	**h**ead, a**h**ead	ʒ	mea**s**ure, divi**si**on	oʊ	r**ow**, g**o**
j	**y**es, **y**ear	**Vowels**		ʊ	f**oo**t
k	**ch**ord, fa**c**t, **k**ey	ɑ	f**a**ther	ʌ	**o**f, n**u**mber
l	**l**ow, s**l**ow	ɑr	**ar**c, b**ar**n	ɜr	c**ur**ve, c**ir**cle
m	**m**iddle, ti**m**e	ɒ	s**o**ng, s**o**lid	u	contin**ue**
n	**n**ot, i**n**	ɒr	b**o**rrow	y	c**u**be.
ŋ	thi**ng**, lo**ng**	æ	**a**dd, **a**ngle	**Reduced vowels**	
ŋg	fi**ng**er, a**ng**le	ær	**ar**row, m**arr**y	ə	c**o**mma (if small, is barely pronounced)
θ	**th**ird, ma**th**	aɪ	b**y**, s**i**gn		
p	**p**i, ca**p**	aʊ	**ou**t, h**ow**	ɚ	cent**er**
r	**r**ow, f**r**om	aʊər	h**our**	i	happ**y**
s	**s**ide, ba**s**e	ɛ	b**e**ll	o	g**o**ld
		ɛr	**e**rror		

Notation

Numbers

14	integer
1.5	real number
2.$\overline{6}$	repeating decimal
n^{th}	item n in a list, ordinal number
$3 + 4i$	complex number
$r(\cos\theta + i\sin\theta)$	complex number
$2.2i$	pure imaginary number
$z, a+bi$	complex number
$\bar{z}, \overline{a+bi}$	complex conjugate
$\Im, \text{Im}$	imaginary part of a complex number
$\Re, \text{Re}$	real part of a complex number
$\frac{1}{2}$	rational number, fraction
I	Roman numeral for 1
V	Roman numeral for 5
X	Roman numeral for 10
L	Roman numeral for 50
C	Roman numeral for 100
D	Roman numeral for 500
M	Roman numeral for 1,000
∞	infinity, unbounded
$-a$	negative a
$+a$	positive a
$a\%$	a percent, a parts per hundred
3.77×10^4	scientific notation
37.7×10^3	engineering notation
2.64E05	E notation
$a < b$	a is less than b
$a \leq b$	a is less than or equal to b
$a = b$	a is equal to b
$a \neq b$	a is not equal to b
$a \geq b$	a is greater than or equal to b
$a > b$	a is greater than b
$x \mid y$	x divides evenly into y
$x \nmid y$	x does not divide evenly into y
$y \mod q$	the remainder when y is divided by q, modulo
$x \equiv y \mod q$	x is congruent with y modulo q

Money

¢	cent (United States)
p	pence (United Kingdom)
$	dollar
US$	United States dollar
USD	United States dollar
CA$	Canadian dollar
CAD	Canadian dollar
£	British pound
GBP	British pound
€	European Euro

Arithmetic

$a + b$	addition, add a to b
$a - b$	subtraction; subtract b from a
$-b$	negation; negative b
$a \pm b$	a plus or minus b
$a \mp b$	a minus or plus b
$a \times b$	multiply a by b

$a \cdot b$	multiply a by b
ab	multiply a by b
$a * b$	1) an arbitrary operation on a and b
	2) multiply a by b in some computer languages
a^b	exponentiation: a raised to the b power; a multiplied times itself b times
$a \wedge b$	exponentiation in some computer languages (a raised to the b power)
$a**b$	exponentiation in some computer languages (a raised to the b power)
$\sqrt{n}$	square root of n
$\sqrt[3]{m}, \sqrt[4]{m}, \sqrt[n]{m}$	cube root of m, fourth root of m, n^{th} root of m
$\frac{a}{b}$	fraction, a divided by b
$a \div b$	a divided by b
a/b	a divided by b
$a : b$	ratio of a to b, divided by
$a \cdots z, A \cdots Z$	variables
$a_1, a_2, \cdots$	indexed variables
$a \equiv b$	1) a is identical to b
	2) a is equivalent to b
$c \equiv a \mod b$	c is congruent to a modulo b
$\rightarrow$	1) approaches
	2) implies
$\Rightarrow$	implies
$x \rightarrow \infty$	x is unbounded in the positive direction
$x \rightarrow -\infty$	x is unbounded in the negative direction
$a \propto b$	a varies as b, a is proportional to b
∞	infinity
$f \circ g(x)$	composition of functions f and g, $f(g(x))$
$f^{-1}(x)$	inverse of function f(x)
( )	parenthesis, grouping of operations
[ ]	brackets, grouping of operations
{ }	1) braces, grouping of operations
	2) beginning and ending of a set
$n°$	n degrees
n'	1) n arc minutes (1/60th degree)
	2) n feet
n''	1) n arc seconds (1/60th minute)
	2) n inches
Δx	change in x, delta x
$\sum$	sum of a sequence
$\prod$	product of a sequence
$f(x)$	function f with independent variable x
$n!$	n factorial, $1 \cdot 2 \cdot 3 \cdots n$
$|x|$	absolute value of x, magnitude of x
$\log_b x$	logarithm
$\ln x$	natural logarithm
$\lceil x \rceil$	ceiling function of x
$\lfloor x \rfloor$	floor function of x
$\lim_{x \rightarrow a} f(x)$	the limit of f(x) as x approaches a

Geometry

$\approx$	1) is congruent with (geometry)
	2) is approximately equal to (algebra)
$\cong$	is congruent with
$\not\approx$	is not congruent with
$\not\cong$	is not congruent with
$\sim$	is similar to
$\overline{AB}$	line segment AB
AB	length of line segment AB
$\overleftrightarrow{AB}$	line AB
$\overrightarrow{AB}$	ray AB with endpoint A
$\angle \alpha$	angle alpha
$m\angle \alpha$	the measure of angle alpha
$\triangle ABC$	triangle ABC
$l \parallel m$	l is parallel to m
$l \nparallel m$	l is not parallel to m
$l \perp m$	l is perpendicular to m
$l \not\perp m$	l is not perpendicular to m
$\widehat{JK}$	minor arc with endpoints J and K
$\widehat{ABC}$	major arc containing point B
(θ, γ, z)	cylindrical coordinates
(r, θ, γ)	polar coordinates
$n°$	n degrees
n'	n arc minutes
n''	n arc seconds (1/60th minute)
ϵ	eccentricity of a conic section

Logic

P, Q	propositions
$P, \sim P, !P$	negation, NOT P
$P \vee Q, P + Q$	disjunction, P OR Q
$P \wedge Q, P \cdot Q$	conjunction, P AND Q
$P \oplus Q$	exclusive disjunction, P XOR Q
$P \rightarrow Q$	P implies Q
$P \Rightarrow Q$	P implies Q
$P \leftrightarrow Q$	equivalence, biconditional, if and only if
$P \Leftrightarrow Q$	equivalence
$P \equiv Q$	equivalence, identity
iff	if and only if
0, F	false
1, T	true
$\therefore$	therefore, in conclusion
QED	End of proof
∎	End of proof

Set Theory

$A, B, C, \cdots$	set
$a, b, c, \cdots$	element of a set; member of a set
$x \in A$	x is an element of set A
$x \notin A$	x is not an element of set A
$A \subset B$	set A is a subset of set B
$A \subseteq B$	set A is a subset of or equal to set B
$A \subsetneq B$	set A is a proper subset of set B
$B \supset A$	set B is a superset of set A
$A \not\subset B$	set A is not a subset of set B

$A \not\subseteq B$ .... set A is neither a subset of nor equal to set B
$A \cup B, A + B$ .. union of set A and set B
$A \cap B, A \cdot B$ .. intersection of set A and set B
$A - B$ .... difference of set A and set B
$\emptyset, \{\}$ .... empty set, null set
$A', \overline{A}$ .... complement of set A
A/S .... complement of set A in set S
$\{x : P(x)\}$ ...... the set of all x with property P
$\{a, b, c, \cdots\}$ .... set
$(a, b, c, \cdots)$ ..... ordered set
$\langle a, b, c, \cdots \rangle$ ..... ordered set
$A \times B$ .... Cartesian product, A cross B
$f \circ g(x)$ .... composition of functions f and g: $f(g(x))$
$f(X)$ .... image of set X
one-to-one ...... one-to-one correspondence
$|X|$ .... cardinality of set X
$\aleph_0$ .... denumerable infinity
$\aleph_1, \aleph_2, \aleph_3, \cdots$ ..... nondenumerable infinities
$\mathcal{P}(A)$ .... power set of A
$n(A)$ .... number of elements of set A

Sets of Numbers

$\mathbb{N}, \mathbb{Z}^+$ .... natural numbers, the set of positive integers
$\mathbb{Z}$ .... the set of all integers
$\mathbb{R}$ .... the set of all real numbers
$\mathbb{C}$ .... the set of all complex numbers
$[m, n]$ .... closed interval from m to n, $m \leq x \leq n$
$(m, n),]m, n[$ .. open interval from m to n, $m < x < n$
$(m, n],]m, n]$ .. half open interval on the left from m to n, $m < x \leq n$
$[m, n), [m, n[$ .. half open interval on the right from m to n, $m \leq x < n$
$(-\infty, \infty)$ .... the interval of all real numbers
$\cdots$ .... ellipsis, continued in the same pattern
sup .... supremum
inf .... Infimum
$\overline{X}$ .... arithmetic mean of the set of numbers X
$\sum_{i=1}^{n} a_i$ .... sum of a set of numbers
$\prod_{i=1}^{n} a_i$ .... product of a set of numbers

Matrices

$\begin{bmatrix} 1 & 3 \\ 0 & 2 \end{bmatrix}$ .... matrix
$A, B, C, \cdots, Z$ matrix identifier
$A[i, j], A_{i,j}$ ..... element at row i and column j
$|A|$ .... determinate of a matrix A
$\det(A)$ .... determinate of matrix A
A^T .... transpose of matrix A
$\text{adj}(A)$ .... adjoint of matrix A
A^{-1} .... inverse of square matrix A
I_n .... $n \times n$ identity matrix
$Z_{n \times m}$ .... $n \times m$ zero matrix

Vectors

$u, v, w, \cdots$ .... vectors
$\vec{u}, \vec{v}, \vec{w}$ .... vectors
$\langle a, b \rangle, \langle a, b, c \rangle$. vectors
$a\hat{i} + b\hat{j} + c\hat{k}$. vector in unit vector notation
$\begin{pmatrix} 2 \\ 4 \end{pmatrix}$ .... vector
$u + v$ .... vector addition
$u - v$ .... vector subtraction
$u \times v$ .... cross product of u and v
$u \cdot v$ .... dot product of u and v
$kv, k \cdot v$ .... scalar k multiplied by vector v
$u \parallel v$ .... u is parallel to v
$u \not\parallel v$ .... u is not parallel to v
$u \perp v$ .... u is perpendicular to v
$u \not\perp v$ .... u is not perpendicular to v
$|v|$ .... magnitude of vector v
$\|v\|$ .... norm of vector v
$\langle u, v \rangle$ .... inner product of u and v
$\text{proj}_v u$ .... projection of v on u

Probability and Statistics

$P(e)$ .... probability of event e
$P(e_1, e_2)$ .... conditional probability of e_1 given e_2
$P(A|B)$ .... probability of A given condition B
$E(x)$ .... expectation of X
$E(X, c)$ .... conditional expectation of X given condition c
e' .... complement of event e
$\overline{A}$ .... mean of sample A
$nPr, P(n, r)$ ... the selection of r objects, chosen from n distinct objects where $r \leq n$ and there is no replacement.
$nCr, C(n, r)$ ... the selection of r objects from a set of n objects with replacement.
$\text{var}(X)$ .... variance of X
$\text{cov}(X, Y)$ .... covariance of X and Y

Calculus

ϵ .... epsilon, very small number
e .... e constant, Euler's number
y' .... derivative
y'' .... second derivative
$y^{(n)}$ .... n^th derivative
f_x .... derivative of f with respect to x.
$\frac{dy}{dx}$ .... derivative
$\frac{d^2y}{dx^2}$ .... second derivative

$\frac{d^n y}{dx^n}$ .... nth derivative
$D_x y$ .... derivative
$D_x^2 y$ .... second derivative
$\frac{\partial f(x,y)}{\partial x}$ .... partial derivative
$\int$ .... integral
$\iint$ .... double integral
$\iiint$ .... triple integral
$\oint$ .... closed contour, line integral
$\oiint$ .... closed surface integral
$\oiiint$ .... closed volume integral
$\nabla f(x, y, z)$ .... gradient

Numbers

0, division by NOUN /ˈzɪə.roʊ dɪˈvɪ.ʒən baɪ/ division by 0 is undefined; division by zero has no mathematical meaning. Math definition: $\frac{a}{0}$ is undefined, $a \div 0$ is undefined.

0 exponent NOUN /ˈzɪə.roʊ ˈɛks.poʊ.nənt/ anything to the zero power, except zero, equals one. $b^0 = 1, b \neq 0$. 0^0 is undefined.

0, Property of Addition by NOUN /ˈzɪə.roʊ ˈprɒ.pər.ti ʌv əˈdɪ.ʃən baɪ/ if zero is added to any number, the sum is equal to that number. $0 + a = a + 0 = a$.

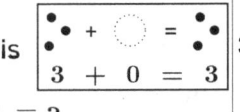
$3 + 0 = 3$

0, Property of Multiplication by NOUN /ˈzɪə.roʊ ˈprɒ.pər.ti ʌv ˌmʌl.tə.plɪˈkeɪ.ʃən baɪ/ any number times zero equals zero. Example: $0 \cdot a = a \cdot 0 = 0$.

0 to the 0 power NOUN /ˈzɪə.roʊ tu ðə ˈzɪə.roʊ ˈpaʊ.ər/ 0^0 is undefined.

1-D ABBREVIATION one-dimensional; has one dimension. Example: line.

1, Property of Division by NOUN /wʌn ˈprɒ.pər.ti ʌv dɪˈvɪ.ʒən baɪ/ any number divided by one equals itself: $\frac{a}{1} = a$.

$3 \div 1 = 3$

1, Property of Multiplication by NOUN /wʌn ˈprɒ.pər.ti ʌv ˌmʌl.tə.plɪˈkeɪ.ʃən baɪ/ any number times one equals itself. $1 \cdot a = a \cdot 1 = a$.

$5 \times 1 = 5$

2-D ABBREVIATION two-dimensional; has two dimensions.

2-space NOUN /tu speɪs/ a geometric space with 2 dimensions. Example: rectangular coordinate plane. The Euclidean geometry of 2-space is called plane geometry.

3-D ABBREVIATION three-dimensional; has three dimensions.

3-space NOUN /θri speɪs/ a geometric space with 3 dimensions. The Euclidean geometry of 3-space is called solid geometry.

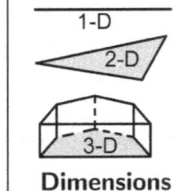
Dimensions

4-cube NOUN /fɔr kjub/ see *hypercube* (p 58).

4-space NOUN /fɔr speɪs/ a geometric space with 4 dimensions.

10^{100} NOUN a googol is a large number.

10^{googol} NOUN a googolplex, or $10^{10^{100}}$, is a very large number.

n-space NOUN /ən speɪs/ a geometric space with n dimensions.

n-tuple NOUN /ɛnˈtu.pəl/ a set of n coordinates written like $(x_1, x_2, x_3, \cdots, x_n)$. Example: 3-tuple $(3, 0, 2)$.

A

a ABBREVIATION atto- (p 14) 10^{-18}. Example: 7.2 attoseconds $= 7.2 \times 10^{-18}$ seconds. Synonym: quintillionth (p 94).

A ABBREVIATION ampere (p 9).

a- PREFIX not. Example: asymmetric.

AAA similarity NOUN /eɪ eɪ eɪ ˌsɪ.məˈlæ.rɪ.ti/ (angle-angle-angle similarity) See *AA similarity* (p 6).

AAS congruence NOUN /eɪ eɪ ɛs kənˈgru.əns/ (angle-angle-side congruence) two triangles are congruent if and only if two adjacent angles and a side not between the angles are congruent with the corresponding angles and side of the other triangle. Math definition: Given $\triangle ABC$ and $\triangle A'B'C'$, $\triangle ABC \cong \triangle A'B'C'$ if and only if $\angle CAB \cong \angle C'A'B'$, $\angle ABC \cong \angle A'B'C'$ and $BC \cong B'C'$.

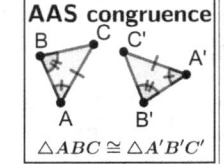
AAS congruence
$\triangle ABC \cong \triangle A'B'C'$

AA similarity NOUN /eɪ eɪ ˌsɪ.məˈlæ.rɪ.ti/ (angle-angle similarity) two triangles are similar if and only if two pair of corresponding angles are congruent. Math definition: Given $\triangle ABC$ and $\triangle A'B'C'$, $\triangle ABC \sim \triangle A'B'C'$ if and only if $\angle CAB \cong \angle C'A'B'$ and $\angle ABC \cong \angle A'B'C'$. Synonym: AAA similarity. Corollary: AAA similarity.

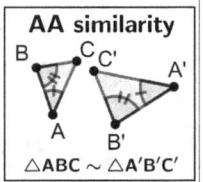
AA similarity
$\triangle ABC \sim \triangle A'B'C'$

abacus NOUN /ˈæ.bə.kəs/ a device used for counting and arithmetic that has sliders and beads. Plural: abacuses /ˈæ.bə.kəs.əz/ or abaci /ˈæb.ə.kaɪ/.

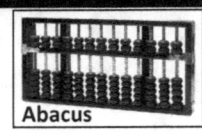
Abacus

abbreviation NOUN /əˈbri.viˈeɪ.ʃən/ a short way to write a word or phrase. Example: A is the abbreviation for ampere.

Abelian ADJECTIVE /əˈbi.li.ən/ see *commutative* (p 23).

Abelian group NOUN /əˈbi.li.ən grup/ see *commutative group* (p 24).

abscissa NOUN /æbˈsɪs.sə/
1) the horizontal coordinate of a point, the x-coordinate of a point. The distance between a point and the y-axis, measured parallel to the x-axis. Example: (abscissa, ordinate).
2) the value of the independent variable in a relation or function. Plural: abscissae /æbˈsɪs.i/ Synonym: x-coordinate (p 122). Antonym: ordinate (p 84).

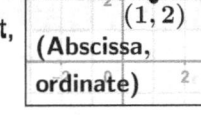
(Abscissa, ordinate)

absolute ADJECTIVE /ˈæb.səˌlut/
1) having to do with absolute value.
2) exact.
3) global.

absolute change NOUN /ˈæb.səˌlut tʃeɪndʒ/ the change in one variable without considering any other variables.

absolute convergence NOUN /ˈæb.səˌlut kənˈvɜr.dʒəns/ the property of converging absolutely. See also *converge*

absolutely (p 29). Antonym: *conditional convergence* (p 27).

absolute convergence test NOUN /æb.sə'lut kən'vɜr.dʒəns test/ if the absolute values of the terms of a sequence converge, then the original sequence converges. Math definition: if $\{|a_1|, |a_2|, |a_3|, \cdots\}$ converges then $\{a_1, a_2, a_3, \cdots\}$ converges.

absolute deviation NOUN /æb.sə'lut ˌdi.vi'eɪ.ʃən/ the distance between a data point and a center of all data points in a dataset. Formula: $D_i = |x_i - m(X)|$ where x_i is the value of data point i, $m(X)$ is the center of the dataset, and D_i is the absolute deviation of data point i. See also *deviation* (p 37). See also *average absolute deviation* (p 14).

absolute error NOUN /æb.sə'lut 'ɛr.ər/ the difference between a measured or estimated value and the actual value.

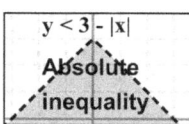

absolute extremum NOUN /æb.sə'lut ɪk'stri.məm/ an absolute minimum or an absolute maximum. Plural: *absolute extrema*.

absolute frequency NOUN /æb.sə'lut 'fri.kwən.si/
1) (probability) the total number of times an event happened during a set of experiments.
2) (statistics) an exact count of elements of a dataset that share a particular property.
Antonym: *relative frequency* (p 98).

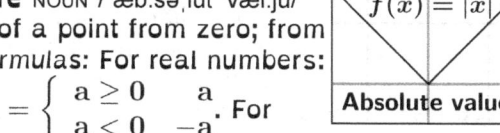

absolute inequality NOUN /æb.sə'lut ˌɪn.ɪ'kwɒ.lɪ.ti/ an inequality that has at least one absolute value containing a variable. Example: $y < 3 - |x|$.

absolute magnitude NOUN /'æb.sə.lut 'mæg.nɪ.tud/ see *absolute value* (p 7).

absolute maximum NOUN /'æb.sə.lut 'mæk.sə.məm/ see *global maximum* (p 54).

absolute mean deviation NOUN /'æb.sə.lut min ˌdi.vi'eɪ.ʃən/ see *mean deviation* (p 73).

absolute minimum NOUN /'æb.sə.lut 'mɪ.nə.məm/ see *global minimum* (p 54).

absolute value NOUN /'æb.sə.lut 'væl.ju/ the distance of a point from zero; from the origin. Formulas: For real numbers: $|a| = \sqrt{a^2}$; $|a| = \begin{cases} a & a \geq 0 \\ -a & a < 0 \end{cases}$. For complex numbers: $|a + bi| = \sqrt{a^2 + b^2}$. Synonyms: *magnitude* (p 71), *modulus*.

absolute value equation NOUN /'æb.sə.lut 'væl.ju ɪ'kweɪ.ʃən/ an equation containing the absolute value of a variable. Example: $y = |x - 2|$.

absolute value inequality NOUN /'æb.sə.lut 'væl.ju ˌɪn.ɪ'kwɒ.lɪ.ti/ an inequality containing the absolute value of a variable. Example: $y < |x - 2|$.

absolute value function NOUN /'æb.sə.lut 'væl.ju 'fʌŋk.ʃən/ see *absolute value equation* (p 7).

absolute zero NOUN /'æb.sə.lut 'zɪə.roʊ/ the theoretical temperature at which all movement stops: $-273.15°C$, $-459.67°F$, $0K$.

abstract algebra NOUN /æb'strækt 'æl.dʒə.brə/ algebra generalized to any set and operations on that set, and not just numbers. Elements of the set can be matrices, equations or abstract mathematical objects. An operation is some mapping of one or more elements of a set that gives another element. See also *modern algebra* (p 76).

absurd ADJECTIVE /əb'sɜrd/
1) inconsistent with reason.
2) contradictory.
3) illogical or untrue.

abundant number NOUN /ə'bʌn.dənt 'nʌm.bər/ an integer where the sum of its proper divisors is greater than the integer itself. Example: $1 + 2 + 3 + 4 + 6 > 12$. Antonyms: *deficient number* (p 35); *perfect number* (p 87).

acceleration NOUN /æk.sɛl.ə'reɪ.ʃən/ speeding up or slowing down; the rate of change of velocity with respect to time. Units of measure: m/s^2 (meters per second squared) or km/h^2 (kilometers per hour squared). Formula: $a = \frac{d}{t^2}$ where a is acceleration, d is distance traveled and t is time.

accidental sample NOUN /ˌæk.sɪ'dɛn.tl 'sæm.pəl/ see *convenience sample* (p 29).

account VERB /ə'kaʊnt/ to verify usage or explanation of.

accumulation factor NOUN /əˌkju.mju'leɪ.ʃən 'fæk.tər/ the quantity $\left(1 + \frac{i}{n}\right)^n$ in the formula for compound interest $P = P_0\left(1 + \frac{i}{n}\right)^{n \cdot m}$. Accumulation factor measures the rate at which principal grows. See also *compound interest* (p 26).

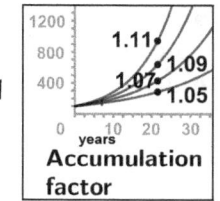

accuracy NOUN /'æ.kjər.ə.si/
1) how close a calculated or estimated number is to an actual value. Synonym: *precision* (p 91).
2) the level of freedom from error. Synonym: *error level*.

accurate ADJECTIVE /'æ.kjər.ət/
1) exact.
2) without error.
3) having error less than a specified tolerance.
Example: accurate to two decimal places.

acos ABBREVIATION arccosine.

acosh ABBREVIATION arc hyperbolic cosine.

acot ABBREVIATION arccotangent.

acoth ABBREVIATION arc hyperbolic cotangent.

acre NOUN /'eɪ.kər/ a unit of measure of land surface equal to $43{,}560$ square feet or $\frac{1}{640}$ of a square mile. Formula: 640 acres $= 1$ square mile. 1 acre $\approx 4{,}047$ m^2.

acsc ABBREVIATION arccosecant.

acsch ABBREVIATION arc hyperbolic cosecant.

actual ADJECTIVE /'æk.tju.l/
1) not estimated or measured; exact.
2) real or factual.

actual value NOUN /'æk.tju.l 'væl.ju/ a value which is exact and not estimated or measured.

acute ADJECTIVE /ə'kjut/ having one or more angles that measure less than a right angle.

acute angle NOUN /ə'kjut 'æŋ.gəl/ an angle that measures less than $90°$. Math definition: $\angle\alpha$ is an acute angle if

3rd Dyslexic's Edition

and only if $0° < \alpha < 90°, 0 < \alpha < \frac{\pi}{2}$.

acute triangle NOUN /əˈkjut ˈtraɪ.æŋ.gəl/ a triangle that has three acute angles.

add VERB /æd/
1) to join two or more quantities together into a sum.
2) to count objects in two or more groups.
Inverse: subtract (p 110). Synonym: sum (p 111).

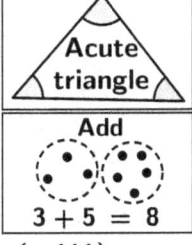

addend NOUN /ˈæ.dɛnd/ a number or expression that is to be added. Formula: **addend** + **addend** = **sum**. Example: $\underbrace{3}_{\text{addend}} + \underbrace{2}_{\text{addend}} = \underbrace{5}_{\text{sum}}$.

addition NOUN /əˈdɪ.ʃən/ the joining of two or more quantities together into a sum. Notation: +. Inverse: subtraction (p 110). Example: $1 + 3 = 4$. See also Properties of Addition (p 125).

addition fact NOUN /əˈdɪ.ʃən fækt/ two integers and their sum. Example: $1 + 1 = 2$. See also Addition Facts (p 124).

addition of polynomials NOUN /əˈdɪ.ʃən ʌv ˌpɒ.ləˈnoʊ.mi.əls/ joining two or more polynomials together into a sum. Adding like terms of polynomials.

	$3x^3$	$+4x^2$	$-7x$	
+	$2x^3$		$+6x$	$+2$
	$5x^3$	$+4x^2$	$-x$	$+2$

addition postulate NOUN /əˈdɪ.ʃən ˈpɒs.tʃə.lɪt/ see Angle Addition Postulate (p 10).

Addition Principle of Counting NOUN /əˈdɪ.ʃən ˈprɪn.sə.pəl ʌv ˈkaʊn.tɪŋ/ given $n(A)$ is the number of elements of set A, if $n(A \cap B) = 0$, then $n(A \cup B) = n(A) + n(B)$. See also General Addition Principle of Counting (p 52).

Addition Property of Equality NOUN /əˈdɪ.ʃən ˈprɒ.pər.ti ʌv ɪˈkwɒl.ɪ.ti/ the same number can be added to both sides of an equation without changing the truth value of the equation. Math definition: if $a = b$ then $a + c = b + c$, and if $a \ne b$ then $a + c \ne b + c$.

Addition Property of Inequality NOUN /əˈdɪ.ʃən ˈprɒ.pər.ti ʌv ˌɪn.ɪˈkwɒ.lɪ.ti/ the same number can be added to both sides of an inequality without changing the truth value of the inequality. Math definition: if $a > b$ then $a + c > b + c$. If $a < b$ then $a + c < b + c$.

Addition Property of Zero NOUN /əˈdɪ.ʃən ˈprɒ.pər.ti ʌv ˈzɪə.roʊ/ see additive identity (p 8).

addition sign NOUN /əˈdɪ.ʃən saɪn/ the symbol '+' is used to show addition. Example: $3 + 2 = 5$.

additive ADJECTIVE /ˈæ.dɪ.tɪv/ having to do with addition. Example: additive inverse.

additive identity NOUN /ˈæ.dɪ.tɪv aɪˈdɛn.tɪ.ti/ the additive identity for real and complex numbers is 0 since $a + 0 = 0 + a = a$.

additive inverse NOUN /ˈæ.dɪ.tɪv ɪnˈvɜrs/ two numbers that, when added together, equals zero. The additive inverse of any real or complex number a is $-a$, since $a + (-a) = 0$. Example: $3 + (-3) = 0$. Synonym: opposite number (p 83).

adjacent ADJECTIVE /əˈdʒeɪ.sənt/
1) next to. Synonym: consecutive (p 27).
2) having a common endpoint or boundary.
See also Adjacent in Geometric Figures (p 139).

adjoint NOUN /ˈæd.ʒɔɪnt/ the adjoint of a square matrix is another matrix that, when multiplied by the original matrix, gives an identity matrix times the determinant of the original matrix. Math definition: B is the adjoint of A if and only if $A \cdot B = \det(A) \cdot I$. Notation: $\text{adj}(B)$. Synonym: adjugate.

adjugate see adjoint (p 8).

admissible hypothesis NOUN /ædˈmɪ.sə.bəl haɪˈpɒ.θə.sɪs/ a hypothesis that has not been proven true, has not been proven false, and is self-consistent. Synonym: conjecture (p 27).

affine cipher NOUN /əˈfaɪn ˈsaɪ.fər/ a cipher where each letter is converted to a number, then that number is encrypted to a different number by a function. Example: 'hello' becomes '11-8-12-12-15'.

affine transformation NOUN /əˈfaɪn ˌtræns.fərˈmeɪ.ʃən/ any transformation or combination of transformations where lines are preserved, but not necessarily angles or parallelism.

after PREPOSITION /ˈæf.tər/
1) coming in back of. Example: 't' comes after 'a' in 'cat'.
2) coming later in order or in time. Example: 5 comes after 3.
Antonym: before (p 16).

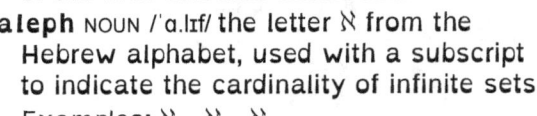

Agnesi, Maria Gaetana PERSON /ˌmɑrˈi.ə ˌgɛtˈɑn.ɑ ɑːnˈjeɪz.i/ (1718—1799) known for having written Instituzioni Analitiche, one of the first calculus textbooks.

aleph NOUN /ˈɑ.lɪf/ the letter $\aleph$ from the Hebrew alphabet, used with a subscript to indicate the cardinality of infinite sets. Examples: $\aleph_0, \aleph_1, \aleph_2, \ldots$.

aleph null NOUN /ˈɑ.lɪf nʌl/ the symbol $\aleph_0$ representing the cardinality of a denumerable set, a set with a one-to-one correspondence with the natural numbers. See cardinal number (p 19). Synonym: aleph-naught.

algebra NOUN /ˈæl.dʒə.brə/ the study of relations, the use of variables to represent values, and the rules for manipulating those variables.

algebraic ADJECTIVE /ˌæl.dʒəˈbreɪ.ɪk/
1) having to do with algebra. Example: algebraic identity.
2) having to do with addition, subtraction, multiplication, division, exponentiation and taking of roots. Example: algebraic expression.

algebraically ADVERB /ˌæl.dʒəˈbreɪ.ɪk.li/ using algebra. Example: solve the equation algebraically. Antonym: geometrically (p 53).

algebraic equation NOUN /ˌæl.dʒəˈbreɪ.ɪk ɪˈkweɪ.ʃən/ an equation that uses only the operations of addition, subtraction, multiplication, division, exponentiation and taking of roots. Example: $y = 3 + 2 \div x$.

algebraic expression NOUN /ˌæl.dʒəˈbreɪ.ɪk ɪkˈsprɛ.ʃən/ an expression that uses only the operations of addition, subtraction, multiplication, division, exponentiation and taking of roots. Example: $3xy + 1 \div y - 7$.

algebraic function NOUN /ˌæl.dʒəˈbreɪ.ɪk ˈfʌŋk.ʃən/ a function that uses only the operations of addition, subtraction, multiplication, division, exponentiation and taking of roots. Example: $f(x) = 3 \times 2 + 7$.

algebraic identity NOUN /ˌæl.dʒəˈbreɪ.ɪk aɪˈdɛn.tɪ.ti/ an equation that uses only the operations of addition, subtraction, multiplication, division, and exponentiation, and is true for all possible values of the variables. Notation: ≡. Example: $(x+y)(x-y) \equiv x^2 - y^2$.

algebraic number NOUN /ˌæl.dʒəˈbreɪ.ɪk ˈnʌm.bər/ any number that is a root of a single variable, non-zero, real-valued polynomial with rational coefficients. Examples: $5, -\frac{3}{2}, \sqrt{17}$. Antonym: *transcendental number* (p 115).

algebraic operating system NOUN /ˌæl.dʒəˈbreɪ.ɪk ˌɒ.pəˈreɪ.tɪŋ ˈsɪs.təm/ see *order of operations* (p 83). Abbreviation: AOS.

algebraic operation NOUN /ˌæl.dʒəˈbreɪ.ɪk ˌɒ.pəˈreɪ.ʃən/ one of the operations of addition, subtraction, multiplication, division, exponentiation and taking of roots. Examples: $+, -, \times, \div, a^b, \sqrt{a}$.

algebraic representation NOUN /ˌæl.dʒəˈbreɪ.ɪk ˌrɛ.prɪ.zɛnˈteɪ.ʃən/ a representation that uses algebra, such as an equation. Example: If the price of gasoline is $4.70 per gallon, the equation C = 4.70g is an algebraic representation of the cost of purchasing g gallons.

algebra tile NOUN /ˈæl.dʒə.brə taɪl/ a square or rectangular tile used to represent algebraic operations.

algorithm NOUN /ˈæl.ɡəˌrɪ.ðəm/ a set of instructions for doing a procedure or solving a problem. Example: (cross multiplication) $\frac{a}{b} = \frac{c}{d} \rightarrow ad = bc$. Synonym: *method* (p 74). Antonym: *heuristic method* (p 56).

align VERB /əˈlaɪn/ to arrange in a straight line; to make line up.

al-Khwārizmī, Muḥammad ibn Mūsā PERSON (c 780—850) (محمد بن موسى وارزمی) an Arab mathematician whose works introduced Arabic numerals to Europe.

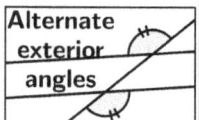
Muḥammad al-Khwārizmī

all together PREPOSITION /ɔl təˈɡɛð.ər/ added together; summed. Keyword for addition.

alpha NOUN /ˈæl.fə/ the Greek letter α is often used to represent angles. See also *Greek Letters* (p 135).

alternate
1) ADJECTIVE /ˈɔl.tər.nɪt/ on opposites sides.
2) ADJECTIVE /ˈɔl.tər.nɪt/ changing signs.
3) ADJECTIVE /ˈɔl.tər.nɪt/ one then the other, back and forth.
4) VERB /ˈɔl.tər.neɪt/ to change from one to another, back and forth.

alternate angles NOUN /ˈɔl.tər.nɪt ˈæŋ.ɡəlz/ vertical angles on opposites sides of a transversal.

alternate exterior angles NOUN /ˈɔl.tər.nɪt ɪkˈstɪər.i.ər ˈæŋ.ɡəlz/ angles that are on different sides of a transversal and are outside the transversed lines.

Alternate Exterior Angles Theorem NOUN /ˈɔl.tər.nɪt ɪkˈstɪər.i.ər ˈæŋ.ɡəlz ˈθɪ.ə.rəm/ if two parallel lines are cut by a transversal, then each pair of alternate exterior angles is congruent.

alternate interior angle NOUN /ˈɔl.tər.nɪt ɪnˈtɪər.i.ər ˈæŋ.ɡəl/ one of two angles that are on different sides of a transversal that intersects two other lines. The angles are between the two intersected lines.

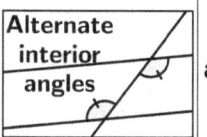

Alternate Interior Angles Theorem NOUN /ˈɔl.tər.nɪt ɪnˈtɪər.i.ər ˈæŋ.ɡəlz ˈθɪ.ə.rəm/ if two parallel lines are cut by a transversal, then each pair of alternate interior angles is congruent.

alternating ADJECTIVE /ˈɔl.tərˌneɪ.tɪŋ/ changing between one and another, back and forth.

alternating series NOUN /ˈɔl.tərˌneɪ.tɪŋ ˈsɪər.iz/ a series which changes back and forth between negative and positive terms. Example: $\frac{1}{2} - \frac{1}{3} + \frac{1}{4} - \frac{1}{5} + \cdots$. Plural: *alternating series* /ˈɔl.tərˌneɪ.tɪŋ ˈsɪər.iz/.

altitude NOUN /ˈæl.tɪˌtud/
1) the height of an object from a reference point, usually sea level or ground level.
2) a line segment from the top of a figure to the bottom that is perpendicular to both the top and the bottom.
3) a line segment from the base of a geometric figure to the apex, that is perpendicular to the base. See also *Altitudes of Geometric Figures* (p 139).

am ABBREVIATION /eɪ ɛm/ ante meridiem; a time after midnight and before noon. Example: 10:00 AM is 10 o'clock in the morning. Notation: AM, a.m..

ambiguous ADJECTIVE /æmˈbɪ.ɡju.əs/ open to more than one possibility, especially when only one possibility can be true at a time. Example: ambiguous case.

ambiguous case NOUN /æmˈbɪ.ɡju.əs keɪs/ a case where the result cannot be uniquely identified. Example: Given one side and two angles, the law of sines sometimes gives two possibilities, only one of which can be true.

amount NOUN /əˈmaʊnt/
1) a quantity. Example: the amount of money in my wallet.
2) a total or sum of two or more quantities.

amp ABBREVIATION ampere (p 9).

ampere NOUN /ˈæm.pɪər/ a unit of measure of electrical current. Abbreviations: A, amp.

Ampère, André-Marie PERSON /ˈæm.pɪər ɑnˈdreɪ məˈri/ (1775—1836) a French physicist, who was one of the original discoverers of electromagnetism. The unit of measure of electric current, the ampere, is named after him.

André-Marie Ampère

amplify VERB /ˈæm.pləˌfaɪ/
1) to increase; make larger. Synonym: *enlarge* (p 44).
2) to make louder.

amplification NOUN /ˌæm.plə.fɪˈkeɪ.ʃən/
1) the act of increasing; making larger. Synonym: *enlargement* (p 44).
2) the act of making louder.

amplitude NOUN /ˈæm.plɪˌtud/ half the distance from a minimum to a maximum value of a periodic function. In nature, the amplitude of many waves is related to the energy of the waves. Formula: amp. = $\frac{\max(f(x)) - \min(f(x))}{2}$.

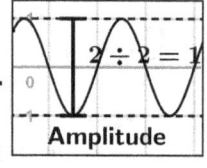
Amplitude

analog ADJECTIVE /ˈæ.nəˌlɒɡ/ having to do with a mechanism that shows data continuously; that shows data on a dial or by other non-digital means.

Antonym: digital (p 38).

analog clock NOUN /ˈæ.nə.lɔg klɒk/ a clock with a minute hand and an hour hand that turn in a circle. *Antonym: digital clock* (p 38).

Analog Clock

analogy NOUN /əˈnæ.lə.dʒi/ a type of reasoning that assumes that two situations are similar and draws conclusions about one based on the other. An analogy is not a mathematical proof. *Example: Life is like an onion.*

analysis NOUN /əˈnæl.ɪ.sɪs/
1) use of the principles of algebra as opposed to geometry.
2) a branch of mathematics that includes differentiation, integration, infinite series, and analytic functions.
3) (statistics) the processing of raw data to create information.

analytic ADJECTIVE /ˌæ.nəˈlɪ.tɪk/ having to do with analysis.

analytical ADJECTIVE /ˌæ.nəˈlɪ.tɪ.kəl/ see *analytic* (p 10).

analytic geometry NOUN /ˌæ.nəˈlɪ.tɪk dʒiˈɒ.mɪ.tri/ the study of geometry using coordinate systems and the methods of algebra. *Synonym: Cartesian geometry.*

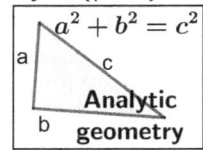
Analytic geometry

analytic method NOUN /ˌæ.nəˈlɪ.tɪk ˈmɛ.θəd/
1) any method that uses algebra or numeric methods as the main way to solve a problem.
2) a method of breaking down a problem into parts, then reassembling the parts to find a solution.

analytic proof NOUN /ˌæ.nəˈlɪ.tɪk pruf/
1) a proof that assumes the conclusion is true, then works backwards to show the proposition is true.
2) a proof that uses algebra, and not geometry.

analytic values of trigonometric functions NOUN /ˌæ.nəˈlɪ.tɪk ˈvæl.juz ʌv ˌtrɪ.gə.nəˈmɛ.trɪk ˈfʌŋk.ʃənz/ see *exact values of trigonometric functions* (p 46).

analyze VERB /ˈæ.nəˌlaɪz/ to look at methodically in order to discover fact.

anchor ring NOUN /ˈæŋ.kər rɪŋ/ see *torus* (p 114).

and CONJUNCTION /ænd/ see *conjunction* (p 27).

anecdotal ADJECTIVE /ˌæ.nɪkˈdoʊ.təl/ based on personal experience, rather than systematic scientific evaluation. *Antonyms: empirical* (p 43), *theoretical* (p 114).

angle NOUN /ˈæŋ.gəl/ the rotation between two rays or line segments with a common endpoint. Angles are measured in degrees (360 degrees = 1 full circle), radians (2π radians = 1 full circle) or gradians (400 gradians = 1 full circle). *Notation:* ∠.

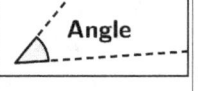
Angle

Angle Addition Postulate NOUN /ˈæŋ.gəl əˈdɪ.ʃən ˈpɒs.tʃə.lɪt/ adjacent angles can be added together to form a larger angle. *Math definition:* Given noncollinear points **A**, **B**, **C** and a point **D** in the interior of ∠BAC, m∠BAD + m∠DAC = m∠BAC.

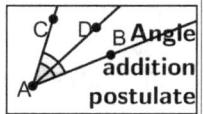
Angle addition postulate

angle-angle-angle similarity NOUN /ˈæŋ.gəl ˈæŋ.gəl ˈæŋ.gəl ˌsɪ.məˈlær.ɪ.ti/ see *AA similarity* (p 6).

angle-angle-side congruence NOUN /ˈæŋ.gəl ˈæŋ.gəl saɪd kənˈgru.əns/ see *AAS congruence* (p 6).

angle-angle similarity NOUN /ˈæŋ.gəl ˈæŋ.gəl ˌsɪ.məˈlær.ɪ.ti/ see *AA similarity* (p 6).

angle between vectors NOUN /ˈæŋ.gəl bɪˈtwin ˈvɛk.tərz/ the angle between two vectors **u** and **v** is $\theta = \arccos \frac{\mathbf{u} \cdot \mathbf{v}}{|\mathbf{u}||\mathbf{v}|}$.

angle bisection NOUN /ˈæŋ.gəl baɪˈsɛk.ʃən/ the act of dividing an angle into two equal angles. See also *bisect an angle* (p 17).

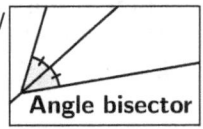
Angle bisector

angle bisector NOUN /ˈæŋ.gəl baɪˈsɛk.tər/ a ray or line that divides an angle into two equal angles. See also *bisect an angle* (p 17).

angle bracket noun /ˈæŋ.gəl ˈbræ.kɪt/ the symbols '<' (left angle bracket) and '>' (right angle bracket) used to indicate an ordered set, or vector inner product.

angle of depression NOUN /ˈæŋ.gəl ʌv dɪˈprɛ.ʃən/ the angle at which an observer must look below a line of sight to see an object.

Angle of depression

angle of elevation NOUN /ˈæŋ.gəl ʌv ˌɛl.əˈveɪ.ʃən/ the angle at which an observer must look above the line of sight to see an object.

Angle of elevation

angle of incidence NOUN /ˈæŋ.gəl ʌv ˈɪn.sɪ.dəns/ the angle at which an object strikes a surface, measured from a line perpendicular to the surface at the point of reflection. *Antonym: angle of reflection* (p 10).

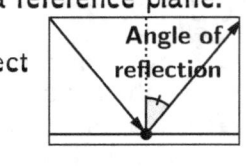
Angle of incidence

angle of inclination noun /ˈæŋ.gəl ʌv ˌɪn.kləˈneɪ.ʃən/
1) either an angle of depression or an angle of elevation.
2) an angle on a graph measured from the positive x-axis.
3) the angle between a plane and a reference plane.

Angle of inclination

angle of reflection NOUN /ˈæŋ.gəl ʌv rɪˈflɛk.ʃən/ the angle at which an object 'bounces' off a surface, measured from a line perpendicular to the surface at the point of reflection. *Antonym: angle of incidence* (p 10).

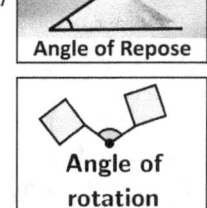
Angle of reflection

angle of repose NOUN /ˈæŋ.gəl ʌv rəˈpoʊz/ the maximum angle of a stable slope of granular materials, such as sand.

Angle of Repose

angle of rotation NOUN /ˈæŋ.gəl ʌv roʊˈteɪ.ʃən/ the angle though which an object is rotated about a fixed point.

Angle of rotation

angle-side-angle congruence NOUN /ˈæŋ.gəl saɪd ˈæŋ.gəl kənˈgru.əns/ see *ASA congruence* (p 14).

angle sum NOUN /ˈæŋ.gəl sʌm/ the sum of all of the interior angles of a polygon.

Angle Sum Theorem NOUN /ˈæŋ.gəl sʌm ˈθɪ.ə.rəm/ in Euclidean geometry, the sum of the measures of the angles of a triangle is $180°$ or π radians. *Formula:* $\alpha + \beta + \gamma = 180°$.

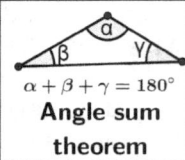
$\alpha + \beta + \gamma = 180°$
Angle sum theorem

angular ADJECTIVE /ˈæŋ.gjə.lər/
1) having to do with an angle.
2) measured using an angle. *Example: angular distance.*

angular distance NOUN /ˈæn.gjə.lər ˈdɪs.təns/ the measure of the angle between two objects from a reference point.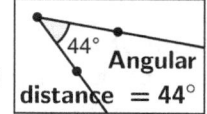

angular speed NOUN /ˈæn.gjə.lər spid/ see angular velocity (p 11).

angular velocity NOUN /ˈæn.gjə.lər vəˈlɒ.sɪ.ti/ 1) how many times an object goes around a center point during a time interval. Example: An automobile engine turns at about 2000 revolutions per minute. 2) the angle passed through in a unit of time. Example: 1 radian per second. Formula: angular velocity $= \frac{\theta}{t}$ where θ is the angle moved through in time t. Synonym: angular speed.

annexing zeros NOUN /əˈnɛk.sɪŋ ˈzɪə.roʊs/ a strategy for multiplication and division that adds extra zeros. Example: $2 \times 3 = 6, 20 \times 3 = 60, 200 \times 3 = 600$.

annual ADJECTIVE /ˈæn.ju.əl/
1) once a year. Example: annual company picnic.
2) during a whole year. Example: annual rainfall.

annual interest rate NOUN /ˈæn.ju.əl ˈɪn.trɪst reɪt/ see annual percentage rate (p 11).

annualize VERB /ˈæn.ju.əˌlaɪz/ to convert an interest rate to another rate that would generate the same interest amount if compounded once in a year; to calculate for a whole year. Formula: $r_a = \left(1 + \frac{r}{n}\right)^n - 1$ where r_a is the annual interest rate, r is the stated interest rate and n is the number of times per year the interest is compounded. Example: 10% compounded 12 times a year: $r_a = \left(1 + \frac{0.10}{12}\right)^{12} - 1 = 1.0083^{12} - 1 \approx 1.1047 - 1 = 0.1047 = 10.47\%$.

annually ADVERB /ˈæn.ju.əˌli/ once a year; each year. Example: compounded annually.

annual percentage rate NOUN /ˈæn.ju.əl pərˈsɛn.tɪdʒ reɪt/ an interest rate that, if compounded once a year, would produce the same amount of interest as the nominal (stated) interest rate. Synonym: annual interest rate. Abbreviation: APR. See also annualize (p 11).

annual percent yield NOUN /ˈæn.ju.əl pərˈsɛnt yild/ see annual percentage rate (p 11).

annuity NOUN /əˈnu.ɪ.ti/ an income payable at stated intervals. Formula: present value of an annuity: $A_p = P \frac{1 - (i+1)^n}{i}$ where P is the principal, i is the interest rate, and n is the number of periods.

annulus NOUN /ˈæn.jə.ləs/ the region between two concentric circles. Formula: Area $= \pi \left(r_1^2 - r_2^2\right), r_1 > r_2$. Example: the cross section of a pipe is an annulus. Plural: annuli /ˈæn.jəˌlaɪ/.

answer NOUN /ˈæn.sər/ a correct response to a problem.

ante- PREFIX /ˈæn.tə/ before. Example: antecedent.

antecedent NOUN /ˌæn.təˈsi.dnt/ the first of two statements in an "if-then" relationship (an implication). Notation: **antecedent → consequent**. Example: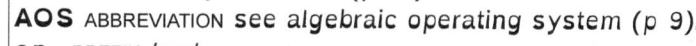

anti- PREFIX /ˈæn.tɪ/
1) opposite of. Example: anticlockwise.
2) inverse of. Example: antilogarithm.
3) opposed to.

anticlockwise ADJECTIVE /ˌæn.tɪˈklɒk.waɪz/ (British English) see counterclockwise (p 31).

antiderivative NOUN /ˌæn.tɪ.dɪˈrɪ.və.tɪv/ an indefinite integral. Math definition: a function F is called an antiderivative of f on an interval I if $F'(x) = f(x)$ for all x in I.

antilogarithm NOUN /ˌæn.tɪˈlɒ.gəˌrɪ.ðəm/ a number for which the given number is the logarithm. In $y = \log_b x$, x is the antilogarithm of y to the base b.

antipode NOUN /ˈæn.tɪˌpoʊd/ an exact or direct opposite.

antipodal ADJECTIVE /ænˈtɪ.paʊ.dl/ being exactly opposite each other; being on the opposite ends of a diameter of a circle or sphere. Synonym: diametrically opposed (p 37).

antipodal points NOUN /ænˈtɪ.paʊ.dl pɔɪntz/ two points that are endpoints on the same diameter of a circle or sphere.

antiprism NOUN /ˌæn.tɪˈprɪ.zəm/ a 3-dimensional geometric shape having congruent polygons for bases and isosceles triangles for lateral faces.

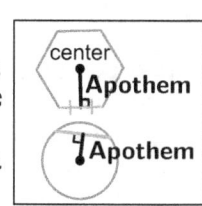

any ADJECTIVE /ˈɛ.ni/ it does not matter which. Antonym: certain (p 11).

AOS ABBREVIATION see algebraic operating system (p 9).

ap- PREFIX /æp/
1) before.
2) away from.

apex NOUN /ˈeɪ.pɛks/ the vertex at the top of a cone or pyramid; the highest point of a figure when that figure comes to a point.

aphelion NOUN /əˈfi.li.ən/ for an object in an elliptical orbit, the point in the orbit that is farthest from the focus that the object is orbiting around. Antonym: perihelion (p 87).

apothem NOUN /ˈæ.pəˌθɛm/
1) a line segment from the center of a regular polygon to the midpoint of one of the sides of the polygon.
2) a line segment from the center of a circle to the midpoint of a chord of a circle.

apparent ADJECTIVE /əˈpɛər.ənt/
1) obvious. Example: It is apparent that the angle is a right angle.
2) seems to be. May be or may not be. Example: apparent solution.

apparent solution NOUN /əˈpɛər.ənt səˈlu.ʃən/ a solution that may or may not be a valid solution. A solution that may be an extraneous solution. See also extraneous solution (p 48).

applied mathematics NOUN /əˈplaɪd ˌmæθˈmæ.tɪks/ mathematics that is applied to real-world problems. Antonym: pure mathematics (p 93). Examples: accounting, statistics, physics.

3rd Dyslexic's Edition

apply VERB /əˈplaɪ/ to use to help solve a problem. Example: apply the property of addition by zero.

appreciate VERB /əˈpriː.ʃiˌeɪt/ to go up in value. Synonym: *increase* (p 60). Antonym: *depreciate* (p 36).

appreciation NOUN /əˌpriː.ʃiˈeɪ.ʃən/
1) an increase in the value of assets.
2) the amount of increase in the value of assets.
Synonym: *increase* (p 60). Antonym: *depreciation* (p 36).

approach /əˈproʊtʃ/
1) VERB to get close to. Notation: →. Example: x → a, x approaches a.
2) NOUN a way to accomplish a task.

approximate
1) ADJECTIVE /əˈprɒk.sə.mɪt/ an estimated value. Antonym: *exact* (p 46).
2) VERB /əˈprɒk.sə.meɪt/ to find a number close to the actual number. Example: approximate the square root of 2.

approximately ADJECTIVE /əˈprɒk.sə.mɪt.li/
1) close to the actual value. Examples: π is approximately 3.14, $\pi \approx 3.14$.
2) estimated to be.
3) changes, but is close to. Example: The distance between the moon and the earth is approximately 3.85×10^5 km.
Notation: $\approx$. Antonym: *exactly* (p 46).

approximation NOUN /əˌprɒk.səˈmeɪ.ʃən/
1) a value found by approximating.
2) the process of finding an approximate value.

APR ABBREVIATION annual percentage rate.

Arabic ADJECTIVE /ˈæ.rə.bɪk/ having to do with Arabs or Arabia.

Arabic numerals NOUN /ˈæ.rə.bɪk ˈnum.rəlz/ numerals that use the digits 0, 1, 2, 3, 4, 5, 6, 7, 8, 9. Example: 23.5. Synonym: *Hindu-Arabic numerals*. See also *decimal numeration* (p 34).

arbitrary ADJECTIVE /ˈar.bɪˌtrɛr.i/ any value may be chosen, without restriction. Example: an arbitrary integer.

arc NOUN /ark/
1) a smooth, unbroken curve joining two points; a finite curve. See also *circular arc* (p 21).
2) of a chord, the smallest arc of the circle that intersects the chord.

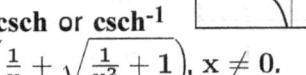

arc- PREFIX /ark/ an inverse trigonometric function or an inverse hyperbolic function. Example: the arcsine function is the inverse of the sine function.

arccos ABBREVIATION arccosine.

arccosecant NOUN /ar.koʊˈsi.kænt/ an angle that has a cosecant equal to a given value. Notation: **acsc** or $\csc^{-1}$. Math definition: $\theta = \csc^{-1} x$ if and only if $x = \csc \theta$, $x \leq -1$ or $x \geq 1$, $-90° \leq \theta < 0°$ or $0° < \theta \leq 90°$, $-\frac{1}{2}\pi \leq \theta < 0$ or $0 < \theta \leq \frac{1}{2}\pi$.

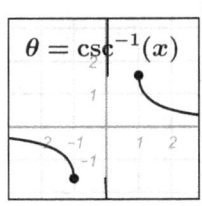

arccosine NOUN /arˈkoʊ.saɪn/ an angle that has a cosine equal to a given value. Notation: **acos** or $\cos^{-1}$. Math definition: $\theta = \cos^{-1} x$ if and only if $x = \cos \theta$, $-1 \leq x \leq 1$, $0° \leq \theta \leq 180°$,

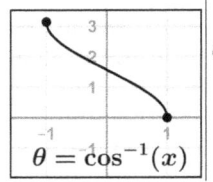

$0 \leq \theta \leq \pi$.

arccot ABBREVIATION arccotangent.

arccotangent NOUN /ar.koʊˈtæn.dʒənt/ an angle that has a cotangent equal to a given value. Notation: **acot** or $\cot^{-1}$. Math definition: $\theta = \cot^{-1} x$ if and only if $x = \cot \theta$, $x \in \mathbb{R}$, $0° < \theta < 180°$, $0 < \theta < \pi$.

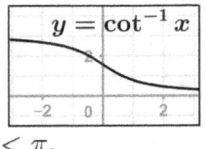

arccsc ABBREVIATION arccosecant.

Archimedean solid NOUN /ˌar.kəˈmi.di.ən ˈsɒ.lɪd/ one of 13 possible polyhedra whose faces are regular polygons. Synonym: *semi-regular solid*.

Archimedes' axiom NOUN /ˌar.kəˈmi.diz ˈæk.si.əm/ see *Axiom of Archimedes* (p 15).

Archimedes of Syracuse PERSON /ˌar.kəˈmi.diz ʌv ˈsɪr.əˌkjuz/ (287 BCE—212 BCE) an inventor and geometer after whom the Archimedean solids and the axiom of Archimedes are named.

arc hyperbolic cosecant NOUN /ark ˌhaɪ.pərˈbɒl.ɪk koʊˈsi.kænt/ an angle that has a hyperbolic cosecant equal to a given value. Notation: **acsch** or csch^{-1}. Formula: $\text{acsch } x = \ln\left(\frac{1}{x} + \sqrt{\frac{1}{x^2} + 1}\right)$, $x \neq 0$. Inverse: *hyperbolic cosecant*.

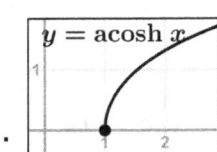

arc hyperbolic cosine NOUN /ark ˌhaɪ.pərˈbɒl.ɪk ˈkoʊ.saɪn/ an angle that has a hyperbolic cosine equal to a given value. Notation: **acosh** or $\cosh^{-1}$. Formula: $\text{acosh} = \ln\left(x + \sqrt{x^2 - 1}\right)$, $x \geq 1$. Inverse: *hyperbolic cosine*.

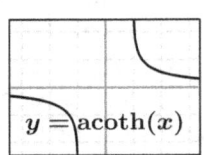

arc hyperbolic cotangent NOUN /ark ˌhaɪ.pərˈbɒl.ɪk ˈkoʊˌtæn.dʒənt/ an angle that has a hyperbolic cotangent equal to a given value. Notation: **acoth** or $\coth^{-1}$. Formula: $\text{acoth } x = \frac{1}{2}\ln\left(\frac{x+1}{x-1}\right)$, $x < -1$ or $x > 1$. Inverse: *hyperbolic cotangent*.

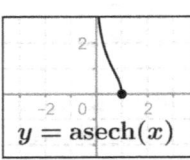

arc hyperbolic secant NOUN /ark ˌhaɪ.pərˈbɒl.ɪk ˈsi.kænt/ an angle that has a hyperbolic secant equal to a given value. Notation: **asech** or sech^{-1}. Formula: $\text{asech } x = \ln\left(\frac{1}{x} + \sqrt{\frac{1}{x^2} - 1}\right)$, $0 < x \leq 1$. Inverse: *hyperbolic secant*.

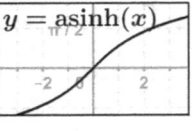

arc hyperbolic sine NOUN /ark ˌhaɪ.pərˈbɒl.ɪk saɪn/ an angle that has a hyperbolic sine equal to a given value. Notation: **asinh** or $\sinh^{-1}$. Formula: $\text{asinh } x = \ln\left(x + \sqrt{x^2 + 1}\right)$, $x \in \mathbb{R}$. Inverse: *hyperbolic sine*.

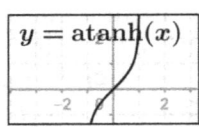

arc hyperbolic tangent NOUN /ark ˌhaɪ.pərˈbɒl.ɪk ˈtæn.dʒənt/ an angle that has a hyperbolic tangent equal to a given value. Notation: **atanh** or $\tan^{-1}$. Formula: $\text{atanh } x = \frac{1}{2}\ln\left(\frac{1+x}{1-x}\right)$, $-1 < x < 1$. Inverse: *hyperbolic tangent*.

arc length NOUN /ark lɛŋθ/ the linear length of an arc as if measured along the edge of the curve. Formula: (circular arcs) $l = r\theta$ where r is the

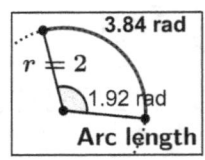

radius of the circle and θ is the subtended angle in radians. Math definition: (curves) if f' is continuous on $[a, b]$, then the length of the curve $y = f(x)$, $a \leq x \leq b$ is $L = \int_a^b \sqrt{1 + [f'(x)]^2} dx$.

arc minute NOUN /ark ˈmɪ.nɪt/ see minute, definition 2, (p 75).

arc of a chord NOUN /ark ʌv ə kɔrd/ an arc with the same endpoints as a given chord.

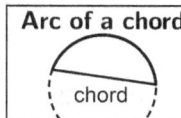

arcosh ABBREVIATION arc hyperbolic cosine.

arcoth ABBREVIATION arc hyperbolic cotangent.

arcsch ABBREVIATION arc hyperbolic cosecant.

arcsec ABBREVIATION arcsecant.

arcsecant NOUN /ark ˈsi.kənt/ an angle that has a secant equal to a given value. Notation: **asec** or **sec^{-1}**. Math definition: $\theta = \sec^{-1} x$ if and only if $x = \sec\theta$, $x \leq -1$ or $1 \leq x$.

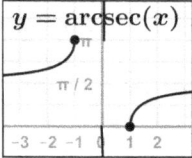

arc second NOUN /ark ˈsɛk.ənd/ see second, definition 2, (p 102).

arcsin ABBREVIATION arcsine.

arcsine NOUN /ˈark.saɪn/ an angle that has a sine equal to a given value. Notation: **asin** or **sin^{-1}**. Math definition: $\theta = \sin^{-1} x$ if and only if $x = \sin\theta$, $-1 \leq x \leq 1$.

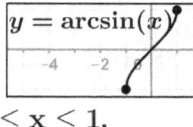

arctan ABBREVIATION arctangent.

arctangent NOUN /ark ˈtæn.dʒənt/ an angle that has a tangent equal to a given value. Notation: **atan** or **tan^{-1}**. Math definition: $\theta = \tan^{-1} x$ if and only if $x = \tan\theta$, $x \in \mathbb{R}$.

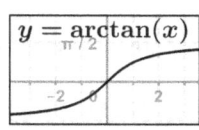

area NOUN /ˈɛər.i.ə/
1) the number of square units contained in a 2-dimensional object.
2) the measure of space in a 2-dimensional figure; the measure of a surface of a 3-dimensional figure. See also surface area (p 111). See also Units of Measure of Area (p 136).

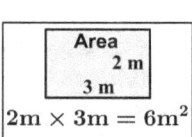

area between curves NOUN /ˈɛər.i.ə bɪˈtwin kɜrvs/ the area between two curves. Formula: $A = \int_a^b |f(x) - g(x)| dx$.

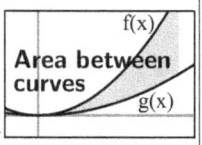

area model of multiplication NOUN /ˈɛər.i.ə ˈmɒ.dl ʌv ˌmʌl.tə.plɪˈkeɪ.ʃən/ a method of multiplying using rectangles to represent the two integers being multiplied.

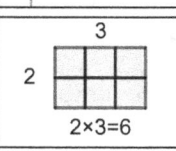

area problem NOUN /ˈɛər.i.ə ˈprɒb.ləm/ the problem of finding the area under a curve $f(x)$ on the interval $[a, b]$ where, for all values of x in $[a, b]$, $f(x) \geq 0$.

area under a curve NOUN /ˈɛər.i.ə ˈʌn.dər ə kɜrv/ the area under a curve $f(x)$ on interval $[a, b]$ where, for all values of x in $[a, b]$, $f(x) \geq 0$. Formula: $\lim_{n \to \infty} \sum_{i=1}^{n} f(u_i) \Delta x = \int_a^b f(x) dx$. Synonym: area under a graph.

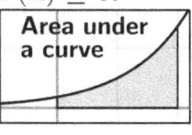

area under a graph NOUN /ˈɛər.i.ə ˈʌn.dər ə græf/ see area under a curve (p 13).

Argand diagram NOUN /arˈgand ˈdaɪ.əˌɡræm/ see complex plane (p 25).

Argand plane NOUN /arˈgand pleɪn/ see complex plane (p 25).

argument NOUN /ˈar.gjə.mənt/
1) an independent variable passed to a function. Example: x in $f(x)$.
2) a justification given in a proof. See also logical argument (p 70).
3) (complex number) the angle between the positive real axis and the ray passing through the origin and a complex number.
4) (vector) the angle between a reference axis and the vector.

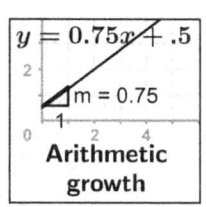

arithmetic
1) NOUN /əˈrɪθ.mə.tɪk/ addition, subtraction, multiplication, division, and the taking of roots. Synonym: computation (p 26).
2) ADJECTIVE /ˌær.ɪθˈmɛt.ɪk/ having to do with addition, subtraction, multiplication, division, and the taking of roots.

arithmetic average NOUN /ˌær.ɪθˈmɛt.ɪk ˈæ.vrɪdʒ/ see arithmetic mean (p 13).

arithmetic fact NOUN /əˈrɪθ.mə.tɪk fækt/ an addition, subtraction, multiplication, or division operation on two whole numbers and the correct answer. Example: $1 + 3 = 4$. See also fact family (p 49).

arithmetic growth NOUN /ˌær.ɪθˈmɛt.ɪk ɡroʊθ/ growth that happens at a constant rate each time period. Formula: $y = ax + b$ where b is the initial value and a is the growth rate per time period. Synonyms: linear growth (p 69), constant growth (p 28).

arithmetic mean NOUN /ˌær.ɪθˈmɛt.ɪk min/ the sum of a set of numbers divided by the number of elements in the set. Formula: for the set $A = \{a_1, a_2, \cdots, a_n\}$, $\overline{A} = \frac{a_1 + a_2 + \ldots + a_n}{n}$. Example: mean of $\{1, 2, 4, 8\}$ is $\frac{1 + 2 + 4 + 8}{4} = \frac{15}{4} = 3\frac{3}{4}$. Notation: $\overline{X}, \overline{A}$. Synonym: arithmetic average.

arithmetic precision NOUN /ˌær.ɪθˈmɛt.ɪk prɪˈsɪ.ʒən/ the number of digits that are accurate. Example: if, given the number 32.567325, the arithmetic precision is 4, only the first four digits, 32.56, are accurate.

arithmetic progression NOUN /ˌær.ɪθˈmɛt.ɪk prəˈɡrɛ.ʃən/ a sequence of numbers with a common difference. To get the next number in the sequence, add the common difference to the previous number. Formula: for the kth term: $a_k = a_0 + dk$ where a_0 is the value of the first term, d is the common difference. Example: $1, 3, 5, 7, 9, \ldots$. Synonym: arithmetic sequence.

arithmetic sequence NOUN /ˌær.ɪθˈmɛt.ɪk ˈsi.kwəns/ see arithmetic progression (p 13).

arithmetic series NOUN /ˌær.ɪθˈmɛt.ɪk ˈsɪər.iz/ the sum of a finite arithmetic sequence. Formula: $s_n = \frac{1}{2} n (a_1 + a_n)$ where n is the number of terms, a_1 is the first term and a_n is the last term. Plural: arithmetic series.

arm NOUN /arm/ one ray that defines an angle. Synonym: leg (p 68).

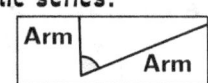

3rd Dyslexic's Edition

arrange VERB /əˈreɪndʒ/ to place in a particular order.

arrangement NOUN /əˈreɪndʒ.mənt/ a particular ordering of objects.

array NOUN /əˈreɪ/ an arrangement of objects in rows and columns. Synonym: *matrix* (p 72).

$\begin{matrix} 2 & -1 & 3 & 2 \\ 4 & 0 & 2 & 5 \end{matrix}$
Array

arrow SYMBOL /ˈær.oʊ/
1) a vector. Example: $\vec{ab}$.
2) implies. Example: $P \rightarrow Q$
3) ray. Example: $\overrightarrow{AB}$.
4) line. Example: $\overleftrightarrow{AB}$.
5) a directed path in a network graph.
6) maps to.
7) translation. Example: $(a, b) \rightarrow (c, d)$.

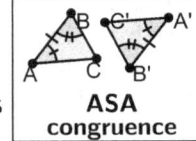
Arrow - maps to

arrow diagram NOUN /ˈær.oʊ ˈdaɪ.ə.græm/ see *flow chart* (p 50).

arsech ABBREVIATION arc hyperbolic cosecant

arsinh ABBREVIATION arc hyperbolic sine

artanh ABBREVIATION arc hyperbolic tangent

ASA congruence NOUN /eɪ es eɪ kənˈgru.əns/ (angle-side-angle congruence) two triangles are congruent if two corresponding angles and the side they contain are congruent. Math definition: Given two triangles $\triangle ABC$ and $\triangle A'B'C'$, $\triangle ABC \cong \triangle A'B'C'$ if and only if $\angle BAC \cong \angle B'A'C'$, $\angle CBA \cong \angle C'B'A'$ and $AB \cong A'B'$.

ASA congruence

ascend VERB /əˈsɛnd/
1) to go up; to increase.
2) to slant upwards.
Antonym: *descend* (p 37).

ascending ADJECTIVE /əˈsɛn.dɪŋ/ going up; increasing. Example: sort in ascending numerical order: 1, 5, 6, 7, 7, 10, 12. Antonym: *descending* (p 37).

asec ABBREVIATION arc secant.

asech ABBREVIATION arc hyperbolic secant.

asin ABBREVIATION arc sine.

asinh ABBREVIATION arc hyperbolic sine.

assert VERB /əˈsɜrt/ to make a statement that one thinks is true.

assertion NOUN /əˈsɜr.ʃən/
1) a statement that is presented as true.
2) a statement that a particular Boolean variable is true or false.

asset NOUN /ˈæ.sɛt/ something which has value. Example: a building is an asset of a company.

associative ADJECTIVE /əˈsoʊ.si.ə.tɪv/ having the same result no matter how the operations are grouped. Math definition: a binary operator * is associative over a set A if and only if, for all $a, b, c \in A$, $a * (b * c) = (a * b) * c$.

Associative Property of Addition NOUN /əˈsoʊ.si.ə.tɪv ˈprɒ.pər.ti ʌv əˈdɪ.ʃən/ addition of real and complex numbers can be grouped in any order without changing the sum. Math definition: $a + (b + c) = (a + b) + c$.

Associative Property of Multiplication NOUN /əˈsoʊ.si.ə.tɪv ˈprɒ.pər.ti ʌv ˌmʌl.tə.plɪˈkeɪ.ʃən/ multiplication of real and complex numbers can be grouped in any order without changing the product. Math definition: $a \cdot (b \cdot c) = (a \cdot b) \cdot c$.

associativity NOUN /əˌsoʊ.si.əˈtɪ.vɪ.ti/ having to do with whether or not an operation is associative.

assumption NOUN /əˈsʌmp.ʃən/
1) a statement that is taken to be true without proof. Synonym: *axiom* (p 15).
2) a criterion. Example: let $\angle a \cong \angle b$.

asymmetric ADJECTIVE /ˌeɪ.səˈmɛ.trɪk/ not symmetric about any line or point. Antonym: *symmetric* (p 111).

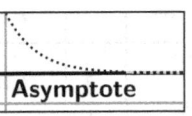
Asymmetric

asymmetry NOUN /ˌeɪ.səˈmɛ.tri/ not symmetric about any line or point. Antonym: *symmetry* (p 112).

asymptote NOUN /ˈæ.sɪmˌtoʊt/ a straight line to which a curve get closer and closer, but never reaches.

Asymptote

atan( ) COMPUTERS the arctangent function in many computer languages.

atan ABBREVIATION arctangent.

atanh ABBREVIATION arc hyperbolic tangent.

at least ADJECTIVE /æt list/ that many or more. Example: at least one.

atto- PREFIX /ˈæ.toʊ/ 10^{-18}. Example: 3 attometer = 3×10^{-18} meters. Abbreviation: a. Synonym: *quintillionth* (p 94).

attracting ADVERB /əˈtrækt.ɪŋ/ points near $\vec{x}^*$ move toward $\vec{x}^*$. Formula: $\vec{x}^*$ is attracting if and only if $\left|\frac{d}{dx}f(x)\right| < 1$. Antonym: *repelling* (p 98).

attribute NOUN /ˈæ.trɪˌbjut/ see *property* (p 93).

augmented matrix NOUN /ˈɒg.mɛn.təd ˈmæ.trɪks/ a square matrix with one column added on the right, usually separated by a line. Plural: augmented matrices.

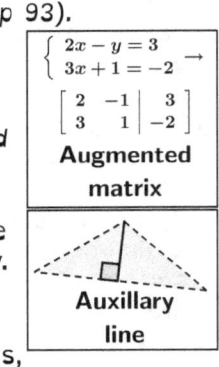
Augmented matrix

auxiliary line NOUN /ɒgˈzɪl.jə.ri laɪn/ a line or line segment added to a figure to illustrate a relationship or property. Synonym: *helping line*.

Auxillary line

average /ˈæ.vrɪdʒ/
1) NOUN the center of a set of numbers, usually the arithmetic mean (p 13).
2) VERB to take the average of a set of numbers.
3) ADJECTIVE having to do with a center of a set, especially an arithmetic mean.

average absolute deviation NOUN /ˈæ.vrɪdʒ æb.səˈlut ˌdi.viˈeɪ.ʃən/ the arithmetic mean of the absolute deviations of a dataset. Formula: $D = \frac{|d_1| + |d_2| + \ldots + |d_n|}{n}$ where $d_1, d_2, \ldots$ are the deviations of each data item, and n is the total number of data items. Synonyms: *mean absolute deviation, mean absolute residual*. See also *absolute deviation* (p 7).

average expected payoff NOUN /ˈæ.vrɪdʒ ɛkˈspɛkt.əd ˈpeɪ.ɒf/ the amount one can expect to win on average from a gambling bet. Synonym: *expected value* (p 47).

average rate of change NOUN /ˈæ.vrɪdʒ reɪt ʌv tʃeɪndʒ/
1) the arithmetic mean of the amounts of change from one period to another.
2) between two points on a curve, the

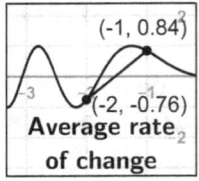
Average rate of change

rise over the run. *Formula:* average rate of change = $\frac{\Delta y}{\Delta x} = \frac{f(b)-f(a)}{b-a}$, $a \neq b$ where **a** and **b** are the x-values between which to find the average change. *Synonym:* slope (p 106) for linear functions.

axial ADJECTIVE /ˈæk.si.əl/ having to do with an axis. *Example:* axial symmetry.

axial plane NOUN /ˈæk.si.əl pleɪn/ a plane in a 3-dimensional coordinate system that contains two of the three axes. The axial plane containing the x-axis and the y-axis is called the x-y axial plane.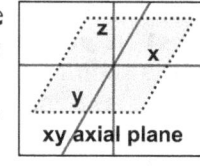

axial symmetry NOUN /ˈæk.si.əl ˈsɪ.mɪ.tri/ see line symmetry (p 69).

axiom NOUN /ˈæk.si.əm/ a statement that is taken to be true without proof. *Synonyms:* postulate, assumption (p 14).

axiomatic ADJECTIVE /ˌæk.si.əˈmæt.ɪk/ based on axioms. *Example:* axiomatic system.

axiomatic system NOUN /ˌæk.si.əˈmæt.ɪk ˈsɪs.təm/ a logical system that is based on axioms, primitives, definitions, plus theories proved from those bases. *Example:* Euclidean geometry.

Axiom of Archimedes NOUN /ˈæk.si.əm ʌv ˌɑr.kəˈmi.diz/ there is always at least one more number. *Math definition:* For every real number x, there exists a real number n such that n > x. *Synonym:* Archimedes' Axiom.

Axiom of Choice NOUN /ˈæk.si.əm ʌv tʃɔɪs/ a set can be created from an infinite collection of infinite sets.

Axiom of Extension NOUN /ˈæk.si.əm ʌv ɪkˈstɛn.ʃən/ set **A** equals set **B** if and only if they contain exactly the same elements.

Axiom of Parallels NOUN /ˈæk.si.əm ʌv ˈpær.əˌlɛlz/ see Parallel Postulate (p 85).

axis NOUN /ˈæk.sɪs/
1) a line, possibly with tick marks, that is used to define a metric space. *Example:* x-axis.
2) a line that is used as a reference. *Example:* axis of reflection.
3) a line about which a geometric object is symmetric. *Example:* axis of symmetry. *Plural:* **axes** /ˈæk.siz/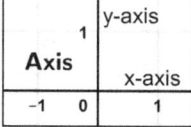

axis of abscissas NOUN /ˈæk.sɪs ʌv æbˈsɪs.əz/ see x-axis (p 122).

axis of an ellipse NOUN /ˈæk.sɪs ʌv ən ɪˈlɪps/ one of two line segments about which an ellipse is symmetric. *Plural:* **axes of an ellipse**.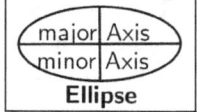

axis of ordinates NOUN /ˈæk.sɪs ʌv ˈɔr.dəˌnɪts/ see y-axis (p 123).

axis of reflection NOUN /ˈæk.sɪs ʌv rɪˈflɛk.ʃən/ a line across which an object is reflected. *Plural:* **axes of reflection**. *Synonym:* line of reflection.

axis of rotation NOUN /ˈæk.sɪs ʌv roʊˈteɪ.ʃən/ a line about which an object rotates. *Example:* the Earth rotates around an imaginary axis passing through the North Pole and the South Pole. *Plural:* **axes of rotation**.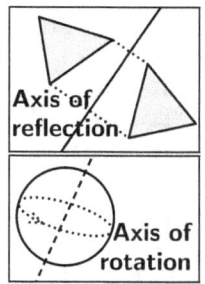

axis of symmetry NOUN /ˈæk.sɪs ʌv ˈsɪ.mɪ.tri/ see line of symmetry (p 69). *Plural:* **axes of symmetry**.

azimuth NOUN /ˈæ.zɪ.məθ/ the angle from north or south of the equator an object in the sky would be if it were on the horizon. See also zenith (p 123).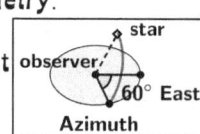

B

back substitution NOUN /bæk ˌsʌb.stɪˈtu.ʃən/ the process of substituting known values back into an equation to find the values of other unknowns. *Example:* $3x + y = 1$, $y = 2 \rightarrow 3x + 2 = 1 \rightarrow 3x = -1 \rightarrow x = -\frac{1}{3}$.

back-to-back stem and leaf plot NOUN /bæk tu bæk stɛm ənd lif plɒt/ two leaf plots placed on opposite sides of a stem so one can be compared with the other. See also stemplot (p 109).

1		1
36	2	5
124788	3	389
379	4	2458
6	5	34

Back to back stem and leaf plot

backwards ADVERB /ˈbæk.wərdz/ in the opposite direction from normal.

balance /ˈbæ.ləns/
1) NOUN a state where two things are equal in some way; a state of equilibrium.
2) NOUN a device for comparing the weights of two objects. *Synonym:* beam balance (p 16).
3) NOUN the current amount in an account. *Example:* the balance in a checking account.
4) VERB to adjust so that both sides are even.
5) VERB (equation) to keep both sides equal by adding, subtracting or multiplying both sides of the equation by the same amount, or by dividing both sides of the equation by the same nonzero amount. *Example:* $a + 5 = 6 \rightarrow a + 5 - 5 = 6 - 5 \rightarrow a = 1$.

bar NOUN /bɑr/
1) a rectangular figure used to represent data in a bar graph.
2) a line segment over or under text. *Example:* $3.\overline{6} = 3.666666\cdots$. *Synonyms:* overbar (p 85), vinculum (p 122).

bar chart NOUN /bɑr tʃɑrt/ a graph that uses parallel lines or rectangles to represent data. *Synonym:* bar graph.

bar graph NOUN /bɑr græf/ see bar chart (p 15).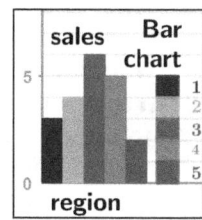

bar notation NOUN /bɑr noʊˈteɪ.ʃən/ a line segment over a part of a real number indicating a repeating decimal. *Example:* $3.\overline{6} = 3.666666\cdots$.

base /beɪs/
1) NOUN (exponents and logarithms) a number or variable being raised to a power. The bases in the following expressions are '**b**': b^e, $\log_b x$.
2) NOUN (number systems) the number of different digits that can be used to make a numeral. The decimal number system is base 10. *Synonym:* radix.
3) NOUN (geometric figures) the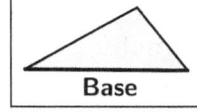

3rd Dyslexic's Edition 15

'bottom' and/or 'top' of a geometric figure.
4) ADJECTIVE (time) a period of time from which all other periods of time are relative, usually the first period of time in which measurements are made. Example: base year.
5) VERB to be the basis for.

base angle NOUN /beɪs ˈæŋ.gəl/ one of two angles that are adjacent to the base of a 2-dimensional figure.

Base Angle Congruence Theorem NOUN /beɪs ˈæŋ.gəl kənˈgru.əns ˈθi.ə.rəm/ if two angles of a triangle are equal, the sides opposite the equal angles are also equal; ∠a ≅ ∠b if and only if a ≅ b.

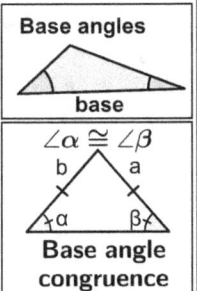

base area NOUN /beɪs ˈɛər.i.ə/ the area of the base of a geometric solid.

base change NOUN /beɪs tʃeɪndʒ/ see change of base formula (p 20).

base edge NOUN /beɪs ɛdʒ/ an edge of a polyhedron that is adjacent to a base.

base period NOUN /beɪs ˈpɪər.i.əd/ a period from which indexed periods are calculated. The first period of a study.

Base Period Example	
Period	Month
Base	Jan. 2002
1	Feb. 2002
2	Mar. 2002

base surface area NOUN /beɪs ˈsɜr.fɪs ˈɛər.i.ə/ see base area (p 16).

base ten block NOUN /beɪs tɛn blɑk/ a set of blocks used to represent base 10 operations numbers and operations.

base unit NOUN /beɪs ˈju.nɪt/ see fundamental unit (p 52).

base year NOUN /beɪs jɪər/ see base period (p 16).

basic ADJECTIVE /ˈbeɪ.sɪk/ the property of being a base on which other objects or methods are built.

basic fact NOUN /ˈbeɪ.sɪk fækt/ an addition, subtraction, multiplication or division problem of one or two digits.

basis NOUN /ˈbeɪ.sɪs/ something on which other things are based.

basis vectors NOUN /ˈbeɪ.sɪs ˈvɛk.tərz/ a set of mutually perpendicular vectors where any vector in a vector space can be written as a linear combination of the basis vectors.

beam balance NOUN /bim ˈbæ.ləns/ a device with a bar from which objects are placed to compare their weights. Synonym: balance (p 15).

bearing NOUN /ˈbɛər.ɪŋ/ the direction to one object from another, as measured from true north or true south.

before PREPOSITION /bɪˈfor/
1) earlier in order or time.
2) coming previous to.
Antonym: after (p 8).

bell curve NOUN /bɛl kɜrv/ see normal curve (p 80).

bell shaped curve NOUN /bɛl ʃeɪpt kɜrv/ see normal curve (p 80).

benchmark NOUN /ˈbɛntʃ.mɑrk/ something that is a standard of comparison.

benchmark number NOUN /ˈbɛntʃ.mɑrk ˈnʌm.bər/ a number that is used as a standard of comparison in studies and tests.

Bernoulli trial NOUN /bərˈnu.li ˈtraɪ.l/ one instance of a probability experiment where the output is random and can be one of two possibilities. Example: the flip of a coin can be heads or tails.

best fit NOUN /bɛst fɪt/ comes the closest to the values in a dataset.

best fit curve NOUN /bɛst fɪt kɜrv/ a curve that comes the closest to a set of data points. Best fit curves can be polynomial or trigonometric.

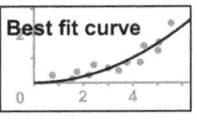

best fit line NOUN /bɛst fɪt laɪn/ a line that comes the closest to a set of data points.

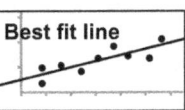

beta NOUN /ˈbeɪ.tə/ (American English) or /ˈbi.tə/ (British English) the Greek letter β, often used to represent an angle. See also Greek Letters (p 135).

between PREPOSITION /bɪˈtwin/ having something on both sides. Math definition: given three points a, b, and c, point c is between points a and b if and only if $ac + cb = ab$. Synonym: Segment Addition Postulate (p 103).

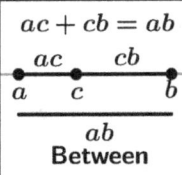

Bézier curve NOUN /beɪˈzyeɪ kɜrv/ see spline (p 108).

Bhāskara II PERSON /bɑsˈkɛr.ʌ/ (c. 1114—1185) an Indian mathematician and astronomer, known for an ingenious geometric proof of the Pythagorean theorem.

bi- PREFIX /baɪ/ two. Example: binary, having two parts.

bias NOUN /ˈbaɪ.əs/ a systematic distortion of a sample.

biased ADJECTIVE /ˈbaɪ.əst/ having, showing or causing a distortion.

biased question NOUN /ˈbaɪ.əst ˈkwɛs.tʃən/ a question that influences the answer one way or another. Example: "Have you stopped hitting your brother yet?"

biased sample NOUN /ˈbaɪ.əst ˈsæm.pəl/ a sample that is distorted by a non-scientific selection of the sample.

biconditional ADJECTIVE /ˌbaɪ.kənˈdɪ.ʃə.nl/ two propositions are either both true or both false. Notation: **P if and only if Q**, $P \Leftrightarrow Q$, or $P \equiv Q$. Synonym: if and only if.

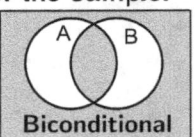

bifurcate VERB /ˈbaɪ.fərˌkeɪt/ to divide into two branches.

bifurcation NOUN /ˈbaɪ.fərˌkeɪ.ʃən/ a dividing into two branches.

bijection NOUN /baɪˈdʒɛk.ʃən/ a relation between sets where each member of two sets is related to exactly one member of the other set. Synonyms: one-to-one correspondence (p 82), one-to-one function (p 83).

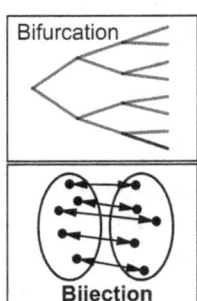

bilateral ADJECTIVE /baɪˈlæ.tər.l/ having two sides.

bilateral symmetry NOUN /baɪˈlæ.tər.l ˈsɪ.mɪ.tri/ symmetry about a line or plane that bisects the figure. Synonym: line symmetry (p 69).

billion NOUN /ˈbɪl.jən/ the number $10^9 = 1,000,000,000$. Synonym: giga-. Important: The term 'billion' is not used the same in all countries or in all languages. In the

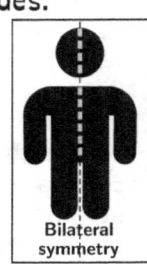

short scale, **1 billion** = 10^9. Canada, United Kingdom and the United States use the short scale. In the long scale, **1 billion** = 10^{12}.

billionth ADJECTIVE, NOUN /'bɪl.jənθ/ 10^{-9} = **0.000 000 001**. Synonym: **nano-** (p 78).

bimodal distribution NOUN /ˌbaɪˈmoʊ.dəl ˌdɪs.trəˈbju.ʃən/ a distribution of statistical data that has two 'humps'.

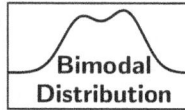

binary ADJECTIVE /'baɪ.nɛr.i/
1) having two parts. Example: binary operation.
2) (sets) having exactly two elements. Example: $\{0, 1\}$.
3) having 2 as a base. Example: binary number.

binary digit NOUN /'baɪ.nɛr.i 'dɪ.dʒɪt/ one of two digits, 0 or 1.

binary logarithm NOUN /'baɪ.nɛr.i 'lɒ.gə.rɪ.ðəm/ a logarithm in base 2. Example: $\log_2 14 \approx 3.81$.

binary notation NOUN /'baɪ.nɛr.i noʊˈteɪ.ʃən/ see **binary numeral** (p 17).

binary number NOUN /'baɪ.nɛr.i 'nʌm.bər/ see **binary numeral** (p 17).

binary numeral NOUN /'baɪ.nɛr.i 'nu.mər.əl/ a number written in a base 2 numeration system which uses the binary digits **0** and **1** as the only digits. Example: $101_2 = 1 \times 2^2 + 0 \times 2^1 + 1 = 4 + 0 + 1 = 5_{10}$.

binary operation NOUN /'baɪ.nɛr.i ˌɒp.əˈreɪ.ʃən/ an operation that takes two operands. Example: In $a + b$ the binary operation is addition.

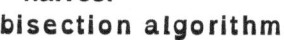

binary operator NOUN /'baɪ.nɛr.i ˌɒp.əˈreɪ.tər/ an operator that takes two operands as arguments. Example: $a + b$ where '+' is a binary operator, **a** and **b** are the two operands.

binomial /baɪˈnoʊ.mi.əl/
1) NOUN a polynomial with exactly two terms. Example: $m + n$.
2) ADJECTIVE an outcome space where there are exactly two possible outcomes.

binomial coefficient NOUN /baɪˈnoʊ.mi.əl ˌkoʊ.əˈfɪ.ʃənt/ a coefficient of a term of a polynomial created by raising a binomial to a positive integer power. Example: For $(a + b)^3 = a^3 + 3a^2b + 3ab^2 + b^3$, the binomial coefficients are **1, 3, 3, 1**, respectively.

binomial distribution NOUN /baɪˈnoʊ.mi.əl ˌdɪs.trəˈbju.ʃən/ the probability distribution of a binomial experiment. Formula: The probability of **k** successes in **n** trials where the probability of success in each trial is **p**: $P(n, k) = \binom{n}{k} p^{n-k} (1-p)^k$.

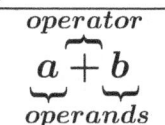

binomial expansion NOUN /baɪˈnoʊ.mi.əl ɪkˈspæn.ʃən/ an expansion of a binomial using the Binomial Theorem. Example: $(a + b)^3 = a^3 + 3a^2b + 3ab^2 + b^3$.

binomial experiment NOUN /baɪˈnoʊ.mi.əl ɪkˈspɛr.ə.mənt/ an experiment in probability where the outcome will be one of exactly two possibilities. Example: flipping a coin has two possible outcomes: heads or tails.

binomial series NOUN /baɪˈnoʊ.mi.əl ˈsɪər.iz/ the series $\sum_{k=0}^{\infty} \binom{a}{k} x^k = 1 + ax + \frac{a(a-1)}{2!}x^2 + \frac{a(a-1)(a-2)}{3!}x^3 + \ldots$

Binomial Theorem NOUN /baɪˈnoʊ.mi.əl ˈθi.ə.rəm/ a rule for expanding $(a + b)^n$ which predicts the coefficient of a term of a binomial raised to an integer power. Math definition: $(a+b)^n = \sum_{k=0}^{n} \binom{n}{k} a^{n-k} b^k = \binom{n}{0}a^n + \binom{n}{1}a^{n-1}b^1 + \binom{n}{2}a^{n-2}b^2 + \ldots + \binom{n}{n-1}a^1 b^{n-1} + \binom{n}{n}b^n$ where $\binom{n}{m} = \frac{n!}{(n-m)!m!}$. See also **Pascal's triangle** (p 86).

biquadratic NOUN /ˌbaɪ.kwɒˈdræ.tɪk/ see **quartic** (p 94).

birectangular ADJECTIVE /ˌbaɪ.rɛkˈtæŋ.gjə.lər/ (spherical geometry) having two right angles.

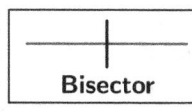

bisect VERB /baɪˈsɛkt/ to cut into two equal halves.

bisection algorithm NOUN /baɪˈsɛk.ʃən ˈæl.gəˌrɪð.əm/ a method for approximating a root of an equation by bisecting an interval, then selecting the subinterval which contains the root.

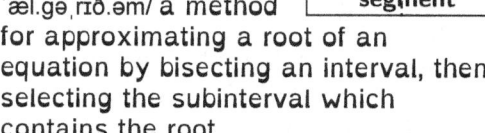

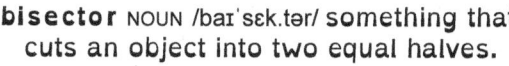

bisector NOUN /baɪˈsɛk.tər/ something that cuts an object into two equal halves.

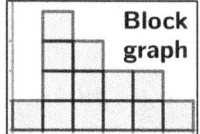

bit NOUN /bɪt/ one of the digits **0** or **1** in a binary numeral.

bivariate ADJECTIVE /baɪˈvɛər.i.eɪt/ having to do with two variables.

bivariate data NOUN /baɪˈvɛər.i.eɪt ˈdeɪ.tə/ data that has two variables.

block graph NOUN /blɒk græf/ a graph made up of squares or cubes where each square or cube represents one item.

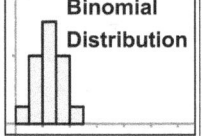

Boolean ADJECTIVE /ˈbu.li.ən/ having to do with Boolean algebra.

Boolean algebra NOUN /ˈbu.li.ən ˈæl.dʒə.brə/ an algebra where each variable can take only one of two values and that has the operations **AND**, **OR** and **NOT**. The two values are usually **0** and **1**, **false** and **true**, or **off** and **on**.

Boolean function NOUN /ˈbu.li.ən ˈfʌŋk.ʃən/ a function that takes one or more Boolean values and returns a Boolean value. Example: **AND(P, Q)** means **P** and **Q**.

Boolean operation table NOUN /ˈbu.li.ən ˌɒ.pəˈreɪ.ʃən ˈteɪ.bəl/ see **truth table** (p 117).

Boolean operator NOUN /ˈbu.li.ən ˌɒ.pəˈreɪ.tər/
1) the operators **AND** ($\wedge$), **OR** ($\vee$), and **NOT** ($\neg$) and any operator that can be written as a combination of **AND**, **OR**, and **NOT**.
2) an operator that takes one or more Boolean values and returns a Boolean value.

Boolean value NOUN /ˈbu.li.ən ˈvæl.ju/ either **0** or **1**, or **false** or **true**. In some computer languages Boolean values are integers where **0** represents false, and all nonzero integers represent true.

Boole, George PERSON /bul dʒɔrdʒ/ (1815—1864) an English mathematician most noted for discovering and describing Boolean logic.

borrow VERB /ˈbɒ.roʊ/ (obsolete) see regroup (p 98).

bound NOUN /baʊnd/
1) a number that is either greater than every number in a set or less than every number in a set. Synonyms: *supremum* (p 111), *infimum* (p 62), *upper bound* (p 120), *lower bound* (p 71), *least upper bound* (p 68), *greatest lower bound* (p 55).
2) see *boundary* (p 18).

boundary NOUN /ˈbaʊn.dri/ all points that are between the interior points and the exterior points of a geometric figure. Synonyms: *edge* (2-d); *face* (3-d); *surface* (3-d); *frontier*.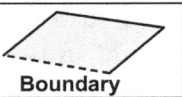

boundary point NOUN /ˈbaʊn.dri pɔɪnt/ a point on the boundary of a figure or a set. A boundary point may or may not be a member of the set. Math definition: A point is a boundary point of a set if and only if every neighborhood of the point contains at least one point in the set and at least one point not in the set.

bounded ADJECTIVE /ˈbaʊn.dɪd/ not infinite in extent; having a boundary in all directions; having an end. Synonym: *finite* (p 50). Antonym: *unbounded* (p 118).

bounded function NOUN /ˈbaʊn.dɪd ˈfʌŋk.ʃən/ a function whose range has an upper and a lower bound.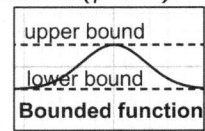

bounded sequence NOUN /ˈbaʊn.dɪd ˈsi.kwəns/ a sequence that has an upper bound and a lower bound. Example: $\{-2, -1, 0, 1, 2\}$.

box NOUN /bɒks/
1) a rectangle used to enclose a figure.
2) a rectangle used to represent data.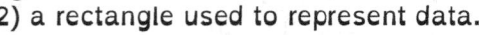

box and whisker plot NOUN /bɒks ənd ˈhwɪs.kər plɒt/ a way to graph data that shows the distribution of the data. The 1st and 4th quartiles are drawn as a line segment, the 2nd and 3rd quartiles are drawn as boxes. Synonym: *boxplot*.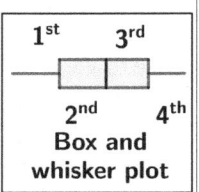

boxplot NOUN /bɒks.plɒt/ see *box and whisker plot* (p 18).

brace NOUN /breɪs/ one of a pair of marks '{}' used to group operations and to define sets. Synonym: *curly brace, grouping symbol*.

brachistochrone NOUN /brəˈkɪs.təˌkroʊn/ a downward hanging cycloid where an object sliding down the curve will reach the bottom faster than from any point on the curve quicker than any other curve. Synonym: *curve of quickest descent*. See also *cycloid* (p 33). Formula: $x = a(\theta - \sin\theta) + x_0$, $y = -a(1 - \cos\theta) + y_0$.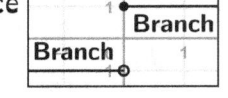

bracket NOUN /ˈbræ.kɪt/ one of a pair of marks '[ ]' used to group operations and to mark the beginning and end of matrices. Synonyms: *square brace, grouping symbol*.

branch NOUN /brɑntʃ/ each individual piece of a disconnected graph.

breadth NOUN /brɛdθ/ see *width* (p 122).

budget /ˈbʌ.dʒɪt/
1) VERB to estimate expected income and expenses for a given period of time.
2) NOUN an estimate of expected income and expenses for a given period of time.

budgeting ADJECTIVE /ˈbʌ.dʒɪ.tɪŋ/ the process of estimating income and expenses for a future period of time.

by inspection NOUN /baɪ ɪnˈspɛk.ʃən/ to find the answer to a simple problem simply by looking at it.

byte NOUN /baɪt/ eight bits of ones and zeros, an eight digit number in base 2. Example: 10010111_2.

C

c ABBREVIATION
1) centi-. 10^{-2}. Example: 1 centimeter = 0.01 meters. Synonym: *hundredth*.
2) cup.

C
1) ABBREVIATION degree Celsius (p 35).
2) SYMBOL 100 in Roman numerals.

cal ABBREVIATION *calorie* (p 18).

Cal ABBREVIATION *kilocalorie* (p 66).

calculate VERB /ˈkæl.kjəˌleɪt/ to compute values. Example: calculate the sum of five and seven: $5 + 7 = 12$. Synonym: *compute* (p 26).

calculator NOUN /ˈkæl.kjəˌleɪ.tər/ a device that performs calculations.

calculus NOUN /ˈkæl.kjə.ləs/ a branch of mathematics that deals with integration, differentiation and infinitesimals.

calendar NOUN /ˈkæl.ən.dər/ a table showing dates laid out in rows and columns.

calorie NOUN /ˈkæ.lə.ri/ the amount of energy equal to 4.184 joules. Abbreviation: cal.

Calorie NOUN /ˈkæ.lə.ri/ a kilocalorie (p 66), an amount of energy equal to 4184 joules. Abbreviation: Cal.

cancel VERB /ˈkæn.səl/ to simplify by removing. Synonym: *eliminate* (p 43).

cancellation NOUN /ˈkæn.səl.eɪ.ʃən/ the process of simplifying expressions by removing common factors or by removing sums equal to zero. Examples:
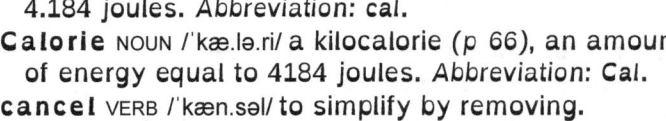

candela NOUN /kænˈdɛ.lə/ an SI unit of measure of the brightness of light; luminous intensity. Abbreviation: cd.

canonical ADJECTIVE /kəˈnɒ.nɪ.kəl/ in simplest or standard form. Example: a canonical equation.

Cantor, Georg Ferdinand Ludwig Philipp PERSON /ˈkæn.tɔr dʒɔrdʒ ˈfɜr.dn ænd ˈlʌd.wɪg ˈfil.ip/ (1845—1918) a Russian mathematician known for proving that the set of rational numbers is countable.

Georg Cantor

Cantor's Axiom NOUN /ˈkæn.tɔrz ˈæk.si.əm/ see Ruler Postulate (p 101).

cap NOUN /kæp/ the symbol ∩ used to show intersection of sets. Notation: $A \cap B$.

capital NOUN /ˈkæp.ɪ.təl/ assets such as money or property.

capacity NOUN /kʌˈpæ.sɪ.ti/ how much a container can hold; a volume.

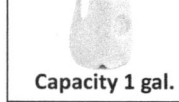
Capacity 1 gal.

cardinal ADJECTIVE /ˈkard.nəl/
1) of an integer, used in counting. Antonym: ordinal (p 84).
2) having to do with the size of a set.

cardinality NOUN /ˌkar.dəˈnæl.ɪ.ti/ the size of a set. For finite sets, the number of members in the set. For infinite sets, one of $\aleph_0, \aleph_1, \aleph_2, \cdots$, where $\aleph_0$ is the cardinality of any set with a one-to-one correspondence with the set of natural numbers.

cardinal number NOUN /ˈkard.nəl ˈnʌm.bər/ the number of elements in a set such as $1, 2, 3, \cdots$ for finite sets, or $\aleph_0, \aleph_1, \aleph_2, \cdots$ for infinite sets.

cardioid NOUN /ˈkar.di.ɔɪd/ a figure that can be drawn by tracing a point on the edge of a circle that is rolling around the outside of another circle of the same size. Equation:
$x = a(2\cos t - \cos 2t)$,
$y = a(2\sin t - \sin 2t)$.

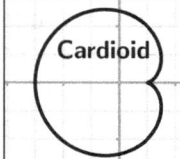
Cardioid

Carroll diagram NOUN /ˈkɛər.əl ˈdaɪ.ə.græm/ a diagram that groups things into yes/no groups.

carry VERB /ˈkɛə.ri/ when adding numbers, to add the upper digits from the sum of a column of digits to the next column. Synonym: regroup (p 98).

Cartesian ADJECTIVE /karˈti.ʒən/
1) having to do with a rectangular coordinate system.
2) attributed to or named after René Descartes.

Cartesian axis NOUN /karˈti.ʒən ˈæk.sɪs/ see x-axis (p 122) and y-axis (p 123).

Cartesian coordinate NOUN /karˈti.ʒən koʊˈɔr.də.nɪt/ see rectangular coordinate (p 96).

Cartesian coordinate system NOUN /karˈti.ʒən koʊˈɔr.də.nɪt ˈsɪs.təm/ see rectangular coordinate system (p 96).

Cartesian geometry NOUN /karˈti.ʒən dʒiˈɒ.mə.tri/ see analytic geometry (p 10).

Cartesian plane NOUN /karˈti.ʒən pleɪn/ see coordinate plane (p 30).

Cartesian product NOUN /karˈti.ʒən ˈprɒ.dʌkt/ a set of ordered pairs made of each and every member of set A paired with each and every member of set B. Notation: $A \times B$, or $A \times A = A^2$. Example: $A = \{a_1, b_2\}$, $B = \{b_1, b_2, b_3\}$. $A \times B = \{(a_1, b_1), (a_1, b_2), (a_1, b_3), (a_2, b_1), (a_2, b_2), (a_2, b_3)\}$.

Cartesian space NOUN /karˈti.ʒən speɪs/ an n-dimensional metric space based on Euclidean geometry.

case NOUN /keɪs/ one of several situations into which a problem can be divided. Example: case 1: $a < b$; case 2: $a = b$; case 3: $a > b$.

casting out nines NOUN /ˈkæ.stɪŋ aʊt naɪnz/ a method of checking the correctness of the sum of a list of numbers.

categorical ADJECTIVE /ˌkæ.tɪˈgɔr.ɪ.kəl/ having to do with a division into categories.

categorical data NOUN /ˌkæ.tɪˈgɔr.ɪ.kəl ˈdeɪ.tə/ (probability and statistics) data which has been divided into categories. Example: data divided into age groupings. Synonym: qualitative data (p 94).

categorical variable NOUN /ˌkæ.tɪˈgɔr.ɪ.kəl ˈvɛər.i.ə.bəl/ a variable that is divided into categories.

category NOUN /ˌkæ.tɪˈgɔr.i/ a distinct class into which data items are divided. Example: age 12-16.

catenary NOUN /ˈkæ.tə.nɛr.i/ (British English) /kəˈti.nə.ri/ the shape a wire or rope makes when hanging from two poles. Equation: $f(x) = a \cosh\left(\frac{x-h}{a}\right) + k$ where **a** affects the steepness of the catenary, **h** moves the catenary left and right and **k** moves the catenary up and down.

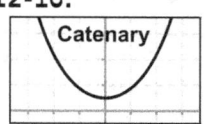
Catenary

Cavalieri, Bonaventura Francesco PERSON /ˌka.vaˈli.ɛr.i boʊn.æv.ənˈtɛrr.ʌ frænˈtʃes.koʊ/ (1598—1647) an Italian mathematician who is known for his work in infinitesimals, including Cavalieri's principle.

Bonaventura Cavalieri

Cavalieri's principle NOUN /ˌka.vaˈli.ɛr.iz ˈprɪn.sə.pəl/ given two solids, if the areas of each cross section and the heights are equal, then the volumes are equal. Example: A stack of pennies. Even if one slides a penny over, the total volume of the stack remains constant.

Cavalieri's Principle

Cayley, Arthur PERSON /ˈkeɪ.li ˈar.θər/ (1821—1895) a British mathematician credited with the invention of matrices.

Arthur Cayley

cd ABBREVIATION candela (p 18).

ceil(), ceiling() COMPUTERS represents the ceiling function in some computer languages.

ceiling NOUN /ˈsil.ɪŋ/ an upper limit.

ceiling function NOUN /ˈsil.ɪŋ ˈfʌŋk.ʃən/ returns the smallest integer greater than or equal to a real number. Notation: $\lceil x \rceil$.

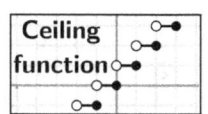
Ceiling function

cell NOUN /sɛl/ a single box in a table containing data.

Celsius NOUN /ˈsɛl.si.əs/ see degree Celsius (p 35).

Celsius, Anders PERSON /ˈsɛl.si.əs ˈan.dərs/ (1701—1744) a Swedish astronomer who invented the Celsius temperature scale.

Anders Celsius

census NOUN /ˈsɛn.səs/ data from an entire population, rather than a sample. Antonym: sample (p 101).

cent NOUN /sɛnt/ an amount of money equal to $\frac{1}{100}$ of a dollar. Notation: ¢. Formula: 1¢ = $0.01. Synonym: penny (p 86).

center NOUN /ˈsɛn.tər/
1) a point that has a symmetric relationship to a geometric figure. See also Centers of Geometric Figures (p 140).
2) an element that has a symmetric relationship to a

set.

centered difference NOUN /'sɛn.tərd 'dɪf.rəns/ a method for approximating the derivative of a function. Formula: $f'(x) \approx \frac{f(x+\Delta x) - f(x-\Delta x)}{2\Delta x}$. Synonym: *finite difference* (p 50).

centi- PREFIX /'sɛn.tə/ $10^{-2} = 0.01$. Abbreviation: c. Example: 4 centimeters = 4×10^{-2} meters = 0.04 meters. Synonym: *hundredth*.

centigrade NOUN /'sɛn.tə.greɪd/ see *degree Celsius* (p 35).

centimeter NOUN /'sɛn.tə.mi.tər/ a unit of measure of distance. Abbreviation: cm. Formulas: 100 cm = 1 meter, 2.54 cm ≈ 1 inch.

central ADJECTIVE /'sɛn.trəl/
1) being at or near a center. Example: central angle.
2) having to do with a center. Example: central tendency.

central angle NOUN /'sɛn.trəl 'æŋ.gəl/
1) (of a circle) an angle inscribed in a circle with the vertex at the center of the circle.
2) (of a regular polygon) the angle between two line segments extending from the center of the polygon to two adjacent vertices.

central box NOUN /'sɛn.trəl bɒks/ a rectangle at the center of a hyperbola with two sides passing through $(a, 0)$ and $(-a, 0)$, and two sides passing through $(0, b)$ and $(0, -b)$.

Central Limit Theorem NOUN /'sɛn.trəl 'lɪ.mɪt 'θi.ə.rəm/ as a dataset grows larger, the probability density for a dataset tends to approach a normal distribution.

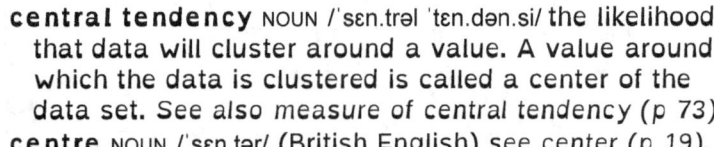

central tendency NOUN /'sɛn.trəl 'tɛn.dən.si/ the likelihood that data will cluster around a value. A value around which the data is clustered is called a center of the data set. See also *measure of central tendency* (p 73).

centre NOUN /'sɛn.tər/ (British English) see *center* (p 19).

centroid NOUN /'sɛn.trɔɪd/
1) the center of area of a 2-dimensional figure.
2) the center of mass of a 3-dimensional figure.
3) the point where the medians of a triangle intersect.
Formula: for a simple n-sided polygon with vertices $(x_1, y_1), (x_2, y_2), \ldots, (x_n, y_n)$, the centroid is $\left(\frac{x_1+x_2+\ldots+x_n}{n}, \frac{y_1+y_2+\ldots+y_n}{n}\right)$. Synonyms: *center of gravity, center of mass*.

century NOUN /'sɛn.tʃər.i/ one hundred years. Formula: 100 years = 1 century.

certain ADJECTIVE /'sɜr.tən/
1) sure to happen. Example: a certain event. Antonym: *impossible* (p 60).
2) a specific item or element. Example: a certain triangle. Antonym: *any* (p 20).

certain event NOUN /'sɜr.tən ɪ'vɛnt/ an event that will always happen. Math definition: e is a certain event if and only if $P(e) = 1$. Antonym: *impossible event* (p 60).

Ceva's Theorem NOUN /'sɛv.ʌz 'θi.ə.rəm/ given a triangle **ABC**, and points **D, E,** and **F** that lie on line segments **AB, BC,** and **CA** respectively, lines **AE, BF** and **DC** are concurrent if and only if $\frac{AD}{DB} \cdot \frac{BE}{EC} \cdot \frac{CF}{FA} = 1$.

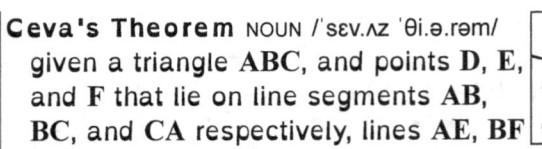

cevian NOUN /'si.vi.ən/ any line passing through a vertex of a triangle and the side opposite the vertex.

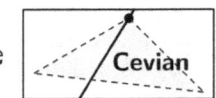

chain NOUN /tʃeɪn/ a group of objects that are linked one to the next to the next and so on.

chain rule NOUN /tʃeɪn rul/
1) (logic) if two propositions each imply a third proposition, then they imply each other. If $P \to Q$ and $Q \to R$ then $P \to R$ Example: A square has four congruent sides. Any quadrilateral with four congruent sides has diagonals that bisect each other. Therefore, a square has diagonals that bisect each other.
2) (calculus) given differentiable functions $f(x)$ and $g(x)$, $\frac{d}{dx}[f(g(x))] = f'(g(x))g'(x)$.

chance NOUN /tʃæns/ the likelihood, probability, or odds that an event will happen.

change /tʃeɪndʒ/
1) NOUN the difference between two objects.
2) NOUN money received back when paying.
3) VERB (with object) to make something different.
4) VERB (without object) to become different in some way.

change of base formula NOUN /tʃeɪndʒ ʌv beɪs 'fɔr.mjə.lə/ a formula used to change the base of a logarithm: $\log_a x = \frac{\log_b x}{\log_b a}$. Example: $\log_{11} 5 = \frac{\log_{10} 5}{\log_{10} 11} \approx \frac{0.6990}{1.041} \approx 0.6712$.

chaos NOUN /'keɪ.ɒs/
1) the tendency of chaotic functions to have a large change in output given a small change in input.
2) the inherent unpredictability of many natural systems.

chaos theory NOUN /'keɪ.ɒs 'θɪər.i/ the study of systems that generate widely differing output from small changes in input.

chaotic ADJECTIVE /keɪ'ɒ.tɪk/ having a tendency to generate widely differing output given small changes in input. Example: weather is a chaotic system.

characteristic NOUN /kɛər.ək.tər.ɪ.stɪk/
1) the whole part of a base 10 logarithm. Example: the characteristic of $\log_{10} 642 \approx 2.80754$ is 2.
2) a graph or other property that defines a class of object.
3) see *property* (p 93).

charge NOUN /tʃɑrdʒ/ what must be paid for goods or services.

chart NOUN /tʃɑrt/ a table, graph or diagram describing data. Synonym: *graph* (p 54), *bar graph* (p 15), *pie chart* (p 88).

check VERB /tʃɛk/
1) to verify correctness; to look over. Synonym: verify (p 121).
2) to compare results with the original problem. Example: check the solution. Synonym: validate (p 120).

check a solution VERB /tʃɛk eɪ səˈluː.ʃən/ to substitute a solution back into the original equation or inequality to verify that it is a valid solution. If the resulting equation or inequality is true, then the solution is valid. Example: Is $x = 3$ a solution of $x^2 - x - 6 = 0$? Check $3^2 - 3 - 6 \stackrel{?}{=} 0 \rightarrow 9 - 3 - 6 \stackrel{?}{=} 0 \rightarrow 0 = 0$. Yes, $x = 3$ is a solution.

chord NOUN /kɔrd/ a line segment connecting two different points on a curve.

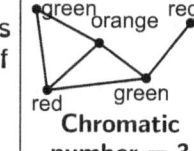
Chord

chromatic number NOUN /kroʊˈmæ.tɪk ˈnʌm.bər/ the smallest number of colors that can be used to color the nodes of a graph so that no two same-colored nodes are connected by an edge.

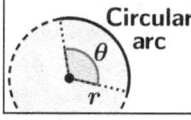
Chromatic number = 3

chronological ADJECTIVE /krɒˈnɒ.lə.dʒɪ.kəl/
1) arranged in the order of the time that things happened. Example: chronological order.
2) measured or calculated in units of time. Example: chronological age.

chronological order noun /krɒˈnɒ.lə.dʒɪ.kəl ˈɔr.dər/ ordered by the time that things happened.

cipher NOUN /ˈsaɪ.fər/ (American English)
1) a method of converting plain text to enciphered text.
2) a message that has been enciphered.
3) a key used to encipher a message.
Synonym: cypher (British English).

circle NOUN /ˈsɜr.kəl/ the set of all points in a plane that are a given distance from a center point. Formula: $(x - h)^2 + (y - k)^2 = r^2$ where (h, k) is the center of the circle and r is the radius of the circle. In general form $x^2 + y^2 + ax + by + c = 0$. See also Properties of a Circle (p 137).

circle graph NOUN /ˈsɜr.kəl græf/ see pie chart (p 88).

circular ADJECTIVE /ˈsɜr.kjə.lər/
1) having to do with a circle. Example: circular motion.
2) shaped like a circle.
3) being part of a circle. Example: circular arc.

circular arc NOUN /ˈsɜr.kjə.lər ɑrk/ an arc that is a portion of the circumference of a circle. Formula: $l = r\theta$ where l is the length of the arc, r is the radius of the circle, and θ is the angle in radians between the initial line and terminal line.

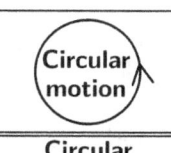
Circular arc

circular function NOUN /ˈsɜr.kjə.lər ˈfʌŋk.ʃən/ see trigonometric function (p 116).

circular motion NOUN /ˈsɜr.kjə.lər ˈmoʊ.ʃən/ movement around a circle.

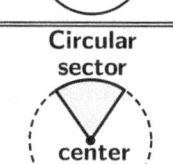
Circular motion

circular sector NOUN /ˈsɜr.kjə.lər ˈsɛk.tər/ the portion of a circle between two radii. Formula: $\text{Area} = \frac{1}{2}\theta r^2 \theta$ in radians, not degrees.

Circular sector

circum- PREFIX /ˈsɜr.kəm/
1) around the outside.
2) surrounding.

circumcenter NOUN /ˈsɜr.kəm.sɛn.tər/ the center of the circle that intersects all vertices of a triangle, a regular polygon or a cyclic polygon.

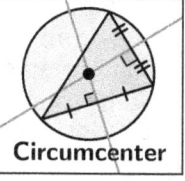
Circumcenter

circumcircle NOUN /ˈsɜr.kəm.sɜr.kəl/ the circle that intersects all of the vertices of a triangle, a regular polygon or a cyclic polygon.

circumference NOUN /sɜrˈkʌm.frəns/
1) the edge of a circle.
2) the length of the edge of a circle. Formula: where r is the radius of the circle. $C = 2\pi r$

Circumference

circumradius NOUN /ˌsɜr.kəmˈreɪ.di.əs/
1) the radius of a circumcircle.
2) the length of the radius of a circumcircle.
Plural: circumradii /ˌsɜr.kəmˈreɪ.di.aɪ/.

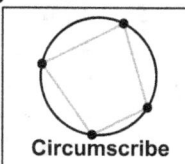
Circumradius

circumscribable ADJECTIVE /ˌsɜr.kəmˈskraɪ.bə.bl/ of a polygon, a circle can be drawn that intersects all of its vertices exactly once.

circumscribe VERB /ˈsɜr.kəm.skraɪb/ to draw a circle around a geometric figure that intersects as many of the figure's vertices as possible.

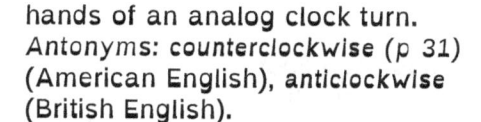
Circumscribe

cis FUNCTION a shorthand for $\cos\theta + i\sin\theta$. Formula: $\text{cis}\,\theta = \cos\theta + i\sin\theta = e^{i\theta}$.

claim NOUN /kleɪm/ see proposition (p 93).

class NOUN /klæs/ a set of objects having a particular property in common. Example: acute angles are a class of angles whose measure is less than a right angle. Synonym: subset (p 110).

classification NOUN /ˌklæs.ə.frˈkeɪ.ʃən/
1) one class into which objects are sorted.
2) the act of sorting into classes.

classify VERB /ˈklæs.ə.faɪ/ to sort into classes.

class interval NOUN /klæs ˈɪn.tər.vəl/ (statistics) an interval of values that are assigned to a class. Example: ages 3-8.

clock arithmetic NOUN /ˈklɒk əˈrɪθ.mə.tɪk/ see modular arithmetic (p 76).

clockwise ADJECTIVE, ADVERB /ˈklɒk.waɪz/ a rotation in the same direction that the hands of an analog clock turn. Antonyms: counterclockwise (p 31) (American English), anticlockwise (British English).

Clockwise

closed ADJECTIVE /kloʊzd/
1) (figure) having a boundary that completely encloses an area; having a boundary that can be traced from any point by any path and always return to the original point without retracing. Antonym: open (p 83).
2) (set) given a set and an operation on the members of the set, the result of the operation is still in the set. Example: the set of integers is open with respect to addition. Antonym: open (p 83).

Closed figure   open figure

open interval
Closed interval
half-open interval

3rd Dyslexic's Edition

3) (interval) both the endpoints of the interval are included in the interval. Example: $0 \leq x \leq 9$.
Antonym: open (p 83).
4) (curve) the end point of the curve is the same as the start point. A curve that completely encloses an area.
Antonym: open (p 83).

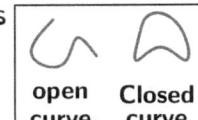
open curve   Closed curve

5) (dot) having the interior filled in, showing a closed side of an interval. Example: •.
6) (math sentence) a mathematical sentence with no variables. Example: $3 + 2 = 5$.

closure NOUN /ˈkloʊ.ʒər/
1) the condition of being closed or not closed.
2) a mathematical property that the result of an operation on any two members of a set is itself in the set.

closure property NOUN /ˈkloʊ.ʒər ˈprɒ.pər.ti/ given a set and an operation on members of the set, the result of the operation is a member of the set. Math definition: Given an operation $*$ on set G, if for every $a, b \in G$, $a * b = c$ if and only if $c \in G$, then set G is closed with respect to $*$. Example: Since the set of real numbers is closed with respect to addition, given two real numbers a and b, then $a + b$ is always a real number.

cluster /ˈklʌs.tər/
1) NOUN a subset of data whose values crowd together.
2) NOUN a natural grouping in a population.
3) VERB to crowd together.
4) ADJECTIVE considered in groups.

Clusters

clustering noun /ˈklʌs.tər.ɪŋ/
1) a tendency for some data to crowd together.
2) a method of estimating a sum when a group of values are close. Example: $6.2 + 5.7 + 5.9 \approx 6.0 + 6.0 + 6.0 = 18$.

cluster sampling NOUN /ˈklʌs.tər ˈsæm.plɪŋ/ a sample taken randomly from within natural groupings in a population. Example: a population is divided into age groupings, then random samples are taken from each age grouping.

cm ABBREVIATION centimeter (p 20).

co- PREFIX /koʊ/
1) with.
2) together.
3) jointly.

code NOUN /koʊd/
1) information that has been encrypted.
2) a method or key for encryption.

coefficient NOUN /ˌkoʊ.əˈfɪ.ʃənt/
1) a number in a term that may be multiplied by one or more variables.
Example: In $3x^2 + x - 2$ the

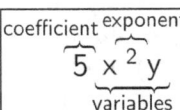
coefficient^{exponent}
$5 x^2 y$
variables

coefficients are 3, 1, and -2 respectively. 1 is an implied coefficient, -2 is the constant term.
2) a number that gives a measure of some property. Example: correlation coefficient (p 30).

coefficient matrix NOUN /ˌkoʊ.əˈfɪ.ʃənt ˈmeɪ.trɪks/ a matrix that represents the coefficients of a linear system. Example: the coefficient matrix for the linear system $\begin{matrix} 3x + 4y = 1 \\ -2x + y = 3 \end{matrix}$ is $\left[\begin{array}{cc|c} 3 & 4 & 1 \\ -2 & 1 & 3 \end{array}\right]$.

coefficient of correlation noun /ˌkoʊ.əˈfɪ.ʃənt ʌv ˌkɔ.rəˈleɪ.ʃən/ see correlation coefficient (p 30).

cofactor NOUN /ˈkoʊˌfæk.tər/ the signed minor of an element of a matrix. If the sum of the row number and column number is odd, the sign is positive, otherwise it is negative. Example:
$\begin{bmatrix} 3 & \cancel{-2} & 1 \\ \cancel{0} & \cancel{3} & \cancel{-1} \\ -2 & \cancel{-1} & 4 \end{bmatrix} \xrightarrow{\text{cofactor}_{2,2}} \begin{vmatrix} 3 & 1 \\ -2 & 4 \end{vmatrix} =$
$3 \cdot 4 - 1 \cdot (-2) = 12 + 2 = 14$.

cofactor matrix NOUN /ˈkoʊˌfæk.tər ˈmeɪ.trɪks/ the cofactor matrix of a matrix **A** is a matrix with the same dimensions as **A** where each element of the matrix is replaced by the cofactor of that element.

cofunction NOUN /ˈkoʊˌfʌŋk.ʃən/ one of pair of related trigonometric functions such as sine and cosine, or secant and cosecant where the value of one function for a certain angle is equal to the value of the other function for the complement of the angle.

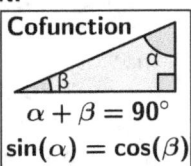
Cofunction
$\alpha + \beta = 90°$
$\sin(\alpha) = \cos(\beta)$

Cofunction Identity NOUN /ˈkoʊˌfʌŋk.ʃən aɪˈdɛn.tɪ.ti/ a trigonometric identity that relates cofunctions. See also Trigonometric Identities (p 143).

coincide VERB /ˌkoʊ.ɪnˈsaɪd/
1) to occupy the same place.
2) to have one or more points in common.

coincidental NOUN /ˌkoʊ.ɪn.sɪˈdɛn.tl/
1) occupying the same place.
2) sharing one or more points.

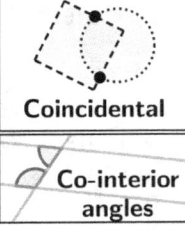
Coincidental

co-interior angles NOUN /ˌkoʊ.ɪnˈtɪə.ri.ər ˈæŋ.gəlz/ two angles on the same side of a transversal that intersects two lines. If the two lines are parallel, the sum of the two angles is $180°$.

Co-interior angles

collect VERB /kəˈlɛkt/ to gather together in one group.

collection NOUN /kəˈlɛk.ʃən/ a group of objects; an identifiable group of objects. Synonym: set (p 104).

collinear ADJECTIVE /koʊˈlɪ.ni.ər/ contained by the same line. Antonym: noncollinear (p 79).

A   B
Collinear
• non-collinear

collinearity NOUN /ˌkoʊ.lɪn.i.ɛər.ɪ.ti/ whether or not objects are contained by the same line.

collinear vectors NOUN /koʊˈlɪ.ni.ər ˈvɛk.tərz/ vectors that go in the same direction or in opposite directions; vectors that are non-zero scalar multiples of each other. Math definition: Vector **u** is collinear with vector **v** if and only if, for some nonzero real number a, $\mathbf{u} = a \cdot \mathbf{v}$.

Collinear vectors

column NOUN /ˈkɒl.əm/ a set of values arranged vertically.

column addition NOUN /ˈkɒl.əm əˈdɪ.ʃən/ a strategy for addition where the addends are arranged in columns according to place value.

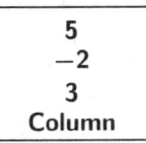
5
−2
3
Column

column graph NOUN /ˈkɒl.əm græf/ see bar graph (p 15).

column matrix NOUN /ˈkɒl.əm ˈmeɪ.trɪks/ a matrix with exactly one column. *Synonym: column vector.*

$$\begin{bmatrix} 5 \\ -2 \\ 3 \end{bmatrix}$$
Column matrix

column operation NOUN /ˈkɒl.əm ˌɒ.pərˈeɪ.ʃən/ one of a set of rules for manipulating the columns of a matrix without changing the solution of the linear system represented by the matrix: • Any two columns can be swapped. • Any column can be multiplied by a nonzero scalar. • Any column can be added to another column. *See also row operation (p 101).*

column rank NOUN /ˈkɒl.əm ræŋk/ the number of linearly independent columns in a matrix.

column subtraction NOUN /ˈkɒl.əm səbˈtræk.ʃən/ a strategy for subtraction where the operands are arranged in columns according to place value.

column vector NOUN /ˈkɒl.əm ˈvɛk.tər/ see *column matrix* (p 23).

com- PREFIX /kɒm/
1) with.
2) together.
3) jointly.

combination NOUN /ˌkɒm.bəˈneɪ.ʃən/
1) (probability) the number of different ways a certain number of members of a set can be arranged when order is not important. The combinations of $\{a, b, c\}$ taken two at a time are $\{a, b\}, \{a, c\}, \{b, c\}$. Formula: $C(n, r) = nCr = \binom{n}{r} = \frac{n!}{(n-r)!r!}$ where n is the total number of objects, r is the number of objects selected, and $r \leq n$.
2) the selection of objects from a set when order is not important.
3) (linear algebra) see *linear combination (p 69)*.

combination notation NOUN /ˌkɒm.bəˈneɪ.ʃən noʊˈteɪ.ʃən/ a notation for combinations in the form **nCr** where **n** is the total number of objects that can be selected and **r** is the number of objects that are selected.

combinatorial analysis NOUN /kɒmˌbə.nəˈtɔr.i.əl əˈnæl.ə.sɪs/ the study of counting, combination and permutation, particularly for statistics and probability. *Synonym: combinatorics.*

combinatorics NOUN /kɒm.bə.nəˈtɔr.ɪks/ see *combinatorial analysis (p 23)*.

combine VERB /kəmˈbaɪn/ to put together, or add together. *Synonym: compound (p 25).*

comma separator NOUN /ˈkɒm.ə ˈsɛp.əˌreɪ.tər/ a comma used to group digits of a number. *Examples: 3,203.15.* *Synonym: thousands separator (p 114).*

commission NOUN /kəˈmɪ.ʃən/ a fee charged for performing work, often a percentage of a transaction. *Formula:* **total × rate = commission**. *Example: The auctioneer receives a* **10%** *commission on everything sold at an auction.*

common ADJECTIVE /ˈkɒ.mən/
1) the same for all instances. *Example: common factors.*
2) sharing something. *Example: common point.*
3) accepted, familiar.

common denominator NOUN /ˈkɒ.mən dɪˈnɒ.məˌneɪ.tər/ a number that is a multiple of two or more denominators; a number that can be evenly divided by two or more denominators. *Example: common denominators of the fractions $\frac{3}{6}$ and $\frac{4}{5}$ are 30, 60, 90, …: ($6 \times 5 \times 1 = 30, 6 \times 5 \times 2 = 60, 6 \times 5 \times 3 = 90, \cdots$). See also least common denominator (p 67).*

common difference NOUN /ˈkɒ.mən ˈdɪf.rəns/ in an arithmetic sequence, the constant difference between a term and the term before it. *Formula:* $d = a_n - a_{n-1}$. *Example: the common difference of $\{1, 3, 5, 7, \cdots\}$ is 2.*

$\overbrace{1,3,5,7}^{5-3=2}$
$\underbrace{}_{3-1=2 \ \ 7-5=2}$
Common difference

common endpoint NOUN /ˈkɒ.mən ˈɛnd.pɔɪnt/ a point at an end of two or more objects that is shared by all of the objects. *Synonym: vertex (p 121).*

Common endpoint

common external tangent NOUN /ˈkɒ.mən ɪkˈstɜr.nl ˈtæn.dʒənt/ a line that is tangent to two circles and does not intersect the line segment between the centers of the circles.

Common external tangents

common factor NOUN /ˈkɒ.mən ˈfæk.tər/
1) an integer that is a factor of two or more other integers. *Example: the common factors of* **4** *and* **12** *are* **1, 2,** *and* **4**.
2) an expression that is a factor of two or more other expressions. *Example: $x - 1$ is a common factor of $(x - 1)(x + 2)$ and $(x - 4)(x - 1)$.*

common fraction NOUN /ˈkɒ.mən ˈfræk.ʃən/ a fraction whose numerator and denominator are integers. *Examples: $\frac{3}{7}, \frac{9}{4}$. Synonym: vulgar fraction.*

common internal tangent NOUN /ˈkɒ.mən ɪnˈtɜr.nl ˈtæn.dʒənt/ a line that is tangent to two circles and intersects the line segment between the centers of the circles.

Common internal tangents

common logarithm NOUN /ˈkɒ.mən ˈlɒ.gəˌrɪð.əm/ a logarithm with base 10. *Abbreviation: log. Math definition: $\log a \equiv \log_{10} a$. See also Properties of Logarithms (p 128).*

common multiple NOUN /ˈkɒ.mən ˈmʌl.tə.pəl/ a number or expression that is a multiple of two or more other numbers or expressions. *Example: the first three common multiples of* **2** *and* **3** *are* **6, 12, 18,** ….

common point NOUN /ˈkɒ.mən pɔɪnt/ a point that is shared by two or more objects.

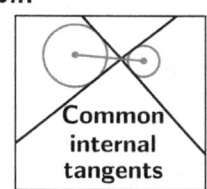
Common point

common ratio NOUN /ˈkɒ.mən ˈreɪ.ʃoʊ/ in a geometric sequence, the constant ratio between any term and the term after it. *Example: the common ratio of the geometric sequence $\{2, 6, 18, \cdots\}$ is* **3** *since $2 \times 3 = 6, 6 \times 3 = 18, \cdots$.*

$\overbrace{2, 6, 18, 54}^{6 \times 3 = 18}$
$\underbrace{}_{2 \times 3 = 6 \ \ 18 \times 3 = 54}$
Common ratio

common side NOUN /ˈkɒ.mən saɪd/ a ray or line segment that is shared by two objects.

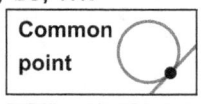
Common side

common tangent NOUN /ˈkɒ.mən ˈtæn.dʒənt/ a line that is tangent to two circles or curves.

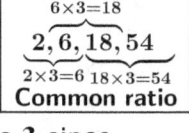
Common tangents

commutative ADJECTIVE /ˈkɒ.mjuˌtə.tɪv/ it doesn't matter the order in which an operation is performed. *Math definition: a binary operation $*$ on members of a set A is commutative if and only if for every $a, b \in A$,*

3rd Dyslexic's Edition

$a * b \equiv b * a$. Example: addition of real numbers is commutative since $a + b \equiv b + a$.

commutative group NOUN /'kɒ.mju̇ˌtə.tɪv grup/ a group where the operation on the group is commutative. Example: the set of odd numbers under addition is a commutative group. Synonym: *Abelian group*.

Commutative Property of Addition NOUN /'kɒ.mju̇ˌtə.tɪv 'prɒ.pər.ti ʌv ə'dɪ.ʃən/ addition can be performed in any order. Math definition: for any real or complex numbers a and b, $a + b \equiv b + a$. Example: $2 + 3 = 5 = 3 + 2$.

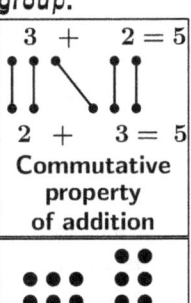
Commutative property of addition

Commutative Property of Multiplication NOUN /'kɒ.mju̇ˌtə.tɪv 'prɒ.pər.ti ʌv ˌmʌl.tə.plɪ'keɪ.ʃən/ multiplication can be performed in any order. Math definition: for any real or complex numbers a and b, $ab \equiv ba$. Example: $2 \cdot 3 = 6 = 3 \cdot 2$.

Commutative property of multiplication

compare VERB /kʌm'pɛər/ to look at in order to note what is the same and what is different.

comparison NOUN /kʌm'pɛər.ɪ.sən/ a statement of what is different and what is the same.

comparison test NOUN /kʌm'pɛər.ɪ.sən tɛst/ see *comparison theorem* (p 24).

Comparison Theorem NOUN /kʌm'pɛər.ɪ.sən 'θɪ.ə.rəm/ determines if an integral is convergent or divergent based on the relative values of the function. Math definition: Let f and g be continuous functions and $f(x) \geq g(x) \geq 0$ for all $x \geq a$. If $\int_a^\infty f(x)dx$ is convergent, then $\int_a^\infty g(x)dx$ is convergent. If $\int_a^\infty g(x)dx$ is divergent, then $\int_a^\infty f(x)dx$ is divergent. Synonyms: *comparison test, direct comparison test*.

compass NOUN /'kʌm.pəs/ a tool that can draw a circle and copy a distance.

compatible ADJECTIVE /kəm'pæ.tə.bəl/ can be used together. Antonym: *Incompatible* (p 60).

compatible matrices NOUN /kəm'pæ.tə.bəl 'meɪ.trɪ.siz/ matrix A is compatible with matrix B if the number of columns of matrix A is the same as the number of rows of matrix B. If matrices A and B are compatible, then the multiplication of A by B is defined. Antonym: *incompatible matrices*.

compatible numbers NOUN /kəm'pæ.tə.bəl 'nʌm.bərz/ two numbers that, when divided, give an integer. Example: 6 and 3 are compatible numbers since $6 \div 3 = 2$.

compensation and change method NOUN /ˌkɒm.pən'seɪ.ʃən ənd 'tʃeɪndʒ 'mɛ.θəd/ a strategy that uses rounding to make mental addition or subtraction easier. Example: $42 + 37 = 42 + 40 - 3 = 82 - 3 = 79$.

complement NOUN /'kɒm.plə.mənt/
1) (sets) all elements that are not members of a set. Notation: A', A.
2) (sets) the complement of set A in set S is the set of all elements that are members of set S, but not members of set A. Notation: spoken "the complement of A in S"; written A/S.
3) (events) given an event e, one or more other events that will happened if and only if event e does not happen. Example: when flipping a coin, heads is the complement of tails.
4) (angle) given angle α, another angle β such that $m\angle\alpha + m\angle\beta = 90° = \frac{\pi}{2}$ rad..

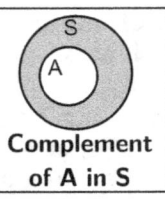
Complement of A in S

complementary ADJECTIVE /ˌkɒm.plə'mɛn.tər.i/ having the property of being complements of each other.

complementary angle NOUN /ˌkɒm.plə'mɛn.tər.i 'æŋ.gəl/ one of two angles that, when taken together, make a right angle. Angles do not have to be next to each other to be complementary. Math definition: $\angle\alpha$ is complementary to $\angle\beta$ if and only if $m\angle\alpha + m\angle\beta = 90° = \frac{\pi}{2}$ rad..

Complementary angles

Complementary Angle Congruence Theorem NOUN /ˌkɒm.plə'mɛn.tər.i 'æŋ.gəl 'kɒn.gru.əns 'θɪ.ə.rəm/ angles that are complementary to the same angle or to congruent angles are congruent. Math definition: if $\angle\alpha$ is complementary to $\angle\beta$ and $\angle\alpha$ is complementary to $\angle\gamma$, then $\angle\beta \cong \angle\gamma$.

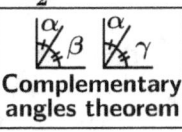
Complementary angles theorem

complementary event NOUN /ˌkɒm.plə'mɛn.tər.i ɪ'vɛnt/ one of a set of events where exactly one of the events must happen in any single trial. Notation: e' (read "complement of e"). Formulas: $P(e) = 1 - P(e')$ and $P(e') = 1 - P(e)$. Example: when flipping a coin, either a heads or a tails must happen. Heads and tails are complementary events.

Complement Theorems NOUN /'kɒm.plə.mənt 'θɪ.ə.rəmz/
1) the complement of the intersection of two sets equals the union of the complements of the sets. $(A \cap B)' = (A' \cup B')$ (de Morgan's Theorem).
2) the complement of the union of two sets equals the intersection of the complements of the sets. $(A \cup B)' = (A' \cap B')$ (de Morgan's Theorem).
3) $A/(B \cap C) = (A/B) \cup (A/C)$.
4) $A/(B \cup C) = (A/B) \cap (A/C)$.

complete /kəm'plit/
1) ADJECTIVE (axiomatic system) every statement can be proved to be true or false.
2) ADJECTIVE (network) a network where each node is connected to every other node by a unique edge.
3) ADJECTIVE (graph) a graph where the view window indicates the path of the graph for the part of the graph not in the view window.
4) ADJECTIVE finished; lacking nothing.
5) VERB to finish.
Antonym: *incomplete* (p 60).

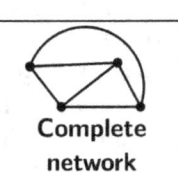
Complete network

Complete Factorization Theorem NOUN /kəm'plit 'fæk.tər.aɪ.zeɪ.ʃən 'θɪ.ə.rəm/ if $P(x)$ is a polynomial of degree $n \geq 1$, then there exists complex numbers

$a, c_1, c_2, \cdots, c_n, a \neq 0$, such that $P(x) = a(x - c_1)(x - c_2) \cdots (x - c_n)$.

complete the square VERB /kəmˈplit ðə skwɛər/ an algorithm used to transform a quadratic equation into vertex form, or solve a quadratic equation.

complex ADJECTIVE /kəmˈplɛks/
1) not simple. Example: complex curve. Antonym: simple (p 105).
2) made up of two or more parts. Example: complex fraction. Synonym: compound (p 25).
3) having to do with a complex number. Antonym: real (p 96).

complex conjugate NOUN /kəmˈplɛks ˈkɒn.dʒə.gət/ one of two complex numbers in the form $a + bi$ and $a - bi$. Notation: $\overline{a + bi}$. Formula: $\overline{a + bi} = a - bi$. Example: $\overline{-3 + 2i} = -3 - 2i$. See also Properties of Complex Conjugates (p 130).

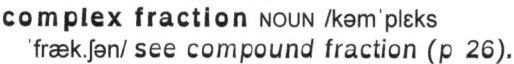

complex curve NOUN /kəmˈplɛks kɜrv/ a curve that crosses itself. Antonym: simple curve (p 105).

complex fraction NOUN /kəmˈplɛks ˈfræk.ʃən/ see compound fraction (p 26).

complex inequality NOUN /kəmˈplɛks ˌɪn.ɪˈkwɒl.ɪ.ti/ see compound inequality (p 26).

complex integer NOUN /kəmˈplɛks ˈɪn.tɪ.dʒər/ see Gaussian integer (p 52).

complex number NOUN /kəmˈplɛks ˈnʌm.bər/ a number that has a real part and an imaginary part; a number in the form $a + bi$ where $i \equiv \sqrt{-1}$ and a and b are real numbers. Notations: $a + bi$, z, $r(\cos \theta + i \sin \theta)$. Formula: $z = a + bi = \sqrt{a^2 + b^2}(\cos(\arctan \frac{b}{a}) + i \sin(\arctan \frac{b}{a}))$. Example: $5 - 3i = 5 - 3\sqrt{-1}$. See also Operations on Complex Numbers (p 129).

complex plane NOUN /kəmˈplɛks pleɪn/ a rectangular coordinate system on which complex numbers are plotted. The horizontal axis represents the real part of the complex number. The vertical axis represents the imaginary part of the complex number. Synonym: Argand diagram.

complex polygon NOUN /kəmˈplɛks ˈpɒ.lɪˌgɒn/ a polygon whose sides intersect each other. Antonym: simple polygon (p 105).

complex solution NOUN /kəmˈplɛks səˈlu.ʃən/ a solution that may contain at least one complex number. Antonym: real solution (p 96).

Complex Polynomial Zeros Theorem NOUN /kəmˈplɛks ˌpɒ.ləˈnoʊ.mi.əl ˈzɪə.roʊz ˈθɪ.ə.rəm/ every complex polynomial function of degree $n \geq 1$ can be factored into n linear factors (not necessarily distinct) in the form $f(x) = a(x - r_1)(x - r_2) \cdots (x - r_n)$.

complex valued ADJECTIVE /kəmˈplɛks ˈvæl.jud/ having variables that can represent complex numbers. Antonym: real-valued (p 96).

complex variable NOUN /kəmˈplɛks ˈvɛər.i.ə.bəl/ a variable that can have a complex number for a value.

component NOUN /kəmˈpoʊ.nənt/
1) a distinct part of a whole.
2) one of two vectors parallel to mutually perpendicular axes whose sum equals the given vector. In $\langle a, b \rangle$, $\langle a, 0 \rangle$ is the horizontal component and $\langle 0, b \rangle$ is the vertical component.

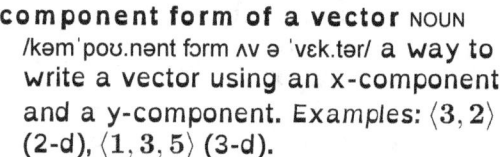

component form of a vector NOUN /kəmˈpoʊ.nənt fɔrm ʌv ə ˈvɛk.tər/ a way to write a vector using an x-component and a y-component. Examples: $\langle 3, 2 \rangle$ (2-d), $\langle 1, 3, 5 \rangle$ (3-d).

component of a vector on a vector NOUN /kəmˈpoʊ.nənt ʌv ə ˈvɛk.tər ɒn ə ˈvɛk.tər/ the part of a vector that 'fits' onto another vector. Math definition: the component of $\mathbf{u}$ on $\mathbf{v}$ is $|\mathbf{u}|\cos\theta$, where θ is the angle between the vectors. Formula: component of $\mathbf{u}$ on $\mathbf{v}$ is $\frac{\mathbf{u} \cdot \mathbf{v}}{|\mathbf{v}|}$.

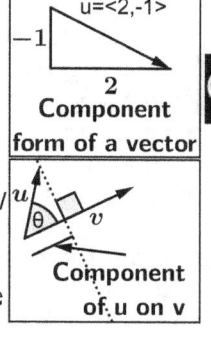

compose VERB /ˈkəm.poʊz/
1) to combine together by a rule. Antonym: decompose (p 34).
2) (functions) to form a composite function. Notation: $f \circ g(x) = f(g(x))$ (compose $f(x)$ and $g(x)$).

composite ADJECTIVE /kɒmˈpɒ.zɪt/
1) not prime; can be factored. Example: composite number.
2) made from more than one distinct part. Example: composite function.

composite figure NOUN /kɒmˈpɒ.zɪt ˈfɪg.jər/ a figure made up of more than one simpler figures.

composite function NOUN /kɒmˈpɒ.zɪt ˈfʌŋk.ʃən/ the function of a function; if $f(x)$ and $g(x)$ are functions, $f(g(x))$ is a function composed of $f(x)$ and $g(x)$. Notation: $f \circ g(x) = f(g(x))$. Synonym: compound function.

composite number NOUN /kɒmˈpɒ.zɪt ˈnʌm.bər/ an integer that is not a prime number. Example: 12 is a composite integer since $12 = 2 \cdot 2 \cdot 3$. Synonym: rectangular number (p 97). Antonym: prime number (p 91).

composite of reflections NOUN /kɒmˈpɒ.zɪt ʌv rɪˈflɛk.ʃənz/ two or more reflections performed in a certain order.

composition NOUN /ˌkɒm.pəˈzɪ.ʃən/ the act of combining together by a rule. Antonym: decomposition (p 34).

composition of functions NOUN /ˌkɒm.pəˈzɪ.ʃən ʌv ˈfʌŋk.ʃənz/ the act of forming a composite function. Notations: $f \circ g(x)$, $f(g(x))$. In both of the notations, $g(x)$ is the inner function and $f(x)$ is the outer function.

composition operator NOUN /ˌkɒm.pəˈzɪ.ʃən ˈɒ.pəˌreɪ.tər/ the operator indicating composition of functions. Notation: $f \circ g$.

compound /ˈkɒm.paʊnd/
1) ADJECTIVE more than one parts combined together,

perhaps by a rule. *Example:* compound inequality. *Synonym:* complex (p 25). *Synonym:* combine (p 23).
2) VERB to add interest to the principal of a loan.

compound event NOUN /ˈkɒm.paʊnd ɪˈvɛnt/ one of two or more events taken together. *Example:* a blue ball is picked (event 1) then a red ball is picked (event 2).

compound fraction NOUN /ˈkɒm.paʊnd ˈfræk.ʃən/ a fraction that has at least one other fraction in the numerator or denominator. *Synonym:* complex fraction.

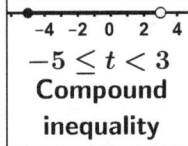
Compound fraction

compound function /ˈkɒm.paʊnd ˈfʌŋk.ʃən/ see composite function (p 25).

compound inequality NOUN /ˈkɒm.paʊnd ˌɪn.ɪˈkwɒl.ɪ.ti/ an inequality that has more than one inequality operator. *Example:* $-5 \leq t < 3$ means $-5 \leq t$ and $t < 3$. *Synonym:* complex inequality.

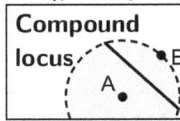
Compound inequality

compound interest NOUN /ˈkɒm.paʊnd ˈɪn.trɪst/ interest that is added to the principal of a loan, so that future interest is calculated on prior interest plus principal. *Formula:* $\mathbf{P} = \mathbf{P_0}\left(1 + \frac{\mathbf{i}}{\mathbf{n}}\right)^{\mathbf{t} \cdot \mathbf{n}}$ where $\mathbf{P_0}$ is the initial principal, $\mathbf{i}$ is the nominal interest rate, $\mathbf{n}$ is the number of compounding periods per year, and $\mathbf{t}$ is the number of years. *Antonym:* simple interest (p 105).

compound locus NOUN /ˈkɒm.paʊnd ˈloʊ.kəs/ a locus with more than one condition. *Example:* The illustration shows a compound locus with the conditions: 1) all points equidistant from $\mathbf{A}$ and $\mathbf{B}$ that 2) lie in the disk centered at $\mathbf{A}$ with radius $\mathbf{AB}$. *Plural:* compound loci /ˈkɒm.paʊnd ˈloʊ.saɪ/.

compound measure NOUN /ˈkɒm.paʊnd ˈmɛʒ.ər/ a measure made up of two or more simpler measures. *Examples:* velocity $= \frac{\text{distance}}{\text{time}}$, 5 km in 1 hour $= \frac{5 \text{ km}}{1 \text{ hr}} = 5$ km/hr.

compound sentence NOUN /ˈkɒm.paʊnd ˈsɛn.tns/ see compound statement (p 26).

compound statement NOUN /ˈkɒm.paʊnd ˈsteɪt.mənt/ two or more statements connected with logical operators such as 'and' and 'or'. *Example:* a square is a quadrilateral **and** a square is equilateral.

compress VERB /kəmˈprɛs/ to make smaller. *Synonym:* shrink. *Antonyms:* enlarge (p 44), stretch.

compression NOUN /kəmˈprɛ.ʃən/
1) (geometry) a dilation where the image is smaller than the preimage. *Synonym:* contraction. *Antonym:* enlargement (p 44).
2) (algebra) a transformation of a function that decreases the output. *Example:* $y = \frac{1}{2}f(x)$.
3) (graph) a transformation on a graph that makes the $\mathbf{x}$ values or $\mathbf{y}$ values smaller. *Example:* The graph of $y = f(2x)$ is a horizontal compression of $y = f(x)$.

computation NOUN /ˌkɒm.pjuˈteɪ.ʃən/ a calculation, usually with numbers. *Synonym:* arithmetic.

compute VERB /kəmˈpjut/ to calculate a result, usually with an electronic or mechanical device. *Example:* compute the difference of 5 and 3: $5 - 3 = 2$. *Synonym:* calculate (p 18).

computer NOUN /kəmˈpju.tər/ a device used to calculate, usually with an electronic processor.

Computer

con- PREFIX /kɒn/
1) with.
2) together.
3) jointly.

concave ADJECTIVE /ˈkɒn.keɪv/ arched in. *Math definition:* A shape is concave if a line segment can be drawn between two points in the shape and the line segment is not completely contained within the shape. *Antonym:* convex (p 30).

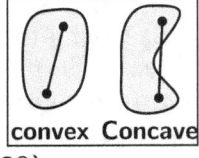
convex Concave

concave down ADJECTIVE /ˈkɒn.keɪv daʊn/ the slopes of the tangents to the function on a range are decreasing; the rate of change is increasing; a line segment drawn between any two points will be entirely below the curve. *Antonym:* concave up.

concave up ADJECTIVE /ˈkɒn.keɪv ʌp/ the slopes of the tangents to the function on a range are increasing; the rate of change is decreasing; a line segment drawn between any two points will be entirely above the curve. *Antonym:* concave down.

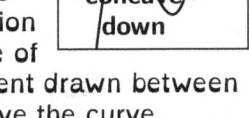
concave up / concave down

concavity NOUN /kənˈkæ.vɪ.ti/
1) the property of being concave or not concave.
2) the property of being concave up or concave down.

concavity test NOUN /kənˈkæ.vɪ.ti tɛst/ if $f''(x) > 0$ on an interval, then f is concave up on that interval. If $f''(x) < 0$ on an interval, then f is concave down on that interval.

concentration NOUN /ˌkɒn.sənˈtreɪ.ʃən/ a measure of the amount of a substance in a solution, compared to the whole. *Unit of measure:* molarity. *Notation:* $\mathbf{M}$.

concentric ADJECTIVE /kənˈsɛn.trɪk/ having the same center. *Antonym:* eccentric (p 42).

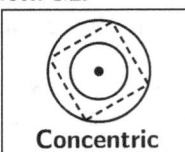
Concentric

conclude VERB /kənˈklud/ to arrive at a logical result.

conclusion NOUN /kənˈklu.ʒən/ a statement proved or supported by a set of mathematical arguments. *Notation:* "If **proposition** and **proposition** then **conclusion**." *Example:* **if** a shape is a rectangle **and** the sides are congruent, **then** the shape is also a square.

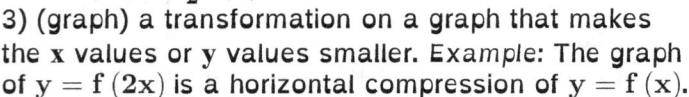

concrete graph NOUN /ˈkɒn.krɪt græf/ see pictograph (p 88).

concrete object NOUN /ˈkɒn.krɪt ˈɒb.dʒɛkt/ see manipulative (p 72).

concurrence NOUN /kənˈkɜr.əns/ the meeting of geometric figures at a common point.

concurrency NOUN /kənˈkɜr.ən.si/ having to do with whether or not one or more points are shared. *Example:* point of concurrency.

concurrent ADJECTIVE, NOUN /kənˈkɜr.ənt/ sharing one or more points. A point that is shared is called a *point of concurrency* (p 89).

condition NOUN /kənˈdɪ.ʃən/
1) a requirement that is imposed. Example: let α be an angle less than 90°. Synonym: *criterion* (p 32).
2) a context for judging truth.

conditional ADJECTIVE /kənˈdɪ.ʃə.nl/ dependent upon a condition.

conditional convergence NOUN /kənˈdɪ.ʃə.nl kənˈvɜr.dʒəns/ a convergent series is conditionally convergent if, when its terms are replaced with their absolute values, the new series diverges. Example: $1 - \frac{1}{2} + \frac{1}{3} - \frac{1}{4} + \cdots$ is conditionally convergent since $1 + \frac{1}{2} + \frac{1}{3} + \frac{1}{4} + \cdots$ diverges. Antonym: *absolute convergence* (p 27).

conditional equation NOUN /kənˈdɪ.ʃə.nl ɪˈkweɪ.ʃən/ an equation that is true only for some values of the variables. Example: $3 + x = 2$ is true only when $x = -1$. Antonym: *identity* (p 59).

conditional probability NOUN /kənˈdɪ.ʃə.nl ˌprɒ.bəˈbɪl.ɪ.ti/ the probability of an outcome of an event where the outcome is dependent on another event. Notation: $P(a|b)$, read 'the probability of **a** given **b**'. Example: A jar contains 5 red balls and 3 blue balls. A red ball is picked and not put back. What is the probability that the next ball is also a red ball?

conditional statement NOUN /kənˈdɪ.ʃə.nl ˈsteɪt.mənt/ a statement that a claim is true if certain criteria are met. Format: **if criterion then claim**. Example: if a quadrilateral is a rectangle then the sides meet at right angles.

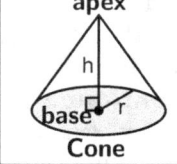

cone NOUN /koʊn/ a 3-dimensional geometric figure with either a circle or an ellipse for a base and a side that comes to a point.

configuration NOUN /kənˌfɪg.jəˈreɪ.ʃən/ an arrangement of objects.

configure VERB /kənˈfɪg.jər/ to arrange objects according to a rule.

congruence NOUN /kənˈgru.əns/
1) the state of being congruent or not congruent.
2) having the same remainder when divided by a particular integer.

congruence transformation NOUN /kənˈgru.əns ˈtræns.fərˌmeɪ.ʃən/ a geometric transformation where the preimage is congruent with the image. Examples: Reflection, translation and rotation.

congruent ADJECTIVE /kənˈgru.ənt/
1) coinciding at all points when one is placed on top of the other. Notation: ≅.
2) having the same measure.
3) (modulo) having the same remainder when divided by a given integer. Example: 10 and 20 are congruent modulo 5.

Congruent Corresponding Angles Postulate NOUN /kənˈgru.ənt ˌkɔr.əˈspɒn.dɪŋ ˈæŋ.gəlz ˈpɒs.tʃə.lɪt/ see *Corresponding Angles Postulate* (p 31).

conic /ˈkɒn.ɪk/
1) ADJECTIVE having to do with a cone.
2) ADJECTIVE cone-like in shape.
3) NOUN a conic section. See *conic section* (p 6).

conical ADJECTIVE /ˈkɒn.ɪ.kl/ cone-like in shape.

conic NOUN /ˈkɒn.ɪk/ see *conic section* (p 6).

conical frustum NOUN /ˈkɒn.ɪ.kl ˈfrʌs.təm/ a cone with its top cut off parallel to the base. Synonym: *truncated cone*.

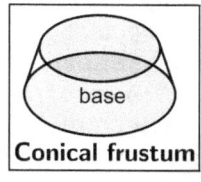

conic section NOUN /ˈkɒn.ɪk ˈsɛk.ʃən/ a figure formed by intersecting the surface of a double cone with a plane. Examples: circle, ellipse, hyperbola and parabola. Formula: $Ax^2 + Bxy + Cy^2 + Dx + Ey + F = 0$.

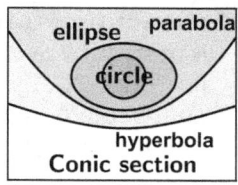

conjecture NOUN /kənˈdʒɛk.tʃər/ a statement that is consistent with known data, has not been proved true, and has not been proved false. Synonym: *admissible hypothesis* (p 8).

conjugate ADJECTIVE /ˈkɒn.dʒəˌgɪt/ having one or more properties in common, but some property the opposite. Examples: conjugate axis, conjugate roots.

conjugate angles NOUN /ˈkɒn.dʒəˌgɪt ˈæŋ.gəlz/ two angles that, taken together, make one full circle: 360° or 2π rad. Synonym: *explementary angles*.

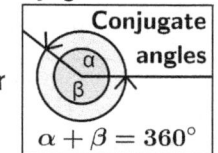

conjugate axis NOUN /ˈkɒn.dʒəˌgɪt ˈæk.sɪs/ the minor axis of an ellipse or a hyperbola. Synonym: *minor axis* (p 75). Antonym: *transverse axis* (p 115).

conjugate of a complex number NOUN /ˈkɒn.dʒəˌgɪt ʌv ə kəmˈplɛks ˈnʌm.bər/ see *complex conjugate* (p 25).

conjugate pair NOUN /ˈkɒn.dʒəˌgɪt pɛər/ two complex numbers in the form $a + bi, a - bi$.

Conjugate Pairs Theorem NOUN /ˈkɒn.dʒəˌgɪt pɛərz ˈθɪər.əm/ given a polynomial with real coefficients, any complex roots come in conjugate pairs. Example: $y = x^2 + x + 5$ has roots $\frac{1}{2} + \frac{1}{2}\sqrt{19}i, \frac{1}{2} - \frac{1}{2}\sqrt{19}i$. Synonym: *Conjugate Zeros Theorem*.

conjugate roots NOUN /ˈkɒn.dʒəˌgɪt ruts/ two related complex conjugate roots of a polynomial with real coefficients in the form $a + bi$ and $a - bi$. Example: $3 + 2i, 3 - 2i$.

Conjugate Zeros Theorem NOUN /ˈkɒn.dʒəˌgɪt ˈzɪə.roʊz ˈθɪ.ə.rəm/ see *Conjugate Pairs Theorem* (p 27).

conjunction NOUN /kənˈdʒʌŋk.ʃən/ two statements joined by an AND operator that is true if and only if both of the statements are true. Notation: ∧. Synonym: *and*.

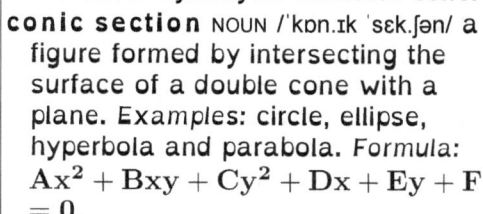

connect VERB /kəˈnɛkt/
1) to join two objects by sharing a point with each.
2) to join two objects by drawing a line segment between them.

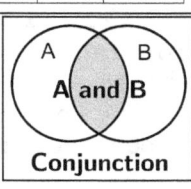

connected ADJECTIVE /kəˈnɛk.tɪd/ sharing at least one point. Antonym: *disconnected* (p 39).

consecutive ADJECTIVE /kənˈsɛk.jə.tɪv/
1) immediately following one another. Example: 1, 2, 3

3rd Dyslexic's Edition

and 4 are consecutive integers.
2) see adjacent (p 8).

consecutive angles NOUN /kənˈsɛk.jə.tɪv ˈæŋ.gəlz/
1) see consecutive interior angles (p 28).
2) angles that share a side. Synonym: **adjacent angles**.

consecutive interior angles NOUN /kənˈsɛk.jə.tɪv ɪnˈtɪər.i.ər ˈæŋ.gəlz/ if two lines are cut by a transversal, the consecutive interior angles are a pair of interior angles on the same side of the transversal.

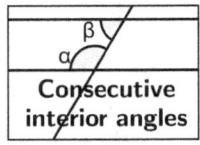
Consecutive interior angles

Consecutive Interior Angles Theorem NOUN /kənˈsɛk.jə.tɪv ɪnˈtɪə.ri.ər ˈæŋ.gəlz ˈθɪ.ə.rəm/ if two parallel lines are cut by a transversal, then each pair of consecutive interior angles are supplementary, their angles total $180°$.

consecutive sides NOUN /kənˈsɛk.jə.tɪv saɪdz/ two sides of a polygon that share a vertex. Synonym: **adjacent sides**.

Consecutive sides

consequent NOUN /ˈkɒn.sɪˌkwɛnt/ the conclusion of a logical statement; the second of two statements in an if-then relationship: **If antecedent then consequent**. Example: if you like carrots then you will like my salad. See also implication (p 59).

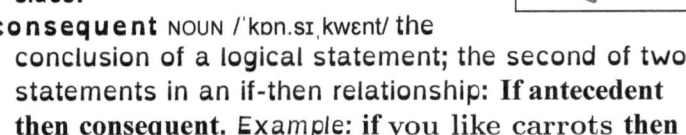

conservation NOUN /kɒn.sərˈveɪ.ʃən/ keeping some attribute the same. Example: conservation of distance.

conserve VERB /kɒnˈsɜrv/ to keep some attribute the same.

conservative ADJECTIVE /kənˈsɜr.və.tɪv/ keeps some attribute the same. Example: conservative field.

conservative field NOUN /kənˈsɜr.və.tɪv fild/ see conservative vector field (p 28).

conservative vector field NOUN /kənˈsɜr.və.tɪv ˈvɛk.tər fild/ a vector field that is the gradient of some function. Conservative vector fields have the property that the line integral is path independent.

consistent ADJECTIVE /kənˈsɪs.tənt/
1) having parts that agree with each other.
2) (set of equations) at least one solution exists that satisfies all equations in the set.
3) (logic) does not generate contradictions.
Antonym: **inconsistent** (p 60).

constant /ˈkɒn.stənt/
1) ADJECTIVE unchanging.
2) ADJECTIVE uniform. Example: constant growth.
3) NOUN a value that does not change. Example: the speed of light in a vacuum.
4) NOUN a letter representing a value that does not change. Example: $\pi \approx 3.14159$.

constant function NOUN /ˈkɒn.stənt ˈfʌŋk.ʃən/ a function that returns the same constant value for all values of the independent variable. Formula: $f(x) = a$. Example: $f(x) = 1.5$.

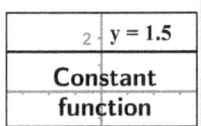
Constant function

constant growth NOUN /ˈkɒn.stənt groʊθ/ growth that happens at a constant rate each time period. Formula:

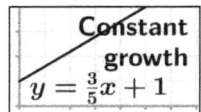
Constant growth

$y = at + y_0$ where $a > 0$ is the constant of growth and y_0 is the initial value at time $t = 0$. Synonyms: **arithmetic growth** (p 13), **linear growth** (p 69).

constant of proportion NOUN /ˈkɒn.stənt ʌv prəˈpɔr.ʃən/ see constant of variation (p 28).

constant of variation NOUN /ˈkɒn.stənt ʌv ˌvɛər.iˈeɪ.ʃən/ the ratio by which the input and output vary in direct variation and constant growth. **m** in $y = mx + b$. Synonyms: **constant of proportion**, **slope** (p 106).

constant term NOUN /ˈkɒn.stənt tɜrm/ the term of a polynomial that has no variables.

constrain VERB /kənˈstreɪn/ to limit or restrict.

constraint NOUN /kənˈstreɪnt/ a limitation or restriction. Example: $x > 0$. Synonym: **criterion** (p 32), **condition** (p 27).

construct VERB /kənˈstrʌkt/ to build according to a set of rules. Example: use a compass to construct a circle.

construction NOUN /kənˈstrʌk.ʃən/ an object built according to a set of rules. Example: a construction of a square.

contain VERB /kənˈteɪn/
1) to include within a volume, area or set. Synonym: **subset**.
2) to enclose on both sides.

A contains B

contained angle NOUN /kənˈteɪnd ˈæŋ.gəl/ an angle between two adjacent sides. In the illustration, $\angle \alpha$ is contained by sides **a** and **b**.

Contained angle

contained side NOUN /kənˈteɪnd saɪd/ a side between two adjacent vertices. In the illustration, side **a** is contained by angles $\angle \alpha$ and $\angle \beta$.

Contained side

context NOUN /ˈkɒn.tɛkst/ a particular situation; the circumstances in which an event happens.

continued ADJECTIVE /kənˈtɪn.jud/ going on without interruption.

continued fraction NOUN /kənˈtɪn.jud ˈfræk.ʃən/ the sum of a number and a fraction whose denominator is the sum of a number and a fraction and so on.

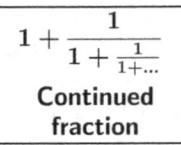
Continued fraction

continued product NOUN /kənˈtɪn.jud ˈprɒ.dʌkt/ the product of three or more factors, including infinite products. Examples: $1 \cdot 2 \cdot 3 \cdots$; $a_1 \cdot a_2 \cdot a_3 \cdots$.

continued sum NOUN /kənˈtɪn.jud sʌm/ the sum of three or more addends, including infinite sums. Examples: $1 + 2 + 3 + \ldots$; $a_1 + a_2 + a_3 + \ldots$. See also sigma notation (p 104).

continuity NOUN /ˌkɒn.tnˈu.ɪ.ti/ having to do with whether or not something is continuous.

continuous ADJECTIVE /kənˈtɪn.ju.əs/
1) without break; uninterrupted.
2) not discrete or discontinuous.
Antonyms: **discrete** (p 39), **discontinuous** (p 39).

continuous compounding NOUN /kənˈtɪn.ju.əs ˈkɒm.paʊn.dɪŋ/ compounding interest on a continuous basis. Formula: $P = P_0 e^{rt}$ where P_0 is the initial principal, e is Euler's number, r is the interest rate per

time period, and **t** is the number of time periods.

continuous data NOUN /kənˈtɪn.ju.əs ˈdeɪ.tə/ data that can take on any value in an interval. Example: height, but not age. Antonym: *discrete data* (p 39).

continuous from the left NOUN /kənˈtɪn.ju.əs frʌm ðə lɛft/ a function $f(x)$ is continuous from the left at $x = a$ if $\lim_{x \to a^-} f(x) = f(a)$.

continuous from the right NOUN /kənˈtɪn.ju.əs frʌm ðə raɪt/ a function $f(x)$ is continuous from the right at $x = a$ if $\lim_{x \to a^+} = f(a)$.

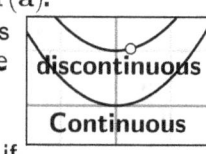
Continuous from the left/right; discontinuous; Continuous

continuous function NOUN /kənˈtɪn.ju.əs ˈfʌŋk.ʃən/ a function that does not have any breaks in it; a function that is defined on the entire domain. A function is continuous on an interval if it has no breaks on that interval. Math definition: function **f** is continuous at **a** if $f(a)$ is defined and $f(x) \to f(a)$ as $x \to a$. Antonym: *discontinuous function* (p 39).

continuous growth NOUN /kənˈtɪn.ju.əs groʊθ/ growth that happens on a continuous basis. Formula: $f(x) = ae^{rx}$ where **a** is the starting value, and **r** is the growth rate.

Continuous growth

continuously ADVERB /kənˈtɪn.ju.əs.li/
1) without stopping.
2) without gaps.

continuously compounded interest NOUN /kənˈtɪn.ju.əs.li ˈkɒm.paʊnd.əd ˈɪn.trɪst/ see *continuous compounding* (p 28).

continuous on an interval NOUN /kənˈtɪn.ju.əs ɒn ən ˈɪn.tər.vəl/ a function is continuous on an interval if it is continuous on any point in the interval. For endpoints, this can be continuous from the right or left.

continuous variable NOUN /kənˈtɪn.ju.əs ˈvɛər.i.ə.bəl/ a variable that can take on any value of continuous data, as opposed to discrete data. Antonym: *discrete variable* (p 39).

continuum NOUN /kənˈtɪn.ju.əm/ an unbroken, continuous set. A set where, between any two elements of the set, there is at least one other element. Examples: The set of real numbers is a continuum. Space-time is called "the continuum". Plural: *continua* /kənˈtɪn.ju.ə/.

contra- PREFIX /ˈkɒn.trə/ against; opposite.

contraction NOUN /kənˈtræk.ʃən/ see *compression* (p 26).

contradict VERB /ˌkɒn.trəˈdɪkt/ to state two things, both of which cannot be true. Example: The statement "a is an integer" contradicts the statement "a is not an integer."

contradiction NOUN /ˌkɒn.trəˈdɪk.ʃən/ a statement that cannot be true if prior statements are true. Example: the line is straight (statement); the line is not straight (contradiction). Synonym: *paradox* (p 85).

contraposition NOUN /ˌkɒn.trə.pəˈzɪ.ʃən/ the inference drawn from a contrapositive statement.

contrapositive NOUN /ˌkɒn.trə.pɒˈzɪ.tɪv/ the contrapositive of the statement 'if P then Q' is 'if not P then not Q'. Example: 'If the house is green then (P →) it must be mine' is the contrapositive of the statement 'If the house is not green then (NOT P →) it must not be mine' (NOT Q).

control group NOUN /kənˈtrɒl grup/ a group that is not affected by an experiment; a group that receives a placebo. Antonym: *experimental group* (p 47).

convenience sample NOUN /kənˈvin.jəns ˈsæm.pəl/ a sample taken from a part of a population that is easy to sample. A convenience sample is not a scientific sample. Example: A sample taken from people in a shopping mall. Synonym: *accidental sample*.

convention NOUN /kənˈvɛn.ʃən/
1) a way things are usually done.
2) an accepted way of doing things. Example: by convention, polynomials are written with the highest degree term on the left.

conventional ADJECTIVE /kənˈvɛn.ʃə.nl/ goes along with the way things are usually done.

converge VERB /kənˈvɜrdʒ/
1) to come closer and closer to a fixed value. Example: $\frac{1}{2}, \frac{1}{4}, \frac{1}{8}, \frac{1}{16}, \cdots$ converges to zero since each term is closer to zero than the last.
2) to come closer and closer together. Example: two lines converging.
Antonym: *diverge* (p 40), *oscillate* (p 84).

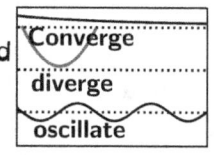
Converge; diverge; oscillate

converge absolutely VERB /kənˈvɜrdʒ ˌæb.səˈlut.li/ a series is said to converge absolutely if the sum of the absolute values of the terms is convergent. Math definition: $\sum_{n=0}^{\infty} a_n$ converges absolutely if $\sum_{n=0}^{\infty} |a_n|$ converges.

convergence NOUN /kənˈvɜr.dʒəns/ having to do with whether or not something converges.

convergent ADJECTIVE /kənˈvɜr.dʒənt/
1) draws closer and closer to a fixed value.
2) draws closer and closer one to another.
Antonym: *divergent* (p 40).

convergent function NOUN /kənˈvɜrdʒ.ənt ˈfʌŋk.ʃən/ the value of the function draws close to a numeric value as the argument tends towards positive or negative infinity. Example: The function $f(x) = x^{-1} + 1$ is convergent since its value approaches 1 as x approaches positive or negative infinity. Antonyms: *divergent function* (p 40), *oscillating function* (p 84).

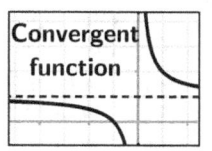
Convergent function

convergent sequence NOUN /kənˈvɜrdʒ.ənt ˈsi.kwəns/ a sequence that converges; an ordered list of numbers where the numbers get closer and closer to a particular value. Example: the sequence $\{1, \frac{1}{2}, \frac{1}{3}, \frac{1}{4}, \cdots\}$ converges to 0. Antonym: *divergent sequence* (p 40).

convergent series NOUN /kənˈvɜrdʒ.ənt ˈsɪər.iz/ a series that converges; as more and more numbers are added to the partial sum, the partial sum gets closer and closer to a particular value. Example: The series $\frac{1}{2} + \frac{1}{4} + \frac{1}{8} + \cdots$ converges to 1. Antonym: *divergent series* (p 41). Plural: *convergent series*.

converse NOUN /ˈkɒn.vɜrs/ the converse of the statement *if P then Q* is the statement *if Q then P*. If a statement and its converse are both true, the relationship is an implication. Example: If *it is an apple* (P) *then* (→) *it is sweet* (Q) is the converse of If *it is sweet* (Q) *then* (→) *it is an apple* (P).

converse of the Pythagorean Theorem NOUN /ˈkɒn.vɜrs ʌv θə pɪˌθæ.gəˈri.ən ˈθɪ.ə.rəm/ if A, B and C are the lengths of sides of a triangle and $A^2 + B^2 = C^2$ then the triangle is a right triangle and the side with length C is the hypotenuse.

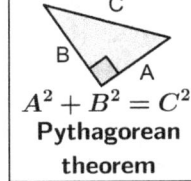
Pythagorean theorem

conversion NOUN /kənˈvɜr.ʒən/
1) the act of changing from one form to another, related, form.
2) the act of changing a unit of measure to a related unit of measure. Example: conversion of degrees Fahrenheit to kelvin.

conversion factor NOUN /kənˈvɜr.ʒən ˈfæk.tər/ a ratio that is multiplied by a quantity that changes the unit of measure of that quantity. Example: the conversion factor to change inches to feet is $\frac{1\,\text{ft}}{12\,\text{in}}$. So $36\,\text{in} = \frac{36\,\text{in}}{1} \cdot \frac{1\,\text{ft}}{12\,\text{in}} = \frac{36}{12}\,\text{ft} = 3\,\text{ft}$. Synonym: conversion ratio.

conversion graph NOUN /kənˈvɜr.ʒən græf/ a graph that can be used to convert between units of measure.

Conversion graph

conversion ratio NOUN /kənˈvɜr.ʒən ˈreɪ.ʃoʊ/ see conversion factor (p 30).

conversion table NOUN /kənˈvɜr.ʒən ˈteɪ.bəl/ a table containing representative values of units of measure used to convert from one unit of measure to another.

°F	°C
32°	0°
77°	25°
122°	50°
167°	75°
212°	100°

Conversion table

convert VERB /kənˈvɜrt/
1) to change from one form to another, usually equivalent, form. Example: convert a fraction to a decimal. Synonym: transform (p 115).
2) to change from one unit of measure to another, related unit of measure. Example: convert meters to kilometers.

convex ADJECTIVE /kɒnˈvɛks/ arching out. Math definition: A shape is convex if any line segment drawn between any two points in the shape is completely contained within the shape. Antonym: concave (p 26).

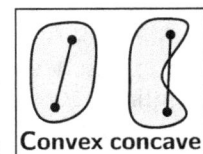
Convex concave

coordinate /koʊˈɔr.də.nɪt/
1) NOUN a location in a coordinate system. Example: In a 2-dimensional rectangular coordinate system, the coordinate $(2, 1)$ refers to the location at $x = 2$ and $y = 1$.
2) ADJECTIVE having to do with a coordinate system.

coordinate axis NOUN /koʊˈɔr.də.nɪt ˈæk.sɪs/ an axis in a coordinate system. Examples: x-axis, y-axis, z-axis. Plural: coordinate axes /koʊˈɔr.dnɪt ˈæk.siz/

Coordinated Universal Time NOUN /koʊˈɔr.dnˌeɪt.ɪd ˌju.nəˈvɜr.səl taɪm/ a time standard that includes addition or subtraction of leap seconds each year. Abbreviation: CUT. Synonym: Zulu time. See also Greenwich Mean Time (p 55).

coordinate geometry NOUN /koʊˈɔr.də.nɪt dʒiˈɒ.mɪ.tri/ see analytic geometry (p 10).

coordinate plane NOUN /koʊˈɔr.də.nɪt pleɪn/ a plane defined by two number lines usually intersecting at right angles. Synonym: Cartesian plane.

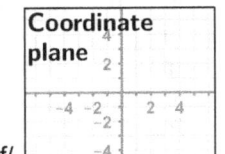
Coordinate plane

coordinate proof NOUN /koʊˈɔr.də.nɪt pruf/ a proof that uses figures in a coordinate system and algebra.

coordinate system NOUN /koʊˈɔr.də.nɪt ˈsɪs.təm/ a geometric space where a location is identified by a coordinate. See also rectangular coordinate system (p 96), polar coordinate system (p 90).

coplanar ADJECTIVE /koʊˈpleɪ.nər/ contained in the same plane. Example: In the figure e, d, and G are coplanar. f is not coplanar with e, d, and G. Antonym: noncoplanar (p 79).

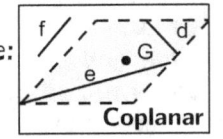
Coplanar

coprime ADJECTIVE /ˈkoʊ.praɪm/ having no common factors other than 1. Example: 10 and 21 are coprime. Synonym: relatively prime.

corner /ˈkɔr.nər/
1) NOUN where two or more intersecting line segments or three surfaces meet. Synonym: vertex.
2) ADJECTIVE on a corner.

corner point NOUN /ˈkɔr.nər pɔɪnt/ a point formed by the intersection of boundary lines or surfaces. Synonym: vertex (p 121).

Corner Point Principle NOUN /ˈkɔr.nər pɔɪnt ˈprɪn.sə.pəl/ a maximum or minimum of a feasible region of a linear system of inequalities will always be a corner point.

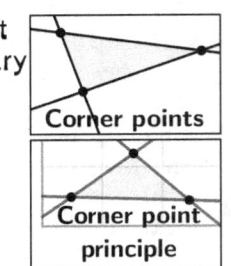
Corners / Corner points / Corner point principle

corner view NOUN /ˈkɔr.nər vju/ see perspective view (p 88).

corollary NOUN /ˈkɔr.əˌlɛr.i/ (British English) /kərˈɒl.ə.ri/ a theorem that can be proved easily from a more important theorem.

correction NOUN /kəˈrɛk.ʃn/ an adjustment to an estimate or measurement that makes the estimate more accurate.

correlate VERB /ˌkɔr.əˈleɪt/ to find relations between two variables in a dataset.

correlation NOUN /ˌkɔ.rəˈleɪ.ʃən/ a measure of the strength and direction of a relation between two variables in a dataset.

correlation coefficient NOUN /ˌkɔ.rəˈleɪ.ʃən ˌkoʊ.əˈfɪ.ʃənt/ a number that measures how close of a relationship exists between two variables. A correlation coefficient close to 1 indicates a strong positive correlation. A correlation coefficient close to -1 indicates a strong negative correlation. A correlation coefficient close to 0 indicates a weak correlation.

correspond VERB /ˌkɔr.əˈspɒnd/
1) to have a relationship such that a change in one

predicts a change in the other.
2) to be in the same relative position on two figures or two parts of the same figure.

correspondence NOUN /ˌkɔr.əˈspɒn.dəns/ a relationship between two objects or variables.

corresponding ADJECTIVE /ˌkɔr.əˈspɒn.dɪŋ/
1) having the same relationship with respect to the whole.
2) being in the same relative position on two figures or two parts of the same figure.
3) being related one to another. Example: the output corresponding to an input.

Corresponding Angles Postulate NOUN /ˌkɔr.əˈspɒn.dɪŋ ˈæŋ.gəlz ˈpɒs.tʃə.lɪt/ if two parallel lines are cut by a transversal, then each pair of corresponding angles is congruent.

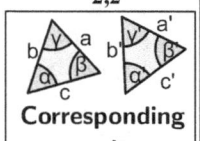
Corresponding angles postulate

corresponding elements of matrices NOUN /ˌkɔr.əˈspɒn.dɪŋ ˈɛ.lə.mənts ʌv ˈmeɪ.trɪ.siz/ elements at the same row and column of two or more matrices. $a_{1,1}$ corresponds with $b_{1,1}$; $a_{2,1}$ corresponds with $b_{2,1}$; $a_{1,2}$ corresponds with $b_{1,2}$; $a_{2,2}$ corresponds with $b_{2,2}$.

corresponding parts NOUN /ˌkɔr.əˈspɒn.dɪŋ pahrts/ parts of two similar figures that are each in the same relative positions as the other.

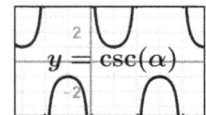
Corresponding parts

Corresponding Parts of Congruent Figures are Congruent NOUN /ˌkɔr.əˈspɒn.dɪŋ pahrts ʌv kənˈgru.ənt ˈfɪg.jərz ɑr kənˈgru.ənt/ if two geometric figures are congruent, then each pair of corresponding parts of those figures are congruent. Acronym: **CPCFC**.

Corresponding Parts of Congruent Triangles are Congruent NOUN /ˌkɔr.əˈspɒn.dɪŋ pahrts ʌv kənˈgru.ənt ˈtraɪˌæŋ.gəlz ɑr kənˈgru.ənt/ if two triangles are congruent, then each pair of corresponding parts of those triangles are congruent. Acronym: **CPCTC**.

corresponding parts of geometric figures NOUN /ˌkɔr.əˈspɒn.dɪŋ pahrts ʌv ˌdʒi.əˈmɛ.trɪk ˈfɪg.jərz/ parts of two geometric figures that are in the same relative positions.

cos ABBREVIATION cosine (p 31).

cos() COMPUTERS the cosine function in most computer languages. Example: $y = \cos(x)$. See also cosine (p 31).

cos⁻¹ ABBREVIATION see arccosine (p 12).

cosecant NOUN /kouˈsi.kænt/ the multiplicative inverse of the sine. Formula: $\csc \alpha = \frac{1}{\sin \alpha} = \frac{\text{hypotenuse}}{\text{opposite}}$. Abbreviation: **csc**.

cosh ABBREVIATION see hyperbolic cosine (p 58).

cosh() COMPUTERS represents the hyperbolic cosine function in most computer languages. Example: $y = \cosh(x)$.

cosine NOUN /ˈkou.saɪn/ for a right triangle, the ratio of the adjacent side to the hypotenuse. Formula: $\cos x = \frac{\text{adjacent}}{\text{hypotenuse}}$. Abbreviation: **cos**.

cosine rule NOUN /ˈkou.saɪn rul/ see Law of Cosines (p 67).

cost NOUN /kɒst/ an amount paid for something. Synonym: wholesale price (p 122).

cost of goods sold NOUN /kɒst ʌv gʊdz sould/ the direct cost to buy items sold.

cot ABBREVIATION see cotangent (p 31).

cot() COMPUTERS represents the cotangent function in most computer languages. Example: $y = \cot(x)$. See also cotangent (p 31).

cot⁻¹ ABBREVIATION see arccotangent (p 12).

cotangent NOUN /ˈkou.tæn.dʒənt/ the multiplicative inverse of the tangent. Formula: $\cot x = \frac{1}{\tan x} = \frac{\text{adjacent}}{\text{opposite}}$. Abbreviation: **cot**.

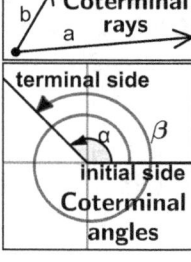

coterminal ADJECTIVE /ˌkouˈtɜr.mə.nl/
1) having a common ending boundary.
2) of two angles, having the same initial line and the same terminal line. The measures of coterminal angles differ by a multiple of a full turn. Formula: $m\angle \beta = 2\pi k + m\angle \alpha, k \in \mathbb{Z}$.
3) of rays, having a common end point.
Synonym: coterminous.

coterminous ADJECTIVE /ˌkouˈtɜr.mə.nəs/ see coterminal (p 31).

coth ABBREVIATION see hyperbolic cotangent (p 58).

coth() COMPUTERS represents the hyperbolic cotangent function on most computer languages. Example: $y = \coth(x)$;

count VERB /kaʊnt/
1) to associate natural numbers with a collection of objects starting with 1. Example: count the number of apples. Synonym: enumerate (p 44).
2) to recite the natural numbers in order. Example: count from 1 to 10.

countable ADJECTIVE /ˈkaʊn.tə.bəl/ can be placed in a one-to-one correspondence with the natural numbers. Example: the set of integers. Synonym: denumerable (p 36). Antonyms: uncountable (p 118), nondenumerable (p 79).

count back VERB /kaʊnt bæk/ to count backwards on a number line, usually for subtraction.

Count back 2

count by VERB /kaʊnt baɪ/ to count every n^{th} number. Example: count by 2's: 2, 4, 6, ... Synonym: skip count (p 106).

Count by 2's

counter- PREFIX /ˈkaʊn.tər/ going against; opposite. Example: counterexample.

counterclockwise ADJECTIVE /ˌkaʊn.tərˈklɒk.waɪz/ (American English) in the opposite direction that the hands of an analog clock turn. Synonym: anticlockwise (British English). Antonym: clockwise (p 21).

Counter clockwise

counterexample NOUN /ˈkaʊn.tər.ɪgˌzæm.pəl/ an example that disproves a proposition.

3rd Dyslexic's Edition

Counting Formula NOUN /ˈkaʊnt.ɪŋ ˈfɔr.mjə.lə/ where $n(A)$ is the number of elements in the set A, $n(A \cup B) = n(A) + n(B) - n(A \cup B)$.

counting number NOUN /ˈkaʊnt.ɪŋ ˈnʌm.bər/ see *natural number* (p 78).

counting principle NOUN /ˈkaʊnt.ɪŋ ˈprɪn.sə.pəl/ the size of the sample space of a set of independent events is the product of the size of the sample space of each of the events. Formula: $S(e_1, e_2, \cdots, e_n) = S(e_1) \cdot S(e_2) \cdot \ldots \cdot S(e_n)$. Example: the sample space of 3 blue balls and 2 red balls is $3 \cdot 2 = 6$. Synonym: *fundamental counting principle*.

count on VERB /kaʊnt ɒn/ to continue counting on a number line, as in addition.

CPCFC ACRONYM see *Corresponding Parts of Congruent Figures are Congruent* (p 31).

CPCTC ACRONYM see *Corresponding Parts of Congruent Triangles are Congruent* (p 31).

cps ABBREVIATION see *cycles per second* (p 33).

Cramer's rule NOUN /ˈkreɪ.mərz rul/ an algorithm for solving square linear systems using determinants. Example: For the system of linear equations $\begin{cases} ax + by = c \\ dx + ey = f \end{cases}$, in matrix form $\begin{bmatrix} a & b & | & c \\ d & e & | & f \end{bmatrix}$, the solution of the system is
$x = \dfrac{\begin{vmatrix} c & b \\ f & e \end{vmatrix}}{\begin{vmatrix} a & b \\ d & e \end{vmatrix}}, y = \dfrac{\begin{vmatrix} a & c \\ d & f \end{vmatrix}}{\begin{vmatrix} a & b \\ d & e \end{vmatrix}}$.

create VERB /kriˈeɪt/ to bring into being.

crest NOUN /krɛst/ the very top of a wave.

criterion NOUN /kraɪˈtɪər.i.ən/ a condition that must be true for the rest to apply. Example: If $\underbrace{\text{the radius of a circle is 1}}_{\text{criterion}}$ then $\underbrace{\text{the circle is a unit circle}}_{\text{consequent}}$. Plural: *criteria* /kraɪˈtɪər.i.ə/. Synonyms: *condition*, *constraint*. See also *assumption* (p 14).

critical ADJECTIVE /ˈkrɪt.ɪ.kl/ indispensable, vital.

critical point ADJECTIVE /ˈkrɪt.ɪ.kl pɔɪnt/ a point on a function that is a stationary point, rough point, or endpoint.

cross multiplication NOUN /krɔs ˌmʌl.tə.plɪˈkeɪ.ʃən/ multiplying each numerator by the denominator on the other side of the equal sign. Math definition: if $\frac{a}{b} = \frac{c}{d}$ then $ad = bc$. $b \neq 0, d \neq 0$. Example: $\frac{3y}{4} = \frac{3}{2} \to 3y \cdot 2 = 3 \cdot 4 \to 6y = 12 \to y = 2$.

cross product NOUN /krɔs ˈprɒ.dʌkt/
1) a method of multiplying 3-dimensional vectors that gives a third vector that is orthogonal to both **u** and **v**. Notation: $\mathbf{u} \times \mathbf{v}$. Formula: $\langle a_1, a_2, a_3 \rangle \times \langle b_1, b_2, b_3 \rangle = \langle a_2 b_3 - a_3 b_2, a_3 b_1 - a_1 b_3, a_1 b_2 - a_2 b_1 \rangle$. Example: $\langle -1, 2, 3 \rangle \times \langle 2, -3, 1 \rangle = \langle 2 \cdot 1 - 3(-3), 3 \cdot 2 - (-1) \cdot 1, (-1) \cdot (-13) - 2 \cdot 2 \rangle = \langle 2 + 9, 6 + 1, 3 + 4 \rangle = \langle 11, 7, -1 \rangle$. Corollary: If θ is the angle between vectors $\vec{a}$ and $\vec{b}$ and $\vec{n}$ is the unit vector perpendicular to both $\vec{a}$ and $\vec{b}$, then $a \times b = \|a\| \|b\| n \sin \theta$. Synonym: *vector product*.
2) (fractions) the result of cross multiplication.

Cross Product Theorem NOUN /krɔs ˈprɒ.dʌkt ˈθɪ.ə.rəm/ the vector product of $a \times b$ is orthogonal to both $\vec{a}$ and $\vec{b}$. Math definition: if $c = a \times b$, then $c \perp a$ and $c \perp b$.

cross section NOUN /krɔs ˈsɛk.ʃən/
1) (geometry) a 2-dimensional figure formed by intersecting a 3-dimensional figure with a plane, often at right angles to an axis.
2) (statistics) a representative sample.

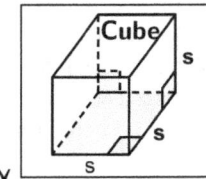
Cross section

csc ABBREVIATION see *cosecant* (p 31).

csc() COMPUTERS represents the cosecant function in most computer languages. Example: `y = csc(x);`

csc⁻¹ ABBREVIATION see *arccosecant* (p 12).

csch ABBREVIATION see *hyperbolic cosecant* (p 58).

csch() COMPUTERS represents the hyperbolic cosecant function in most computer languages. Example: `y = csch(x);`

cu ABBREVIATION *cubic* (p 32).

cub- PREFIX /kjub/
1) having to do with a cube (geometric figure).
2) having an exponent of 3.

cube /kjub/
1) NOUN (geometry) a solid figure whose edges are all the same length and whose faces are congruent squares.
2) NOUN (algebra) a value multiplied by itself three times; a value raised to the power of 3. Example: $t^3 = t \cdot t \cdot t$.
3) VERB (algebra) to multiply a value by itself three times; to raise to the power of 3.
4) ADJECTIVE having to do with a cube.
5) ADJECTIVE shaped like a cube.
6) ADJECTIVE multiplied by itself three times.

cube function NOUN /kjub ˈfʌŋk.ʃən/ the function $f(x) = x^3$.

cube root NOUN /kjub rut/ a number that, when multiplied by itself three times, equals the original value. Notation: $\sqrt[3]{x}$ or $x^{\frac{1}{3}}$. Math definition: $y = \sqrt[3]{x}$ if and only if $y^3 = x$. Example: $\sqrt[3]{8} = 2$ since $2^3 = 8$.

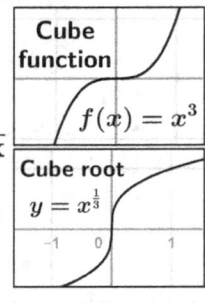
Cube function $f(x) = x^3$
Cube root $y = x^{\frac{1}{3}}$

cubic /ˈkju.bɪk/
1) ADJECTIVE having to do with an exponent of 3. Example: x^3; ft^3 (cubic feet). Abbreviation: cu.
2) ADJECTIVE having to do with a cube.
3) NOUN a cubic equation.

cubic equation NOUN /ˈkju.bɪk ɪˈkweɪ.ʃən/ an equation of a cubic polynomial. Example: $y = 2x^3 - 2x + 1$.

cubic function NOUN /ˈkju.bɪk ˈfʌŋk.ʃən/ a function of a cubic polynomial. Example: $f(x) = x^3 + 2x^2 - 3$.

cubic measure NOUN /ˈkju.bɪk ˈmɛʒ.ər/ a unit of measure of volume; distance cubed.

cubic meter NOUN /ˈkju.bɪk ˈmi.tər/ a unit of measure of volume measuring 1

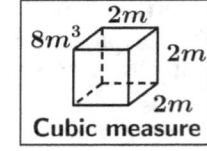
Cubic measure

meter on each side. Example: 1 m^3.

cubic polynomial NOUN /'kju.bɪk ˌpɒl.ə'nou.mi.əl/ a polynomial of degree 3. Example: $3x^3 - 4x^2 + 2x + 1$

cubic unit NOUN /'kju.bɪk 'ju.nɪt/ a unit of measure of volume. Example: $1 \text{ cm} \times 1 \text{ cm} \times 1 \text{ cm} = 1 \text{ cm}^3$.

cuboctahedron NOUN /'kjub ˌɒk.tə.hi.drən/ a polyhedron whose faces are six congruent squares and eight congruent equilateral triangles. Plural: cuboctahedra /'kjub ˌɒk.tə.hi.drə/.

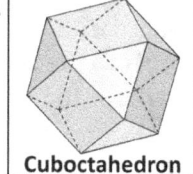
Cuboctahedron

cuboid NOUN /'kju.bɔɪd/ see rectangular solid (p 97).

cumulative ADJECTIVE /'kju.mjə.lə.tɪv/ adding up over time; combined effect. Example: the cumulative effect of a lifetime of illegal drug use.

cumulative error NOUN /'kju.mjə.lə.tɪv 'ɛr.ər/
1) an error that does not decrease with additional observations.
2) the combined effect of multiple errors, especially in computing.

cumulative frequency NOUN /'kju.mjə.lə.tɪv 'fri.kwən.si/ (statistics) the sum of the frequencies below or equal to a certain value.

cup NOUN /kʌp/
1) (sets) the symbol $\cup$ which represents union of sets.
2) (measure) a unit of measure of volume. Formulas: $1 \text{ cup} = 8 \text{ fluid ounces}$. $2 \text{ cups} = 1 \text{ pint}$. $4 \text{ cups} = 1 \text{ quart}$. $1 \text{ cup} \approx 0.237 \text{ liters}$. Abbreviation: c.

curly brace NOUN /'kɜr.li breɪs/ see brace (p 18).

currency NOUN /'kɜr.ən.si/ something that is used as money.

curvature NOUN /'kɜr.və.tʃər/ how much something curves; how fast the slope of a line tangent to a curve changes as the point of tangency moves along the curve. Notation: κ. Formulas: $\kappa = \left| \frac{dT}{ds} \right|$ where $\mathbf{T}$ is the unit tangent vector; or $\kappa(t) = \frac{|\mathbf{r}'(t) \times \mathbf{r}''(t)|}{|\mathbf{r}'(t)|^3}$ where $\mathbf{r}$ is the vector function defining the curve.

Curvature

curve /kɜrv/
1) NOUN a continuous, one-dimensional set of points.
2) VERB to move on a path that is not straight.

Curve

curve fitting NOUN /kɜrv 'fɪt.ɪŋ/ any method of calculating an equation that best fits a set of data points.

Curve fitting

cusp NOUN /kʌsp/ a place on a graph that comes to a point. Functions are not differentiable at a cusp.

Cusp

customary ADJECTIVE /'kʌs.tə.mɛ.ri/ based on common practice. Example: gallon is a customary unit of measure.

customary measurement system NOUN /'kʌs.tə.mɛ.ri 'mɛ.ʒər.mənt 'sɪs.təm/ the measurement system based on feet, miles, gallons and cups still in use in the United States.

customary unit NOUN /'kʌs.tə.mɛr.i 'ju.nɪt/ one of the units of measure from the customary measurement system. Examples: feet, miles and gallons.

cut VERB /kʌt/
1) to intersect.
2) to divide into two or more parts.

cut off VERB /kʌt ɑf/ to remove a part of a larger object by intersecting it with a plane. Everything on one side of the plane is 'cut off'.

cycle NOUN /'saɪ.kəl/
1) the period of time over which a set of events repeats. Example: annual weather cycle.
2) of a periodic function, the smallest part that repeats.
3) a system that repeats over time. Example: water cycle.

1 Cycle

cycles per second NOUN /'saɪ.kəlz pɜr 'sɛk.ənd/ the number of times a complete cycle happens each second. Abbreviation: cps. Formula: $\text{CPS} = \frac{\text{no. cycles}}{\text{no. seconds}}$. Synonym: frequency (p 51).

3 cycles per sec.

cyclic ADJECTIVE /'sɪk.lɪk/
1) having to do with a circle.
2) repeating at regular intervals.

cyclic polygon NOUN /'sɪk.lɪk 'pɒ.li.gɒn/ a polygon whose vertices lie on a common circle; a polygon that can be circumscribed.

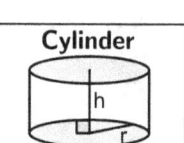
Cyclic polygon

cycloid NOUN /'saɪ.klɔɪd/ a curve generated by a point on the circumference of a circle as it rolls along a line. Equation: $x = r(t - \sin t)$, $y = r(1 - \cos t)$.

Cycloid

cylinder NOUN /'sɪl.ɪn.dər/ a 3-dimensional geometric figure with circular, congruent and parallel bases and straight sides.

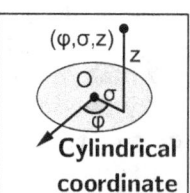
Cylinder

cylindrical ADJECTIVE /sʌ'lɪn ˌdrɪ.kəl/
1) shaped like a cylinder.
2) having to do with a cylinder.

cylindrical coordinate NOUN /sʌ'lɪn ˌdrɪ.kəl kou'ɔr.dn.ɪt/ a coordinate using polar coordinates in the x-y axial plane and a height parallel with the z-axis. Notation: (φ, σ, z) where φ is the angle in the x-y axial plane, σ is the radius and z is the height.

Cylindrical coordinate

cypher NOUN /'saɪ.fər/ (British English) see cipher (American English) (p 21).

D

d ABBREVIATION deci-.

D SYMBOL 50 in Roman numerals.

da ABBREVIATION deka-. Example: $5 \text{ decagrams} = 50 \text{ grams}$. Synonym: ten.

damped harmonic motion NOUN /dæmpd hɑr'mɒ.nɪk 'mou.ʃən/ the motion of an oscillating spring that slows down due to friction. Formulas: $f(t) = ab^t \sin(Bt) + k$ or $f(t) = ae^{rt} \sin(Bt) + k$.

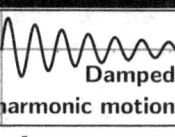
Damped harmonic motion

dash NOUN /dæʃ/ a short line segment that may be repeated to form a line or curve.

dashed ADJECTIVE /dæʃt/ drawn with dashes. Example: dashed line.

Dashed line

data NOUN /ˈdeɪ.tə/ a set of facts used in analysis or associated with a study of a population. Singular: *datum* /ˈdeɪ.tʌm/.

data analysis NOUN /ˈdeɪ.tə əˈnæ.lə.sɪs/ performing calculations on data in order to arrive at conclusions about a population. Plural: *data analyses* /ˈdeɪ.tə əˈnæ.lə.siz/.

data item NOUN /ˈdeɪ.tə ˈaɪ.təm/ a single row in a dataset.

data point NOUN /ˈdeɪ.tə pɔɪnt/ a single item of data in a dataset.

dataset NOUN /ˈdeɪ.tə.sɛt/ a collection of related numbers and facts, usually organized into rows and columns.

data type NOUN /ˈdeɪ.tə taɪp/ there are two main data types in statistics: qualitative (or categorical) and quantitative (or numerical).

date NOUN /deɪt/ a day, month and year. Dates are written in years since a reference date, months since the start of the year, and days since the start of the month. Example: 25 January 1964.

day NOUN /deɪ/ the period of time it takes for the Earth to rotate once on its axis. Formulas: $365\frac{1}{4}$ days ≈ 1 year, 24 hours ≈ 1 day.

day of the week NOUN /deɪ ʌv ðə wik/ Sunday, Monday, Tuesday, Wednesday, Thursday, Friday or Saturday.

de- PREFIX /dɪ/ undo, not, reverse.

deca- PREFIX /ˈdɛ.kə/ ten. See also *deka-* (p 36).

decade NOUN /ˈdɛ.keɪd/
1) a period of time equal to 10 years.
2) a period of ten years beginning with a year whose last digit is zero.

decagon NOUN /ˈdɛ.kəˌgɒn/ any ten-sided polygon.

Decagon

decahedron NOUN /ˌdɛ.kəˈhi.drən/ any polyhedron with 10 faces. Plural: *decahedra* /ˌdɛ.kəˈhi.drə/.

Decahedron

decay NOUN /dɪˈkeɪ/ the gradual breaking down of a substance. Antonym: *growth* (p 55).

decay factor NOUN /dɪˈkeɪ ˈfæk.tər/ a number that shows how fast decay is happening. Example: In $y = ab^x$, $0 < b < 1$, the decay factor is b. Antonym: *growth factor* (p 55). Synonym: *decay rate* (p 34).

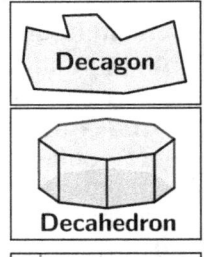
Decay factor

decay rate NOUN /dɪˈkeɪ reɪt/ a rate that determines the decrease of a function. For linear equations, $m < 0$ in $y = mx + b$. For exponential equations, $0 < r < 1$ in $y = ae^{rx}$. Over any subdomain where $f''(x) < 0$, the rate of decay is decreasing. Antonym: *growth rate* (p 55). Synonym: *decay factor* (p 34).

deci- PREFIX /ˈdɛ.sə/ one tenth of; $\frac{1}{10} = 0.1 = 10^{-1}$. Example: **2 decigram = 2×10^{-1} grams = 0.2 grams**. Abbreviation: *d*.

decile NOUN /ˈdɛ.sɪl/ one of nine values that divides a dataset into ten parts.

decimal /ˈdɛs.məl/
1) NOUN a number written in base 10.
2) NOUN a decimal separator '.' or ','.
3) ADJECTIVE having do with numbers written in base 10.
4) ADJECTIVE based on the number 10.

decimal digit NOUN /ˈdɛs.məl ˈdɪ.dʒɪt/ one of the digits **0, 1, 2, 3, 4, 5, 6, 7, 8,** and **9** used to write decimal numerals.

decimal fraction NOUN /ˈdɛs.məl ˈfræk.ʃən/ a fraction where the denominator is a power of 10. Example: $\frac{37}{10^2} = \frac{37}{100}$.

decimal number NOUN /ˈdɛs.məl ˈnʌm.bər/ a numeral written in base 10.

decimal numeration NOUN /ˈdɛs.məl ˌnu.məˈreɪ.ʃən/ a real number in base 10 that may use a decimal separator. Examples: 532.4, 5, 12.3, 1,003.72.

decimal part NOUN /ˈdɛs.məl pɑrt/ the part of a decimal number to the right of the decimal separator. Example: 47 in 53.47.

Whole part | Decimal part
367.532
Decimal point

decimal place NOUN /ˈdɛs.məl pleɪs/
1) the position of a digit to the right of a decimal separator. Synonym: *digit position*.
2) the number of digits to the right of a decimal separator kept when rounding. Example: round to 3 decimal places.

$\underset{1^{st}}{1}\ \underset{}{5} . \underset{2^{nd}}{6}\ \underset{3^{rd}}{3}$ — 2nd, 1st, 3rd
Decimal place

decimal point NOUN /ˈdɛs.məl pɔɪnt/ see *decimal separator* (p 34).

decimal representation NOUN /ˈdɛs.məl ˌrɛ.prɪ.zɛnˈteɪ.ʃən/ a number put in decimal form.

decimal separator NOUN /ˈdɛs.məl ˈsɛp.əˌreɪ.tər/ a period or comma in a decimal number separating the whole part from the decimal part. In United Kingdom, Canada and the United States, a period, called a decimal point, is used.

Whole part | Decimal part
367.532
Decimal separator

decipher VERB /dɪˈsaɪ.fər/ to convert from enciphered text to plain text using a method such as transposition of letters. Antonym: *encipher* (p 43). Synonym: *decypher* (British English).

decipherment NOUN /dɪˈsaɪ.fər.mənt/ the act of deciphering. Antonym: *encipherment* (p 43).

declination NOUN /ˌdɛ.kləˈneɪ.ʃən/ the slope of a line or plane from a vertical or horizontal reference line or plane.

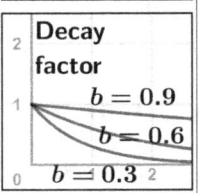
Declination

decompose VERB /ˌdi.kɒmˈpoʊz/ to break into parts by a rule. Antonym: *compose* (p 25).

decomposition NOUN /ˌdi.kɒm.pəˈzɪ.ʃən/
1) the act of breaking into parts by a rule.
2) the result of breaking into parts by a rule. Antonym: *composition* (p 25).

decomposition method NOUN /ˌdi.kɒm.pəˈzɪ.ʃən ˈmɛ.θəd/ a strategy for subtracting when the digit for the minuend is smaller than the digit for the subtrahend. Synonym: *regroup* (p 98), *borrow* (obsolete).

decrease /dɪˈkris/
1) VERB to reduce by a certain amount. Keyword for subtraction. Synonym: *subtract* (p 110).
2) VERB to become smaller and smaller; to become less and less. Synonyms: *shrink*, *compress* (p 26).

3) NOUN the amount, proportion or percentage by which a value decreases. Antonym: *increase* (p 60).

decrease by PREPOSITION /dɪˈkris baɪ/ reduce by a given quantity or percentage. Key phrase for subtraction.

decreasing ADJECTIVE /dɪˈkris.ɪŋ/ going down; becoming less. Antonym: *increasing* (p 60).

decreasing function NOUN /dɪˈkris.ɪŋ ˈfʌŋk.ʃən/ a function whose values become less as the function argument increases. Math definitions: for all a, b in the domain of f, if $a > b$, then $f(a) < f(b)$; or $\frac{d}{dx} f(x) < 0$. Antonym: *increasing function* (p 60).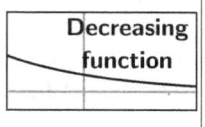

decreasing on an interval ADJECTIVE /dɪˈkris.ɪŋ ɒn ən ˈɪn.tər.vəl/ a function whose values become less as the independent variable increases on a subdomain. Antonym: *increasing on an interval* (p 60).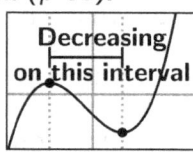

decreasing sequence NOUN /dɪˈkris.ɪŋ ˈsi.kwəns/ a sequence of real numbers where each term is less that its preceding term. Example: $1, \frac{1}{2}, \frac{1}{4}, \frac{1}{8}, \cdots$. Antonym: *increasing sequence* (p 60).

decreasing test NOUN /dɪˈkri.sɪŋ tɛst/ a test that reveals if a function is decreasing on an interval. Math definition: if $f'(x) < 0$ on an interval, then f is decreasing on that interval. Antonym: *increasing test* (p 60).

decrypt VERB /diˈkrɪpt/ to convert encrypted text to plain text using an encryption key. Antonym: *encrypt* (p 44).

decryption NOUN /diˈkrɪp.ʃən/ the act of decrypting. Antonym: *encryption* (p 44).

decypher VERB /diˈsaɪ.fər/ (British English) see *decipher* (p 34).

deduce VERB /dɪˈdus/ to arrive at a conclusion by deduction.

deduct VERB /dɪˈdʌkt/
1) to subtract from. Keyword for subtraction.
2) to come to a conclusion using premises and logic.

deduction NOUN /dɪˈdʌk.ʃən/
1) using agreed upon premises to support a conclusion.
2) the conclusion of an argument.
3) an amount subtracted from a total.

deductive ADJECTIVE /dɪˈdʌk.tɪv/ based on deduction. Example: deductive reasoning.

deductive reasoning NOUN /dɪˈdʌk.tɪv ˈriz.nɪŋ/ a form of logic that starts with premises and proceeds to conclusions based on those premises. Example: • All people are mortal (premise). • Socrates is a person (premise). • So, Socrates is mortal (conclusion or deduction).

deficient number NOUN /dəˈfɪ.ʃənt ˈnʌm.bər/ an integer whose sum of its proper divisors is less than the integer itself. Example: $1 + 2 + 5 < 10$. Antonyms: *abundant number* (p 7); *perfect number* (p 87).

define VERB /dəˈfaɪn/ to state the properties that belong to a particular object or class of objects, especially necessary properties. Example: A line segment is defined as a continuous portion of a line between two points on that line.

defined ADJECTIVE /dəˈfaɪnd/ having an explicit definition. Antonym: *undefined* (p 118).

definite ADJECTIVE /ˈdɛ.fə.nɪt/ over a specified, non-infinite range. Antonym: *indefinite* (p 61).

definite integral NOUN /ˈdɛ.fə.nɪt ˈɪn.tɛ.grəl/ an integral over a specified, non-infinite range, which gives a number. Formula: $\int_a^b f(x) dx = \lim_{n \to \infty} \sum_{i=1}^n f(x_i) \Delta x$. Antonym: *indefinite integral* (p 61).

definition NOUN /ˌdɛ.fəˈnɪ.ʃən/ a statement of the properties that belong to a mathematical object. Example: a square is a: • quadrilateral (property) • with congruent sides (property) • whose sides meet at right angles (property).

degenerate
1) ADJECTIVE /dɪˈdʒɛ.nə.rɪt/ changed to a simpler form. Example: a line segment is a degenerate case of a rectangle with a zero width.
2) VERB /dɪˈdʒɛ.nəˌreɪt/ to change to a simpler form. Example: as the radius of a circle approaches 0, the circle degenerates into a point.

degenerate conic NOUN /dɪˈdʒɛ.nər.ɪt ˈkɒn.ɪk/ a point, line, or pair of intersecting lines generated when a plane intersects a double cone through its vertex.

degree NOUN /dəˈgri/
1) (of an angle) a unit of measure of angles. $360°$ equals one full circle. Notation: $°$.
2) (of a variable) the exponent of a variable.
3) (of a term) the sum of the degrees of variables in the term.
4) (of an expression, polynomial) the greatest degree of terms in the expression. Example: The polynomial $x^4 - 3x^2 + 2x$ has a degree of 4.
5) (of a node) the number of paths that meet at a node of a network graph.
6) (temperature) a unit of measure of temperature. One of degree Fahrenheit, degree Celsius, or kelvin. Notation: $°F$, $°C$, K.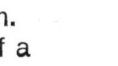

degree Celsius NOUN /dəˈgri ˈsɛl.si.əs/ a unit of measure of temperature. $0°C$ is the freezing temperature of water at sea level. $100°C$ is the boiling temperature of water at sea level. Formulas: $C = \frac{5}{9}(F - 32)$, $F = \frac{9}{5}C + 32$ where F is degrees Fahrenheit. Notation: $°C$. Synonym: *degree centigrade* (obsolete).

degree Fahrenheit NOUN /dəˈgri ˈfær.ənˌhaɪt/ a unit of measure of temperature. $32°F$ is about the freezing temperature of pure water at sea level. $212°F$ is about the boiling temperature of pure water at sea level. Formulas: $F = \frac{9}{5}C + 32$, $C = \frac{5}{9}(F - 32)$ where C is degrees Celsius. Notation: $°F$.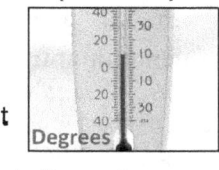

degree kelvin NOUN /dəˈgri ˈkɛl.vɪn/ see *kelvin* (p 66).

degree of accuracy NOUN /dəˈgri ʌv æˈkjə.rə.si/ the number of significant digits in a measurement.

degrees of freedom NOUN /dəˈgriz ʌv ˈfri.dʌm/ the number of parameters that may vary independently.

deka- PREFIX /ˈdɛ.kə/ 10. Example: 7 dekagrams = 70 grams; 7 dag = 70g. Abbreviation: da. See also deca- (p 34).

deleted neighborhood NOUN /dɪˈli.təd ˈneɪ.bɔr.hʊd/ a neighborhood around a point, not including the point itself.

delineate VERB /dɪˈlɪ.ni.eɪt/
1) to form a boundary around;
2) to show the beginning and the end.

delta NOUN /ˈdɛl.tə/ the Greek letter Δ, used to represent incremental change. Example: 'Δx' means 'change in x'. See also Greek Letters (p 135).

delta- PREFIX /ˈdɛl.tə/ having to do with equilateral triangles.

delta function NOUN /ˈdɛl.tə fʌŋk.ʃən/ a function describing the slope of a step function; a function that is a derivative of the step function.

deltahedron NOUN /ˈdɛl.təˌhi.drən/ any polyhedron whose faces are congruent equilateral triangles. Plural: deltahedra /ˈdɛl.təˌhi.drə/.

deltoid NOUN /ˈdɛl.tɔɪd/ see kite (p 66).

deltoidal ADJECTIVE /dɛlˈtɔɪ.dl/ containing or constructed from deltoids (kite).

denote VERB /dɪˈnoʊt/ is a representation of a mathematical operations. See also Notation (p 3).

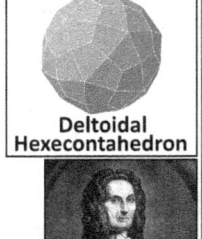
Deltoidal Hexecontahedron

de Moivre, Abraham PERSON /də mwɑvr ˈeɪ.brəˌhæm/ (1667—1754) a French mathematician known for his contributions to probability and for de Moivre's formula.

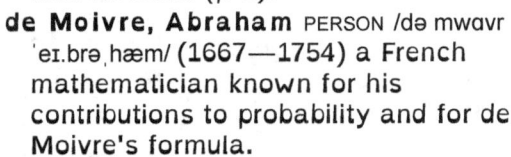
Abraham de Moivre

de Moivre's formula NOUN /də mwɑvrz ˈfɔr.mjə.lə/ a formula for the exponentiation of complex numbers in trigonometric form. Formula: $z^n = (r(\cos\theta + i\sin\theta))^n = r^n(\cos n\theta + i\sin n\theta)$

de Morgan, Augustus PERSON /dɪ ˈmɔr.gən ɔˈgʌs.təs/ (1806—1871) an India born British mathematician who advanced, among other things, Boolean algebra.

de Morgan's Theorem NOUN /dɪ ˈmɔr.gənz ˈθɪ.ə.rəm/ a set of identities relating the complements of unions and intersections of sets: • $(A \cap B)' = A' \cup B'$; • $(A \cup B)' = A' \cap B'$; • $\neg(P \wedge Q) \Leftrightarrow (\neg P) \vee (\neg Q)$; • $\neg(P \vee Q) \Leftrightarrow (\neg P) \wedge (\neg Q)$.

Augustus de Morgan

denominator NOUN /dɪˈnɒm.əˌneɪ.tər/ the bottom part of a fraction. Notation: $\frac{\text{numerator}}{\text{denominator}}$ = numerator ÷ denominator. Example: In $\frac{3}{7}$, the denominator is 7. Synonym: divisor (p 41).

denote VERB /diˈnoʊt/ to represent using a symbol; stand as a symbol for.

density NOUN /ˈdɛn.sɪ.ti/ how closely a set of objects are crowded together.

density function NOUN /ˈdɛn.sɪ.ti fʌŋk.ʃən/ a function of a continuous random variable whose integral over an interval gives the probability that its value will fall within the interval.

density property NOUN /ˈdɛn.sɪ.ti ˈprɒ.pər.ti/ a property of many ordered sets where, between any two members of a set, there exists at least one other member of the set. Example: real numbers.

denumerable ADJECTIVE /dɪˈnu.mər.ə.bəl/ see countable (p 31).

depend VERB /dɪˈpɛnd/ to be conditioned on.

dependent ADJECTIVE /dɪˈpɛn.dənt/ depending on one or more other math objects. Antonym: Independent (p 61).

dependent axiom NOUN /dɪˈpɛn.dənt ˈæk.si.əm/ an axiom that can be proven from other axioms in an axiomatic system. Antonym: Independent axiom (p 61).

dependent event NOUN /dɪˈpɛn.dənt ɪˈvɛnt/ an event depends on the outcome of another event. Antonym: Independent event (p 61).

dependent linear equation NOUN /dɪˈpɛn.dənt ˈlɪ.ni.ər ɪˈkweɪ.ʒən/ a linear equation having solutions identical to another linear equation; a linear equation that is a linear combination of one or more other linear equations.

dependent system of linear equations NOUN /dɪˈpɛn.dənt sɪs.təm ʌv ˈlɪ.ni.ər ɪˈkweɪ.ʒənz/ a system of linear equations having infinite solutions. Example: $x + y = 3, 2x + 2y = 6$.

dependent variable NOUN /dɪˈpɛn.dənt ˈvɛər.i.ə.bəl/ having values that depend on one or more independent variable(s). Example: in $y = \sin x$, y is the dependent variable. Synonym: output (p 84). Antonyms: Independent variable (p 61), input (p 62).

deposit NOUN /dəˈpɑz.ɪt/
1) money paid to reserve goods or services.
2) money placed in an interest bearing account.

depreciate VERB /dɪˈpri.ʃiˈeɪt/ to decrease in value. Antonym: appreciate (p 6).

depreciation NOUN /dɪˌpri.ʃiˈeɪ.ʃən/ a decrease in value, usually due to wear. Antonym: appreciation (p 12).

depth NOUN /dɛpθ/ a distance below a surface. Example: a depth of 10 feet.

derivation NOUN /ˌdær.əˈveɪ.ʃən/ 1) how a formula is found.
2) how a conclusion is reached.

derivative NOUN /dɪˈrɪ.və.tɪv/ the instantaneous change of the output of a relation compared to the input. Formula: $f'(h) = \lim_{x \to h} \frac{f(x) - f(h)}{x - h}$. Example: $\frac{d}{dx} x^a = ax^{a-1}$. Synonyms: differential coefficient (British, p 38), instantaneous rate of change (p 63), differential quotient.

derive VERB /dəˈraɪv/
1) to trace how a formula is found. Example: the quadratic formula is derived using the complete the squares algorithm.
2) to obtain from a more fundamental measure.

derived unit NOUN /dəˈraɪvd ˈju.nɪt/ a unit of measure that is obtained from one of the fundamental units of measure. Example: velocity in meters per second squared.

Descartes, René PERSON /deɪˈkɑrt rəˈneɪ/ (1596—1650) a French philosopher and mathematician who formalized the basic concepts of analytic geometry, including the rectangular coordinate system.

René Descartes

Descartes' Rule of Signs NOUN /deɪˈkɑrtz rul ʌv saɪnz/ a rule for determining the maximum number of different types of zeros of a polynomial. Math definition: Let P be a polynomial with real coefficients. Then, 1) The number of positive real zeros of $P(x)$ is either equal to the number of variations in the sign of $P(x)$ or less than that by an even whole number. 2) The number of negative real zeros of $P(-x)$ is either equal to the number of variations in the sign of $P(-x)$ or less than that by an even whole number.

descend VERB /dɪˈsɪnd/ to go down; to reduce in quantity. Antonym: ascend (p 14).

descending ADJECTIVE /dɪˈsɪn.dɪŋ/ going down; reducing in quantity. Example: sort into descending numerical order: 9, 8, 6, 4, 1, -1. Antonym: ascending (p 14).

descriptive variable NOUN /dɪˈskrɪp.tɪv ˈvɛər.i.ə.bəl/ a variable whose name describes in some way the value it represents. Example: h for height.

descriptive statistics NOUN /dɪˈskrɪp.tɪv stəˈtɪs.tɪks/ the organization and summarization of data.

designed experiment NOUN /dɪˈsaɪnd ɪkˈspɛr.ə.mənt/ a statistical study that studies the effect of applying a change to a group. Synonym: experimental study.

determinant /dɪˈtɜr.mə.nənt/
1) NOUN a scalar generated from the elements of a square matrix. Notation: $|A|$, $\det(A)$. Example:
$\begin{vmatrix} 3 & 1 & 0 \\ 2 & 4 & 2 \\ 2 & 3 & 1 \end{vmatrix} = 3(4 \cdot 1 - 2 \cdot 3) - 1(2 \cdot 1 - 2 \cdot 2) + 0(2 \cdot 3 - 4 \cdot 2) = 3 \cdot (-2) - 1 \cdot (-2) + 0 \cdot (-2) = -6 + 2 + 0 = 4$. See also Properties of Determinants (p 134).
2) ADJECTIVE having a finite number of solutions. Antonym: indeterminate (p 61).

determinate equation NOUN /dɪˈtɜr.mə.nət ɪˈkweɪ.ʃən/ an equation that has a finite number of solutions. Example: $0 = x^2 - 4$ is a determinate equation. Its solution set is $\{2, -2\}$. Antonym: indeterminate equation (p 61).

determine VERB /dɪˈtɜr.mɪn/ to define an object is such a way that no other unique object can be defined this way. Example: two points determine a line.

determined ADJECTIVE /dɪˈtɜr.mɪnd/ no other object of the same type can fulfill the given condition. Example: a line is determined by two points on the line.

developable surface NOUN /dɪˈvɛl.ə.pə.bl ˈsɜr.fɪs/ a surface of a 3-dimensional object that can be 'rolled flat' without changing the surface area. Synonym: geometric net.

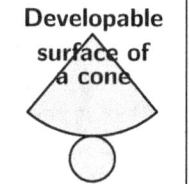
Developable surface of a cone

deviation NOUN /ˌdi.viˈeɪ.ʃən/ the difference of a mean of a data set and a data value in the data set. Math definition: $D(n) = M_x - d_n$ where $D(n)$ is the deviation for item n, M_x is the mean of the data set, and d_n is the data value for item n.

di- PREFIX /daɪ/
1) divided into two pieces that may be equal. Example: diagonal.
2) two. Example: dihedral.

diagonal NOUN /daɪˈæ.gə.nl/
1) (of a matrix) the diagonals of an $n \times n$ square matrix A are the elements $A[1,1], A[2,2], A[3,3], \ldots, A[n,n]$ (main diagonal), or the elements $A[1,n], A[2, n-1], \ldots, A[n, 1]$.
2) (of a polygon) a line segment between any two nonadjacent vertices of a polygon.
3) (of a polyhedron) a line segment between two vertices that are not on the same face.

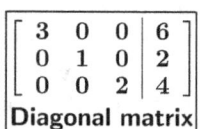
Diagonal of a matrix

Diagonal

diagonalize VERB /daɪˈæ.gə.nlˌaɪz/ to convert a square matrix into a diagonal matrix using matrix row operations.

diagonal matrix NOUN /daɪˈæ.gə.nl ˈmeɪ.trɪks/ a matrix with zeros in all elements except the main diagonal and the optional augmented column: Plural: diagonal matrices /daɪˈæ.gə.nl ˈmeɪ.trɪˌsiz/

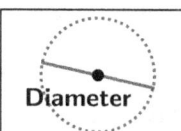
Diagonal matrix

diagram NOUN /ˈdaɪ.əˌgræm/ a figure, especially a line drawing, that outlines and explains a principle or problem.

diameter NOUN /daɪˈæm.ɪ.tər/
1) a line segment extended from one edge of a circle or a sphere to the other edge that passes through the center of the circle.
2) the length of such a line segment.

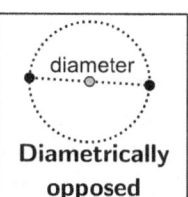
Diameter

diametrically ADVERB /ˌdaɪ.əˈmɛ.trɪ.kli/ having to do with a diameter.

diametrically opposed NOUN /ˌdaɪ.əˈmɛ.trɪ.kli əˈpoʊzd/ two points on a circle or a sphere that are on opposite sides of a diameter of that circle or sphere. Synonym: antipodal (p 11).

diamond NOUN /ˈdaɪˌmənd/ see rhombus (p 99).

dice NOUN /daɪs/ see die (p 37).

die NOUN /daɪ/ a small polyhedron with dots or numbers on each side. Plural: dice /daɪs/. Synonym: number cube (p 81).

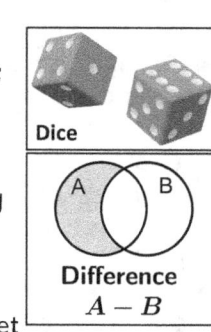
Diametrically opposed

Dice

difference NOUN /ˈdɪf.rəns/
1) (numbers) the result of subtracting one number from another. Formula: **minuend − subtrahend = difference**. Antonym: sum (p 111).
2) (sets) all of the elements of one set that do not belong to another set. Notation: $A - B$.

Difference $A - B$

Difference of Cubes NOUN /ˈdɪf.rəns ʌv kjubz/ a polynomial identity useful in solving certain cubic equations. Formula: $a^3 - b^3 \equiv (a - b)(a^2 + ab + b^2)$.

Difference of Squares NOUN /ˈdɪf.rəns ʌv skwɛərz/ a polynomial identity useful in solving certain quadratic equations. Formula: $a^2 - b^2 \equiv (a + b)(a - b)$.

difference quotient NOUN /ˈdɪf.rəns ˈkwoʊ.ʃənt/ an essential building block of calculus. Formula: $\frac{f(x+h) - f(x)}{h}$ where h is a very small number.

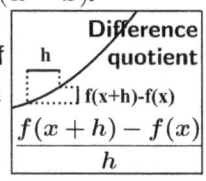
Difference quotient

different ADJECTIVE /ˈdɪ.frənt/
1) not like each other.
2) not identical.

differentiable ADVERB /ˌdɪ.fərˈɛn.ʃə.bəl/ a function **f** is differentiable at **a** if $f'(a)$ exists. A function **g** is differentiable on the interval $[b, c]$ if it is differentiable at every value in the interval.

differential /ˌdɪ.fərˈɛn.ʃəl/
1) ADJECTIVE having to do with taking derivatives.
2) NOUN a math equation that allows one to find the area under a curve. Notation: $\frac{dy}{dx}$.
3) NOUN the result of solving a differential equation.
4) NOUN either dy or dx in the equation $\frac{dy}{dx} = f'(x) \Rightarrow dy = f'(x)dx$.

differential calculus NOUN /ˌdɪ.fərˈɛn.ʃəl ˈkæl.kjə.ləs/ a branch of calculus that deals with differentiation and derivatives.

differential coefficient NOUN /ˌdɪ.fərˈɛn.ʃəl ˌkoʊ.əˈfɪ.ʃənt/ see derivative (p 36).

differentiation NOUN /ˌdɪ.fərˌɛn.ʃiˈeɪ.ʃən/ the act or processes of finding a differential or derivative, such as the area under a curve. Antonym: integration (p 63).

digit NOUN /ˈdɪ.dʒɪt/ a single symbol used to represent a part of a number. Example: the decimal digits are 0, 1, 2, 3, 4, 5, 6, 7, 8 and 9.

digital ADJECTIVE /ˈdɪ.dʒɪ.tl/
1) having to do with the digits of a numeral.
2) having to do with or containing discrete numeric values.
3) displays numerical digits rather than a pointer or hands on a dial.
Antonym: analog (p 9).

digital clock NOUN /ˈdɪ.dʒɪ.tl klɒk/ a clock that uses changing numbers to show the time instead of hands. Antonym: analog clock (p 10).

Digital Clock

digital root NOUN /ˈdɪ.dʒɪ.tl rut/
1) an algorithm for adding the digits of a decimal number to get a single digit. Each of the digits is added together. If the result has more than one digit, each of those digits is added together until a single digit is found. Example: given $329 \to 3 + 2 + 9 = 14 \to 1 + 4 = 5$.
2) the result of such an algorithm.

digit position NOUN /ˈdɪ.dʒɪt pəˈzɪ.ʃən/ see decimal place (p 34).

dihedral ADJECTIVE /daɪˈhi.drəl/ having to do with two intersecting planes.

dihedral angle NOUN /daɪˈhi.drəl ˈæŋ.gəl/ the angle made by two intersecting planes. Dihedral angles are measured between lines in each plane that are perpendicular to the line formed by the intersection of the planes.

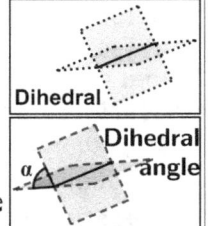
Dihedral
Dihedral angle

dihedron NOUN /daɪˈhi.drən/ a figure formed by two intersecting planes. Plural: dihedra /daɪˈhi.drə/.

diletation NOUN /ˌdɪl.əˈteɪ.ʃən/ see dilation (p 38).

dilation NOUN /daɪˈleɪ.ʃən/ a geometric transformation where each point of a figure is moved a certain ratio of its distance from a center point.
Synonyms: diletation, enlargement (p 44).

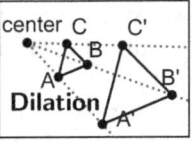
Dilation

dime NOUN /daɪm/ (U.S.) a coin valued at ten cents or $\frac{1}{10}$ of a dollar.

dimension NOUN /dɪˈmɛn.ʃən/
1) an extension in a direction. Example: a plane has 2 dimensions.
2) a size or length.
3) one element of a measurement. Example: meters in meters per second.
4) (of a matrix) the number of rows and columns in a matrix. Example: $\dim \left(\begin{bmatrix} 1 & 0 & 1 \\ 4 & 1 & -1 \end{bmatrix} \right) = 2 \times 3$ (2 rows, 3 columns).
5) (of a geometric space) the number of coordinates needed to define a location in that space.

dimensional ADJECTIVE /dɪˈmɛn.ʃə.nl/
1) contained within a certain number of dimensions. Example: 1-dimensional.
2) having to do with dimensions.

dimensional analysis NOUN /dɪˈmɛn.ʃə.nl əˈnæ.lə.sɪs/ a process for verifying an equation using dimensions. Example: $5\frac{m}{s^2} = a\frac{m^2}{s^2}$ is invalid because $\frac{m}{s^2} \neq \frac{m^2}{s^2}$.

dimensionless ADJECTIVE /dɪˈmɛn.ʃən.ləs/
1) having no dimensions. Examples: a point is dimensionless; the equation $L = 5$ is dimensionless.
2) a ratio that has no dimensions. Example: a ratio of length to width.

Diophantine equation NOUN /ˌdaɪ.oʊˈfæn.taɪn ɪˈkweɪ.ʃən/ a polynomial equation with integer coefficients and integer values for variables. Example: $0 = 3x^2 - 2x + 1, x \in \mathbb{Z}$.

Diophantus of Alexandria PERSON /ˌdaɪ.oʊˈfæn.təs ʌv ˌæ.lɪɡˈzæn.dri.ə/ (about 200 AD—about 284 AD) the first person known to have developed algebraic notation and who is considered the father of algebra. Author of the book *Arithmetica*.

direct
1) ADJECTIVE /dɪˈrɛkt/ proceeding in a straight line, without deviation. Antonym: indirect (p 61).
2) ADJECTIVE /dɪˈrɛkt/ being proportional one to another; involves multiplication and not division. Example: direct variation. Antonym: inverse (p 64).
3) ADJECTIVE /dɪˈrɛkt/ proceeding from the premises to the conclusion. Example: direct proof.
4) ADJECTIVE /dɪˈrɛkt/ preserves one or more attributes. Example: direct isometry.
5) VERB /dɪˈrɛkt/ to guide.

direct comparison test NOUN /dɪˈrɛkt kʌmˈpɛər.ɪ.sən tɛst/ see comparison test (p 24).

directed ADJECTIVE /dɪˈrɛk.tɪd/ having a direction; for which direction is important. Examples: positive or negative, clockwise or counterclockwise.

directed angle NOUN /dɪˈrɛk.tɪd ˈæŋ.gəl/ an angle for which the direction of rotation is important (clockwise or counterclockwise).

Directed angle

directed distance NOUN /dɪˈrɛk.tɪd ˈdɪs.təns/ a distance that includes a direction. Examples: negative or positive, east or west.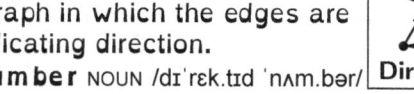

directed graph NOUN /dɪˈrɛk.tɪd græf/ a network graph in which the edges are arrows indicating direction.

directed number NOUN /dɪˈrɛk.tɪd ˈnʌm.bər/ see signed number (p 105).

directed quantity NOUN /dɪˈrɛk.tɪd ˈkwɒn.tɪ.ti/ a quantity that has a magnitude and a direction. Vectors are usually used to represent directed quantities. Examples: velocity, force.

direction NOUN /dɪˈrɛk.ʃən/
1) a path something follows.
2) (number line) positive or negative.
3) left or right, up or down, backwards or forwards.
4) (angle) clockwise or counterclockwise.
5) (2-dimensional) angle of rotation from the positive x-axis.
6) (3-dimensional) two angles of rotation, one from the positive x-axis, and one from the positive y-axis.
7) (of a vector) the rotation from the positive x-axis. Formula: Given vector $\langle x, y \rangle$, $\alpha = \tan^{-1} \frac{y}{x}$.
8) (of a curve) the slope of a non-vertical line that is tangent to the curve at a point.
9) north, south, east or west.

directional derivative NOUN /dɪˈrɛk.ʃə.nl dɪˈrɪ.və.tɪv/ gives the rate of change of a function in a particular direction. Formula: the directional derivative of **f** at (x_0, y_0) in the direction of unit vector $u = \langle a, b \rangle$ is $D_u f(x_0, y_0) = \lim_{h \to 0} \frac{f(x_0 + ha, y_0 + hb) - f(x_0, y_0)}{h}$; $D_u f(x, y) = f_x(x, y) a + f_y(x, y) b$.

direction angle NOUN /dɪˈrɛk.ʃən ˈæŋ.gəl/ direction angles of a vector uniquely determine the vector's direction, but not its length. Math definition: if $z = a\hat{i} + b\hat{j} + c\hat{k}$ is a vector in space, the direction angles are $\alpha = \arccos \frac{a}{|z|}$, $\beta = \arccos \frac{b}{|z|}$, $\gamma = \arccos \frac{c}{|z|}$. Formula: $\cos^2 \alpha + \cos^2 \beta + \cos^2 \gamma = 1$.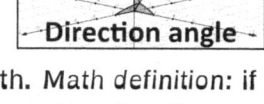

direct isometry NOUN /dɪˈrɛkt aɪˈsɒm.ɪ.tri/ an isometry that preserves orientation and order. Examples: dilation, translation. Antonym: indirect isometry (p 61). See also isometry (p 65).

directly proportional ADJECTIVE /dɪˈrɛkt.li prəˈpɔʊr.ʃə.nl/ having a relationship of direct variation (p 39). Formula: $y = ax$ where **a** is the constant of proportion.

direct proof NOUN /dɪˈrɛkt pruf/ a proof that builds on axioms, definitions and previously proved theorems. Antonym: proof by contradiction (p 93).

direct proportion NOUN /dɪˈrɛkt prəˈpɔʊr.ʃən/ see direct variation (p 39).

direct reasoning NOUN /dɪˈrɛkt ˈriz.nɪŋ/ see direct proof (p 39).

directrix NOUN /dɪˈrɛk.trɪks/ a fixed line used to determine a curve, particularly a conic section. Example: a parabola is the locus of all points equidistant from a directrix and a focus.

direct variation NOUN /dɪˈrɛkt ˌvɛə.riˈeɪ.ʃən/ one variable is equal to a constant times another variable. Formula: $y = ax$ where **a** is the constant of variation. Synonym: direct proportion.

dis- PREFIX /dɪs/
1) not. Example: discontinuous.
2) undo. Example: discover.
3) opposite of. Example: disjoint.

disc NOUN /dɪsk/ (British English) see disk (p 40).

disconnected ADJECTIVE /ˈdɪs.kəˌnɛk.tɪd/ does not share any points. Antonym: connected (p 27).

discontinuity NOUN /ˌdɪs.kɒn.tɪˈnu.ɪ.ti/ a point where a function is not continuous. See also essential discontinuity (p 45), jump discontinuity (p 66), removable discontinuity (p 98).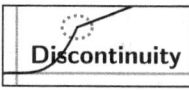

discontinuous ADJECTIVE /ˈdɪs.kənˌtɪn.ju.əs/ not continuous; not all in one piece. Antonym: continuous (p 28).

discontinuous function NOUN /ˈdɪs.kənˌtɪn.ju.əs fʌŋk.ʃən/ a function that is not continuous; a function that has one or more 'holes' in it. Antonym: continuous function (p 29).

discount NOUN /ˈdɪs.koʊnt/
1) an amount subtracted from a total. Formula: **total − discount = net**.
2) a percentage of the total amount which is subtracted from the total. Formula: **gross×(1 − discount%) = net**.

discover VERB /dɪˈskʌ.vər/
1) to notice or realize.
2) to find out.

discovery NOUN /dɪˈskʌ.vər.i/ something that is noticed or realized.

discrete ADJECTIVE /dɪˈskrit/
1) isolated. Example: The set of integers is a discrete set.
2) having a finite number of elements. Example: discrete function.
Antonyms: continuous (p 28), discontinuous (p 39).

discrete data NOUN /dɪˈskrit ˈdeɪ.tə/ data that takes only isolated values. Example: age as opposed to height. Antonym: continuous data (p 29).

discrete graph NOUN /dɪˈskrit græf/ a graph of individual, non-connected points.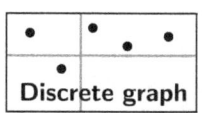

discrete mathematics NOUN /dɪˈskrit ˌmæθ.məˈtɪks/ a branch of mathematics dealing with discrete, and not continuous, objects such as integers.

discrete variable NOUN /dɪˈskrit ˈvɛər.i.ə.bəl/ a variable that can take on values of discrete data, as opposed to continuous data. Example: age of participant. Antonym: continuous variable (p 29).

discriminant NOUN /dɪsˈkrɪ.mə.nənt/ an expression that gives information about the properties of a mathematical object. Example: discriminant of a quadratic equation.

discriminant of a conic NOUN /dɪˈskrɪ.mə.nənt ʌv ə ˈkɒn.ɪk/ given a conic with the equation $Ax^2 + Bxy + Cy^2 + Dx + Ey + F = 0$, the discriminant is $G = B^2 - 4AC$. If $G < 0$, the equation represents an ellipse. If $G = 0$, the equation represents a parabola. If $G > 0$, the equation represents a hyperbola.

discriminant of a quadratic equation NOUN /dɪˈskrɪ.mə.nənt ʌv ə kwɒˈdræ.tɪk ɪˈkweɪ.ʒən/ the expression $D = b^2 - 4ac$ where $ax^2 + bx + c = 0$. If the discriminant $D > 0$, the quadratic equation has two unequal real roots. If $D = 0$, the quadratic equation has one real root with a multiplicity of two. If $D < 0$ the quadratic equation has two complex roots, conjugates of each other.

disjoint ADJECTIVE /dɪsˈdʒɔɪnt/ (sets) having no members in common. Synonym: **exclusive** (p 46). Antonym: **equivalent** (p 45).

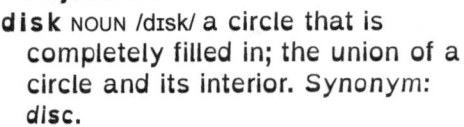

disjoint events NOUN /dɪsˈdʒɔɪnt ɪˈvɛntz/ see **exclusive events** (p 47).

disjunction NOUN /dɪsˈdʒʌŋk.ʃən/ two logical statements connected with an 'or'. A disjunction is true if either or both of its arguments are true. Notation: ∨. Synonym: **or, inclusive disjunction**.

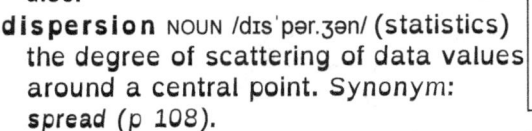

disk NOUN /dɪsk/ a circle that is completely filled in; the union of a circle and its interior. Synonym: **disc**.

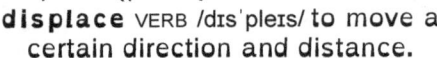

dispersion NOUN /dɪsˈpər.ʒən/ (statistics) the degree of scattering of data values around a central point. Synonym: **spread** (p 108).

displace VERB /dɪsˈpleɪs/ to move a certain direction and distance.

displacement NOUN /dɪsˈpleɪs.mənt/
1) the direction and distance of a movement. Synonym: **translation** (p 115).
2) the amount of liquid replaced by a solid.
3) an event where an object is moved without rotation.

displacement vector NOUN /dɪsˈpleɪs.mənt ˈvɛk.tər/ a vector used to show the direction and distance of movement.

display window NOUN /dɪsˈpleɪ ˈwɪn.doʊ/ see **viewing rectangle** (p 121).

disproof NOUN /dɪsˈpruf/ a set of statements that show a proposition is false.

disprove VERB /dɪsˈpruv/ show by logical argument that a statement is false. Most disproofs show that at least one case exists that contradicts the proposition.

dissimilar /dɪsˈsɪ.mə.lər/
1) not similar.
2) unlike.
Antonym: **similar** (p 105).

dissimilar terms NOUN /dɪsˈsɪ.mə.lər tɜrmz/ see **unlike terms** (p 119).

distance NOUN /ˈdɪs.təns/
1) how far apart two locations are.
2) a measurement of space in one dimension. Formula: distance between **a** and **b** is $|a - b|$.

distance formula NOUN /ˈdɪs.təns ˈfɔr.mjə.lə/ a formula used to calculate distance. See also **Distance Formulas** (p 142).

distance-time graph NOUN /ˈdɪs.təns taɪm græf/ a graph with distance on the vertical axis and time on the horizontal axis.

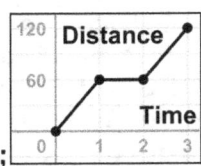

distinct ADJECTIVE /dɪˈstɪŋkt/ not the same; not identical; separate from.

distort VERB /dɪˈstɔrt/ to make a change such that something no longer accurately represents the original.

distortion NOUN /dɪˈstɔr.ʃən/ a change such that something no longer accurately represents the original. Example: shear.

distribute VERB /dɪˈstrɪ.bjut/ to expand an expression by multiplying through parentheses. Example: $a(b+c) = a \cdot b + a \cdot c$.

distribution NOUN /dɪˈstrɪ.bju.ʃən/
1) (dataset) the frequency of data in a dataset over the range of the dataset. Synonym: **spread** (p 108).
2) (operations) the performance of operations through parentheses. Example: $3(5+2) = 3 \cdot 5 + 3 \cdot 2$.

distributive ADJECTIVE /dɪˈstrɪ.bju.tɪv/ having the property of performing operations through parentheses.

distributive property NOUN /dɪˈstrɪ.bju.tɪv ˈprɒ.pər.ti/ a property of operations that can be performed through parentheses. Example: distributive property of multiplication over addition and subtraction $a(b+c) = ab + ac$.

diverge VERB /dɪˈvɜrdʒ/
1) to not get closer and closer to a fixed value.
2) to not approach each other.
3) (series) having no limits.
Antonym: **converge** (p 29), **oscillate** (p 84).

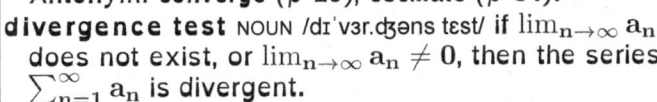

divergence test NOUN /dɪˈvɜr.dʒəns tɛst/ if $\lim_{n \to \infty} a_n$ does not exist, or $\lim_{n \to \infty} a_n \neq 0$, then the series $\sum_{n=1}^{\infty} a_n$ is divergent.

divergence theorem NOUN /dɪˈvɜr.dʒəns ˈθɪ.ə.rəm/ the flux $\mathbf{F} = M\hat{\mathbf{i}} + N\hat{\mathbf{j}} + P\hat{\mathbf{k}}$ through the boundary surface $\mathbf{S}$ equals the integral of the divergence of $\mathbf{F}$ in the neighborhood of $\mathbf{V}$. $\oiint_S (\mathbf{F} \cdot \mathbf{n}) ds = \iiint_V (\nabla \cdot \mathbf{F}) dv = \int \int \int \left(\frac{\partial M}{\partial x} + \frac{\partial N}{\partial y} + \frac{\partial P}{\partial z} \right) dx\, dy\, dz$.

divergent ADJECTIVE /dɪˈvɜr.dʒənt/ having no finite limit. Example: the geometric sequence 1, 2, 4, 8, 16, ... is divergent. Antonym: **convergent** (p 29).

divergent function NOUN /dɪˈvɜr.dʒənt fʌŋk.ʃən/ a function that increases or decreases without bounds. Antonyms: **convergent function** (p 29), **oscillating function** (p 84).

divergent sequence NOUN /dɪˈvɜr.dʒənt ˈsi.kwəns/ an infinite sequence that increases or decreases without bounds. Example: the geometric sequence 1, 2, 4, 8, 16, ... is divergent. Antonym: **convergent sequence** (p 29).

divergent series NOUN /dɪˈvɜr.dʒənt ˈsɪər.iz/ an infinite series whose partial sums do not approach a particular value. Plural: divergent series /dɪˈvɜr.dʒənt ˈsɪər.iz/. Antonym: convergent series (p 29).

divide VERB /dɪˈvaɪd/
1) to calculate how many times a value is contained in another value; repeated subtraction. Example: $10 ÷ 3 = 3r1$. Inverse: multiply. Notations: $÷, /,)$. Math definitions: (integers) $a ÷ b = cRd$ if and only if $b · c + d = a$; (real numbers) $a ÷ b = c$ if and only if $b · c = a$.
2) to separate into two or more parts.

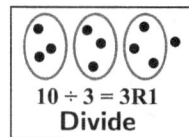
Divide

divided bar graph NOUN /dɪˈvaɪ.dəd bɑr græf/ a bar graph where each bar is divided into sections showing a proportion to the whole.

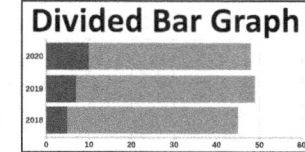
Divided Bar Graph

divide evenly VERB /dɪˈvaɪd ˈi.vən.li/ (integer division) to divide into with no remainder. Example: 4 divides evenly into 16 since $16 ÷ 4 = 4R0$.

dividend NOUN /ˈdɪ.vɪˌdɛnd/ a number or expression that is divided in a division problem. Notation: $\text{divisor} \overline{)\text{dividend}}^{\text{quotient}}$; $\frac{\text{dividend}}{\text{divisor}} = \text{quotient}$; dividend ÷ divisor = quotient. Synonym: numerator (p 81).

divine proportion NOUN /dɪˈvaɪn prəˈpɔr.ʃən/ see golden ratio (p 54).

divisibility NOUN /dɪˌvɪz.əˈbɪl.ɪ.ti/ the capacity to be evenly divided.

divisibility rules NOUN /dɪˌvɪz.əˈbɪl.ɪ.ti rulz/ a set of rules for determining if an integer is divisible by a smaller integer. See also Divisibility Rules (p 135).

divisible ADJECTIVE /dɪˈvɪz.ə.bəl/ can be evenly divided. Math definition: given integers a and b, a is divisible by b if $a ÷ b$ has a remainder of 0. Notation: $b \mid a$ (b divides a, a is divisible by b); $b \nmid a$ (b does not divide a, a is not divisible by b). Examples: 12 is divisible by 4: $(4 \mid 12)$; 14 is not divisible by 5: $(5 \nmid 14)$.

division NOUN /dɪˈvɪ.ʒən/ the act of dividing; the opposite of multiplication; repeated subtraction. Math definition: $a ÷ b = c$ if and only if $a = b · c, b \neq 0$. Inverse: multiplication (p 77).

division algorithm NOUN /dɪˈvɪ.ʒən ˈæl.gəˌrɪ.ðəm/
1) (integers) see Division With Remainder Theorem (p 41).
2) (polynomials) given the rational polynomial $\frac{P(x)}{Q(x)}$, where the degree of $P(x)$ is more than the degree of $Q(x)$, the division algorithm transforms the fraction to $r(x) = ax + b + \frac{R(x)}{Q(x)}$ where $a \neq 0$ and the degree of $R(x)$ is one less than the degree of $P(x)$. $y = ax + b$ is the equation for the slant asymptote of the ratio.

division by zero NOUN /dɪˈvɪ.ʒən baɪ ˈzɪə.roʊ/ division by zero is undefined.

division modulo NOUN /dɪˈvɪ.ʒən ˈmɒ.dʒu.loʊ/ finding the remainder when dividing one integer by another. Example: $13 \mod 5 = 3$ since $13 ÷ 5 = 2R3$. Abbreviation mod. Formula: **number mod. modulo = residue**.

Division Property of Equality NOUN /dɪˈvɪ.ʒən ˈprɒ.pər.ti ʌv ɪˈkwɒl.ɪ.ti/ both sides of an equation can be divided by a nonzero value without changing the truth value of the equation. Math definition: For any real or complex numbers a, b and $c \neq 0$; if $a = b$ then $a ÷ c = b ÷ c$ and if $a ÷ c = b ÷ c$ then $a = b$; if $a \neq b$ then $a ÷ c \neq b ÷ c$ and if $a ÷ c \neq b ÷ c$ then $a \neq b$.

Division Property of Inequality NOUN /dɪˈvɪ.ʒən ˈprɒ.pər.ti ʌv ˈɪn.ɪ.kwɒl.ɪ.ti/ if both sides of an inequality are divided by the same positive value, the truth value of the inequality does not change. If both sides of an inequality are divided by the same negative value, '>' flips to '<' and '<' flips to '>'. Example: if $a < b$ then $a ÷ 3 < b ÷ 3$ and $a ÷ (-3) > b ÷ (-3)$.

division sign NOUN /dɪˈvɪ.ʒən saɪn/ the symbol '÷', used to show division. Notation: 'x ÷ y' is read 'x divided by y'. Synonym: obelus (p 81).

Division With Remainder Theorem NOUN /dɪˈvɪ.ʒən wɪθ rɪˈmeɪn.dər ˈθɪə.rəm/
1) (integers) division of any two integers equals an integer with an integer remainder. Math definition: given two integers a and d, with $d \neq 0$, there exist unique integers q and r such that
$$\overbrace{a}^{\text{dividend}} = \overbrace{q}^{\text{divisor}} \times \overbrace{d}^{\text{quotient}} + \overbrace{r}^{\text{remainder}}$$
and $0 \leq r < |d|$.
2) (polynomials) given polynomials $P(x)$ and $D(x) \neq 0$, there exists unique polynomials $Q(x)$ and $R(x)$, where $R(x)$ is a polynomial of degree less than $D(x)$, such that
$$\overbrace{P(x)}^{\text{dividend}} = \overbrace{D(x)}^{\text{divisor}} · \overbrace{Q(x)}^{\text{quotient}} + \overbrace{R(x)}^{\text{remainder}}$$
. Synonym: division algorithm.

divisor NOUN /dɪˈvaɪ.zər/ an expression that is used to divide into the dividend in a division problem. Notation: $\text{divisor} \overline{)\text{dividend}}^{\text{quotient}}$; $\frac{\text{dividend}}{\text{divisor}} = \text{quotient}$; dividend ÷ divisor = quotient. Synonym: denominator (p 36).

dodeca- PREFIX /doʊˈdɛ.kə/ twelve.

dodecagon NOUN /doʊˈdɛ.kəˌgɒn/ any twelve-sided polygon.

dodecahedron NOUN /doʊˌdɛ.kəˈhi.drən/ any twelve-faced polyhedron. Plural: dodecahedra /doʊˌdɛ.kəˈhi.drə/.

dollar NOUN /ˈdɒ.lər/ a unit of currency used in many countries around the world. Notations: $ (U.S. dollar), USD (U.S. dollar), CAD (Canadian dollar).

domain NOUN /doʊˈmeɪn/ all input values of a function; the values for which a function is defined. Antonym: range (p 95).

domain of definition NOUN /doʊˈmeɪn ʌv dɛ.fəˈnɪ.ʃən/ all values for which a function is defined without additional restrictions. Example: the domain of definition of the function is $x \geq 0$.

dot NOUN /dɒt/ a point drawn on a paper. A solid dot indicates the point is included in the set. A hollow dot indicates that the point is not included in the set. Examples: •, ◦.

dot plot NOUN /dɒt plɒt/ a graph where each data point is plotted as a single dot. Synonym: *scatter plot* (p 102).

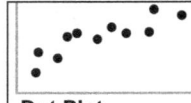
Dot Plot

dot product NOUN /dɒt ˈprɒ.dʌkt/ given two vectors $X = \langle x_1, x_2 \rangle$ and $Y = \langle y_1, y_2 \rangle$, the dot product is $X \cdot Y = x_1y_1 + x_2y_2$. In 3-D, $X = \langle x_1, x_2, x_3 \rangle$, $Y = \langle y_1, y_2, y_3 \rangle$, $X \cdot Y = x_1y_1 + x_2y_2 + x_3y_3$. Formula: $u \cdot v = |u| \, |v| \cos\theta$, where θ is the angle between the two vectors. Example: $\langle 3, 2 \rangle \cdot \langle 1, 1 \rangle = 3 \cdot (-1) + (-2) \cdot 1 = -3 + -2 = -5$. Notation: '·'. Synonyms: *inner product, scalar product*.

dotted ADJECTIVE /ˈdɒt.ɪd/ made of dots. Example: dotted line.

Dotted line

double /ˈdʌ.bəl/
1) ADJECTIVE twice as much. Example: double of 3 is 6. Antonym: *half* (p 55).
2) ADJECTIVE two. Antonym: *half* (p 55).
3) VERB increase by a factor of two. Antonym: *halve* (p 56).

Double Angle Identities NOUN /ˈdʌ.bəl ˈæŋ.gəl aɪˈdɛn.tɪ.tiz/ trigonometric identities involving double angles. See also Trigonometric Identities (p 143).

double bar graph NOUN /ˈdʌ.bəl bɑr græf/ a bar graph with two sets of bars placed next to each other to compare related data.

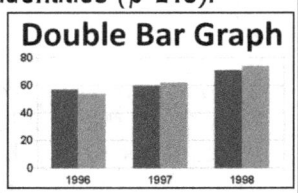
Double Bar Graph

double blind NOUN /ˈdʌ.bəl blaɪnd/ a study where neither the administrators nor the subjects know to which group subject belongs.

double box and whisker plot NOUN /ˈdʌ.bəl bɒks ənd ˈhwɪs.kər plɒt/ two adjacent box and whisker plots drawn using the same scale.

Double Box and Whisker Plot

double cone NOUN /ˈdʌ.bəl koʊn/ two cones placed apex to apex whose altitudes lie in the same line.

Double Cone

double integral NOUN /ˈdʌ.bəl ˈɪn.tɛ.grəl/ the integral of an integral. Formula: The double integral of $f(x, y)$ over rectangle R is $\int\int_R f(x, y)dA = \lim_{m,n \to \infty} \sum_{i=1}^{m} \sum_{j=1}^{n} f\left(x_{i,j}^*, y_{i,j}^*\right) \Delta A$.

double minus one VERB /ˈdʌ.bəl ˈmaɪn.əs wʌn/ to multiply a number by 2, then subtract 1. Math definition: $2a - 1$. Example: double 3 minus $1 = 2 \cdot 3 - 1 = 6 - 1 = 5$.

double negative NOUN /ˈdʌ.bəl ˈnɛ.gə.tɪv/
1) the negative of a negative number. Formula: $-(-a) = a$.
2) the negative of a negative of a proposition. Notation: $\neg\neg P$. In most systems of logic, $\neg\neg P \equiv P$.

double plus one VERB /ˈdʌ.bəl plʌs wʌn/ to multiply a number by 2, then add 1. Math definition: $2a + 1$. Example: double 3 plus 1 is $2 \cdot 3 + 1 = 6 + 1 = 7$. Synonym: *near double*.

double root NOUN /ˈdʌ.bəl rut/ a root of a polynomial that is repeated exactly twice. Given the polynomial $(x + 2)(x + 2)(x - 1)$, the root -2 is a double root. Synonym: *double zero*.

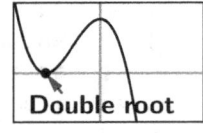
Double root

double zero NOUN /ˈdʌ.bəl ˈzɪə.roʊ/ see *double root* (p 42).

doubling time NOUN /ˈdʌ.blɪŋ taɪm/ the time it takes for the output of an exponential function to double. Doubling time remains constant for all intervals of the same length of an exponential function. Formula: $y = a \cdot 2^{\frac{t}{d}}$ where a is the initial value at $t = 0$, t is the elapsed time, and d is the doubling time.

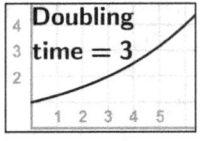
Doubling time = 3

down ADVERB /daʊn/
1) a vertical direction moving towards the center of the earth.
2) in a negative direction.
3) decreasing in size or quantity.
Antonym: *up* (p 119).

dozen ADJECTIVE /ˈdʌ.zən/ exactly 12.

draw VERB /drɔ/
1) to create a figure freehand without using tools such as a compass or a ruler.
2) to infer from a sample. Example: draw a conclusion.

drawing NOUN /ˈdrɔ.ɪŋ/ a sketch or design that uses lines to represent an object or idea.

duodecimal system NOUN /ˌdu.oʊˈdɛs.məl sɪs.təm/ a base 12 numeration system. Example: $3B7_{12} = 3 \cdot 12^2 + 11 \cdot 12 + 7 = 432 + 132 + 7 = 571_{10}$.

dynamic geometry software NOUN /daɪˈnæm.ɪk dʒiˈɒ.mɪ.tri ˈsɒft.wɛər/ computer software that allows a user to explore geometric concepts by creating and manipulating geometric drawings. See http://www.geogebra.org for free dynamic geometry software.

E

e NOUN /i/ a constant that is the base of the natural logarithm; $e \approx 2.71827$. Synonym: *Euler's number*. Math definition: $e = \lim_{n \to +\infty} \left(1 + \frac{1}{n}\right)^n$, $e = \sum_{n=0}^{\infty} \frac{1}{n!} = 1 + \frac{1}{1} + \frac{1}{1 \cdot 2} + \frac{1}{1 \cdot 2 \cdot 3} + \ldots$.

E ABBREVIATION exa-.

ϵ SYMBOL /ˈɛp.sɪ.lɒn/ the Greek letter epsilon, used to represent eccentricity in geometry; and to represent a very small, positive quantity in calculus. See also Greek Letters (p 135).

eccentric ADJECTIVE /ˌɛkˈsɛn.trɪk/
1) not having the same center. Antonym: *concentric* (p 26).
2) deviating from a circular path.

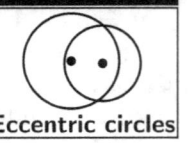
Eccentric circles

eccentricity NOUN /ˌɛk.sənˈtrɪ.sɪ.ti/ a ratio defining the shape of a conic; a number that tells how much a conic section is different from a circle; the ratio of the distance of any point on a conic section from a focus and the corresponding directrix.

Notation: ϵ (epsilon). Formula: $\epsilon = \frac{c}{a}$ where **c** is the distance between the center and either of the foci, and **a** is the length of the semi-major axis.

echelon ADJECTIVE /ˈɛ.ʃəˌlɒn/ arranged in parallel rows and columns at a diagonal to the direction of travel.

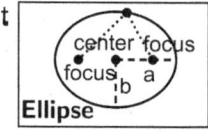
Echelon

echelon form NOUN /ˈɛ.ʃəˌlɒn fɔrm/ see row-echelon form (p 101).

echelon matrix NOUN /ˈɛ.ʃəˌlɒn ˈmeɪ.trɪks/ a matrix in row-echelon form.

edge NOUN /ɛdʒ/
1) (of a polygon) see side, definition 1 (p 104).
2) (of a polyhedron) a line segment where two faces of the polyhedron meet.
3) (of a figure) see boundary (p 18).
4) (graph theory) see path (p 86).

effective APR NOUN /əˈfɛk.tɪv eɪ pi ɑr/ the annual percentage rate with the effects of compounding added in. Formula: effective $\mathrm{APR} = \left(1 + \frac{i}{n}\right)^n - 1$ where **i** is the nominal interest rate, and **n** is the number of periods in one year. Example: 9% interest compounded monthly $\left(1 + \frac{0.09}{12}\right)^{12} - 1 = (1 + 0.0075)^{12} - 1 = 1.0075^{12} - 1 \approx 1.0938 - 1 = 0.0938 = 9.38\%$.

effective interest rate NOUN /əˈfɛk.tɪv ˈɪn.trɪst reɪt/ see effective APR (p 43).

Eigenvalue NOUN /ˈaɪ.gənˌvæl.yu/ a factor by which an Eigenvector is scaled. Notation: λ. Synonym: characteristic value.

Eigenvector NOUN /ˈaɪ.gənˌvɛk.tər/ a vector for which there exists a scalar, called an Eigenvalue, such that the value of the vector under a given transformation is equal to the scalar times the vector. Synonym: characteristic vector.

eight ADJECTIVE, NOUN /eɪt/ the number or digit 8.

eighteen ADJECTIVE, NOUN /eɪˈtin/ the number 18.

eighth ADJECTIVE /eɪtθ/
1) coming in position 8 in an ordered list. Notation: 8th.
2) one of eight equal parts; $\frac{1}{8}$.

eighty ADJECTIVE, NOUN /ˈeɪ.ti/ the number 80.

elapsed time NOUN /əˈlæpsd taɪm/ the amount of time between two events.

element NOUN /ˈɛ.lə.mənt/
1) a uniquely identifiable component of a mathematical object.
2) (of a set) an object belonging to a set. Notation: $x \in A$. Synonym: member.
3) (of a matrix) one item at a particular row and column. Synonym: member.
4) (geometry) a fundamental object such as a point, line or plane.

eleven ADJECTIVE, NOUN /ɪˈlɛ.vən/ the number 11.

eleventh ADJECTIVE /ɪˈlɛ.vənθ/
1) coming in position 11 in an ordered list. Notation: 11th.
2) one of eleven equal parts; $\frac{1}{11}$.

eliminate VERB /ɪˌlɪ.məˈneɪt/
1) to remove.
2) to get rid of; to cause to disappear.

Synonym: cancel (p 18).

elimination NOUN /ɪˌlɪ.məˈneɪ.ʃən/ simplification by removing variables. Example: elimination of a variable in a system of equations.

elimination method NOUN /ɪˌlɪ.məˈneɪ.ʃən ˈmɛ.θəd/ a method for solving linear systems of equations by eliminating variables one by one until only one variable is left, solving for that variable, then back substituting.

ellipse NOUN /ɪˈlɪps/ all points equidistant from two focal points; a closed curve with an equation in the form $\frac{(x-h)^2}{a^2} + \frac{(y-k)^2}{b^2} = 1$ or $\frac{(x-h)^2}{b^2} + \frac{(y-k)^2}{a^2} = 1$ where (h, k) is the coordinate of the center of the ellipse, **a** is half the length of the horizontal axis and **b** is half the length of the vertical axis. See also Equations of an Ellipse (p 138).

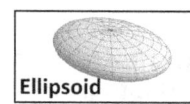
Ellipse

ellipsis SYMBOL /ɪˈlɪp.sɪs/ three dots (...) placed in a sequence of objects to indicate that there are more objects in the same pattern. An ellipsis at the beginning or the end of a sequence indicates that the sequence is infinite. Example: 1, 2, 3, ... is the set of all positive integers.

ellipsoid NOUN /ɪˈlɪp.sɔɪd/ a 3-dimensional solid whose cross sections are ellipses. An ellipsoid can be formed by rotating an ellipse about one of its axes.

Ellipsoid

elliptic ADJECTIVE /ɪˈlɪp.tɪk/
1) having to do with an ellipse.
2) in the shape of an ellipse.

elliptical ADJECTIVE /ɪˈlɪp.tɪ.kəl/ see elliptic (p 43).

elliptic geometry NOUN /ɪˈlɪp.tɪk dʒiˈɒ.mɪ.tri/ a non-Euclidean geometry that can be visualized as taking place on the surface of a sphere or an ellipsoid. Synonym: spherical geometry (p 107).

empirical ADJECTIVE /ˈɛm.pɪr.ɪ.kl/ based on scientific observation and experiment, not theory. Antonyms: theoretical (p 114), anecdotal (p 10).

empirical data NOUN /ˈɛm.pɪr.ɪ.kl ˈdeɪ.tʌ/ data obtained through observation and experiment and not generated from theory.

empirical model NOUN /ˈɛm.pɪr.ɪ.kl ˈmɒ.dl/ a model based on empirical data.

empty ADJECTIVE /ˈɛmp.ti/
1) having no members.
2) containing nothing.

empty set NOUN /ˈɛmp.ti sɛt/ the unique set containing no members. Notation: $\emptyset$ or $\{\}$. Synonym: null set.

en- PREFIX /ɛn/
1) to make. Example: enlarge (to make larger).
2) to transform. Example: encrypt.

encipher VERB /ɛnˈsaɪ.fər/ to convert plain data to enciphered data using a method such as transposition of letters. Example: 'encipher this text' becomes 'neich preht siett x'. Antonym: decipher (p 34).

enciphered text NOUN /ɛnˈsaɪ.fərd tɛkst/ text that has been enciphered. Antonym: plain text (p 88).

encipherment NOUN /ɛnˈsaɪ.fər.mənt/ the process of rendering data unreadable using a cipher. Antonym:

decipherment (p 34).

encrypt VERB /ɛnˈkrɪpt/ to convert plain data to encrypted data using a key. Example: 'George' becomes '10-6-18-18-12-14'. Antonym: decrypt (p 35).

encryption NOUN /ɛnˈkrɪp.ʃən/ the act of encrypting. Antonym: decryption (p 35).

end NOUN /ɛnd/ the first or final part; the first or last of something.

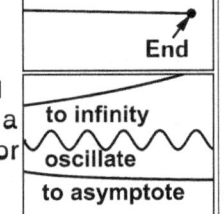

end behavior of a function NOUN /ɛnd bɪˈheɪ.vjər ʌv eɪ ˈfʌŋk.ʃən/ the behavior of a function as the input goes to infinity or negative infinity. The function can:
• go to positive infinity or negative infinity, • approach a horizontal asymptote, or
• oscillate.

endecagon NOUN /ɛnˈdɛ.kəˌgɒn/ any eleven-sided polygon.

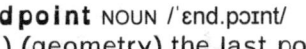

end of proof NOUN /ɛnd ʌv pruf/ a statement that the proof is finished. Notations: QED, ■.

endpoint NOUN /ˈɛnd.pɔɪnt/
1) (geometry) the last point where a ray, line segment, or other curve stops.

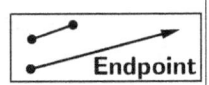

2) (statistics) a boundary between categories.

endpoint convention NOUN /ˈɛnd.pɔɪnt kənˈvɛn.ʃən/ (histogram) the category to which a data value on the boundary between two categories is assigned.

energy NOUN /ˈɛn.ər.dʒi/ the capacity to do work. Example: energy of position.

engineering notation NOUN /ˌɪn.dʒəˈnɪər.ɪŋ noʊˈteɪ.ʃən/ a way to write real numbers that are very large or very small. Notation: **mantissa×10^{exponent}** where $1 \leq \text{mantissa} < 1000$ and exponent is a multiple of 3. Example: 25.5×10^6. Synonym: e notation (p 44).

enlarge VERB /ɛnˈlɑrdʒ/ to make bigger. Synonyms: amplify (p 9), stretch. Antonyms: compress (p 26), shrink.

enlargement NOUN /ɛnˈlɑrdʒ.mənt/
1) (geometry) any dilation that increases the size of objects. Antonym: compression (p 26). Synonyms: dilation (p 38), stretch, amplification (p 10).

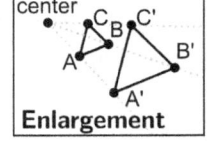

2) (algebra) a transformation of a function that increases the value of the output. Example: $f'(x) = 2 \cdot f(x)$.
3) an image of a transformation that is larger than the preimage.

e notation NOUN /i noʊˈteɪ.ʃən/ a way to represent real numbers that are very large or very small that is used by many calculators and computer programs. Notation: **mantissaE±nn** where $1 \leq \text{mantissa} < 10$, ± is either + or −, and **nn** is an unsigned integer.
Example: $\mathbf{2.749\text{E-}08 = 2.749 \times 10^{-8}}$. Synonyms: scientific notation (p 102), engineering notation (p 44).

enumerate VERB /ɪˈnu.mə.reɪt/ to count instances; to associate objects in a set with the set of natural numbers starting at 1. Synonym: count (p 31).

enumeration NOUN /ɪˌnu.məˈreɪ.ʃən/ the act of counting instances.

envelope NOUN /ˈɛn.vəˌloʊp/ a curve that is tangent to a family of lines or other geometric shapes.

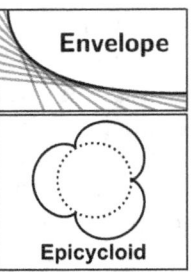

epicycloid NOUN /ˌɛ.pɪˈsaɪ.klɔɪd/ a plane curve made by tracing a point on a circle that is rolling around the outside of another circle. Formula: $x(\theta) = (R+r)\cos\theta - r\cos\left(\frac{R+r}{r}\theta\right)$, $y(\theta) = (R+r)\sin\theta - r\sin\left(\frac{R+r}{r}\theta\right)$ where r is the radius of the smaller circle and R is the radius of the larger circle.

epsilon SYMBOL /ˈɛp.sɪˌlɒn/ the Greek letter ϵ, used to represent eccentricity in geometry; and to represent a very small, positive quantity in calculus. See also Greek Letters (p 135).

equal ADJECTIVE /ˈi.kwəl/
1) has the same value as. Example: $a = b$, say "**a equals b.**"
2) satisfies an equivalence relation. Example: $5 \mod 2 = 7 \mod 2$.
3) means the same thing mathematically. Synonym: congruent (p 27). Antonym: unequal (p 118). See also equal sign (p 44).

equality NOUN /ɪˈkwɒl.ɪ.ti/ the state of being equal or not.
1) (of numbers) $a = b$ if and only if **a** has the same numeric value as **b**.
2) (of ordered pairs) $(a_1, b_1) = (a_2, b_2)$ if and only if $a_1 = a_2$ and $b_1 = b_2$.
3) (of sets) two sets are equal if they contain exactly the same members. Math definition: $A = B$ if and only if $A \subseteq B$ and $B \subseteq A$.
4) (of vectors) has the same components. Math definition: $\langle a_1, b_1 \rangle = \langle a_2, b_2 \rangle$ if and only if $a_1 = a_2$ and $b_1 = b_2$.
5) (of matrices) two matrices are equal if and only if they have the same dimensions and if their corresponding elements are the same.

equally ADJECTIVE /ˈi.kwəl.i/ having the property of sameness or of equality.

equally likely ADJECTIVE /ˈi.kwəl.i ˈlaɪk.li/ having the same chances of happening. Math definition: events e_1 and e_2 are equally likely if and only if $P(e_1) = P(e_2)$. Example: when flipping a coin, heads and tails are equally likely events.

equal parts NOUN /ˈi.kwəl pɑrtz/
1) congruent parts.
2) parts containing the same amount or having the same size.

equal sign NOUN /ˈi.kwəl saɪn/ the symbol '=' which represents equality. Example: $2 + 3 = 5$.

equate VERB /ɪˈkweɪt/ to state algebraically that two expressions are, perhaps conditionally, equal to each other. Example: equate $y + 2$ and $x - 3$:
$y + 2 = x - 3$.

equation NOUN /ɪˈkweɪ.ʒən/ a mathematical statement that two expressions are, perhaps conditionally, equal. Notation: **expression = expression**. Example: $x + 3 = 2x - 4$.

equation in n variables NOUN /ɪˈkweɪ.ʒən ɪn ən ˈvɛər.i.ə.bəlz/ an equation that has **n** different variables. Example: equation in 2 variables: $x + y = 0$; equation in 3 variables: $x^2 + y + z = 1$.

Equation to Inequality Property NOUN /ɪˈkweɪ.ʒən tu ˌɪn.ɪˈkwɒl.ɪ.ti ˈprɒp.pər.ti/ if $a > 0$ and $b > 0$ and $a + b = c$, then $c > a$ and $c > b$. If $a < 0$ and $b < 0$ and $a + b = c$, then $c < a$ and $c < b$.

equi- PREFIX /ˈi.kwə/
1) equal.
2) the same.

equiangular ADJECTIVE /ˌi.kwəˈæŋ.gyə.lər/ having angles that are the same measure. Synonym: congruent angles.

Equiangular

equiangular triangle ADJECTIVE /ˌi.kwəˈæŋ.gyə.lər ˈtraɪˌæŋ.gəl/ a triangle whose angles are all congruent. Synonym: equilateral triangle (p 45).

equidistant ADJECTIVE /ˌi.kwəˈdɪs.tənt/ having the same distance.

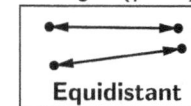
Equidistant

equilateral ADJECTIVE /ˌi.kwəˈlæ.tər.əl/
1) (polygon) having sides that are the same length.
2) (polyhedron) having faces that are congruent.

equilateral triangle NOUN /ˌi.kwəˈlæ.tər.əl ˈtraɪˌæŋ.gəl/ a triangle whose sides and angles are all congruent. Synonym: equiangular triangle (p 45).

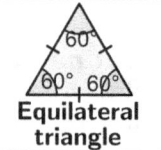
Equilateral triangle

equilibrium NOUN /ˌi.kwəˈlɪ.bri.əm/ a state of balance when opposing forces are equal.

equilibrium point NOUN /ˌi.kwəˈlɪ.bri.əm pɔɪnt/
1) a point where two forces are equal.
2) a point where two graphs representing opposing forces intersect.

Equilibrium point

equilibrium price NOUN /ˌi.kwəˈlɪ.bri.əm praɪs/ a price where supply and demand are in equilibrium.

equinox NOUN /ˈɛ.kwəˌnɒks/ one of two days each year when the length of night and day are the closest to equal length.

equivalence NOUN /ɪˈkwɪ.və.ləns/ the state of being equivalent or not equivalent.

Equivalence of Congruence of Angles Theorem NOUN /ɪˈkwɪ.və.ləns ʌv ˈkɒn.gru.əns ʌv ˈæŋ.gəlz ˈθɪ.ə.rəm/ congruence of angles is reflexive, symmetric and transitive. See also equivalence relation (p 45).

Equivalence of Congruence of Segments Theorem NOUN /ɪˈkwɪv.ə.ləns ʌv ˈkɒn.gru.əns ʌv ˈsɛg.məntz ˈθɪ.ə.rəm/ congruence of line segments is reflexive, symmetric and transitive. See also equivalence relation (p 45).

equivalence relation NOUN /ɪˈkwɪ.və.ləns rɪˈleɪ.ʃən/ a relation that shows if two elements are equal and is reflexive, symmetric and transitive. Example: equality of real numbers is an equivalence relation. See also equal (p 44).

equivalent ADJECTIVE /ɪˈkwɪ.və.lənt/
1) has the same amount.
2) possessing the properties of an equivalence relation: reflexive, symmetric and transitive.
3) identical to; the same as.
4) has the same meaning as.
5) (logic) either all of the equivalent statements are true or all are false.
6) (sets) having the same number of members or having a one-to-one correspondence. Antonym: disjoint.
7) (decimals) two or more decimals, perhaps written differently, that have the same value. Example: $5 = 5.0$.
8) (equations) two or more equations that have exactly the same solution set. Example: $y = x + 2$ is equivalent to $2y = 2x + 4$.
9) (fractions) two or more fractions that have the same value. Example: $\frac{1}{2} = \frac{2}{4} = \frac{3\pi}{6\pi}$.
10) (ratios) two or more ratios that have the same values. Example: $1:2 = 2:4 = 3:6$.

Eratosthenes of Cyrene PERSON /ˌɛr.əˈtɒs.θəˌniz ʌv saɪˈri.ni/ (276 BCE—194 BCE) a Libyan mathematician who measured the circumference of the Earth with astonishing accuracy and for whom the Sieve of Eratosthenes (p 104) is named.

Eratosthenes' sieve NOUN /ˌɛr.əˈtɒs.θəˌniz sɪv/ see Sieve of Eratosthenes (p 104).

error NOUN /ˈɛr.ər/
1) the difference between a measured or computed value and the actual or theoretical value.
2) something which causes an inaccurate result.

error analysis NOUN /ˈɛr.ər əˈnæ.lɪ.sɪs/ the process of discovering errors and what caused an error.

error correcting NOUN /ˈɛr.ər kəˈrɛk.tɪŋ/ a process for reducing or eliminating error.

escapee NOUN /ɛsˈkeɪ.pi/ a value in a Julia set or a Mandelbrot set that grows larger with each iteration. Antonym: prisoner (p 92).

essential discontinuity NOUN /əˈsɛn.ʃəl ˌdɪs.kɒn.tnˈu.ɪ.ti/ a discontinuity where the limit of the function does not exist. Antonyms: removable discontinuity (p 98), step discontinuity (p 109), vertical asymptote (p 121).

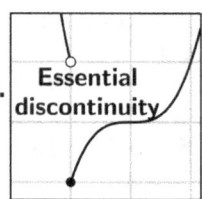
Essential discontinuity

estimate
1) VERB /ˈɛs.təˌmeɪt/ to approximate a value by making an educated guess. Example: estimate the number of jelly beans in a jar.
2) VERB /ˈɛs.təˌmeɪt/ to approximate a value using an inexact algorithm. Example: estimate the circumference of the Earth.
3) NOUN /ˈɛs.təˌmɪt/ a value arrived at by estimating. Example: Jana's estimate of the number of marbles in the jar was spot on.

estimation NOUN /ˈɛs.təˌmeɪ.ʃən/
1) the process of estimating.
2) a value arrived at by estimating.

Euclidean ADJECTIVE /juˈklɪ.di.ən/
1) having to do with Euclidean geometry.
2) being attributed to or named after Euclid of Alexandria.

Euclidean algorithm NOUN /juˈklɪ.di.ən ˈæl.gəˌrɪ.ðəm/ a method for calculating a greatest common divisor: Take the two numbers, and subtract the smaller from the larger. If difference is not zero, repeat with the smallest two of the three numbers. When the difference is zero, the subtrahend is the greatest common divisor. Example: Take 186 and 124.
$186 - 124 = 62; 124 - 62 = 62; 62 - 62 = 0$; So, $\gcd(186, 124) = 62$.

Euclidean geometry NOUN /juˈklɪ.di.ən dʒiˈɒ.mɪ.tri/ the geometry based on Euclid's landmark work *Elements*. Euclidean geometry is distinguished from other geometries by the Parallel Postulate. (p 85). Antonym: *non-Euclidean geometry* (p 79).

Euclidean n-space NOUN /juˈklɪ.di.ən ən speɪs/ an n-dimensional geometric space where objects follow the rules of Euclidean geometry. Example: Euclidean 3-space.

Euclid of Alexandria PERSON /ˈju.klɪd ʌv ˌæl.ɪgˈzæn.dri.ə/ (325 BCE—265 BCE) a mathematician famous for collecting and formalizing the knowledge of mathematics, particularly geometry. Euclid is the earliest known writer to publish an axiomatic system.

Euler characteristic NOUN /ˈɔɪ.lər ˌkær.ɪk.təˈrɪs.tɪk/ see *Euler-Descartes polyhedron formula* (p 46).

Euler-Descartes polyhedron formula NOUN /ˈɔɪ.lər deɪˈkɑrt ˌpɒ.liˈhi.drən ˈfɔr.mjə.lə/ a formula relating the number of faces, edges and vertices of convex polyhedra. Formula: $V - E + F = 2$. Synonym: *Euler characteristic*.

Euler, Leonhard PERSON /ˈɔɪ.lər ˈlɪn.ɑrd/ (1707—1783) a Swiss mathematician considered by some to be the greatest mathematician ever. Leonhard Euler is credited with, among other things, Euler's formula and discovering the constant e.

Leonhard Euler

Euler line NOUN /ˈɔɪ.lər laɪn/ a line that passes through a triangle's orthocenter, centroid and circumcenter.

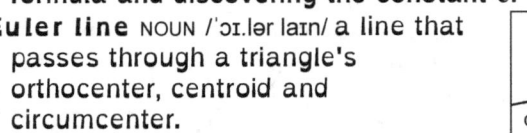

Euler's formula NOUN /ˈɔɪ.lərz ˈfɔr.mjə.lə/ $e^{i\theta} = \cos\theta + i\sin\theta$. Euler's formula relates exponents, complex numbers, and trigonometric functions.

Euler's number NOUN /ˈɔɪ.lərz ˈnʌm.bər/ see *e* (p 42).

evaluate VERB /ɪˈvæl.juˌeɪt/
1) to find the value of an expression given specific values for the variables. Example: evaluate $3x - 4$ when $x = -2$: $3(-2) - 4 = -6 - 4 = -10$.
2) to find the output value(s) of a relation given an input value. Example: evaluate $f(x)$ at $x = 4$.

even ADJECTIVE /ˈi.vən/
1) having a property associated with multiples of 2. Example: even number. Antonym: *odd* (p 82).
2) balanced. Example: even function.
3) having a property related to evenness.
4) equal in quantity.

even function NOUN /ˈi.vən ˈfʌŋk.ʃən/ a function that is symmetric about the y-axis; a function for which $f(x) = f(-x)$. Examples: $f(x) = x^2$, $f(x) = \cos x$.

Even function

even node NOUN /ˈi.vən noʊd/ a node of a network graph that has an even number of paths connecting it to other nodes. Antonym: *odd node* (p 82).

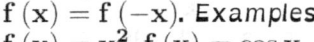
Even node

even number NOUN /ˈi.vən ˈnʌm.bər/ an integer that is divisible by 2. Math definition: $\{\cdots, -4, -2, 0, 2, 4, \cdots\}$, or $\{x : x = 2k, k \in \mathbb{Z}\}$. Antonym: *odd number* (p 82).

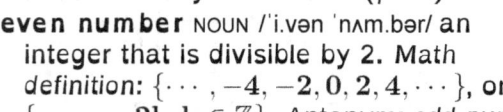
Even numbers

Even-Odd Trigonometric Identities NOUN /ˈi.vən ɒd ˌtrɪg.ə.nəˈmɛ.trɪk aɪˈdɛn.tɪ.tiz/ trigonometric identities resulting from the evenness or oddness of trigonometric functions. Synonym: *negative angle identities*. See also *Trigonometric Identities* (p 143).

event NOUN /ɪˈvɛnt/ any outcome or related group of outcomes of a probability experiment. Notation: e, e_n. Examples: flip of a coin; roll of a die.

ex- PREFIX /ɪks/
1) out of; from. Example: expand.
2) utterly, sometimes used to emphasize a concept, particularly uniqueness. Example: exact.
3) outside of. Example: exterior.
Antonym: *inter-* (p 63).

exa- PREFIX /ˈɪg.zə/ 10^{18}. Abbreviation: E. Example: 5 exameters = 5×10^{18} meters. Synonym: *quintillion*.

exact ADJECTIVE /ɪgˈzækt/
1) precise.
2) accurate or correct.
Antonyms: *inexact* (p 61), *approximate* (p 12).

exactly ADJECTIVE /ɪgˈzækt.li/ precisely; no more no less. Example: a line segment has exactly two end points. Antonym: *approximately* (p 12).

exact number NOUN /ɪgˈzækt ˈnʌm.bər/ a number arrived at by counting or by theory and not by measurement or inexact calculation. Antonym: *measurement* (p 73).

exact values of trigonometric functions NOUN /ɪgˈzækt ˈvæl.juz ʌv ˌtrɪg.əˈnɒ.mə.trɪk ˈfʌŋk.ʃənz/ values of trigonometric functions at certain angles that can be written exactly using expressions containing integers, radicals of integers and pi. See *Exact Values of Trigonometric Functions* (p 144).

example NOUN /ɪgˈzæm.pl/ an instance that illustrates a whole.

exceed VERB /ɪkˈsid/
1) to increase beyond a limit. Example: their expenses exceed their income.
2) to go beyond a boundary.

except PREPOSITION /ɛkˈsɛpt/ not including. Example: all prime numbers are odd except 2. Antonym: *including*.

exception NOUN /ɛkˈsɛp.ʃən/ something that is not included. Example: all prime numbers are odd with the exception of 2.

exchange /ɛkˈtʃeɪndʒ/
1) VERB to trade one thing for another. Synonym: *interchange* (p 63).
2) NOUN a market where stocks, bonds or commodities are traded.

exclude VERB /ɪkˈsklud/ to not include; to remove from consideration. Antonym: *include* (p 60).

exclusive ADJECTIVE /ɛkˈsklu.sɪv/
1) if one happens, others can not happen. Example: exclusive events.
2) not including the endpoints, only the middle. Example: the interval from 1 to 3, exclusive. Antonym: *inclusive* (p 60), Synonym: *disjoint* (p 40).

exclusive disjunction NOUN /ɛkˈsklu.sɪv dɪsˈdʒʌŋk.ʃən/ $P \oplus Q$ is true if and only if P is true or Q is true, but not both. Notation: $\oplus$. Synonym: *exclusive or*; *XOR*.

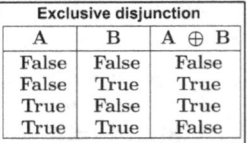

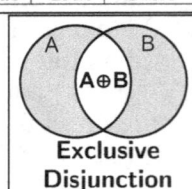
Exclusive Disjunction

exclusive events NOUN /ɛkˈsklu.sɪv ɪˈvɛntz/ two or more events where only one of the events can happen in any single trial. Example: When flipping a coin, heads and tails are exclusive events. Synonym: *mutually exclusive events*.

exclusive or NOUN /ɛkˈsklu.sɪv ɔr/ see *exclusive disjunction* (p 46).

exist VERB /ɛgˈzɪst/ to have actual or theoretical being. Example: there exists exactly one line through two points.

existence NOUN /ɛgˈzɪs.təns/ having the property of being. Example: the existence of extraterrestrials has not been proven.

existence theorem NOUN /ɛgˈzɪs.təns ˈθiə.rəm/ any theorem that proves the existence of an object without necessarily telling how to find the object.

exp() COMPUTER the natural exponential function in some computer languages. Example: **exp(x)** means e^x.

expand VERB /ɛkˈspænd/ to multiply through parentheses or raise an expression in parentheses to an exponent. Example: $(x + 2)^2 = x^2 + 4x + 4$. See also *FOIL method* (p 51).

expanded form NOUN /ɛkˈspænd.ɪd fɔrm/ a form where multiplication has been expanded through parentheses. Example: the expanded form of $(a + b)^2$ is $a^2 + 2ab + b^2$. Synonym: *expansion*.

expanded notation NOUN /ɛkˈspænd.ɪd noʊˈteɪ.ʃən/ writing out the digits of a number showing the digits multiplied by the place value. Example: $324 = 3 \times 100 + 2 \times 10 + 4$.

expansion NOUN /ɛkˈspæn.ʃən/
1) something that has been expanded. Example: the expansion of $(a + b)^2$ is $a^2 + 2ab + b^2$.
2) any mathematical series that converges to a function is an expansion of that function.
3) the act of expanding.
4) a function that is expressed as an infinite product or sum of terms.

expansion by cofactors NOUN /ɛkˈspæn.ʃən baɪ ˈkoʊˌfæk.tərz/ a method for finding the determinant of a matrix. One row or column of a square matrix is selected, then each element of the selected row or column is multiplied by its cofactor. Example:

$$\begin{vmatrix} 2 & 0 & 1 \\ -1 & 2 & -1 \\ 3 & 1 & 1 \end{vmatrix} = \underline{2} \begin{vmatrix} 2 & -1 \\ 1 & 1 \end{vmatrix} - \underline{0} \begin{vmatrix} -1 & -1 \\ 3 & 1 \end{vmatrix} +$$
$$\underline{1} \begin{vmatrix} -1 & 2 \\ 3 & 1 \end{vmatrix} = 2(2 - (-1)) - 0(-1 - (-3)) +$$
$$1(-1 - 6) = 6 - 0 - 7 = -1.$$

expect VERB /ɛkˈspɛkt/ to think that something will happen. Example: expect night to follow day.

expected frequency NOUN /ɛkˈspɛkt.ɛd ˈfri.kwən.si/ the theoretical frequency of an event.

expected value NOUN /ɛkˈspɛkt.ɛd ˈvæl.ju/ the sum of the value of each possible outcome multiplied by the probability of the outcome. Formula: $e_1 \cdot P(e_1) + e_2 \cdot P(e_2) + \cdots + e_n \cdot P(e_n)$. Example: the expected value of the roll of a single die roll is:
$1 \cdot \frac{1}{6} + 2 \cdot \frac{1}{6} + 3 \cdot \frac{1}{6} + 4 \cdot \frac{1}{6} + 5 \cdot \frac{1}{6} + 6 \cdot \frac{1}{6} = \frac{21}{6} = 3.5$.

experiment NOUN /ɛɪkˈspɛr.ə.mənt/ making an event happen and recording the outcome. Example: one flip of a coin is an experiment.

experimental ADJECTIVE /ɛkˌspɛr.əˈmɛn.tl/ having to do with making events happen. Example: experimental data. Antonyms: *observational* (p 81), *theoretical* (p 114).

experimental data NOUN /ɛkˌspɛr.əˈmɛn.tl deɪ.tʌ/ data obtained through a controlled experiment. Example: flip a coin 100 times and record the result. Antonym: *observational data* (p 82).

experimental group NOUN /ɛkˌspɛr.əˈmɛn.tl grup/ a group that is affected by an experiment. Antonym: *control group* (p 29).

experimental probability NOUN /ɛkˌspɛr.əˈmɛn.tl ˌprɑ.bəˈbɪl.ɪ.ti/ a probability arrived at by experimentation. Formula: $P(a) = \frac{f}{n}$ where **f** is the count of the outcome being measured and **n** is the total number of trials. Example: if event **a** happened 10 times out of 50 trials, the experimental probability of **a** is $P(a) = \frac{10}{50} = 0.2 = 20\%$. Antonym: *theoretical probability* (p 114).

experimental study NOUN /ɛkˌspɛr.əˈmɛn.tl ˈstʌ.di/ see *designed experiment* (p 37).

explain VERB /ɛkˈspleɪn/ tell how something is known or what is known. Example: explain AAS triangle congruence.

explanation NOUN /ˌɛk.spləˈneɪ.ʃən/ a statement of how a conclusion is reached or what is known. Example: the big bang theory is an explanation of the origin of the universe.

explementary angles NOUN /ˈɛk.splə.mən.tər.i ˈæŋ.gəlz/ see *conjugate angles* (p 27).

explicit ADJECTIVE /ɪkˈsplɪs.ɪt/ leaving nothing implied. Antonym: *implicit* (p 59).

explicit formula of a sequence NOUN /ɪkˈsplɪs.ɪt ˈfɔr.mjə.lə ʌv ə ˈsi.kwəns/ a formula that returns the value of an element of the sequence, given the order number of the sequence. Example: for the sequence $\{1, 2, 4, 8, \cdots\}$, the explicit formula is $a_0 = 1$, $a_n = 2 \cdot a_{n-1}$.

explicit function NOUN /ɪkˈsplɪs.ɪt ˈfʌŋk.ʃən/ a function having the dependent variable expressed directly in terms of the independent variable(s). Example: $y = 3x + 2$. Antonym: *implicit function* (p 59).

exploration NOUN /ˌɛk.splɔrˈeɪ.ʃən/ the act of exploring.

explore VERB /ɛkˈsplɔr/ to investigate systematically for the purpose of discovery. Example: explore the properties of triangles.

exponent NOUN /ˈɛks.poʊ.nənt/ notation for repeated multiplication. Example: $x^3 = x \cdot x \cdot x$. Notations: $a^b = \underbrace{a \cdot a \cdots \cdot a}_{\text{Exponent } b \text{ times}}$; **base**^{exponent}; Computers: **base^exponent**, **base**exponent**. Synonym: *power*. British English: *index*. Inverse: *logarithm* (p 70). See also *Properties of Exponents* (p 127).

exponential ADJECTIVE /ˌɛk.spoʊˈnɛn.ʃəl/
1) having to do with exponents. Example: exponential graph.
2) having a variable that is part of an exponent. Example: exponential equation.

3rd Dyslexic's Edition

exponential decay NOUN /ˌɛk.spoʊˈnɛn.ʃəl dɪˈkeɪ/ a decreasing exponential function in the form $y = ab^x, a > 0, 0 < b < 1$ where **a** is the initial value and **b** is the decay factor.

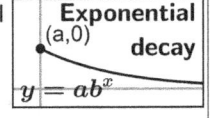

exponential identity NOUN /ˌɛk.spoʊˈnɛn.ʃəl aɪˈdɛn.tɪ.ti/ 1 is the exponential identity, since $a^1 \equiv a$.

exponential function NOUN /ˌɛks.poʊ.nɛn.ʃəl ˈfʌŋk.ʃən/ a function with a variable in an exponent. Formula: $f(x) = a \cdot b^{x-x_0} + y_0$.

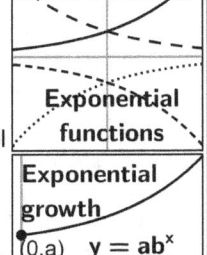

exponential growth NOUN /ˌɛk.spoʊˈnɛn.ʃəl groʊθ/ an increasing function in the form $y = ab^x, a > 0, b > 1$ where **a** is the initial value and **b** is the growth factor. Synonym: *geometric growth*. Formula: $A(t) = A_0 e^{kt}$ where A_0 is the initial population, $k \neq 0$ is the constant of growth, and $t \geq 0$ is elapsed time.

exponential notation NOUN /ˌɛk.spoʊˈnɛn.ʃəl noʊˈteɪ.ʃən/ see *e notation* (p 44).

exponential series NOUN /ˌɛk.spoʊˈnɛn.ʃəl ˈsɪər.iz/ an infinite series that equals e^x. Formula: $e^x = \frac{1}{0!} + \frac{x}{1!} + \frac{x^2}{2!} + \frac{x^3}{3!} + \cdots = \sum_{k=0}^{\infty} \frac{x^k}{k!}$.

exponentiation NOUN /ˌɛk.spoʊˌnɛn.ʃiˈeɪ.ʃən/ multiplying a number by itself a certain number of times: $a^b = \underbrace{a \cdot a \cdot \ldots \cdot a}_{b \text{ times}}$. Raising a number or expression to an exponent. Notation: a^b, a^b (computers). Example: x^4. Inverse: *take a logarithm*.

expression NOUN /ɪkˈsprɛ.ʃən/
1) a group of symbols that make a mathematical statement.
2) any mathematical formula without equals or inequalities. Examples: $x^3 + 3xy - y^3, \sin 2x$.

extend VERB /ɪkˈstɛnd/ to make longer in one or more dimensions. Example: extend a line segment.

extended line NOUN /ɪkˈstɛn.dɪd laɪn/ a line that contains a given line segment or ray.

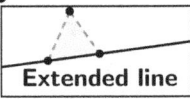

extended side NOUN /ɪkˈstɛn.dɪd saɪd/ see *extended line* (p 48).

extension NOUN /ɪkˈstɛn.ʃən/ something added on.

exterior ADJECTIVE /ɪkˈstɪər.i.ər/
1) (geometry) lying outside a boundary.
2) (angle) not lying on the interior of the angle.
Synonym: *outside* (p 84). Antonym: *interior* (p 63).

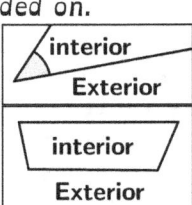

exterior angle NOUN /ɪkˈstɪər.i.ər ˈæŋ.gəl/
1) (of polygons) an angle between an extended side and an adjacent side of the polygon.
2) (of transversals) the angle between a transversal and one of a pair of transversed lines that is not between the transversed lines.

Exterior Angle Theorem NOUN /ɪkˈstɪər.i.ər ˈæŋ.gəl ˈθɪ.ə.rəm/ the measure of an exterior angle of a triangle is equal to the sum of the measures of the two remote interior angles. In the illustration, $\alpha + \beta = \gamma$.

exterior point NOUN /ɪkˈstɪər.i.ər pɔɪnt/ a point in the exterior of a figure; not a boundary point or an interior point.

external secant segment NOUN /ɪkˈstɜr.nl ˈsi.kænt ˈsɛg.mənt/ the part of a secant segment that is on the exterior of a circle. See also *secant segment* (p 102).

extract VERB /ˈɛk.strækt/
1) to calculate. Example: extract a root.
2) to approximate from a known value.

extract a root VERB /ˈɛk.strækt ʌ rut/ to approximate the value of a root. Example: $\sqrt{2} \approx 1.414$.

extraneous ADJECTIVE /ɪkˈstreɪ.ni.əs/
1) extra; not needed. Example: extraneous solution.
2) impracticable.

extraneous solution NOUN /ɪkˈstreɪ.ni.əs səˈlu.ʃən/ a solution that is not useful or is invalid. An extraneous solution can be a false solution that was introduced while solving a problem, or a solution that does not make sense in the practical context of the problem. See also *apparent solution* (p 11).

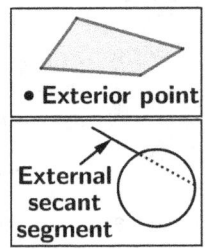

extrapolate VERB /ɪkˈstræ.pəˌleɪt/ to estimate by extending data to values not in the dataset or to values outside the known range. Example: extrapolate life expectancy.

extrapolation NOUN /ɪkˈstræ.pəˌleɪ.ʃən/ an estimation arrived at by extending data to values not in the dataset or to values outside the known range.

extreme ADJECTIVE /ɪkˈstrim/ a maximum or a minimum. Example: extreme value.

Extreme Value Theorem NOUN /ɪkˈstrim ˈvæl.ju ˈθɪ.ə.rəm/ if **f** is a continuous function whose domain is a closed interval $[a, b]$, then **f** has an absolute maximum value and an absolute minimum value on $[a, b]$.

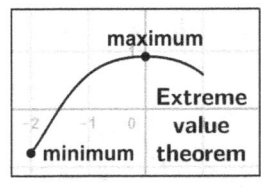

extremum NOUN /ɪkˈstri.məm/ a maximum or minimum value of a function. Plural: *extrema* /ɪkˈstri.mə/.

F

f ABBREVIATION **femto-**. $10^{-15} = 0.000\,000\,000\,000\,001$. Synonym: *quadrillionth* (p 94).

F ABBREVIATION **degree Fahrenheit**.

face NOUN /feɪs/ a flat, 2-dimensional polygon on the surface of a polyhedron.

fact NOUN /fækt/
1) a true statement.
2) a widely accepted truth.

fact family NOUN /fækt ˈfæm.li/ three integers and the addition and subtraction problems that connect them. Example: The fact family for 1, 4 and 5 is: $1 + 4 = 5$; $4 + 1 = 5$; $5 - 1 = 4$; $5 - 4 = 1$.

factor /ˈfæk.tər/
1) NOUN each of two or more integers or expressions that, when multiplied together, gives a particular product. Math definition: given integers **a** and **b**; **a** is a factor of **b** if and only if an integer **c** can be found such that $a \cdot c = b$. Example: $3 \cdot 2 = 6$. 3 and 2 are factors of 6.
2) NOUN a number that is multiplied by an expression in a function or equation, usually determining the form of the equation. Example: decay factor.
3) VERB to divide an integer or an expression into parts that, when multiplied together, equal the original expression.

factor completely VERB /ˈfæk.tər kəmˈplit.li/ to find irreducible factors whose product equals the original expression. See also irreducible (p 65).

factored form NOUN /ˈfæk.tərd form/ any polynomial written as the product of irreducible polynomials. Examples: $(x+1)(x-2)$, $(x-2)(x^2+x+7)$.

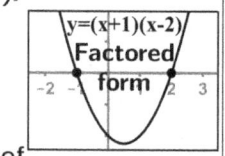

factorial NOUN /fækˈtʊr.i.əl/ the product of all integers between **1** and **n**, inclusive. Math definition: $n! \equiv 1 \cdot 2 \cdot 3 \cdot \ldots \cdot n$, $0! \equiv 1$. Example: $3! = 1 \cdot 2 \cdot 3 = 6$.

factoring formula NOUN /ˈfæk.tər.ɪŋ ˈfor.mjə.lə/ one of several formulas useful for factoring polynomials. See also Factoring Formulas (p 129).

factorization NOUN /ˌfæk.tʊr.aɪˈzeɪ.ʃən/
1) the results of finding factors. Example: a factorization of 12 is $2 \cdot 2 \cdot 3$.
2) the act of factoring.

factorize VERB /ˈfæk.tʊr.aɪz/ to find the factors of a number or expression.

factor pair NOUN /ˈfæk.tər pɛər/ two numbers or expressions that are multiplied together to get a particular product.

factor out VERB /ˈfæk.tər aʊt/ to find common factors, which are then eliminated.

Factor Theorem NOUN /ˈfæk.tər ˈθɪ.ə.rəm/ $x - a$ is a factor of polynomial $P(x)$ if and only if $P(a) = 0$. Example: $(x+3)$ is a factor of $P(x) = x^2 + 5x + 6$ since $P(-3) = (-3)^2 + 5(-3) + 6 = 9 - 15 + 6 = 0$.

factor tree NOUN /ˈfæk.tər tri/ an algorithm for finding the prime factors of an integer.

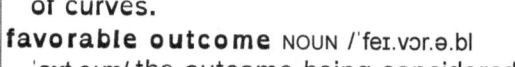

Fahrenheit NOUN /ˈfær.ənˌhaɪt/ see degree Fahrenheit (p 35).

Fahrenheit, Gabriel Daniel PERSON /ˈfɑr.ənˌhaɪt ˈɡɑ.briˌɛl ˈdɑ.niˌɛl/ (1686—1736) a German physicist who invented the Fahrenheit temperature scale.

fair ADJECTIVE /fɛər/ a probability experiment is called fair if all outcomes are equally likely. Example: when flipping a coin, if heads is just as likely as tails, then the flip of a coin is a fair experiment.

fallacy NOUN /ˈfæ.lə.si/ an argument that does not meet the standards of a logical argument. Example: Premise 1: Most birds can fly. Premise 2: A penguin is a bird. Conclusion: Therefore most penguins can fly.

falling body NOUN /ˈfɔ.lɪŋ ˈbɒ.di/ see projectile motion (p 92).

false ADJECTIVE /fals/ not true; one of two truth values. False is often written 0, especially in computer programs. Antonym: true (p 117). See also truth value (p 117).

family NOUN /ˈfæm.li/ a set of related objects. Examples: fact family; family of curves.

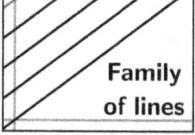

favorable outcome NOUN /ˈfeɪ.vər.ə.bl ˈaʊt.kʌm/ the outcome being considered.

feasible ADJECTIVE /ˈfi.zə.bəl/
1) can be done; can be accomplished.
2) satisfies the criteria. Example: feasible region.

feasible point NOUN /ˈfi.zə.bəl pɔɪnt/ a point in the feasible region of a system of linear inequalities.

feasible region NOUN /ˈfi.zə.bəl ˈri.dʒən/ in linear programming, the region of values that satisfy a system of linear inequalities.

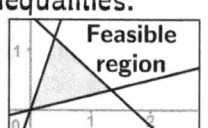

feasible solution NOUN /ˈfi.zə.bəl soʊˈlu.ʃən/ in linear programming, a solution that satisfies a system of linear inequalities.

feet per second NOUN /fit pər ˈsɛk.ənd/ a unit of measure of speed. Abbreviation: ft/s. Formulas: 1 ft/s ≈ 0.68 mph. 1 ft/s ≈ 1.10 kph. Example: an average person walks at about 4.4 ft/s.

femto- PREFIX /ˈfɪm.toʊ/ 10^{-15}. Example: 5 femtometers = 5×10^{-15} meters. Abbreviation: f. Synonym: quadrillionth.

Fermat, Pierre de PERSON /fɛrˈmɑ pjɛr də/ (1601—1665) a French mathematician famous for writing proofs in the margins of books, and claiming to have proved things, but not having written down the proof.

Fermat's last theorem NOUN /fɛrˈmɑz læst ˈθɪ.ə.rəm/ of the theorems claimed to be proved by Fermat, the last to be actually proved. Theorem: given integers **i**, **j**, **k** and an integer $n > 2$, no solutions exist for the equation $i^n + j^n = k^n$.

few ADJECTIVE /fju/
1) more than one but not many. Example: a few friends came over. Synonym: many (p 72).
2) more than zero.

fewer PRONOUN /ˈfju.ər/ less in quantity; a keyword for subtraction. Example: there are three fewer red bricks than tan bricks. Synonym: less (p 26).

fewer than PREPOSITION /ˈfju.ər ðæn/ has less than. Keyword for subtraction.

Fibonacci PERSON /fɪ.boʊˈnɑ.tʃi/ see Pisano, Leonardo (p 88).

Fibonacci numbers NOUN /ˌfɪ.boʊˈnɑ.tʃi ˈnʌm.bərz/ a sequence starting with 1, 1 where each

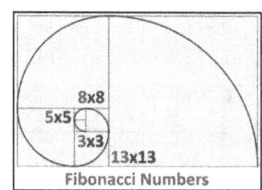

additional term is the sum of the previous two terms. Math definition: $F(0) = 1$, $F(1) = 1$, $F(n) = F(n-2) + F(n-1)$, $n > 1$. Example: first few Fibonacci numbers are **1, 1, 2, 3, 5, 8, 13, 21, 34, 55, 89, ...**

Fibonacci sequence NOUN /ˌfɪ.boʊˈnɑ.tʃi ˈsi.kwəns/ see *Fibonacci numbers* (p 49).

fifteen ADJECTIVE, NOUN /fɪfˈtin/ the number **15**. Synonym: *pentadeca-*.

fifth ADJECTIVE /fɪfθ/
1) coming in position **5** in an ordered list. Notation: **5th**.
2) one of five equal parts; $\frac{1}{5}$.

fifty ADJECTIVE, NOUN /ˈfɪf.ti/ the number **50**.

figurate number NOUN /ˈfɪg.jər.ət ˈnʌm.bər/ a number generated from the edges of regular polygons. Examples: triangular number, pentagonal number. See also *Figurate Numbers* (p 137).

finance /ˈfaɪ.nəns/
1) NOUN practices associated with money management and lending. Example: personal finance.
2) ADJECTIVE having to do with lending, money or the management of money.

finance charge NOUN /ˈfaɪ.nəns tʃɑrdʒ/ a fee paid to a lender for the use of money. Formula: **amount borrowed + finance charge = amount owed.**

find VERB /faɪnd/ to discover using mathematics.

finite ADJECTIVE /ˈfaɪ.naɪt/ ends; does not go on forever. Antonym: *infinite* (p 62).

finite difference NOUN /ˈfaɪ.naɪt ˈdɪf.rəns/
1) an expression in the form $f(x+h) - f(x)$. The finite difference divided by **h** is the difference quotient. Synonym: *centered difference* (p 20).
2) the difference between two consecutive numbers in a table.

finite sequence NOUN /ˈfaɪ.naɪt ˈsi.kwəns/ a sequence that has a first and last term. Example: $\{1, 3, 9, 27\}$. Antonym: *infinite sequence* (p 62).

first ADJECTIVE /fɜrst/
1) coming before all others. Antonym: *last* (p 67).

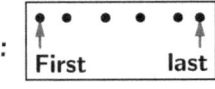

2) coming in position **1** in an ordered list. Notation: **1st**.

first degree ADJECTIVE /fɜrst dəˈgri/ containing only one variable, and that variable has no exponent. Example: **3x**.

first derivative test NOUN /fɜrst dɪˈrɪ.və.tɪv tɛst/ a test that determines if a local minimum or local maximum exists at a point. Math definition: Suppose that **c** is a critical number of a continuous function **f**. If the derivative of **f** (**f'**) changes from positive to negative at **c**, then **c** is a local maximum of **f**. If **f'** changes from negative to positive at **c**, then **c** is a local minimum of **f**. If **f'** stays positive or stays negative around **c**, then **f** does not have a local minimum or a local maximum at **c**.

fit /fɪt/
1) VERB to find an equation that best matches a data set. Example: fit an exponential equation to the data.
2) NOUN an equation that best matches a data set.

five ADJECTIVE, NOUN /faɪv/ the number or digit **5**. Synonym: *penta-*.

five frames NOUN /faɪv freɪmz/ five boxes on a paper to put marks in, useful in learning how to count.

five number summary NOUN /faɪv ˈnʌm.bər ˈsʌm.ri/ a summary of a dataset containing the minimum, the first quartile, the median, the third quartile, and the maximum of the dataset.

fixed ADJECTIVE /fɪkst/
1) does not change. Example: a fixed value.
2) does not move. Example: a fixed point. Synonym: *stationary* (p 109).

flat ADJECTIVE /flæt/
1) level and even; not curved.
2) exists in a single plane.

flip VERB /flɪp/
1) to reflect across a line or around a point.
2) to make turn over in the air. Example: flip a coin.

flip a coin VERB /flɪp ə kɔɪn/ to toss a coin in the air and see which side lands up. Synonym: *toss a coin*.

floor /flɔr/
1) ADJECTIVE having a lower limit.
2) NOUN a lower limit.

floor() COMPUTERS the representation of the floor function in many computer languages. Example: `y = floor(x);`

floor function NOUN /flɔr ˈfʌŋk.ʃən/ see *greatest integer function* (p 55).

flow /floʊ/
1) VERB to move from one place to another in a smooth and predictable fashion.
2) NOUN a smooth uninterrupted movement.

flowchart NOUN /ˈfloʊ.tʃɑrt/ a diagram showing the steps in solving a problem. Synonym: *arrow diagram*.

flow proof NOUN /floʊ pruf/ a proof where each statement and its justification are placed in a box, and whose arrows show the logical flow from one box to another.

fluid ADJECTIVE /ˈflu.ɪd/ liquid. Example: water.

fluid ounce NOUN /ˈflu.ɪd aʊns/ a unit of measure of volume. **1 fl oz ≈ 1.8047 cubic in. 8 fl oz = 1 cup. 128 fl oz = 1 gal. 1 fl oz ≈ 29.6 milliliters.** Abbreviation: **fl oz**.

flux NOUN /flʌks/
1) the rate of flow of fluid, particles, or energy.
2) a quantity expressing the strength of a field of force in a given area.

focus NOUN /ˈfoʊ.kəs/ one or two points related to the construction and properties of conic sections. Plural: *foci* /ˈfoʊ.saɪ/.

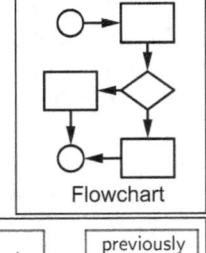

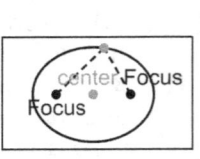

FOIL method NOUN /fɔɪl ˈmɛ.θəd/ an algorithm for expanding the product of two binomials: First, Outer, Inner, Last.

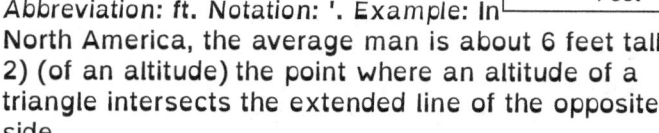

foot NOUN /fʊt/
1) a unit of measure of distance. **12 in = 1 ft; 3 ft = 1 yd; 5280 ft = 1 mile; 1 foot ≈ 0.3048 meters.** Abbreviation: ft. Notation: '. Example: In North America, the average man is about 6 feet tall.
2) (of an altitude) the point where an altitude of a triangle intersects the extended line of the opposite side.
Plural: feet /fit/.

force NOUN /fɔrs/ something that causes an object to move, or keeps it from moving; a push or pull. Example: the force of gravity.

form /fɔrm/
1) NOUN how something in written. Example: vertex form of a quadratic equation.
2) NOUN how something is expressed. Example: degree Fahrenheit is a form of temperature.
3) VERB to bring into being. Example: a line formed by two intersecting planes.

formula NOUN /ˈfɔr.mjə.lə/ a rule, usually an equation, used to calculate a value. Example: the formula for the area of a circle is $A = \pi r^2$.

fortnight NOUN /ˈfɔrt.naɪt/ a period of **14 days = 2 weeks.**

forty ADJECTIVE, NOUN /ˈfɔr.ti/ the number **40.**

four ADJECTIVE, NOUN /fɔr/ the number or digit **4.**

four-color problem NOUN /fɔr ˈkʌlər ˈprɑb.ləm/ regions on a map can be colored using exactly four colors without adjacent regions having the same color.

fourteen ADJECTIVE, NOUN /fɔrˈtin/ the number **14.**

fourth ADJECTIVE /fɔrθ/
1) coming in position 4 in an ordered list. Notation: **4th**.
2) one of four equal parts; $\frac{1}{4}$.

fractal NOUN /ˈfræk.tl/ a geometric object that has an irregular boundary and is self-similar at all scales. Example: the Sierpiński triangle.

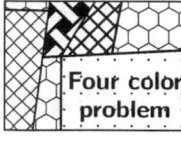

fractal geometry NOUN /ˈfræk.tl dʒiˈɒ.mɪ.tri/ a branch of geometry based on fractals.

fraction NOUN /ˈfræk.ʃən/
1) an expression divided by another expression. Math definition: $\frac{numerator}{denominator} \equiv numerator \div denominator$. Examples: $\frac{5}{16}, \frac{x+3}{x-2}$.
2) part of a whole. Example: a fraction of a second.

fractional ADJECTIVE /ˈfræk.ʃə.nl/
1) having to do with fractions. Example: fractional exponent.
2) less than a whole. Example: fractional part.

fractional exponent NOUN /ˈfræk.ʃə.nl ˈɛks.poʊ.nənt/ an exponent written as a fraction where the numerator is a power and the denominator is a root. Formula: $x^{\frac{a}{b}} = \left(\sqrt[b]{x}\right)^a = \sqrt[b]{x^a}$. Example: $9^{\frac{3}{2}} = \left(\sqrt{9}\right)^3 = 3^3 = 27.$

fractional part NOUN /ˈfræk.ʃə.nl pɑrt/
1) the part of a number that is less than one. Examples: the fractional part of **3.15** is **0.15**. The fractional part of $1\frac{3}{4}$ is $\frac{3}{4}$.
2) any part that is less than a whole.

fractional power NOUN /ˈfræk.ʃə.nl ˈpaʊ.ər/ an exponent that is a fraction. Formula: $x^{\frac{a}{b}} = \left(\sqrt[b]{x}\right)^a = \sqrt[b]{x^a}$. Example: $x^{\frac{2}{3}} = \left(\sqrt[3]{x}\right)^2$.

fraction bar NOUN /ˈfræk.ʃən bɑr/ the line segment between the numerator and denominator in a fraction. Notation: $\frac{numerator}{denominator}$ ← fraction bar.

fraction rules NOUN /ˈfræk.ʃən rulz/ algebraic rules for computing with fractions. See also Properties of Fractions (p 126).

frame NOUN /freɪm/ a list of all individuals of a population being studied.

frequency NOUN /ˈfri.kwən.si/
1) (periodic functions) the number of cycles that happen each time period.
2) (probability) the number of times an event happens compared to the total number of events. Synonym: quantity (p 94).
3) (statistics) the number of occurrences in a category or an interval compared to the total sample. Synonym: quantity (p 94).

frequency distribution NOUN /ˈfri.kwən.si dɪˈstrɪ.bju.ʃən/
1) a graph showing how many events happened in each category or interval.
2) the number of events happening in each category or interval.

Height range	# stud.	Cum. #
less than 5.0 feet	25	25
5.0–5.5 feet	35	60
5.5–6.0 feet	20	80
6.0–6.5 feet	20	100

Frequency distribution, Frequency table

frequency table NOUN /ˈfri.kwən.si ˈteɪ.bəl/ a table that shows the frequency of occurrence of data values by category or interval.

frequent ADJECTIVE /ˈfri.kwənt/
1) happening often.
2) happening at short intervals.

frequently ADVERB /ˈfri.kwənt.li/
1) often.
2) at short intervals. Example: disruption happens frequently.

front end digits NOUN /frʌnt ɛnd ˈdɪ.dʒɪts/ the first one or more digits of a numeral. Example: In **1643.2**, the three front end digits are **164**.

front view NOUN /frʌnt vju/ the view from the front of an object.

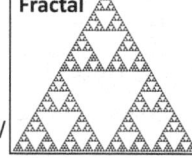

frustum NOUN /ˈfrʌs.təm/
1) a cone or pyramid with the top cut off parallel to the base.
2) the part of a solid between two parallel planes.

f/s ABBREVIATION feet per second.

ft. ABBREVIATION foot.

fulcrum NOUN /ˈfʊl.krəm/ the point on which a lever turns.

full angle NOUN /fʊl ˈæŋ.gəl/ an angle that measures a full circle. A full angle measures 360° and 2π radians.

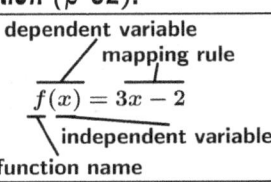
Full angle

full circle NOUN /fʊl ˈsɜr.kəl/ all the way around a circle. 360° or 2π rad.

function NOUN /ˈfʌŋk.ʃən/ a relation that has exactly one output for each input; a rule that relates input and output. Examples: $f(x) = \sin(x)$, $\{(1,3),(-2,1)\}$. Synonym: *injection* (p 62).

function notation NOUN /ˈfʌŋk.ʃən noʊˈteɪ.ʃən/ a way to write a function that clarifies the name of the function, the independent variables, and the dependent variables.

$f(x) = 3x - 2$ with labels: dependent variable, mapping rule, independent variable, function name.

function operations NOUN /ˈfʌŋk.ʃən ˌɒ.pərˈeɪ.ʃənz/ operations that can be performed on functions:
• $f(x) + g(x)$: add like terms; • $f(x) - g(x)$: subtract like terms; • $f(x) \cdot g(x)$: multiply each term of f by each term of g; • $f(x) \div g(x)$: write f and g as a fraction, then reduce; • $f(x) \circ g(x)$: replace each instance of x if f with g(x).

function rule NOUN /ˈfʌŋk.ʃən rul/ a method of transforming an independent variable into a dependent variable. Synonym: *mapping rule*.

fundamental ADJECTIVE /ˌfʌn.dəˈmɛn.tl/ forming a base on which a larger part depends. Example: Fundamental Theorem of Arithmetic.

Fundamental Counting Principle NOUN /ˌfʌn.dəˈmɛn.tl ˈkaʊnt.ɪŋ ˈprɪn.sə.pəl/ see *counting principle* (p 32).

Fundamental Theorem of Algebra NOUN /ˌfʌn.dəˈmɛn.tl ˈθi.ə.rəm ʌv ˈæl.dʒə.brə/ every non-constant single-variable polynomial with complex coefficients has at least one complex root.

Fundamental Theorem of Arithmetic NOUN /ˌfʌn.dəˈmɛn.tl ˈθi.ə.rəm ʌv əˈrɪθ.mə.tɪk/ for all positive integers except 1, there exists a unique prime factorization. Example: the prime factorization of 12 is $2^2 \cdot 3$. There is no other number has the same prime factorization as 12.

Fundamental Theorem of Calculus NOUN /ˌfʌn.dəˈmɛn.tl ˈθi.ə.rəm ʌv ˈkæl.kjə.ləs/ an indefinite integral, say f′, of some function f may be obtained as the integral of f with a bounded variable of integration. Math definition: Let f be continuous on $[a, b]$. If $g(x) = \int_a^x f(t)dt$, then $g'(x) = f(x)$. $\int_a^b f(x)dx = F(b) - F(a)$, where $F' = f$.

fundamental unit NOUN /ˌfʌn.dəˈmɛn.tl ˈju.nɪt/ one of the units of measure from which all other units of measure are derived: meter, kilogram, second, ampere, kelvin, candela, mole. See *International System of Units* (p 145).

furlong NOUN /ˈfɜr.lɒŋ/ a unit of measure of distance. Formulas: 1 furlong = 220 yards = 1/8 mile. 1 furlong ≈ 201 m.

future /ˈfju.tʃər/
1) NOUN a period of time after now.
2) ADJECTIVE having to do with things that are to come.

past ← Future → present

future value NOUN /ˈfju.tʃər ˈvæl.ju/ the value of an investment at a particular time in the future.

G

g ABBREVIATION
1) gram.
2) force of gravity. $g \approx 9.81 m/s^2$. Example: the force of gravity at the surface of the earth is 1g.

G ABBREVIATION
1) giga-. 10^9. Example: 5 gigagrams = 5×10^9 grams. Synonym: *billion*.
2) the universal gravitational constant. $G \approx 6.67384 \times 10^{-11} m^3/kg \cdot s^2$.

gain NOUN /geɪn/ an increase of value of an investment. Keyword for addition. Formula: investment + gain = new value. Example: post a gain of $100.

gal ABBREVIATION gallon.

gallon NOUN /ˈgæ.lən/ a unit of measure of Abbreviation: gal. 1 gal = 4 quarts. 1 gal 128 fluid ounces. 1 gal ≈ 3.78 liters.

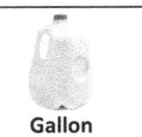
Gallon

Gaussian ADJECTIVE /ˈgaʊ.zi.ən/ credited to or named after Johann Carl Friedrich Gauss.

Gaussian curve NOUN /ˈgaʊ.zi.ən kɜrv/ see *normal curve* (p 80).

Gaussian distribution NOUN /ˈgaʊ.zi.ən dɪˈstrɪ.bju.ʃən/ see *normal distribution* (p 80).

Gaussian elimination NOUN /ˈgaʊ.zi.ən ɪˌlɪm.əˈneɪ.ʃən/ a method for solving linear systems in matrices by:
1) putting the matrix in row-echelon form, and
2) using back substitution.

Gaussian integer NOUN /ˈgaʊ.zi.ən ˈɪn.tɪ.dʒər/ a complex number $a + bi$ where a and b are both integers. Example: $3 - 2i$. Synonym: *complex integer*.

Gauss, Johann Carl Friedrich PERSON /gaʊs ˈyoʊ.hɑn kɑrl ˈfri.drɪk/ (1777—1855) a German mathematician and physicist. A unit of measure of magnetism (the Gauss) and two similar methods for solving linear equations (Gaussian elimination and Gauss-Jordan elimination) are named after him.

Johann Gauss

Gauss-Jordan elimination NOUN /gaʊs ˈdʒɔr.dn ɪˌlɪm.əˈneɪ.ʃən/ a method for solving linear systems in matrices by putting the matrix in reduced row-echelon form.

gcd ABBREVIATION see *greatest common divisor* (p 54).

gcf ABBREVIATION see *greatest common factor* (p 54).

general ADJECTIVE /ˈdʒɛ.nə.rəl/ applying to an entire class of objects. Example: general case.

General Addition Principle of Counting NOUN /ˈdʒɛ.nə.rəl əˈdɪ.ʃən ˈprɪn.sə.pəl ʌv ˈkaʊn.tɪŋ/ where $n(A)$ is the number of elements of set A, given disjoint sets $A_1, A_2, \cdots, A_n$, $n(A_1 \cup A_2 \cup \cdots \cup A_n) = n(A_1) + n(A_2) + \cdots + n(A_n)$. See also *Addition Principle of Counting* (p 8).

general case NOUN /ˈdʒɛ.nə.rəl keɪs/ a formula or principle that applies to an entire class of objects.

general term NOUN /ˈdʒɛ.nə.rəl tɜrm/ the definition of an arbitrary n^{th} term of a sequence. Example: $a_0 = 1$,

$a_n = \frac{1}{2}a_{n-1}$, $n > 0$ defines the sequence $1, \frac{1}{2}, \frac{1}{4}, \frac{1}{8}, \ldots$

generalization NOUN /ˌdʒɛ.nə.rəl.aɪˈzeɪ.ʃən/ using a specific result to describe a larger case.

generalize VERB /ˈdʒɛ.nə.rəˌlaɪz/ to take specific results and apply them to a larger class of objects.

Generalized Mean Value Theorem NOUN /ˈdʒɛ.nə.rəlˌaɪzd min ˈvæl.ju ˈθɪ.ə.rəm/ if f(x) and g(x) are continuous on [a, b] and differentiable on (a, b), then there is a point $c \in (a, b)$ where $[f(b) - f(a)]\, g'(c) = [g(b) - g(a)]\, f'(c)$.

Generalized Pythagorean Theorem NOUN /ˈdʒɛ.nə.rəlˌaɪzd pɪˌθæ.gəˈri.ən ˈθɪ.ə.rəm/ see Law of Cosines (p 67).

generate VERB /ˈdʒɛ.nə.reɪt/ to create based on one or more rules. Example: generate the first ten Fibonacci numbers.

generator NOUN /ˈdʒɛ.nə.reɪ.tər/
1) a line that, when given a specific movement, generates a figure.
2) (fractals) a figure that replaces an initiator in one iteration of a classical fractal.

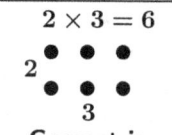
Generator

geo- PREFIX /ˈdʒi.oʊ/
1) having to do with the Earth.
2) having to do with geometry.

geoboard NOUN /ˈdʒi.oʊ.bɔrd/ a board with pegs on it on which geostrips or rubber bands are strung to demonstrate geometric principles.

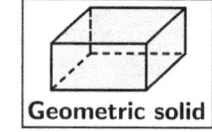
Geoboard

geodesic ADJECTIVE /ˌdʒi.əˈdɛs.ɪk/ having to do with the shortest distance between two points on a non-planar surface.

GeoGebra NOUN /ˌdʒiˈoʊ.dʒə.brə/ free interactive geometry software. See also http://www.geogebra.org.

Geodesic

geometric ADJECTIVE /ˌdʒi.əˈmɛ.trɪk/
1) having to do with geometry. Example: geometric net.
2) having to do with multiplication. Example: geometric sequence.
3) having to do with exponentiation. Example: geometric growth.

geometrically ADVERB /ˌdʒi.əˈmɛ.trɪk.li/ using geometry. Antonym: algebraically (p 8).

geometric average NOUN /ˌdʒi.əˈmɛ.trɪk ˈæ.vrɪdʒ/ see geometric mean (p 53).

geometric figure NOUN /ˌdʒi.əˈmɛ.trɪk ˈfɪg.jər/ a set of one or more points in n-space.

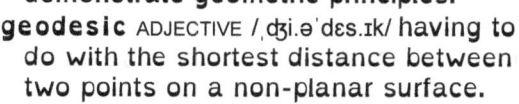
Geometric figure

geometric growth NOUN /ˌdʒi.əˈmɛ.trɪk groʊθ/ see exponential growth (p 48).

geometric mean NOUN /ˌdʒi.əˈmɛ.trɪk min/ the nth root of the product of all of the numbers in a set. Formula: $\text{mean}_{\text{geometric}}(a_1, a_2, \ldots, a_n) = \sqrt[n]{a_1 \cdot a_2 \cdot \ldots \cdot a_n}$. Example: $\text{mean}_{\text{geometric}}(1, 4, 6, 7) = \sqrt[4]{1 \cdot 4 \cdot 6 \cdot 7} = \sqrt[4]{168} \approx 3.6002$. Synonym: geometric average.

geometric net NOUN /ˌdʒi.əˈmɛ.trɪk nɛt/ a 2-dimensional shape that folds into a 3-dimensional shape. Synonym: developable surface (p 37).

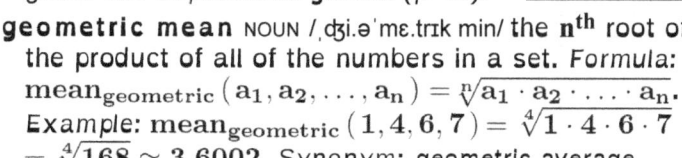
Geometric net

geometric probability NOUN /ˌdʒi.əˈmɛt.rɪk ˌprɒ.bəˈbɪ.lɪ.ti/ uses the principles of area to find the probability of an event. Example: the probability of a 2×2 cm piece of paper being hit by a raindrop.

geometric progression NOUN /ˌdʒi.əˈmɛ.trɪk proʊˈgrɛ.ʃən/ see geometric sequence (p 53).

geometric representation NOUN /ˌdʒi.əˈmɛ.trɪk ˌrɛ.prɪ.zɛnˈteɪ.ʃən/ a drawing based on geometry that illustrates or clarifies a mathematical truth.
Example: A geometric representation of multiplication of integers is rows and columns of dots.

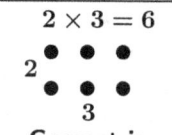
Geometric representation

geometric sequence NOUN /ˌdʒi.əˈmɛ.trɪk ˈsi.kwəns/ a sequence of numbers that have a common ratio. Formula: $n_i = r \cdot n_{i-1}$ where n_i is the ith term, r is the common ratio, and n_{i-1} is the term before the ith term. Example: $\{1, 3, 9, 27, 81, \cdots\}$ has a common ratio of 3: $(1 \cdot 3 = 3, 3 \cdot 3 = 9, \cdots)$. Synonym: geometric progression.

geometric series NOUN /ˌdʒi.əˈmɛ.trɪk ˈsɪər.iz/ the sum of all the terms of a geometric sequence. Formula: A geometric sequence with a common ratio greater than 0 and less than 1 converges to the value $s = a \frac{1}{1-r}$ where a is the value of the first term of the series and r is the common ratio. Example: the sum of the geometric sequence $1, \frac{1}{2}, \frac{1}{4}, \frac{1}{8}, \ldots$ is $s = 1 \cdot \frac{1}{1-\frac{1}{2}} = 1 \cdot \frac{1}{\frac{1}{2}} = 1 \cdot \frac{1 \cdot 2}{\frac{1}{2} \cdot 2} = 1 \cdot \frac{2}{1} = \frac{2}{1} = 2$.
Plural: geometric series.

geometric solid NOUN /ˌdʒi.əˈmɛ.trɪk ˈsɒ.lɪd/ a bounded 3-dimensional geometric figure.

geometric space NOUN /ˌdʒi.əˈmɛ.trɪk speɪs/ see space (p 107).

geometric transformation NOUN /ˌdʒi.əˈmɛ.trɪk ˈtræns.fərˌmeɪ.ʃən/ see transformation (p 115).

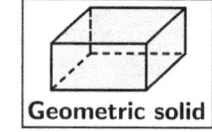
Geometric solid

geometry NOUN /dʒiˈɒ.mɪ.tri/ the study of points, lines and other shapes in space.

geostrip NOUN /ˈdʒi.oʊ.strɪp/ a straight piece of plastic with holes in it that fits on a geoboard.

Germain, Sophie PERSON /ˈsoʊ.fi ˈdʒɛr.mɑ/ (1776—1831) not allowed to study math because she was female, she became a self-taught mathematician, publishing works under the pseudonym Monsieur LeBlanc.

Sophie Germain

giga- PREFIX /ˈgɪ.gə/ $10^9 = 1,000,000,000$.
Example: 3 gigahertz = 3×10^9 hertz. Abbreviation: G.

given /ˈgɪ.vən/
1) PREPOSITION knowing that the criterion is true. Example: given a = b ….
2) NOUN a known value.
3) NOUN a criterion.

glide /glaɪd/
1) VERB to slide along a straight line for a certain distance.
2) NOUN see translation (p 115).

glide reflection NOUN /glaɪd rɪˈflɛk.ʃən/ a transformation that "flips" an object over a line, then slides the object along the same line. See also reflection (p 97).

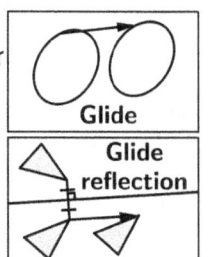
Glide
Glide reflection

3rd Dyslexic's Edition

glide reflection symmetry NOUN /glaɪd rɪˈflɛk.ʃən ˈsɪ.mɪ.tri/ two objects have glide reflection symmetry if a glide reflection will place one exactly on top of the other.

global ADJECTIVE /ˈgloʊ.bəl/ applying to a whole. Example: global maximum. Antonym: local (p 70).

global maximum NOUN /ˈgloʊ.bəl ˈmæk.sə.məm/ the greatest value that a function can take. Math definition: $f(a)$ is a global maximum for f if and only if for all x in the domain of f, $f(a) \geq f(x)$. Antonym: global minimum (p 54). Synonym: absolute maximum.

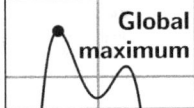

global minimum NOUN /ˈgloʊ.bəl ˈmɪ.nə.məm/ the least value that a function can take. Math definition: $f(a)$ is a global minimum for f if and only if for all x in the domain of f, $f(a) \leq f(x)$. Antonym: global maximum (p 54). Synonym: absolute minimum.

GMT ACRONYM see Greenwich Mean Time (p 55).

Goldbach's conjecture NOUN /ˈgold.bɑks kənˈdʒɛk.tʃər/ every even integer greater than 2 can be written as the sum of two prime numbers. This conjecture has not been proved nor disproved. Examples: $1 + 2 = 3$, $2 + 2 = 4, 2 + 3 = 5, \ldots$.

golden ratio NOUN /ˈgoʊl.dən ˈreɪ.ʃoʊ/ a ratio between two numbers such that the ratio between the sum of the numbers and the larger number is equal to the ratio between the larger number and the smaller. Formulas: $\varphi \rightarrow \frac{a+b}{a} = \frac{a}{b}, \varphi = \frac{1+\sqrt{5}}{2} \approx 1.6180339887$. Synonyms: golden section, golden mean, golden proportion, golden number.

golden rectangle NOUN /ˈgoʊl.dən ˈrɛk.tæŋ.gəl/ a rectangle where the ratio of the length of the sides is equal to the golden ratio: $\varphi = \frac{1+\sqrt{5}}{2} \approx 1.618$.

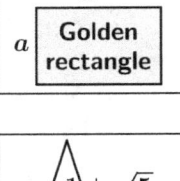

golden section NOUN /ˈgoʊl.dən ˈsɛk.ʃən/ see golden ratio (p 54).

golden triangle NOUN /ˈgoʊl.dən ˈtraɪ.æŋ.gəl/ an isosceles triangle where the ratio of the length of the sides to the base is equal to the golden ratio: $\varphi = \frac{1+\sqrt{5}}{2} \approx 1.618$.

goniometer NOUN /ˌgoʊ.niˈɒ.mɪ.tər/ an instrument that measures angles.

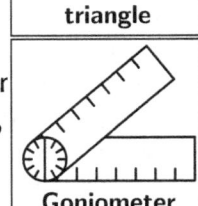

googol NOUN /ˈgu.gɒl/ a very large number equaling 10^{100}=10,000,000,000,000,000, 000,000,000,000,000,000,000,000, 000,000,000,000,000,000,000,000, 000,000,000,000,000,000,000,000, 000.

googolplex NOUN /ˈgu.gɒlˌplɛks/ an extremely large number. Formula: 1 googolplex $= 10^{\text{googol}} = 10^{10^{100}}$.

gradian NOUN /ˈgreɪ.di.n/ a unit of measure of an angle. Formula: 1 gradian $= \frac{1}{400}$ of a full circle.

gradient NOUN /ˈgreɪ.di.ənt/
1) see slope (p 106).
2) the gradient of a scalar-valued differentiable function f of several variables is the vector field ∇f whose value at a point p is the vector whose components are the partial derivatives of f at p.

graduated ADJECTIVE /ˈgræ.dju.eɪ.təd/ having marks used for measurement.

gram NOUN /græm/ a unit of measure of mass. Abbreviation: gr. Formulas: **1000 grams = 1 kilogram. 1 gram ≈ 0.0022 pounds.**

graph /græf/
1) NOUN a drawing showing an algebraic relation.
2) NOUN a set of lines and points that represent a geometric network. Synonym: geometric net (p 53).
3) NOUN a visual representation of data. Synonym: chart (p 20).
4) VERB to draw a graph.

graphical ADJECTIVE /ˈgræ.fɪ.kl/ having to do with a graph.

graphical method NOUN /ˈgræ.fɪ.kl ˈmɛ.θəd/ a method for solving systems of equations by graphing each equation, then finding intersection points.

graphing ADJECTIVE /ˈgræf.ɪŋ/ having to do with the construction of a graph.

graphing calculator NOUN /ˈgræf.ɪŋ ˈkæl.kjəˌleɪ.tər/ a calculator that plots graphs of functions on a screen.

graphing window NOUN /ˈgræf.ɪŋ ˈwɪn.doʊ/ the portion of a graph that is visible, especially in graphing calculators and graphing software.

graph theory NOUN /græf ˈθɪər.i/ the study of nodes and the paths that connect those nodes.

gravity NOUN /ˈgræv.ɪ.ti/ the attraction between two objects. Formula: $F = G\frac{m_1 m_2}{r^2}$ where F is the force of gravity, $G \approx 6.67384 \times 10^{-11} \frac{m^3}{kg \cdot s^2}$ is the gravitational constant, m_1, m_2 are the masses of the two objects, and r is the distance between the centers of the objects.

gravitational constant NOUN /ˌgræv.ɪˈteɪ.ʃə.nl ˈkɒn.stənt/ a constant used to calculate the pull of gravity between two objects. $G \approx 6.67384 \times 10^{-11} \frac{m^3}{kg \cdot s^2}$.

great ADJECTIVE /greɪt/ large or important.

great circle NOUN /greɪt ˈsɜr.kəl/ a circle on the surface of a sphere that divides the sphere into two half-spheres. Antonym: small circle (p 106).

greater ADJECTIVE /ˈgreɪ.tər/
1) more positive than. Notation: >. Example: $5 > 3$.
2) larger.
3) more important than.
Synonym: higher (British English).

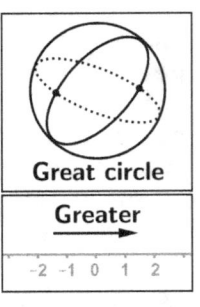

greatest ADJECTIVE /ˈgreɪt.əst/
1) most positive.
2) largest.
3) most important.
Synonym: highest (British English).

greatest common divisor NOUN /ˈgreɪt.əst ˈkɒ.mən dɪˈvaɪ.zər/ (American English) the greatest common factor of two divisors. Abbreviation: gcd. Synonym: highest common divisor (British English). See also greatest common factor (p 54).

greatest common factor NOUN /ˈgreɪt.əst ˈkɒ.mən ˈfæk.tər/ the largest number or expression of highest degree that divides evenly into two or more numbers or expressions. Abbreviation: gcf. Examples: gcf $(12, 16) = 4$, gcf $((x + 2)(x - 3), (x - 4)(x - 3)) = x - 3$. Synonym: highest common factor (British English).

greatest integer function NOUN /ˈgreɪt.est ˈɪn.tɪ.dʒər ˈfʌŋk.ʃən/ the function that returns the largest integer less than or equal to the argument. Notation: $\lfloor x \rfloor$. Synonym: floor function (p 50).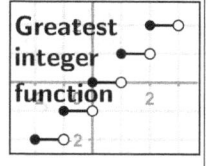

greatest lower bound NOUN /ˈgreɪt.est ˈloʊ.ər baʊnd/ the greatest number that is less than or equal to all members of a set of numbers. Synonym: infimum.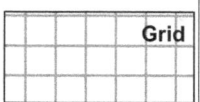

greatest possible error NOUN /ˈgreɪt.est ˈpɑs.ɪ.bəl ˈɛər.ər/ half of the smallest measurement division on a measuring instrument. Example: if a ruler is marked in centimeters, the greatest possible error is $\frac{1}{2}$ centimeter.

Greek letters NOUN /grik ˈlɛt.ərz/ ancient Greek letters are used for special variables and constants. Examples: α, β, π, θ. See also Greek Letters (p 135).

Green's Theorem NOUN /grinz ˈθɪ.ə.rəm/ suppose the region **R** is bounded by the simple closed piecewise smooth curve **C**. Then an integral over **R** equals a line integral around **C**. Formula: $\oint_C M dx + N dy = \iint_R \left(\frac{\partial N}{\partial x} - \frac{\partial M}{\partial y} \right) dx\, dy$.

Greenwich Mean Time NOUN /ˈgrɪn.ɪdʒ min taɪm/ the mean solar time at the Royal Observatory in Greenwich, England. This standard has been replaced by the Coordinated Universal Time (CUT) (p 30). Acronym: GMT.

grid NOUN /grɪd/ regularly spaced lines at right angles used as guide lines for graphs and figures.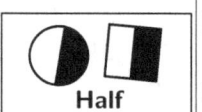

grid paper NOUN /grɪd ˈpeɪ.pər/ paper with grid lines printed on it used for drawing graphs and figures.

gross NOUN /groʊs/
1) an amount before deductions.
2) 12 dozen; 144 items.

gross profit NOUN /groʊs ˈprɑ.fɪt/ profit on sales before any deductions not directly related to the sales. Formula: **gross profit − expenses = net profit**.

gross weight NOUN /groʊs weɪt/ the weight of a container including its packaging and contents. Formula: **gross weight − tare = net weight**.

group /grup/
1) NOUN (set theory) a set with an operation defined on members of the set. The operation must meet the requirements of closure, associativity, identity and invertibility. Example: the set of real numbers under addition is a group.
2) NOUN (statistics) a sample of a population used in a study. Example: control group.
3) VERB to gather things into sets based on some criterion.
4) NOUN a collection of objects. Synonym: set (p 104).

grouped data NOUN /grupd ˈdeɪ.tʌ/ data that has been sorted into categories.

grouping /ˈgrup.ɪŋ/
1) ADJECTIVE how objects are grouped together.
2) NOUN a set of objects that have been grouped together.

grouping property of addition NOUN /ˈgrup.ɪŋ ˈprɑ.pər.ti ʌv əˈdɪ.ʃən/ see associative property of addition (p 14).

grouping property of multiplication NOUN /ˈgrup.ɪŋ ˈprɑ.pər.ti ʌv ˌmʌl.tə.plɪˈkeɪ.ʃən/ see associative property of multiplication (p 14).

grouping symbol NOUN /ˈgrup.ɪŋ ˈsɪm.bəl/ one of parenthesis (), brackets [] or braces { }.

growth NOUN /groʊθ/ an increase in quantity. Keyword for addition, multiplication, or exponentiation. Example: arithmetic growth. Antonym: decay (p 34).

growth factor NOUN /groʊθ ˈfæk.tər/ a factor indicating the speed of growth in an exponential equation. b in $y = ab^x$ where $a > 0$ and $b > 1$. Antonym: decay factor (p 34). Synonym: growth rate (p 55).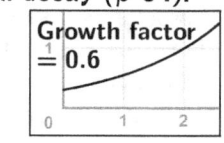

growth rate NOUN /groʊθ reɪt/ the rate of increase of a function. For linear equations, $m > 0$ in $y = mx + b$. For exponential equations, $r > 1$ in $y = ae^{rx}$. Over any subdomain where $f'(x) > 0$, the rate of growth is increasing. Antonym: decay rate (p 34). Synonym: growth factor (p 55).

guess and check NOUN /gɛs ənd tʃɛk/ see trial and error (p 116).

H

h ABBREVIATION
1) hecto-. Example: **2.3 hectometers = 230 m**. Synonym: hundred.
2) hour

ha ABBREVIATION hectare.

half /hæf/
1) NOUN one of two equal portions. Notation: $\frac{1}{2}$.
2) ADJECTIVE an amount divided by 2. Antonym: double (p 42). Plural: halves /hævz/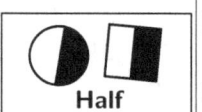

Half-Angle Identities NOUN /ˈhæf.æŋ.gəl aɪˈdɛn.tɪ.tiz/ trigonometric identities for half-angles. See also Trigonometric Identities (p 143).

half closed interval NOUN /hæf kloʊzd ˈɪn.tər.vəl/ an interval that is open on one side and closed on the other. Example: $\{x : x \geq 3\}$. Synonym: half open interval (p 56).

half-dollar NOUN /ˈhæf ˌdɑ.lər/ a coin worth $\frac{1}{2}$ of a dollar or **50 cents**.

half-hour NOUN /ˈhæf.aʊr/ $\frac{1}{2}$ of an hour or **30 minutes**.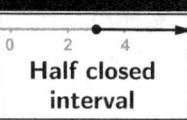

half-life NOUN /ˈhæf.laɪf/ the amount of time in which $\frac{1}{2}$ of a substance is decayed, metabolized, or used up. Formula: $h(t) = I_0 \left(\frac{1}{2}\right)^{\frac{t}{h}}$ where I_0 is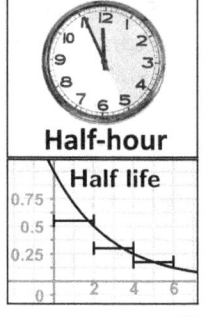

3rd Dyslexic's Edition

the initial quantity, t is the elapsed time and h is the half-life. t and h must use the same units of time. Plural: half-lives /'hæf,laɪvz/.

half-line NOUN /'hæf.laɪn/ see ray (p 96).

half open interval NOUN /hæf 'oʊ.pən 'ɪn.tər.vəl/ an interval that is open on one side and closed on the other. Example: $\{x : 0 < x \leq 2\}$. Synonym: half closed interval (p 55).

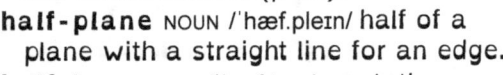
Half open interval

half-plane NOUN /'hæf.pleɪn/ half of a plane with a straight line for an edge.

half-turn NOUN /'hæf.tɜrn/ a rotation through half of a circle. An 180° turn.

halve VERB /hæv/
1) see bisect (p 17)
2) to divide by two. Antonym: double (p 42).

handspan NOUN /'hænd.spæn/ a measure of distance used in ancient Greece measuring about 9 in, or 22 cm.

harmonic ADJECTIVE /har'mɒ.nɪk/
1) having to do with the sequence $1, \frac{1}{2}, \frac{1}{3}, \frac{1}{4}, \dots$.
2) having to do with a motion similar to an oscillating spring. Example: harmonic motion.

harmonic mean NOUN /har'mɒ.nɪk min/ Formula: for the set $\{x_1, x_2, \cdots, x_n\}$, the harmonic mean is $H = \frac{n}{\frac{1}{x_1} + \frac{1}{x_2} + \dots + \frac{1}{x_n}}$.

harmonic motion NOUN /har'mɒ.nɪk 'moʊ.ʃən/ a motion similar to the motion of an oscillating spring. Formula: $f(t) = a \sin(Bt) + k$.

harmonic progression NOUN /har'mɒ.nɪk proʊ'gɹɛʃ.ən/ see harmonic sequence (p 56).

harmonic sequence NOUN /har'mɒ.nɪk 'si.kwəns/ the sequence $1, \frac{1}{2}, \frac{1}{3}, \frac{1}{4}, \dots$.

harmonic series NOUN /har'mɒ.nɪk 'sɪər.iz/ the divergent series $\sum_{n=1}^{\infty} \frac{1}{n} = 1 + \frac{1}{2} + \frac{1}{3} + \frac{1}{4} + \dots$.

hash mark NOUN /hæʃ mark/ see tally mark (p 112).

hcf ABBREVIATION highest common factor (British English). See greatest common factor (p 54).

head NOUN /hɛd/ the end of a vector with the arrow. Synonym: terminal point (p 113). Antonyms: tail (p 112), initial point (p 62).

heading NOUN /'hɛ.dɪŋ/ the angle between the imaginary line running from the front to the back of a conveyance and true north or true south.

hectare NOUN /'hɛk.tɛər/ a unit of measure of area equaling 10,000 square meters. Formula: 1 hectare ≈ 2.47 acres.

hecto- PREFIX /'hɛk.tə/ $10^2 = 100$. Abbreviation: h. Example: 3 hectograms = 3×10^2 grams = 300 grams. Synonym: hundred (p 57).

heft /hɛft/
1) NOUN weight; heaviness.
2) VERB to estimate weight by lifting.

height NOUN /haɪt/
1) any vertical measure of distance.
2) the length of an altitude of a

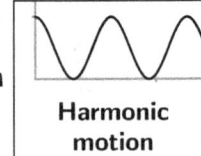
Half plane

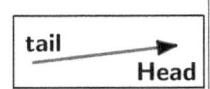
Half turn

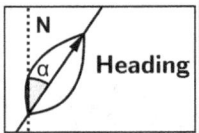
Harmonic motion

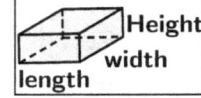
Head (tail → Head)

Heading

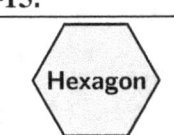
Height, width, length

geometric figure.
3) a measurement of distance at right angles to length and width.

helping line NOUN /'hɛl.pɪŋ laɪn/ see auxiliary line (p 14).

helix NOUN /'hi.lɪks/ a curve formed by wrapping a wire around a cylinder. Equations: $x = a \sin \theta$, $y = a \cos \theta$, $z = b\theta$.

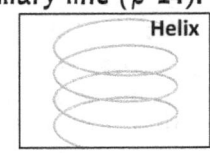
Helix

hemi- PREFIX /'hɛ.mɪ/ half. Example: hemisphere.

hemisphere NOUN /'hɛ.mɪ.sfɪər/ exactly one half of a sphere; a sphere cut in two by a plane passing through the center of the sphere.

Hemisphere

hepta- PREFIX /'hɛp.tə/ seven. Example: heptahedron.

heptagon NOUN /'hɛp.tə.gɒn/ any seven-sided polygon.

Heptagon

heptahedron NOUN /,hɛp.tə'hi.drən/ any polyhedron with seven faces. Example: pentagonal prism. Plural: heptahedra /,hɛp.tə'hi.drə/.

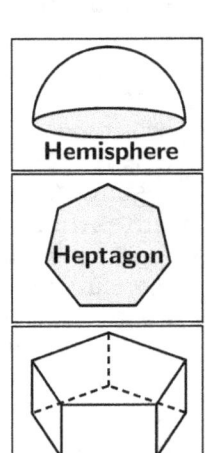
Heptahedron

Heron of Alexandria PERSON /'hɛ.rən ʌv ˌæl.ɪg'zæn.dri.ə/ (ca. 10 CE—ca. 75 CE) a mathematician from Alexandria, Egypt who discovered Heron's formula for the area of a triangle.

Heron's formula NOUN /'hɛ.rənz 'fɔr.mjə.lə/ a formula for the area of a triangle given the lengths of the sides. Formula: $s = \frac{l+m+n}{2}$, $A = \sqrt{s(s-l)(s-m)(s-n)}$. Synonym: Hero's formula.

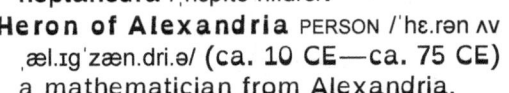
Heron's formula

Hero's formula NOUN /'hɪə.roʊz 'fɔr.mjə.lə/ see Heron's formula (p 56).

heuristic ADJECTIVE /hyʊr'ɪs.tɪk/ involving trial and error; involving guess and check.

heuristic method NOUN /hyʊr'ɪs.tɪk 'mɛ.θəd/ a method of solving a problem that involves trial and error. Antonym: algorithm (p 9).

hex ABBREVIATION hexadecimal (p 56).

hexa- prefix /'hɛk.sə/ six. Example: hexagon.

hexadec- PREFIX /,hɛk.sə'dɛs/ sixteen. Example: hexadecimal.

hexadecimal /,hɛk.sə'dɛs.məl/
1) ADJECTIVE having to do with a base 16 numeration system. Example: $2F0B_{16} = 2 \times 16^3 + 15 \times 16^2 + 0 \times 16 + 11 = 12043_{10}$.
2) NOUN the hexadecimal numeration system. Abbreviation: hex.

hexadecimal digit NOUN /,hɛk.sə'dɛs.məl 'dɪ.dʒɪt/ a digit used in hexadecimal numeration: 0, 1, 2, 3, 4, 5, 6, 7, 8, 9, A=10, B=11, C=12, D=13, E=14, F=15.

hexagon NOUN /'hɛk.sə.gɒn/ any six-sided polygon.

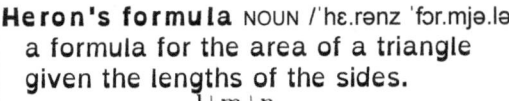
Hexagon

hexagonal ADJECTIVE /'hɛk.sə.gɒ.nl/
1) having to do with a hexagon.
2) including a hexagon. Example: hexagonal pyramid.
3) shaped like a hexagon.

hexahedron NOUN /ˌhɛk.səˈhi.drən/ any polyhedron with six faces and six vertices. A regular hexahedron is a cube. Plural: hexahedra /ˌhɛk.səˈhi.drə/.

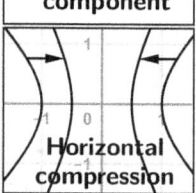
Hexahedron

higher ADJECTIVE /ˈhaɪ.ər/ see greater (p 54).

highest ADJECTIVE /ˈhaɪ.ɛst/ see greatest (p 54).

highest common factor NOUN /ˈhaɪ.ɛst ˈkɒ.mən ˈfæk.tər/ (British English) see greatest common factor (p 54).

Hilbert, David PERSON /ˈhɪl.bərt ˈdeɪ.vɪd/ (1862—1943) a Prussian mathematician who reorganized Euclidean Geometry into what is now called Modern Geometry.

David Hilbert

Hindu NOUN /ˈhɪn.du/ having to do with the people of northern India.

Hindu-Arabic numerals NOUN /ˈhɪn.du ˈæ.rə.bɪk ˈnum.rəlz/ see Arabic numerals (p 12).

histogram NOUN /ˈhɪs.tə.ɡræm/ a bar graph where the height of a rectangle shows frequency or quantity.

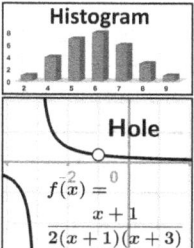
Histogram

hole NOUN /hoʊl/ a point of a function where the function is undefined. This can happen if both the numerator and denominator of a rational function are zero. Example: in $f(x) = \frac{x-2}{2(x-2)(x+3)}$, $f(x)$ is undefined when $x = 2$ or $x = -3$.

Hole
$$f(x) = \frac{x+1}{2(x+1)(x+3)}$$

homo- PREFIX /ˈhoʊ.moʊ/ the same in some way.

homogeneous ADJECTIVE /ˌhoʊ.məˈdʒi.ni.əs/ having some property in common.

$2x - 4y = 0$
$-x + 2y = 0$
$x + y = 0$
Homogeneous

homogeneous system of equations NOUN /ˌhoʊ.məˈdʒi.ni.əs ˈsɪs.təm ʌv ɪˈkweɪ.ʒənz/ a system of equations where the constant terms are zero.

horizon NOUN /həˈraɪ.zən/ the apparent boundary between the Earth and the sky.

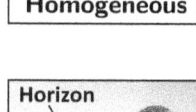
Horizon

horizon line NOUN /həˈraɪ.zən laɪn/ a line used in perspective view where objects seem to disappear into the distance.

horizontal /ˌhɔr.əˈzɒn.tl/
1) ADJECTIVE parallel with the x-axis.
2) ADJECTIVE parallel with the horizon.
3) ADJECTIVE goes from left to right or from right to left, not up and down.
4) NOUN a horizontal line or a horizontal line segment. Antonym: vertical (p 121).

Horizontal

horizontal asymptote NOUN /ˌhɔr.əˈzɒn.tl ˈæ.sɪm.toʊt/ a type of essential discontinuity where x goes to positive or negative infinity on both sides of the point of discontinuity. Formula: for polynomials, the equation of an asymptote is $y = \frac{\text{leading coefficient of the numerator}}{\text{leading coefficient of the denominator}}$. Math definition: The line L is a horizontal asymptote of f if $\lim_{x \to \pm\infty} f(x) = L$. Antonyms: oblique asymptote (p 81), vertical asymptote (p 121).

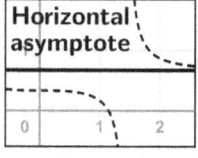
Horizontal asymptote

horizontal axis NOUN /ˌhɔr.əˈzɒn.tl ˈæk.sɪs/ in a rectangular coordinate system, the axis that goes from side to side. Synonyms: x-axis (p 122),

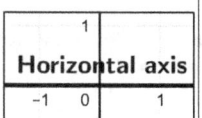
Horizontal axis

real axis (p 96). Antonym: vertical axis (p 121).

horizontal component NOUN /ˌhɔr.əˈzɒn.tl kəmˈpoʊ.nənt/ the part of a vector that is horizontal. Antonym: vertical component (p 121).

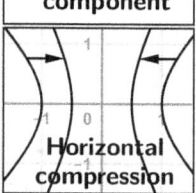
vertical component, vector, Horizontal component

horizontal compression NOUN /ˌhɔr.əˈzɒn.tl kəmˈprɛ.ʃən/ a transformation of a function that shrinks the function horizontally. Example: $f'(x) = f(2x)$. Antonym: horizontal enlargement (p 57).

Horizontal compression

horizontal dilation NOUN /ˌhɔr.əˈzɒn.tl daɪˈleɪ.ʃən/ see horizontal enlargement (p 57).

horizontal enlargement NOUN /ˌhɔr.əˈzɒn.tl ɛnˈlɑrdʒ.mənt/ a transformation of a function that stretches the function horizontally. Example: $f'(x) = f(\frac{1}{2}x)$. Antonym: horizontal compression (p 57).

Horizontal enlargement

horizontal intercept NOUN /ˌhɔr.əˈzɒn.tl ˈɪn.tərˌsɛpt/ see x-intercept (p 122).

horizontal line NOUN /ˌhɔr.əˈzɒn.tl laɪn/
1) a line that is parallel with the x-axis. Equation: $y = a$. Example: $y = 5$.
2) a line that is parallel with the horizon.

$y = 1$
Horizontal line

horizontal line test NOUN /ˌhɔr.əˈzɒn.tl laɪn tɛst/ a way to see if a function is a one-to-one function: If all horizontal lines in the range of a function cross the graph of the function no more than once, and the function passes the horizontal line test, then it is a one-to-one function.

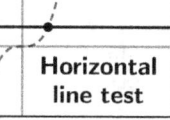
Horizontal line test

horizontal reflection NOUN /ˌhɔr.əˈzɒn.tl rɪˈflɛk.ʃən/ a reflection in which a plane figure flips over horizontally. The axis of reflection for a horizontal reflection is a vertical line. Formula: $f'(x) = -f(x)$.

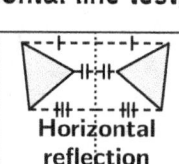
Horizontal reflection

horizontal shift NOUN /ˌhɔr.əˈzɒn.tl ʃɪft/ a shift of a function either right or left horizontally. Formula: $f'(x) = f(x + a)$ (shift left by a). Synonym: phase shift (p 88).

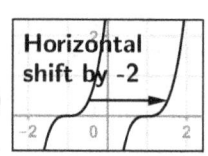
Horizontal shift by -2

horizontal shrink NOUN /ˌhɔr.əˈzɒn.tl ʃrɪŋk/ see horizontal compression (p 57)

horizontal stretch NOUN /ˌhɔr.əˈzɒn.tl strɛtʃ/ see horizontal enlargement (p 57).

horizontal translation NOUN /ˌhɔr.əˈzɒn.tl trænzˈleɪ.ʃən/ see horizontal shift (p 57).

hour NOUN /aʊər/ a unit of measure of time. Abbreviation: h. Formulas: 1 day ≈ 24 hours; 1 hour = 60 minutes.

hour hand NOUN /aʊər hænd/ the smaller hand on an analog clock that indicates the current hour.

Hour hand

hundred NOUN /ˈhʌn.drɛd/ 100. Synonym: hecto- (p 56).

hundredth NOUN /ˈhʌn.drɛθ/
1) coming in position 100 in an ordered list. Notation: 100th.
2) one of one hundred parts. $\frac{1}{100}$. Synonym: centi-

(p 20).

Hypatia of Alexandria PERSON /hɪˈpi.ʃʌ ʌv ˌæl.ɪgˈzæn.dri.ə/ (born c. 350—370CE; died 415CE) the first well-known woman mathematician, who worked at the famed Library of Alexandria. She is known for translating mathematical texts and for her commentary on writings by other mathematicians.

hyper- PREFIX /haɪˈpɜr/
1) over.
2) above.
3) beyond.
4) an extension of a 3-dimensional figure to 4 or more dimensions. Example: hypersphere.

hyperbola NOUN /haɪˈpɜr.bə.lə/ a conic section formed by intersecting a plane with both halves of a right double cone; all points in a plane where the difference of the distances between two points is constant. Formula: $\frac{x^2}{a} - \frac{y^2}{b} = 1$ where **a** is half the length of the transverse axis, and **b** is half the length of the conjugate axis. See also Equations for a Hyperbola (p 142).

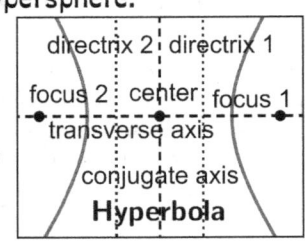

hyperbolic ADJECTIVE /ˌhaɪ.pərˈbɒl.ɪk/
1) having to do with a hyperbola. Example: hyperbolic function.
2) having to do with a geometric space where two distinct parallel lines can pass through the same point. Example: hyperbolic geometry.

hyperbolic cosecant NOUN /ˌhaɪ.pərˈbɒl.ɪk ˈkoʊ.si.kænt/ a function based on the ratios of line segments between the origin and a unit hyperbola; the multiplicative inverse of the hyperbolic sine. Abbreviation: csch. Equation: $\operatorname{csch} x = \frac{1}{\sinh x} = \frac{2}{e^x - e^{-x}}$. Inverse: arc hyperbolic cosecant.

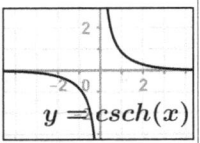

hyperbolic cosine NOUN /ˌhaɪ.pərˈbɒl.ɪk ˈkoʊ.saɪn/ a function based on the ratios of line segments between the origin and a unit hyperbola. Abbreviation: cosh. Equation: $\cosh x = \frac{e^x + e^{-x}}{2}$. Inverse: arc hyperbolic cosine.

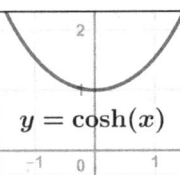

hyperbolic cotangent NOUN /ˌhaɪ.pərˈbɒl.ɪk ˈkoʊ.tæn.dʒənt/ a function based on the ratios of line segments between the origin and a unit hyperbola; the multiplicative inverse of the hyperbolic tangent. Abbreviation: coth. Equation: $\coth x = \frac{\cosh x}{\sinh x} = \frac{e^{2x}+1}{e^{2x}-1}$. Inverse: arc hyperbolic cotangent.

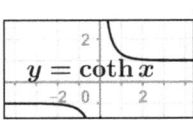

hyperbolic function NOUN /ˌhaɪ.pərˈbɒl.ɪk ˈfʌŋk.ʃən/ a function based on the hyperbola similar to the trigonometric functions. Examples: hyperbolic sine, hyperbolic cosine.

hyperbolic geometry NOUN /ˌhaɪ.pərˈbɒl.ɪk dʒiˈɒ.mɪ.tri/ a geometry where two distinct parallel lines can both pass through the same point.

hyperbolic secant NOUN /ˌhaɪ.pərˈbɒl.ɪk ˈsi.kænt/ a function based on the ratios of line segments between the origin and a unit hyperbola; the multiplicative inverse of the hyperbolic cosine. Abbreviation: sech. Equation: $\operatorname{sech} x = \frac{1}{\cosh x} = \frac{2}{e^x + e^{-x}}$. Inverse: arc hyperbolic secant.

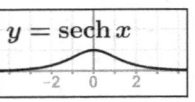

hyperbolic sine NOUN /ˌhaɪ.pərˈbɒl.ɪk saɪn/ a function based on the ratios of line segments between the origin and a unit hyperbola. Abbreviation: sinh. Equation: $\sinh x = \frac{e^x - e^{-x}}{2}$. Inverse: arc hyperbolic sine.

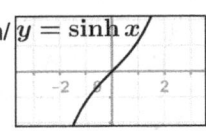

hyperbolic tangent NOUN /ˌhaɪ.pərˈbɒl.ɪk ˈtæn.dʒənt/ a function based on the ratios of line segments between the origin and a unit hyperbola. Abbreviation: tanh. Equation: $\tanh x = \frac{\sinh x}{\cosh x} = \frac{e^{2x}-1}{e^{2x}+1}$. Inverse: arc hyperbolic tangent.

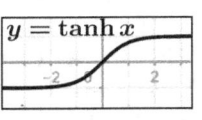

hyperbolic trigonometry NOUN /ˌhaɪ.pərˈbɒl.ɪk ˌtrɪ.gəˈnɒ.mɪ.tri/ a trigonometry where the trigonometric functions are defined in terms of the constant e. Important: hyperbolic trigonometry is unrelated to hyperbolic geometry.

hyperboloid NOUN /haɪˈpɜr.bəˌlɔɪd/ a 3-dimensional figure created by rotating a hyperbola around its axis.

hypercube NOUN /haɪˈpər.kjub/ a cube extended to a fourth dimension; a four-dimensional figure bounded by 6 cubes. Synonyms: tesseract (p 113), 4-cube.

hyperplane NOUN /ˈhaɪ.pərˌpleɪn/ a plane extended to three or more dimensions. Formula: $ax + by + cz = d$ (3-dimensional).

hypersphere NOUN /ˈhaɪ.pərˌsfɪər/ a sphere extended to four or more dimensions; the set of all points in four or more dimensions that are equidistant from a center point.

hypo- PREFIX /ˈhaɪ.poʊ/ under.

hypocycloid NOUN /ˈhaɪ.poʊˌsaɪ.klɔɪd/ a curve generated by tracing a fixed point on a circle as it rolls around the inside of another circle.

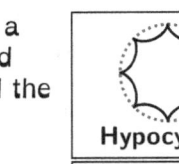

hypotenuse NOUN /haɪˈpɒ.tn.us/
1) the side of a right triangle opposite the right angle. Antonym: side (p 104).
2) the length of a hypotenuse.

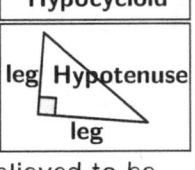

hypothesis NOUN /haɪˈpɒ.θə.sɪs/
1) (mathematics) a statement that is believed to be true, and is to be proved.
2) (statistics and science) a proposal or an educated guess to be investigated.
Plural: hypotheses /haɪˈpɒ.θə.siz/.

I

i SYMBOL /aɪ/ see imaginary unit (p 59).

I SYMBOL
1) 1 in Roman numerals.

2) see *identity* (p 59).

I_n SYMBOL an identity matrix with dimensions $n \times n$. See also *identity matrix* (p 59). Example: $I_2 = \begin{bmatrix} 1 & 0 \\ 0 & 1 \end{bmatrix}$.

icosa- PREFIX /aɪˈkoʊ.sə/ twenty. Example: icosahedron.

icosahedron NOUN /aɪˌkoʊ.səˈhi.drən/ any polyhedron with 20 faces. A regular icosahedron has 20 congruent sides all of which are equilateral triangles. Plural: icosahedra /aɪˌkoʊ.səˈhi.drə/.

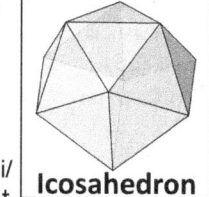
Icosahedron

idempotency ADJECTIVE /ˌaɪ.dəmˈpoʊ.tən.si/ having to do with whether or not a set has an idempotent element.

idempotent ADJECTIVE, NOUN /ˌaɪ.dəmˈpoʊ.tnt/
1) an element and a binary operation such that if the operation is applied using the same element for both operands, the result is the original element. Examples: $1 \cdot 1 = 1, 0 \cdot 0 = 0, 0 + 0 = 0$.
2) an element of a set that is idempotent with respect to that set.

identical ADJECTIVE /aɪˈdɛn.tɪ.kəl/ exactly the same.

identify VERB /aɪˈdɛn.tə.faɪ/ to recognize as being a particular thing. Example: identify the variable.

identity NOUN /aɪˈdɛn.tɪ.ti/
1) an equation that is true for all values of the variables. Notation: $\equiv$. Example: $\sin^2 \theta + \cos^2 \theta \equiv 1$.
2) a value that returns the same value after an operation. Math definition: **i** is an identity for the operation $*$ on the set **A** if and only if, for every element **a** of **A**, $a * i = a$ and $i * a = a$. Example: $a + 0 = a, 0 + a = a$. Synonym: *identity element*. See also *additive identity* (p 8), *multiplicative identity* (p 77), *Algebraic Identities* (p 136).

identity function NOUN /aɪˈdɛn.tɪ.ti fʌŋk.ʃən/ the function $f(x) = x$.

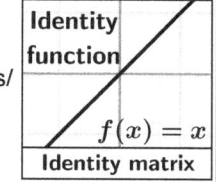
Identity function $f(x) = x$
Identity matrix

identity matrix NOUN /aɪˈdɛn.tɪ.ti meɪ.trɪks/ a square matrix containing all zeros, except for the main diagonal which contains all ones. Notation: I_n represents an $n \times n$ identity matrix.

identity property of 0 NOUN /aɪˈdɛn.tɪ.ti ˈprɒ.pər.ti ʌv ˈzɪə.roʊ/ see *additive identity* (p 8).

identity property of 1 NOUN /aɪˈdɛn.tɪ.ti ˈprɒ.pər.ti ʌv wʌn/ see *multiplicative identity* (p 77).

identity property of addition NOUN /aɪˈdɛn.tɪ.ti ˈprɒ.pər.ti ʌv əˈdɪ.ʃən/ see *additive identity* (p 8).

identity property of multiplication NOUN /aɪˈdɛn.tɪ.ti ˈprɒ.pər.ti ʌv ˌmʌl.tə.plɪˈkeɪ.ʃən/ see *multiplicative identity* (p 77).

if PREPOSITION /ɪf/ based on a condition. Example: if a rectangle has congruent sides, then it is also a square.

if and only if /ɪf ænd ˈoʊn.li ɪf/ see *biconditional* (p 16). Notation: iff.

iff CONJUNCTION if and only if. see *biconditional* (p 16).

if ... then ... /ɪf ðɛn/ see *implication* (p 59).

im- PREFIX /ɪm/ not. Example: impossible.

image NOUN /ˈɪ.mɪdʒ/
1) a copy of an object; the result of a geometric transformation.
2) the result of a mapping of a set.

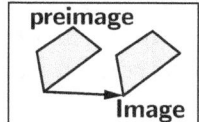
preimage
Image

imaginary ADJECTIVE /ɪˈmæ.dʒəˌnɛr.i/ having to do with the part of a complex number multiplied by $\sqrt{-1}$.

imaginary axis NOUN /ɪˈmæ.dʒəˌnɛr.i ˈæk.sɪs/ the vertical axis in a complex plane that represents the imaginary part of a complex number.

Imaginary axis
real axis

imaginary number NOUN /ɪˈmæ.dʒəˌnɛr.i ˈnʌm.bər/ a complex number that has no real part. Example: $3i = 0 + 3i$. Synonym: *pure imaginary number*.

imaginary part NOUN /ɪˈmæ.dʒəˌnɛr.i pɑrt/ the part of a complex number that is multiplied by the imaginary unit $i \equiv \sqrt{-1}$ Notation: $\Im$ or **Im**. Formula: $\Im(a + bi) = b$. Example: $\Im(2 + 3i) = +3$.

imaginary unit NOUN /ɪˈmæ.dʒəˌnɛr.i ˈju.nɪt/ the square root of negative one. Notation: **i**. Math definition: $i \equiv \sqrt{-1}$.

imperial ADJECTIVE /ɪmˈpɛr.i.l/ having to do with an empire, especially the British Empire.

imperial system NOUN /ɪmˈpɛr.i.l ˈsɪs.təm/ a set of units of measures once used in the United Kingdom. Synonym: *imperial unit* (p 59).

imperial unit NOUN /ɪmˈpɛr.i.l ˈju.nɪt/ one of several units of measure once used in United Kingdom. Examples: foot, mile and gallon.

implication NOUN /ˌɪm.plɪˈkeɪ.ʃən/ if ... then .... Math definition: if **P** implies **Q**, then if **P** is true, **Q** must be true, and if **P** is false, **Q** must be false. Notation: $P \rightarrow Q$. Synonym: *if ... then ...*. Example: if the sides of a rhombus meet at a right angle then the rhombus is also a square.
$\underbrace{\text{the sides of a rhombus meet at a right angle}}_{P}$
$\underset{\rightarrow}{\text{then}} \underbrace{\text{the rhombus is also a square}}_{Q}$.

implicit ADJECTIVE /ɪmˈplɪ.sɪt/ implied, rather than stated. Antonym: *explicit* (p 47).

implicit differentiation NOUN /ɪmˈplɪ.sɪt ˌdɪ.fərˌɛn.ʃiˈeɪ.ʃən/ a method for finding the derivative of an implicitly defined function or relation. Example: $\frac{d}{dx}(x^2 + y^2 = r^2) \Rightarrow ((y')^2 + 1)^3 = (ry'')^2$.

implicit function NOUN /ɪmˈplɪ.sɪt ˈfʌŋk.ʃən/ a function where the dependent variable is not explicitly written as a function of the independent variable. Example: $xy = 1$. Antonym: *explicit function* (p 47).

implicit relation NOUN /ɪmˈplɪ.sɪt rɪˈleɪ.ʃən/ a relation where the dependent variable is not explicitly written as a function of the independent variable. Example: $x^2 + xy - y^2 = 1$.

implied coefficient NOUN /ɪmˈplaɪd ˌkoʊ.əˈfɪ.ʃənt/ a term without an explicit coefficient has an implied coefficient of 1. Example: x^2y has an implied coefficient of 1 since $x^2y = 1x^2y$. See also *1, Property of Multiplying by* (p 6).

implied multiplication NOUN /ɪmˈplaɪd ˌmʌl.tə.plɪˈkeɪ.ʃən/ in the term ax, the multiplication of **a** by **x** is implied. Example: $2x \equiv 2 \cdot x$.

imply VERB /ɪmˈplaɪ/
1) if one is true the other is true. If one is false the other is false. Example: aRb implies bRa. Notations: $\equiv, \rightarrow, \Rightarrow$.
2) to suggest without stating explicitly. Example: implied coefficient.

impossible ADJECTIVE /ɪmˈpɒ.sə.bəl/ cannot happen; will not happen. Antonyms: certain (p 20), possible (p 91).

impossible event NOUN /ɪmˈpɒ.sə.bəl ɪˈvɛnt/ an event that will never happen. Math definition: e is an impossible event if and only if $P(e) = 0$. Antonym: certain event (p 20).

improper ADJECTIVE /ɪmˈprɒ.pər/ not in standard or reduced form. Antonym: proper (p 93).

improper fraction NOUN /ɪmˈprɒ.pər ˈfræk.ʃən/
1) a numeric fraction where the absolute value of the numerator is greater than the absolute value of the denominator. Example: $\frac{16}{7}$.
2) a rational polynomial where the degree of polynomial in the numerator is greater than or equal to the degree of the polynomial in the denominator. Example: $\frac{x^3-1}{x+1}$.
Antonym: proper fraction (p 93).

improper integral NOUN /ɪmˈprɒ.pər ˈɪn.tɛ.grəl/ the limit of a definite integral as an endpoint of the interval(s) of integration approaches either a specified real number, ∞, $-\infty$, or in some instances as both endpoints approach limits. Math definition: if $\int_a^t f(x)dx$ exists for every number $t \geq a$, then $\int_a^\infty f(x)dx = \lim_{t \to \infty} \int_a^t f(x)dx$. If $\int_t^b f(x)dx$ exists for every number $t \geq b$, then $\int_{-\infty}^b f(x)dx = \lim_{t \to \infty} \int_t^b f(x)dx$. If both $\int_a^\infty f(x)dx$ and $\int_{-\infty}^a f(x)dx$ are convergent, then $\int_{-\infty}^\infty f(x)dx = \int_{-\infty}^a f(x)dx + \int_a^\infty f(x)dx$.

in ABBREVIATION inch.

in- PREFIX /ɪn/
1) in, inside.
2) not.

inaccurate ADJECTIVE /ɪnˈæ.kyə.rɪt/ not free of error; not exact.

incenter NOUN /ˈɪnˌsɛn.tər/ the center of the circle that intersects each side of a triangle or a regular polygon exactly once. The incenter of a triangle is located at the intersection of the angle bisectors of the triangle.

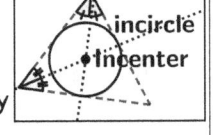

inch NOUN /ɪntʃ/ a unit of measure of distance. Abbreviation: in. Notation: ". Formulas: 1 foot = 12 inches = 12"; 1 inch ≈ 2.54 centimeters.

incircle NOUN /ˈɪnˌsɜr.kəl/ the circle that is tangent to all the sides of a triangle or of a regular polygon. The center of the incircle of is located at the intersection of the angle bisectors of the figure.

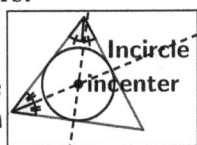

inclination NOUN /ˌɪn.kləˈneɪ.ʃən/
1) a plane-like figure that is not parallel with a reference plane.
2) the dihedral angle between a reference plane and another plane.

incline /ɪnˈklaɪn/
1) NOUN the slope of a plane-like figure measured from the horizontal.
2) NOUN an inclined plane.
3) VERB to place at an incline.

inclined plane NOUN /ɪnˈklaɪnd pleɪn/ a plane that is sloped compared to the horizontal. Synonym: incline (p 60).

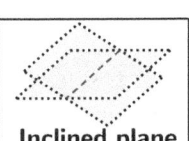

include VERB /ɪnˈklud/
1) to contain.
2) to make part of a whole.
Antonym: exclude (p 46).

included angle NOUN /ɪnˈklu.dɪd ˈæŋ.gəl/ see contained angle (p 28).

included side NOUN /ɪnˈklu.dɪd saɪd/ see contained side (p 28).

inclusion relation NOUN /ɪnˈklu.ʒən rɪˈleɪ.ʃən/ see subset (p 110).

inclusive ADJECTIVE /ɪnˈklu.sɪv/ includes all parts; includes limits or extremes. Example: the interval from 1 to 3, inclusive is $\{x \mid 1 \leq x \leq 3\}$. Antonym: exclusive (p 46).

incompatible ADJECTIVE /ˌɪn.kəmˈpæ.tə.bəl/ cannot be used together. Antonym: compatible (p 24).

incomplete ADJECTIVE /ˌɪn.kəmˈplit/ of a network graph, at least one pair of nodes is not connected by a path. Antonym: complete (p 24).

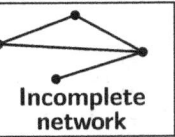

in conclusion IDIOM /ɪn kənˈklu.ʒən/ it can be concluded that; the preceding arguments lead to the following conclusion. Synonym: therefore (p 114).

inconsistent ADJECTIVE /ˌɪn.kənˈsɪs.tənt/
1) (system of equations) having no common solution.
2) (axiomatic system) generates at least one contradiction; both a proposition and its negation can be proved.
Antonym: consistent (p 28).

increase /ˈɪn.kris/
1) VERB to go up; to become more or larger. Keyword for addition. Synonym: add (p 8), appreciate (p 12).
2) NOUN the amount, proportion or percentage by which a value increases. Synonym: appreciation (p 12).
Antonym: decrease (p 34).

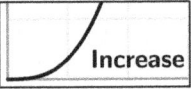

increase by PREPOSITION /ˈɪn.kris baɪ/ add to. Keywords for addition. Example: 5 increased by 2 is $5 + 2 = 7$.

increasing ADJECTIVE /ɪnˈkri.sɪŋ/ the property of having an increase. Example: increasing sequence. Antonym: decreasing (p 35).

increasing function NOUN /ɪnˈkri.sɪŋ ˈfʌŋk.ʃən/ a function whose output increases as the input increases. Math definition: for all **a**, **b**, if $a > b$, then $f(a) > f(b)$; or $\frac{d}{dx}f(x) > 0$. Antonym: decreasing function (p 35).

increasing on an interval ADJECTIVE /ɪnˈkri.sɪŋ ɒn ən ˈɪn.tər.vəl/ a function whose output increases as the input increases on a continuous subdomain. Antonym: decreasing on an interval (p 35).

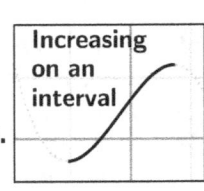

increasing sequence NOUN /ɪnˈkri.sɪŋ ˈsi.kwəns/ a sequence of real numbers where each term is greater that its preceding term. Example: $\frac{2}{2}, \frac{3}{2}, \frac{4}{2}, \frac{5}{2}, \ldots$. Antonym: decreasing sequence (p 35).

increasing test NOUN /ɪnˈkri.sɪŋ tɛst/ a test that reveals if a function is increasing on an interval. Math definition: if $f'(x) > 0$ for all **x** on an interval, then **f** is increasing on that interval. Antonym: *decreasing test* (p 35).

increment /ˈɪn.krəˌmənt/
1) VERB to increase by a small quantity.
2) NOUN a usually small quantity by which something is increased each iteration.

incremental ADJECTIVE /ˌɪn.krəˈmən.tl/
1) added in small amounts each iteration. Example: incremental increase.
2) in small steps.

indefinite ADJECTIVE /ɪnˈdɛf.nɪt/ over a specified, non-infinite range. Antonym: *definite* (p 35).

indefinite integral NOUN /ɪnˌdɛf.nɪt ˈɪn.tɛ.grəl/ a function that is an integral of a given function. Antonym: *definite integral* (p 35).

independent ADJECTIVE /ˌɪn.dɪˈpɛn.dənt/ not relying on anything else. Example: independent events. Antonym: *dependent* (p 36).

independent axiom NOUN /ˌɪn.dɪˈpɛn.dənt ˈæk.si.əm/ an axiom that cannot be proven from other axioms in an axiomatic system. Antonym: *dependent axiom* (p 36).

independent axis NOUN /ˌɪn.dɪˈpɛn.dənt ˈæk.sɪs/ see *x-axis* (p 122).

independent events NOUN /ˌɪn.dɪˈpɛn.dənt ɪˈvɛntz/ an event that is not affected by another event. Antonym: *dependent event* (p 36).

independent variable NOUN /ˌɪn.dɪˈpɛn.dənt ˈvɛər.i.ə.bəl/ a variable whose value can change without regard to other variables; an input to a function. By convention, x is often used to represent an independent variable. Antonym: *dependent variable* (p 36), *output* (p 84). Synonym: *input* (p 62).

indeterminate ADJECTIVE /ˌɪn.dɪˈtɜr.mə.nət/
1) having an infinite number of solutions. Example: indeterminate equation. Antonym: *determinate* (p 37).
2) undefined. Example: indeterminate expression.

indeterminate equation NOUN /ˌɪn.dɪˈtɜr.mə.nət ɪˈkweɪ.ʃən/ an equation that has infinite solutions. Example: $y = x^2 - 2$. Antonym: *determinate equation* (p 37).

indeterminate expression NOUN /ˌɪn.dɪˈtɜr.mə.nət ɪkˈsprɛ.ʃən/ one of the undefined expressions $\frac{0}{0}, \frac{\infty}{\infty}, \infty \cdot 0, 1^\infty, 0^0, \infty^0, \infty - \infty$.

index /ˈɪn.dɛks/
1) NOUN (British English) the number of times a number is multiplied by itself: $base^{index}$. Synonym: *exponent* (p 47).
2) NOUN the number to the left of a radical that indicates which root to extract. Example: the 3 in $\sqrt[3]{x}$.
3) NOUN a subscript indicating order. Example: a_1, a_2, a_3.
4) NOUN an integer indicating the current step in a repeated sum or product. Example: n in $\sum_{n=1}^{\infty}$. Synonym: *iterator* (p 65).
5) VERB to order by assigning a number to each item.

indexed ADJECTIVE /ˈɪn.dɛksd/ ordered by assigning a nominal number to each item, usually starting with 1 or 0.

indexed variable NOUN /ˈɪn.dɛksd ˈvɛər.i.ə.bəl/ a variable with a subscript. Indexed variables are used when a set of variables are related. Examples: $a_1, a_2, a_3, \cdots$.

index laws NOUN /ˈɪn.dɛks lɔz/ (British English) see *Properties of Exponents* (p 127).

indirect ADJECTIVE /ˌɪn.dəˈrɛkt/
1) not by a direct route.
2) using a contradiction to lead to a conclusion. Antonym: *direct* (p 38).

indirect argument NOUN /ˌɪn.dəˈrɛkt ˈɑr.gjə.mənt/ see *proof by contradiction* (p 93).

indirect isometry NOUN /ˌɪn.dəˈrɛkt aɪˈsɒ.mɪ.tri/ an isometry that does not preserve either orientation or order. Antonym: *direct isometry* (p 39). See *isometry* (p 65).

indirect measurement NOUN /ˌɪn.dəˈrɛkt ˈmɛ.ʒər.mənt/ a way to measure something when it cannot be directly measured. Example: using triangulation to find the height of a mountain.

indirect proof NOUN /ˌɪn.dəˈrɛkt pruf/ see *proof by contradiction* (p 93).

indirect reasoning NOUN /ˌɪn.dəˈrɛkt ˈriz.nɪŋ/ see *proof by contradiction* (p 93).

individual /ˌɪn.dɪˈvɪ.dju.əl/
1) NOUN a single person or entity.
2) NOUN a single member of a population being studied.
3) ADJECTIVE considered one at a time.

induction NOUN /ɪnˈdʌk.ʃən/ going from specific cases to an infinite, general case, possibly using a recursive definition. Important: Mathematical induction is not the same as either logical induction or inductive reasoning. For contrast see *mathematical induction* (p 72).

inductive ADJECTIVE /ɪnˈdʌk.tɪv/ using mathematical or logical induction. Example: inductive reasoning.

inductive proof NOUN /ɪnˈdʌk.tɪv pruf/ a proof that uses mathematical induction. The steps of an inductive proof are: 1) Show that the first case is true; 2) Show that if an arbitrary case n is true, then case $n + 1$ must be true.

inductive reasoning NOUN /ɪnˈdʌk.tɪv ˈriz.nɪŋ/ coming to a general conclusion from a limited number of specific cases. Important: Inductive reasoning is not accepted as a mathematical proof. Example: all the apples in my orchard are red, so all apples must be red.

inequality NOUN /ˌɪn.ɪˈkwɒl.ɪ.ti/ a mathematical statement comparing two values using $<, \leq, \neq, \geq,$ or $>$. Example: $x < 5$.

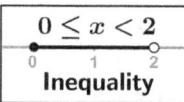
Inequality

inequality operator NOUN /ˌɪn.ɪˈkwɒl.ɪ.ti ˈɒ.pəˌreɪ.tər/ one of the operators $<, \leq, \neq, \geq,$ or $>$.

inequality sign NOUN /ˌɪn.ɪˈkwɒl.ɪ.ti saɪn/ see *inequality operator* (p 61).

inertia NOUN /ɪˈnɜr.ʃə/ a property of matter where it remains at rest or in uniform motion in the same straight line unless acted upon by some external force.

inexact ADJECTIVE /ˌɪn.ɪgˈzækt/
1) containing an error.
2) arrived at by measurement or estimation, or by a calculation that introduces error. Antonym: *exact* (p 46).

3rd Dyslexic's Edition

infer VERB /ɪnˈfɜr/ to come to a conclusion based on logical arguments.

inference NOUN /ˈɪn.fər.əns/ a conclusion based on strict logical arguments.

inferential statistics NOUN /ˌɪn.fəˈrɛn.ʃəl stəˈtɪs.tɪks/ the extension of the summary results of a sample to a population with a measure of reliability.

infimum NOUN /ɪnˈfi.mʌm/ see *greatest lower bound* (p 55).

infinite ADJECTIVE /ˈɪn.fə.nɪt/
1) goes on forever; does not end.
2) increases without bound.
3) larger than any arbitrary value.
Notation: ∞. Synonym: *unbounded* (p 118). Antonyms: *finite* (p 50), *bounded* (p 18).

infinite decimal NOUN /ˈɪn.fə.nɪt ˈdɛs.məl/ see *nonterminating decimal* (p 80).

infinite limit NOUN /ˈɪn.fə.nɪt ˈlɪ.mɪt/ a limit as **x** approaches **a** where $f(x)$ increases or decreases infinitely; $f(x)$ is unbounded at **a**. Synonym: *unbounded* (p 118).

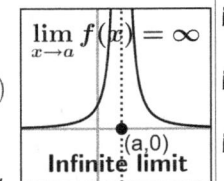

infinite product NOUN /ˈɪn.fə.nɪt ˈprɒ.dʌkt/ a product with an infinite number of factors. Notation: $\prod_{i=1}^{\infty} a_i = a_1 \cdot a_2 \cdots$.

infinite sequence NOUN /ˈɪn.fə.nɪt ˈsi.kwəns/ a sequence that does not have a last term. Example: $\{1, 2, 4, 8, \cdots\}$. Antonym: *finite sequence* (p 50).

infinite series NOUN /ˈɪn.fə.nɪt ˈsɪər.iz/ a sum that has an infinite number of terms.

infinite set NOUN /ˈɪn.fə.nɪt sɛt/ a set that has no end. Example: the set of natural numbers.

infinitesimal /ˌɪn.fɪ.nɪˈtɛs.ə.məl/
1) ADJECTIVE immeasurably small; approaches zero, usually without reaching zero.
2) NOUN a variable having zero as a limit.
3) NOUN a value that is very close to zero, but not equal to zero.

infinity NOUN /ɪnˈfɪ.nɪ.ti/ never having an end; being unbounded. Notation: ∞. Important: infinity is a concept, and not a number.

inflection point NOUN /ɪnˈflɛk.ʃən pɔɪnt/ a point where a graph changes from concave up to concave down or from concave down to concave up; a point where $f''(a) = 0$.

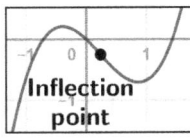

information NOUN /ˌɪn.fərˈmeɪ.ʃən/
1) knowledge gained through an analysis of data.
2) knowledge received.

information processing NOUN /ˌɪn.fərˈmeɪ.ʃən ˈprɒ.sɛ.sɪŋ/ the analysis of data to produce information.

in general PREPOSITION /ɪn ˈdʒɛ.nə.rəl/ a generalization of a specific case or cases. Example: $\cdots, (-1)^2 > 0, 0^2 = 0, 1^2 > 0, \cdots$. In general, $a^2 \geq 0, a \in \mathbb{R}$. See also *generalization* (p 53).

initial ADJECTIVE /ɪˈnɪ.ʃəl/
1) at the start; beginning with. Example: initial line.
2) the first of several. Example: initial value.

initial line NOUN /ɪˈnɪ.ʃəl laɪn/ see *initial side* (p 62).

initial point NOUN /ɪˈnɪ.ʃəl pɔɪnt/ a starting point. Example: initial point of a vector. Synonym: *tail* (p 56). Antonyms: *head* (p 62), *terminal point* (p 113).

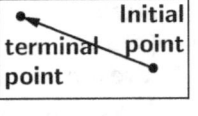

initial side NOUN /ɪˈnɪ.ʃəl saɪd/ the line segment or ray from which an angle is measured. Synonym: *initial line*. Antonym: *terminal side* (p 113).

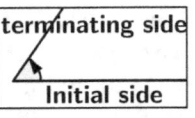

initial value NOUN /ɪˈnɪ.ʃəl ˈvæl.ju/ the starting value, usually of an independent variable or index.

initiator NOUN /ɪˈnɪ.ʃiˌeɪ.tər/ the starting figure when drawing a classical fractal.

injection NOUN /ɪnˈdʒɛk.ʃən/ a relation having exactly one output for each input. Synonym: *function* (p 52), *one-to-one correspondence* (p 82).

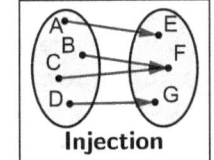

injective ADJECTIVE /ɪnˈdʒɛk.tɪv/ having exactly one output for each input.

inner product NOUN /ˈɪ.nər ˈprɒ.dʌkt/ see *dot product* (p 42).

input NOUN /ˈɪn.pʊt/ a set of values supplied to a function. Synonym: *independent variable* (p 61), *abscissa* (p 6). Antonym: *output* (p 84).

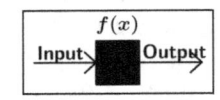

inradius NOUN /ˈɪn.reɪ.di.əs/ the radius of an incircle. Plural: inradii /ˈɪn.reɪ.diˌaɪ/.

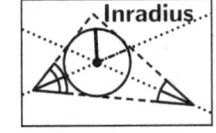

inscribe VERB /ɪnˈskraɪb/ to draw inside of, touching as many points as possible.

inscribed angle NOUN /ɪnˈskraɪbd ˈæŋ.gəl/ an angle drawn inside a circle.

inscribed circle NOUN /ɪnˈskraɪbd ˈsɜr.kəl/ a circle drawn inside another figure, usually intersecting all sides of the figure exactly once.

inscribed polygon NOUN /ɪnˈskraɪbd ˈpɒ.liˌgɒn/ a polygon drawn inside a circle where the circle intersects all vertices of the polygon.

inside ADJECTIVE /ˈɪn.saɪd/ in the interior of. Antonym: *outside* (p 84). Synonym: *interior* (p 63).

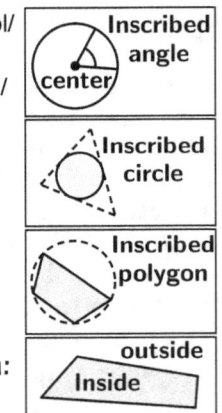

insignificant ADJECTIVE /ˌɪn.sɪgˈnɪ.fɪ.kənt/
1) not needed; does not make a difference.
2) so small it doesn't matter.

insignificant zero NOUN /ˌɪn.sɪgˈnɪ.fɪ.kənt ˈzɪə.roʊ/ a zero in a numeral that is not needed. Examples: 02.7, 3.250.

installment NOUN /ɪnˈstɔl.mənt/ a single part of something that happens at regular intervals.

installment loan NOUN /ɪnˈstɔl.mənt loʊn/ a loan where a number of regular payments of the same amount each time are made. Formula: $R = \frac{i \cdot P}{1-(1+i)^{-n}}$ where **R** is the installment payment, **i** is the interest rate, **P** is the total value of the purchase, and **n** is the number of installments.

instance NOUN /ˈɪn.stəns/
1) a case or example.
2) one of a set of objects.

instant NOUN /ˈɪn.stənt/ an infinitesimal or very short period of time.

instantaneous ADJECTIVE /ˌɪn.stənˈteɪ.ni.əs/
1) occurring, done, or completed in an instance.
2) existing at or pertaining to a particular instance.

instantaneous rate of change NOUN /ˌɪn.stənˈteɪ.ni.əs reɪt ʌv tʃeɪndʒ/ the slope of a curve at a point. Formula: $f'(c) = \lim_{x \to c} \frac{f(x) - f(c)}{x - c}$. Synonyms: derivative (p 36), differential coefficient (p 38).

integer NOUN /ˈɪn.tɪ.dʒər/ a positive or negative whole number or zero having no decimal part. Notation: $\mathbb{Z}$. Math definition: $\mathbb{Z} = \{\cdots, -3, -2, -1, 0, 1, 2, 3, \cdots\}$. Synonym: whole number.

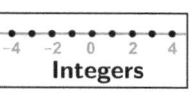
Integers

Integer Roots Theorem NOUN /ˈɪn.tɪ.dʒər ruts ˈθɪ.ə.rəm/ for a polynomial with integer coefficients and a leading coefficient of 1, any rational roots of the polynomial are integers. Example: $x^2 - 2x - 3$.

integral /ˈɪn.tɪ.grəl/
1) ADJECTIVE having to do with integrals.
2) NOUN a tool used to find the area under a curve in a specific range.

integral calculus NOUN /ˈɪn.tɪ.grəl ˈkæl.kjə.ləs/ a branch of mathematics about the theory and applications of integrals and integration.

integral test NOUN /ˈɪn.tɪ.grəl tɛst/ if f is a continuous, positive, decreasing function on $[1, \infty]$ and $a_n = f(N)$, then the series $\sum_{n=N}^{\infty} a_n$ is convergent if and only if $\int_n^{\infty} f(x)dx$ is convergent.

integrated ADJECTIVE /ˈɪn.tɪˌgreɪ.tɪd/ two or more elements are combined into one whole.

integrated integral NOUN /ˈɪn.tɪˌgreɪ.tɪd ˈɪn.tɛ.grəl/ the result of applying integrals to a function of more than one variable in such a way that each of the integrals considers some of the variables as given constants.

integration NOUN /ˌɪn.tɪˈgreɪ.ʃən/
1) the operation of finding a function whose differential is known.
2) the operation of solving a differential equation. Antonym: differentiation (p 38).

integration by parts NOUN /ˌɪn.tɪˈgreɪ.ʃən baɪ pɑrtz/ a process that finds the integral of a product of functions using the integral of the product of their derivative and antiderivative. Formula: $\int u\,dv = uv - \int v\,du$.

integration by substitution NOUN /ˌɪn.tɪˈgreɪ.ʃən baɪ ˈsʌb.stɪˌtu.ʃən/ a method for finding an integral that involves substituting equivalent expressions.

inter- PREFIX /ɪn.tər/
1) inside of. Example: interior.
2) between. Example: interactive.
3) together. Example: intercept.
Antonym: ex- (p 46).

interactive geometry software NOUN /ˌɪn.tərˈæk.tɪv dʒiˈɒm.ɪ.tri ˈsɒft.wɛər/ computer software that allows the user to create and manipulate geometric drawings. See also GeoGebra (p 53).

intercept NOUN /ˈɪn.tərˌsɛpt/
1) a point where a graph crosses an axis.
2) a point where two geometric figures cross.
Synonym: intersection (p 64).

intercepted arc NOUN /ˌɪn.tərˌsɛp.tɪd ɑrk/ part of a circle between two rays that start inside or on the circle and intercept the circle.

intercept form NOUN /ˈɪn.tərˌsɛpt fɔrm/
1) a linear equation in the form $\frac{x}{a} + \frac{y}{b} = 1$ where **a** is the x-intercept, and **b** is the y-intercept.
2) a quadratic equation the form $y = a(x - x_1)(x - x_2)$ where x_1 and x_2 are the x-intercepts. Synonym: factored form (p 49).

intercept method NOUN /ˈɪn.tərˌsɛpt ˈmɛ.θəd/ an algorithm for graphing a linear equation using the **x** and **y** intercepts: 1) Plot the x-intercept. 2) Plot the y-intercept. 3) Draw the line containing the intercepts.

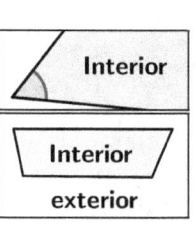

interchange VERB /ˌɪn.tərˈtʃeɪndʒ/ to exchange places. Synonym: exchange (p 46).

interest NOUN /ˈɪn.trɪst/ an amount paid for the use of the money. Interest is based on the principle of the loan. Formula: **Interest + Principal = Total Payments**. Example: If you borrow £100 and pay £110 at the end of the loan, the interest is £10.

interest rate NOUN /ˈɪn.trɪst reɪt/ the portion of the principal that is charged as interest. Example: if the principal of the loan is €140 and the interest rate is 12%, the interest amount is €140 × 0.12 = €16.8. Formula: **principle × interest rate = interest amount**. Synonym: rate of interest.

interior /ɪnˈtɪə.ri.ər/
1) ADJECTIVE lying inside a boundary.
2) NOUN the inside of an object.
3) NOUN all points that are a part of a figure, but are not boundary points.
Synonym: inside (p 62). Antonyms: outside (p 84), exterior (p 48).

interior angle NOUN /ɪnˈtɪə.ri.ər ˈæŋ.gəl/
1) an angle at a vertex of a polygon that is inside the polygon.
2) an angle between two lines that are intersected by a transversal.

interior of an angle NOUN /ɪnˈtɪə.ri.ər ʌv ən ˈæŋ.gəl/ the area between the initial side and the terminal side.

interior point NOUN /ɪnˈtɪə.ri.ər pɔɪnt/ a point in the interior of a figure; not a boundary point nor an exterior point.

intermediate ADJECTIVE /ˌɪn.tərˈmi.di.ɪt/
1) being between.
2) temporarily used to simplify an equation or process.

intermediate variable NOUN /ˌɪn.tərˈmi.di.ɪt ˈvɛər.i.ə.bəl/ a variable that is not a dependent or independent variable that is used to simplify an equation or process.

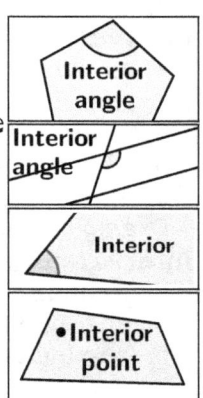

Intermediate Value Theorem NOUN /ˌɪn.tərˈmi.di.ɪt ˈvæl.yu ˈθɪ.ə.rəm/ If f is a function that is continuous on the interval [a, b], then it takes on all values between f (a) and f (b) at some point within the interval. *Corollary:* if f (a) and f (b) have opposite signs, then there is at least one root of f (x) in the interval [a, b].

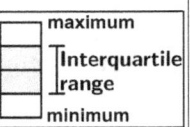

International System of Units NOUN /ˌɪn.tərˈnæ.ʃə.nl ˈsɪs.təm ʌv ˈju.nɪtz/ an international convention for naming units of measure. *Examples:* meter, nanometer. *See also* International System of Units (p 145).

interpolate VERB /ɪnˈtɜr.pəˈleɪt/ to approximate a value starting with known values nearby. *Example:* interpolate the value of $\sqrt{2}$ to six decimal places.

interpolation NOUN /ɪnˌtɜr.pəˈleɪ.ʃən/ a process of approximating a value starting with known values nearby.

interpret VERB /ɪnˈtɜr.prɪt/ to give the meaning of, usually verbally.

interquartile range NOUN /ɪn.tɜrˈkwɔr.taɪl reɪndʒ/ the difference between the first and the third quartiles of a dataset; a measure of the spread of the middle half of the dataset.

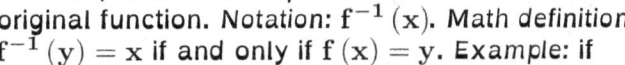

intersect VERB /ɪn.tərˈsɛkt/
1) to cross each other; to coincide at least one point.
2) to overlap.

Intersecting Planes Postulate NOUN /ˌɪn.tərˈsɛkt.ɪŋ pleɪnz ˈpɒs.tʃə.lɪt/ if two planes intersect, then their intersection is a line.

intersection NOUN /ˌɪn.tərˈsɛk.ʃən/
1) (geometry) one or more points at which geometric figures meet.
2) (sets) the set containing all the elements that are in each of the sets. *Synonym:* intercept (p 63).

intersection point NOUN /ˌɪn.tərˈsɛk.ʃən pɔɪnt/ *see* point of concurrency (p 89).

interval NOUN /ˈɪn.tər.vəl/
1) an unbroken range of values. *Example:* **1 to 5**. Numeric intervals can be written using an inequality: $1 \leq x \leq 5$, interval notation: $[1, 5]$, set notation: $\{x : 1 \leq x \leq 5, x \in \mathbb{R}\}$.
2) a period of time with a beginning and an end. *Example:* two second interval.

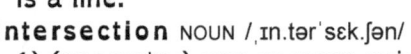

interval notation NOUN /ˈɪn.tər.vəl noʊˈteɪ.ʃən/ a convention for writing intervals. A square bracket '[]' means the end value is included. A parenthesis '()' means the end value is not included. *Examples:* $(-\infty, \infty)$ is the set of all real numbers, $[3, 12) = \{x : 3 \leq x < 12\}, (-2, 1] = \{x : -2 < x \leq 1\}, [3, 49] = \{x : 3 \leq x \leq 49\}$.

interview /ˈɪn.tər.vju/
1) NOUN a meeting where the interviewer asks questions of the person being interviewed.
2) VERB to conduct an interview as the interviewer.

interviewer error NOUN /ˈɪn.tər.vju.ər ˈɛr.ər/ a statistical error caused when an interviewer does not get truthful responses.

intuition NOUN /ˌɪn.tuˈɪ.ʃən/ quick insight; an ability to discern.

intuitive ADJECTIVE /ɪnˈtu.ɪ.tɪv/ able to be discerned by intuition.

invalid ADJECTIVE /ɪnˈvæ.lɪd/
1) not well founded. *Example:* an invalid reason.
2) not justifiable.
Antonym: valid (p 120).

invariant ADJECTIVE /ɪnˈvɛər.i.ənt/
1) unchanging, perhaps under specific conditions.
2) of a property of a geometric figure undergoing a transformation that is unchanged by the transformation. *Example:* the measure of an angle is invariant under dilation.

inverse NOUN /ɪnˈvɜrs/
1) when one increases, the other decreases. *Antonym:* direct (p 38).
2) (of a function) another function that, for every output of the original function, returns the input of the original function. *Notation:* $f^{-1}(x)$. *Math definition:* $f^{-1}(y) = x$ if and only if $f(x) = y$. *Example:* if $f(x) = 2x + 2$ then $f^{-1}(x) = \frac{1}{2}x - 1$.
3) (of an operation) another operation that 'undoes' the original operation. *Math definition:* given an element and an operation, another element when combined under the operation with the first gives the identity element. *Examples:* The inverse of addition is subtraction: $(x + 5) - 5 = x$. The inverse of multiplication is division: $5 \cdot x \div 5 = x$.
4) (of a logical statement) the negation of a statement. *Notation:* the inverse of the statement **'P'** is the statement **'not P'** or **'¬P'**. *Example:* 'the ball is blue' is the inverse of 'the ball is not blue'.
5) (of a square matrix) a matrix A^{-1} such that $A \cdot A^{-1} = I$ and $A^{-1} \cdot A = I$. *Important:* not all square matrices have an inverse.

inverse element NOUN /ɪnˈvɜrs ˈɛ.lə.mənt/ an element that undoes an operation on another element. *Example:* the inverse element of **a** under addition is -a since $a + (-a) = 0$.

inverse function property NOUN /ɪnˈvɜrs ˈfʌŋk.ʃən ˈprɒ.pər.ti/ if $f^{-1}(x)$ is the inverse of $f(x)$, then $f^{-1}(f(x)) = x$ for every x in the domain of $f(x)$, and $f(f^{-1}(y)) = y$ for all y in the range of $f(x)$. Conversely, if these properties apply then $f^{-1}(y)$ and $f(x)$ are inverses of each other.

inversely ADJECTIVE /ɪnˈvɜr.sli/ having or using an inverse. *Example:* inversely proportional.

inversely proportional ADJECTIVE /ɪnˈvɜr.sli prəˈpour.ʃə.nl/ *see* inverse variation (p 65).

inversely proportional to the square adjective /ɪnˈvɜr.sli prəˈpour.ʃə.nl tu ðə skwɛər/ having a relationship of $f(x) = \frac{d}{x^2}$ where **d** is the constant of proportionality.

inverse operation NOUN /ɪnˈvɜrs ˌɒ.pərˈeɪ.ʃən/ an operation that 'undoes' another operation. *Example:* the inverse of addition is subtraction, since $a + b - b = a$. *See also* Inverse Operations (p 129).

inverse property of addition NOUN /ɪnˈvɜrs ˈprɒ.pər.ti ʌv əˈdɪ.ʃən/ *see* additive inverse (p 8).

inverse property of multiplication NOUN /ɪnˈvɜrs ˈprɒ.pər.ti ʌv mʌl.tə.plɪˈkeɪ.ʃən/ see *multiplicative inverse* (p 77).

inverse trigonometric function NOUN /ɪnˈvɜrs ˌtrɪ.ɡə.nəˈmɛ.trɪk ˈfʌŋk.ʃən/ a function that takes a ratio as an input and returns an angle as an output. Examples: $\sin^{-1}$, arccos.

inverse variation NOUN /ɪnˈvɜrs ˌvɛə.riˈeɪ.ʃən/ a relation between two variables such that $y = \frac{a}{x} = ax^{-1}$ or $xy = a$ where **a** is the constant of variation.

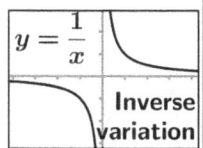

Inverse variation

invert VERB /ɪnˈvɜrt/
1) to turn upside down. Example: invert the fraction.
2) to find the inverse of. Example: invert the function.
3) to reverse in position.
4) to find the reciprocal of. Example: invert $\frac{x}{y}$: $\frac{y}{x}$.

invertibility NOUN /ˈɪn.vɜr.tɪ.bɪl.ɪ.ti/ the state of whether or not an inverse exists.

invertible ADJECTIVE /ˈɪn.vɜr.tə.bl/ (square matrix) having the property that an inverse exists. Example: Matrix **A** is invertible if the determinant of **A** is not zero. Antonym: *noninvertable* (p 79).

invertible matrix NOUN /ɪnˈvɜr.tə.bl ˈmeɪ.trɪks/ a square matrix that has an inverse; that can be inverted. Antonym: *noninvertable matrix* (p 79).

investigate VERB /ɪnˈvɛ.stɪˌɡeɪt/ to make a methodical exploration in order to discover truth. Example: investigate the properties of a triangle.

investigation NOUN /ɪnˌvɛ.stɪˈɡeɪ.ʃən/
1) the process of exploring.
2) an act of exploration. Example: an investigation of the properties of triangles.
Synonym: *study* (p 110).

ir- PREFIX /ɪr/ not.

irrational /ɪˈræ.ʃə.nl/
1) ADJECTIVE cannot be written exactly as a ratio of integers.
2) NOUN an irrational number.
Antonym: *rational*.

irrational number NOUN /ɪˈræ.ʃə.nl ˈnʌm.bər/ a real number that cannot be written exactly as the ratio of two integers. Examples: $\sqrt{2}$, π. Synonym: *surd*. Antonym: *rational number* (p 96).

irrationals NOUN /ɪˈræ.ʃə.nlz/ the set of irrational numbers. Notation: $\mathbb{R}/\mathbb{Q}$ or $\mathbb{R} - \mathbb{Q}$.

irreducible ADJECTIVE /ˌɪr.ɪˈdu.sə.bəl/ having no factors other than 1 and itself. Examples: $7, x + 2$. Antonym: *reducible* (p 97).

irreducible polynomial NOUN /ˌɪr.ɪˈdu.sə.bəl ˌpɒ.ləˈnoʊ.mi.əl/ a polynomial that cannot be factored using expressions containing only real numbers. Examples: $x + 2$, $x^2 + x + 7$. Antonym: *reducible polynomial* (p 97). See also *factor completely* (p 49).

irregular ADJECTIVE /ˌɪˈrɛ.ɡjə.lər/ without symmetry; having an uneven shape. Example: irregular polygon. Antonym: *regular* (p 98).

irregular fractal NOUN /ˌɪˈrɛ.ɡjə.lər ˈfræk.tl/ a complex fractal whose dimensions are often difficult to determine and in some cases are unknown.

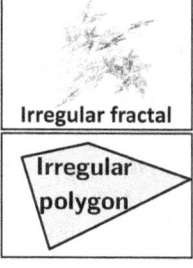

Irregular fractal

Irregular polygon

irregular polygon NOUN /ˌɪˈrɛ.ɡjə.lər ˈpɒ.li.ɡɒn/ a polygon that is concave or that has unequal sides. Antonym: *regular polygon* (p 98).

iso- PREFIX /ˈaɪ.sə/ the same, equal. Example: isometric: having the same measure.

isometric ADJECTIVE /ˌaɪ.səˈmɛ.trɪk/ having the property of equality in measure. Example: isometric projection.

isometric drawing NOUN /ˌaɪ.səˈmɛ.trɪk ˈdrɔ.ɪŋ/ see *isometric projection* (p 65).

isometric projection NOUN /ˌaɪ.səˈmɛ.trɪk proʊˈdʒɛk.ʃən/ a 2-dimensional drawing of a 3-dimensional shape where the angles between the axes are equal. See also *perspective view* (p 88).

Isometric projection

isometry NOUN /aɪˈsɒm.ɪ.tri/ a geometric transformation that preserves distance and length. Examples: reflection, rotation and translation.

isosceles right triangle NOUN /aɪˈsɒ.səˌliz raɪt ˈtraɪˌæŋ.ɡəl/ a right triangle whose legs are the same length.

Isosceles right triangle

isosceles trapezoid NOUN /aɪˈsɒ.səˌliz ˈtræ.pəˌzɔɪd/ a trapezoid whose legs are congruent.

Isosceles trapezoid

isosceles triangle NOUN /aɪˈsɒ.səˌliz ˈtraɪˌæŋ.ɡəl/ a triangle where exactly two of the sides are congruent. The base angles of an isosceles triangle are also congruent.

Isosceles triangle

iterate VERB /ˈɪ.tərˌeɪt/ to repeat steps of an iterative algorithm. Example: iterate through all the values.

iteration NOUN /ˌɪ.təˈreɪ.ʃən/
1) a single step in a repeating algorithm.
2) the process of iterating.
Synonym: *recursion* (p 97).

Iteration

iterative ADJECTIVE /ˈɪ.tər.ə.tɪv/ repeats all or part of itself. Example: iterative algorithm. Synonym: *recursive* (p 97).

iterative algorithm NOUN /ˈɪ.tər.ə.tɪv ˈæl.ɡəˌrɪ.ðəm/ an algorithm where part or all of the algorithm is repeated.

iterative process NOUN /ˈɪ.tər.ə.tɪv ˈprɒ.sɛs/ a process where part or all of the process is repeated.

iterator NOUN /ˈɪ.təˈreɪ.tər/ a parameter that is used to cycle through iterations. Example: **i** in $\sum_{i=1}^{\infty}$. Synonym: *index* (p 61).

J

J ABBREVIATION joule.

jerk NOUN /dʒɜrk/ the third derivative of the position function, which is also the derivative of the acceleration function. Formula: $\mathbf{j} = \frac{da}{dt} = \frac{d^3s}{dt^3}$.

join /dʒɔɪn/
1) NOUN see *union* (p 118).

2) VERB to bring together into one.
3) VERB to connect one to another.

joint ADJECTIVE /dʒɔɪnt/ two or more math objects working together.

joint proportion NOUN /dʒɔɪnt prə'pɔr.ʃən/ see *joint variation* (p 66).

joint variation NOUN /dʒɔɪnt ˌvɛə.ri'eɪ.ʃən/ a relationship between two independent variables **x** and **y** and a dependent variable **z** where $z = axy$.

Jordan, Wilhelm PERSON /'dʒɔr.dn 'wɪl.hɛlm/ (1842 — 1899) a surveyor who extended the Gaussian elimination method into the Gauss-Jordan method in order to find squaring errors in surveying.

joule NOUN /dʒul/ a unit of measure for work or energy. *Abbreviation: J*.

jump discontinuity NOUN /'dʒʌmp ˌdɪs.kɒn.tn'u.ɪ.ti/ a type of essential discontinuity that "jumps" up or down at the point of discontinuity. *Synonym: step discontinuity* (p 109).

jump strategy NOUN /'dʒʌmp 'stræ.tə.dʒi/ a strategy for using a number line where one 'jumps' by tens or hundreds.

junction NOUN /'dʒʌŋk.ʃən/ see *node* (p 79).

justifiable adjective /ˌdʒʌ.stə'faɪ.ə.bəl/ can be defended as valid; can be justified. *Example: the conclusion is justifiable.*

justification NOUN /ˌdʒʌs.tə.fɪ'keɪ.ʃən/ why something is true; a statement justifying a step in a proof. *Example: The justification for the claim is ....*

justify VERB /'dʒʌ.stə.faɪ/ to defend as valid.

K

k ABBREVIATION kilo-. *Example: 1 kilogram = 1000 grams. Synonym: thousand.*

K ABBREVIATION kelvin.

Kcal ABBREVIATION kilocalorie.

kelvin NOUN /'kɛl.vɪn/ a unit of measure of temperature based on absolute zero, the theoretical least possible temperature. $273.16 K$ is the triple point of water. *Formulas:* $K = C + 273.15$, $C = K - 273.15$ where C is degrees Celsius. *Notation:* **K**.

Kelvin, William Thomson, 1st Barron PERSON /'kɛl.vɪn 'wɪl.jəm 'tɒm.sən/ (1824 — 1907) an English physicist and mathematician after whom the kelvin temperature scale is named.

Kepler's laws NOUN /'kɛp.lərz lɒz/ three rules that describe the orbit of planets about the sun. 1) A planet revolves around the sun in an elliptical orbit with the sun at one focus. 2) The line joining the sun to a planet sweeps out equal areas in equal times. 3) The square of the period of revolution of a planet is proportional to the cube of the length of the major axis of its orbit.

key NOUN /ki/
1) something that enables decryption of an encrypted message. *Example: a 64-bit encryption key.*
2) a note that explains symbols on a graph.
3) something that serves as an indicator. *Example: keyword.*

keyword NOUN /'ki.wɜrd/ a word that shows how to write a word problem as an equation. *Example: decrease is a keyword for subtraction.*

kg ABBREVIATION kilogram.

kilo- PREFIX /'kɪ.loʊ/ $10^3 = 1000$. *Abbreviation: k. Example:* $4.7 \text{ kilogram} = 4.7 \times 10^3 \text{ grams} = 4700 \text{ grams}$. *Synonym: thousand* (p 114).

kilocalorie NOUN /'kɪ.loʊ ˌkæl.ə.ri/ 1000 calories. *Abbreviation: Kcal.* See *calorie* (p 18).

kilogram NOUN /'kɪ.loʊ ˌgræm/ a unit of measure of mass. *Abbreviation: kg. Formulas: 1 kilogram = 1000 grams. 1 kilogram ≈ 2.2 pounds* on the Earth's surface.

kilometer NOUN /kɪ'lɒ.mɪ.tər/ a unit of measure of distance. *Formulas: 1 kilometer = 1000 meters. 1 kilometer ≈ 0.62 miles. Abbreviation km.*

kilometers per hour NOUN /kɪ'lɒ.mɪ.tərz pər 'aʊ.ər/ a unit of measure of speed. *Abbreviation: kph. Formulas: 1 kph ≈ 0.2778 m/s. 1 kph ≈ 0.6214 mph.*

kite NOUN /kaɪt/ a geometric figure formed by two perpendicular line segments, one of which is bisected by the other. *Synonym: deltoid.*

km ABBREVIATION kilometer.

kn ABBREVIATION knot (nautical speed).

knot NOUN /nɒt/ a unit of measure of speed on water equal to one nautical mile per hour. *Abbreviation: kn. Formulas: 1 knot = 1.852 kph, 1 knot ≈ 1.51 mph.*

known /noʊn/
1) ADJECTIVE specified or discovered. *Example: the known world.*
2) NOUN a quantity that has been identified. *Synonym: known value. Antonym: unknown* (p 119).

known value NOUN /noʊn 'væl.ju/ see *known* (p 66).

Kovalevskaya, Sofia PERSON /ˌkɒv.ə'lɛf.ski səʊ'faɪə/ (1850—1891) a Russian-born German mathematician who was the first woman to receive a full professorship in northern Europe. She wrote a number of works and won two coveted mathematics prizes.

kph ABBREVIATION kilometers per hour.

L

l ABBREVIATION liter.

L SYMBOL **50** in Roman numerals.

λ LETTER lambda.

label /'leɪ.bəl/
1) NOUN a letter, letters or symbol used to identify an object. *Examples:* A, d, ℑ, ℘, β, ∈, ∠. *Synonym: symbol* (p 111).
2) VERB to mark an object with a symbol, letter or letters so that it can be identified.

lambda SYMBOL /ˈlæm.də/ the Greek letter λ, used as a variable for wavelength. See also Greek Letters (p 135).

last ADJECTIVE /læst/ after any other. Antonym: first (p 50).

lateral ADJECTIVE /ˈlæ.tər.əl/
1) having to do with a side or sides. Example: lateral area.
2) being part of the surface of a 3-dimensional object that is not a base.
Synonym: of the side(s).

lateral area NOUN /ˈlæ.tər.əl ˈɛər.i.ə/ the combined surface area of the faces of a polyhedron not including the bases.

lateral edge NOUN /ˈlæ.tər.əl ɛdʒ/ an edge between two adjacent lateral faces.

lateral face NOUN /ˈlæ.tər.əl feɪs/ a face of a polyhedron that is not a base.

lateral surface NOUN /ˈlæ.tər.əl ˈsɜr.fɪs/ the surface of a polyhedron excluding the bases.

lateral surface area NOUN /ˈlæ.tər.əl ˈsɜr.fɪs ˈɛər.i.ə/ the surface area of a polyhedron excluding the bases.

latitude NOUN /ˈlæ.tɪ.tud/ an angular distance north or south of the equator of a point on the Earth's surface.

latus rectum NOUN /ˈlæ.təs ˈrɛk.təm/ a chord perpendicular to the major axis and passing through a focus of an ellipse, parabola, or hyperbola.

law NOUN /lɑ/ a property or rule that does not change. Example: law of sines. Synonyms: axiom (p 15), theorem (p 113).

Law of Cosines NOUN /lɑ ʌv ˈkoʊ.saɪnz/ a rule relating the lengths of the sides of a triangle: $c^2 = a^2 + b^2 - 2ab\cos\gamma$.

Law of Detachment NOUN /lɑ ʌv dɪˈtætʃ.mənt/ if **P** implies **Q**, and **P** is true, then **Q** must be true. Notation: $P \to Q$. Example:

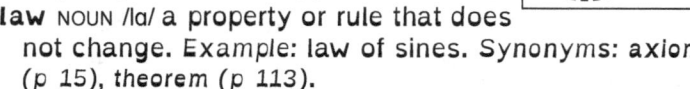

Law of Exponents NOUN /lɑ ʌv ˈɛk.spoʊ.nəntz/ see Properties of Exponents (p 127).

Law of Logarithms NOUN /lɑ ʌv ˈlɔ.gə.rɪð.əmz/ see Properties of Logarithms (p 128).

Law of Signs NOUN /lɑ ʌv saɪnz/ if a negative and a positive number are multiplied, the product is negative. If two negative numbers or two positive numbers are multiplied, the product is positive. Formulas: for $a, b > 0$: $a \cdot b = ab$; $-a \cdot b = -ab$; $a \cdot -b = -ab$; $-a \cdot -b = ab$.

Law of Sines NOUN /lɑ ʌv saɪnz/ a rule relating the lengths of the sides of a triangle. Formula: $\frac{a}{\sin\alpha} = \frac{b}{\sin\beta} = \frac{c}{\sin\gamma}$.

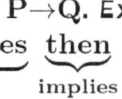

Law of Syllogism NOUN /lɑ ʌv ˈsɪl.ə.dʒɪz.əm/ if **P** implies **Q** and **Q** implies **R**, then **P** implies **R**. This is the logical equivalent of the transitive property of equality.

Law of Tangents NOUN /lɑ ʌv ˈtæn.dʒəntz/ a rule relating the lengths of the sides of a triangle. Formula: $\frac{a-b}{a+b} = \frac{\tan\left(\frac{1}{2}(\alpha-\beta)\right)}{\tan\left(\frac{1}{2}(\alpha+\beta)\right)}$.

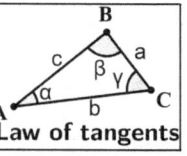

laws of exponents NOUN /lɑz ʌv ɪkˈspoʊ.nənts/ see properties of exponents (p 127).

lb ABBREVIATION pound (weight).

LCD ACRONYM least common denominator (p 67).

LCM ACRONYM least common multiple (p 67).

lead VERB /lid/
1) to go in front of.
2) to go first.

leading ADJECTIVE /ˈli.dɪŋ/
1) in front of.
2) going first. Example: leading term.

leading coefficient NOUN /ˈli.dɪŋ ˌkoʊ.əˈfɪ.ʃənt/ in a polynomial, the coefficient of the term with the highest degree. Example: in $3x^2 + 2x - 4$, the leading coefficient is 3.

leading entry NOUN /ˈli.dɪŋ ˈɛn.tri/ the first column of any row of a matrix.

leading term NOUN /ˈli.dɪŋ tɜrm/ in a polynomial, the term with the highest degree; the first term of a polynomial in standard form.

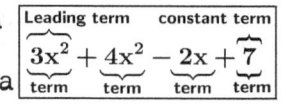

leading variable NOUN /ˈli.dɪŋ ˈvɛər.i.ə.bəl/ the variable corresponding to the first column of a matrix.

leading zero NOUN /ˈli.dɪŋ ˈzɪə.roʊ/ a zero on the left of a numeral; a zero with no nonzero digits in a higher place value. Example: the numeral 00152.7 has two leading zeros.

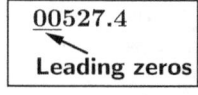

leap year NOUN /lip jɪər/ a year when February has 29 days. In the Gregorian calendar, a year is a leap year if it is divisible by 4, but not divisible by 100, unless it is divisible by 400.

lease NOUN /lis/ a contract that transfers use of an object in exchange for a rent payment. Example: lease a car.

least ADJECTIVE /list/
1) the smallest.
2) the closest to negative infinity.
3) one number from a set of numbers that is less than all the other numbers in the set. Example: the least value of $\{-3, -2, 0, 1, 3\}$ is -3.

least common denominator NOUN /list ˈkɒ.mən dɪˈnɒ.mə.neɪ.tər/ the least common multiple of two or more denominators. Example: $\text{lcd}\left(\frac{3}{2}, \frac{5}{6}\right) = \text{lcm}(2, 6) = 6$. Abbreviation: LCD. Synonym: least common multiple (p 67).

least common divisor NOUN /list ˈkɒ.mən dɪˈvaɪ.zər/ the least common multiple of two or more divisors. Example: $\text{lcd}(2, 5) = 10$. Synonym: least common multiple (p 67).

least common multiple NOUN /list ˈkɒ.mən ˈmʌl.tə.pl/ the smallest integer or expression that is a multiple of two or more integers or expressions. Example: $\text{lcm}(12, 10) = 60$ since $12 = 2 \cdot 2 \cdot 3$, $10 = 2 \cdot 5$ and $60 = 2 \cdot 2 \cdot 3 \cdot 5$. Abbreviation: LCM.

least integer function NOUN /list ˈɪn.tɪ.dʒər ˈfʌŋk.ʃən/ see ceiling function (p 19).

least squares line NOUN /list skwɛərz laɪn/ a line generated by a linear least squares regression method that minimizes the distance between the data points it represents and the line itself.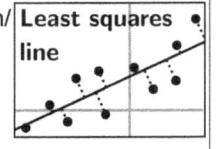

least squares method NOUN /list skwɛərz ˈmɛ.θəd/ see least squares regression (p 68).

least squares regression noun /list skwɛərz rɪˈɡrɛ.ʃən/ a method of finding a best fit solution for a dataset that minimizes the sum of the squares of the distance from data points to the generated line or curve.

least upper bound NOUN /list ʌpər baʊnd/ the least value that is greater than or equal to all members of a set. Synonym: *supremum*.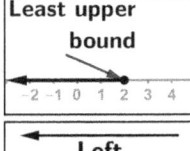

left NOUN /lɛft/ in the opposite direction of right. Antonym: *right* (p 99).

left-hand limit noun /lɛft hænd ˈlɪ.mɪt/ the limit of a function as x approaches c from the left (lower side). Notation: $\lim_{x \to c^-} f(x)$. Math definition: $\lim_{x \to a^-} = L$ if, for every number $\epsilon > 0$, there exits a number $\delta > 0$ such that $|f(x) - L| < \epsilon$ whenever $a - \delta < x < a$. Antonym: *right limit* (p 100).

leftover NOUN /ˈlɛft.oʊ.vər/ anything remaining.

left to right PREPOSITION /lɛft tu raɪt/ starting on the left and moving to the right.

leg NOUN /lɛɡ/
1) (of an angle) one of the line segments or rays that define the angle. Synonyms: *side* (p 104), *arm* (p 13).
2) of a triangle, one of the sides of a triangle. Synonym: *side* (p 104).
3) of an isosceles triangle, one of the congruent sides of an isosceles triangle.
4) of a right triangle, one of the sides of a right triangle that is not the hypotenuse.

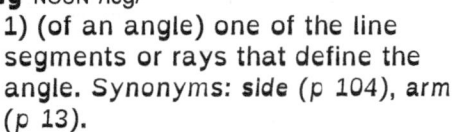

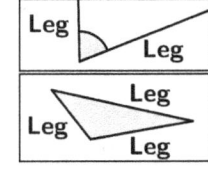

legend NOUN /ˈlɛ.dʒənd/ a list of symbols or colors that gives information about the meaning of those symbols or colors.

lemma NOUN /ˈlɛ.mə/ a theorem that is used as a stepping stone to prove a more important theorem.

lemniscate NOUN /ˈlɛm.nɪˌskeɪt/ a geometric figure shaped like an infinity sign. Equations: (rectangular coordinates): $(x^2 + y^2)^2 = 2a^2(x^2 - y^2)$; (polar coordinates): $r^2 = a^2 \cos 2\theta$, $r^2 = a^2 \sin 2\theta$.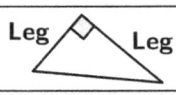

length NOUN /lɛŋkθ/
1) the measure of a 1-dimensional object from one end to the other.
2) the longest measure of distance of a multidimensional object.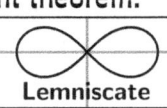

less /lɛs/
1) ADJECTIVE smaller, more negative, less positive. Notation: <. Example: 1 is less than 3. Synonym: *fewer* (p 49).
2) PREPOSITION subtract. Keyword for subtraction. Example: 4 less 1 is 3.

level curve NOUN /ˈlɛ.vəl kɜrv/ a curve showing the level or altitude of a 3-dimensional function. Synonyms: *contour line*, *isothermal*.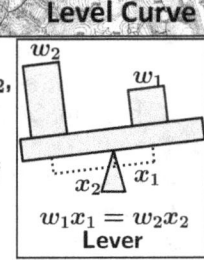

lever NOUN /ˈlɛ.vər/ a device for moving heavy objects. Formula: $w_1 x_1 = w_2 x_2$, where w_1 and w_2 are the weights of objects on the lever, and x_1 and x_2 are the respective distance of each of the objects from the fulcrum.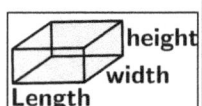

L'Hôpital's rule NOUN /ˈlo.pi.talz rul/ a technique to evaluate limits of indeterminate forms. Math definition: for functions **f** and **g** which are differentiable on an open interval **I** except possibly at a point $c \in I$, if $\lim_{x \to c} f(x) = \lim_{x \to c} g(x)$ equals either **0** or $\pm\infty$; and $g'(x) \neq 0$ for all $x \in I$ where $x \neq c$ and $\lim_{x \to c} \frac{f'(x)}{g'(x)}$ exists, then $\lim_{x \to c} \frac{f(x)}{g(x)} = \lim_{x \to c} \frac{f'(x)}{g'(x)}$.

like ADJECTIVE /laɪk/ the same in some way. Example: like terms. Antonym: *unlike* (p 119).

like fractions NOUN /laɪk ˈfræk.ʃənz/ fractions with the same denominator. Example: $\frac{3}{5}$ and $\frac{2}{5}$. Antonym: *unlike fractions* (p 119).

likely ADJECTIVE /ˈlaɪk.li/ has a good chance of happening. Example: It is likely that the sun will rise tomorrow. Antonym: *unlikely* (p 119).

likelihood ADJECTIVE /ˈlaɪk.li.hʊd/ see likely (p 68).

like terms NOUN /laɪk tɜrmz/ terms that have the same variables with the same exponents. Examples: x^2 and $-2x^2$ are like terms; $3y^2$ and $2y^3$ are unlike terms. Synonym: *similar terms*. Antonym: *unlike terms* (p 119).

limaçon NOUN /ˈlɪ.məˌsɒn/ a geometric figure that can be shaped like an oval, a heart, or having an inner and outer loop. Equations: (rectangular coordinates) $(x^2 + y^2 - ax)^2 = b^2(x^2 + y^2)$, (polar coordinates) $r = b + a \cos \theta$.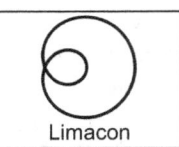

limit NOUN /ˈlɪ.mɪt/ a value that a sequence or function gets closer and closer to, perhaps without ever reaching. Notation: $\lim_{n \to a} f(n)$: is read "the limit of $f(n)$ as **n** approaches **a**." See also *Properties of a Limit* (p 134). Math definition: $\lim_{x \to a} f(n) = L$ if, for every small number $\epsilon > 0$, there exists a number $\delta > 0$ such that $|f(x) - L| < \epsilon$ whenever $0 < |x - a| < \delta$.

limit comparison test NOUN /ˈlɪ.mɪt kʌmˈpɛər.ɪ.sən tɛst/ given $a_n \geq 0$, $b_n > 0$ for all **n**, if the ratio $\lim_{n \to \infty} \frac{a_n}{b_n} = c$, $0 < c < \infty$, then the series either both diverge or both converge.

line NOUN /laɪn/ a straight, one-dimensional figure that does not end. See also *Properties of a Line* (p 140), *Equations of a line* (p 141).

linear ADJECTIVE /ˈlɪ.ni.ər/
1) the degree of each term is **0** or **1**.

2) having to do with a line. Example: linear equation. Antonym: nonlinear (p 79).

3) having only one dimension.

linear algebra NOUN /ˈlɪ.ni.ər ˈæl.dʒə.brə/ an algebra of structures such as linear systems, matrices and vectors.

linear approximation NOUN /ˈlɪ.ni.ər əˌprɒk.səˈmeɪ.ʃən/ the approximation of the equation of a line tangent to a curve. Formula: $y = f(a) + f'(a)(x - a)$. Synonym: tangent line approximation.

Linear and Irreducible Quadratic Factors Theorem NOUN /ˈlɪ.ni.ər ænd ˌɪr.ɪˈdu.sə.bəl kwɒdˈræ.tɪk ˈfæk.tərz ˈθɪ.ə.rəm/ any polynomial with real coefficients may be written as a product of linear factors and irreducible quadratic factors. The sum of the degrees of these component factors is the degree of the polynomial.

Linear and Quadratic Factors Theorem NOUN /ˈlɪ.ni.ər ænd kwɒdˈræ.tɪk ˈfæk.tərz ˈθɪ.ə.rəm/ see Linear and Irreducible Quadratic Factors Theorem (p 69).

linear combination NOUN /ˈlɪ.ni.ər ˌkɒm.bəˈneɪ.ʃən/ a linear combination of A and B is $a \cdot A + b \cdot B$, where a and b are nonzero numbers.

linear equation NOUN /ˈlɪ.ni.ər ɪˈkweɪ.ʒən/ an equation that, when graphed, makes a line; a polynomial equation of degree 1. Formula: $ax + by = c$. Example: $x + 3y = 2$. Antonym: nonlinear equation (p 79).

linear factor NOUN /ˈlɪ.ni.ər ˈfæk.tər/ a factor of a polynomial that is a linear expression in the form $x - a$.

linear fit NOUN /ˈlɪ.ni.ər fɪt/ see regression line (p 97).

linear function NOUN /ˈlɪ.ni.ər fʌnk.ʃən/ a function that, when graphed, makes a line; a polynomial function of degree 1. Formula: $f(x) = mx + b$. Example: $f(x) = 3x + 4$.

linear growth NOUN /ˈlɪ.ni.ər groʊθ/ growth that happens at a constant rate each time period. Formula: $y = mx + b$ where $m > 0$ is the growth rate and b is the initial value. Synonym: constant growth (p 13).

linear inequality NOUN /ˈlɪ.ni.ər ˌɪn.ɪˈkwɒl.ɪ.ti/ an inequality with one or more variables that do not have exponents. Example: $y > 2x + 1$.

linearization NOUN /ˌlɪn.i.ər.aɪˈzeɪ.ʃən/ the linearization of a curve $f(x)$ at $x = a$ is $L(x) \approx f(a) + f'(a)(x - a)$.

linearize VERB /ˈlɪ.ni.ər.aɪz/ to change into a linear form, usually using a log graph or a log/log graph. This is used to determine which function type might fit the data best.

linearly dependent ADJECTIVE /ˈlɪ.ni.ər.li dɪˈpɛn.dənt/ at least one linear combination of the elements equals zero. Math definition: Linear equations A, B are linearly dependent if, for some $a \neq 0$, $b \neq 0$, $aA + bB = 0$. Antonym: linearly independent (p 69).

linearly independent ADJECTIVE /ˈlɪ.ni.ər.li ˌɪn.dɪˈpɛn.dənt/ no linear combination of the elements equals zero. Math definition: Linear equations A, B are linearly independent if there exists **no** $a \neq 0$, $b \neq 0$ such that $aA + bB = 0$. Antonym: linearly dependent (p 69).

linear objective function NOUN /ˈlɪ.ni.ər ɒbˈdʒɛk.tɪv fʌnk.ʃən/ a function $z = Ax_1 + Bx_2 + \cdots + Zx_n$ where at least one of $A \cdots Z$ is not zero.

linear pair NOUN /ˈlɪ.ni.ər pɛər/ a pair of adjacent angles whose non-common legs are opposite rays. The angles in a linear pair are supplementary.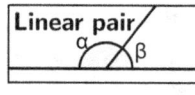

linear programming NOUN /ˈlɪ.ni.ər ˈproʊ.græ.mɪŋ/ a method for determining the best outcome using a set of linear equations or linear inequalities to represent a real-life situation.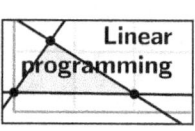

linear programming problem NOUN /ˈlɪ.ni.ər ˈproʊ.græ.mɪŋ ˈprɒ.bləm/ a linear programming problem of n variables consists of minimizing or maximizing a linear objective function $z = Ax_1 + Bx_2 + \cdots + Zx_n$ where at least one of $A \cdots Z$ is not zero.

linear regression NOUN /ˈlɪ.ni.ər rɪˈgrɛ.ʃən/ any method of finding a best fit line for a set of data. See also best fit line (p 16).

linear relation NOUN /ˈlɪ.ni.ər rɪˈleɪ.ʃən/ a relation between two variables that has a linear shape. Antonym: nonlinear relation (p 79).

linear speed NOUN /ˈlɪ.ni.ər spid/ speed along a curve. Formula: (circle) $l = \frac{r\theta}{t}$.

linear system NOUN /ˈlɪ.ni.ər ˈsɪs.təm/ a set of linear objects that may all be simultaneously true. Example: $3x + 2y = 1$, $x - 2y = 5$.

linear velocity NOUN /ˈlɪ.ni.ər vəˈlɒ.sɪ.ti/ the speed of an object along a curve. Example: An automobile can travel at 65 miles per hour.

line chart NOUN /laɪn tʃɑrt/ a graph that shows data as a set of points connected by line segments. Synonym: line graph.

line graph NOUN /laɪn græf/ see line chart (p 69).

line integral NOUN /laɪn/ an integral where a scalar field or vector field to be integrated is evaluated along a curve.

line of fit NOUN /laɪn ʌv fɪt/ see best fit line (p 16).

line of reflection NOUN /laɪn ʌv rɪˈflɛk.ʃən/ see axis of reflection (p 15).

line of sight NOUN /laɪn ʌv saɪt/ a straight line from the observer's eye to a distant point.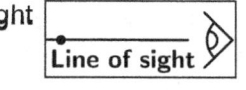

line of symmetry NOUN /laɪn ʌv ˈsɪ.mɪ.tri/ a line about which an object or multiple objects are symmetric. Synonym: axis of symmetry.

line plot NOUN /laɪn plɒt/ see line chart (p 69).

line segment NOUN /laɪn ˈsɛg.mənt/ a continuous portion of a straight line with two endpoints.

line symmetry NOUN /laɪn ˈsɪ.mɪ.tri/ if a geometric figure can be rotated about some line without changing the figure, the figure is said to have line symmetry. The line about which the figure is rotated is called the line of symmetry. Synonym: axial symmetry.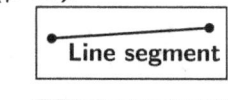

list /lɪst/

1) NOUN item by item entries of objects, usually in a

3rd Dyslexic's Edition

particular order.
2) VERB to show entries of objects item by item, usually in a particular order.

liter NOUN /ˈli.tər/ a unit of measure of volume. Abbreviation: l. Math definition: $1 l \equiv 1000 \text{ cm}^3$. Formulas: 1000 milliliters = 1 liter. 1 liter ≈ 0.264 US gallons. 1 liter ≈ 1 US quart.

literal NOUN /ˈlɪ.tər.əl/ any object written as an explicit value, and not as a variable. Example: 5 is a literal number.

ln ABBREVIATION natural logarithm. Formula: $\ln a \equiv \log_e a$.

ln() COMPUTERS the natural logarithmic function in most computer languages.

loan /loʊn/
1) NOUN an agreement to borrow and repay money.
2) NOUN money that is borrowed.
3) VERB to lend money.

local ADJECTIVE /ˈloʊ.kəl/ restricted to a finite region; not global. Antonym: global (p 54).

local extrema of a polynomial NOUN /ˈloʊ.kəl ɪkˈstri.mə ʌv ə ˌpɒ.ləˈnoʊ.mi.əl/ local minimum or local maximum values of a polynomial.

local extremum NOUN /ˈloʊ.kəl ɪkˈstri.məm/ either a local maximum or a local minimum. Math definition: $f(a)$ is a local minimum or maximum for f if and only if $f'(a) = 0$. Plural: local extrema /ˈloʊ.kəl ɪkˈstri.mə/.

local maximum NOUN /ˈloʊ.kəl ˈmæk.sə.məm/ the greatest value of a function in a local subdomain. Math definition: $f(a)$ is a local maximum for f if and only if for all x near a, $f(a) > f(x)$; if $f'(a) = 0$ and $f''(a) < 0$. Synonym: relative maximum, constrained maximum. Plural: local maxima.

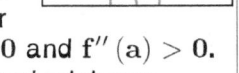

local minimum NOUN /ˈloʊ.kəl ˈmɪ.nə.məm/ the least value of a function in a local subdomain. Math definition: $f(a)$ is a local minimum for f if and only if for all x near a, $f(a) < f(x)$; if $f'(a) = 0$ and $f''(a) > 0$. Synonym: relative minimum, constrained minimum. Plural: local minima.

local subdomain NOUN /ˈloʊ.kəl ˌsʌbˈdoʊ.meɪn/ a continuous, finite subset of a domain; a subdomain that does not extend to either negative infinity or positive infinity.

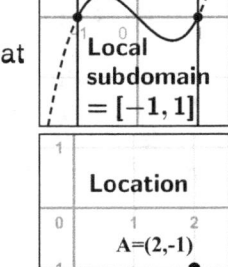

location NOUN /loʊˈkeɪ.ʃən/ where an object exists in a geometric space. Example: the location of point A is $(2, -1)$.

Location of the Solution of a Linear Programming Problem Theorem NOUN a solution point of a linear programming problem will be at a vertex of the feasible region.

locus NOUN /ˈloʊ.kəs/ a continuous set of points that satisfy one or more conditions. Example: a circle is the locus of all points equidistant from a center point. Plural: loci /ˈloʊ.saɪ/.

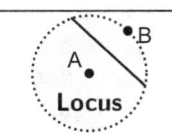

log ABBREVIATION logarithm. If the base is not shown, either base 10 (business, social sciences) or base e (physics, engineering) is assumed. Math definition: $\log_b c = a$ if and only if $b^a = c$. Examples: $\log_{12} 3.6$, $\log 6$, $\ln 7$.

log() COMPUTERS the common logarithmic function ($\log_{10} x$) for most computer languages. In some computer languages, log() represents the natural logarithm ($\log_e x$).

logarithm NOUN /ˈlɒ.gəˌrɪ.ðəm/ the value of an exponent; the inverse of exponentiation. Math definition: $\log_b c = a$ if and only if $b^a = c$. Inverse: exponent (p 47). Synonyms: common logarithm (p 23), natural logarithm (p 78). See also Properties of Logarithms (p 128).

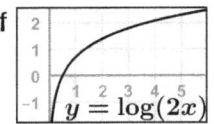

logarithmic ADJECTIVE /ˌlɒ.gəˈrɪð.mɪk/ having to do with logarithms. Example: logarithmic equation.

logarithmic differentiation NOUN /ˌlɒ.gəˈrɪð.mɪk ˌdɪ.fər.ɛnˌʃiˈeɪ.ʃən/ a method for differentiating functions using the logarithmic derivative of a function f. Example: $\frac{d}{dx}\ln(x^2 + 1) = \frac{2x}{x^2+1}$.

logarithmic equation NOUN /ˌlɒ.gəˈrɪð.mɪk ɪˈkweɪ.ʒən/ an equation that contains a logarithm of a variable. Example: $y = \log_{10} x$.

logarithmic function NOUN /ˌlɒ.gəˈrɪð.mɪk fʌŋk.ʃən/ a function that contains a logarithm of a variable. Example: $f(x) = \log_{10} x$.

logarithmic scale NOUN /ˌlɒ.gəˈrɪð.mɪk skeɪl/ a scale of a graph where the value is multiplied by a given factor each tick mark.

Logarithmic scale
$\frac{1}{2}$ 1 2 4 8 16...

logic NOUN /ˈlɒ.dʒɪk/
1) the study of sound reasoning.
2) a series of statements that make use of the science of logic.

logical ADJECTIVE /ˈlɒ.dʒɪ.kəl/
1) having to do with logic. Example: logical value.
2) following the rules of logic. Example: logical argument.

logical argument NOUN /ˈlɒ.dʒɪ.kəl ˈɑr.gjə.mənt/ one or more premises followed by one or more valid conclusions. Example: Socrates is a man. (premise). All men are mortal (premise). So, Socrates is mortal (conclusion).

logically ADVERB /ˈlɒ.dʒɪ.kə.li/ in agreement with the rules of logic.

logical value NOUN /ˈlɒ.dʒɪ.kəl ˈvæl.ju/
1) see truth value (p 117).
2) see Boolean value (p 17).

logistic curve NOUN /ləˈdʒɪ.stɪk kɜrv/ see logistic growth (p 70).

logistic function NOUN /ləˈdʒɪ.stɪk ˈfʌŋk.ʃən/ see logistic growth (p 70).

logistic growth NOUN /ləˈdʒɪ.stɪk groʊθ/ growth in natural populations where there is a limiting factor to growth. Formula: $P(t) = \frac{c}{1+ae^{-bt}}$ where $a > 0$, $c > 0$, $0 < b < 1$ for decay, $b > 1$ for growth.

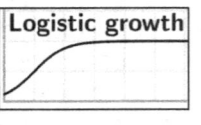

log graph NOUN /lɒg græf/ a graph where one axis uses a logarithmic scale. Synonym: semi-log graph (p 103).

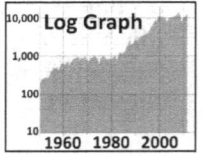

log-log graph NOUN /lɔg lɔg græf/ a graph where both axes use a logarithmic scale. Synonym: *log-log plot*.

log-log plot NOUN /lɔg lɔg plɒt/ see *log-log graph* (p 71).

log plot NOUN /lɔg plɒt/ see *log graph* (p 70).

long division NOUN /lɒŋ dɪˈvɪ.ʒən/ an algorithm for dividing real numbers or polynomials where each step is shown in detail.

$$14\overline{)274} \quad \begin{array}{r} 19r8 \\ \hline 14 \\ \hline 134 \\ 126 \\ \hline 8 \end{array}$$

longitude NOUN /ˈlɒn.dʒɪ.tud/ the angle of a point on the Earth's surface measured from the meridian that passes through Greenwich, England to the meridian on which the point lies.

Longitude

long run behavior NOUN /lɒŋ rʌn bɪˈheɪ.vjər/ see *end behavior of a function* (p 44).

long scale NOUN /lɒŋ skeɪl/ a standard for naming multiples of powers of 10 where $10^{12} = 1$ billion. Antonym: *short scale* (p 104).

loss NOUN /lɒs/
1) a decrease in amount. Keyword for negative and for subtraction.
2) an amount by which expenses are more than income. Formula: **Expenses − Income = Loss, Expenses > Income**.

Lovelace, Ada, Countess /ˈlʌv.læs ˈeɪ.də/ PERSON (1815—1852) a mathematician who advanced the theory of the computing by

Ada Lovelace

outlining an algorithm to calculate Bernoulli numbers.

lower ADJECTIVE /ˈloʊ.ər/ less than; below. Example: lower bound. Antonym: *upper* (p 120).

lower bound NOUN /ˈloʊ.ər baʊnd/ a number that is less than all numbers in a set. Antonym: *upper bound* (p 120). See also *greatest lower bound* (p 55).

Lower bound

lower extreme NOUN /ˈloʊ.ər ɪkˈstrim/ the least value of a variable in a dataset. Synonym: *minimum* (p 75).

lower quartile NOUN /ˈloʊ.ər ˈkwɔr.taɪl/ the first quartile of a dataset.

lower triangular matrix NOUN /ˈloʊ.ər traɪˈæn.gjə.lər ˈmeɪ.trɪks/ a matrix having all zeros below and to the left of the main diagonal.

$$\left[\begin{array}{ccc|c} 3 & -1 & 2 & 1 \\ 0 & 2 & 1 & 2 \\ 0 & 0 & -2 & -2 \end{array}\right]$$
Lower triangular matrix

lowest ADJECTIVE /ˈloʊ.ɛst/
1) (numbers) see *least* (p 67).
2) (geometry) closest to the bottom.

lowest common denominator NOUN /ˈloʊ.ɛst ˈkɑ.mən dɪˈnɒ.məˌneɪ.tər/ see *least common denominator* (p 67).

lowest common multiple NOUN /ˈloʊ.ɛst ˈkɑ.mən ˈmʌl.tə.pəl/ see *least common multiple* (p 67).

lurking variable NOUN /ˈlɜr.kɪŋ ˈvɛər.i.ə.bəl/ a variable that is not identified in a study, but may affect the result.

M

μ ABBREVIATION micro- 10^{-6}. Example: **2.5 micrometers = 2.4×10^{-6} meters = 0.000 002 4 meters**. Synonym: *millionth*.

m ABBREVIATION
1) meter.
2) milli- 10^{-3}. Example: **5 millimeters = 5×10^{-3} meters = 0.005 meters**. Synonym: *thousandths*.
3) minute.

M
1) ABBREVIATION mega- 10^6. Example: **5 megameters = 5×10^6 meters**. Synonym: *million*.
2) SYMBOL Roman numeral for 1,000.
3) ABBREVIATION million.

MAB block NOUN /ɛm eɪ bi blɒk/ see *base ten block* (p 16).

Maclaurin series NOUN /məkˈlɔr.ɪn ˈsɪər.iz/ a special case of a Taylor series that is calculated around the point $(0, f(0))$. See also *Taylor series* (p 113).

macro- PREFIX /ˈmæ.kroʊ/ very large in scale.

magic square NOUN /ˈmæ.dʒɪk skwɛər/ a square matrix containing integers where the rows and columns all add up to the same number.

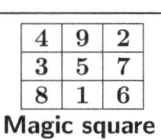
Magic square

magnetic north NOUN /mægˈnɛt.ɪk nɔrθ/ the direction towards the north magnetic pole along magnetic flux lines, and not the actual north pole. Antonym: *magnetic south* (p 71).

magnetic south NOUN /mægˈnɛt.ɪk saʊθ/ the direction towards the south magnetic pole along magnetic flux lines, and not the actual south pole. Antonym: *magnetic north* (p 71).

magnitude NOUN /ˈmæg.nɪˌtud/
1) the distance of a point from zero. The distance formula is used to calculate magnitudes. Notation: $|x|$. Formulas: $|a| = \sqrt{a^2}$, $|a + bi| = \sqrt{a^2 + b^2}$. Example: $|-3 + 4i| = \sqrt{(-3)^2 + 4^2} = \sqrt{9 + 16} = \sqrt{25} = 5$.
2) (vector) the length of a vector disregarding direction. Notation: $|\langle x, y \rangle|$. Formulas: $|\langle x, y \rangle| = \sqrt{x^2 + y^2}$ (2-d); $|\langle x, y, z \rangle| = \sqrt{x^2 + y^2 + z^2}$ (3-d).
3) a number that is a relative quantity, particularly of a unit of measure. Example: magnitude of a star. Synonym: *absolute value* (p 7).

main ADJECTIVE /meɪn/ the longest or most important. Example: main diagonal. Synonym: *major* (p 71).

main diagonal NOUN /meɪn daɪˈæ.gə.nl/ the diagonal of a matrix going from the upper left to the lower right. Synonym: *principle diagonal*.

$$\begin{bmatrix} 2 & 2 & 1 \\ 1 & 3 & 2 \\ 2 & 6 & 1 \end{bmatrix}$$
Main diagonal

major ADJECTIVE /ˈmeɪ.dʒər/
1) larger or largest; greater or greatest. Example: major sector.
2) most important. Synonym: *main* (p 71). Antonym: *minor* (p 75).

major arc NOUN /ˈmeɪ.dʒər ɑrk/ an arc of a circle that is longer than a semicircle of the same circle. Antonym: *minor arc* (p 75).

major axis NOUN /ˈmeɪ.dʒər ˈæk.sɪs/ the longer of two axes. Plural: major axes /ˈmeɪ.dʒər ˈæk.siz/. Antonym: *minor axis* (p 75).

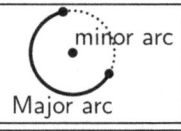
Major axis

majority NOUN /məˈdʒɔr.ɪ.ti/ more than one half of a population. Example: the bill passed the legislature by a majority vote. Antonym: *minority* (p 75).

major sector NOUN /ˈmeɪ.dʒər ˈsɛk.tər/ the larger of two circular sectors into which a circle has been divided. Antonym: *minor sector* (p 75).

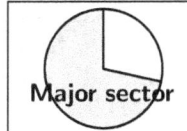
Major sector

make VERB /meɪk/
1) to bring into existence.
2) to produce.

Mandelbrot, Benoît B. PERSON /ˈmæn.dl.brɔt bɛnˈwɑ/ (1924—2010) a Poland-born Franco-American mathematician known for his work with fractals and credited for creation of the Mandelbrot set.

Mandelbrot set NOUN /ˈmæn.dl.brɔt sɛt/ a set of points in a complex plane generated by iterating through the complex polynomial $z_{n+1} = z_n^2 + c$.

Mandelbrot Set

manipulative NOUN /mænˈɪ.pju.lə.tɪv/ a physical or virtual object that can be handled or changed. Example: Algebra tiles. Synonym: *concrete object*.

mantissa NOUN /mænˈtɪs.ə/
1) the part of a number written in scientific notation or e notation that contains the significant digits of the number. Example: In 3.529×10^5, the mantissa is 3.529. Synonym: *significand*.
2) the decimal part of a logarithm. Example: $\log_{10} 12.2 \approx 1.08636$ the mantissa is .08636.

many ADJECTIVE /ˈmɛn.i/
1) more than one.
2) more than a few. Antonym: *few* (p 49).

many to one correspondence NOUN /ˈmɛn.i tu wʌn ˌkɔ.rəˈspɒn.dəns/ a mapping or relation where each object in the dataset can map to multiple objects.

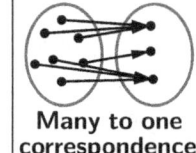
Many to one correspondence

mapping NOUN /ˈmæp.ɪŋ/ see *relation* (p 98).

map scale NOUN /mæp skeɪl/ the ratio of distances in a map to the actual distances in the thing being mapped. Example: a 1:20 map scales means that real objects are 20 times bigger than shown on the map. See also *representative fraction* (p 99).

margin NOUN /ˈmɑr.dʒɪn/
1) the boundary of a figure.
2) the difference between two quantities. Example: margin of error.

marginal ADJECTIVE /ˈmɑr.dʒɪ.nl/
1) having to do with a border, or a margin.
2) having to do with a ratio. Example: marginal rate.

marginal rate NOUN /ˈmɑr.dʒɪ.nl reɪt/ the ratio of the change in the input as compared to the change in the output over a particular range.

margin of error NOUN /ˈmɑr.dʒɪn ʌv ˈɛr.ər/ (statistics) a measure of the expected accuracy of a result. Example: a margin of error of 3% means that the actual value is most likely to vary from 0.97 to 1.03 times the measured result.

markdown NOUN /ˈmɑrkˌdaʊn/ an amount or percentage that is subtracted from a cost to get the final price. Formula: **price − markdown = final price**. Antonym: *markup* (p 72).

markup NOUN /ˈmɑrk.ʌp/ an amount or percentage that is added to a cost to get the retail price. Formula: **cost + markup = retail price**. Antonym: *markdown* (p 72).

mass NOUN /mæs/ the amount of matter contained in a substance as determined by Newton's second law of motion. Example: the mass of the moon is about 7.36×10^{22} kg.

math NOUN /mæθ/ see *mathematics* (p 72).

mathemagically ADVERB /ˌmæθ.əˈmæ.dʒɪ.kli/ doing something according to the principles of mathematics that seems like magic.

mathematical ADJECTIVE /ˌmæθˈmæ.tɪ.kəl/ having to do with mathematics. Example: mathematical logic.

mathematical expectation NOUN /ˌmæθˈmæ.tɪ.kəl ˌɛk.spɛkˈteɪ.ʃən/ see *expected value* (p 47).

mathematical induction NOUN /ˌmæθˈmæ.tɪ.kəl ɪnˈdʌk.ʃən/ a method for proving a proposition involving an infinite sequence of elements. The steps of mathematical induction are: 1) Show the first case is true; 2) Show that, if an arbitrary case **n** is true, then the next case, **n + 1**, must be true. For contrast see *induction* (p 61).

mathematical logic NOUN /ˌmæθˈmæ.tɪ.kəl ˈlɒ.dʒɪk/ a subset of logic used in mathematics based on axiomatic systems, deductive logic and mathematical induction. Mathematical logic is more rigorous than standard logic.

mathematical model NOUN /ˌmæθˈmæ.tɪ.kəl ˈmɒ.dl/ see *model* (p 61).

mathematical reasoning NOUN /ˌmæθˈmæ.tɪ.kəl ˈriz.nɪŋ/ formation of conclusions using mathematical logic.

mathematical situation NOUN /ˌmæθˈmæ.tɪ.kəl ˌsɪ.tʃuˈweɪ.ʃən/ a mathematical problem where the context is not known. Example: Solve the equation $0 = x + 2$. Antonym: *practical situation* (p 91).

mathematician NOUN /ˌmæθ.məˈtɪ.ʃən/ one who studies or practices mathematics.

mathematics NOUN /ˌmæθˈmæ.tɪks/
1) the study of numbers, shapes, patterns and relationships.
2) the science of necessary conditions. Synonym: *math*.

matrix NOUN /ˈmeɪ.trɪks/ values arranged in rows and columns, usually enclosed in square brackets. Values can be any math object that can be added and multiplied by other objects of the same kind. Plural: **matrices** /ˈmeɪ.trɪˌsiz/. Synonym: *array* (p 14).

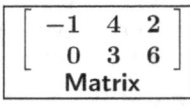
$\begin{bmatrix} -1 & 4 & 2 \\ 0 & 3 & 6 \end{bmatrix}$
Matrix

matrix addition NOUN /ˈmeɪ.trɪks əˈdɪ.ʃən/ addition of corresponding elements of matrices with the same dimensions. Example:
$$\begin{bmatrix} 2 & -2 \\ 3 & 0 \\ -1 & 2 \end{bmatrix} + \begin{bmatrix} 1 & 3 \\ -1 & 0 \\ -1 & -3 \end{bmatrix} = \begin{bmatrix} 2+1 & -2+3 \\ 3-1 & 0+0 \\ -1-1 & 2-3 \end{bmatrix} = \begin{bmatrix} 3 & 1 \\ 2 & 0 \\ -2 & -1 \end{bmatrix}.$$

matrix algebra NOUN /ˈmeɪ.trɪks ˈæl.dʒə.brə/ an algebra for manipulating matrices. Matrix algebra includes addition, subtraction, multiplication, multiplicative identities and additive identities.

matrix dimension NOUN /ˈmeɪ.trɪks dɪˈmɛn.ʃən/ the number of rows and columns in a matrix. Notation: $\dim(A) = m \times n$ (matrix **A** has **m** rows and **n** columns)

$$\begin{bmatrix} -1 & 4 & 2 \\ 0 & 3 & 6 \end{bmatrix}$$
Dimension 2×3

matrix element NOUN /ˈmeɪ.trɪks ˈɛ.lə.mənt/ a matrix entry at a particular row and column. Notation: $a_{r,c}$ where **r** is the row, **c** is the column.

$$\begin{bmatrix} A_{1,1} & A_{1,2} & A_{1,3} \\ A_{2,1} & A_{2,2} & A_{2,3} \end{bmatrix}$$
Matrix elements

matrix inverse NOUN /ˈmeɪ.trɪks ɪnˈvɜrs/ a square matrix A^{-1} such that $A \cdot A^{-1} = I$ and $A^{-1} \cdot A = I$ where **I** is the identity matrix with the same dimensions as **A**. A square matrix with a determinant of zero has no inverse.

matrix of cofactors NOUN /ˈmeɪ.trɪks ʌv ˈkoʊˌfæk.tərz/ see cofactor matrix (p 22).

matrix multiplication NOUN /ˈmeɪ.trɪks ˌmʌl.tə.pləˈkeɪ.ʃən/ multiplication of the rows of the first matrix by the columns of the second matrix. Example:
$$\begin{bmatrix} 0 & 1 & 4 \\ 3 & 2 & 5 \end{bmatrix} \cdot \begin{bmatrix} 2 & -2 \\ 3 & 0 \\ 1 & 4 \end{bmatrix} =$$
$$\begin{bmatrix} 0 \cdot 2 + 1 \cdot 3 + 4 \cdot 1 & 0 \cdot -2 + 1 \cdot 0 + 4 \cdot 4 \\ 3 \cdot 2 + 2 \cdot 3 + 5 \cdot 1 & 3 \cdot -2 + 2 \cdot 0 + 5 \cdot 4 \end{bmatrix} =$$
$$\begin{bmatrix} 0+3+4 & 0+0+16 \\ 6+6+5 & -6+0+20 \end{bmatrix} = \begin{bmatrix} 7 & 16 \\ 17 & 14 \end{bmatrix}.$$

matrix row operation NOUN /ˈmeɪ.trɪks roʊ ˌɒ.pərˈeɪ.ʃən/ see row operation (p 101).

matrix subtraction NOUN /ˈmeɪ.trɪks səbˈtræk.ʃən/ subtraction of corresponding elements of two matrices that have the same dimensions. Example:
$$\begin{bmatrix} 4 & 5 \\ -1 & 1 \\ 0 & 3 \end{bmatrix} - \begin{bmatrix} 2 & 3 \\ -1 & 3 \\ -1 & 4 \end{bmatrix} =$$
$$\begin{bmatrix} 4-2 & 5-3 \\ -1-(-1) & 1-3 \\ 0-(-1) & 3-4 \end{bmatrix} = \begin{bmatrix} 2 & 2 \\ 0 & -2 \\ 1 & -1 \end{bmatrix}.$$

matrix transposition NOUN /ˈmeɪ.trɪks ˌtræns.pəˈzɪ.ʃən/ swapping the rows of a matrix with the columns.
Example: $A = \begin{bmatrix} 4 & 5 \\ -1 & 1 \\ 0 & 3 \end{bmatrix}, A_T = \begin{bmatrix} 4 & -1 & 0 \\ 5 & 1 & 3 \end{bmatrix}.$

maximize VERB /ˈmæk.səˌmaɪz/ to increase to the greatest possible amount or degree. Antonym: minimize (p 75).

maximum NOUN, ADJECTIVE /ˈmæk.sə.məm/
1) the greatest of several quantities.
2) the greatest value of a function on a possibly infinite interval.
Antonym: minimum (p 75). Plural: maxima /ˈmæk.səˌmə/.

maximum of a function NOUN /ˈmæk.sə.məm ʌv ə ˈfʌŋk.ʃən/ the largest value of a function. Synonym: global maximum (p 54), local maximum (p 70).

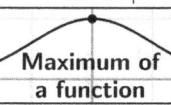
Maximum of a function

maximum point NOUN /ˈmæk.sə.məm pɔɪnt/ see local maximum (p 70).

mean NOUN /min/
1) an average; a value that is a center of a set of values. Example: arithmetic mean.
2) (statistics) the arithmetic mean of a set of numbers.

mean absolute deviation NOUN /min ˌæb.səˈlut ˌdi.viˈeɪ.ʃən/ see average absolute deviation (p 14).

mean absolute residual NOUN /min ˌæb.səˈlut rɪˈzɪ.dʒu.əl/ see average absolute deviation (p 14).

mean deviation NOUN /min ˌdi.viˈeɪ.ʃən/ the arithmetic average of the absolute values of deviations in a dataset. Formula: $D_m = \frac{|d_1| + |d_2| + \ldots + |d_n|}{n}$ where d_i is the deviation of the ith item and **n** is the number of values in the dataset.

mean proportional NOUN /min prəˈpoʊr.ʃə.nl/ see geometric mean (p 53).

mean square deviation NOUN /min skwɛər ˌdi.viˈeɪ.ʃən/ see variance (p 120).

Mean Value Theorem NOUN /min ˈvæl.ju ˈθɪ.ə.rəm/ if $f(x)$ is continuous on $[a, b]$ and differentiable on (a, b), then there is a point $c \in (a, b)$ where $f'(c) = \frac{f(b) - f(a)}{b - a}$.

measure /ˈmɛ.ʒər/
1) NOUN a distance, quantity, volume or other dimension associated with an object.
2) VERB to find a distance, quantity, volume or other dimension of an object.
3) VERB compare a dimension of an object to a unit of measure.
4) VERB assign a number to a location based upon a unit of measure.

measurement NOUN, ADJECTIVE /ˈmɛ.ʒər.mənt/
1) a measure associated with an object.
2) the act of measuring.

measurement system NOUN /ˈmɛ.ʒər.mənt ˈsɪs.təm/ a collections of units of measure and the rules relating them.

measure of an angle NOUN /ˈmɛ.ʒər ʌv ən ˈæŋ.gəl/ the portion of a full circle formed by an angle, measured in degrees, radians, or gradians. Notation: $m\angle\alpha$ is read 'the measure of angle alpha.'

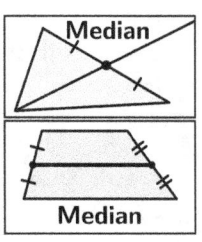
Measure of an angle

Measure of an Angle					
Unit of Measure	Notation	Conversion			
		$\frac{1}{4}$ Circle	$\frac{1}{2}$ Circle	$\frac{3}{4}$ Circle	Full
Degree	°	90°	180°	270°	360°
Radian	rad.	$\frac{\pi}{2}$ rad.	π rad.	$\frac{3\pi}{2}$ rad.	2π rad.
Gradian	grad.	100 grad.	200 grad.	300 grad.	400 grad.

measure of central tendency NOUN /ˈmɛ.ʒər ʌv ˈsɛn.trəl ˈtɛn.dən.si/ any formula that identifies a center of a set of numbers. Examples: mean, median and mode.

Mechanic's Rule NOUN /məˈkæn.ɪks rul/ an iterative algorithm for approximating $\sqrt{x}$. Start with an estimate **n**. Apply the iterative formula $n' = \frac{1}{2}\left(n + \frac{x}{n}\right)$ until the desired accuracy is achieved.

median NOUN /ˈmi.di.ən/
1) (numbers) the middle value of a set of numbers. If there are an even number of elements in the set, the median is the mean of the middle two numbers. Examples: The median of

$\{-4, 3, 7, 14, 27\}$ is 7. The median of $\{-6, -2, 3, 5, 7, 9\}$ is $\frac{3+5}{2} = 4$.
2) (triangle) a line through the vertex of a triangle and the midpoint of the opposite side.
3) (trapezoid) a line segment between midpoints of the non-parallel sides.

median point NOUN /ˈmi.di.ən pɔɪnt/ see *centroid* (p 20).

mediator NOUN /ˈmi.di.eɪ.tər/ see *perpendicular bisector* (p 87).

mega- PREFIX /ˈmɛ.gə/ million; $10^6 = 1,000,000$.
Abbreviation: M. Formula: **2 megawatts = 2×10^6 watts.** Synonym: *million* (p 75).

member NOUN /ˈmɛm.bər/ an object belonging to a set. Notation: $\in$. Example: $x \in A$. Synonym: *element* (p 43).

Menelaus of Alexandria PERSON /ˌmɛn.əˈleɪ.əs ʌv ˌæl.ɪgˈzæn.dri.ə/ (70—130 CE) an Egyptian astronomer and mathematician.

Menelaus Theorem NOUN /ˌmɛn.əˈleɪ.əs ˈθɪ.ə.rəm/ given points **A, B,** and **C** that are vertices of a triangle and points **P** on **AC**, **Q** on **AB** and **R** on the extended line **BC**, then points **P, Q,** and **R** are collinear if and only if $\frac{AP}{PC} \cdot \frac{CR}{BR} \cdot \frac{BQ}{QA} = 1$.

mensuration NOUN /ˌmɛn.sərˈeɪ.ʃən/
1) measurement of distance, area and volume.
2) using analytic geometry to calculate measurements from other measurements including angles.

mental ADJECTIVE /ˌmɛn.təl mæθ/ done in the head without writing anything down.

mental computation NOUN /ˌmɛn.təl ˌkɒm.pjuˈteɪ.ʃən/ see *mental math* (p 74).

mental math NOUN /ˌmɛn.təl mæθ/ math calculations that are done in the head without aid of pencils, calculators or other devices.

meridian NOUN /mərˈɪd.i.ən/ any great circle passing through the north and south poles.

meter NOUN /ˈmi.tər/ a unit of measure of distance. Abbreviation: m. Formulas:
1 meter = 100 centimeters.
1 kilometer = 1000 meters. 1 meter ≈ 3.28 feet. Example: a baseball bat is about 1 meter long.

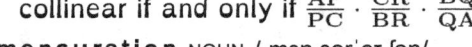
Meridians

meters per second NOUN /ˈmi.tərz pər ˈsɛ.kənd/ a unit of measure of speed. How many meters something moves in one second. Abbreviation: m/s. Formulas:
1 m/s = 3.6 kph. 1 m/s ≈ 3.218 f/s. Example: an average person walks at about **1.8 m/s**.

method NOUN /ˈmɛ.θəd/ a systematic way to do something. Synonym: *algorithm* (p 9).

method of exhaustion NOUN /ˈmɛ.θəd ʌv ɪgˈzɔs.tʃən/ a method of finding the area of a circle involving inscribing polygons with increasingly smaller sides until the desired accuracy is reached.

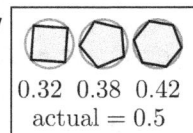
0.32 0.38 0.42
actual = 0.5
Method of exhaustion

metric /ˈmɛ.trɪk/
1) ADJECTIVE having to do with measurement. Example: metric geometry.
2) ADJECTIVE having to do with the metric system of measurement. Example: metric ton.
3) NOUN a non-negative measure of distances.

metric geometry NOUN /ˈmɛ.trɪk dʒiˈɒ.mɪ.tri/ a geometry in which distances can be measured relative to one or more units of measure.

metric space NOUN /ˈmɛ.trɪk speɪs/ a geometric space: 1) that has a unit of measure for each dimension, 2) that has an origin, and 3) where the distance between any two points can be calculated. Example: Cartesian 2-space.

metric system NOUN /ˈmɛ.trɪk ˈsɪs.təm/ a set of units of measures and notations that form the basis of the International System of Units. Metric units of measure include kilogram, meter, and second. See also *International System of Units* (p 145).

metric ton NOUN /ˈmɛ.trɪk tʌn/ **1000 kilogram.** Abbreviation: t. Formula: **1 metric ton ≈ 1.1 tons.** Example: an average mid-sized car weighs about **1.6 metric tons.** Synonym: *tonne*.

metric unit NOUN /ˈmɛ.trɪk ˈju.nɪt/ one of the units of measure of the metric system. Examples: meter, liter, and gram.

mi ABBREVIATION mile.

micro- PREFIX /ˈmaɪ.kroʊ/ $10^{-6} = 0.000\,001$. Abbreviation: μ. Examples: **2.4 micrometer = 2.4×10^{-6} meters.** The diameter of a human hair is about **50-100 μm.** Synonym: *millionth*.

mid- PREFIX /mɪd/ in the middle.

midday NOUN /ˈmɪd.deɪ/ see *noon* (p 80).

midline NOUN /ˈmɪd.laɪn/
1) the line at the exact center of the oscillations of a periodic function.
2) see *midsegment* (p 74).

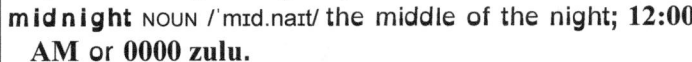
Midline

midnight NOUN /ˈmɪd.naɪt/ the middle of the night; **12:00 AM or 0000 zulu.**

midpoint NOUN /ˈmɪd.pɔɪnt/
1) the center point of a line segment.
2) a point between two other points that is equidistant from both points.
Formula: The midpoint of (x_1, y_1) and (x_2, y_2) is $\left(\frac{x_1+x_2}{2}, \frac{y_1+y_2}{2}\right)$.

Midpoint
(x_1, y_1) (x_2, y_2)
$\left(\frac{x_1+x_2}{2}, \frac{y_1+y_2}{2}\right)$

Midpoint Rule NOUN /ˈmɪd.pɔɪnt rul/ Riemann sums tend to be closer to the actual integral when using the midpoint of each rectangle. Math definition:
$\int_a^b f(x)dx \approx \sum_{i=1}^n f(\overline{x}_i)\Delta x = \Delta x[f(\overline{x}_1) + \ldots + f(\overline{x}_n)]$ where $\Delta x = \frac{b-a}{n}$ and $\overline{x}_i = \frac{x_{i-1}+x_i}{2}$ = midpoint of $[x_{i-1}, x_i]$.

Midpoint Theorem NOUN /ˈmɪd.pɔɪnt ˈθɪ.ə.rəm/ M is the midpoint of **AB** if and only if $AM \cong MB$ and $AM = MB$.

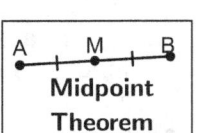
Midpoint Theorem

midsegment NOUN /ˈmɪd.sɛg.mənt/ a line segment joining midpoints of two sides of a triangle. Synonym: *midline*.

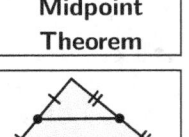
Midsegment

mile NOUN /maɪl/ a unit of measure of distance. Abbreviation: mi. Formulas:
1 mile = 5280 feet. 1 mile ≈ 1.61 kilometers.
1 kilometer ≈ 0.621 miles. Example: 1 mile is about 8-10 city blocks. See *nautical mile* (p 78).

mileage NOUN /ˈmaɪl.ɪdʒ/ the number of miles traveled per gallon of gas consumed. Notation: mpg. Synonym: *miles per gallon*.

miles per gallon NOUN /maɪlz pər ˈgæl.ən/ the average number of miles that can be traveled while using a gallon of gas. Abbreviation: mi/gal. Synonym: *mileage*.

miles per hour NOUN /maɪlz pər ˈaʊ.ər/ a unit of measure of speed; how many miles are traveled each hour. Abbreviation: mph. Formulas: **1 mph ≈ 1.467 f/s, 1 mph ≈ 1.609 kph.** Example: an average human adult walks at about 3-4 mph.

millennium NOUN /mɪˈlɛ.ni.əm/ a period of 1000 years.

milli- PREFIX /ˈmɪ.lə/ one thousandth; $10^{-3} = 0.001$. Abbreviation: m. Examples: 3 millimeters = 3×10^{-3} meters = 0.003 meters. A human fingernail is about 0.3-0.5mm thick. Synonym: *thousandth*.

milligram NOUN /ˌmɪ.ləˈgræm/ a unit of measure of mass. Abbreviation: mg. Formulas: **1000 milligrams = 1 gram. 1 milligram = 0.001 gram.** Example: a honey bee weighs about 90 mg.

milliliter NOUN /ˌmɪ.ləˈli.tər/ a unit of measure of volume. Abbreviation: ml. Formulas: **1000 milliliters = 1 liter. 1 milliliter = 0.001 liter. 1 milliliter = 1 cm³.**

millimeter NOUN /ˌmɪ.ləˈmi.tər/ a unit of measure of distance. Abbreviation: mm. Formulas: **1000 millimeters = 1 meter. 1 millimeter = 0.001 meter. 1 millimeter = 0.03937008 inches.** Example: Ants are between **3 mm-12 mm** long.

million NOUN /ˈmɪl.jən/ $1,000,000 = 10^6$. Abbreviations: **M, MM**. Synonym: *mega* (p 74).

min ABBREVIATION minute.

min- PREFIX /mɪn/ smaller or smallest.

minimize VERB /ˈmɪn.əˌmaɪz/ to reduce to the smallest possible amount or degree. Antonym: *maximize* (p 73).

minimum NOUN, ADJECTIVE /ˈmɪ.nə.məm/
1) the least of several quantities.
2) the least value of a function on an interval.
Plural: *minima* /ˈmɪn.ə.mʌ/. Antonym: *maximum* (p 73).

Minimum Line Postulate NOUN /ˈmɪ.nə.məm laɪn ˈpɒs.tʃə.lɪt/ a line contains at least two distinct points.

minimum of a function NOUN /ˈmɪ.nə.məm ʌv ə ˈfʌŋk.ʃən/ the smallest (closest to negative infinity) value a function can take.

Minimum Plane Postulate NOUN /ˈmɪ.nə.məm pleɪn ˈpɒs.tʃə.lɪt/ a plane contains at least three distinct points not on the same line (noncollinear).

minimum point NOUN /ˈmɪ.nə.məm pɔɪnt/ see *local minimum* (p 70).

minor /ˈmaɪ.nər/
1) ADJECTIVE smaller or less important. Antonym: *major* (p 71).
2) NOUN (of a matrix) the determinant of a smaller matrix obtained by eliminating the row and column of the selected element from the original matrix. See also *cofactor* (p 22). Example:

$$\begin{bmatrix} 3 & -2 & 0 \\ 1 & 4 & -1 \\ -3 & 2 & 1 \end{bmatrix} \xrightarrow{\text{minor}_{2,2}} \begin{vmatrix} 3 & 0 \\ -3 & 1 \end{vmatrix} =$$
$3 \cdot 1 - (-3) \cdot 0 = 3.$

minor arc NOUN /ˈmaɪ.nər ɑrk/ an arc of a circle that is shorter than a semicircle of the same circle. Antonym: *major arc* (p 71).

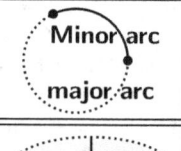

minor axis NOUN /ˈmaɪ.nər ˈæk.sɪs/
1) the smaller of two axes. Synonym: *conjugate axis* (p 27).
2) (hyperbola) the axis that does not intersect the foci.
Plural: *minor axes*. Antonym: *major axis* (p 71).

minority NOUN /maɪˈnɔr.ɪ.ti/ less than half of a population. Example: a minority of voters voted against the proposition. Antonym: *majority* (p 72).

minor sector NOUN /ˈmaɪ.nər ˈsɛk.tər/ the smaller of two circular sectors into which a circle has been divided. Antonym: *major sector* (p 72).

minuend NOUN /ˈmɪn.juˌɛnd/ a number or expression from which a value is subtracted. Formula: **minuend − subtrahend = difference.**

minus /ˈmaɪ.nəs/
1) PREPOSITION subtract from. Example: **5 minus 2** means $5 - 2$.
2) ADJECTIVE negative. Example: **minus 5** means -5.

minus or plus PREPOSITION /ˈmaɪ.nəs ɔr plʌs/ an operator than can be either addition or can be subtraction. If the first $\pm$ is taken to be addition, then the $\mp$ is taken to be subtraction. If the first $\pm$ is taken to be subtraction, then the $\mp$ is taken to be addition. Notation: $\mp$. Example: $3 \mp 4 = -1$ or 7. See also *plus or minus* (p 89).

minus sign NOUN /ˈmaɪ.nəs saɪn/ the symbol '−' which represents subtraction (Example: $3 - 1 = 2$) or negation (Example: -5).

minute NOUN /ˈmɪ.nɪt/
1) a unit of measure of time. Abbreviation: m, min. Formulas: **1 minute = 60 seconds. 1 hour = 60 minutes.**
2) a unit of measure of rotation. Formulas: **60 arc minutes = 1 arc degree. 1 arc minute = 60 arc seconds.** Synonym: *arc minute*. Notation: '.

minute hand NOUN /ˈmɪ.nɪt hænd/ the longer hand on an analog clock that points to the number of minutes after the hour.

mirror VERB /ˈmɪr.ər/ see *reflect* (p 97).

mirror image NOUN /ˈmɪr.ər ˈɪ.mɪdʒ/ reversed from left to right as if seen in a mirror. Synonym: *reflection* (p 97).

mixed ADJECTIVE /mɪkst/ containing more than one type of object.

mixed decimal NOUN /mɪkst ˈdɛs.məl/ a decimal numeral with a whole part and a decimal part. Example: 3.69.

mixed number NOUN /mɪkst ˈnʌm.bər/ a whole number and a proper fraction together. Example: $1\frac{1}{2} = 1.5$.

ml ABBREVIATION milliliter.

mm ABBREVIATION millimeter.

MM ABBREVIATION million.

mnemonic NOUN /nɪˈmɒ.nɪk/ a mental device designed to help people remember something. Example: SOHCAHTOA (p 106).

mo ABBREVIATION month.

Möbius, August Ferdinand PERSON /ˈmœ.bi.ʊs ɔˈgʌst ˈfɜr.dn.ˌænd/ (1790—1868) a German mathematician remembered for the Möbius strip.

August Möbius

Möbius band NOUN /ˈmœ.bi.əs bænd/ see *Möbius strip* (p 76).

Möbius strip NOUN /ˈmœ.bi.əs strɪp/ a 3-dimensional geometric figure with one side and one edge. Synonym: *Möbius band*.

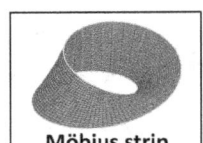
Möbius strip

mod. ABBREVIATION modulo n.

mod- PREFIX /mɒd/ modular.

mode NOUN /moʊd/ the value(s) that appear most frequently in a dataset. Example: The mode of $\{-4, 3, 3, 7, 14, 14, 27, 27, 27\}$ is 27. The number 27 appears three times in the set, more than any other number.

model /ˈmɒ.dl/
1) NOUN a graph, table, function or other device that approximates real world data or situations, or helps visualize a mathematical relationship. Example: an exponential growth equation models unrestricted bacteria growth.
2) VERB to make a graph, table, function or other device that approximates real world data or situations, or helps visualize a mathematical relationship.

model breakdown NOUN /ˈmɒ.dl ˈbreɪk.ˌdaʊn/ a point after which a model no longer accurately reflects the data.

modeling NOUN /ˈmɒ.dəl.ɪŋ/ the act or process of making a graph, table, function or other device that approximates real world data or situations, or helps visualize a mathematical relationship.

modeling process NOUN /ˈmɒ.dəl.ɪŋ ˈprɒ.sɛs/ (British English) /ˈmɒd.əl.ɪŋ ˈproʊ.sɛs/ a process for finding a solution by creating a mathematical formula. The steps of the modeling process are: 1) verify the real world problem, 2) create a verbal description, 3) translate the verbal description into mathematics language, 4) state the problem in mathematical terms.

modern ADJECTIVE /ˈmɒ.dərn/ based on complete axiomatic system(s). Example: modern geometry.

modern algebra NOUN /ˈmɒ.dərn ˈæl.dʒə.brə/ algebra based on set theory, including groups. See *abstract algebra* (p 7).

modern geometry NOUN /ˈmɒ.dərn dʒiˈɒm.ɪ.tri/ geometry based on complete axiomatic systems.

modular ADJECTIVE /ˈmɒdʒ.ə.lər/ having to do with modular arithmetic.

modular arithmetic NOUN /ˈmɒ.dʒə.lər əˈrɪθ.mə.tɪk/ an arithmetic on numbers that wraps around and begins again at 0; an arithmetic that uses the remainders after division. Example: $(3 + 4) \mod 5 = 7 \mod 5 = 2$. Synonym: *clock arithmetic*.

modulo PREPOSITION /ˈmɒ.dʒə.ˌloʊ/ having to do with modular arithmetic.

modulo n NOUN /ˈmɒ.dʒə.ˌloʊ ən/ the remainder of division by n. Notation: *mod*. Math definition: Given integers $a \neq 0$, $n \neq 0$ and $c \geq 0$, $a \mod n = c$ if and only if $c < |n|$ and for some integer d, $a \div n = dRc$. Example: $17 \mod 5 = 2$ since $17 \div 5 = 3R2$. Synonym: *remainder* (p 98).

modulus NOUN /ˈmɒ.dʒə.ləs/
1) the base used to compute congruence modulo n. Example: the 5 in $7 \mod 5 = 2$.
2) (British English) see *absolute value* (p 7).
3) (complex numbers) see *absolute value* (p 7).

mol ABBREVIATION mole.

mole NOUN /moʊl/ a unit of measure of the amount of a substance. Abbreviation: *mol*.

moment NOUN /ˈmoʊ.mənt/ see *moment of inertia*.

moment of inertia NOUN /ˈmoʊ.mənt ʌv ɪˈnɜr.ʃə/ a value describing the torque required to produce a specific circular acceleration of a solid.

mon- PREFIX /mɒn/ one; single.

monic ADJECTIVE /ˈmɒ.nɪk/ having a leading (implied) coefficient of 1. Example: monic polynomial; $x^3 - 2x + 3$.

monic equation NOUN /ˈmɒ.nɪk ɪˈkweɪ.ʃən/ a monic polynomial set equal to either zero or a dependent variable. Example: $x^2 - 3 = 0$.

monic polynomial NOUN /ˈmɒ.nɪk ˌpɒl.əˈnoʊ.mi.əl/ a polynomial where the leading coefficient is 1. Example: $x^2 + 3x - 3$.

monomial NOUN /mɒˈnoʊ.mi.əl/ a polynomial with only one term; any polynomial expression that does not include addition or subtraction. Formula: ax^n, $n > 0$, $n \in \mathbb{N}$. Examples: $3x^2$, $4x^2y^3z$. Antonym: *multinomial* (p 76).

monotonic ADJECTIVE /ˌmɒ.noʊˈtɒn.ɪk/ increasing or decreasing throughout, and does not oscillate. Example: monotonic sequence.

monotonic sequence NOUN /ˌmɒ.noʊˈtɒn.ɪk ˈsi.kwəns/ a sequence that continually increases or decreases, and does not oscillate. Example: 1, 2, 4, 8, ...

month NOUN /mʌnθ/ a unit of measure of time. Formulas: 1 month = 28, 29, 30, or 31 days. 12 months = 1 year. 1 month ≈ 4.3 weeks. Abbreviation: *mo*.

more ADJECTIVE /moʊr/
1) in addition to. Keyword for addition. Example: Ray has ten more.
2) greater than. Example: Lucia has more apples than Jeff.

most ADJECTIVE /moʊst/ greatest amount. Example: Who has the most apples?

motion NOUN /ˈmoʊ.ʃən/ the act of changing location.

mph ABBREVIATION miles per hour.

m/s ABBREVIATION meters per second.

multi- PREFIX /ˈmʌl.tɪ/
1) many. Example: multilateral.
2) more than one. Example: multiple bar graph.
3) more than two.
4) having to do with multiplication. Example: multiple.

multilateral ADJECTIVE /ˌmʌl.tɪˈlæ.tər.l/ having many sides.

multinomial NOUN /ˌmʌl.tɪˈnoʊ.mi.əl/ a polynomial with two or more terms. Example: $2x + 1$. Antonym: *monomial* (p 76).

multiple /ˈmʌl.tə.pəl/
1) NOUN the product of two quantities, especially integers. Example: 15 is a multiple of 5 since $5 \cdot 3 = 15$.
2) ADJECTIVE more than one. Example: multiple bar graph.
3) NOUN many times.

multiple bar graph NOUN /ˈmʌl.tə.pəl bɑr græf/ a bar graph with multiple bars grouped together that is useful for comparing data.

multiple line graph NOUN /ˈmʌl.tə.pəl laɪn græf/ a line graph with multiple lines that is useful for comparing data.

multiple root NOUN /ˈmʌl.tə.pəl rut/ a root that happens more than once. Since the roots of $(x-1)(x-1)(x+2)$ are 1, 1, and -2; 1 is a multiple root.

multiplicand NOUN /ˌmʌl.tə.plɪˈkænd/ a number or expression that is to be multiplied. Formula: **multiplicand × multiplier = product**. Example: $a \times b = c$, a is the multiplicand.

multiplication NOUN /ˌmʌl.tə.plɪˈkeɪ.ʃən/ the process of repeated addition. Notation: '×' and '·'. Formula: **multiplicand × multiplier = product**. Example: $2 \times 3 = 2 + 2 + 2 = 6$.
Inverse: division (p 41). See also Properties of Multiplication (p 125), Multiplication Facts (p 124).

multiplication fact NOUN /ˌmʌl.tə.plɪˈkeɪ.ʃən fækt/ two integers and the result of their multiplication. Example: $2 \times 3 = 6$. See also Multiplication Facts (p 124).

multiplication of polynomials NOUN /ˌmʌl.tə.plɪˈkeɪ.ʃən ʌv ˌpɒ.ləˈnoʊ.mi.əlz/ to multiply two polynomials, multiply each term of the first polynomial by each term of the second polynomial, then add like terms.

multiplication principle NOUN /ˌmʌl.tə.plɪˈkeɪ.ʃən ˈprɪn.sə.pəl/ see counting principle (p 32).

Multiplication Principle of Counting NOUN /ˌmʌl.tə.plɪˈkeɪ.ʃən ˈprɪn.sə.pəl ʌv ˈkaʊn.tɪŋ/ see counting principle (p 32).

Multiplication Property of Equality NOUN /ˌmʌl.tə.plɪˈkeɪ.ʃən ˈprɒ.pər.ti ʌv ɪˈkwɒl.ɪ.ti/ both sides of an equation can be multiplied by the same nonzero value without changing the truth value of the equation. Math definition: For any real or complex numbers a, b and $c \neq 0$; if $a = b$ then $ac = bc$ and if $a \neq b$ then $ac \neq bc$.

Multiplication Property of Inequality NOUN /ˌmʌl.tə.plɪˈkeɪ.ʃən ˈprɒ.pər.ti ʌv ˌɪn.ɪˈkwɒ.lɪ.ti/ if both sides of an inequality are multiplied by the same positive value, the truth value of the inequality does not change. If both sides of an inequality are multiplied by the same negative value, '>' flips to '<' and '<' flips to '>'. Math definition: For any real or complex numbers a, b; if $a < b$ and $c > 0$ then $a \cdot c < b \cdot c$; if $a > b$ and $c > 0$ then $a \cdot c > b \cdot c$. If $a < b$ and $c < 0$ then $a \cdot c > b \cdot c$; if $a > b$ and $c < 0$ then $a \cdot c < b \cdot c$.

multiplication sign NOUN /ˌmʌl.tə.plɪˈkeɪ.ʃən saɪn/ one of the symbols '×' or '·', used to indicate multiplication. Important: In multiplication of vectors, '×' has a different meaning than '·'. Synonym: *times sign*.

multiplicative ADJECTIVE /ˈmʌl.tə.plɪˌkeɪ.tɪv/ having to do with multiplication. Example: multiplicative identity.

multiplicative identity NOUN /ˈmʌl.tə.plɪˌkeɪ.tɪv aɪˈdɛn.tɪ.ti/ the number 1 that, when multiplied by any real number, gives a product equal to the original number. Formula: $a \cdot 1 = 1 \cdot a = a$.

multiplicative inverse NOUN /ˈmʌl.tə.plɪˌkeɪ.tɪv ˈɪn.vɜrs/ a number that, when multiplied by its inverse, gives 1. The multiplicative inverse of a is $\frac{1}{a}$, $a \neq 0$, because $a \cdot \frac{1}{a} = \frac{a}{a} = 1$. Synonym: *reciprocal* (p 96).

multiplicity NOUN /ˌmʌl.təˈplɪ.sɪ.ti/
1) the state of being a multiple.
2) the number of times an object occurs. Example: If an object occurs 3 times, it has a multiplicity of 3.

multiplier NOUN /ˈmʌl.təˌplaɪ.ər/ a number by which another number is multiplied. Formula: **multiplicand × multiplier = product**. Example: $3 \times 2 = 6$.

multiply VERB /ˈmʌl.təˌplaɪ/ add repeatedly; to find a product of two or more factors. Example: $2 \times 4 = \underbrace{2+2+2+2}_{4 \text{ times}} = 8$. Notation: · or ×.
Inverse: *divide*.

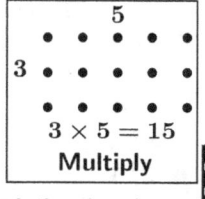

multiplying by 0 See 0, Property of Multiplication by (p 6).

multiplying by 1 See 1, Property of Multiplication by (p 6).

multistage sampling NOUN /ˌmʌl.tɪˈsteɪdʒ ˈsæm.plɪŋ/ a sampling that uses multiple sampling methods.

multistep ADJECTIVE /ˌmʌl.tiˈstɛp/ requiring more than two steps to solve.

multistep equation NOUN /ˌmʌl.tiˈstɛp ɪˈkweɪ.ʒən/ an equation that takes more than 2 steps to solve. Example: $2x - 2 = x + 4 \longrightarrow 2x = x + 6 \longrightarrow x = 6$.

multivariable ADJECTIVE /ˌmʌl.tiˈvɛər.i.ə.bəl/ input is made up of multiple numbers. Example: $f(x, y) = 2xy$.

multivariate ADJECTIVE /ˌmʌl.tɪˈvɛər.i.ɪt/ (statistics) having more than one variate or variable.

mutually exclusive ADJECTIVE /ˈmju.tʃu.ə.li ɪkˈsklu.sɪv/
1) (sets) none of the sets includes any of the others.
2) (events) if one of the events happens the others cannot happen. Example: in a single flip of a coin, heads and tails are mutually exclusive events.

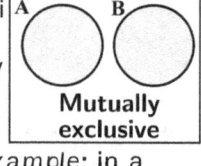

N

n ABBREVIATION nano-. 10^{-9}. Example: $5 \text{ ns} = 5 \times 10^{-9}$ seconds. Synonym: *billionth*.

n- PREFIX /ən/
1) any positive integer can be substituted. Example: n-gon.
2) not. Example: nand.

nand NOUN /nænd/ a combination of **not** and **and**. Notation: ↑. Math definition:
$A \uparrow B \equiv \neg (A \wedge B)$,
$A \text{ nand } B \equiv \text{not} (A \text{ and } B)$.

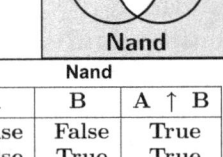

Nand

A	B	A ↑ B
False	False	True
False	True	True
True	False	True
True	True	False

nano- PREFIX /ˈnæ.noʊ/ one billionth. $10^{-9} = 0.000000001$. Abbreviation: n. Example: **6 nanometers = 6×10^{-9} meters**. Synonym: billionth (p 17).

natural ADJECTIVE /ˈnæ.tʃrəl/
1) related to nature.
2) existing in nature. Example: natural number.
3) based on Euler's number e.

natural exponential function NOUN /ˈnæ.tʃrəl ˌɛks.poʊˈnɛn.ʃəl ˈfʌŋk.ʃən/ an exponential function with base e. Formula: $y = e^x$.

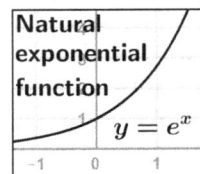

natural logarithm NOUN /ˈnæ.tʃrəl ˈlɔ.gə.rɪð.əm/ a logarithm with base e. Abbreviation: ln. Notation: $\ln x$, or $\log_e x$. Important: In engineering, the natural log is written $\log x$. Math definition: $\ln x \equiv \log_e x$, $\ln x = \int_1^x \frac{1}{x} dx$.

natural number NOUN /ˈnæ.tʃrəl ˈnʌm.bər/ a positive whole number. Notation: $\mathbb{N}, \mathbb{Z}^+$. Math definition: $\mathbb{N} \equiv 1, 2, 3, 4, \cdots$. Synonyms: counting number, positive integer (p 90).

nautical mile NOUN /ˈnɔ.tɪ.kəl maɪl/ a unit of measure of distance used for ocean-going vessels. Formulas: **1 nautical mile = 1.852 kilometers. 1 nautical mile ≈ 1.15 miles.**

n-dimensional ADJECTIVE /ɛn dɪˈmɛn.ʃə.nl/ having **n** dimensions. Example: a 3-dimensional solid.

near ADVERB /nɪər/ close to in distance, time, or value.

near double NOUN /nɪər ˈdʌ.bəl/ see double plus one (p 42).

nearest ADJECTIVE /ˈnɪər.ɪst/ the one closest to something in distance, time or value.

necessary ADJECTIVE /ˈnɛ.sə.sɛr.i/
1) must be true for the rest to be valid.
2) required.

necessary condition NOUN /ˈnɛ.sə.sɛr.i kənˈdɪ.ʃən/ a condition that must be true; a condition that is required.

negate VERB /nɪˈgeɪt/
1) to take the negative of a number.
2) to perform logical negation (**not P**).

negation NOUN /nɪˈgeɪ.ʃən/
1) taking the negative of a number. Example: the negation of a is $-a$.
2) logical not; change the truth value of a logical or Boolean value. Notation: '¬' or 'not'. Synonym: not (p 80).

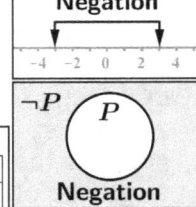

Negation

A	¬A
False	True
True	False

negative /ˈnɛ.gə.tɪv/
1) NOUN additive inverse of. Example: negative x is $-x$.
2) NOUN a number less than zero. Example: -5. Antonym: nonnegative (p 79).
3) ADJECTIVE expressing negation. Example: negative number.
4) ADJECTIVE in a negative direction.
5) ADJECTIVE an angle measured in a clockwise direction. Notation: -. Antonym: positive (p 90).

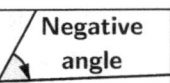

Negative Angle Identities NOUN /ˈnɛ.gə.tɪv æŋ.gəl aɪˈdɛn.tɪ.tiz/ see Even-Odd Identities (p 46).

negative correlation NOUN /ˈnɛ.gə.tɪv ˌkɔr.əˈleɪ.ʃən/ a relationship between variables such that when one increases, the other tends to decrease. Antonym: positive correlation (p 90).

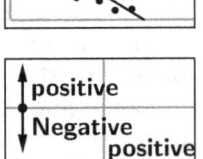

negative direction NOUN /ˈnɛ.gə.tɪv dɪˈrɛk.ʃən/ a direction opposite of positive. Example: depth is the negative of height. Antonym: positive direction (p 78).

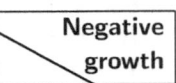

negative exponent NOUN /ˈnɛ.gə.tɪv ɪkˈspoʊ.nənt/ the reciprocal of. Math definition: $x^{-b} \equiv \frac{1}{x^b}$, $x \neq 0$. Example: $2^{-3} \equiv \frac{1}{2^3} = \frac{1}{8} = 0.125$.

negative growth NOUN /ˈnɛ.gə.tɪv groʊθ/ decreases at a constant rate each time period. Formula: $y = mx + b$ where $m < 0$ is the growth rate and b is the initial value when $x = 0$. See constant growth (p 28).

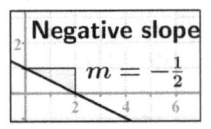

negative reciprocal NOUN /ˈnɛ.gə.tɪv rɪˈsɪp.rə.kəl/ the negative reciprocal of a is $-\frac{1}{a}$. See also: reciprocal (p 96).

negative sign NOUN /ˈnɛ.gə.tɪv saɪn/ the symbol '−' which indicates negation. Examples: $-x$, -5.

negative slope NOUN /ˈnɛ.gə.tɪv sloʊp/ a slope that slants downward from left to right; a slope that can be described by a negative number. Antonym: positive slope (p 90).

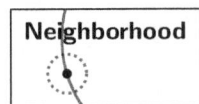

neighborhood NOUN /ˈneɪ.bɔr.hʊd/ everything contained in a small disk whose center is a particular point.

net /nɛt/
1) NOUN see geometric net (p 53).
2) NOUN see network (p 78).
3) ADJECTIVE what is left after a deduction. Example: net profit.

Net Change Theorem NOUN /nɛt tʃeɪndʒ ˈθɪ.ə.rəm/ the integral of a rate of change equals the net change. Math definition: $\int_a^b F'(x) dx = F(b) - F(a)$.

net profit NOUN /nɛt ˈprɑ.fɪt/ profit left after all expenses are paid.

net weight NOUN /nɛt weɪt/ the weight of product not including the packaging material.

network NOUN /ˈnɛt.wɜrk/ a set of objects that are connected together. Each object is called a node and each connection is called a path.

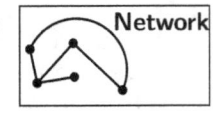

network graph NOUN /ˈnɛt.wɜrk græf/ a drawing of a network where dots represent nodes and curved or straight line segments represent paths.

Newton, Sir Isaac PERSON /ˈnu.tn sɜr ˈaɪ.sək/ (1642—1726) an English mathematician, physicist, astronomer, theologian, and author who is widely recognized as one of

Sir Isaac Newton

the most influential scientists of all time and as a key figure in the scientific revolution.

Newton's law of cooling NOUN /'nu.tnz lɑ ʌv 'ku.lɪŋ/ describes the rate of cooling of an object in a constant environment. *Formula:*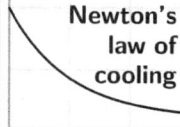
$T(t) = T_{env} + (T_0 - T_{env})e^{\frac{-t}{r}}$ where T is the temperature of the object, T_0 is the initial temperature of the object, r is the cooling rate of the object, and T_{env} is the temperature of the environment.

Newton's law of universal gravitation NOUN /'nu.tnz lɑ ʌv ˌyu.nəˈvɜr.səl ˌgræ.vɪˈteɪ.ʃən/ every particle attracts every other particle in the universe with a force that is directly proportional to the product of their masses and inversely proportional to the square of the distance between their centers. *Formula:* $F = G\frac{m_1 m_2}{r^2}$

Newton's method NOUN /'nu.tnz 'mɛ.θəd/ a root-finding algorithm which produces successively better approximations to the roots (zeroes) of a real-valued function. *Synonym: Newton-Raphson method. Formula:* $x_{n+1} = x_n + \frac{f(x_n)}{f'(x_n)}$.

n-gon NOUN /'ɛn.gɒn/ an n-sided polygon. *Example:* a 14-gon is a 14-sided polygon.

nickel NOUN /'nɪ.kəl/ (USA) a coin with a value of five cents, $\frac{1}{20}$ of a dollar. *Synonym: half-dime.*

nine ADJECTIVE, NOUN /naɪn/ the number or digit 9.

nineteen ADJECTIVE, NOUN /naɪnˈtin/ the number 19.

ninety ADJECTIVE, NOUN /'naɪn.ti/ the number 90.

ninth ADJECTIVE /naɪnθ/
1) coming in position 9 in an ordered list. *Notation:* 9th.
2) one of nine equal parts; $\frac{1}{9}$.

no correlation ADJECTIVE /noʊ ˌkɔ.rəˈleɪ.ʃən/ no significant relations exists between two variables. A value of one of the variables cannot be used to predict the value of the other.

node NOUN /noʊd/ an object in a network that may be connected to other nodes by a path. Nodes are usually drawn as dots. *Synonym: junction.*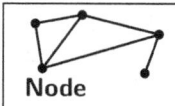

Noether, Amalie Emmy PERSON /'nø:tɐ ɑˈmɑl.iə ˈɪ.mi/ (1882—1935) a mathematician and physicist known for her work on the calculus of variations, which lead to Noether's Theorem.

nominal ADJECTIVE /'nɒ.mə.nl/
1) in name only. *Example:* nominal number.
2) stated. *Example:* nominal interest rate.

nominal APR NOUN /'nɒ.mə.nl eɪ pi ɑr/ annualized interest rate without the effect of any fees.

nominal interest rate NOUN /'nɒ.mə.nl 'ɪn.trɪst reɪt/ the stated interest rate before the effects of compounding are added in.

nominal number NOUN /'nɒ.mə.nl 'nʌm.bər/ a number that is used for identification only; a number that does not represent a quantity. *Examples:* zip codes; postal codes.

non- PREFIX /nɒn/ not. *Example:* noncollinear.

nona- PREFIX /'nɒ.nə/ nine. *Example:* nonagon.

nonagon NOUN /'nɒ.nəˌgɒn/ any polygon with 9 sides and 9 angles.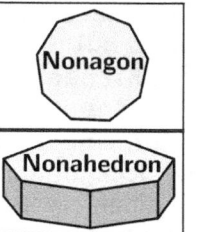

nonahedron NOUN /nɒ.nəˈhi.drən/ any polyhedron with nine faces. *Synonym: enneahedron. Plural:* nonahedra /nɒ.nəˈhi.drə/.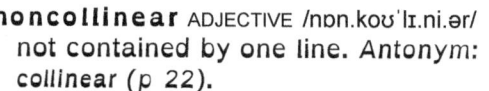

noncollinear ADJECTIVE /nɒn.koʊˈlɪ.ni.ər/ not contained by one line. *Antonym:* collinear (p 22).

noncoplanar ADJECTIVE /nɒn.koʊˈpleɪ.nər/ does not exist in a single plane. In the illustration, the line segment f is noncoplanar with e, d, and G. *Antonym:* coplanar (p 30).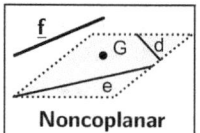

nondenumerable ADJECTIVE /nɒn.dɪˈnu.mər.ə.bəl/ see uncountable (p 118).

nonary ADJECTIVE /'noʊ.nə.ri/ having to do with the number 9. *Example:* a nonary numeration system.

none PRONOUN /nʌn/
1) nothing.
2) not even one.
3) zero.

non-Euclidean geometry NOUN /nɒn.juˈklɪ.di.ən dʒiˈɒm.ɪ.tri/ one of several geometries that are not based on all of the basic five postulates of Euclidean geometry or their modern equivalents. *Examples:* elliptic geometry and hyperbolic geometry. *Antonym:* Euclidean geometry (p 46).

noninvertible ADJECTIVE /nɒn.ɪnˈvɜr.tɪ.bl/ cannot be inverted. *Antonym:* invertible (p 65).

noninvertible matrix NOUN /nɒn.ɪnˈvɜr.tɪ.bl ˈmeɪ.trɪks/ a square matrix that has no inverse, that has a determinate of zero. *Antonym:* invertible matrix (p 65).

nonlinear ADJECTIVE /nɒnˈlɪ.ni.ər/
1) having terms with a degree greater than 1 or having operations other than arithmetic operations. *Examples:* $y = x^2$, $\sin x$.
2) not linear; not associated with a line. *Example:* nonlinear curve.
Antonym: linear (p 68).

nonlinear equation NOUN /nɒnˈlɪ.ni.ər ɪˈkweɪ.ʒən/ an equation that has terms with a degree greater than 1 or that has operations other than arithmetic operations. *Examples:* $y = 2x^2$, $y = \sin x$. *Antonym:* linear equation (p 69).

nonlinear relation NOUN /nɒnˈlɪ.ni.ər rɪˈleɪ.ʃən/ a relation between two variables that does not have a linear shape. *Antonym:* linear relation (p 69).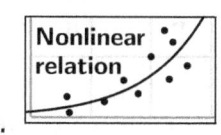

nonnegative ADJECTIVE /nɒnˈnɛ.gə.tɪv/ zero or positive; Math definition: $\{x \mid x \geq 0\}$ *Antonym:* negative (p 78).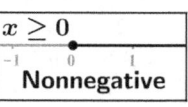

nonplanar ADJECTIVE /ˌnɒnˈpleɪ.nər/ not contained within a single plane. *Antonym:* planar (p 88).

nonplanar graph NOUN /ˌnɒnˈpleɪ.nər græf/ a network graph that cannot be drawn in a plane without the paths crossing. *Antonym:* planar graph (p 89).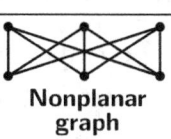

nonpositive NOUN /nɒnˈpɒ.zɪ.tɪv/ negative or zero. $\{x \mid x \leq 0\}$. Antonym: positive (p 90).

nonrepeating ADJECTIVE /nɒn.rɪˈpit.iŋ/ does not repeat. Antonym: repeating (p 98).

nonrepeating decimal NOUN /nɒn.rɪˈpit.iŋ ˈdɛs.məl/ a decimal that does not repeat a series of digits infinitely. Examples: an integer; an irrational number, **14.227**. Antonym: repeating decimal (p 98).

nonresponse NOUN /nɒn.rɪˈspɒns/ not returning a survey; not answering a question.

nonsampling error NOUN /nɒnˈsæm.plɪŋ ˈɛr.ər/ an error that results from a problem in the survey process. Examples: nonresponse, poorly worded question.

nonsingular matrix NOUN /nɒnˈsɪŋ.gjə.lər ˈmeɪ.trɪks/ a matrix that has an inverse; a matrix that can be inverted. Plural: nonsingular matrices. Antonym: singular matrix (p 106).

nonstandard ADJECTIVE /nɒnˈstæn.dərd/
1) not described in an accepted standard.
2) uncommon.
3) not generally accepted.
Antonym: standard (p 108).

nonstandard unit NOUN /nɒnˈstæn.dərd ˈju.nɪt/ a unit of measure that is not one of the custom or standard units of measure. Example: 3 fingers wide.

nonterminating ADJECTIVE /nɒnˈtɜr.mə.neɪt.iŋ/ not having an end. Example: nonterminating decimal. Antonym: terminating (p 113).

nonterminating decimal NOUN /nɒnˈtɜr.mə.neɪt.iŋ ˈdɛs.məl/ a decimal number whose digits go on forever; a decimal number that is a repeating decimal or an irrational number. Examples: $3.\overline{1} = 3.1111\cdots$, $\pi = 3.14159\ldots$. Antonym: terminating decimal (p 113).

nontrivial NOUN /nɒnˈtrɪ.vi.əl/ (linear systems) at least one of the variables has a nonzero solution.

nonzero ADJECTIVE /nɒnˈzɪə.roʊ/ either positive or negative, but not zero. Notation: $x \neq 0$. Math definition: $x < 0$ or $x > 0$ Antonym: zero (p 123).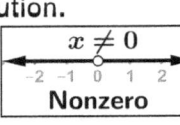

noon NOUN /nun/ the middle point of the day. 12:00 PM or 1200 zulu. Synonym: midday.

nor NOUN /nɔr/ NOT OR. A Boolean operator that returns true only when both operands are false. Notation: $A \downarrow B$. Math definition:
$A \text{ nor } B = A \downarrow B =$
$\text{not}\,(A \text{ or } B) =$
$\text{not } A \text{ and not } B = \neg(A \vee B)$.

Nor		
A	B	A ↓ B
False	False	True
False	True	False
True	False	False
True	True	False

norm NOUN /nɔrm/ see magnitude, definition 2 (p 71).

normal ADJECTIVE /ˈnɔr.məl/
1) perpendicular to. Example: normal to a curve. Synonym: perpendicular (p 87).
2) most common or regular. Example: normal distribution.

normal curve NOUN /ˈnɔr.məl kɜrv/ a curve shaped like a bell that shows the normal distribution of populations. Formula: $f(x) = \frac{1}{\rho\sqrt{2\pi}} e^{-\frac{1}{2}\left(\frac{x-\mu}{\rho}\right)^2}$ where μ is the mean of the distribution, and ρ is the 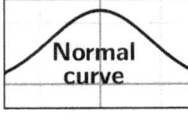 standard deviation of the distribution. Synonyms: bell curve, bell shaped curve, Gaussian curve.

normal distribution NOUN /ˈnɔr.məl dɪs.trɪˈbju.ʃən/ a distribution of statistical data that follows the shape of a normal curve. Synonym: Gaussian distribution, symmetric distribution (p 111). Antonym: bimodal distribution, skewed distribution (p 106). See also normal curve (p 80), standard normal distribution (p 109).

normalize VERB /ˈnɔr.mə.laɪz/ (vectors) to find a unit vector with the same direction as the given vector by dividing it by its magnitude. Notation: $\|\mathbf{v}\|$. Formula: $\|\mathbf{v}\| = \frac{\mathbf{v}}{|\mathbf{v}|}$.

normal line NOUN /ˈnɔr.məl laɪn/ see normal to a curve (p 80).

normal magic square NOUN /ˈnɔr.məl ˈmæ.dʒɪk skwɛər/ a magic square using the sequential numbers $1\ldots n$ where **n** is the number of cells. In a magic square, the rows, columns and diagonals of the magic square all add up to the same number. See also magic square (p 71).

normal to a curve NOUN /ˈnɔr.məl tu ə kɜrv/ a line that passes through a curve and is perpendicular to the tangent to the curve at that point.

north NOUN /nɔrθ/ in a direction towards the north pole, or the north magnetic pole. Antonym: south (p 107).

no solution ADJECTIVE /noʊ səˈlu.ʃən/ (system of equations) there exists no solution that satisfies all of the equations.

not ADVERB /nɒt/ a unary Boolean operator that returns false if the operand is true and true if the operand is false. Notation: $\neg$. Synonym: negation (p 78).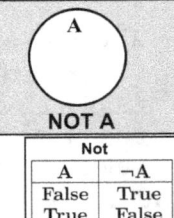

notation NOUN /noʊˈteɪ.ʃən/ a way to write things down using special signs or symbols. Example: interval notation. See Notations (p 3).

nothing NOUN /ˈnʌ.θɪŋ/
1) not one.
2) zero.

naught NOUN /nɔt/ zero.

n-space NOUN /ɛn speɪs/ an n-dimensional geometric construct in which other geometric objects can be placed. Example: 3-space is a 3-dimensional space that can contain geometric solids.

nth partial sum NOUN /ɛnθ ˈpar.ʃəl sʌm/ the sum of the first **n** terms of an infinite series.

nth root NOUN /ɛnθ rut/ a value that, when multiplied by itself **n** times, equals the number. Formula: $\sqrt[n]{x} = x^{\frac{1}{n}}$. Math definition: $y = \sqrt[n]{x}$ if and only if $y^n = x$, $y \geq 0$ if **n** is even, $y \in \mathbb{Z}$ if **n** is odd. Example: $\sqrt[3]{27} = 3$ since $3^3 = 27$.

nth term rule NOUN /ɛnθ tɜrm rul/ a formula for determining the nth term of a linear sequence. If **n** is the term number (starting at zero), **d** is the constant difference, and **b** is the value of term **0**, then

$term_n = d \cdot n + b$.

n-tuple NOUN /ɛn'tu.pəl/ a set of **n** coordinates written like $(x_1, x_2, x_3, \cdots, x_n)$. Example: 3-tuple $(3, 0, 2)$.

null ADJECTIVE /nʌl/
1) having to do with zero. Example: null vector.
2) empty; has zero elements or members. Example: null set.

null element NOUN /nʌl 'ɛ.lə.mənt/ an element of a set that, when multiplied by any member of the set, returns itself. Example: $a \cdot 0 = 0$; 0 is the null element for integers and real numbers.

null matrix NOUN /nʌl 'meɪ.trɪks/ see zero matrix (p 123).

null set NOUN /nʌl sɛt/ see empty set (p 43).

null vector NOUN /nʌl 'vɛk.tər/ see zero vector (p 123).

number NOUN /'nʌm.bər/ how many or how much; a quantity. Important: A number is an abstract quantity. A numeral is a representation of a number.

number cube NOUN /'nʌm.bər kjub/ see die (p 37).

number line NOUN /'nʌm.bər laɪn/ a line where each point on the line represents a real number. See also Ruler Postulate (p 101).

Number of Real Zeros Theorem NOUN /'nʌm.bər ʌv riəl 'zɪə.roʊz 'θɪ.ə.rəm/ a polynomial function cannot have more real zeros than its degree.

number pattern NOUN /'nʌm.bər pæt.ərn/ see sequence (p 103).

number sense NOUN /'nʌm.bər sɛns/ an understanding of numbers, their characteristics and operations on numbers.

number sentence NOUN /'nʌm.bər sɛn'tɛns/ an expression or equation that contains only numbers and operators. Example: $3 + 6 = 9$.

number theory NOUN /'nʌm.bər 'θɪər.i/ the study of the properties of integers, including divisibility.

numeral NOUN /'nu.mər.əl/ symbols used together to represent a number. Example: **124.3**.

numeration NOUN /ˌnu.məˈreɪ.ʃən/
1) how numbers are written; the representation of numbers. Example: decimal numeration.
2) the act of counting.

numeration system NOUN /ˌnu.məˈreɪ.ʃən 'sɪs.təm/ a way to represent numbers. Example: decimal numeration system.

numerator NOUN /'nu.məˌreɪ.tər/ the top half of a fraction; the dividend. Math definition: $\frac{\text{numerator}}{\text{denominator}} = \text{numerator} \div \text{denominator}$. Notation: $\frac{\text{numerator}}{\text{denominator}}$. Example: in $\frac{3}{7}$, the numerator is 3. Synonym: dividend (p 41).

numeric ADJECTIVE /nu'mɛr.ɪk/ having to do with or containing numbers. Example: numeric data. Synonym: numerical.

numerical ADJECTIVE /nu'mɛr.ɪ.kəl/ see numeric (p 81).

numerical analysis NOUN /nu'mɛr.ɪ.kəl æ'næ.lɪ.sɪs/ a branch of mathematics that deals with approximation and error.

numerically ADVERB /nu'mɛr.ɪ.kli/ using numbers.

numeric data NOUN /nu'mɛr.ɪk 'deɪ.tʌ/ data whose values are numbers. Singular: numeric datum /nu'mɛr.ɪk deɪ.tʌm/.

numeric expression NOUN /nu'mɛr.ɪk ɪk'sprɛ.ʃən/ an expression with numbers, but no variables. Example: $3(4 + 2)$.

numerical integration NOUN /nu'mɛr.ɪ.kəl ˌɪn.tɪˈgreɪ.ʃən/ algorithms for calculating the numerical value of a definite integral. Notation: $\int_a^b f(x)dx$.

O

ob- PREFIX /ɒb/, /oʊb/
1) towards
2) inversely.

obelus NOUN /'ɒb.ə.ləs/ the symbol for division. Notation: $\div$. Synonym: division sign (p 41).

object NOUN /'ɒb.dʒɛkt/ something being considered; an arbitrary entity.

objective NOUN /'ɒb.dʒɛk.tɪv/ a goal; what one is trying to accomplish.

oblate ADJECTIVE /'ɒ.bleɪt/ being flattened at the top and bottom; being flattened at the poles. Example: because of centrifugal force caused by its spin, the Earth is slightly oblate.

oblate spheroid NOUN /'ɒ.bleɪt 'sfɪər.ɔɪd/ a sphere that is flattened at the poles; an ellipsoid that can be made by rotating an ellipse around its minor axis. Antonym: prolate spheroid (p 92).

oblique ADJECTIVE /oʊ'blik/
1) (angles) not a right angle nor a multiple of a right angle. Antonym: right angle (p 100).
2) neither perpendicular nor parallel. Example: oblique lines.
3) neither vertical nor horizontal.
4) (geometric solid) having an altitude that does not pass through the center of the base(s). Example: oblique cone.
5) slanting or sloping. Synonym: skew (p 106). Synonym: slant (p 81). Antonym: right (p 99).

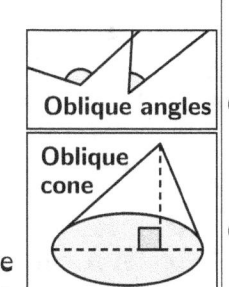

oblique asymptote NOUN /oʊ'blik 'æ.sɪmˌtoʊt/ an asymptote that approaches a line $y = mx + b, m \neq 0$. Antonyms: horizontal asymptote (p 57), vertical asymptote (p 121).

oblique coordinate system NOUN /oʊ'blik koʊ'ɔr.dn.ɪt 'sɪs.təm/ a coordinate system whose axes are not perpendicular to each other. Antonym: rectangular coordinate system (p 96).

oblique line NOUN /oʊ'blik laɪn/ see skew line (p 106).

oblong /'ɑb.lɔŋ/
1) NOUN a rectangle that is not a square.
2) ADJECTIVE in the shape of a rectangle, but not a square.

observation NOUN /'ɑb.sərˌveɪ.ʃən/
1) watching what happens and writing down the results without trying to influence what happens.
2) a single row of data.

observational ADJECTIVE /'ɑb.sərˌveɪ.ʃə.nl/ based on watching what happens without trying to influence what happens. Example: observational data.

Antonym: experimental (p 47).

observational data NOUN /ˈɑb.sərˌveɪ.ʃə.nl ˈdeɪ.tʌ/ data collected by watching what happens without trying to influence what happens. *Example:* Watching a gorilla and writing down the gorilla's behavior. *Antonym: experimental data* (p 47).

observational study NOUN /ˈɑb.sərˌveɪ.ʃə.nl ˈstʌ.di/ a study where the administrators watch what happens without trying to influence what happens.

observe VERB /ˌəbˈsərv/ to watch with attention to detail.

observed frequency NOUN /ˌəbˈsərvd fri.kwɪn.si/ the number of times an event happened in a probability experiment.

observer NOUN /ˌəbˈsər.vər/
1) a person or object from whose point of view an angle or distance is measured.
2) a person collecting data in an observational study.

obtuse ADJECTIVE /əbˈtus/ being or having an angle between 90° and 180° exclusive, between $\frac{\pi}{2}$ rad. and π rad exclusive.

obtuse angle NOUN /əbˈtus ˈæŋ.gəl/ an angle that measures between 90° and 180°. *Math definition:* angle θ is obtuse if and only if $90° < \theta < 180°, \frac{\pi}{2} < \theta < \pi$.

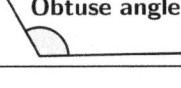

obtuse triangle NOUN /əbˈtus ˈtraɪ.æŋ.gəl/ a triangle that has exactly one obtuse angle.

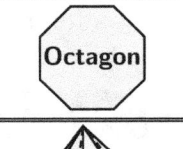

o'clock ADVERB /əˈklɑk/ hour of day according to a clock. *Example:* 5 o'clock in the evening.

octa- PREFIX /ˈɑk.tə/ eight.

octagon NOUN /ˈɑk.təˌgɑn/ any eight-sided polygon.

octahedron NOUN /ˌɑk.təˈhi.drən/ any eight-faced polyhedron. *Example:* heptagonal pyramid. *Plural:* octahedra /ˌɑk.təˈhi.drə/.

octal ADJECTIVE /ˈɑk.tl/ having to do with a base 8 numeration system. *Example:* octal digit.

octal digit NOUN /ˈɑk.tl ˈdɪ.dʒɪt/ one of eight digits used in an octal numeration system: 0, 1, 2, 3, 4, 5, 6, 7.

octal numeration system NOUN /ˈɑk.tl ˌnu.məˈreɪ.ʃən ˈsɪs.təm/ a base 8 numeration system that uses the digits 0-7 and whose place values are exponents of 8. *Example:* $213_8 = 2 \times 8^2 + 1 \times 8 + 3 = 128 + 8 + 3 = 139_{10}$.

octant NOUN /ˈɑk.tənt/ in a 3-dimensional rectangular coordinate system, one of eight sections into which the coordinate space is divided by the perpendicular planes containing the x, y, and z axes.

odd ADJECTIVE /ɑd/
1) (integers) not divisible by 2.
2) having to do with an integer that is not a multiple of 2.
3) (figures) having reflective symmetry about a point.
4) having a property related to oddness.
Antonym: even (p 46).

Odd Degree Real Root Theorem NOUN /ɑd dəˈgri riəl rut ˈθɪ.ə.rəm/ if a polynomial has real coefficients and has a degree that is odd, then it has at least one real root. *Example:* $3x^3 - x^2 + x - 3$.

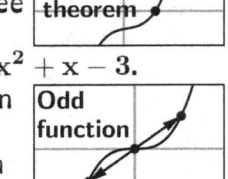

odd function NOUN /ɑd ˈfʌŋk.ʃən/ function that is symmetric about the origin; a function where $f(-x) = -f(x)$. *Math definition:* $f(x)$ is an odd function if and only if $f(-x) = -f(x)$ for all x in the domain of $f(x)$. *Example:* $f(x) = x^3, (-x)^3 = -x^3 \to -x^3 = -x^3$, so $f(-x) = -f(x)$.

odd node NOUN /ɑd noʊd/ a node of a network graph that has an odd number of paths connecting it to other nodes. *Antonym: even node* (p 46).

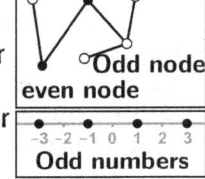

odd number NOUN /ɑd ˈnʌm.bər/ an integer that is not divisible by 2. *Math definition:* $\{x \mid x = 2k - 1, k \in \mathbb{Z}\}$. *Examples:* 1, –3, 11, 27. *Antonym: even number* (p 46).

odd polynomial NOUN /ɑd ˌpɑl.əˈnoʊ.mi.əl/ a polynomial that is an odd function. All odd polynomials have an odd degree, but not all polynomials with an odd degree are odd functions. *Example:* x^3.

odds NOUN /ɑdz/
1) the likelihood of an event happening.
2) an estimate of the probability that an event will happen.

odometer NOUN /oʊˈdɑm.ɪ.tər/ a device that shows or records distance traveled, usually on a car or truck.

omit VERB /oʊˈmɪt/ to leave out.

on average PHRASE /ɑn ˈæ.vrɪdʒ/ while the results of single experiments may differ, the more experiments one performs, the closer the average gets to that amount.

one ADJECTIVE, NOUN /wʌn/ the number or digit 1.

one and only one ADJECTIVE /wʌn ænd ˈoʊn.li wʌn/ unique; no other object exists with the same properties. *Synonym: exactly one.*

one-dimensional ADJECTIVE /wʌn dɪˈmɛn.ʃə.nl/ having only one dimension; having length, but not width or height. *Example:* a line is one-dimensional. *Abbreviation:* 1-D.

one point perspective ADJECTIVE /wʌn pɔɪnt pərˈspɛk.tɪv/ a perspective drawing with one vanishing point.

one-sided limit NOUN /wʌn ˈsaɪ.dɪd ˈlɪ.mɪt/ a limit that exists on one side of a discontinuity, but not the other. *Notation:* $\lim_{x \to -c} f(x)$ (from the left), $\lim_{x \to +c} f(x)$ (from the right).

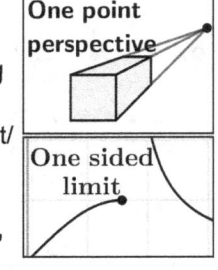

one step equation NOUN /wʌn stɛp ɪˈkweɪ.ʒən/ an equation that can be solved using one operation. *Example:* $x + 1 = 3 \to x + 1 - 1 = 3 - 1 \to x = 3 - 1 \to x = 2$.

one-to-one correspondence NOUN /wʌn tu wʌn ˌkɔr.əˈspɑn.dəns/ a correspondence where every member of set A can be matched with exactly one member of set B and every

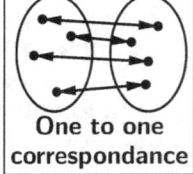

member of set **B** can be matched with exactly one member of set **A**. Synonym: bijection (p 16).

one-to-one function NOUN /wʌn tu wʌn ˈfʌŋk.ʃən/ a function that has exactly one output for each input, and exactly one input for each output. Math definition: $f(x)$ is one-to-one if and only if, for all distinct x_1, x_2 in the domain of $f(x)$, $f(x_1) \neq f(x_2)$ when $x_1 \neq x_2$. Synonym: bijection (p 16). Example: $y = x^3$.

one-to-one mapping see one-to-one correspondence (p 82).

op- PREFIX /ɒp/, /oʊp/
1) toward.
2) inversely.

open ADJECTIVE /ˈoʊ.pən/
1) (figure) a figure whose boundary cannot be traced from any point by any path and always return to the starting point without retracing.
2) (sets) a set is open if any part of the boundary of the set is not contained in the set.
3) (dot) having a hollow dot showing that a point is not included in the set.
4) (intervals) an interval that does not include both endpoints. Example: $-3 \geq x > 1$ is open since it does not include the endpoint 1.
5) a mathematical sentence with one or more numbers that are missing and are replaced with symbols. Example: $1 + ? = 5$.
Antonym: closed (p 21).

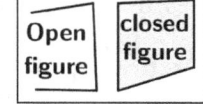

operand NOUN /ˈɒ.pər.ænd/ something on which an operation is performed. Example: In $3 + 4$, the operands are 3 and 4.

operation NOUN /ˌɒ.pərˈeɪ.ʃən/ a mathematical function performed on one or more operands. Example: in $3+4$, the operation is **addition**. Synonym: algebraic operation (p 9).

operations on functions NOUN /ˈfʌŋk.ʃən ˌɒ.pərˈeɪ.ʃənz/ see function operations (p 52).

operator NOUN /ˈɒ.pər.eɪ.tər/ a symbol representing a mathematical operation. Examples: '+', '−', '×', '÷'.

opposed ADJECTIVE /ɒˈpoʊzd/ on opposite sides of.

opposite /ˈɒ.pə.sɪt/
1) ADJECTIVE situated directly across from. Example: opposite side.
2) NOUN inverse of. Example: the opposite of a is -a.

Opposite Angle Congruence Theorem NOUN /ˈɒ.pə.sɪt ˈæn.gəl ˈkɒn.gru.əns ˈθɪ.ə.rəm/ if two angles of a triangle are congruent, then the sides opposite the congruent angles are also congruent.

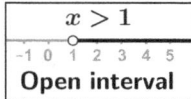

opposite isometry NOUN /ˈɒ.pə.sɪt aɪˈsɒm.ɪ.tri/ see indirect isometry (p 61).

opposite number NOUN /ˈɒ.pə.sɪt ˈnʌm.bər/ the negative of a number. Example: the opposite of 5 is -5; the opposite of -3 is 3. Synonym: additive inverse (p 8).

opposite rays noun /ˈɒ.pə.sɪt reɪz/ two rays with a common endpoint going in opposite directions.

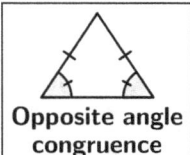

opposites NOUN /ˈɒ.pə.sɪts/ two things that are opposite each other.

opposite transformation NOUN /ˈɒ.pə.sɪt ˈtræns.fərˌmeɪ.ʃən/ a transformation that changes the orientation of a figure so that if the order of the points in the preimage is clockwise, the order of the points in the image is counterclockwise. Examples: reflection and glide reflection.

optical ADJECTIVE /ˈɒp.tɪ.kl/ having to do with the eye or with vision.

optical illusion NOUN /ˈɒp.tɪk.l ɪˈlu.ʃən/ a drawing or picture that 'tricks' the eye.

or CONJUNCTION /ɔr/ see disjunction (p 40).

orbit /ˈɔr.bɪt/
1) NOUN one revolution around an object.
2) VERB going around an object.

order /ˈɔr.dər/
1) NOUN the sequence in which events happen or operations are performed. Example: order of operations.
2) NOUN an arrangement of a set such that, for any element, it is known if another element comes before or after that element. Example: alphabetical order.
3) NOUN a relative ranking. Example: order of magnitude.
4) NOUN a number assigned to a property of an object indicating magnitude. Example: order of rotational symmetry.
5) VERB to place a set in order.
6) VERB to declare the order of the set.

ordered ADJECTIVE /ˈɔr.dərd/ having an order. A set is ordered if, for every distinct pair of elements a and b, exactly one of $a < b$, $a = b$ or $a > b$ is always true. Notation: $(a, b, c, \cdots)$ or $\langle a, b, c, \cdots \rangle$.

ordered list NOUN /ˈɔr.dərd lɪst/ a list of objects placed in a specific order.

ordered pair NOUN /ˈɔrd.ərd pɛər/ a set of two values where the order has a specific meaning: $(x, y) \neq (y, x)$. Example: $(8, 4)$.

ordered triple NOUN /ˈɔrd.ərd ˈtrɪ.pəl/ a set of three values where the order has a specific meaning. Example: $(-2, 3, 7)$.

ordering NOUN /ˈɔr.dər.ɪŋ/ the specific order of a set. Example: an alphabetic ordering.

order of accuracy NOUN /ˈɔr.dər ʌv æˈkjə.rə.si/ quantifies the rate of convergence of a numerical approximation of a differential equation to the exact solution into first order of accuracy, second order of accuracy, ... n^{th} order of accuracy.

order of magnitude NOUN /ˈɔr.dər ʌv ˈmæg.nɪˌtud/ the relative size of a number measured by the exponent of ten used for that number in scientific notation. Example: 6.4×10^5 is 3 orders of magnitude less than 2.7×10^8, since $8 - 5 = 3$.

order of operations NOUN /ˈɔr.dər ʌv ˌɒ.pərˈeɪ.ʃənz/ the order in which arithmetic operations are performed on expressions: 1) parenthesis, 2) exponents, 3) multiplication and division (left to right), 4) addition and subtraction (left to right). Mnemonic: **'please**

excuse my dear aunt sally', representing parentheses, exponentiation, multiplication and division, addition and subtraction.

order of rotational symmetry NOUN /ˈɔr.dər ʌv roʊˈteɪ.ʃə.nl ˈsɪ.mɪ.tri/ the number of distinct angles of rotation that show symmetry. Example: the order of rotational symmetry of a square about its center is 4.

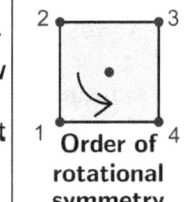

order property of addition NOUN /ˈɔr.dər ˈprɒ.pər.ti ʌv əˈdɪ.ʃən/ see Commutative Property of Addition (p 24).

order property of multiplication NOUN /ˈɔr.dər ˈprɒ.pər.ti ʌv ˌmʌl.tə.plɪˈkeɪ.ʃən/ see Commutative Property of Multiplication (p 24).

ordinal NOUN /ˈɔr.dn.əl/ an integer giving position in a list. Antonym: cardinal (p 19).

ordinal number NOUN /ˈɔr.dn.əl ˈnʌm.bər/ first, second, third, ...; 1st, 2nd, 3rd, ... used to describe the position of entries in an ordered set.

ordinate NOUN /ˈɔr.dɪ.nɑt/
1) the second entry in an ordered pair: (abscissa, ordinate); the y-value of a coordinate. Synonym: y-coordinate (p 123).
2) the value of a dependent variable. Antonym abscissa (p 6).

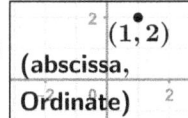

or function NOUN /ɔr ˈfʌŋk.ʃən/ see disjunction (p 40).

organize VERB /ˈɔr.gə.naɪz/ to arrange in a pattern.

orient VERB /ˈɔr.i.ənt/ to rotate an object so that it lies in a particular direction.

orientation NOUN /ˌɔr.i.ənˈteɪ.ʃən/ the rotation of an object relative to a space. Example: The orientation of a line can be vertical, horizontal, or oblique.

origin NOUN /ˈɔr.ɪ.dʒɪn/ the point at $(0, 0)$ in a 2-D rectangular coordinate system; an arbitrary point from which all locations in a metric space are measured. Notation: O (zero).

or rule NOUN /ɔr rul/ when it has been established that either P or Q is true, but not both, and P is known to be not true, then Q is true. Math definition: $(P \oplus Q) \wedge (\neg P) \to Q$.

ortho- PREFIX /ˈɔrθ.oʊ/
1) straight. Example: orthogonal.
2) right (especially right angle); perpendicular.

orthocenter NOUN /ˈɔr.θoʊˌsɛn.tər/ the point where the altitudes of the triangle coincide.

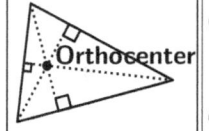

orthogonal ADJECTIVE /ɔrˈθɒ.gə.nl/
1) perpendicular. Example: orthogonal line.
2) right angled.
3) having no common dimensional measure; at right angles to each other. Example: orthogonal vector.
4) vertical.

orthogonal curves NOUN /ɔrˈθɒ.gə.nl kɜrvz/ two curves are orthogonal if all of the tangents of one curve are perpendicular to the tangents of the other curve.

orthogonal lines NOUN /ɔrˈθɒ.gə.nl laɪnz/ see perpendicular lines (p 88).

orthogonal matrix NOUN /ɔrˈθɒ.gə.nl ˈmeɪ.trɪks/ a square matrix that, when multiplied by its transpose, gives an identity matrix. Formula: $\mathbf{A} \cdot \mathbf{A^T} = \mathbf{I}$.

orthogonal trajectories NOUN /ɔrˈθɒ.gə.nl trəˈdʒɛk.tə.riz/ given a family of curves, an orthogonal trajectory is a curve that intersects each curve of the family orthogonally.

orthogonal vectors NOUN /ɔrˈθɒ.gə.nl ˈvɛk.tərz/ vectors that have an inner product of zero; have no common components; and are perpendicular to each other. Notation: $\vec{u} \perp \vec{v}$. Math definition: $\vec{u} \perp \vec{v}$ if and only if $\vec{u} \cdot \vec{v} = 0$. Antonym: parallel vectors (p 85).

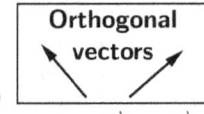

orthographic drawing NOUN /ˌɔr.θoʊˈgræ.fɪk ˈdrɔ.ɪŋ/ a drawing of a 3-dimensional object on a 2-dimensional surface from a particular viewpoint.

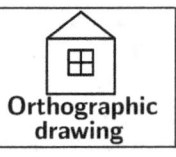

oscillate VERB /ˈɒs.əˌleɪt/ to change in value back and forth. Synonyms: converge (p 29), diverge (p 40).

oscillating function NOUN /ˌɒ.səˈleɪ.tɪŋ ˈfʌŋk.ʃən/ a function that has no limit, including no infinite limit. The output of an oscillating function does not 'settle down' as the input approaches positive or negative infinity. Antonyms: convergent function (p 29), divergent function (p 40).

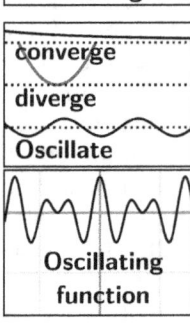

oscillating series NOUN /ˌɒ.səˈleɪ.tɪŋ ˈsɪər.iz/ a series that does not 'settle down'; a series that does not approach a specific value or infinity. Example: $\{1, -1, 1, -1, \cdots\}$.

oscillation NOUN /ˌɒ.səˈleɪ.ʃən/
1) the act of oscillating.
2) a single instance of going back and forth.

ounce NOUN /aʊns/ a unit of measure of weight. Abbreviation: oz. Formulas: 16 ounces $= 1$ pounds. 1 ounce ≈ 28.4 grams.

outcome NOUN /ˈaʊtˌkʌm/ the result of a probability experiment. Example: Given a flip of a coin, the outcome is either heads or tails.

outcome space NOUN /ˈaʊtˌkʌm speɪs/ all of the possible outcomes of an experiment. Example: of the roll of a single die: $\{1, 2, 3, 4, 5, 6\}$.

outlier NOUN /ˈaʊtˌlaɪ.ər/ an element of data which lies well outside the rest of the dataset.

output NOUN /ˈaʊt.pʊt/ the set of values generated by a function. Synonym: dependent variable (p 36). Antonym: input (p 62).

outside ADJECTIVE /ˈaʊt.saɪd/
1) the exterior of an object.
2) the space past the boundary of an object.
  Antonym: inside (p 62). Synonym: exterior (p 48).

oval /ˈoʊ.vəl/
1) ADJECTIVE egg shaped.
2) NOUN an object that is egg shaped.
Formula: $\frac{(ax)^2}{9} + \frac{e^{0.2x}(by)^2}{4} = 1$.

overbar NOUN /ˈoʊ.vər.bɑr/ a line segment over a symbol, which changes the meaning of the symbol. Example: $5.\overline{143} = 5.143143143\cdots$. Synonyms: bar (p 15), vinculum (p 122).

overestimate VERB /ˌoʊ.vərˈɛs.tɪ.meɪt/
1) to estimate larger than the actual value.
2) to intentionally estimate too large.
Antonym: underestimate (p 118).

oz ABBREVIATION ounce.

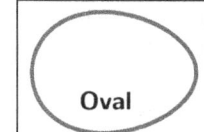
Oval

P

p ABBREVIATION pico-; 10^{-12}. Example: 5.3 picograms = 5.3×10^{-12} grams. Synonym: trillionth.

P ABBREVIATION peta-; 10^{15}. Example: 4.7 petameters = 4.7×10^{15} meters. Synonym: quadrillion.

pair NOUN /pɛər/ two associated objects. Example: ordered pair.

palindrome NOUN /ˈpæl.ɪnˌdroʊm/ a word, phrase or number that reads the same forward as backwards. Example: 101.

Pappus' form of a quadratic equation NOUN /ˈpæ.pəs fɔrm ʌv ə kwɒˈdræt.ɪk ɪˈkweɪ.ʃən/ a quadratic equation in the form $(x - h)^2 = 4p(y - k)$ where (h, k) is the location of the focus and p describes the directrix.

parabola NOUN /pərˈæ.bə.lə/ the shape made when graphing a quadratic equation; a shape that reflects light from a source at its focus straight ahead; all points equidistant from a directrix and its focus. See also Equations for a Parabola (p 142).

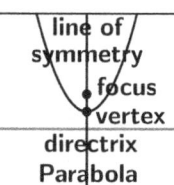
Parabola

parabolic ADJECTIVE /ˌpær.əˈbɒl.ɪk/ having to do with a parabola. Example: parabolic segment.

parabolic segment NOUN /ˌpær.əˈbɒl.ɪk ˈsɛg.mənt/ the region contained by a parabola and a line.

paraboloid NOUN /pərˈæ.bə.lɔɪd/ a 3-dimensional geometric figure whose cross sections through its axis of symmetry are parabolas; a shape made by rotating a parabola about its axis.

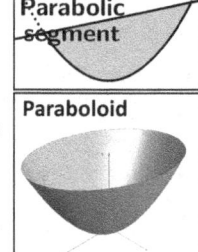
Parabolic segment

Paraboloid

paradox NOUN /ˈpær.əˌdɒks/
1) a statement that contradicts itself. Example: up is down.
2) a set of statements that cannot all be true at the same time. Synonym: contradiction (p 29).

paragraph proof NOUN /ˈpær.əˌgræf pruf/ a proof written in paragraph form, as opposed to a two-column proof or a flow proof.

parallel ADJECTIVE /ˈpær.əˌlɛl/
1) having parallel lines or line segments.
2) having the property of all points being equidistant and do not intersect.

parallelepiped NOUN /ˌpær.əˈlɛl.əˌpaɪ.pɪd/ a hexahedron whose faces are all parallelograms.

Parallelpiped

parallel lines NOUN /ˈpær.əˌlɛl laɪnz/ two distinct lines are parallel if the distance between the lines is constant. Two lines are parallel if and only if their slopes are equal. Two lines that lie on the same plane and do not intersect are parallel.

Parallel lines
b $a||b$
a

parallel line segments NOUN /ˈpær.əˌlɛl laɪn ˈsɛg.məntz/ two line segments that lie on the same line or that lie on parallel lines.

parallelogram NOUN /ˌpær.əˈlɛl.əˌgræm/ a four-sided polygon whose opposite sides are parallel.

parallelogram law NOUN /ˌpær.əˈlɛl.əˌgræm lɔ/ see parallelogram property of vectors (p 85).

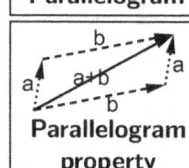
$a||c$, $b||d$
Parallelogram

Parallelogram Property of Vectors NOUN /ˌpær.əˈlɛl.əˌgræm ˈprɒp.ər.ti ʌv ˈvɛk.tərz/ the addition of one vector to another can be visualized as placing the tail of vector $\vec{b}$ at the head of the vector $\vec{a}$. The vector sum extends from the tail of $\vec{a}$ to the head of $\vec{b}$. Synonym: parallelogram law.

Parallelogram property

parallel planes NOUN /ˈpær.əˌlɛl pleɪnz/ planes that are a constant distance apart. Two planes are parallel if a line that is perpendicular to one is also perpendicular to the other.

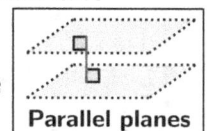
Parallel planes

Parallel Postulate NOUN /ˈpær.əˌlɛl ˈpɒs.tʃəˌlɪt/ guarantees the uniqueness of a line parallel to a given line through a point. Math definition: If L is a line in a plane and P is a point in the plane not on L, then there is exactly one line passing through P that is parallel to L.

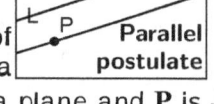
Parallel postulate

parallel rays NOUN /ˈpær.əˌlɛl reɪz/ two or more rays contained by the same line or by parallel lines.

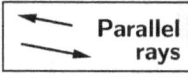
Parallel rays

Parallel Slope Postulate NOUN /ˈpær.əˌlɛl sloʊp ˈpɒs.tʃəˌlɪt/ two non-vertical lines that lie in the same plane have the same slope if and only if they are parallel.

parallel vectors NOUN /ˈpær.əˌlɛl ˈvɛk.tərz/ two vectors are parallel if one is a non-zero scalar multiple of the other.

Parallel vectors

Math definition: **u** is parallel with **v** if and only if there exists a real, nonzero number **a** such that $u = av$.
Formula: Two nonzero vectors **u** and **v** are parallel if and only if $u \times v = 0$. Antonym: orthogonal vectors (p 84).

parameter NOUN /pəˈræ.mɪ.tər/
1) a value that can be changed, usually determining the exact form of an equation. Example: in $y = ax^2 + bx + c$ the parameters are a, b, and c.
2) an independent variable in a parametric equation. Example: t in $x = \sin t$, $y = \cos t$.
3) (statistics) a value to be discovered. Example: the mean height of all six-year-olds.

parameterize VERB /pəˈræ.mɪ.təˌraɪz/ to change into parametric form.

parametric ADJECTIVE /ˌpær.əˈmɛ.trɪk/ containing or made of parameters.

parametric equation NOUN /ˌpær.əˈmɛ.trɪk ɪˈkweɪ.ʃən/ a set of two or more equations that share an independent variable. Example: $y = 2\cos 3t$, $x = 3\cos 2t$. t is the independent variable, x and y are dependent variables.

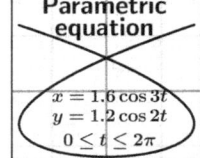

parametric form NOUN /ˌpær.əˈmɛ.trɪk fɔrm/ in the form of a parametric equation.

parent function NOUN /ˈpær.ənt ˈfʌŋk.ʃən/ a function that is used to build a more complex function. Examples: $f(x) = x^2$ and $g(x) = \sin x$ can be used to create the equation $h(x) = f(g(x)) = \sin^2 x$. Synonym: *toolkit function*.

parenthesis NOUN /pərˈɛn.θə.sɪs/ a set of marks '()' used to group operations or enclose dependent variables in a function notation. '(' is called the open parenthesis. ')' is called the close parenthesis. Example: $(3 + 2) \cdot 4 = 5 \cdot 4 = 20$. Plural: *parentheses* /pərˈɛn.θə.siz/. Synonym: *grouping symbol*.

parity NOUN /ˈpær.ɪ.ti/ two integers have the same parity if they are both even or if they are both odd. Example: 5 and 7 have the same parity, 4 and 8 have the same parity.

part NOUN /pɑrt/ a piece of a whole.

partial ADJECTIVE /ˈpɑr.ʃəl/
1) having to do with a part of a whole. Example: partial product.
2) incomplete.

partial derivative NOUN /ˈpɑr.ʃəl dɪˈrɪ.və.tɪv/ (of a function of several variables) the derivative with respect to one of the variables, with the others unchanged.

partial fraction decomposition NOUN /ˈpɑr.ʃəl ˈfræk.ʃən ˌdi.kɒm.pəˈzɪ.ʃən/ a method for reducing improper rational expressions to a polynomial plus a proper rational expression. Example: Let Q be a polynomial: $Q = (x - a_1)(x^2 + b_2x + a_2)\cdots(x - a_n)$ where each term is a non-reducible linear or quadratic. The partial fraction decomposition of $\frac{P}{Q}$ is $\frac{P(x)}{Q(x)} = \frac{A_1}{x-a_1} + \frac{A_2}{x^2+b_2x+-a_2} + \cdots + \frac{A_n}{x-a_n}$.

partial product NOUN /ˈpɑr.ʃəl ˈprɒ.dʌkt/ the product of the first n terms of an infinite product. Example: $\frac{1}{2} \cdot \frac{1}{4} \cdot \frac{1}{8} = \frac{1}{64}$.

partial product model of multiplication NOUN /ˈpɑr.ʃəl ˈprɒ.dʌkt ˈmɒ.dl ʌv ˌmʌl.tə.plɪˈkeɪ.ʃən/ a model that reduces numbers to their factors or place values to make multiplication easier.

partial sum NOUN /ˈpɑr.ʃəl sʌm/ the sum of the first n terms of a geometric sequence or series. Example: For $\frac{1}{2}, \frac{1}{4}, \frac{1}{8}, \cdots$, the third partial sum is $\frac{1}{2} + \frac{1}{4} + \frac{1}{8} = \frac{4}{8} + \frac{2}{8} + \frac{1}{8} = \frac{7}{8}$.

partition /pɑrˈtɪ.ʃən/
1) NOUN one of a set of parts that make up an entire whole.
2) VERB to split a whole into parts.

part-part ratio NOUN /pɑrt pɑrt ˈreɪ.ʃoʊ/ a ratio of two parts of the same whole.

part-whole ratio NOUN /pɑrt hoʊl ˈreɪ.ʃoʊ/ a ratio of a part of a whole compared to the whole.

Pascal, Blaise PERSON /pɑˈskɑl bleɪz/ (1623—1662) a French mathematician who designed the first digital calculator and popularized the triangle of numbers that came to be known as Pascal's Triangle.

Pascal's triangle NOUN /pɑˈskɑlz ˈtraɪˌæŋ.gəl/ a simplified version of the Binomial Theorem invented by French mathematician Blaise Pascal. See *Binomial Theorem* (p 17).

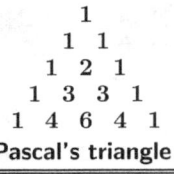

path /pɑθ/ NOUN
1) a way to move along a linear boundary.
2) a line connecting two points.
3) a connection between nodes of a network graph. Paths are drawn using line segments or curves. Synonym: *edge*.

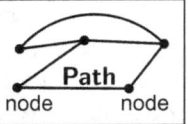

path-connected ADJECTIVE /pɑθ kəˈnɛk.tɪd/ in a geometric figure, there is a path starting at one point and ending at the other that does not leave the figure.

pattern NOUN /ˈpat.ərn/ a repeating arrangement of objects.

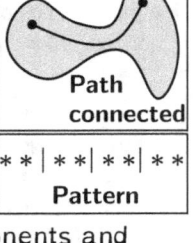

PENDOS MNEMONIC a mnemonic for the order of operations: Parentheses, Exponents and roots, Multiplication, Division, Addition, Subtraction.

pencil of lines NOUN /ˈpɛn.səl ʌv laɪnz/ a set of lines passing through a common point.

pendulum NOUN /ˈpɛn.du.lʌm/ a weight on a string or cable that swings back and forth.

penny NOUN /ˈpɛn.i/
1) $\frac{1}{100}$ of a base unit of currency for many currencies.
2) the coin valued at $\frac{1}{100}$ of a base unit of currency.
Symbols: ¢. (US), p (UK). Plural: *pennies* /ˈpɛn.iz/ (American English), *pence* /pɛns/ (British English). Synonym: *cent* (p 19).

penta- PREFIX /ˈpɛn.tə/ five. Example: pentagon.

pentadeca- PREFIX /ˌpɛn.təˈdɛ.kə/ fifteen. Example: pentadecagon.

pentadecagon NOUN /ˌpɛn.təˈdɛ.kə.gɒn/ a polygon with fifteen sides and fifteen vertices.

pentagon NOUN /ˈpɛnt.ə.gɒn/ a polygon with five sides and five vertices.

pentagonal ADJECTIVE /ˈpɛn.təˌgɒ.nl/
1) having to do with a pentagon.
2) includes a pentagon.
3) shaped like a pentagon.

pentagonal number NOUN /ˈpɛn.təˌgɒ.nl ˈnʌm.bər/ the number of dots in the edges of pentagons starting with 1 and increasing the number dots in each side by 1. The first few pentagonal numbers are 1, 5, 12, 22 and 35. Formula: $P(n) = \frac{n(3n - 1)}{2}$.

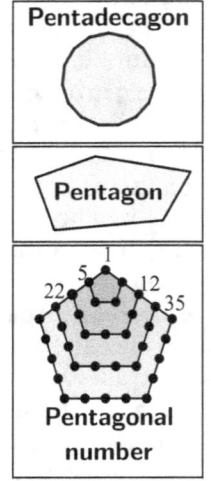

pentagonal prism NOUN /ˈpɛn.tə.ɡɒ.nl ˈprɪz.əm/ a seven-faced polyhedron with congruent parallel pentagons for bases and rectangles for sides.

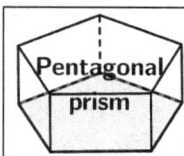

pentagonal pyramid NOUN /ˈpɛn.tə.ɡɒ.nl ˈpɪr.ə.mɪd/ a six-faced polyhedron with a pentagonal base and isosceles triangles for sides that come to a point at the apex.

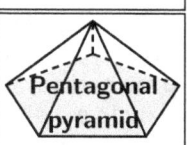

pentahedron NOUN /ˌpɛn.təˈhi.drən/ a five-faced polyhedron. Examples: square pyramid, triangular prism. Plural: pentahedra /ˌpɛn.təˈhi.drə/.

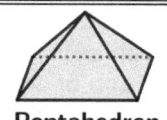

pentomino NOUN /ˌpɛn.təˈmi.noʊ/ a shape made of five connected, congruent squares that share sides.

per PREPOSITION /pər/
1) for every.
2) each. Example: per annum.

per- PREFIX /pər/
1) for every. Example: percent.
2) each.

per annum NOUN /pərˈæn.əm/ each year. Example: a 10% annual interest rate is 10% per annum.

percent NOUN, ADJECTIVE /pərˈsɛnt/ a value written in parts per hundred. Notation: $\%$. Formula: $a\% = \frac{a}{100}$. Example: $25\% = \frac{25}{100} = 0.25$.

percentage NOUN /pərˈsɛnt.ɪdʒ/ portion out of 100.

percent decrease NOUN /pərˈsɛnt dɪˈkris/ a decrease written as a percentage of the original amount. Formula: Quantity A decreased by B: $\frac{100 \cdot B}{A}\%$ decrease. Example: Originally \$20, decreased by \$5. $\frac{100 \cdot 5}{20}\% = \frac{500}{20}\% = 25\%$ decrease.

percentile NOUN, ADJECTIVE /pərˈsɛn.taɪl/ the nth percentile of a dataset is the value of the element that is just greater than $n\%$ of all the elements of the dataset. Synonym: percentile ranking /pərˈsɛn.taɪl ˈræŋ.kɪŋ/.

percent increase NOUN /pərˈsɛnt ˈɪn.kris/ an increase written as a percentage of the original amount. Formula: Quantity A increased by B: $\frac{100 \cdot B}{A}\%$ increase. Example: Originally \$20, increased by \$5. $\frac{100 \cdot 5}{20}\% = \frac{500}{20}\% = 25\%$ increase.

perfect ADJECTIVE /ˈpər.fɪkt/
1) exactly.
2) conforming to an ideal.

perfect cube NOUN /ˈpər.fɪkt kjub/
1) an integer that is the cube of another integer. Examples: $1 = 1^3, 8 = 2^3, 27 = 3^3, 64 = 4^3, \ldots$.
2) a binomial raised to the third power. Formulas: $(a+b)^3 = a^3 + 3a^2b + 3ab^2 + b^3$, $(a-b)^3 = a^3 - 3a^2b + 3ab^2 - b^3$.

perfect number NOUN /ˈpər.fɪkt ˈnʌm.bər/ an integer whose proper divisors add up to exactly that number. The first three perfect numbers are: $1 + 2 + 3 = 6$, $1 + 2 + 4 + 7 + 14 = 28$, and $1 + 2 + 4 + 8 + 16 + 31 + 62 + 124 + 248 = 496$. Antonyms: abundant number (p 7); deficient number (p 35).

perfect square NOUN /ˈpər.fɪkt skwɛər/
1) an integer that is a square of another integer. Examples: $1 = 1^2, 4 = 2^2, 9 = 3^2, 16 = 4^2, \ldots$. Synonym: square number (p 108).
2) see perfect square trinomial (p 87).

perfect square trinomial NOUN /ˈpər.fɪkt skwɛər traɪˈnoʊ.mi.əl/ a trinomial generated from the square of a binomial. Formulas: $(a+b)^2 = a^2 + 2ab + b^2$; $(a-b)^2 = a^2 - 2ab + b^2$.

perhaps ADVERB /pərˈhæps/ possibly; maybe or maybe not.

perihelion NOUN /ˌpɛ.rəˈhi.li.ən/ for an object in an elliptical orbit, the point closest to the focus around which the object orbits. Antonym: aphelion (p 11).

peri- PREFIX /ˈpɛr.ɪ/ around. Example: perimeter.

perimeter NOUN /pərˈɪm.ɪ.tər/
1) the edges of a closed 2-dimensional figure.
2) the sum of the lengths of the edges of a closed 2-dimensional figure.

period NOUN /ˈpɪər.i.əd/
1) (periodic function) the smallest interval over which the values of a periodic function repeat.
2) (interest) the amount of time after which interest is charged on a loan.
3) (waves) the distance from crest to crest. See wavelength (p 122).
4) (time) a constant interval of time. Example: a period of one second. Synonym: time interval.

periodic ADJECTIVE /ˌpɪər.iˈɒd.ɪk/ repeating at regular intervals. Example: periodic function.

periodic function NOUN /ˌpɪər.iˈɒd.ɪk ˈfʌŋk.ʃən/ a function whose values repeat at regular intervals. Example: the sine function.

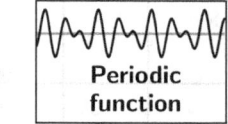

periodicity NOUN /ˌpɪər.i.əˈdɪs.ɪ.ti/ the property of repeating at regular intervals.

periodic motion NOUN /ˌpɪər.iˈɒd.ɪk ˈmoʊ.ʃən/ motion that repeats itself over time. Example: waves, the swinging of a pendulum.

permutation NOUN /ˌpər.mjuˈteɪ.ʃən/ a selection of objects in a particular order. n objects can be selected in n! different orders. Formula: $nPr = \frac{n!}{(n-r)!} = n(n-1)(n-2) \cdot \ldots \cdot (n-(r-1))$. Notation: nPr where n is the number of objects from which to choose and r is the number of objects to choose. Example: there are $3! = 6$ permutations of $\{abc\}$: $\{abc\}, \{acb\}, \{bac\}, \{bca\}, \{cab\}, \{cba\}$.

permutation notation NOUN /ˌpər.mjuˈteɪ.ʃən noʊˈteɪ.ʃən/ nPr where n is the number of objects from which to choose and r is the number of objects to choose.

perpendicular /ˌpər.pənˈdɪk.jə.lər/
1) ADJECTIVE meeting at right angles. Example: perpendicular bisector. Synonym: normal (p 80).
2) NOUN a line that is at right angles to a given object.

perpendicular bisector NOUN /ˌpər.pənˈdɪk.jə.lər ˈbaɪ.sɛk.tər/ an object, usually a line, that bisects a line segment and is perpendicular to that line segment.

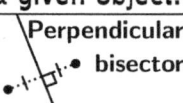

Perpendicular Bisector Concurrence Theorem NOUN /ˌpɚ.pənˈdɪk.jə.lɚ ˈbaɪ.sɛk.tɚ kənˈkɚ.əns ˈθɪ.ə.rəm/ the perpendicular bisectors of the sides of a triangle are concurrent.

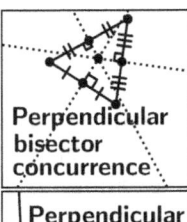
Perpendicular bisector concurrence

perpendicular lines NOUN /ˌpɚ.pənˈdɪk.jə.lɚ laɪnz/ lines that intersect at right angles. Math definition: Two lines are perpendicular if the relationship between the slopes is $m_1 \cdot m_2 = -1 \rightarrow m_1 = -\frac{1}{m_2}$. See also Perpendicular Slope Postulate (p 88).

Perpendicular lines

perpendicular planes NOUN /ˌpɚ.pənˈdɪk.jə.lɚ pleɪnz/ planes that intersect at a right angle.

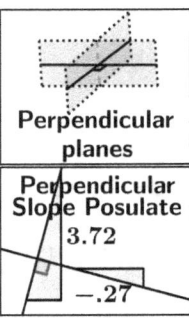
Perpendicular planes

Perpendicular Slope Postulate NOUN /ˌpɚ.pənˈdɪk.jə.lɚ sloʊp ˈpɒs.tʃə.lɪt/ two non-vertical lines are perpendicular if and only if the product of their slopes is -1: $m_1 m_2 = -1 \rightarrow m_1 = -\frac{1}{m_2}$.

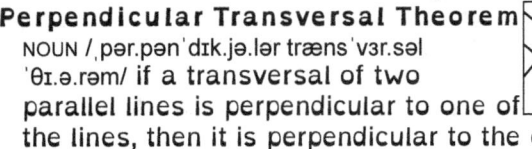
Perpendicular Slope Posulate 3.72 −.27

Perpendicular Transversal Theorem NOUN /ˌpɚ.pənˈdɪk.jə.lɚ trænsˈvɚ.səl ˈθɪ.ə.rəm/ if a transversal of two parallel lines is perpendicular to one of the lines, then it is perpendicular to the other.

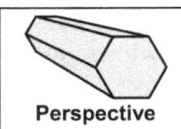
Perpendicular Transversal Theorem

perspective NOUN /pɚˈspɛk.tɪv/
1) a technique for drawing three dimensions on a flat surface where the object appears to get smaller in the distance.
2) a figure using this technique.

Perspective

perspective drawing NOUN /pɚˈspɛk.tɪv ˈdrɑ.ɪŋ/ see perspective view (p 88).

perspective view NOUN /pɚˈspɛk.tɪv vju/ a view from a corner of a figure. Synonyms: perspective drawing, isometric projection (p 65).

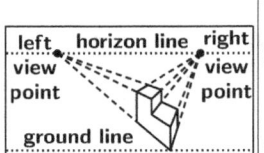
Perspective view

peta- PREFIX /ˈpɛ.tə/ 10^{15}. Example: 5 petameters = 5×10^{15} meters. Abbreviation: P. Synonym: quadrillion.

phase NOUN /feɪz/ a fractional part of a cycle through which a periodic function has passed.

phase shift NOUN /feɪz ʃɪft/ the horizontal movement of an entire periodic function when the angle is changed. Such a movement 'shifts' the phase. Synonym: horizontal shift (p 57).

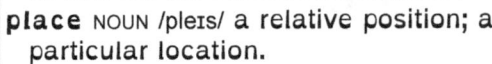
Phase shift

phi SYMBOL /fi/ the Greek letter ϕ, used to represent the golden ratio or a portion of a 3-dimensional angle. See also Greek Letters (p 135).

pi NOUN /paɪ/ the Greek letter π, used for the constant ratio of the circumference of a circle to the diameter of that circle. Formulas: $\pi \approx 3.14159$. $\pi \equiv \frac{C}{D}$ where C is the circumference of a circle and D is the diameter. See also Greek Letters (p 135).

pico- PREFIX /ˈpi.koʊ/ 10^{-12}. Example: 7.2 picometers = 7.2×10^{-12} meters. Abbreviation: p. Synonym: trillionth (p 117).

picto- PREFIX /ˈpɪk.toʊ/ having to do with pictures.

pictogram NOUN /ˈpɪk.toʊ.græm/ see pictograph (p 88).

pictograph NOUN /ˈpɪk.toʊ.græf/ graph that uses pictures to show quantity. Each picture represents a particular quantity. Synonyms: pictogram, concrete graph.

Attendance at the Book Fair: Children 40, Adults 15, = 10 people

picture graph NOUN /ˈpɪk.tʃɚ græf/ see pictograph (p 88).

piece NOUN /pis/ a single part of a whole.

piecewise ADJECTIVE /ˈpisˌwaɪz/ having some property over a finite number of subdomains. Example: piecewise function.

piecewise continuous function NOUN /ˈpisˌwaɪz kənˈtɪn.ju.əs ˈfʌŋk.ʃən/ a function that is continuous over each of a finite number of intervals.

piecewise function NOUN /ˈpisˌwaɪz ˈfʌŋk.ʃən/ a function that is defined differently over more than one subdomain. Example:
$$f(x) = \begin{cases} \text{if } x < 1: & \frac{1}{2}x + \frac{1}{2} \\ \text{if } x \geq 1: & x^2 - 2x + 2 \end{cases}$$

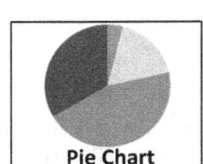
Piecewise function

pie chart NOUN /paɪ tʃɑrt/ a graph in the shape of a circle, divided into sectors, where each sector represents a proportion of a whole. Synonyms: circle graph, pie graph.

Pie Chart

pie graph NOUN /paɪ græf/ see pie chart (p 88).

pint NOUN /paɪnt/ a unit of measure of volume. Abbreviation: pt. Formulas: 1 pint = 2 cups. 2 pints = 1 quart. 1 pint ≈ 0.473 liters.

Pisano, Leonardo PERSON /piˈzɑ.noʊ ˌli.oʊˈnɑr.doʊ/ (1170—1250) an Italian mathematician nicknamed Fibonacci known for the Fibonacci numbers.

Leonardo Pisano

place NOUN /pleɪs/ a relative position; a particular location.

placebo NOUN /pləˈsi.boʊ/ a non-active pill, such as a sugar pill, used to test the validity of the results of a study. Synonym: sugar pill.

placeholder NOUN /ˈpleɪsˌhoʊl.dɚ/ something that 'reserves' a place. Example: Zero is a placeholder in numerals. It adds no value to a numeral, but is important in telling the difference between numerals such as 204 and 24.

place value NOUN /pleɪs ˈvæl.ju/ a value by which a digit in a particular place in a numeral is multiplied to find the value of the numeral. Example: $312.7 = 3 \times 10^2 + 1 \times 10^1 + 2 \times 10^0 + 7 \times 10^{-1}$.

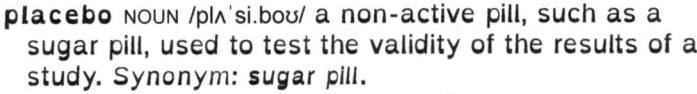
hundreds ones hundredths 125.76 tens tenths Place value

plain text NOUN /pleɪn tɛkst/ text that can be read without decrypting or deciphering. Synonym: human readable text. Antonyms: enciphered text (p 43), encrypted text.

plan NOUN /plæn/
1) NOUN a diagram showing a view from above; a scale drawing of a structure.
2) NOUN a way to accomplish a task.
3) VERB to figure out a way to accomplish a task.

Plan

planar ADJECTIVE /ˈpleɪ.nɚ/
1) contained within a single plane. Example: planar curve.

2) involving two dimensions.
Antonym: *non-planar* (p 79).

planar graph NOUN /ˈpleɪ.nər græf/ a network graph whose paths do not cross when drawn in two dimensions. Antonym: *non-planar graph* (p 79).

plane /pleɪn/
1) NOUN a flat, 2-dimensional space with infinite length and width and no thickness. Equation: $a(x - x_0) + b(y - y_0) + c(z - z_0) = 0$ where $n = a\hat{i} + b\hat{j} + c\hat{k}$ is a vector normal (perpendicular) to the plane and (x_0, y_0, z_0) is any point in the plane.
2) ADJECTIVE existing in only one plane.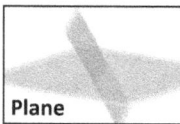

plane, complex see *complex plane* (p 25).

plane curve NOUN /pleɪn kɜrv/ a curve that exists entirely within a single plane. Counterexample: helix.

plane figure NOUN /pleɪn ˈfɪg.jər/ a geometric figure than can exist within a single plane. See *planar* (p 88).

plane geometry NOUN /pleɪn dʒiˈɒ.mɪ.tri/ the study of objects in a flat, 2-dimensional space.

plane shape NOUN /pleɪn ʃeɪp/ see *plane figure* (p 89).

plane trigonometry NOUN /pleɪn ˌtrɪ.gəˈnɒm.ɪ.tri/ the branch of mathematics that deals with right triangles, unit circles and the calculations and relationships between the sides and angles of right triangles in a plane.

Plato PERSON /ˈpleɪ.toʊ/ (427 BCE—347 BCE) a Greek philosopher and mathematician who made important contributions to geometry and to the science of logic.

Platonic ADJECTIVE /pləˈtɒn.ɪk/ credited to or named after Plato.

Platonic solid NOUN /pləˈtɒn.ɪk ˈsɒ.lɪd/ see *regular polyhedron* (p 98).

please excuse my dear aunt sally MNEMONIC a mnemonic for remembering the order of operations: parentheses, exponents, multiplication and division (left to right), addition and subtraction (left to right).

plot VERB /plɒt/
1) to mark on a graph.
2) to draw a figure by marking points in a coordinate plane.
3) to cause a graph to be drawn.

plus PREPOSITION /plʌs/
1) added to; increased by. Keyword for addition.
2) in addition to.
Notation: $+$.

plus or minus PREPOSITION /plʌs ɔr ˈmaɪ.nəs/ an operator than can be either plus or minus. Notation: $\pm$. Example: $3 \pm 4 = 7 \text{ or } -1$. Antonym: *minus or plus* (p 75).

plus sign NOUN /plʌs saɪn/ the symbol '+' used to show addition or to indicate a positive number.

pm ABBREVIATION post meridiem, which means after noon. Example: 3:00 pm is 3 hours after noon

point NOUN /pɔɪnt/
1) a point has a location but no width, length or height. A point is drawn as a dot and/or written as a coordinate.
2) a dot in a drawing.

point of concurrency NOUN /pɔɪnt ʌv kənˈkɜr.ən.si/ see *point of intersection* (p 89).

point of contact NOUN /pɔɪnt ʌv ˈkɒn.tækt/ where one object touches another without crossing. See also *point of intersection* (p 89).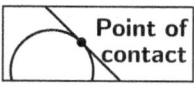

point of division formula NOUN /pɔɪnt ʌv dɪˈvɪ.ʒən ˈfɔr.mju.lə/ a formula for getting the coordinates of a point that is partway between two points. Formula: $(x_1 + t(x_2 - x_1), y_1 + t(y_2 - y_1))$ where (x_1, y_1) and (x_2, y_2) are two points, and $0 < t < 1$ is the portion of the distance between the from point 1 to point 2.

point of intersection NOUN /pɔɪnt ʌv ˌɪn.tərˈsɛk.ʃən/ a point where two or more geometric objects intersect. Synonym: *point of concurrency*.

point of reflection NOUN /pɔɪnt ʌv rɪˈflɛk.ʃən/ a point about which a reflection is performed. Math definition: Given point P and a reflection point Q, point R is the reflection of P about Q if and only if Q is the midpoint of line segment PR.

point of rotation NOUN /pɔɪnt ʌv rouˈteɪ.ʃən/ see *center* (p 19).

point of symmetry NOUN /pɔɪnt ʌv ˈsɪ.mɪ.tri/ a point about which an object has radial or reflective symmetry.

point of tangency NOUN /pɔɪnt ʌv ˈtæn.dʒən.si/ a point where a tangent line touches a circle or a curve without crossing it.

point-slope form NOUN /pɔɪnt sloʊp fɔrm/ a way to write a linear equation given the coordinates of a point on a line and the slope of the line. Formula: $y = m(x - x_0) + y_0$, or $y - y_0 = m(x - x_0)$ where m is the slope and (x_0, y_0) is the coordinate of any point on the line.

point symmetry NOUN /pɔɪnt ˈsɪ.mɪ.tri/ an image that, when reflected across a point, is identical to the preimage has point symmetry about that point.

polar ADJECTIVE /ˈpoʊ.lər/ where location in a plane is determined by an angle and a distance from the endpoint of a fixed ray.

polar angle NOUN /ˈpoʊ.lər ˈæŋ.gəl/ the second coordinate in a 2-dimensional polar coordinate system: (r, θ). A polar angle is measured from a horizontal ray extending to the right of the origin.

polar axis NOUN /ˈpoʊ.lər ˈæk.sɪs/ the horizontal ray extended from the origin to the right. All angles are measured from the polar axis.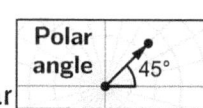

polar conversion formulas NOUN /ˈpoʊ.lər kənˈvɜr.ʒən ˈfɔr.mju.lə/ formulas for converting polar coordinates to rectangular coordinates and from rectangular coordinates to polar coordinates: To polar coordinates, $r = \sqrt{x^2 + y^2}, \theta = \arctan \frac{y}{x}$; To rectangular coordinates: $x = r \cos \theta, y = r \sin \theta$.

polar coordinate NOUN /ˈpoʊ.lər koʊˈɔr.dn.ɪt/ for 2-dimensional systems, a distance from the origin and an angle from the positive x-axis, written (r, θ) where **r** is the distance from the origin and θ is the angle from the standard position. For 3-dimensional systems, a distance and two angles, written (r, θ, ρ).

polar coordinate plane NOUN /ˈpoʊ.lər koʊˈɔr.dn.ɪt pleɪn/ a plane containing a polar coordinate system.

polar coordinate system NOUN /ˈpoʊ.lər koʊˈɔr.dn.ɪt ˈsɪs.təm/ coordinate system that uses an angle and a distance to determine the location of a point. A 3-dimensional polar coordinate system uses two angles at right angles to each other and a distance to define the location of a point.

polar equation of conics NOUN /ˈpoʊ.lər ɪˈkweɪ.ʃən ʌv ˈkɒn.ɪks/ a conic section can be described by one of the polar equations $r = \frac{\epsilon d}{1 \pm \epsilon \cos \theta}$ (horizontal directrix), or $r = \frac{\epsilon d}{1 \pm \epsilon \sin \theta}$ (vertical directrix) where **d** is the distance from the directrix and ϵ is the eccentricity of the conic.

polar form NOUN /ˈpoʊ.lər fɔrm/
1) (complex numbers) a complex number in the form (r, θ) where **r** is the magnitude and θ is the rotation from the positive real axis. Formula: the polar form of the complex number $a + bi$ is $\left(\sqrt{a^2 + b^2}, \arctan \frac{b}{a}\right)$.
2) (vectors) a vector in the form (r, θ) where **r** is the magnitude and θ is the rotation from the positive x-axis. Formula: the polar form of vector $\langle x, y \rangle$ is $\left(\sqrt{x^2 + y^2}, \arctan \frac{y}{x}\right)$.
3) (equation) an equation written using polar coordinates, often in the form $r = f(\theta)$. Example: $r = \cos \theta$.

polar origin NOUN /ˈpoʊ.lər ˈɔr.ɪ.dʒɪn/ see pole (p 90).

pole NOUN /poʊl/
1) the origin in a polar coordinate system. Synonym: polar origin.
2) an imaginary line about which a sphere rotates.
3) one of two points at which a pole intersects the surface of a sphere. Example: north pole.

poly- PREFIX /ˈpɒ.li/
1) many. Example: polygon.
2) more than one.
3) more than two.

Pólya, George PERSON /ˈpoʊl.jə dʒɔrdʒ/ (1887—1985) a Hungarian mathematician noted for characterizing how people solve problems. See Polya's Four Step Approach.

Polya's Four Step Approach NOUN /ˈpoʊl.jəz fɔr stɛp əˈproʊtʃ/ a method of solving problems: 1) Read and understand the problem. 2) Plan how to solve the problem. 3) Solve the problem. 4) Review.

polygon NOUN /ˈpɒ.li.gɒn/ a closed n-sided figure in a plane. Each side is a straight line segment.

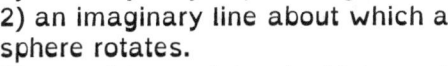

polyhedron NOUN /ˌpɒ.liˈhi.drən/ a 3-dimensional shape with faces made of polygons. Plural: polyhedra /ˌpɒ.liˈhi.drə/.

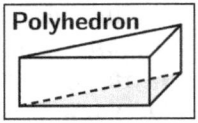
Polyhedron

polynomial NOUN /ˌpɒl.əˈnoʊ.mi.əl/ an expression where each term has a coefficient and zero or more variables raised to a non-negative integer power. Example: $3x^5 - x^2 + 2$.

polyomino NOUN /ˌpɒl.i.oʊˈmi.noʊ/ a plane figure made of two or more identical squares that share sides.

population NOUN /ˌpɒp.juˈleɪ.ʃən/ all of a group of people or objects about which statistical data is collected and analyzed. Example: all frogs in a particular ecosystem.

portion NOUN /ˈpɔr.ʃən/ a part of a whole.

position /ˌpoʊˈsɪ.ʃən/
1) NOUN see location (p 70).
2) NOUN an object's place in an ordered set.
3) VERB to place an object in order or location.

position to term rule NOUN /ˌpoʊˈsɪ.ʃən tu tɜrm rul/ a method for finding the value of a term of an arithmetic sequence given its position. Formula: $t_n = dn + a$ where t_n is the value of term **n**, **d** is the common difference, **n** is the position of the term (starting at zero), and **a** is the value of term 0.

positive ADJECTIVE, NOUN /ˈpɒz.ɪ.tɪv/
1) greater than zero. Not zero or negative. Antonym: nonpositive (p 80).
2) in a positive direction. Antonym: negative (p 78).
3) (angle) in a counterclockwise direction. Antonym: negative (p 78).

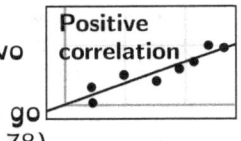

positive correlation NOUN /ˈpɒz.ɪ.tɪv ˌkɔr.əˈleɪ.ʃən/ a correlation between two variables such that as one variable goes up, the other variable tends to go up. Antonym: negative correlation (p 78).

positive direction noun /ˈpɒz.ɪ.tɪv dɪˈrɛk.ʃən/ an arbitrary direction in which values increase. Antonym: negative direction (p 78).

positive integer NOUN /ˈpɒz.ɪ.tɪv ˈɪn.tɪ.dʒər/ a whole number that is greater than zero; a natural number. Notation: $\mathbb{N}$ or $\mathbb{Z}^+$. Math definition: $\mathbb{N} = \{1, 2, 3, 4, \cdots\}$. Synonyms: natural number (p 78), counting number.

positive number NOUN /ˈpɒz.ɪ.tɪv ˈnʌm.bər/ a number greater than zero. Math definition: $\{x : x > 0\}$. Antonym: nonpositive number.

positive sign NOUN /ˈpɒz.ɪ.tɪv saɪn/ the symbol '+' meaning that a number is positive. Example: $+5$. Synonym: plus sign.

positive slope NOUN /ˈpɒz.ɪ.tɪv sloʊp/ a slope that slants upwards from left to right; a slope that can be written as a positive number. Antonym: negative slope (p 78).

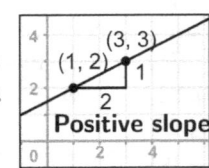

possibility NOUN /ˌpɒ.sɪˈbɪl.ɪ.ti/
1) one of several things that can happen.
2) the state of being possible or impossible.

3) the condition of being possible.
possible ADJECTIVE /ˈpɑ.sɪ.bəl/
1) can happen.
2) can be true.
Antonym: **impossible** (p 60).
postulate NOUN /ˈpɒs.tʃə.lɪt/ see **axiom** (p 15).
potential NOUN /poʊˈtɛn.ʃəl/ the energy possessed by an object.
potential function NOUN /poʊˈtɛn.ʃəl fʌnk.ʃən/ a function that describes potential energy of an object at all points of the object.
pound NOUN /paʊnd/
1) unit of measure of weight. Abbreviation: lb. Formulas: **16 ounces = 1 pound, 2000 pounds = 1 ton, 1 pound ≈ 0.454 kg** on the Earth's surface.
2) see **pound sterling** (p 91).
pound sterling NOUN /paʊnd ˈstɜr.lɪŋ/ the base currency in the United Kingdom. Formula: **100 pence = 1 GBP**. Symbol: **£**. ISO code: **GBP**.
power NOUN /ˈpaʊ.ər/ see **exponent** (p 47).
power function NOUN /ˈpaʊ.ər fʌnk.ʃən/ a function with a variable raised to an integer exponent. Formula: $y = x^n$. Example: $f(x) = x^2$.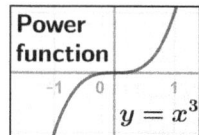
power of a power NOUN /ˈpaʊ.ər ʌv ə ˈpaʊ.ər/ a base raised to a power, the whole of which is raised to another power. Formula: $(b^m)^n = b^{m \cdot n}$. Important: $b^{(m^n)} \neq b^{m \cdot n}$. Synonym: **power rule** (p 91).
Power Property of Logarithms NOUN /ˈpaʊ.ər ˈprɒ.pər.ti ʌv ˈlɒ.gə.rɪð.əmz/ the logarithm of a value to a power is equal to the power times the logarithm of the value: $\log_b M^k = k \log_b M$.
Power Rule NOUN /ˈpaʊ.ər rul/
1) (algebra) a property of exponents such that $(b^m)^n = b^{m \cdot n}$. Important: $b^{(m^n)} \neq b^{m \cdot n}$. Synonym: **power of a power** (p 91).
2) (calculus) given differentiable expression x^n, $\frac{d}{dx}[x^n] = nx^{n-1}$. Example: $\frac{d}{dx}[x^3] = 3x^2$.
power series NOUN /ˈpaʊ.ər ˈsɪər.iz/ an infinite series containing one or more variables in the form $f(x) = a_0 + a_1(x-c) + a_2(x-c)^2 + a_3(x-c)^3 + \cdots$.
power set NOUN /ˈpaʊ.ər sɛt/ the set of all subsets of a particular set. Notation: $\mathcal{P}(A)$. Example: If $A = \{a, b, d\}$ then $\mathcal{P}(A) = \{\emptyset, \{a\}, \{b\}, \{d\}, \{a,b\}, \{a,d\}, \{b,d\}, \{a,b,d\}\}$.
powers of 10 NOUN /ˈpaʊ.ər ʌv tɛn/ ..., $0.01 = 10^{-2}$, $0.1 = 10^{-1}$, $1 = 10^0$, $10 = 10^1$, $100 = 10^2$, ...
powers of i NOUN /ˈpaʊ.ərz ʌv aɪ/ $i^n =$ i, -1, -i, or 1.

Powers of i		
$i^1 = i$	$i^5 = i$	$i^{4k+1} = i, k \in \mathbb{Z}$
$i^2 = -1$	$i^6 = -1$	$i^{4k+2} = -1, k \in \mathbb{Z}$
$i^3 = -i$	$i^7 = -i$	$i^{4k+3} = -i, k \in \mathbb{Z}$
$i^4 = 1$	$i^8 = 1$	$i^{4k+4} = 1, k \in \mathbb{Z}$

practical situation NOUN /ˌpræk.tɪ.kəl ˈsɪ.tʃu.weɪ.ʃən/ a real world mathematical problem. Example: Jeremy has five fewer pencils than Jen. Jen has ten pencils. How many pencils does Jeremy have? Antonym: **mathematical situation** (p 72).

pre- PREFIX /prɪ/
1) before. Example: predict.
2) in front of. Example: precedence.
precedence NOUN /ˈprɛs.ɪ.dəns/ see **order of operations** (p 83).
precise ADJECTIVE /prɪˈsaɪs/ being exact; no more and no less. Synonym: **exact** (p 46).
precision NOUN /prɪˈsɪ.ʒən/
1) how accurate something is. Synonym: **accuracy**.
2) degree of accuracy or correctness.
predecessor NOUN /ˈprɛd.ə.sɛ.sər/ (American English) /ˈpri.də.sɛ.sər/ (British English) one that comes before. Antonym: **successor** (p 111).
predict VERB /prɪˈdɪkt/
1) to tell or estimate in advance.
2) to model. Example: The equation $y = a_0 t^2 + v_0 t + h_0$ predicts the vertical height of a projectile at time **t**.
prediction NOUN /prɪˈdɪk.ʃən/
1) a description of possible future events made in advance.
2) an estimate of a result.
preimage NOUN /ˈpri.ɪm.ɪdʒ/ a geometric figure before a transformation.
premise NOUN /ˈprɛm.ɪs/ one sentence in a logical argument. Example:
• Socrates is a man. (premise) • All men are mortal. (premise) • So Socrates is mortal (conclusion).
present NOUN, ADJECTIVE /ˈprɛs.ənt/ at this time; currently.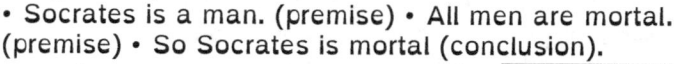
present value NOUN /ˈprɛs.ənt ˈvæl.ju/ the current value of a future payment or payments discounted to reflect the time value of money. Formulas: $P = A\left(1 + \frac{r}{n}\right)^{nt}$, or for continuous compounding $P = Ae^{rt}$, **n** is the number of compounding periods, **r** is the interest rate, and **t** is the number of elapsed periods.
price NOUN /praɪs/ the amount of money paid for something.
primary ADJECTIVE /ˈpraɪ.mɛr.i/
1) first in order or time.
2) greatest or most important.
prime ADJECTIVE /praɪm/ cannot be factored. Example: prime number. Antonym: **composite**.
prime factor NOUN /praɪm ˈfæk.tər/ a factor that is either a prime number or an irreducible expression. Examples: 7, 19, $(x-2)$.
prime factorization NOUN /praɪm ˈfæk.tə.raɪ.zeɪ.ʃən/ a set of factors that are all prime and that, when multiplied together, give a specific number or expression. Example: $12 = 2^2 \cdot 3$. See also **factor tree** (p 49).
prime notation NOUN /praɪm noʊˈteɪ.ʃən/ to show that an object is created from another object, label the new object with the old label plus the prime mark ('). Example: if a new object is created from a, label the new object a'.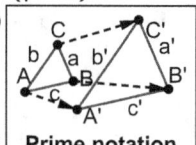
prime number NOUN /praɪm ˈnʌm.bər/ an integer greater than 1 that is evenly divisible only by 1 and itself. Examples: 2, 3, 5, 7, 11, 13, 17, ... Antonym: **composite number** (p 25).

Prime Number Theorem NOUN /praɪm 'nʌm.bər 'θɪ.ə.rəm/ the area of $\int_b^c \frac{dx}{\ln x}$ is approximately equal to the number of primes between **b** and **c**.

primitive NOUN /'prɪm.ə.tɪv/ an object that is defined implicitly by the axioms of an axiomatic system. Example: points and lines are primitives of modern geometry. Synonym: *undefined term*.

principal /'prɪn.sə.pəl/
1) NOUN the amount of a loan on which interest is calculated. Formula: **principal + interest = total payment**.
2) ADJECTIVE major. Example: principal axis.
3) ADJECTIVE most important. Example: principal root.

principal diagonal NOUN /'prɪn.sə.pəl daɪ'æ.gə.nl/ see main diagonal (p 71).

principal root NOUN /'prɪn.sə.pəl rut/ the positive square root of a real number. Example: The principal square root of 25 is 5, and not -5. The principal root of the negative number -n is $i\sqrt{n}$.

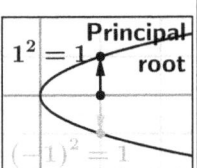

principal value NOUN /'prɪn.sə.pəl 'val.ju/ (trigonometry) the output of an arcsine or arccosine function that lies in a range, usually $\left[-\frac{\pi}{2}, \frac{\pi}{2}\right]$, or the output of an arctangent function that lies in a range, usually $[0, \pi]$.

principle of substitution NOUN /'prɪn.sə.pəl ʌv 'sʌb.stɪ.tu.ʃən/ any value or expression can be substituted for a letter in a formula. Example: substitute $n + 1$ for x in $y = 3x - 2$: $y = 3(n+1) - 2 = 3n + 1$.

prior ADJECTIVE /'praɪ.ər/ coming before in order or in time.

prism NOUN /'prɪz.əm/ a geometric solid whose bases are parallel and congruent polygons, and whose sides are parallelograms.

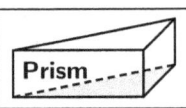

prisoner NOUN /'prɪ.zə.nər/ in a Mandelbrot set or a Julia set, a value that tends to zero. Antonym: *escapee* (p 45).

probability NOUN /ˌprɒ.bə'bɪl.ɪ.ti/
1) the likelihood, chance, or odds of an event happening.
2) the study of chance occurrences.

probability density function NOUN /ˌprɒ.bə'bɪl.ɪ.ti 'dɛn.sɪ.ti 'fʌŋk.ʃən/ a function whose value at any given point in the sample space can be interpreted as providing a relative likelihood that the value of the random variable would equal that sample.

probability model NOUN /ˌprɒ.bə'bɪl.ɪ.ti 'mɒ.dl/ a mathematical model intended to predict the probability outcomes. Notation: **P(event) = probability**. Example: $P(\text{heads}) = 0.5$. Synonym: *statistical model* (p 109).

probable ADJECTIVE /'prɒ.bə.bəl/
1) likely to happen.
2) likely to be true.

problem NOUN /'prɒ.bləm/ a situation or equation to be solved.

problem solving NOUN /'prɒ.bləm sɒl.vɪŋ/ finding a solution to a problem.

process /'prɒ.sɛs/
1) NOUN a way of doing something in a systematic manner to bring about a particular result.
2) VERB to do something in a systematic manner to bring about a particular result.

product NOUN /'prɒ.dəkt/
1) the result of multiplication. Formula: **multiplicand × multiplier = product**. Example: $5 \times 3 = 15$.
2) one or more numbers or expressions multiplied by each other.

Product Property of Exponents NOUN /'prɒ.dəkt 'prɒ.pər.ti ʌv 'ɛks.poʊ.nəntz/ the product of two terms with the same base is the base raised to the sum of the exponents. Math definition: $b^m b^n = b^{m+n}$.

Product Property of Logarithms NOUN /'prɒ.dəkt 'prɒ.pər.ti ʌv 'lɒ.gə.rɪð.əmz/ the log of a product is equal to the sum of logs of the multiplicands. Math definition: $\log_b M \cdot N = \log_b M + \log_b N$.

Product Property of Proportions NOUN /'prɒ.dəkt 'prɒ.pər.ti ʌv prə'poʊr.ʃənz/ if $\frac{a}{b} = \frac{c}{d}$, then $ad = bc$. Conversely, if $ad = bc \neq 0$, then $\frac{a}{b} = \frac{c}{d}$ and $\frac{b}{a} = \frac{d}{c}$.

product rule NOUN /'prɒ.dəkt rul/ the derivative of a product of functions is equal to the sum of the first function times the derivative of the second function plus the second function times the derivative of the first function. Math definition: $\frac{d}{dx}[uv] = u\frac{d}{dx}v + v\frac{d}{dx}u$.

Product to Sum Identities NOUN /'prɒ.dəkt tu sʌm aɪ'dɛn.tɪ.tiz/ trigonometric identities involving the product of two trigonometric functions. See also *Trigonometric Identities* (p 143).

profit /'prɒ.fɪt/
1) NOUN an amount of money gained on one or more transactions or in a certain period of time.
2) VERB to gain money on one or more transactions.

progression NOUN /proʊ'grɛ.ʃən/ see sequence (p 103).

projectile NOUN /prə'dʒɛk.taɪl/ a free falling body that has been projected forward. Example: a ball thrown off a roof, before it hits the ground.

projectile motion NOUN /prə'dʒɛk.taɪl 'moʊ.ʃən/ the vertical motion of a free falling object with respect to time. Formula: $y = \frac{1}{2}at^2 + v_0 t + h_0$ (Cartesian) where **y** is the height at time **t**, **a** is the vertical acceleration due to gravity, v_0 is the initial vertical velocity and h_0 is the initial height. Synonym: *falling bodies*.

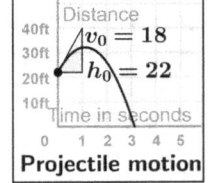

projection NOUN /proʊ'dʒɛk.ʃən/
1) a 2-dimensional drawing of a 3-dimensional object.
2) see vector projection (p 121).

prolate spheroid NOUN /'proʊ.leɪt 'sfɪər.ɔɪd/ an ellipsoid made by rotating an ellipse around its major axis; a sphere 'flattened' at the poles. Antonym: *oblate spheroid* (p 81).

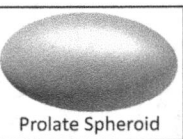

pronumeral NOUN /'proʊ.num.ər.əl/ see variable (p 120).

proof NOUN /pruf/ a series of statements that show a claim is true.

proof by construction NOUN /pruf baɪ kən'strʌk.ʃən/ construction of a specific example with a property that shows the property exists. Synonym: *Proof by example*.

proof by contradiction NOUN /pruf baɪ ˌkɒn.trəˈdɪk.ʃən/ a proof that shows a proposition is true by showing that, if the proposition were false, then there would be a contradiction. Synonym: *indirect proof*. Antonym: *direct proof*.

proof by example NOUN /pruf baɪ ɪɡˈzæm.pəl/ see *proof by construction* (p 92).

proof by exhaustion NOUN /pruf baɪ ɪɡˈzɒs.tʃən/ a proof where a proposition is divided into a number of cases, and each of the cases is individually proved.

proof by induction NOUN /pruf baɪ ɪnˈdʌk.ʃən/ a proof that shows that, if a proposition is true for the first case and for an arbitrary case, it is always true for the case after the arbitrary case. Important: Proof by induction is not the same as logical induction.

proof by transposition NOUN /pruf baɪ ˌtræns.poʊˈzɪ.ʃən/ a proof that shows that the contrapositive of a statement is true. If the contrapositive of a statement is true, then the statement is true. See also *contrapositive* (p 29).

proper ADJECTIVE /ˈprɒ.pər/ in ideal form. Example: proper fraction. Antonym: *improper* (p 60).

proper divisor NOUN /ˈprɒ.pər dɪˈvaɪ.zər/ a divisor that is not the integer itself. Example: the proper divisors of 12 are $1, 2, 3, 4$ and 6.

proper factor NOUN /ˈprɒ.pər ˈfæk.tər/ see *proper divisor* (p 93).

proper fraction NOUN /ˈprɒ.pər ˈfræk.ʃən/
1) a numeric fraction where the absolute value of the numerator is less than the absolute value of the denominator: $\frac{a}{b}$ such that $|a| < |b|$. Examples: $\frac{3}{4}, \frac{-7}{16}$.
2) a rational polynomial such that the degree of the numerator is less than the degree of the denominator: $\frac{P}{Q}$ such that $\deg(P) < \deg(Q)$. Example: $\frac{x-3}{x^2+2}$. Antonym: *improper fraction* (p 60).

proper subset NOUN /ˈprɒ.pər ˈsʌb.sɛt/ a subset that is not equal to the original set. Math definition: A is a proper subset of B if and only if $A \subset B$ and $A \neq B$. Notation: $\subsetneq$. Synonym: *subset* (p 110).

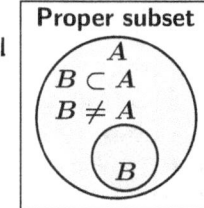
Proper subset
A
$B \subset A$
$B \neq A$
B

property NOUN /ˈprɒ.pər.ti/ an attribute or characteristic shared by a class of objects. Example: length is a property of line segments. Synonyms: *attribute, characteristic* (p 20).

Property of Addition by 0 NOUN /ˈprɒ.pər.ti ʌv əˈdɪ.ʃən baɪ ˈzɪə.roʊ/ see *0, Property of Addition By* (p 6).

Property of Division by 1 NOUN /ˈprɒ.pər.ti ʌv dɪvˈɪ.ʃən baɪ wʌn/ see *1, Property of Division by* (p 6).

Property of Multiplication by 0 NOUN /ˈprɒ.pər.ti ʌv ˌmʌl.tə.plɪˈkeɪ.ʃən baɪ ˈzɪə.roʊ/ see *0, Property of Multiplication by* (p 6).

Property of Multiplication by 1 NOUN /ˈprɒ.pər.ti ʌv ˌmʌl.tə.plɪˈkeɪ.ʃən baɪ wʌn/ see *1, Property of Multiplication by* (p 6).

proportion NOUN /prəˈpoʊr.ʃən/
1) a part compared to a whole.
2) an equation of two ratios in the form $\frac{a}{b} = \frac{c}{d}$.

proportional ADJECTIVE /prəˈpoʊr.ʃə.nl/ having a common ratio. Notation: $\propto$. Formula: $y = ax$ where a is the common ratio. Notation: $x \propto y$ (x is proportional to y).

proportional reasoning NOUN /prəˈpoʊr.ʃə.nl ˈriz.ən.ɪŋ/ an understanding of co-variation and multiple comparisons. The ability to mentally store and process several pieces of mathematical information.

proposition NOUN /ˌprɒ.pəˈzɪ.ʃən/
1) a true statement used to support a conclusion.
2) a statement to be proved. Synonym: *claim*.

protractor NOUN /proʊˈtræk.tər/ a tool used to draw or measure angles.

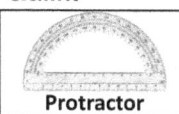
Protractor

Protractor Postulate NOUN /proʊˈtræk.tər ˈpɒs.tʃə.lɪt/ any angle can be paired with a real number.

prove VERB /pruv/ use a mathematically logical argument to show that a proposition is true.

pseudo-random number NOUN /ˈsu.doʊ ˈreɪn.dəm ˈnʌm.bər/ a number from a list of numbers that are not truly random, but are used as if the list is random.

pt. ABBREVIATION pint.

pure ADJECTIVE /pjʊər/ having no other type of component.

pure imaginary number NOUN /pjʊər ɪˈmædʒ.əˌnɛr.i ˈnʌm.bər/ see *imaginary number* (p 59).

pure mathematics NOUN /pjʊər ˌmæθˈmæ.tɪks/ mathematics that is not related to a real-world application; mathematics for the sake of mathematics. Antonym: *applied mathematics* (p 11).

pyramid NOUN /ˈpɪr.ə.mɪd/ a geometric solid with a polygon for a base and triangular sides that meet at a point.

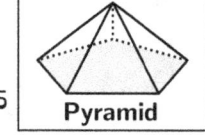
Pyramid

Pythagoras PERSON /pɪˈθæɡ.ər.əs/ (ca 575 B.C.E.—ca. 495 B.C.E.) a Greek mathematician, philosopher, musician and religious leader for whom the Pythagorean Theorem is named.

Pythagorean Identity NOUN /pɪˌθæɡ.əˈri.ən aɪˈdɛn.tɪ.ti/
1) the identity $\cos^2\theta + \sin^2\theta \equiv 1$.
2) one of several trigonometric identities based on the Pythagorean Theorem. See also *Trigonometric Identities* (p 143).

Pythagorean Theorem NOUN /pɪˌθæɡ.əˈri.ən ˈθɪ.ə.rəm/ a theorem relating the lengths of the sides of right triangles. Formula: $A^2 + B^2 = C^2$ where A and B represent the lengths of the legs of the right triangle and C represents the length of the hypotenuse.

$A^2 + B^2 = C^2$
Pythagorean theorem

Pythagorean triple NOUN /pɪˌθæɡ.əˈri.ən ˈtrɪp.əl/ an ordered set of three positive integers which satisfy the Pythagorean Theorem: $A^2 + B^2 = C^2$. Example: $(3, 4, 5)$.

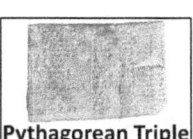
Pythagorean Triple

3rd Dyslexic's Edition

Q

QED ABBREVIATION /kju i di/ Latin for *quod erat demonstrundum* meaning 'that which was to be shown'; an abbreviation placed at the end of a proof. Notation: ∎.

qt. ABBREVIATION see *quart* (p 94).

quad- PREFIX /kwɒd/ four. Example: quadrant.

quadrangle NOUN /ˈkwɒˌdræŋ.ɡəl/ see *quadrilateral* (p 94).

quadrant NOUN /ˈkwɒ.drnt/
1) one of four regions into which the rectangular coordinate plane is divided by the axes.
2) one quarter of a circle.

quadrantal ADJECTIVE /kwɒˈdrən.tl/ having to do with a quadrant.

quadrantal angle NOUN /kwɒˈdrən.tl ˈæn.ɡəl/ any angle that is a multiple of 90°. Examples: 0°, 90°, 180°, 270°.

quadratic /kwɒˈdræ.tɪk/
1) ADJECTIVE involving a 2nd degree polynomial. Example: quadratic formula.
2) NOUN a quadratic equation.

quadratic approximation NOUN /kwɒˈdræ.tɪk əˌprɒk.səˈmeɪ.ʃən/ a way to approximate a function given its first and second derivatives. Formula: given a function $f(x)$ that is smooth near $x = a$, $f(x) \approx f(a) + f'(a)(x-a) + \frac{1}{2}f''(a)(x-a)^2$.

quadratic equation NOUN /kwɒˈdræ.tɪk ɪˈkweɪ.ʃən/ equation of a single variable polynomial that is degree 2. Formulas: $y = ax^2 + bx + c, a \neq 0$; or $f(x) = a(x-h)^2 + k, a \neq 0$. Example: $y = -3x^2 + 2x - 4$.

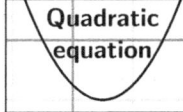

quadratic factor NOUN /kwɒdˈræ.tɪk ˈfæk.tər/ a factor of a polynomial where the factor is degree 2. Example: $x^2 + x - 2$.

quadratic formula NOUN /kwɒdˈræ.tɪk ˈfɔr.mju.lə/ a formula used to solve and find the roots of quadratic equations. Formula: $x = \frac{-b \pm \sqrt{b^2 - 4ac}}{2a}$ where $0 = ax^2 + bx + c$.

quadratic function NOUN /kwɒdˈræ.tɪk ˈfʌŋk.ʃən/ a function of a quadratic polynomial. Formula: $f(x) = ax^2 + bx + c, a \neq 0$, $y = a(x-h)^2 + k, a \neq 0$, (h, k) is the vertex.

quadratic inequality NOUN /kwɒdˈræ.tɪk ˌɪn.ɪˈkwɒl.ɪ.ti/ an inequality with a quadratic polynomial on one side of the inequality and zero or a dependent variable on the other side. Example: $y > x^2 - x - 2$.

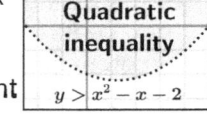

quadrilateral NOUN /ˌkwɒ.drəˈlæ.tər.əl/ a four-sided polygon. Some common types of quadrilaterals are: square, rectangle, rhombus and trapezoid (trapezium in British English).

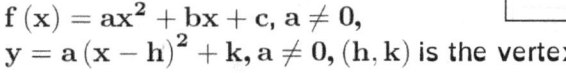

quadrillion ADJECTIVE, NOUN /kwɒˈdrɪl.jən/ $10^{15} = 1,000,000,000,000,000$. Synonym: peta-.

quadrillionth ADJECTIVE, NOUN /kwɒˈdrɪl.jənθ/ $10^{-15} = 0.000\ 000\ 000\ 000\ 001$. Synonym: femto-.

quadruple /ˌkwɒˈdru.pl/
1) VERB multiply by four.
2) NOUN multiplied by four.
3) ADJECTIVE being four times as great.

qualitative data NOUN /ˌkwɒ.lɪˈteɪ.tɪv ˈdeɪ.tʌ/ data that is not numerical data. Examples: gender, color preference. Synonym: categorical data (p 19). Antonym: quantitative data (p 94).

quantitative data NOUN /ˈkwɒn.tɪˈteɪ.tɪv ˈdeɪ.tʌ/ numerical data. Examples: age, height. Antonym: qualitative data (p 94).

quantity NOUN /ˈkwɒn.tɪ.ti/ how many or how much of something there is. Synonym: frequency (p 51).

quar- PREFIX /kwɔr/ four or fourth. Example: quarter.

quart NOUN /kwɔrt/ a unit of measure of volume. Abbreviation: qt. Formula: 1 quart = 4 cups. 1 quart = 32 fluid ounces. 1 quart $\approx$ 0.946 liters.

quarter NOUN /ˈkwɔr.tər/
1) one of four equal parts; $\frac{1}{4}$ or 25%.
2) a coin valued at $\frac{1}{4}$ of a dollar or 25 cents.
3) a period of three months, $\frac{1}{4}$ of a year.

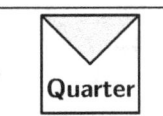

quarterly NOUN /ˈkwɔr.tər.li/
1) once every three months. Example: quarterly meeting.
2) having to do with a three month period. Example: quarterly profit.

quartic /ˈkwɔr.tɪk/
1) NOUN a 4th degree polynomial. Example: $x^4 + 3x^2$.
2) ADJECTIVE having to do with a 4th degree polynomial.

quartile NOUN /ˈkwɔr.taɪl/ one of three values that divide a dataset into four equal parts.

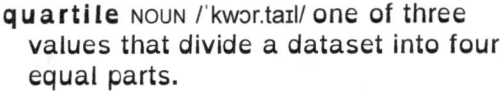

quarternary ADJECTIVE /ˈkwɔr.təˌnær.i/
1) fourth in rank or importance.
2) having to do with the number four.

quin- PREFIX /kwɪn/ five or fifth. Example: quintic.

quinary ADJECTIVE /ˈkwɪnˌnær.i/
1) fifth in order or importance.
2) having to do with the number five.

quintic /ˈkwɪn.tɪk/
1) NOUN a 5th degree polynomial. Example: $x^5 - 4x^2$.
2) ADJECTIVE having to do with a 5th degree polynomial.

quintile NOUN /ˈkwɪn.taɪl/ one of four values that divide a dataset into five equal parts.

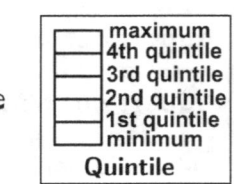

quintillion ADJECTIVE, NOUN /kwɪnˈtɪl.jən/ $10^{18} = 1,000,000,000,000,000,000$. Synonym: exa-.

quintillionth ADJECTIVE, NOUN /kwɪnˈtɪl.jənθ/ $10^{-18} = 0.000\ 000\ 000\ 000\ 000\ 001$. Synonym: atto-.

quotient NOUN /ˈkwoʊ.ʃənt/ the result of a division problem. Notation: $\text{divisor} \overline{)\text{dividend}}^{\text{quotient}}$;

$\frac{\text{dividend}}{\text{divisor}}$ = quotient; dividend ÷ divisor = quotient

Quotient Property of Exponents NOUN /'kwoʊ.ʃənt 'prɒ.pər.ti ʌv 'ɛks.poʊ.nəntz/ the quotient of two values with exponents that have the same base is equal to the base raised to the difference of the exponents. Math definition: $\frac{b^m}{b^n} = b^{m-n}$, $b \neq 0$.

Quotient Property of Logarithms NOUN /'kwoʊ.ʃənt 'prɒ.pər.ti ʌv 'lɒ.gə.rɪð.əmz/ the logarithm of one value divided by another is equal to the logarithm of the numerator minus the logarithm of the denominator. Math definition: $\log_b \frac{M}{N} \equiv \log_b M - \log_b N$, $N \neq 0$.

quotient rule NOUN /'kwoʊ.ʃənt rul/ the differential of a quotient is the differential of the denominator minus the differential of the numerator, all divided by the denominator squared. Math definition: $\frac{d}{dx}\left[\frac{u}{v}\right] = \frac{\frac{d}{dx}v - \frac{d}{dx}u}{v^2}$.

R

R ABBREVIATION
1) remainder. Example: 5R2 (5 remainder 2).
2) relation. Example: aRb is a relation between a and b.

rad. ABBREVIATION radian.

radial ADJECTIVE /'reɪ.di.əl/ having to do with a radius from a central point. Example: radial symmetry.

radial point NOUN /'reɪ.di.əl pɔɪnt/ a point from which multiple rays start.

radial symmetry NOUN /'reɪ.di.əl 'sɪ.mɪ.tri/ a figure has radial symmetry if, when rotated about a center point by a certain angle θ, $0° < \theta < 360°$, the image of the figure lies exactly on top of the preimage.

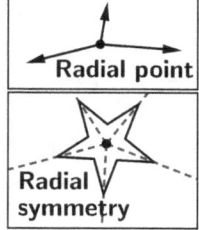
Radial point

Radial symmetry

radian NOUN /'reɪ.diən/ a unit of measure of angles. A full circle equals 2π radians. A radian equals the arc length of a sector of the unit circle from standard position to a terminal side. Formulas: π **radians = 180°. 1 radian ≈ 57.2958°**. Abbreviation: rad.

radical /'ræ.dɪ.kəl/
1) NOUN the root of a quantity. Examples: $\sqrt{5}$ or $\sqrt[3]{x+2}$. Synonym: root (p 100).
2) NOUN the symbol used to indicate root: $\sqrt{}$.
3) ADJECTIVE having to do with or containing roots. Example: radical expression.
See also Properties of Radicals (p 129).

radical expression NOUN /'ræ.dɪ.kəl ɪk'sprɛ.ʃən/ an expression with one or more variables inside a radical. Example: $3 + \sqrt{x}$.

radical function NOUN /'ræ.dɪ.kəl 'fʌŋk.ʃən/ a function with one or more variables in a radical. Example: $f(x) = 2 - \sqrt{x}$.

Radical function
$y = 2 - \sqrt{x}$

radicand NOUN /ˌræ.dɪ'kænd/ the value that appears under a radical sign; the value of which a root is to be taken. Notation: $\sqrt{\text{radicand}}$.

radioactive decay NOUN /ˌreɪ.di.oʊ'æk.tɪv dɪ'keɪ/ the breakdown of radioactive substances. Formula: $f(x) = ae^{bx}$ where $a > 0$ is the initial value, $b < 0$ is the decay factor.

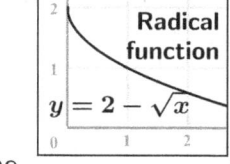
Radioactive decay
$y = 2(\frac{1}{2})^x$

radius NOUN /'reɪ.di.əs/
1) a line segment extending from the center of a circle to the edge of the circle.
2) the length of a radius of a circle.
3) a ray that extends from a central point.
Plural: radii /'reɪ.di.aɪ/.

Radius

radix NOUN /'reɪ.dɪks/ the base number of a numeration system. Example: radix 10. Synonym: base.

raise to a power VERB /reɪz tu ʌ 'paʊ.ər/ to evaluate an exponent. Example: raise 2 to the 3rd power: $2^3 = 8$. See also exponent (p 47).

random ADJECTIVE /'ræn.dəm/ without pattern, nonrepeating. Example: random number.

random event NOUN /'ræn.dəm ɪ'vɛnt/ an event that happens without outside influence on its outcome.

random number NOUN /'ræn.dəm 'nʌm.bər/ a number from a list of numbers that is nonrepeating and satisfies no algorithm.

random number generator NOUN /'ræn.dəm 'nʌm.bər 'dʒɛn.ər.eɪ.tər/ a computer program that produces random or pseudo-random numbers.

random sample NOUN /'ræn.dəm 'sæm.pəl/ a sample taken from a population using a random method to choose the sample.

random selection NOUN /'ræn.dəm sɪ'lɛk.ʃən/ selection from a population using a random process.

random variable NOUN /'ræn.dəm 'vɛər.i.ə.bəl/ a variable that takes on any value in a column of a dataset.

range NOUN /reɪndʒ/
1) (functions) all output values of a function. Antonym: domain (p 41).
2) (of a dataset) the lowest and highest values of the dataset.
3) an interval.

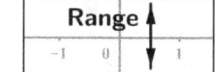
Range

rate NOUN /reɪt/
1) an amount per base unit; a ratio. Example: Prices are increasing at a rate of 3%.
2) a ratio that compares values in different units of measure. Example: dollars per gallon.
3) a ratio. Example: rate of change.

rate of change NOUN /'reɪt ʌv tʃeɪndʒ/
1) (linear) the ratio of change of two variables. Synonym: slope (p 106).
2) (nonlinear) the limit of rates of change between two points on a curve as one approaches the other; the slope of a line tangent to the curve at a point.

rate of interest NOUN /reɪt ʌv 'ɪn.tər.ɛst/ see interest rate (p 63).

ratio NOUN /'reɪ.ʃoʊ/
1) a comparison of two quantities by division.
2) a relative quantity; a proportion. Example: 1 out of 4 people in the United States are obese. 1:4 or $\frac{1}{4}$.

rational ADJECTIVE /'ræʃ.nl/
1) can be written as a ratio. Example: rational number: $\frac{5}{4}$, $\frac{9}{3}$.
2) is written as a ratio. Example: rational expression:

$\frac{x+3}{x^2-2x}$.

rationalize VERB /'ræʃ.nl̩.aɪz/ to remove radicals from the denominator of an expression. Formulas: $\frac{1}{\sqrt{a}} = \frac{1}{\sqrt{a}} \cdot \frac{\sqrt{a}}{\sqrt{a}} = \frac{\sqrt{a}}{a}$, $\frac{1}{\sqrt{a}+\sqrt{b}} = \frac{\sqrt{a}-\sqrt{b}}{a-b}$. Example: $\frac{1}{\sqrt{2}} = \frac{\sqrt{2}}{2}$.

rational number NOUN /'ræʃ.nl̩ 'nʌm.bər/ a real number that can be written as the ratio of two integers. Example: $\frac{2}{3}, \frac{5}{1}$. Antonym: *irrational number* (p 65).

rational root NOUN /'ræʃ.nl̩ rut/ a root that is a rational number.

Rational Roots Theorem NOUN /'ræʃ.nl̩ ruts 'θɪ.ə.rəm/ see *rational zeroes theorem* (p 96).

Rational Zeros Theorem NOUN /'ræʃ.nl̩ 'zɪə.roʊz 'θɪ.ə.rəm/ given a polynomial $a_n x^n + a_{n-1} x^{n-1} + \cdots + a_1 x + a_0$ with integer coefficients, any rational roots of the polynomial have a numerator which is a factor of a_n and a denominator which is a factor of a_0. Example: If $a_n = 6$ and $a_0 = 5$, any rational root of the polynomial will be one of the following: $\frac{1}{1}, \frac{2}{1}, \frac{3}{1}, \frac{6}{1}, \frac{1}{5}, \frac{2}{5}, \frac{3}{5}, \frac{6}{5}$.

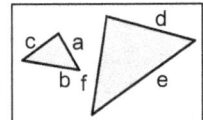
Ratio of sides similarity

Ratio of Sides Similarity NOUN /'reɪ.ʃoʊ ʌv saɪdz ˌsɪ.mə'lær.ɪ.ti/ if the ratios of all three corresponding sides of two triangles are equal, then the triangles are similar. Math definition: given $\triangle ABC$ and $\triangle DEF$, if $\frac{a}{d} = \frac{b}{e} = \frac{c}{f}$ then $\triangle ABC \sim \triangle DEF$.

ratio test NOUN /'reɪ.ʃoʊ tɛst/ a test for convergence used when terms of a series contain factorials and/or an integer exponent. The ratio test makes use of the number $L = \lim_{n \to \infty} \left| \frac{a_{n-1}}{a_n} \right|$. If $L < 1$, the series converges. If $L > 1$, the series diverges. If $L = 1$, or the limit does not exist, the test is inconclusive.

raw data NOUN /rɔ 'deɪ.tə/ data that has been collected, but not processed or sorted.

ray NOUN /reɪ/ a straight half-line starting at an endpoint and going on forever in one direction. Notation: $\overrightarrow{ab}$ (ray ab), where a is the endpoint and b is any point on the ray other than the endpoint. Synonym: *half-line*.

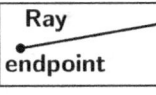
Ray endpoint

re- PREFIX /ri/ again. Example: recur.

real ADJECTIVE /riəl/ having to do with real numbers. Antonym: *complex* (p 25).

real axis NOUN /riəl 'æk.sɪs/ the horizontal axis in the complex plane which represents the real part of a complex number.

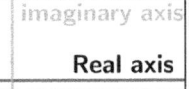
Real axis

real line NOUN /riəl laɪn/ see *number line* (p 81).

real number NOUN /riəl 'nʌm.bər/ a number that can be found on the real number line. Examples: $14, \frac{6}{5}, \pi$.

real number line NOUN /riəl 'nʌm.bər laɪn/ see *number line* (p 81).

real part NOUN /riəl pɑrt/ the part of a complex number that is not multiplied by $i = \sqrt{-1}$: a in $a + bi$. Notation: $\Re$, RE. Examples: $\Re(3 + 2i) = 3$, $RE(4 - i) = 4$.

real solution NOUN /riəl sɑ'lu.ʃən/ a solution that contains only real numbers. Antonym: *complex solution* (p 25).

real valued ADJECTIVE /riəl 'væl.jud/ having variables that represent real numbers and not complex numbers. Antonym: *complex valued* (p 25).

real variable NOUN /riəl 'vɛər.i.ə.bəl/ a variable that represents a real number and not a complex number.

reason /'ri.zən/
1) VERB to form conclusions based on fact or evidence.
2) NOUN why something is true; a justification.
3) NOUN an explanation of why something is.

reasonable ADJECTIVE /'riz.nə.bəl/
1) makes sense.
2) justified.
Antonym: *unreasonable* (p 119).

reasonableness ADJECTIVE /'riz.nə.bəl.nəs/ whether or not something is reasonable. Example: reasonableness test.

reasonableness test NOUN /'riz.nə.bəl.nəs tɛst/ an algorithm for checking reasonableness of a result.

reasoning NOUN /'riz nɪŋ/ a process of forming conclusions or inferences from premises.

reciprocal NOUN /rɪ'sɪp.rə.kəl/ multiplicative inverse. The reciprocal of a is $\frac{1}{a}$ Example: the reciprocal of $\frac{3}{4}$ is $\frac{4}{3}$ Synonym: *multiplicative inverse* (p 77).

reciprocal function noun /rɪ'sɪp.rə.kəl 'fʌŋk.ʃən/ a function that has a reciprocal of a variable. Formula: $f(x) = \frac{1}{x}$.

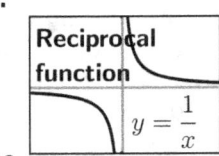
Reciprocal function $y = \frac{1}{x}$

reciprocal rule NOUN /rɪ'sɪp.rə.kəl rul/ the derivative of the reciprocal of a function is equal to the derivative of the function divided by the function squared. Math definition: $\frac{d}{dx}\left[\frac{1}{v}\right] = -\frac{\frac{d}{dx}v}{v^2}$.

recognize VERB /'rɛ.kəg naɪz/ to identify from what is already known.

rectangle NOUN /'rɛk.tæŋ.gəl/ a four-sided polygon whose sides meet at right angles.

Rectangle

rectangular ADJECTIVE /rɛk'tæŋ.gjə.lər/
1) having to do with a rectangle. Example: rectangular number.
2) shaped like a rectangle.
3) having perpendicular axes. Example: rectangular coordinate.
4) including or based on a rectangle. Example: rectangular prism.

rectangular coordinate NOUN /rɛk'tæŋ.gjə.lər koʊ'ɔr.dn.ɪt/ an ordered pair, ordered triple, etc. that represents a location in a rectangular coordinate system. Notation: (x, y) (2-dimensional), (x, y, z) (3-dimensional). Synonym: *Cartesian coordinate*.

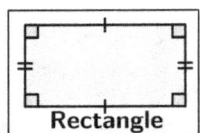
Rectangular coordinate (1, 1.5)

rectangular coordinate plane NOUN /rɛk'tæŋ.gjə.lər koʊ'ɔr.dn.ɪt pleɪn/ a 2-dimensional rectangular coordinate system.

Rectangular coordinate system

rectangular coordinate system NOUN /rɛk'tæŋ.gjə.lər koʊ'ɔr.dn.ɪt 'sɪs.təm/ a metric n-space with perpendicular axes meeting at an origin. Synonym: *Cartesian coordinate system*.

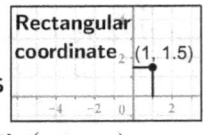
Rectangular hyperbola

rectangular hyperbola NOUN /rɛk'tæŋ.gjə.lər haɪ'pɜr.bə.lə/ a hyperbola with horizontal and vertical asymptotes. *Equation:* $y = \frac{a}{x-h} + k$ where $x = h$ is the vertical asymptote and $y = k$ is the horizontal asymptote.

rectangular number NOUN /rɛk'tæŋ.gjə.lər 'nʌm.bər/ a natural number that can be drawn in the shape of a rectangle; a number that is not a prime number. *Synonym: composite integer (p 25). Antonym: prime number (p 91).*

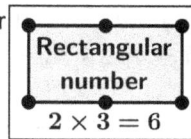
Rectangular number
$2 \times 3 = 6$

rectangular parallelepiped NOUN /rɛk'tæŋ.gjə.lər ˌpær.ə.lɛl.ə'paɪ.pɪd/ see *rectangular solid* (p 97).

rectangular prism NOUN /rɛk'tæŋ.gjə.lər 'prɪz.əm/ see *rectangular solid* (p 97).

rectangular pyramid NOUN /rɛk'tæŋ.gjə.lər 'pɪr.ə.mɪd/ a pyramid whose base is a rectangle.

Rectangular pyramid

rectangular solid NOUN /rɛk'tæŋ.gjə.lər 'sɒ.lɪd/ a geometric solid whose faces are all rectangles. *Synonym: cuboid.*

Rectangular solid

rectilinear ADJECTIVE /ˌrɛk.tə'lɪn.i.ər/
1) moving or forming a straight line or lines.
2) having to do with a straight line.

recur VERB /rɪ'kɜr/
1) to happen again.
2) to repeat.

recurring decimal NOUN /rɪ'kɜr.ɪŋ 'dɛs.məl/ a decimal which has digits that repeat. *Example:* $3.\overline{1} = 3.1111111\cdots$.

recursion NOUN /rɪ'kɜr.ʃən/
1) the process of making repeated use of an algorithm.
2) one step in a repeating algorithm. *Synonym: iteration (p 65).*

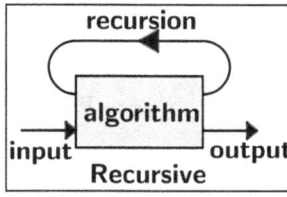
Recursive

recursive ADJECTIVE /rɪ'kɜr.sɪv/ something that is applied repeatedly. *Synonym: iterative (p 65).*

recursive formula NOUN /rɪ'kɜr.sɪv 'fɔr.mju.lə/ a formula that gives the nth element of a sequence. *Example:* $\begin{cases} a_1 = 2 \\ a_{n+1} = 2a_n \end{cases}$ is the formula for the sequence is $\{2, 4, 8, 16, 32, \cdots\}$.

reduce VERB /rɪ'dus/
1) to change to a simpler form. *Example: reduce a fraction.*
2) to find prime factors of. *Example: reduce an integer.*
3) to make smaller.

reduce a fraction VERB /rɪ'dus eɪ 'fræk.ʃən/ to cancel common factors in a fraction. *Formula:* $\frac{a}{b} = \frac{a \div \gcd(a,b)}{b \div \gcd(a,b)}$. *Example:* $\frac{10}{30} = \frac{\cancel{2} \cdot \cancel{5}}{\cancel{2} \cdot 3 \cdot \cancel{5}} = \frac{1}{3}$.

reduced fraction NOUN /rɪ'dusd 'fræk.ʃən/ a fraction whose numerator and denominator have no common factors. See also *simplest form* (p 105).

reduced row echelon form NOUN /rɪ'dus.d roʊ 'ɛʃ.ə.lɒn fɔrm/ an augmented square matrix with zeros in entries to the left of the main diagonal, followed by a one in the main diagonal. See also *row echelon form* (p 101).

$\begin{bmatrix} 1 & 2 & 1 & 3 \\ 0 & 1 & 3 & 2 \\ 0 & 0 & 1 & 1 \end{bmatrix}$
Reduced row echelon form

reducible ADJECTIVE /rɪ'dus.ə.bəl/ can be reduced to a simpler form. *Example:* $\frac{2}{4}$ is reducible to $\frac{1}{2}$. *Antonym: irreducible* (p 65).

reducible polynomial NOUN /rɪ'dus.ə.bəl ˌpɒ.lə'noʊ.mi.əl/ a polynomial that has at least one factor other than 1 and itself. *Antonym: irreducible polynomial* (p 65). See also *factor a polynomial completely* (p 49).

reference ADJECTIVE /'rɛf.rəns/ used for comparison. *Example:* reference line.

reference angle NOUN /'rɛf.rəns 'æŋ.gəl/ an angle between 0° and 90° (0 rad. and $\frac{\pi}{2}$ rad.) that is measured from the closest horizontal axis. *Example:* the reference angle for $157° = 180° - 157° = 23°$. See also *reference number* (p 97).

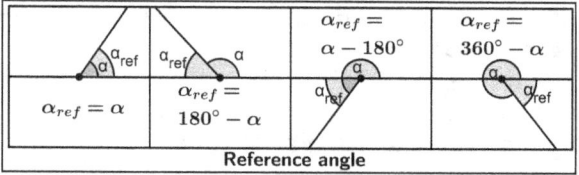
Reference angle

reference number NOUN /'rɛf.rəns 'nʌm.bər/ if t is a real number, the reference number of t is the shortest distance along the unit circle between the terminal point of t and the x-axis. *Notation:* $\bar{t}$. See also *reference angle* (p 97).

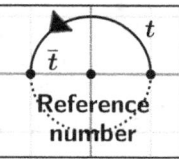
Reference number

reference plane NOUN /'rɛf.rəns pleɪn/ a plane, usually horizontal, to which other objects are compared.

reflect VERB /rɪ'flɛkt/ to 'flip' an object across a line or a point. *Synonym: mirror.*

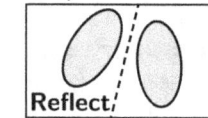
Reflect

reflection NOUN /rɪ'flɛk.ʃən/
1) a geometric transformation made by 'flipping' an object across a line or a point.
2) the result of reflecting an object. *Synonym: mirror image* (p 75).

reflective symmetry NOUN /rɪ'flɛk.tɪv 'sɪ.mɪ.tri/ whether or not the preimage is congruent with the image after a reflection. *Synonyms: line symmetry, mirror symmetry.*

reflex angle NOUN /'ri.flɛks 'æŋ.gəl/ an angle that measures more than 180 degrees and less than 360 degrees.

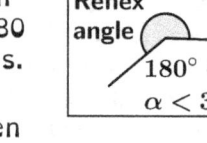
Reflex angle
$180° < \alpha$
$\alpha < 360°$

reflexive adjective /ri'flɛk.sɪv/ if, for a relation R, aRa is always true, then relation R is reflexive. *Example:* $5 = 5$.

Reflexive Property of Equality NOUN /ri'flɛk.sɪv 'prɒ.pər.ti ʌv ɪ'kwɒl.ɪ.ti/ a number is always equal to itself. *Formula:* $a = a$. *Examples:* $-3 = -3$, $1 - i = 1 - i$.

region NOUN /'ri.dʒən/ all points that are part of a shape including boundary points and interior points.

regression ADJECTIVE /rɪ'grɛʃ.ən/ a line or curve determined by regression analysis.

regression analysis NOUN /rɪ'grɛʃ.ən ə'næ.lə.sɪs/ a process used to create an equation that models statistical data. This includes linear regression and nonlinear regression.

regression line NOUN /rɪ'grɛʃ.ən laɪn/ a line used to model data. *Synonym: linear fit.*

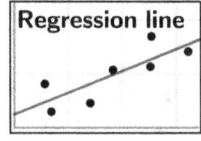
Regression line

regroup VERB /riˈgrup/ to rearrange groups of digits in a numeration system especially in arithmetic operations. Synonyms: *decomposition method* (p 34), *carry* (obsolete), *borrow* (obsolete).

regular ADJECTIVE /ˈrɛ.gjə.lər/
1) uniform; conforming to a standard or a pattern. Example: regular tessellation.
2) symmetric.
Antonym: *irregular* (p 65).

regular interval NOUN /ˈrɛ.gjə.lər ˈɪn.tər.vəl/ one of a group of intervals where the length of each interval is the same.

regular polygon NOUN /ˈrɛ.gjə.lər ˈpɒ.lɪˌgɒn/ a convex polygon whose sides are all the same length. Antonym: *irregular polygon* (p 65).

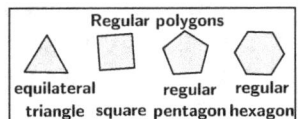

regular polyhedron NOUN /ˈrɛ.gjə.lər ˌpɒ.liˈhi.drən/ any one of five solids whose faces are congruent regular polygons and where the angles between the faces are all congruent. Examples: regular tetrahedron, regular hexahedron, regular octahedron, regular dodecahedron. Plural: regular polyhedra /ˈrɛ.gjə.lər ˌpɒ.liˈhi.drə/.

regular prism NOUN /ˈrɛ.gjə.lər ˈprɪz.əm/ a right prism whose base is a regular polygon.

regular pyramid NOUN /ˈrɛ.gjə.lər ˈpɪr.ə.mɪd/ a right pyramid whose base is a regular polygon.

regular tessellation NOUN /ˈrɛ.gjə.lər ˌtɛs.əˈleɪ.ʃən/ a tessellation made up entirely of regular polygons.

relate VERB /rɪˈleɪt/ to compare using a relationship operator. Example: $x = y + 2$ relates x and y.

related ADJECTIVE /rɪˈleɪ.tɪd/ having a relationship one with another.

related fraction NOUN /rɪˈleɪ.td ˈfræk.ʃən/ one of two or more fractions with the same denominator.

related rates NOUN /rɪˈleɪ.tɪd reɪts/ two rates of change are related if there exists a relation that gives on rate of change in terms of the other. Example: when blowing up a balloon, the rate of change of the volume is related to the rate of change of the diameter.

relation NOUN /rɪˈleɪ.ʃən/
1) a set of ordered pairs, input and output.
2) a property of sets that associates two or more elements. Synonyms: *mapping*, *function* (p 52).
3) a property of sets such that, for any two members of the set a and b, aRb is either true or false. Example: equality.

relationship NOUN /rɪˈleɪ.ʃən.ʃɪp/ how two or more objects relate to each other.

relationship operator NOUN /rɪˈleɪ.ʃən.ʃɪp ˈɒ.pəˌreɪ.tər/ a symbol used to describe a particular relationship between two objects. Examples: $<, \leq, \neq, =, \geq, >, \equiv, \approx$.

relative ADJECTIVE /ˈrɛ.lə.tɪv/
1) compared to. Example: relative frequency.
2) in relation to. Example: relatively prime.
3) local. Example: relative maximum.

relative change NOUN /ˈrɛ.lə.tɪv tʃeɪndʒ/ the ratio of the change of two variables. Formula: $\frac{\Delta y}{\Delta x} = \frac{\text{change in y}}{\text{change in x}}$.

relative error NOUN /ˈrɛ.lə.tɪv ˈɛr.ər/
1) ratio of an absolute error to the actual or theoretical value.
2) the error in proportion to the measurement. Example: if a length measures **2 cm** and the error is ±**0.5 cm**, the relative error is $\frac{0.5}{2} = 0.25 = 25\%$.

relative frequency NOUN /ˈrɛ.lə.tɪv ˈfri.kwɪn.si/
1) (probability) the number of times a particular outcome happened during a set of experiments as a proportion of the total number of trials.
2) (statistics) the number of observations in a particular category divided by the total number of observations.
Antonym: *absolute frequency* (p 7).

relatively prime ADJECTIVE /ˈrɛ.lə.tɪv.li praɪm/ having no common factors except **1**.

relative maximum NOUN /ˈrɛ.lə.tɪv ˈmæk.sə.məm/ see *local maximum* (p 70).

relative minimum NOUN /ˈrɛ.lə.tɪv ˈmɪ.nə.məm/ see *local minimum* (p 70).

remainder NOUN /rɪˈmeɪn.dər/ the amount left over after division. Abbreviation: R. Math definition: $a \div b = cRd$ if and only if $a = bc + d$, $|d| < |b|$. Example: $17 \div 5 = 3R2$. The remainder is **2**. Synonym: *modulo n* (p 76).

Remainder Theorem NOUN /rɪˈmeɪn.dər ˈθɪ.ə.rəm/ if the polynomial $P(x)$ is divided by $x - c$, then the remainder is the value of $P(c)$. Corollary: If a is a root of $P(x)$ then the remainder of the division of $P(x)$ by $x - a$ is **0**. Formula: $\frac{P(x)}{x-a} = P'(x) + \frac{P(a)}{x-a}$.

remaining ADJECTIVE /rɪˈmeɪn.ɪŋ/ not used up; left over.

remote interior angles NOUN /rɪˈmoʊt ɪnˈtɪər.i.ər ˈæŋ.gəlz/ angles of a triangle that are not adjacent to a particular exterior angle.

removable discontinuity NOUN /rɪˈmu.və.bəl ˌdɪs.kɒn.tnˈu.ɪ.ti/ a discontinuity where the discontinuity can be removed by defining the function or relation differently so as to "plug" the hole. Antonym: *essential discontinuity* (p 45).

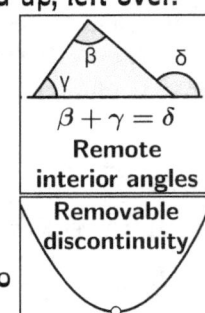

repeat VERB /rɪˈpit/
1) to appear or happen again.
2) to make appear or happen again.

repeating ADJECTIVE /rɪˈpit.ɪŋ/ appearing or happening again. Antonym: *nonrepeating* (p 80). Example: repeating decimal.

repeating decimal NOUN /rɪˈpit.ɪŋ ˈdɛs.məl/ a real number where one or more digits repeat forever. Notation: $5.3\overline{25} = 5.3252525\cdots$. Antonym: *nonrepeating decimal* (p 80).

repelling NOUN /rɪˈpɛl.ɪŋ/ points near x^* move away from x^*. Formula: x^* is repelling if $\left|\frac{d}{dx}f(x)\right| > 1$. Antonym: *attracting* (p 14).

repetition NOUN /ˌrɛ.pɪˈtɪ.ʃən/
1) the act of repeating; the act of appearing or happening again.
2) something that is the result of repeating.

replace VERB /rɪˈpleɪs/
1) (algebra) to substitute objects from one set with objects from another set. Synonym: *substitute* (p 110). Example: Replace **y** with **4** in the equation.
2) (probability) to put back; to allow to be selected again.

replacement NOUN /rɪˈpleɪs.mənt/
1) the property of being used to replace something else.
2) (probability) the property of whether an event can happen a second time. Example: select two balls with replacement: select one ball, put it back, then select another.

replacement set NOUN /rɪˈpleɪs.mənt sɛt/ a set of possible values that can be used in place of an unknown in an open mathematical sentence.

represent VERB /ˌrɛ.prɪˈzɛnt/ use something to stand for or illustrate something else. Example: a variable represents a value that can change.

representation NOUN /ˌrɛ.prɪ.zɛnˈteɪ.ʃən/ something used to represent something else. Example: a bar chart is a representation of data.

representative ADJECTIVE /ˌrɛ.prɪˈzɛn.tə.tɪv/ serving to represent. Example: representative sample.

representative fraction NOUN /ˌrɛ.prɪˈzɛn.tə.tɪv ˈfræk.ʃən/ a fraction that that represents the scale of a map. See also *map scale* (p 72).

representative sample NOUN /ˌrɛ.prɪˈzɛn.tə.tɪv ˈsam.pəl/ a data sample believed to represent an entire population.

research
1) VERB /riˈsɜrtʃ/ to investigate methodically.
2) NOUN /rɪˈsɜrtʃ/ the result of a methodical investigation.

residual NOUN /rɪˈzɪdʒ.u.əl/ the difference between an observation and the mean of the sample from which the observation was taken. Formula: $\mathrm{Residual} = d_n - M_X$ where d_n is the data for item number **n** and M_X is a mean of data set **X**.

residue NOUN /rɛˈzɪ.dju/ the result of a modulo operation. Formula: **dividend mod. divisor = residue**. Example: $14 \bmod 5 = 4$. Synonym: *remainder* (p 98).

respect NOUN /rɪˈspɛkt/ see *with respect to* (p 122).

respectively ADVERB /rɪˈspɛk.tɪv.li/ taken in the same order as the previous list. Example: 'The values of **a**, **b** and **c** are 1, 2 and 3, respectively,' means $a = 1$, $b = 2$ and $c = 3$.

restrict VERB /rɪˈstrɪkt/ to limit in some way. Example: restrict the domain.

restricted domain NOUN /rɪˈstrɪk.tɪd doʊ.meɪn/ a domain where a restriction has been placed on the domain. Example: $x > 2$.

Restricted domain
$y = x^2, x \leq 1$

restricted function NOUN /rɪˈstrɪk.tɪd ˈfʌŋk.ʃən/ a function with a restricted domain.

result NOUN /rɪˈzʌlt/
1) the final answer to a computation. Example: the result of $(5 \times 6) \div 3$ is 10.
2) the outcome of a proof, transformation or other operation.

resultant NOUN /rɪˈzʌl.tnt/ a vector that is the sum of two or more vectors. Example: the resultant of $\langle 3, -1 \rangle + \langle -2, 2 \rangle$ is $\langle 3 - 2, -1 + 2 \rangle = \langle 1, 1 \rangle$.

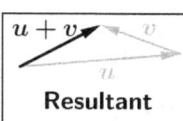
Resultant

retail price NOUN /ˈri.teɪl praɪs/ a price charged retail customers; the price after markup. Formula: **cost + markup = retail price**.

retrace VERB /riˈtreɪs/ to move along a part of a figure that has already been traced over.

reverse /rɪˈvɜrs/
1) VERB to change to the opposite.
2) NOUN the opposite of something.

revise VERB /rɪˈvaɪz/
1) to change.
2) to correct or improve.

revolution NOUN /ˌrɛ.voʊˈlu.ʃən/
1) one complete turn around a circle.
2) one complete orbit around a sphere.

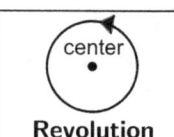
Revolution

revolutions per second NOUN /ˌrɛ.voʊˈlu.ʃənz pər ˈsɛ.kənd/ a unit of measure of rotational speed; the number of times an object rotates a full 360° in one second.

revolve VERB /rɪˈvɒlv/ see *rotate* (p 100).

rewrite VERB /riˈraɪt/ to write in a different form.

Rhind papyrus NOUN /raɪnd pəˈpaɪ.rəs/ an Egyptian mathematical text dating from about 1650 B.C.E. Like a modern textbook, the Rhind papyrus contained a set of math problems and their answers.

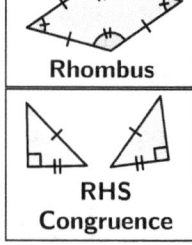
Rhind papyrus

rhombus NOUN /ˈrɒm.bəs/ a quadrilateral with four equal sides. Plural: rhombi /ˈrɒm.baɪ/.

Rhombus

RHS congruence NOUN /ɑr eɪtʃ ɛs ˈkɒŋ.gru.əns/ (right angle-hypotenuse-side congruence) two right triangles are congruent if their hypotenuses and one side are congruent.

RHS Congruence

rhythmic counting NOUN /ˈrɪð.mɪk ˈkaʊn.tɪŋ/ counting while emphasizing certain multiples. Example: 1, 2, **3**, 4, 5, **6**, ...

Riemann, Georg Friedrich Bernhard PERSON /ˈri.mɑn dʒɔrdʒ ˈfri.drɪk bɜrnˈɑrd/ (1826—1866) a German mathematician known for his work with the Dirichlet Principle and the Riemann zeta function.

Georg Riemann

Riemannian geometry NOUN /riˈmɑ.ni.ən dʒiˈɒ.mɪ.tri/ a non-Euclidean geometry that can be visualized as taking place on the surface of a sphere or ellipse, where a line is a great circle. Synonym: *spherical geometry* (p 107).

Riemann sum NOUN /ˈri.mɑn sʌm/ the sum of areas of shapes under a curve. This is a precursor to integrals.

right ADJECTIVE /raɪt/
1) having to do with perpendicular lines. Antonym: *oblique* (p 81).
2) in a direction opposite to left. Antonym: *left* (p 68).

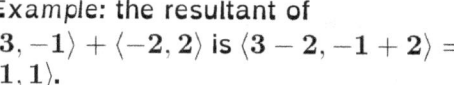
Right angle

right angle NOUN /raɪt ˈæŋ.gəl/ an angle that measures exactly $\frac{1}{4}$ of a full circle. A right angle measures 90° or $\frac{\pi}{2}$ radians. Perpendicular lines form right angles. Antonym: *oblique angle*.

Right Angle Congruence Theorem NOUN /raɪt ˈæŋ.gəl ˈkɒn.gru.əns ˈθɪ.ə.rəm/ a theorem stating that all right angles are congruent.

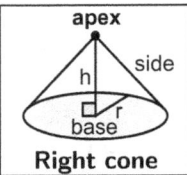
Right Angle Congruence

right-angled triangle NOUN /raɪt ˈæŋ.gəld ˈtraɪˌæŋ.gəl/ see *right triangle*.

right angle-hypotenuse-side congruence NOUN see *RHS congruence* (p 99).

right geometric figure NOUN /raɪt ˌdʒi.əˈmɛ.trɪk ˈfɪg.jər/ a figure whose apex is directly over the center or the base, or a figure where the center of the top is directly over the center of the base. Antonym: *oblique geometry figure*.

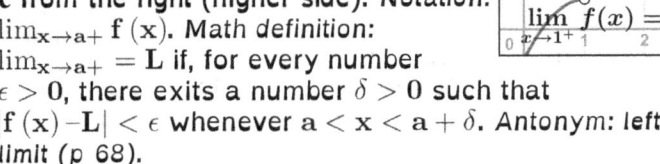
Right cone

right-hand limit NOUN /raɪt hænd ˈlɪ.mɪt/ the limit of a function as x approaches c from the right (higher side). Notation: $\lim_{x \to a+} f(x)$. Math definition: $\lim_{x \to a+} = L$ if, for every number $\epsilon > 0$, there exits a number $\delta > 0$ such that $|f(x) - L| < \epsilon$ whenever $a < x < a + \delta$. Antonym: *left limit* (p 68).

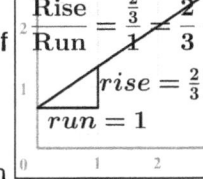
Right limit

rigid ADJECTIVE /ˈrɪ.dʒɪd/
1) not moving.
2) (polygon) angles cannot be continuously changed without changing the lengths of the sides.

rigid motion NOUN /ˈrɪ.dʒɪd ˈmoʊ.ʃən/ movement that does not change the distance between points, and the image and preimage are congruent.

rigorous ADJECTIVE /ˈrɪg.ɔr.əs/
1) logically valid.
2) exact and accurate.
3) precise.
4) allowing no deviation from a standard. Example: rigorous scientific study.

ring NOUN /rɪŋ/ see *annulus* (p 11).

rise NOUN /raɪz/ the vertical component of the slope of a line. Formula: $\text{slope} = \frac{\text{rise}}{\text{run}}$.

Robinson, Julia PERSON /ˈrɒ.bɪn.sən ˈdʒul.yə/ (1919—1985) a mathematician known for finding the conditions under which David Hilbert's tenth problem could be solved.

Julia Robinson

rod NOUN /rɒd/ an old unit of measure of length. Formulas: 1 rod = 5.5 yards, 1 rod ≈ 5.0292 meters, 320 rods = 1 statute mile.

roll a die VERB /roʊl ə daɪ/ to take a die and throw or drop it in such a way as it rolls, revealing a number. Synonym: *toss a die*.

Rolle's Theorem NOUN /ˈrɒlz ˈθɪ.ə.rəm/ a theorem stating that, if the value of f at two endpoints of an interval are equal, then at some point in the interval the slope of the function is zero. Math definition: given function f such that f is continuous on the closed interval $[a, b]$, f is differentiable on the open interval (a, b), and $f(a) = f(b)$, then there exists a number c on the interval (a, b) such that $f'(c) = 0$.

Roman numeral NOUN /ˈroʊ.mən ˈnum.rəl/ a numeral used in ancient Rome constructed from the digits I=1, V=5, X=10, L=50, C=100, D=500, M=1000. Example: 1,640 = MDCXL.

root NOUN /rut/
1) (polynomial) a number that, when substituted into a polynomial, makes the polynomial equal to zero. Example: 2 is a root of $x^2 - x - 2$ since $2^2 - 2 - 2 = 4 - 2 - 2 = 0$. Synonym: *solution*.

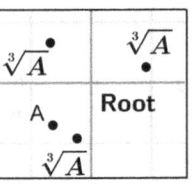
Root

2) (number or expression) a number or expression raised to a fractional power. Synonym *radical* (p 95). Examples: $a^{\frac{1}{2}}$, $\sqrt[n]{x}$.
3) (complex number) a set of n values that, when each is multiplied by itself n times, equals the number. Formula: $z = r(\cos\theta + i\sin\theta)$; $\sqrt[n]{z} = \sqrt[n]{r}\left(\cos\frac{\theta + 2k\pi}{n} + i\sin\frac{\theta + 2k\pi}{n}\right)$, $k = 0, 1, \cdots, n - 1$.

root mean square NOUN /rut min skwɛər/ a measure of central tendency for datasets containing positive and negative numbers. Formula: $R = \sqrt{\frac{a_1^2 + a_2^2 + \ldots + a_n^2}{n}}$. Abbreviation: *RMS*.

rose curve NOUN /roʊz kɜrv/ a curve with multiple "petals" generated by the polar equation $r = a\cos(k\theta)$ where k is any integer representing the number of petals, and a is the radius of each loop. Synonym: *rhodonea curve*.

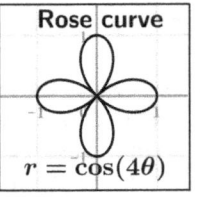
Rose curve
$r = \cos(4\theta)$

rotate VERB /roʊˈteɪt/ to move in a circular direction around a center point (2-D) or line (3-D). Synonym: *revolve*.

rotation NOUN /roʊˈteɪ.ʃən/
1) the measure of angular distance between two intersecting lines.
2) the movement of an object in a circle around a center of rotation.

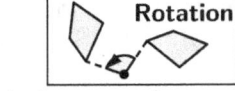
Rotation

rotational NOUN /roʊˈteɪ.ʃə.nl/ having to do with moving an object around a center of rotation.

rotational speed NOUN /roʊˈteɪ.ʃə.nl spid/ how fast something turns in a circle. Rotational speed is usually measured in revolutions per minute or revolutions per second. Synonym: *orbital speed*.

rotational symmetry NOUN /roʊˈteɪ.ʃə.nl ˈsɪ.mɪ.tri/ the image lies on top of the preimage when rotated about a point a certain number of degrees.

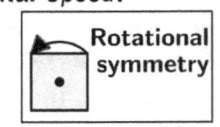
Rotational symmetry

rotation of axes NOUN /roʊˈteɪ.ʃən ʌv ˈæk.sɪz/ a transformation in analytical geometry where the axes are rotated about the origin. Formula: (x, y) becomes $(x\cos\theta - y\sin\theta, x\sin\theta + y\cos\theta)$ where θ is the counterclockwise rotation of the axes.

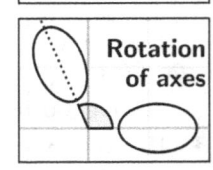
Rotation of axes

rough point NOUN /rʌf pɔɪnt/ a point on a function that has no derivative.

round /raʊnd/
1) VERB to find a number close to a given number, possibly with fewer digits. Example: round 2.57 to 2

significant digits: 2.6. Synonym: *round off*.
2) ADJECTIVE circular or spherical in shape.
See also *Rule for Rounding* (p 129).

round down VERB /raʊnd daʊn/ to round to a lower number. Example: round 6.53 down to 6.5.

rounded ADJECTIVE /ˈraʊn.dɪd/ reduced to fewer digits using a rounding algorithm.

round up VERB /raʊnd ʌp/ to round to a higher number. Example: round 4.59 up to 4.6.

row NOUN /roʊ/ a set of objects arranged horizontally.

row echelon form NOUN /roʊ ˈɛ.ʃə.lɒn form/ an augmented lower triangular matrix. See also *reduced row echelon form* (p 97).

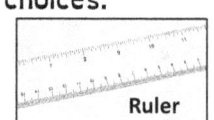
Row echelon form

row matrix NOUN /roʊ ˈmeɪ.trɪks/ any matrix with a single row. Synonym: *row vector*. Plural: *row matrices* /roʊ ˈmeɪ.trɪˌsiz/.

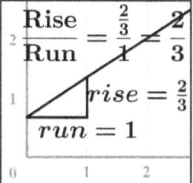
Row matrix

row operation NOUN /roʊ ˌɒ.pərˈeɪ.ʃən/ one of several operations that can be performed on the rows of a matrix without changing the solution of a linear system represented by the matrix: • Any two rows can be swapped. • Any row can be multiplied by a nonzero scalar. • Any row can be added to another row. See also *column operation* (p 23).

row rank NOUN /roʊ ræŋk/ the maximum number of linearly independent rows in a matrix.

row vector NOUN /roʊ ˈvɛk.tər/ see *row matrix* (p 101).

royalty NOUN /ˈrɔɪ.əl.ti/ a portion of sales paid for use of a creative work such as a book.

rule NOUN /rul/
1) an algorithm. Example: rule of 72.
2) a postulate or theorem. Example: rule for rounding.
3) a formula. Example: the formula assigned to a function, $f(x) = \sin x$.
4) a defining statement.

rule of 72 NOUN /rul ʌv ˈsɛ.vən.ti.tu/ a formula for approximating the doubling time of principal at a certain interest rate: $t_d \approx \frac{72}{i}$ where t_d is the estimated doubling time and i is the annualized interest rate. If the interest rate is 10%, use the number 10 for i. Example: the approximate doubling time of an investment that returns 10% annually is $t_d \approx \frac{72}{10} = 7.2$ years.

rule of linearity NOUN /rul ʌv ˌlɪn.iˈær.ɪ.ti/ $\frac{d}{dx}[a \cdot u(x) + b \cdot v(x)] = a\frac{d}{dx}u(x) + b\frac{d}{dx}v(x)$.

rule of sum NOUN /rul ʌv sʌm/ when selecting from two or more sets of events that cannot happen simultaneously, the sample space of each of the events is added together to get the total sample space. Formula: $S(e_1 \text{ and } e_2 \text{ and} \cdots \text{ and } e_n) = S(e_1) + S(e_2) + \cdots + S(e_n)$. Example: Andrea wants one piece of fruit. She can stay home and choose from apples or kiwi. Or she can go to the store and buy bananas. There are 2 choices at home and 1 at the store, making a total of $2 + 1 = 3$ choices.

ruler NOUN /ˈru.lər/ a flat, straight object with tick marks on it that is used for measuring distance.

Ruler Postulate NOUN /ˈru.lər ˈpɒs.tʃə.lɪt/ every point on a line can be paired with a real number. The distance between any two points on a line is the absolute value of the difference of their coordinates. Synonym: *Cantor's axiom*. See also *number line* (p 81).

run NOUN /rʌn/ the horizontal component of a slope. Formula: $\text{slope} = \frac{\text{rise}}{\text{run}}$.

S

s ABBREVIATION second.

saddle point NOUN /ˈsæ.dl pɔɪnt/ a point on the surface of the 3-D graph of a function where the slopes in perpendicular directions are all zero that is not a local extremum of the function.

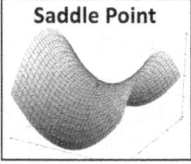
Saddle Point

sagitta NOUN /səˈdʒɪ.tə/ a line segment from the midpoint of a chord to the edge of the circle that is perpendicular to the chord.

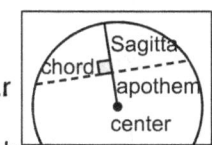

sale price NOUN /seɪl praɪs/ price at which something is sold before sales tax. Formula: **sale price + sales tax = total due**.

sales tax NOUN /seɪlz tæks/ a percentage that is added on to the total of a sale. Formula: **sale price + sales tax = total due**.

same ADJECTIVE /seɪm/
1) being the same thing. Example: Same Plane Postulate.
2) alike; closely similar.

Same Plane Postulate NOUN /seɪm pleɪn ˈpɒs.tʃə.lɪt/ if two points lie on a plane, then the entire line defined by those points lies on the same plane.

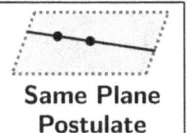
Same Plane Postulate

sample /ˈsam.pəl/
1) NOUN a few objects selected from a set.
2) NOUN a portion of a population being sampled.
3) NOUN a survey of a portion of a population. Antonym: *census* (p 19).
4) VERB to discover data associated with a population.

sample size NOUN /ˈsam.pəl saɪz/ the number of data points in a sample; the number of subjects of a sample.

sample space NOUN /ˈsam.pəl speɪs/
1) (probability) all the possible outcomes of an experiment. Examples: the sample space for the flip of a coin is $\{\text{heads}, \text{tails}\}$. The sample space for the roll of a single six-sided die is $\{1, 2, 3, 4, 5, 6\}$.
2) (statistics) all possible values a sample can take.

sampling NOUN /ˈsam.plɪŋ/
1) data taken from a sample of a population.
2) the process of selecting a sample.

sampling distribution NOUN /ˈsam.plɪŋ ˌdɪs.trɪˈbju.ʃən/ the distribution of a sample within a population.

sampling error NOUN /ˈsam.plɪŋ ˈɛr.ər/ an error that occurs because a sample does not have the exact same characteristics as the population. Example: the average weight of a sample does not exactly match the average weight of a population.

SAS congruence NOUN /es eɪ es kənˈgru.əns/ (side-angle-side congruence) two triangles are congruent if two sides and the enclosed angle of one triangle are congruent with corresponding sides and angle of the other triangle. Math definition: $\triangle ABC \cong \triangle A'B'C'$ if and only if $AB \cong A'B'$, $AC \cong A'C'$, and $\angle BAC \cong \angle B'A'C'$.

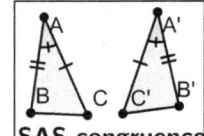
SAS congruence

satisfy VERB /ˈsæ.tɪsˌfaɪ/
1) to make an equation true when substituted in. Example: 5 satisfies $0 = x^2 - 3x - 10$ since $0 = 5^2 - 3 \cdot 5 - 10 = 25 - 15 - 10 = 0$.
2) to fulfill requirements or conditions, particularly of a theorem.

scalar NOUN /ˈskeɪ.lər/
1) a real number that is multiplied by a math object in order to 'scale' the object (make the object larger or smaller). Synonym: **scale factor** (p 102).
2) a value that has only magnitude. Examples: mass, length.

scalar multiplication NOUN /ˈskeɪ.lər ˌmʌl.tə.plɪˈkeɪ.ʃən/
1) (expression) multiply each term of the equation by a real number. Example: $5(-x^2 + 2x + 1) = 5 \cdot -x^2 + 5 \cdot 2x + 5 \cdot 1 = -5x^2 + 10x + 5$.
2) (matrix) multiply each element of the matrix by a number. Formula: $c \cdot \begin{bmatrix} a_{1,1} & a_{1,2} \\ a_{2,1} & a_{2,2} \end{bmatrix} = $
$c \cdot \begin{bmatrix} a_{1,1} & a_{1,2} \\ a_{2,1} & a_{2,2} \end{bmatrix} = \begin{bmatrix} c \cdot a_{1,1} & c \cdot a_{1,2} \\ c \cdot a_{2,1} & c \cdot a_{2,2} \end{bmatrix}$.
3) (vector) multiply each element of a vector by a real number. Formulas: $c \cdot \langle x, y \rangle = \langle c \cdot x, c \cdot y \rangle$, $c \cdot \langle x, y, z \rangle = \langle c \cdot x, c \cdot y, c \cdot z \rangle$.
4) (matrix row) multiply each element in a row of a matrix by a real number. Formula:
$\begin{bmatrix} a_{1,1} & a_{1,2} & a_{1,3} \\ a_{2,1} & a_{2,2} & a_{2,3} \end{bmatrix} \xrightarrow{R2=c \cdot R2} \begin{bmatrix} a_{1,1} & a_{1,2} & a_{1,3} \\ c \cdot a_{2,1} & c \cdot a_{2,2} & c \cdot a_{2,3} \end{bmatrix}$.

scalar triple product NOUN /ˈskeɪ.lər ˈtrɪ.pəl ˈprɒ.dʌkt/ the product of 3 vectors, all of which are 3-dimensional. Formula: $s = A \cdot (B \times C)$.

scalar product NOUN /ˈskeɪ.lər ˈprɒ.dʌkt/ see **dot product** (p 42).

scalar projection NOUN /ˈskeɪ.lər proʊˈdʒɛk.ʃən/ the length of the orthogonal projection of vector **a** on vector **b**. Formula: $\text{comp}_{\mathbf{a}}\mathbf{b} = \frac{\mathbf{a} \cdot \mathbf{b}}{|\mathbf{a}|} = |\mathbf{a}| \cos \theta$.

scale /skeɪl/
1) NOUN the interval that represents '1' on a graph.
2) VERB to make larger or smaller by a ratio.
3) NOUN the ratio between the size of an object and the size of a drawing of the object. Example: **20:1** scale model.
4) NOUN a device for measuring weight.

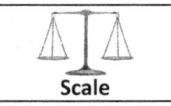
Scale

scale drawing NOUN /skeɪl ˈdrɔ.ɪŋ/ a drawing that is similar to a figure but is drawn smaller or larger than the figure. Example: map.

scale factor NOUN /skeɪl ˈfæk.tər/ a positive number multiplied by a math object to make it larger or smaller. A scale factor greater than 1 makes the object larger, a scale factor between 0 and 1 makes the object smaller. Synonym: **scalar** (p 102).

scale model NOUN /skeɪl ˈmɒ.dl/ a model that is similar to a figure but is built smaller or larger than the figure. Notation: **1:15** (one fifteenth scale).

Scale model 1:2

scalene triangle NOUN /skeɪˈliːn ˈtraɪˌæn.ɡəl/ a triangle where all three sides are different lengths.

Scalene triangle

scatter diagram NOUN /ˈskæ.tər ˈdaɪ.əˌɡræm/ see **scatter plot** (p 102).

scatter plot NOUN /ˈskæ.tər plɒt/ a graph made by plotting discrete data points. Synonyms: **scatter diagram**, **dot plot** (p 42).

Scatter plot

science NOUN /ˈsaɪ.əns/ the process of exploring the natural world and creating systematic knowledge.

scientific ADJECTIVE /ˌsaɪ.ənˈtɪ.fɪk/
1) having to do with science.
2) according to the principles of science.

scientific notation NOUN /ˌsaɪ.ənˈtɪ.fɪk noʊˈteɪ.ʃən/ a way to write real numbers that is very useful for large and small numbers. Format: $\text{mantissa} \times 10^{\text{exponent}}$ where $-10 < \text{mantissa} < 10$ and the exponent is any integer. Example: $2.643 \times 10^{-3} = 0.002643$. Synonyms: **e notation** (p 44), **engineering notation** (p 44), **standard index form**.

scientific sample NOUN /ˌsaɪ.ənˈtɪ.fɪk ˈsæm.pəl/ a sample where the selection of the sample does not influence the information being sampled; a sample where there is no correlation between the selection variable and the variables of interest.

score NOUN /skɔr/
1) a measurement or count, particularly of human performance. Example: score on a test.
2) twenty. Example: four score and seven years ago.

sec ABBREVIATION
1) second.
2) secant.

sec() COMPUTERS the function representing secant in most computer languages.

secant NOUN /ˈsi.kænt/ the multiplicative inverse of the cosine function. Abbreviation: **sec**. Formula: $\text{secant} = \frac{1}{\cosine} = \frac{\text{hypotenuse}}{\text{adjacent}}$.

secant line NOUN /ˈsi.kænt laɪn/ a line that intersects a curve at least twice.

secant segment NOUN /ˈsi.kænt ˈsɛɡ.mənt/ a line segment from a point exterior to a circle through the circle to an endpoint on another part of the circle. See also **external secant segment** (p 48).

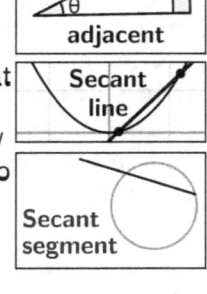

sech ABBREVIATION see **hyperbolic secant** (p 58).

second NOUN, ADJECTIVE /ˈsɛ.kənd/
1) a unit of measure of time. Formula: **60 seconds = 1 minute**. Abbreviation: **s** or **sec**.
2) a unit of measure of angles. Notation: **"**. Formula: **3600 seconds = 1 degree**. Synonym: **arc second**.

3) coming in position 2 in an ordered list. Notation: 2nd.

4) the result of doing an operation twice. Example: second derivative.

secondary ADJECTIVE /ˈsɛ.kənˌdɛ.ri/
1) second in order or time.
2) lesser or less important.

secondary dataset NOUN /ˈsɛ.kənˌdɛ.ri ˈdeɪ.tə sɛt/ a set of data that the researcher did not collect themselves.

second derivative NOUN /ˈsɛ.kɛnd dɪˈrɪ.və.tɪv/ the derivative of a derivative. Math definition: $f'' = (f')'$. Notations: $\frac{d^2y}{dx^2}$, $D^2f(x)$.

second derivative test NOUN /ˈsɛ.kɛnd dɪˈrɪ.və.tɪv tɛst/ let f'' be continuous near c. If $f'(c) = 0$ and $f''(c) > 0$, then f has a local maximum at c. If $f'(c) = 0$ and $f''(c) < 0$, then f has a local minimum at c.

second difference NOUN /ˈsɛ.kɛnd ˈdɪf.rəns/ a method for approximating a second derivative. Formula:
$f''(x) \approx \frac{f(x+\Delta x) - 2f(x) + f(x-\Delta x)}{(\Delta x)^2}$.

section NOUN /ˈsɛk.ʃən/
1) see cross section (p 32).
2) see conic section (p 27).

sector NOUN /ˈsɛk.tər/ see circular sector (p 21).

sector graph NOUN /ˈsɛk.tər græf/ see pie chart (p 88).

segment NOUN /ˈsɛg.mənt/
1) a continuous portion.
2) a continuous portion of a line between two endpoints. Synonym: line segment (p 69).
3) (of a circle) a part of a circle cut off by a chord of the circle.

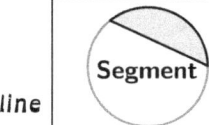

Segment Addition Postulate NOUN /ˈsɛg.mənt əˈdɪ.ʃən ˈpɒs.tʃə.lɪt/ point c is between points a and b if and only if $ac + cb = ab$. Synonym: between (p 16).

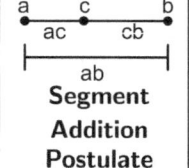

Segment Addition Postulate

segment bisector NOUN /ˈsɛg.mənt ˈbaɪ.sɛk.tər/ see bisector (p 17).

selection NOUN /sɪˈlɛk.ʃən/ one of a group that is chosen.

self-selected sample NOUN /sɛlf sɪˈlɛk.td ˈsæm.pəl/ a person who chooses into a group (not necessarily into a survey) is self-selected. A self-selected sample is a biased sample and not a scientific sample. Synonym: voluntary response sample.

self-similar ADJECTIVE /sɛlf ˈsɪ.mə.lər/ if any part of a figure is similar to the whole, the figure is self-similar. Example: Sierpiński triangle.

self subtraction NOUN /sɛlf səbˈtræk.ʃən/ any number subtracted from itself equals zero. Formula: $a - a \equiv 0$.

semi- PREFIX /ˈsɛ.maɪ/
1) half. Example: semicircle.
2) partially or somewhat. Example: semi-regular.

semiannually ADJECTIVE /ˌsɛm.aɪˈæn.ju.ə.li/ twice a year; every six months.

semicircle NOUN /ˈsɛ.maɪˌsɜr.kəl/ exactly one-half of a circle; an arc cut off from a circle by a diameter of the circle.

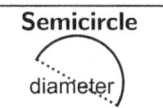

Semicircle

semielliptical ADJECTIVE /ˌsɛ.maɪ.ɪˈlɪp.tɪ.kəl/ being in the shape of half an ellipse.

Semielliptical

semi-log graph NOUN /ˌsɛ.maɪ lɒg græf/ a graph where one axis uses a logarithmic scale and the other axis uses an arithmetic scale. Synonym: log graph (p 70).

semi-log plot NOUN /ˌsɛ.maɪ lɒg plɒt/ see semi-log graph (p 103).

semi-major axis NOUN /ˌsɛ.maɪ ˈmeɪ.dʒər ˈæk.sɪs/ one-half of a major axis.

semi-minor axis NOUN /ˌsɛ.maɪ ˈmaɪ.nər ˈæk.sɪs/ one-half of a minor axis.

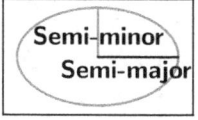

semiperimeter NOUN /ˌsɛ.maɪ.pəˈrɪm.ɪ.tər/ one-half the length of a perimeter.

semiprime ADJECTIVE /ˌsɛ.maɪ.praɪm/ an integer that is the product of two prime numbers. Synonym: biprime.

semi-regular ADJECTIVE /ˌsɛ.maɪ ˈrɛ.gjə.lər/ somewhat regular.

semi-regular polyhedron NOUN /ˌsɛ.maɪ ˈrɛ.gjə.lər ˌpɒ.liˈhi.drən/ see Archimedean solid (p 12).

semi-regular solid NOUN /ˌsɛ.maɪ ˈrɛ.gjə.lər ˈsɒ.lɪd/ see Archimedean solid (p 12).

semi-regular tessellation NOUN /ˌsɛ.maɪ ˈrɛ.gjə.lər ˌtɛ.səˈleɪ.ʃən/ a uniform tessellation made from two or more regular polygons.

Semi-regular tesselation

senary ADJECTIVE /ˈsɛn.ə.ri/
1) sixth in order or importance.
2) having to do with the number six.

sentence NOUN /ˈsɛn.təns/ a statement of a logical relationship. Example: A square has four sides.

separable ADJECTIVE /ˈsɛ.pə.rə.bəl/ can be separated.

separable equation NOUN /ˈsɛ.pə.rə.bəl ɪˈkweɪ.ʃən/ an equation that can be rewritten with each variable on only one side of the equals sign. Example: $x^2 + y^2 = 1 \rightarrow x^2 = 1 - y^2$. See also separation of variables (p 103).

separate
1) VERB /ˈsɛ.pəˌreɪt/ to move apart.
2) ADJECTIVE /ˈsɛ.pər.ɪt/ disconnected, not touching.

separation of variables NOUN /ˈsɛ.pəˌreɪ.ʃən ʌv ˈvɛər.i.ə.bəls/
1) (calculus) any of several methods for solving ordinary and partial differential equations.
2) (algebra) Rewriting an equation so that each of two variables is on a different side of the equation. See also separable equation (p 103).

septillion ADJECTIVE, NOUN /sɛpˈtɪl.jən/ $10^{24} =$ 1,000,000,000,000,000,000,000,000. Synonym: yotta-.

septillionth ADJECTIVE, NOUN /sɛpˈtɪl.jənθ/ $10^{-24} =$ 0.000 000 000 000 000 000 000 001. Synonym: yocto-.

septenary ADJECTIVE /ˈsɛp.təˌnɛər.i/
1) seventh in order or importance.
2) having to do with the number seven.

sequence NOUN /ˈsi.kwəns/ a set of numbers in a specific order with a relation between each element, the element before it, and the element after it. Notation: $a_1, a_2, a_3, \ldots$. Synonyms: arithmetic sequence (p 13), geometric sequence (p 53).

sequence of partial sums NOUN /ˈsi.kwəns ʌv ˈpɑr.ʃəl sʌmz/ a sequence where the nth element of the sequence is the nth partial sum of the original sequence.

series NOUN /ˈsɪər.iz/ the sum of a sequence of numbers. Example: $2 = 1 + \frac{1}{2} + \frac{1}{4} + \frac{1}{8} + \cdots$. Plural: **series** /ˈsɪər.iz/.

set /sɛt/
1) NOUN a well defined group of objects. Notation: upper case letter. Example: $A = \{a, b, c\}$. Synonyms: **class, group** (p 55).
2) VERB to prepare. Example: set up.

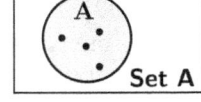
Set A

set builder notation NOUN /sɛt ˈbɪl.dər nouˈteɪ.ʃən/ see set notation (p 104).

set notation NOUN /sɛt nouˈteɪ.ʃən/ a convention for writing sets. Example: $A = \{x \in \mathbf{R} : x < 2\}$: A is the set of all real numbers that are less than 2.

set square NOUN /sɛt skwɛər/ a device for drawing angles.

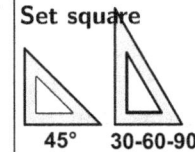
Set square
45° 30-60-90

set theory NOUN /sɛt ˈθɪər.i/ an axiomatic system about sets on which modern mathematics is based.

set up VERB /sɛt ʌp/ to prepare in a particular manner. Example: set up an equation.

seven ADJECTIVE, NOUN /ˈsɛ.vən/ the number or digit 7.

seventeen ADJECTIVE, NOUN /sɛ.vənˈtin/ the number 17.

seventh ADJECTIVE /ˈsɛ.vənθ/
1) coming in position 7 in an ordered list. Notation: 7th.
2) one of seven equal parts: $\frac{1}{7}$.

seventy ADJECTIVE, NOUN /ˈsɛ.vən.ti/ the number 70.

sextillion ADJECTIVE, NOUN /sɛksˈtɪl.jən/ $10^{21} = 1,000,000,000,000,000,000,000$. Synonym: **zetta-**.

sextillionth ADJECTIVE, NOUN /sɛksˈtɪl.jənθ/ $10^{-21} = 0.000\ 000\ 000\ 000\ 000\ 000\ 001$. Synonym: **zepto-**.

shadow stick NOUN /ˈʃæ.dou stɪk/ a stick with one end in the ground used to measure tall objects by comparing the lengths of the shadows.

shape NOUN /ʃeɪp/
1) a figure, form or pattern.
2) what a figure resembles. Example: in the shape of a triangle.

share VERB /ʃɛər/ to have in common.

sharing ADVERB /ˈʃɛər.ɪŋ/ dividing into even groups.

shear /ʃɪər/
1) VERB to transform a space that slants when compared to the original.
2) NOUN the results of a shear.

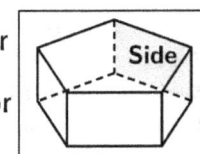
Shear

shell NOUN /ʃɛl/ a thin slice of a solid made by intersecting cylinders of different sizes with the solid.

shift /ʃɪft/
1) VERB (of a graph or function) to move a graph up or down, or left or right. A graph may be shifted left and right by substituting $(x - x_s)$ for x where x_s is the amount of the left-right shift. A graph may be shifted up and down by substituting $(y - y_s)$ for y in the equation where y_s is the amount of the up-down shift.
2) NOUN the results of a shift.
See also Types of Graph Shifts (p 133).

SHM ACRONYM simple harmonic motion (p 105).

short run behavior NOUN /ʃɔrt rʌn bɪˈheɪ.vjər/ the behavior of a function over a limited subdomain.

short scale NOUN /ʃɔrt skeɪl/ a standard for naming multiples of powers of 10 where $10^9 = 1$ billion. Antonym: **long scale** (p 71).

shrink VERB /ʃrɪŋk/ see compress (p 26).

SI ABBREVIATION Système international d'unités (International System of Units). See also International System of Units (p 145).

side NOUN /saɪd/
1) (of a polygon) one of the line segments that make up the boundary of a polygon. Synonyms: **leg** (p 68), **hypotenuse** (p 58).
2) (of an angle) one of the line segments or rays that define the angle. Synonym: **arm** (p 13), **leg** (p 68).
3) (of a polyhedron) a lateral face of a polyhedron.
4) not at the front, top, back or bottom. Example: side view.
5) (of an equation or inequality) either the part of the equation or inequality before the equals or inequality sign, or the part of the equation or inequality after the equals or inequality sign. Example: $\underbrace{x + 2}_{\text{side}} = \underbrace{y - 4}_{\text{side}}$.

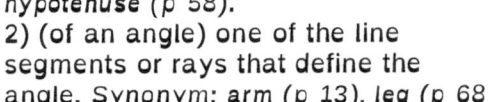

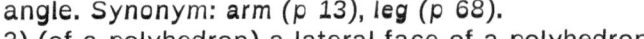

side view NOUN /saɪd vju/ a 2-dimensional drawing of 3-dimensional object from the point of view of a side.

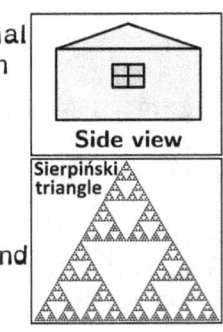
Side view

Sierpiński triangle

Sierpiński triangle NOUN /siˈɛrˈpɪn.ski ˈtraɪˌæŋ.gəl/ a triangle from which the middle $\frac{1}{4}$ is successively removed. With each iteration, the area of the triangle decreases by a factor of $\frac{1}{4}$ and the length of the boundary of the triangle increases by a factor of $\frac{3}{2}$.

Sierpiński, Wacław PERSON /siˈɛrˌpɪn.ski ʰwɑˈklɑ/ (1882—1969) a Polish mathematician known for inventing the Sierpiński triangle.

Sieve of Eratosthenes NOUN /sɪv ʌv ˌɛr.əˈtɒs.θəˌniz/ a method for finding all prime numbers up to a specified value. As each prime number is discovered, all the multiples of that prime number are crossed out until all prime numbers in the range have been found.

sigma SYMBOL /ˈsɪg.mə/
1) the upper case Greek letter Σ, used to indicate repeated addition. See also sigma notation (p 104).
2) the lower case Greek letter σ, used to indicate standard deviation.
See also Greek Letters (p 135).

sigma notation NOUN /ˈsɪg.mə nouˈteɪ.ʃən/ a notation for showing repeated addition of similar terms: $\sum_{i=1}^{n} a_i = a_1 + a_2 + \ldots + a_n$ where $i = 1$ is the starting value of the iterator, n is the final value of the iterator, and a_i is the ith term. n may be infinity. See also continued sum, (p 28).

sign NOUN /saɪn/
1) a symbol used to show an operation or statement. Examples: +, −, =.
2) whether a number is positive or negative.

signed ADJECTIVE /saɪnd/ having a sign. Example: signed number. Antonym: *unsigned* (p 119).

signed number NOUN /saɪnd 'nʌm.bər/
1) a number that has a positive or negative sign. Examples: +5, −3. Synonym: *directed number* (p 39).
2) (computers) a number that can be positive, negative or zero.
Antonym: *unsigned number* (p 119).

significand NOUN /sɪg'nɪ.fɪ.keɪnd/ see *mantissa* (p 72).

significant ADJECTIVE /sɪg'nɪ.fɪ.kənt/
1) having an influence or effect. Example: significant digits.
2) (statistics) unlikely to be caused by chance.
Antonym: *not significant*.

significant digits NOUN /sɪg'nɪ.fɪ.kənt 'dɪ.dʒɪtz/ the number of digits after which an inexact result will happen. If a measurement is accurate to two digits, the number has two significant digits.

similar ADJECTIVE /'sɪ.mə.lər/
1) having the same shape, but possibly different sizes. Example: similar triangles. Notation: ∼.
2) being the same in some way. Example: similar fractions.
Antonym: *dissimilar* (p 40).

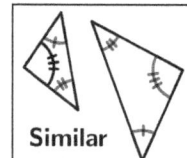
Similar

similar fractions NOUN /'sɪ.mə.lər 'fræk.ʃənz/ fractions having the same denominator. Example: $\frac{3}{4}$, $\frac{1}{4}$ are similar fractions.

similarity ADJECTIVE /ˌsɪ.mə'læ.rɪ.ti/ having to do with whether or not objects are similar. Example: similarity transformation.

similarity ratio NOUN /ˌsɪ.mə'læ.rɪ.ti 'reɪ.ʃoʊ/ the constant ratio of lengths of corresponding parts of two similar figures.

similarity transformation NOUN /ˌsɪ.mə.læ.rɪ.ti 'træns.fər.meɪ.ʃən/ any transformation of a geometric object where the preimage is similar to the image of the transformation.

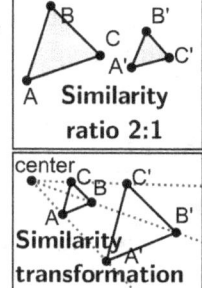
Similarity ratio 2:1
Similarity transformation

similar terms NOUN /'sɪ.mə.lər tərmz/ see *like terms* (p 68).

similar triangles NOUN /'sɪ.mə.lər 'traɪˌæŋ.gəlz/ two triangles whose corresponding angles are congruent, and where the ratios of the corresponding sides are equal to each other. Notation: ∼. Math definition: $\triangle ABC \sim \triangle A'B'C'$ if and only if $\angle\alpha \cong \angle\alpha'$, $\angle\beta \cong \angle\beta'$, $\angle\gamma \cong \angle\gamma'$ and $\frac{a}{a'} = \frac{b}{b'} = \frac{c}{c'}$.

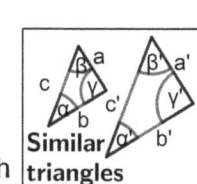
Similar triangles

simple ADJECTIVE /'sɪm.pəl/
1) not complex.
2) not made of multiple parts.
Antonym: *complex* (p 25).

simple closed curve NOUN /'sɪm.pəl kloʊzd kɜrv/ a curve that does not intersect itself and ends on the same point it starts.

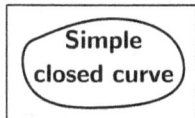
Simple closed curve

simple curve NOUN /'sɪm.pəl kɜrv/ a curve that does not intersect itself. Antonym: *complex curve* (p 25).

Simple curve

simple harmonic motion NOUN /'sɪm.pəl hɑr'mɒ.nɪk 'moʊ.ʃən/ a motion that can be modeled with a sinusoid, such as a back and forth motion. Example: a weight bouncing on a spring. Abbreviation: SHM. Formulas: $\mathbf{x}(t) = \mathbf{x_0}\cos(\omega r) + \frac{\mathbf{v_0}}{\omega}\sin(\omega t)$ where $\omega = \sqrt{\frac{k}{m}}$, $\mathbf{x_0}$ is the initial position, $\mathbf{v_0}$ is the initial velocity, t is time, $\mathbf{k}$ is the spring constant, and $\mathbf{m}$ is the inertial mass of the weight on the spring.

simple interest NOUN /'sɪm.pəl 'ɪn.trɪst/ interest that is not added to the principal of a loan. Formula: $\mathbf{I} = \mathbf{iP}$ where $\mathbf{i}$ is the interest rate and $\mathbf{P}$ is the principal.
Antonym: *compound interest* (p 26).

simple polygon NOUN /'sɪm.pəl 'pɒ.liˌgɒn/ a polygon whose sides do not intersect each other. Antonym: *complex polygon* (p 25).

simple random sample NOUN /'sɪm.pəl 'ræn.dəm 'sæm.pəl/ a sample where any member of the population has an equal chance of being selected.

simplest form NOUN /'sɪm.pləst fɔrm/
1) a fraction where the numerator and denominator have no common factors. Example: $\frac{3}{5}$. See also *reduced fraction* (p 97).
2) an expression where all fractions are in the simplest form and there are no like terms.

simplify VERB /'sɪm.pləˌfaɪ/ convert to a simpler form.

simply connected ADJECTIVE /'sɪm.pli kə'nɛk.tɪd/ of a region, having no holes; is path-connected and every path between two points can be continuously transformed into any other such path while preserving the two endpoints in question.

Simpson's rule NOUN /'sɪmp.sʌnz rul/ one of a set of approximations for definite integrals. Formula: $(\frac{1}{3}$ rule$):\int_a^b f(x)dx \approx \frac{b-a}{6}\left[f(a) + 4f\left(\frac{a+b}{2}\right) + f(b)\right]$.

simulate VERB /ˌsɪm.ju'leɪt/ to generate random events to study a real-life situation. Example: a coin can be flipped and heads can simulate eating a banana, tails eating an apple.

simulation NOUN /ˌsɪm.ju'leɪ.ʃən/ the generation of random events to study a real-life situation. Example: a coin can be flipped and heads can simulate eating a hamburger, tails eating a banana.

simultaneous ADJECTIVE /ˌsaɪ.məl'teɪn.i.əs/ at the same time; all at once. Example: simultaneous equations.

simultaneous equations NOUN /ˌsaɪ.məl'teɪn.i.əs ɪ'kweɪ.ʃənz/ see *system of equations* (p 112).

simultaneous inequalities NOUN /ˌsaɪ.məl'teɪn.i.əs ˌɪn.ɪ'kwɒ.lɪ.tiz/ two or more inequalities that are taken to be true at the same time.

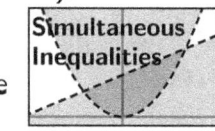
Simultaneous Inequalities

sin ABBREVIATION sine.

sin() COMPUTERS represents the sine function in most computer languages. Example: `y = sin(x)`.

sine NOUN /saɪn/ the ratio between the side of a right triangle opposite a vertex and the hypotenuse. Formula: $sine = \frac{opposite}{hypotenuse}$.

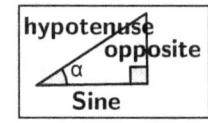
Sine

sine rule NOUN /saɪn rul/ see *Law of Sines* (p 67).

3rd Dyslexic's Edition

singular matrix NOUN /'sɪŋ.gjə.lr 'meɪ.trɪks/ a square matrix for which no inverse exists; a square matrix with a zero determinant. Antonyms: *invertible matrix, nonsingular matrix* (p 80). Plural: **singular matrices** /'sɪŋ.gjə.lr 'meɪ.trɪˌsiz/.

sinh ABBREVIATION see *hyperbolic sine* (p 58).

sinusoid NOUN /'saɪn.ju.sɔɪd/ a curve that is like a sine curve. Formula: $y = A \sin(2\pi rt + P)$ where A is the amplitude, r is the frequency in cycles per second, t is the elapsed time and p is the phase shift.

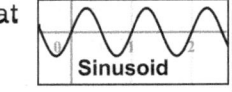
Sinusoid

sinusoidal ADJECTIVE /'saɪn.ju.sɔɪ.dl/ like a sine curve. Example: sinusoidal curve.

SI unit NOUN /əs aɪ 'ju.nɪt/ one of several units of measure documented in the International System of Units (p 145).

six ADJECTIVE, NOUN /sɪks/ the number or digit 6.

sixteen ADJECTIVE, NOUN /sɪks'tin/ the number 16.

sixth ADJECTIVE /sɪksθ/
1) coming in position 6 in an ordered list. Notation: 6th.
2) one of six equal parts $\frac{1}{6}$.

sixty ADJECTIVE, NOUN /'sɪk.sti/ the number 60.

size NOUN /saɪz/ how big or how long.

sketch /skɛtʃ/
1) VERB to draw a rough figure without the use of tools such as a compass or a straightedge.
2) NOUN a rough figure drawn without the use of tools such as compass or straightedge.

skew ADJECTIVE /skju/
1) oblique; not vertical or horizontal. Example: skew line.
2) not perpendicular or parallel. Example: skew lines.
3) slanted to one side or the other. Example: skewed distribution.

skewed distribution NOUN /skjud 'dɪs.trɪ.bu.ʃən/ a distribution that is slanted to the left or right as compared to a normal distribution. Antonym: *symmetric distribution* (p 111).

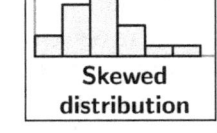
Skewed distribution

skew line NOUN /skju laɪn/
1) a line that is neither vertical nor horizontal.
2) more than one line in 3 or more dimensions that do not intersect and are not parallel. Synonym: *oblique line*.

skip count VERB /skɪp kaʊnt/ to count every 2nd, 3rd, etc. integer. Example: skip count by 2's: 2, 4, 6, ... Synonym: *count by* (p 31).

slant /slænt/
1) NOUN a line segment that is neither vertical nor horizontal. Synonym: *oblique* (p 6).
2) VERB to place at an angle that is neither vertical nor horizontal.

slant asymptote NOUN /slænt 'æ.sɪmˌtoʊt/ see *oblique asymptote* (p 81).

slant height NOUN /slænt haɪt/
1) (right regular pyramid) the length of a lateral face.
2) (right cone) the length of any line segment from the edge of the base to the apex.

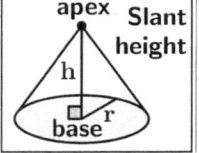
apex Slant height

slice /slaɪs/
1) NOUN the portion of a solid to one side of a plane.
2) NOUN the portion of a solid between two parallel planes.
3) VERB to obtain portions of a solid by intersecting the solid with one or more planes.

slice of a solid NOUN /slaɪs ʌv ə 'sɒ.lɪd/ the part of a solid to one side of a plane that intersects the solid.

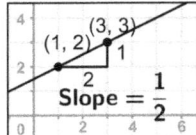
Slice of a solid

slide /slaɪd/
1) NOUN see *translation* (p 115).
2) VERB to move smoothly along a path.
3) VERB to cause to move smoothly along a path.

slide rule NOUN /slaɪd rul/ a computing device with a slider and a stationary part each with a logarithmic scale than can be used to calculate.

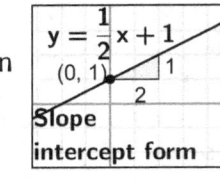
Slide rule

slope NOUN /sloʊp/
1) (of a line) how steep a line is; rise divided by run; vertical change divided by horizontal change. Notation: **m**. Equations: $m = \frac{\Delta y}{\Delta x}$. Given two distinct points on a line, (x_1, y_1) and (x_2, y_2), $m = \frac{y_2 - y_1}{x_2 - x_1}$. Synonyms: *rate of change, gradient*.
2) (of a curve) the slope of a line that is tangent to a curve at a particular point.

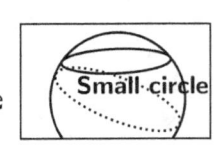

slope-intercept form NOUN /sloʊp 'ɪn.tərˌsɛpt fɔrm/ an equation of a line in the form $y = mx + b$ where **m** is the slope and **b** is the y-intercept.

slope-intercept method NOUN /sloʊp 'ɪn.tərˌsɛpt 'mɛ.θəd/ an algorithm for graphing a line in slope-intercept form ($y = mx + b$): 1) Plot the y-intercept at $(0, b)$. 2) Plot a point one to the right and **m** up (if **m** is positive) or $|m|$ down (if **m** is negative): $(1, b + m)$. 3) Draw the line containing the two points.

small circle NOUN /smɒl 'sɜr.kəl/ a circle on the surface of a sphere that is not a great circle, that does not divide the sphere into two equal halves. Antonym: *great circle* (p 54).

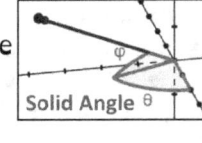
Small circle

smaller ADJECTIVE /'smɒl.ər/ having one or more dimensions that are less.

SOHCAHTOA ACRONYM /'soʊ.kəˌtoʊ.ə/ a mnemonic for remembering the definition of trigonometric functions: SOH stands for Sine equals Opposite over Hypotenuse; CAH stands for Cosine equals Adjacent over Hypotenuse; TOA stands for Tangent equals Opposite over Adjacent.

sol- PREFIX /sɒl/ having to do with the sun.

solid /'sɒ.lɪd/
1) NOUN see *geometric solid* (p 53).
2) ADJECTIVE having to do with three dimensions.

solid angle NOUN /'sɒ.lɪd 'æŋ.gəl/ an angle in three dimensions. (θ, φ) where θ is an angle on a reference plane, and φ is the angle from the reference plane to the point.

Solid Angle θ

solid geometry NOUN /ˈsɒ.lɪd dʒiˈɒ.mɪ.tri/ the study of geometric objects in a 3-dimensional space.

solid of revolution NOUN /ˈsɒ.lɪd ʌv ˌrɛ.voʊˈlu.ʃən/ a solid created by revolving a 2-dimensional figure about a line. Example: a torus can be formed by rotating a circle around a line that does not intersect the circle.

Solid of revolution

solstice NOUN /ˈsɒl.stɪs/ one of two days each year when the Earth is most tilted towards or away from the sun.

Solstice

solution NOUN /soʊˈlu.ʃən/
1) a set of one or more values that, when substituted for variables, make an equation or system of equations true and consistent. Synonym: *solution set*. See also *simultaneous equations* (p 105).
2) (triangle) the measures of the angles and the lengths of the sides of a triangle.
3) (linear programming) a point within the feasible area that minimizes or maximizes the value of the objective function, along with the value of the objective function.

solution set NOUN /soʊˈlu.ʃən sɛt/ see *solution* (p 107).

solve VERB /sɒlv/
1) to find one or more solutions to a problem, equation or a system of equations.
2) (triangle) to find the measures of all the angles and sides of a triangle.

solve analytically VERB /sɒlv ˌæn.ɪˈlɪt.ɪ.kli/ to solve using algebraic and numeric methods.

solve graphically VERB /sɒlv ˈɡræf.ɪ.kli/ find the solution by graphing.

Solve graphically

Somerville, Mary PERSON /ˈmɛər.i ˈsʌ.mərˌvɪl/ (1780—1872) a Scottish science writer and mathematician who was nominated as one of the first female members of the Royal Astronomical Society.

Mary Somerville

sort VERB /sɔrt/ to place in a specific order or grouping. Example: sort numerically.

source error NOUN /sɔrs ˈɛr.ər/ an error that happens while taking a sample.

source free ADJECTIVE /sɔrs fri/ the field $\mathbf{F} = \mathbf{M}(x, y)\mathbf{i} + \mathbf{N}(x, y)\mathbf{j}$ is source-free if it has these equivalent properties: 1. The total flux $\oint \mathbf{F} \cdot \mathbf{n} ds$ through every closed curve is zero. 2. Across all curves from $\mathbf{P}$ to $\mathbf{Q}$, $\int_{\mathbf{P}}^{\mathbf{Q}} \mathbf{F} \cdot \mathbf{n} ds$ is the same. 3. There exists a stream function $\mathbf{g}(x, y)$, for which $\mathbf{M} = \frac{\partial g}{\partial y}$ and $\mathbf{N} = -\frac{\partial g}{\partial x}$. 4. The components satisfy $\frac{\partial M}{\partial x} + \frac{\partial N}{\partial y}$ (the divergence is zero).

south NOUN /saʊθ/ in a direction towards the south pole or south magnetic pole. Antonym: *north* (p 80).

space NOUN /speɪs/
1) (geometry) a mathematical construct with specific properties in which objects may be placed. Example: Euclidean 3-space.
2) (probability) see *sample space* (p 101).

space curve NOUN /speɪs kɜrv/ a curve in three dimensions; a curve that can not exist in two dimensions.

space figure NOUN /speɪs ˈfɪɡ.jər/ see *geometric solid* (p 53).

spatial ADJECTIVE /ˈspeɪ.ʃəl/ having to do with 3-dimensional space. Example: spatial perception.

spatial relationship NOUN /ˈspeɪ.ʃəl rɪˈleɪ.ʃən ˌʃɪp/ the location and relative orientation of objects in a 3-dimensional space.

spatial thinking NOUN /ˈspeɪ.ʃəl ˈθɪŋk.ɪŋ/ the ability to visualize problems.

specific ADJECTIVE /spɪˈsɪf.ɪk/ stated exactly. Example: specific order.

speed NOUN /spid/ distance traveled in a unit of time. If a car is traveling at a speed of 50 kilometers per hour, the car travels a distance of 50 kilometers each hour. Formula: $s = \frac{d}{t}$ where **d** is distance and **t** is time. Synonym: *velocity*.

speedometer NOUN /spiˈdɒm.ɪ.tər/ a device that shows how fast something is going.

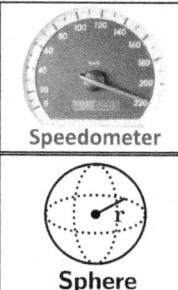
Speedometer

Sphere

sphere NOUN /sfɪər/ a shape like a round ball; all points that are a given distance from the center of the sphere in three dimensions. Formulas: **Volume** $= \frac{4}{3}\pi r^3$, **Surface area** $= 4\pi r^2$. Equation: $(x - h)^2 + (y - k)^2 + (z - l)^2 = r^2$ where (h, k, l) is the center point and **r** is the radius.

spherical ADJECTIVE /ˈsfɪər.ɪ.kl/
1) having to do with a sphere.
2) shaped like a sphere.

spherical cap NOUN /ˈsfɪər.ɪ.kl kæp/ see *spherical sector* (p 107).

spherical geometry NOUN /ˈsfɪər.ɪ.kəl dʒiˈɒ.mɪ.tri/ a non-Euclidean geometry that can be visualized as taking place on the surface of a sphere or ellipse, where a line is a great circle. Synonyms: *Riemannian geometry* (p 99), *elliptic geometry* (p 43).

spherical polar coordinate NOUN /ˈsfɪər.ɪ.kl ˈpoʊ.lər koʊˈɔr.də.nt/ location of a point in a spherical coordinate system, consisting of a radius **r** from the origin, an angle θ on a reference plane, and an angle φ at a right angle to the reference plane. Notation: (r, θ, φ). See also *solid angle* (p 106).

spherical sector NOUN /ˈsfɪər.ɪ.kl sɛk.tər/ a solid created by rotating a sector of a circle about its bisector. Synonym: *spherical cap*.

spherical segment NOUN /ˈsfɪər.ɪ.kəl ˈsɛɡ.mənt/ a portion of a sphere cut off by a plane.

spherical triangle NOUN /ˈsfɪər.ɪ.kəl ˈtraɪ.æŋ.ɡəl/ a triangle formed on the surface of a sphere by three intersecting great circles.

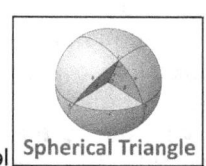
Spherical Triangle

spherical trigonometry NOUN /ˈsfɪər.ɪ.kəl ˌtrɪ.ɡəˈnɒm.ɪ.tri/ a trigonometry dealing with polygons in a spherical geometry and the relationships between lengths of sides and angles.

spheroid NOUN /ˈsfɪər.ɔɪd/ an ellipsoid where two of the axes are equal; a "flattened" sphere; an ellipsoid formed by rotating an ellipse about one of its axes.

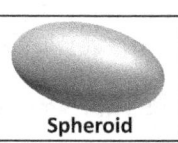
Spheroid

spiral NOUN /ˈspaɪ.rəl/ a shape that revolves around a fixed point while moving away from that point. Formula: $r = a\theta$ (polar coordinates), $x = a\theta \cos\theta$, $y = a\theta \sin\theta$ (parametric).

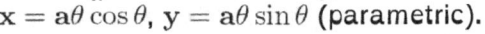

spline NOUN /splaɪn/ a smooth curve that runs through a series of points. Synonym: *Bézier curve*.

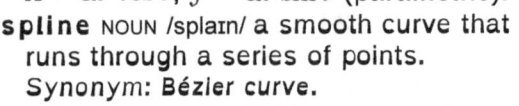

split VERB /splɪt/ to divide or separate.

split strategy NOUN /splɪt ˈstræ.tə.dʒi/ a strategy that splits numbers into smaller addends, factors, or place values to make calculations easier. Synonym: *partitioning*.

spread NOUN /sprɛd/ (statistics) the arrangement and distance of data points from a central point. Synonym: *distribution* (p 40).

spreadsheet NOUN /ˈsprɛd.ʃit/ a computer program that stores data and instructions in rows and columns.

spring scale NOUN /sprɪŋ skeɪl/ a machine that measures weight by tension on a spring.

sq ABBREVIATION square (as in square feet).

square /skwɛər/
1) NOUN a number multiplied by itself. Examples: x^2, $2^2 = 4$.
2) VERB to multiply a number by itself.
3) NOUN a four-sided polygon whose sides are the same length and whose sides intersect at right angles. Synonym: *regular quadrilateral*.
4) ADJECTIVE having to do with a square.
5) ADJECTIVE in the shape of a square.
6) ADJECTIVE containing a square.
7) ADJECTIVE having to do with a number multiplied by itself.
8) ADJECTIVE a number multiplied by another number that both have the same unit of measure. Abbreviation: *sq*.

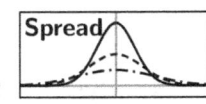

square brace NOUN /skwɛər breɪs/ see *bracket* (p 18).

square bracket NOUN /skwɛər ˈbræ.kɪt/ see *bracket* (p 18).

square function NOUN /skwɛər ˈfʌŋk.ʃən/ the function $f(x) = x^2$.

square matrix NOUN /skwɛər ˈmeɪ.trɪks/ a matrix with the same number of rows as columns. Plural: *square matrices* /skwɛər ˈmeɪ.trɪˌsiz/. Synonym: *augmented matrix* (p 14).

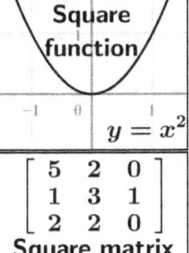

square measure NOUN /skwɛər ˈmɛʒ.ər/ a measure of area; a measure of two dimensions. Example: square meter.

square meter NOUN /skwɛər ˈmi.tər/ a unit of measure of an area that is equal to a square that is one meter on each side. Example: the area of one page of this book is about $0.06 m^2$.

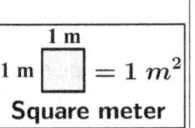

square number NOUN /skwɛər ˈnʌm.bər/ an integer that is the square of another integer. Examples: $1^2 = 1$, $2^2 = 4$, $3^2 = 9$, $4^2 = 16$, $5^2 = 25$, ... Synonym: *perfect square* (p 87).

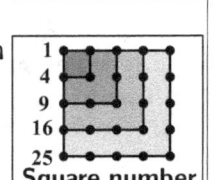

square pyramid NOUN /skwɛər ˈpɪr.ə.mɪd/ a polyhedron with a square base whose sides are triangles meeting at the apex.

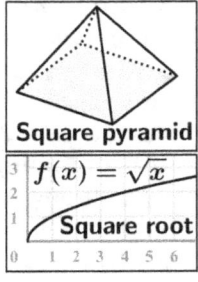

square root NOUN /skwɛər rut/ a number a such that $a^2 = x$. Notation: $\sqrt{}$. Math definition: $y = \sqrt{x}$ if and only if $y^2 = x$. Example: $\sqrt{4} = 2, -2$ because $2^2 = 4$, and $(-2)^2 = 4$.

square root function NOUN /skwɛər rut ˈfʌŋk.ʃən/ the function $f(x) = \sqrt{x}$.

square root method NOUN /skwɛər rut ˈmɛ.θəd/ a method for determining the value of a variable. Math definition: If $x^2 = p$ and $p \geq 0$, then $x = \sqrt{p}$ or $x = -\sqrt{p}$.

square system of equations NOUN /skwɛər ˈsɪs.təm ʌv ɪˈkweɪ.ʃənz/ a system of equations that has as many rows as it has variables.
Example: $\begin{array}{rrrr} 2x & -3y & +2z & = 5 \\ -3x & +2y & +3z & = 7 \\ x & +y & -z & = 2 \end{array}$

square unit NOUN /skwɛər ˈju.nɪt/ a unit of measure where two dimensions having the same unit of measure are multiplied by each other. Example: a 2 meter by 3 meter board covers $2 \times 3 = 6$ square meters.

squaring ADVERB /ˈskwɛər.ɪŋ/
1) the act of transforming something into a square. Example: squaring the circle.
2) the act of multiplying something by itself. Example: squaring an integer.

squaring the circle NOUN /ˈskwɛər.ɪŋ ðə ˈsɜr.kəl/ a problem of constructing a square with the same area as a given circle.

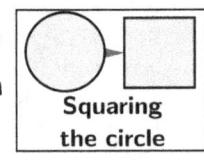

squeeze theorem NOUN /skwiz ˈθɪ.ə.rəm/ if a function is between two other functions, and at some point both functions approach the same value, then the first function approaches the same value. Math definition: Suppose $f(x) \leq g(x) \leq h(x)$ for all x near a. If $\lim_{x \to a} f(x) = L$ and $\lim_{x \to a} h(x) = L$, then $\lim_{x \to a} g(x) = L$.

SSS congruence NOUN /ɛs ɛs ɛs kənˈgru.əns/ (side-side-side congruence) two triangles are congruent if all three corresponding sides are congruent.
Math definition: $\triangle ABC \cong \triangle A'B'C'$ if and only if $a \cong a'$, $b \cong b'$ and $c \cong c'$.

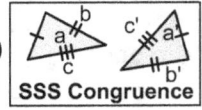

stack VERB /stæk/ to place one on top of another.

stacked bar graph NOUN /stækd bɑr græf/ a bar graph where the bars are stacked on top of each other, showing cumulative values.

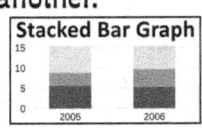

staircase function NOUN /ˈstɛərˌkeɪs ˈfʌŋk.ʃən/ see *step function* (p 109).

standard /ˈstæn.dərd/
1) NOUN a way of doing things that has been decided upon and documented.
2) NOUN something to which other things are compared. Example: kilogram is a standard of mass.
3) ADJECTIVE most usual or common. Example: standard form.

4) ADJECTIVE generally accepted.
Antonym: *nonstandard* (p 80).

standard deviation NOUN /ˈstæn.dərd ˌdi.viˈeɪ.ʃən/ a measure of the 'spread' of a dataset; a way to measure the average distance of a single data element from the center of the dataset. Notation: σ. Formula: $\sigma = \sqrt{v}$ where **v** is the variance (p 120).

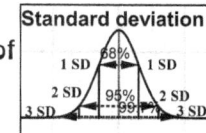

standard form NOUN /ˈstæn.dərd form/ the usual or customary form. Example: the standard form of a linear equation.

standard form of a linear equation NOUN /ˈstæn.dərd form ʌv ə ˈlɪ.ni.ər ɪˈkweɪ.ʃən/ a linear equation in the form $ax + by = c$.

standard form of an exponential equation NOUN /ˈstæn.dərd form ʌv ən ˌɛk.spoʊˈnɛn.ʃəl ɪˈkweɪ.ʃən/ an equation in the form $y = ax^b$ where **a** is the initial value at $x = 0$ and $b > 1$ is the growth factor or $0 < b < 1$ is the decay factor.

standard form of a polynomial NOUN /ˈstæn.dərd form ʌv ə ˌpɒ.ləˈnoʊ.mi.əl/ a polynomial with the terms ordered so higher degree terms are to the left of lower degree terms: $a_0x^n + a_1x^{n-1} + \cdots + a_{n-1}x + a_n$.

standard form of a quadratic equation NOUN /ˈstæn.dərd form ʌv ə kwɒˈdræt.ɪk ɪˈkweɪ.ʃən/ an equation in the form $ax^2 + bx + c = 0$ or $y = ax^2 + bx + c$.

standard index form NOUN /ˈstæn.dərd ˈɪn.dɛks form/ (British English) a way to write real numbers that is very useful for large and small numbers. Format: **mantissa** $\times 10^{\text{exponent}}$ where $-10 <$ **mantissa** < 10 and the exponent is any integer. Example: $2.643 \times 10^{-3} = 0.002\,643$. Synonym: *e notation* (p 44), *engineering notation* (p 44), *scientific notation*.

standardized test NOUN /ˈstæn.dərˌdaɪzd tɛst/ a test that is always administered and scored in the same way.

standard normal distribution NOUN /ˈstæn.dərd ˈnɔr.məl ˌdɪs.trəˈbju.ʃən/ a normal distribution with a mean of 0.

standard position NOUN /ˈstæn.dərd pəˈzɪ.ʃən/ all angles in a circle are measured from the positive horizontal radius of the circle with the center at the origin.

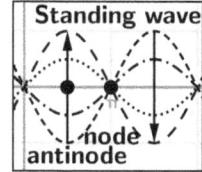

standard unit NOUN /ˈstæn.dərd ˈju.nɪt/ a convention for naming a large or small units of measure. Example: nanometer.

standing wave NOUN /ˈstæn.dɪŋ weɪv/ a wave in a motion that does not move at the nodes, and moves the full amplitude at the anti-nodes. Formula: $f(x, t) = 2A \sin(kx) \cos(kvt)$ where **t** is time, **k** is the period of the wave, **v** is the velocity of the wave.

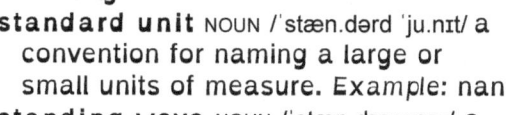

statement NOUN /ˈsteɪt.mənt/ a logical claim; a declaration.

stationary ADJECTIVE /ˈsteɪ.ʃəˌnɛr.i/ not moving. Synonym: *fixed* (p 50).

stationary point NOUN /ˈsteɪ.ʃəˌnɛr.i pɔɪnt/
1) (geometry) a point that does not move. Synonym: *fixed point*.
2) (calculus) a point on a function where $f(x) = 0$; a point where the tangent is a horizontal line.

stationary wave NOUN /ˈsteɪ.ʃəˌnɛr.i weɪv/ see *standing wave* (p 109).

statistic NOUN /stəˈtɪs.tɪk/ a quantity calculated from data elements in a dataset. Example: arithmetic average of heights of members of the population.

statistical model NOUN /stəˈtɪs.tɪ.kl ˈmɒ.dl/ a mathematical model intended to predict statistical outcomes. Synonym: *probability model* (p 92).

statistics NOUN /stəˈtɪs.tɪks/ the science of collection, classification, summarization, analysis and interpretation of data.

steep ADJECTIVE /stip/ the degree of slope. The steeper a slope, the closer it is to vertical. Math definition: if m_1 is the slope of line l_1, and m_2 the slope of line l_2, and $|m_1| > |m_2|$, then l_1 is steeper than l_2.

stellated ADJECTIVE /ˈstɛl.eɪt.əd/
1) (polygon) extended by substituting an isosceles triangle for each side.
2) (polyhedron) extended by substituting a right pyramid for each face. Example: stellated pentagon.

stem and leaf plot NOUN /stɛm ənd lif plɒt/ see *stemplot* (p 109).

stemplot NOUN /ˈstɛm.plɒt/ a graph show numerical data where the stem is the most significant digit of the data, and the leaf contains the second most significant digit. Example: The illustration shows the stemplot for the dataset {12, 12, 13, 15, 17, 21, 21, 23, 24, 24, 24, 25, 28, 30, 32, 35}. See also *back-to-back stem and leaf plot* (p 15).

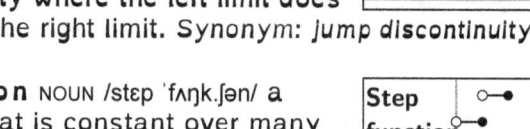

step ADJECTIVE /stɛp/ occurring in sections that are disconnected.

step discontinuity NOUN /stɛp ˌdɪs.kɒn.tnˈuː.ɪ.ti/ a type of essential discontinuity where the left limit does not equal the right limit. Synonym: *jump discontinuity* (p 66).

step function NOUN /stɛp ˈfʌŋk.ʃən/ a function that is constant over many intervals. Synonym: *staircase function*.

step graph NOUN /stɛp græf/ graph of a step function.

steradian NOUN /stəˈreɪ.di.ən/ a solid angle that cuts off a section of the surface of a sphere with an area equal to the radius of the sphere squared.

Stewart's Theorem NOUN /ˈstu.ərtz ˈθɪ.ə.rəm/ a theorem relating the length of the sides of a triangle to a cevian of the triangle. Formula: $b^2 m + c^2 n = a(d^2 + m \cdot n)$ where **a**, **b**, and **c** are lengths of sides of the triangle, **m** and **n** are the lengths of the segments into which **a** is divided by the cevian, and **d** is the length of the cevian.

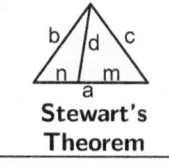

straight ADJECTIVE /streɪt/ does not curve or bend.

straight angle NOUN /streɪt ˈæŋ.gəl/ an angle that measures $\frac{1}{2}$ of a full circle; an angle whose initial and terminal sides lie on the same straight line.

straight edge NOUN /streɪt ɛdʒ/ a tool used to draw straight lines.

straight line NOUN /streɪt laɪn/ line that does not curve or bend.

strategy NOUN /ˈstræ.tə.dʒi/ plan or method for accomplishing a task.

stratified ADJECTIVE /ˈstræ.tə.faɪd/ divided into groups or categories.

stratified sample ADJECTIVE /ˈstræ.tə.faɪd ˈsæm.pəl/ populations are divided into homogeneous categories before sampling. Samples are then taken at random within each stratified group. Example: age groupings. Synonym: *stratified random sample*.

stratify VERB /ˈstræ.tə.faɪ/ to place into groups or categories.

stretch /strɛtʃ/
1) NOUN see *enlargement* (p 44).
2) VERB see *enlarge*.

stretch factor NOUN /strɛtʃ ˈfæk.tər/ a scalar by which a polynomial is multiplied that shows how high and low the 'bumps' of the polynomial go. Example: $0 < a < 1$ in $f(x) = a(x - x_1)(x - x_2)$.

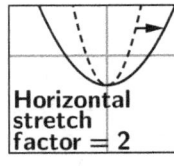

strictly ADJECTIVE /ˈstrɪkt.li/ precisely; no more and no less.

strictly greater than ADJECTIVE /ˈstrɪkt.li ˈgreɪt.ər ðæn/ greater than but not equal to. Notation: $a > b$.

strictly less than ADJECTIVE /ˈstrɪkt.li lɛs ðæn/ less than but not equal to. Notation: $a < b$.

strictly self-similar ADJECTIVE /ˈstrɪkt.li sɛlf ˈsɪ.mə.lər/ a figure is strictly self-similar if any of its parts of any size or location are similar to the whole. Example: Sierpiński triangle.

study /ˈstʌ.di/
1) NOUN the process of examining detail in order to discover fact.
2) NOUN (statistics) the process of collecting data on a population and analyzing that data.
3) NOUN the result of collecting data on a population and analyzing that data.
4) VERB to examine detail in order to discover fact.
5) VERB to collect data on a population and analyze that data.
Synonym: *investigation* (p 65).

sub- PREFIX /sʌb/
1) less than.
2) below. Example: subscript.
3) part of. Example: subdomain.

subdomain NOUN /ˈsʌb.doʊ.meɪn/ a part of the domain; a specific interval of the domain. Example: $f(x)$ is defined on the subdomain $x > 0$.

subitise VERB /ˈsʌb.ɪ.taɪz/ to perceive at a glance; to recognize the number of objects without counting them.

subscript NOUN /ˈsʌb.skrɪpt/ any characters written below and to the right in a smaller font. Notation: f_n where n is the subscript. Synonym: *index* (British English).

subset NOUN /ˈsʌb.sɛt/ part of a set. Notation: $B \subset A$, or $B \subseteq A$ to emphasize that B may be equal to A. Synonym: *inclusion relation*.

substitute VERB /ˈsʌb.stɪ.tut/ to replace a variable or expression with another variable or expression that is equal to the original variable or expression. Example: substitute $x - 2$ for y into the equation $y = 3x$. The result is $x - 2 = 3x \Rightarrow -2 = 2x \Rightarrow x = -1$. Synonym: *replace* (p 99).

substitution NOUN /ˌsʌb.stɪˈtu.ʃən/ the process or act of substituting. Example: substitution property of equality.

substitution method NOUN /ˌsʌb.stɪˈtu.ʃən ˈmɛ.θəd/ a method for solving simultaneous equations involving substituting an expression in for a variable. Example: $y = 3$, $x + y = 1 \Rightarrow x + 3 = 1 \Rightarrow x = -2$.

substitution principle NOUN /ˌsʌb.stɪˈtu.ʃən ˈprɪn.sə.pəl/ see *substitution property of equality* (p 110).

substitution property of equality NOUN /ˌsʌb.stɪˈtu.ʃən ˈprɒ.pər.ti ʌv ɪˈkwɒl.ɪ.ti/ if $a = b$ then b can be substituted for a in any equation without changing the truth value of the equation.

Substitution Rule NOUN /ˌsʌb.stɪˈtu.ʃən rul/
1) if $u = g(x)$ is a differentiable function whose range is I and f is continuous on I, then $\int f(g(x))g'(x)dx = \int f(u)du$.
2) if g' is continuous on $[a, b]$ and f is continuous on the range of $u = g(x)$, then $\int_a^b f(g(x))g'(x)dx = \int_{g(a)}^{g(b)} f(u)du$.

subtended angle NOUN /sʌbˈtɛnd.əd ˈæŋ.gəl/ any angle whose vertex lies on the circumference of a circle and whose legs intersect the end points of a chord or arc of the circle.

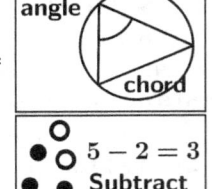

subtract VERB /səbˈtrækt/ to take away from a whole. Notation: −. Example: $5 - 2 = 3$. Synonym: *decrease* (p 34).

subtraction NOUN /səbˈtræk.ʃən/ the process of subtracting. Formula: minuend − subtrahend = difference. Inverse: *addition* (p 8).

subtraction by decomposition NOUN /səbˈtræk.ʃən baɪ ˌdi.kɒm.pəˈzɪ.ʃən/ regrouping a subtraction problem to move a value of 10 from a higher place value.

subtraction of polynomials NOUN /səbˈtræk.ʃən ʌv ˌpɒ.ləˈnoʊ.mi.əlz/ to subtract one polynomial from another, subtract the like terms.

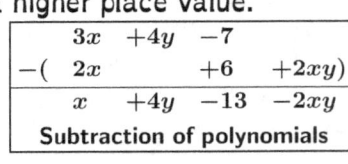

subtraction property of equality NOUN /səbˈtræk.ʃən ˈprɒ.pər.ti ʌv ɪˈkwɒl.ɪ.ti/ a value can be subtracted from both sides of an equation without changing the truth value of the equation. Math definition: for any real or complex numbers a, b and c; if $a = b$ then $a - c = b - c$ and if $a \neq b$ then $a - c \neq b - c$.

subtraction property of inequality NOUN /səbˈtræk.ʃən ˈprɒ.pər.ti ʌv ˌɪn.ɪˈkwɒ.lɪ.ti/ a value can be subtracted from both sides of an inequality without changing the truth value of the inequality. Math definition: for any real numbers **a**, **b** and **c**; if $a < b$ then $a - c < b - c$ and if $a > b$ then $a - c > b - c$.

subtraction sign NOUN /səbˈtræk.ʃən saɪn/ the symbol '−' is used to show subtraction.

subtrahend NOUN /ˈsʌb.trəˌhɛnd/ a number or expression that is subtracted. Formula: **minuend − subtrahend = difference**. Example: $5 - 2 = 3$.

successive NOUN /sʌkˈsɛ.sɪv/ coming one after the other in a specific order with no gaps. Example: successive integers: **5, 6, 7, 8**.

successor NOUN /sʌkˈsɛs.ər/ what comes immediately after in an order. Antonym: *predecessor* (p 91).

sufficient ADJECTIVE /səˈfɪ.ʃənt/ is enough all by itself, usually to show that something is true.

sum /sʌm/
1) NOUN the total of an addition problem. Formula: **addend + addend = sum**. Example: $3 + 2 = 5$. Antonym: *difference* (p 37).
2) VERB see *add* (p 8). Antonym: *subtract* (p 110).

Sum Difference Identities NOUN /sʌm ˈdɪf.rəns aɪˈdɛn.tɪ.tiz/ trigonometric identities involving the sums and differences of angles. See also *Trigonometric Identities* (p 143).

summarize VERB /ˈsʌm.ər.aɪz/ to create a short description of fact or data that gives a good idea of the properties of the data.

summary NOUN, ADJECTIVE /ˈsʌm.ər.i/ a short compilation of fact or data that gives a good idea of the properties of the data. Example: five number summary.

summary statistics NOUN /ˈsʌm.ər.i stəˈtɪs.tɪks/ a short set of statistical information about a dataset.

summation notation NOUN /səˈmeɪ.ʃən noʊˈteɪ.ʃən/ see *sigma notation* (p 104).

summation sign NOUN /səˈmeɪ.ʃən saɪn/ the symbol $\sum$ is used to show repeated addition. Example: $\sum_{n=1}^{5} n = 1 + 2 + 3 + 4 + 5 = 15$.

sum of a geometric sequence NOUN /sʌm ʌv ə ˌdʒi.əˈmɛ.trɪk ˈsi.kwəns/ see *geometric series* (p 53).

Sum of Cubes NOUN /sʌm ʌv kjubz/ a polynomial identity used to factor certain cubic equations. Formula: $a^3 + b^3 = (a + b)(a^2 - ab + b^2)$.

sum rule NOUN /sʌm rul/
1) (probability) see *rule of sum* (p 101).
2) (calculus) the derivative of a sum is the sum of the derivatives. Math definition: $\frac{d}{dx}[u(x) + v(x)] = \frac{d}{dx}u(x) + \frac{d}{dx}v(x)$.

sums of powers NOUN /sʌmz ʌv ˈpaʊ.ərz/ • $\sum_{k=1}^{n} 1 = n$; • $\sum_{k=1}^{n} k = \frac{n(n-1)}{2}$; • $\sum_{k=1}^{n} k^2 = \frac{n(n+1)(2n+1)}{6}$; • $\sum_{k=1}^{n} k^3 = \frac{n^2(n+1)^2}{4}$.

Sum to Product Identities NOUN /sʌm tu ˈprɒd.əkt aɪˈdɛn.tɪ.tiz/ trigonometric identities involving converting sums to products. See also *Trigonometric Identities* (p 143).

super- PREFIX /ˈsu.pər/
1) greater than. Example: superset.
2) above. Example: superscript.

superscript NOUN /ˈsu.pərˌskrɪpt/ text appearing above and to the right in a smaller font. Example: 2 in x^2.

superset NOUN /ˈsu.pərˌsɛt/ a set that contains all of the members of another set, and possibly others. Math definition: If B is a subset of set A then A is a superset of set B; if $A \supset B$ then $B \subset A$. Notation: $A \supset B$.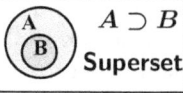

supplementary ADJECTIVE /ˌsʌp.ləˈmɛn.tri/
1) totaling 180°.
2) added to complete something.

supplementary angles NOUN /ˌsʌp.ləˈmɛn.tri ˈæŋ.gəlz/ two angles that, taken together, make a straight angle. Angles do not have to be adjacent to be supplementary.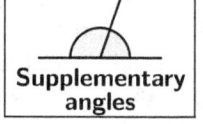

Supplementary Angle Congruence Theorem NOUN /ˌsʌp.ləˈmɛn.tri ˈæŋ.gəl ˈkɒn.gru.əns ˈθɪ.ə.rəm/ angles supplementary to the same angle or to congruent angles are congruent.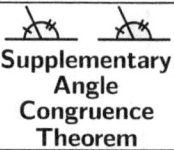

supplementary units NOUN /ˌsʌp.ləˈmɛn.tri ˈju.nɪtz/ the units radian and steradian in SI units.

Supplement Theorem NOUN /ˌsʌp.ləˈmənt ˈθɪ.ə.rəm/ if two angles form a linear pair, then they are supplementary angles.

supremum NOUN /səˈpri.mʌm/ see *least upper bound* (p 68).

surd /sɜrd/
1) NOUN see *irrational number* (p 65).
2) ADJECTIVE see *irrational* (p 65).

surface NOUN /ˈsɜr.fɪs/ the boundary between a geometric solid and the rest of the containing space. Example: the surface of a sphere.

surface area NOUN /ˈsɜr.fɪs ˈɛər.i.ə/ the area of the surface of a 3-dimensional geometric figure. See also *area* (p 13).

surface integral NOUN /ˈsɜr.fɪs ˈɪn.tə.grəl/ a generalization of multiple integrals to integration over surfaces.

surface of revolution NOUN /ˈsɜr.fɪs ʌv ˌrɛ.voʊˈlu.ʃən/ a surface formed by rotating a 2-dimensional figure about a line.

survey /ˈsɜr.veɪ/
1) VERB to sample a population to obtain data.
2) NOUN the process of sampling a population.
3) NOUN the result of sampling a population.

swap VERB /swɒp/ exchange places.

swap rows VERB /swɒp roʊz/ exchange rows in a matrix. Example: Swap rows 1 and 3:
$$\begin{bmatrix} 1 & 3 \\ 2 & 0 \\ 4 & 2 \end{bmatrix} \xrightarrow{\text{Swap R1 and R3}} \begin{bmatrix} 4 & 2 \\ 2 & 0 \\ 1 & 3 \end{bmatrix}$$

symbol NOUN /ˈsɪm.bəl/ a letter, character or other mark used to represent something. Examples: π, **A**. Synonym: *label* (p 66).

symmetric ADJECTIVE /sɪˈmɛ.trɪk/
1) a relation **R** is symmetric if and only if **aRb** always implies **bRa**. Example: if $x = 5$ then $5 = x$.
2) (geometric figures) having a property of symmetry such as symmetry about a line or a point. Synonym: **symmetrical**. Antonym: *asymmetric* (p 14).

symmetric distribution NOUN /sɪˈmɛ.trɪk ˌdɪs.trəˈbju.ʃən/ a distribution that is not skewed to one side or another; a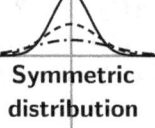

distribution that is symmetric about the mean. Antonym: *skewed distribution* (p 106).

symmetric property of equality NOUN /sɪˈmɛ.trɪk ˈprɒ.pər.ti ʌv ɪˈkwɒl.ɪ.ti/ for real and complex numbers, if a = b, then b = a. Example: if 2 + 3 = 5, then 5 = 2 + 3.

symmetry NOUN /ˈsɪ.mɪ.tri/
1) property of some transformations that leaves an object unchanged under a transformation. Examples: axial, radial and rotational symmetry.
2) a property of geometric objects that they remain unchanged when flipped about a line or point. Antonym: *asymmetry* (p 14).

symmetry principle NOUN /ˈsɪ.mɪ.tri ˈprɪn.sə.pəl/ if a region **R** is symmetric about a line **L**, then the centroid of **R** lies on **L**.

synthetic division NOUN /sɪnˈθɛt.ɪk dɪˈvɪ.ʒən/ an algorithm for quickly dividing one polynomial by another.

synthetic substitution NOUN /sɪnˈθɛt.ɪk ˈsʌb.stɪˌtu.ʃən/ an algorithm for finding the value of a polynomial given a particular value of the independent variable.

system NOUN /ˈsɪs.təm/ a set of objects that work together as a whole.

systematic ADJECTIVE /ˌsɪs.tə'mæt.ɪk/ being ordered and planned.

systematic sample NOUN /ˌsɪs.tə'mæt.ɪk ˈsæm.pəl/ a sample obtained by choosing every k^{th} member of a population. Example: choose every tenth person from a list of names and phone numbers.

system of equations NOUN /ˈsɪs.təm ʌv ɪˈkweɪ.ʒənz/ a set of equations that are taken to be simultaneously true. Synonym: *simultaneous equations*.

system of inequalities NOUN /ˈsɪs.təm ʌv ˌɪn.ɪˈkwɒl.ɪt.iz/ a set of inequalities that are taken to be simultaneously true. See *linear programming* (p 69).

system of linear equations NOUN /ˈsɪs.təm ʌv ˈlɪ.ni.ər ɪˈkweɪ.ʃənz/ a set of linear equations that work together to produce a solution.

Système international d'unités NOUN /ˈsɪs.təm ˌɪn.tər'næ.sio.nal ˈduˌni.teɪ/ International System of Units: an international convention for naming units of measure. Example: nanometer. See also *International System of Units* (p 145).

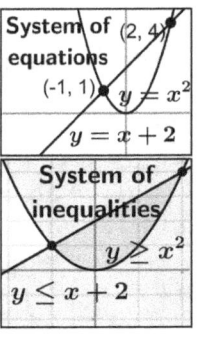

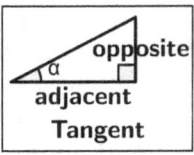

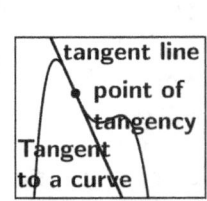

T

t ABBREVIATION metric ton or tonne (1000 kg).

T ABBREVIATION
1) ton (2000 lb.)
2) tera-; 10^{12}. Abbreviation: T. Example: 5 Tbytes = 5×10^{12} bytes. Synonym: *trillion*.

table NOUN /ˈteɪ.bəl/ a set of data in rows and columns.

tabular ADJECTIVE /ˈtæb.jə.lər/
1) taking the form of a table.
2) computed by means of a table.

tabulate VERB /ˈtæb.jə.leɪt/ to organize into a table.

tail NOUN /teɪl/ where a vector starts; the end of a vector without an arrow. Synonym: *initial point* (p 62). Antonyms: *head* (p 56), *terminal point* (p 113).

take VERB /teɪk/
1) can be set to certain values. Example: the variable takes positive values.
2) find by calculating. Example: take a root.
3) remove. Example: 5 take away 3 is 2.

take a logarithm VERB /teɪk eɪ ˈlɒg.əˌrɪð.əm/ find the value of a logarithm. Example: take the logarithm of 2.

take a root VERB /teɪk eɪ rut/ find a root of a number. Example: take the root of 2.

take away PREPOSITION /teɪk əˈweɪ/ subtract. Example: 5 take away 2 is 5 − 2 = 3.

tally /ˈtæl.i/
1) VERB to count using a tally table or tally marks.
2) NOUN a completed set of tally marks; a total. Example: "The tally is 147."

tally mark NOUN /ˈtæl.i mɑrk/ a mark used to count. Synonym: *hash mark*.

tally table NOUN /ˈtæl.i ˈteɪ.bəl/ a set of tally marks placed together.

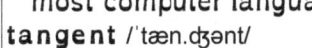

tan ABBREVIATION tangent.

tan() COMPUTERS the tangent function in most computer languages.

tangent /ˈtæn.dʒənt/
1) NOUN of a right triangle, the ratio of the length of the side opposite the angle divided by the length of the side adjacent to the angle. Formula: $\text{tangent} = \frac{\text{opposite}}{\text{adjacent}} = \frac{\text{sine}}{\text{cosine}}$. Inverse: *arctangent*.
2) NOUN a line that touches a curve or conic section exactly once.
3) NOUN a line that touches a curve where the slope of the line is equal to the slope of the curve at that point. Formula of tangent line: $y - f(c) = m_{\tan}(x - c)$, $m_{\tan} = \lim_{x \to c} \frac{x(f) - x(c)}{x - c}$.

tangent circles NOUN /ˈtæn.dʒənt ˈsɜr.kəlz/ circles that intersect exactly once.

tangent line approximation NOUN /ˈtæn.dʒənt laɪn əˌprɒk.səˈmeɪ.ʃən/ see *linear approximation* (p 69).

tangent plane NOUN /ˈtæn.dʒənt pleɪn/ a plane that is tangent to a 3-dimensional curve at a point on the curve. Formula: given the surface $z = f(x, y)$ at the point $P(x_0, y_0, z_0)$ is $z - z_0 = f_x(x_0, y_0)(x - x_0) + f_y(x_0, y_0)(y - y_0)$.

tangent problem NOUN /ˈtæn.dʒənt ˈprɒb.ləm/ how to find the equation for a line that is tangent to a curve. Formula: $y = \left(\lim_{x \to P_x} \frac{f(x) - f(P_x)}{x - P_x}\right)(x - P_x) + P_y$.

tangent segment NOUN /ˈtæn.dʒənt ˈsɛg.mənt/ a line segment that is tangent to a circle where one endpoint of the segment is the point of tangency.

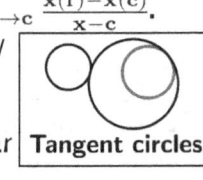

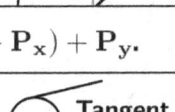

tangram NOUN /ˈtæn.græm/ a Chinese shape puzzle whose pieces can be put together to form different shapes. Traditional tangrams have seven pieces.

tanh ABBREVIATION see *hyperbolic tangent* (p 58).

tanh() COMPUTERS the hyperbolic tangent function in most computer languages.

tape diagram NOUN /teɪp ˈdaɪ.əˌgræm/ a strategy for visualizing the addition of two two-digit integers.

tape measure NOUN /teɪp ˈmɛ.ʒər/ a strip of cloth or metal with tick marks used to measure distance.

tare NOUN /teɪr/
1) packing material including the box.
2) the weight of packaging material. Formula: **gross weight − tare = net weight**.

tautochrone NOUN /ˈtɑ.toʊˌkroʊn/ a cycloid where, if multiple objects slide down the curve from different positions, they will reach the bottom of the cycloid at the same time. Formula: $x = a(\theta - \sin\theta)$, $y = a(1 - \cos\theta)$, $a < 0$.

Taylor polynomial NOUN /ˈteɪ.lər ˌpɒl.əˈnoʊ.mi.əl/ the partial sum formed by the first $n+1$ terms of a Taylor series is a polynomial of degree **n** that is called the nth Taylor polynomial of the function.

Taylor series NOUN /ˈteɪ.lər ˈsɪər.iz/ the Taylor series of a function is an infinite sum of terms that are expressed in terms of the function's derivatives at a single point $x = a$. Formulas: $f(x) = f(a) + f'(a)(x-a) + \frac{1}{2}f''(a)(x-a)^2 + \ldots$, $f(x) = \sum_{n=0}^{\infty} \frac{f^{(n)}(a)}{n!}(x-a)^n$.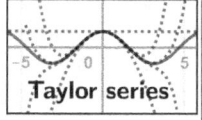

temperature NOUN /ˈtɛm.prəˌtʃər/ how hot or cold something is. See also *degree* (p 35).

template NOUN /ˈtɛm.plɪt/ a pattern used as a guide in making something accurately.

ten NOUN /tɛn/ 10.

tend VERB /tɛnd/ to approach a certain value. Example: the function tends to zero.

tendency NOUN /ˈtɛn.dən.si/ the likelihood that something behaves in a particular way.

ten frames NOUN /tɛn freɪmz/ ten squares arranged in two rows used for visualizing place value and calculation.

tenth ADJECTIVE, NOUN /tɛnθ/
1) one of ten equal parts: $\frac{1}{10}$. Synonym: *deci-*.
2) coming in position 10 in an ordered list. Notation: 10th.

tera- PREFIX /ˈtɛr.ə/ 10^{12}. Abbreviation: T. Example: **5 terameters = 5×10^{12} meters**. Synonym: *trillion* (p 117).

term NOUN /tɜrm/
1) (of a polynomial) a coefficient and zero or more variables multiplied together that are separated from any other terms by addition or subtraction.
2) (of a sequence) a number in a sequence.
3) (in a proof) a concept used in the proof that may or may not be defined.

terminal ADJECTIVE /ˈtɜr.mə.nl/ having to do with an end.

terminal line NOUN /ˈtɜr.mə.nl laɪn/ see *terminal side* (p 113).

terminal point NOUN /ˈtɜr.mə.nl pɔɪnt/ a point where something stops. Example: terminal point on a unit circle. Synonym: *head* (p 56). Antonyms: *initial point* (p 62), *tail* (p 112).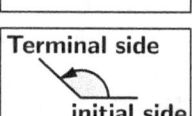

terminal side NOUN /ˈtɜr.mə.nl saɪd/ one of two rays or line segments that define an angle. Antonym: *initial side* (p 62). Synonym: *terminal line*.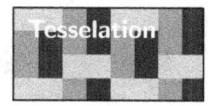

terminate VERB /ˈtɜr.məˌneɪt/
1) to come to an end.
2) to cause to come to an end.

terminating ADJECTIVE /ˈtɜr.məˌneɪt.ɪŋ/ having the property of having an end. Example: terminating decimal. Antonym: *nonterminating* (p 80).

terminating decimal NOUN /ˈtɜr.məˌneɪt.ɪŋ ˈdɛs.məl/ a decimal that has a last digit. Example: 3.52. Antonym: *nonterminating decimal* (p 80).

term to term rule NOUN /tɜrm tu tɜrm rul/ a rule for finding the next number in a sequence. Example: $r_n = 2r_{n-1}$ defines the sequence 1, 2, 4, 8, ….

ternary ADJECTIVE /ˈtɜr.nər.i/ having to do with the number 3.

ternary numeration NOUN /ˈtɜr.nər.i ˌnu.məˈreɪ.ʃən/ a base three numeration system. Example: $201_3 = 2 \times 3^2 + 0 \times 3 + 1 = 18 + 0 + 1 = 19_{10}$.

tertiary ADJECTIVE /ˈtɜr.ʃiˌɛr.i/
1) third in importance.
2) having to do with the number three.

tessellation NOUN /ˌtɛ.səˈleɪ.ʃən/ an arrangement of 2-dimensional geometric figures that completely fills a plane.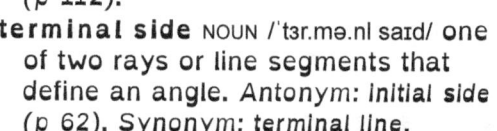

tesseract NOUN /ˈtɛ.səˌrækt/ the extension of a cube into four dimensions. Synonym: *hypercube* (p 58).

test /tɛst/
1) VERB to try something to see if it is true or valid.
2) NOUN a process used to try something or someone, especially to see if knowledge has been acquired.

test point NOUN /tɛst pɔɪnt/ a point used to determine the value of an equation at that point.

test value NOUN /tɛst ˈvæl.ju/ a value substituted into an equation to find the test point.

tetra- PREFIX /ˈtɛ.trə/ four.

tetragon NOUN /ˈtɛ.trəˌgɒn/ see *quadrilateral* (p 94).

tetrahedron NOUN /ˌtɛ.trəˈhi.drən/ any four-sided polyhedron. Synonym: *triangular pyramid* (p 116). Plural: *tetrahedra* /ˌtɛt.rəˈhi.drʌ/.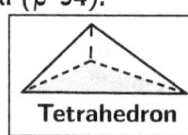

then ADVERB /ðɛn/ see *if … then …* (p 59).

theorem NOUN /ˈθi.ə.rəm/ a proposition that has been proved and generally accepted. Example: Pythagorean Theorem.

theoretic ADJECTIVE /ˌθi.əˈrɛ.tɪk/ see *theoretical* (p 114).

theoretical ADJECTIVE /ˌθi.əˈrɛ.tɪ.kəl/
1) having to do with a theory.
2) calculated, not measured.
3) based on theory, not experiment. Example: theoretical probability.
Antonyms: *anecdotal* (p 10), *empirical* (p 43), *observational* (p 82).

theoretical probability NOUN /ˌθi.əˈrɛt.ɪ.kəl ˌprɒ.bəˈbɪ.lɪ.ti/ a probability based on theory, and not on experimentation. Antonym: *experimental probability* (p 47).

theory NOUN /ˈθɪər.i/
1) a collection of undefined terms, axioms, definitions and theorems that make up a body of mathematical knowledge. Example: set theory.
2) an idea that seems likely, but has been yet been proved. Synonym: *conjecture*.

therefore ADVERB /ˈðɛər.fɔr/ it can be concluded that, the preceding arguments lead to the following conclusion. Notation: ∴. Synonym: *in conclusion* (p 60).

thermometer NOUN /ˌθərˈmɒ.mə.tər/ a device used to measure temperature.

theta SYMBOL /ˈθeɪ.tə/ the Greek letter θ, often used as a variable for angles. See also Greek Letters (p 135).

third NOUN, ADJECTIVE /θɜrd/
1) coming in position 3 in an ordered list. Notation: 3rd.
2) one of three equal parts: $\frac{1}{3}$.
3) the result of three operations. Example: third derivative.

Third Angle Theorem NOUN /θɜrd ˈæŋ.gəl ˈθɪ.ə.rəm/ if two angles of one triangle are congruent to two angles of a second triangle, then the third angles of the triangles are also congruent. Math definition: if $\angle \alpha \cong \angle \alpha'$ and $\angle \beta \cong \angle \beta'$ then $\angle \gamma \cong \angle \gamma'$.

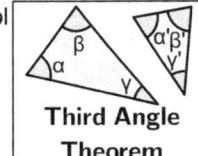

third power NOUN /θɜrd ˈpaʊ.ər/ exponent of 3. Example: x^3 is x to the **third power**.

thirteen ADJECTIVE, NOUN /θɜrˈtin/ the number 13.

thirty ADJECTIVE, NOUN /ˈθɜr.ti/ the number 30.

thousand ADJECTIVE, NOUN /ˈθaʊ.zənd/ 1000. Synonym: *kilo-* (p 66).

thousands separator NOUN /ˈθaʊ.zəndz ˈsɛp.əˌreɪ.tər/ either a comma ',', a period '.' or a space ' ' used to divide large numbers into groups of three. The comma, called a comma separator, is used in U.S., Canada, England, and most of Asia. The period is used in most of Europe. Example: **1,325,602**.

thousandth ADJECTIVE, NOUN /ˈθaʊ.zəndθ/
1) coming in position **1000** in an ordered list. Notation: 1000th.
2) one of one thousand equal parts: $\frac{1}{1000}$. Synonym: *milli-* (p 75).

three ADJECTIVE, NOUN /θri/ the number or digit 3.

three-dimensional ADJECTIVE /θri dɪˈmɛn.ʃə.nl/ having three dimensions, usually length, width and height. Example: solids are three-dimensional. Abbreviation: 3-D.

three space NOUN /θri speɪs/ see *3-space* (p 6).

tick mark NOUN /tɪk mɑrk/ a short line segment used to show the position of values on a number line or axis.

time NOUN /taɪm/
1) the sequence of past, present and future.
2) an interval of time between two events. Example: 15 seconds.
3) time of day. Example: 1:00 PM.

time interval NOUN /taɪm ˈɪn.tər.vəl/ the time that passes between two events. Synonym: *time period* (p 114).

timeline NOUN /ˈtaɪm.laɪn/ a set of events marked on a line showing order in which things happen.

time period NOUN /taɪm ˈpɪər.i.əd/ a specific time interval. Examples: 1 second, 3 hours. Synonyms: *time interval* (p 114), *period of time*.

times PREPOSITION /taɪmz/
1) multiplied by. Notation: ·, ×. Example: $3 \times 5 = 15$.
2) occurs one or more times. Example: a double root is a root that occurs two times.

time series NOUN /taɪm ˈsɪər.iz/ (statistics) data that is gathered over time. Example: population of mice each year for fifty years.

times table NOUN /taɪmz ˈteɪ.bəl/ a table containing integers and their products. See *Multiplication Facts* (p 124).

time table NOUN /taɪm ˈteɪ.bəl/ a table showing the times of events, such as a bus schedule.

time zone NOUN /taɪm zoʊn/ a region throughout which the same standard time is used.

together ADVERB /təˈgɛð.ər/ taken or considered at the same time or place.

tolerance NOUN /ˈtɑl.ər.ɛns/ the maximum allowable error in a measurement.

ton NOUN /tʌn/ a unit of measure of weight. Abbreviation: T. Formulas: 1 ton = 2000 pounds. 1 ton ≈ 0.908 metric tons.

tonne NOUN /tʌn/ a unit of measure of mass. Abbreviation: t. Formulas: 1 tonne = 1 metric ton = 1000 kg ≈ 1.1 tons. Synonym: *metric ton*.

toolkit function NOUN /ˈtuːlˌkɪt/ see *parent function* (p 86).

top NOUN /tɒp/ the upper surface of a geometric figure.

topology NOUN /təˈpɒ.lə.dʒi/ the study of how points are connected together. The study of the properties of the deformation of shapes that do not involve cutting or gluing.

top view NOUN /tɒp vju/ a 2-dimensional figure showing a 3-dimensional object as viewed from the top.

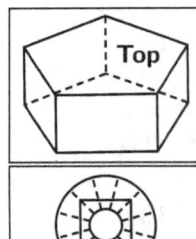

torque NOUN /tɔrk/
1) a force that causes rotation.
2) the measure of a force that causes rotation.

torus NOUN /ˈtɔr.əs/ a doughnut shaped solid.

toss a coin VERB /tɒs ʌ kɔɪn/ see *flip a coin* (p 50).

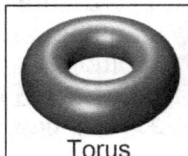

total /ˈtoʊ.tl/
1) VERB to add a list of numbers. Keyword for addition.
2) NOUN the result of adding a list of numbers. Example: the total of 5, 3, and 7 is 15. Synonym: sum.
3) NOUN the whole amount.
4) NOUN all.

to the nth power PREPOSITION /tu ðə nθ ˈpaʊ.ər/ raised to the exponent n. Example: 4 to the **fifth power** is $4^5 = 1024$. See also exponent (p 47).

trace VERB /treɪs/
1) to move along a figure
2) to draw along a figure.

traceable network NOUN /ˈtreɪ.sə.bəl ˈnɛt.wɜrk/ a network graph that can be traced in one continuous path without retracing any edge. A network is traceable if it has all even nodes or exactly two even nodes with the rest of the nodes odd.

trajectory NOUN /trəˈdʒɛk.tər.i/ the path of a projectile.

trans- PREFIX /træns/
1) across. Example: transfinite number.
2) through.

transcendental ADJECTIVE /ˌtræn.sɛnˈdɛn.tl/ not algebraic; having to do with something other than addition, subtraction, multiplication, division or the taking of roots.

transcendental equation NOUN /ˌtræn.sɛnˈdɛn.tl ɪˈkweɪ.ʃən/ an equation that is not an algebraic equation; an equation that has operations other than addition, subtraction, multiplication, division or the taking of roots.

transcendental function NOUN /ˌtræn.sɛnˈdɛn.tl ˈfʌŋk.ʃən/ a function that is not an algebraic function; a function that has operations other than addition, subtraction, multiplication, division or the taking of roots.

transcendental number NOUN /ˌtræn.sɛnˈdɛn.tl ˈnʌm.bər/ a real number that is not an algebraic number; that cannot be a root of a real-valued polynomial with rational coefficients. Antonym: algebraic number (p 9).

transfinite number NOUN /trænsˈfaɪ.naɪt ˈnʌm.bər/ a number that can be finite or infinite; can be a real number or positive or negative infinity.

transform VERB /trænsˈfɔrm/ to change from one form to another, usually by a rule. Example: a translation is a geometric transformation that moves a figure without changing the orientation or size. Synonym: convert (p 30).

transformation NOUN /ˈtræns.fərˌmeɪ.ʃən/
1) a rule for changing the form of an object or function. Common types of transformations: shifting, reflecting, stretching, shrinking.
2) the act of changing the form an object or function.

transformational ADJECTIVE /ˌtræns.fərˈmeɪ.ʃə.nl/ having to do with transformations. Example: transformational geometry.

transformational geometry NOUN /ˌtræns.fərˈmeɪ.ʃə.nl dʒiˈɒ.mɪ.tri/ a branch of geometry that deals with transformations such as translation, reflection, or rotation.

transformational motion NOUN /ˌtræns.fərˈmeɪ.ʃə.nl ˈmoʊ.ʃən/ a motion generated by a transformation such as translation, reflection or rotation.

transformational proof NOUN /ˌtræns.fərˈmeɪ.ʃə.nl pruf/ a proof that uses geometric transformations.

transformation form NOUN /ˈtræns.fərˌmeɪ.ʃən fɔrm/ see vertex form (p 121).

transitive ADJECTIVE /ˈtræn.zɪ.tɪv/ if two objects are related to a third object, then they are related to each other. Math definition: relation R is transitive if and only if aRb and bRc implies aRc. Example: if $a = b$ and $b = c$, then $a = c$.

transitive property of equality NOUN /ˈtræn.zɪ.tɪv ˈprɒ.pər.ti ʌv ɪˈkwɒl.ɪ.ti/ if two numbers are equal to a third number, then they are equal to each other; if $a = b$ and $b = c$, then $a = c$.

transitive property of inequality NOUN /ˈtræn.zɪ.tɪv ˈprɒ.pər.ti ʌv ɪn.ɪˈkwɒl.ɪ.ti/ if $a < b$ and $b < c$, then $a < c$. If $a > b$ and $b > c$ then $a > b$.

translate VERB /trænzˈleɪt/
1) to change from one place to another.
2) to change from one form to another.

translation NOUN /trænzˈleɪ.ʃən/ a geometric transformation where each point of an object is moved a particular direction and distance. Synonyms: glide (p 53), slide.

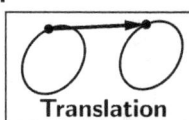

translational ADJECTIVE /trænzˈleɪ.ʃə.nl/ having to do with a translation; having to do with moving an object a certain direction and distance. Example: translational symmetry.

translational symmetry NOUN /trænzˈleɪ.ʃə.nl ˈsɪ.mɪ.tri/ two figures have translational symmetry if a translation exists that will place one object exactly on top of another so that all points of both objects coincide.

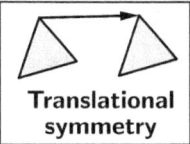

translation of axes NOUN /trænzˈleɪ.ʃən ʌv ˈæk.siz/ exchange of the axes in a coordinate system while leaving the objects in that system unmoved. Example: translate the x and y axes.

transpose VERB /trænsˈpoʊz/ to cause to exchange places.

transpose a matrix VERB /trænsˈpoʊz ə ˈmæ.trɪks/ see matrix transposition (p 73).

transposition NOUN /ˌtræns.pəˈzɪ.ʃən/
1) a process of exchanging places.
2) the result of changing places.

transversal NOUN /trænzˈvɜr.səl/ a line that crosses one or more related lines.

transverse axis NOUN /trænzˈvɜrs ˈæk.sɪs/ the major axis of an ellipse or a hyperbola that passes through the foci. See also hyperbola (p 58). Antonym: conjugate axis (p 27).

transversed line NOUN /trænzˈvɜrsd laɪn/ a line through which a transversal passes.

trapezium NOUN /trəˈpi.zi.əm/
1) (British English) see trapezoid (p 116).

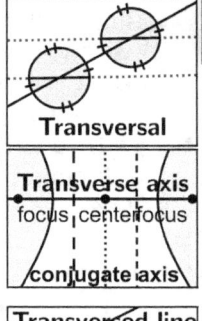

2) (American English) a quadrilateral with no sides that are parallel.

trapezoid NOUN /ˈtræ.pəˌzɔɪd/ (American English) a four-sided quadrilateral where exactly one pair of opposite sides are parallel. Synonym: *trapezium* /trəˈpi.zi.əm/ (British English).

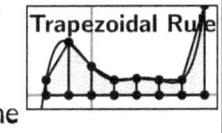
Trapezoid

trapezoidal rule NOUN /ˈtræ.pəˌzɔɪ.dl rul/ an algorithm for approximating the area under a curve. Trapezoids are drawn using points on a curve and the areas of the trapezoids are added together.

travel graph NOUN /ˈtræv.əl græf/ a graph showing the relationship between distance and time traveled.

traveling wave NOUN /ˈtræv.əl.ŋ weɪv/ a wave that moves. *Example*: waves crashing on a beach. *Formula*: $y(x, t) = A \sin k(x - vt)$ where t is time, A is amplitude, v is the linear velocity of the movement, and k controls the period of the wave.

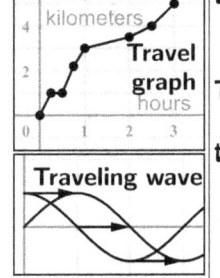

traversable ADJECTIVE /ˈtræ.vərs.ə.bl/ a figure is traversable if the edges can be traced without lifting the pencil from the paper and without going over any part more than once.

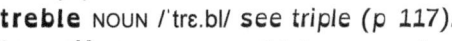
Traversable

treble NOUN /ˈtrɛ.bl/ see *triple* (p 117).

tree diagram NOUN /tri daɪ.ə.græm/ a diagram starting with all possibilities and diagramming all possible combinations. *Example*: Two balls are selected with replacement at random from three red balls and five green balls.

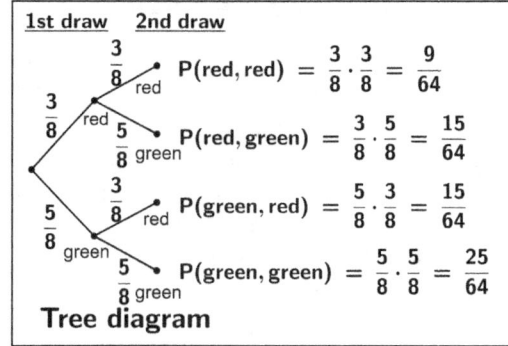
Tree diagram

trend /trɛnd/
1) NOUN the general path of a variable over time. *Example*: linear trend.
2) VERB to tend to go in a particular direction.
3) ADJECTIVE having to do with a tendency to go in a particular direction.

trend line NOUN /trɛnd laɪn/ a line on a graph showing the direction and proportion of a trend, usually a best fit line.

tri- PREFIX /traɪ/ three

trial NOUN /ˈtraɪ.l/
1) one of a series of duplicate experiments. *Example*: one flip of a coin is a trial.
2) an attempt to accomplish a result.

trial and error IDIOM /ˈtraɪ.l ənd ˈɛr.ər/ trying something and, if it doesn't work, trying something else. Synonym: *guess and check*.

triangle NOUN /ˈtraɪˌæn.gəl/ a three-sided polygon. *Formulas*: Area = $\frac{1}{2}$bh, b is the base and h is the height of the vertex opposite the base.

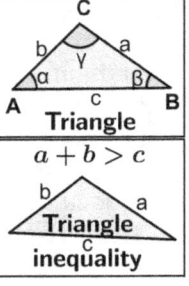

Triangle Inequality Theorem NOUN /ˈtraɪˌæn.gəl ɪn.ɪˈkwɒl.ɪ.ti ˈθɪ.ə.rəm/ the sum of the lengths of any two sides of a triangle is greater than the length of the remaining side. *Formula*: $a + b > c$ where a, b and c are lengths of the sides of a triangle.

triangle inequality with absolute values NOUN /ˈtraɪˌæn.gəl ɪn.ɪˈkwɒl.ɪ.ti wɪθ ˈæb.sə.lut ˈvæl.juz/ $|a + b| \leq |a| + |b|, |a - b| \geq |a| - |b|$.

Triangle Sum Theorem NOUN /ˈtraɪˌæn.gəl sʌm ˈθɪ.ə.rəm/ see *Angle Sum Theorem* (p 10).

triangular ADJECTIVE /traɪˈæn.gjə.lər/
1) having to do with a triangle. *Example*: triangular number.
2) shaped like a triangle. *Example*: triangular matrix.
3) containing a triangle. *Example*: triangular prism.

triangular matrix NOUN /traɪˈæn.gjə.lər ˈmæ.trɪks/ one of an upper triangular matrix or a lower triangular matrix. An upper triangular matrix has all zeros above and to the right of the main diagonal. A lower triangular matrix has all zeros below and to the left of the main diagonal. *Plural*: triangular matrices /traɪˈæn.gjə.lər ˈmæ.trɪ.siz/.

triangular number NOUN /traɪˈæn.gjə.lər ˈnʌm.bər/ one of the numbers 1, 3, 6, 10, 15, ... that can be drawn as points in a triangle. *Formula*: $T_n = \frac{n(n-1)}{2}$, $n > 0$.

triangular prism NOUN /traɪˈæn.gjə.lər ˈprɪz.əm/ a polyhedron whose bases are congruent triangles and sides are rectangles.

triangular pyramid NOUN /traɪˈæn.gjə.lər ˈpɪr.ə.mɪd/ a polyhedron with a base that is a triangle and sides that are triangles. Synonym: *tetrahedron* (p 113).

triangulation NOUN /traɪˌæn.gjə.leɪ.ʃən/ a method of measuring objects indirectly using similar triangles and ratios.

trichotomy NOUN /traɪˈkɒ.tə.mi/ a division into three parts.

trichotomy property of real numbers NOUN /traɪˈkɒ.tə.mi ˈprɒ.pər.ti ʌv riəl ˈnʌm.bərz/ for any two real numbers a and b, exactly one of the following is true: $a < b$, $a = b$ or $a > b$.

trigonometric ADJECTIVE /ˌtrɪ.gə.nəˈmɛ.trɪk/ having to do with trigonometry.

trigonometric equation NOUN /ˌtrɪ.gə.nəˈmɛ.trɪk ɪˈkweɪ.ʃən/ an equation that contains one or more trigonometric functions. *Example*: $y = \sin(x)$.

trigonometric function NOUN /ˌtrɪ.gə.nəˈmɛ.trɪk ˈfʌŋk.ʃən/
1) one of the functions sine, cosine, tangent, secant, cosecant and cotangent.

2) a function that includes trigonometric relationships. Example: $f(x) = \cos^2 x$.
Synonym: circular function.

trigonometric identity NOUN /ˌtrɪ.gə.nəˈmɛ.trɪk aɪˈdɛn.tɪ.ti/ a trigonometric equation that is true for all values of the variable(s). Example: $\sin^2 \theta + \cos^2 \theta \equiv 1$. See also Trigonometric Identities (p 143).

trigonometric ratio NOUN /ˌtrɪ.gə.nəˈmɛ.trɪk ˈreɪ.ʃoʊ/ a ratio of the lengths of two sides of a right triangle.

trigonometric values of special angles NOUN /ˌtrɪg.ə.nəˈmɛ.trɪk ˈvæl.juz ʌv ˈspɛ.ʃəl ˈæŋ.gəlz/ see exact values of trigonometric functions (p 46).

trigonometry NOUN /ˌtrɪ.gəˈnɒ.mɪ.tri/ the branch of mathematics that deals with right triangles, unit circles and the relationships between the sides and angles of right triangles. Synonym: right angle trigonometry. Abbreviation: trig.

trillion NOUN /ˈtrɪl.jun/ $1,000,000,000,000 = 10^{12}$ (short scale). Synonym: tera- (p 113).

trillionth ADJECTIVE, NOUN /ˈtrɪl.junθ/ $10^{-12} = 0.000\,000\,000\,001$. Synonym: pico- (p 88).

trinomial /ˈtraɪ.noʊ.mi.l/
1) NOUN a polynomial with three terms. Example: $x + 3x^2 + x^3$.
2) ADJECTIVE containing a polynomial with three terms.

triple /ˈtrɪ.pəl/
1) NOUN three objects.
2) ADJECTIVE occurs three times.
3) VERB to multiply by 3.
Synonym: treble.

triple product NOUN /ˈtrɪ.pəl ˈprɒ.dʌkt/ see scalar triple product (p 102).

triple root NOUN /ˈtrɪ.pəl rut/ a root of a polynomial that is repeated exactly three times. Given the polynomial $(x+2)(x+2)(x+2)(x-1)$, the root -2 is a triple root. Synonym: triple zero.

triple zero NOUN /ˈtrɪ.pəl ˈzɪə.roʊ/ see triple root (p 117).

trirectangular NOUN /ˌtraɪ.rɛkˈtæŋ.gjə.lər/ a spherical triangle with three right angles.

trisect VERB /traɪˈsɛkt/ to divide into three equal parts. Example: trisect an angle.

trisection NOUN /traɪˈsɛk.ʃən/ division into three equal parts.

trivial ADJECTIVE /ˈtrɪ.vi.əl/
1) immediately clear; obvious.
2) having to do with or containing zero.

trivial solution NOUN /ˈtrɪ.vi.əl səˈlu.ʃən/
1) a solution that is immediately obvious or uninteresting.
2) a solution of zero.

trochoid NOUN /ˈtroʊ.kɔɪd/ the shape made when a point on a disk is traced as the disk rolls along a line. Equation: (parametric) $x = a\theta - b\sin\theta$, $y = a - b\cos\theta$. Synonym: cycloid (p 33).

true ADJECTIVE /tru/
1) (Boolean algebra) one of two truth values. True is sometimes written 1. See also truth value (p 117).
2) (equations) both sides of the equation have the same value.
3) (logic) consistent with fact. Antonym: false (p 49).

trunc() COMPUTERS the truncate function converts a floating point or decimal number (without rounding) to an integer in many computer languages.

truncate VERB /ˈtrʌŋ.keɪt/
1) (numbers) to shorten a numeral by dropping nonsignificant digits. Example: the number 3.5893 truncated to 3 significant digits is 3.58.
2) (geometry) to remove part of a geometric object. Example: truncate a pyramid.

truncated ADJECTIVE /ˈtrʌŋ.keɪ.td/ having part cut off, usually parallel to the base. Example: truncated cone.

truncated icosahedron NOUN /ˈtrʌŋ.keɪ.td aɪˌkoʊ.səˈhi.drən/ a polyhedron with 12 regular pentagonal faces, 20 regular hexagonal faces, 60 vertices and 90 edges. Plural: truncated icosahedra /ˈtrʌŋ.keɪ.td aɪˌkoʊ.səˈhi.drə/.

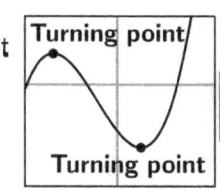
Truncated cone

Truncated Icosahedron

truncation NOUN /ˈtrʌŋ.keɪ.ʃən/
1) the act of truncating.
2) the property of being truncated.

truth NOUN /truθ/ a fact that has been verified.

truth table NOUN /truθ ˈteɪ.bl/ a table showing the arguments and results of a Boolean operation. Synonym: Boolean operation table.

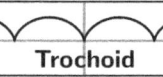

Truth Table		
A	B	A ∧ B
False	False	False
False	True	True
True	False	True
True	True	True

truth value NOUN /truθ ˈvæl.ju/ exactly one of true, false or unknown. Example: the truth value of $5 = 3$ is false. Synonym: logical value.

try /traɪ/
1) VERB to attempt. Example: try a solution.
2) NOUN one trial. Example: I solved it on my third try.

try, test, revise NOUN /traɪ tɛst rɪˈvaɪz/ a method for solving problems: 1) Try a solution; 2) Test the solution to see if it is valid; 3) Revise the solution and repeat until a valid or an accurate enough solution is found.

turn /tɜrn/
1) VERB to change direction, especially vertical direction. Example: turning point.
2) VERB to rotate.
3) NOUN a rotation of 360 degrees; one full rotation.
4) NOUN the act of turning.

turning point NOUN /ˈtɜr.nɪŋ pɔɪnt/ a point at which a graph changes vertical direction; a local minimum or a local maximum. Synonym: vertex (p 121), extremum (p 48).

turning symmetry NOUN /ˈtɜr.nɪŋ ˈsɪ.mɪ.tri/ see rotational symmetry (p 100).

twelfth ADJECTIVE /twɛlfθ/
1) coming in position 12 in an ordered list. Notation: 12th.
2) one of twelve equal parts; $\frac{1}{12}$;

twelve ADJECTIVE, NOUN /twɛlv/ the number 12.

twelve hour time NOUN /twɛlv aʊər taɪm/ a notation for time that goes from 12:00 AM to 12:00 PM for the morning and from 12:00 PM to 12:00 AM for the afternoon and evening.

twenty ADJECTIVE, NOUN /ˈtwɛn.ti/ the number 20.

twenty-four hour time NOUN /ˈtwɛn.ti.fɔr aʊɚ taɪm/ a notation for time that goes from 0000 (midnight) to 2359 (1 minute before midnight). Synonyms: *Zulu time, coordinated universal time.*

twice ADVERB /twaɪs/
1) two times. Example: turn the handle twice.
2) multiplied by two. Example: twice 3 is 6.

twin prime NOUN /twɪn praɪm/ one of two prime numbers that differ by two. Example: 5, 7.

two ADJECTIVE /tu/ the number or digit 2.

two column proof NOUN /tu ˈkɒl.əm pruf/ a notation for proofs in which statements are listed in the first column and the justification of the statements in the second column.

two-dimensional ADJECTIVE /tu dɪˈmɛn.ʃə.nl/ having two dimensions, usually length and width. Abbreviation: 2-D.

two point form NOUN /tu pɔɪnt fɔrm/ a linear equation in the form $y = \frac{y_2 - y_1}{x_2 - x_1}(x - x_1) + y_1$ where (x_1, y_1) and (x_2, y_2) are any two distinct points on the line.

Two point form
$(1,2)$, $(-2,-2)$, $y = \frac{4}{3}(x+2) - 2$

two space NOUN /tu speɪs/ see 2-space (p 6).

two step equation NOUN /tu stɛp ɪˈkweɪ.ʃən/ an equation that takes two steps to solve. Example: $3x - 2 = 4 \rightarrow 3x = 6 \rightarrow x = 2$.

two way table NOUN /tu weɪ ˈteɪ.bəl/ a table that displays the relationship between two categories.

Two way table		
	Apples	Oranges
Adults	140	92
Children	120	112

type NOUN /taɪp/
1) belongs to a particular class of objects. Example: type of factoring.
2) something that belongs to a class of objects; kind; sort.

U

un- PREFIX /ʌn/ not

una- PREFIX /ˈju.nə/ one

unary ADJECTIVE /ˈju.nər.i/ having one. Example: unary operator.

unary operation NOUN /ˈju.nər.i ˌɒp.əˈreɪ.ʃən/ an operation that takes one operand. Example: -x.

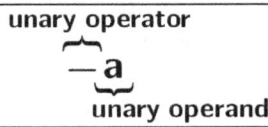

unbounded ADJECTIVE /ʌnˈbaʊn.dɪd/ having no end; infinite. Example: $x > 0$. Antonym: *bounded* (p 18). Synonym: *infinite* (p 62).

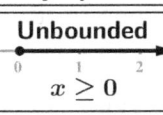

unbounded interval NOUN /ʌnˈbaʊn.dɪd ˈɪn.tɚ.vəl/ an interval that extends to negative infinity, positive infinity or both. Examples: $[3, \infty), (\infty, \infty)$. Antonym: *bounded interval.*

uncountable ADJECTIVE /ʌnˈkaʊn.tə.bəl/ is infinite and does not have a one-to-one correspondence with the set of natural numbers. Example: the set of real numbers. Synonym: *nondenumerable.* Antonyms: *countable, denumerable.*

undecagon NOUN /ʌnˈdɛ.kə.gɒn/ a polygon with eleven sides.

undefined ADJECTIVE /ˌʌn.dɪˈfaɪnd/
1) mathematically meaningless. Example: division by zero is undefined. Any expression or equation containing an undefined element is also undefined.
2) not having an explicit definition. Example: undefined term.
Antonym: *defined* (p 35).

undefined term NOUN /ˌʌn.dɪˈfaɪnd tɚm/
1) a word or phrase that is described rather than defined.
2) a word or phrase whose definition is implied in axioms. Examples: points, lines, and planes. Synonym: *primitive.*

unequal ADJECTIVE /ʌnˈi.kwəl/ not having the same number of objects; not having the same value. Synonym: *not equal.*

underestimate VERB /ˌʌn.dɚˈɛs.tɪ.meɪt/
1) to estimate less than the actual value.
2) to intentionally estimate less than the actual value.
Antonym: *overestimate* (p 85).

underrepresent VERB /ˌʌn.dɚˌrɛp.rɪˈzɛnt/ to use less of a group or partition of a population in a sample than the actual proportion within the entire population being sampled.

undo VERB /ʌnˈdu/ to reverse the doing of.

unequal ADJECTIVE /ʌnˈi.kwəl/ not equal; not having the same value. Notation: $\neq$. Antonym: *equal* (p 44). Example: 5 and 6 are unequal.

uni- PREFIX /ˈju.nə/ one. Example: uniform (having one form).

unicursal ADJECTIVE /ˌju.nəˈkɚ.səl/ a network graph for which a path exists that traces each edge exactly once.

uniform ADJECTIVE /ˈju.nəˌfɔrm/ the same throughout. Example: uniform tessellation.

uniform cross section NOUN /ˈju.nəˌfɔrm krɔs ˈsɛk.ʃən/ a cross section parallel to the base that is similar to the base.

uniform motion NOUN /ˈju.nəˌfɔrm ˈmoʊ.ʃən/ motion that occurs at a constant rate of speed. Formula: $d = rt$ where d is distance, r is rate or speed, and t is time.

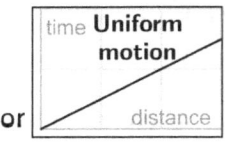

uniform probability model NOUN /ˈju.nəˌfɔrm ˌprɒ.bəˈbɪl.ɪ.ti ˈmɒ.dl/ a model where each outcome is equally likely.

uniform tessellation NOUN /ˈju.nəˌfɔrm ˌtɛs.əˈleɪ.ʃən/ a tessellation that has the same combination of shapes and angles at each vertex.

union NOUN /ˈjun.jən/ a set containing all the members of two or more sets. Notation: $\cup$. Math definition: $A \cup B = \{x \mid x \in A \text{ or } x \in B\}$. Synonym: *join.*

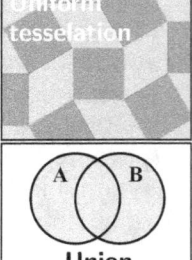

unique ADJECTIVE /juˈnik/ there exists one and only one. Example: two points determine a unique line.

Unique Factorization Theorem NOUN /juˈnik ˈfæk.tərˌaɪ.zeɪ.ʃən ˈθɪ.ə.rəm/ see *Fundamental Theorem of Arithmetic* (p 52).

Unique Line Postulate NOUN /juˈnik laɪn ˈpɒs.tʃə.lɪt/ through any two distinct points there is exactly one line. Two points define a line.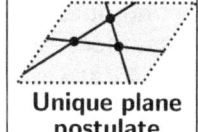

uniqueness ADJECTIVE /juˈnik.nəs/ the property of being the only one.

Unique Plane Postulate NOUN /juˈnik pleɪn ˈpɒs.tʃə.lɪt/ through any three distinct non-collinear points there is exactly one plane; three points define a plane.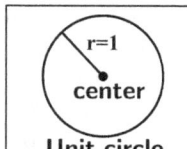

unique solution NOUN /juˈnik səˈlu.ʃən/ a solution that is the only possible solution of a problem or linear system.

unit /ˈju.nɪt/
1) NOUN one of something that is measured or counted. Example: meter.
2) NOUN containing the number 1. Example: unit fraction.
3) NOUN the number 1; the identity element.
4) ADJECTIVE having to do with the number 1. Example: unit circle.

unit circle NOUN /ˈju.nɪt ˈsɜr.kəl/ a circle with a radius of 1, usually centered at the origin. Equation: $x^2 + y^2 = 1$.

unit conversion NOUN /ˈju.nɪt kʌnˈvər.ʃən/ conversion from one unit of measure to a related unit of measure. Example: convert from meters to feet.

unit digit NOUN /ˈju.nɪt ˈdɪ.dʒɪt/ the digit in the one's place; the whole digit with the smallest place value. Example: in the number 543.2, the unit digit is 3.

unit fraction NOUN /ˈju.nɪt ˈfræk.ʃən/ a fraction with a numerator of 1 and a denominator that is a positive integer. Example: $\frac{1}{5}$.

unit matrix NOUN /ˈju.nɪt ˈmæ.trɪks/ see *identity matrix* (p 59).

unit of measure NOUN /ˈju.nɪt ʌv ˈmɛʒ.ər/ the meaning of 1 in a single dimension of a metric space. Examples: 'meter' is a unit of measure of distance; 'second' is a unit of measure of time.

unit price NOUN /ˈju.nɪt praɪs/ the price for a single item. Formula: **unit price × quantity = extended price**.

unit rate NOUN /ˈju.nɪt reɪt/
1) the price or cost for one item.
2) a rate with a denominator of 1.

unit sphere NOUN /ˈju.nɪt sfɪər/ a sphere with a radius of 1.

unit square NOUN /ˈju.nɪt skwɛər/ a square with sides that measure 1.

unit vector NOUN /ˈju.nɪt ˈvɛk.tər/ any vector that has a magnitude of 1.

unity NOUN /ˈju.nɪ.ti/ any mathematical object whose dimension is defined as 1. Example: "Let the length of line segment **m** be unity."

univariate ADJECTIVE /ˌyu.nəˈvɛər.i.ɪt/ having only one variable.

universal ADJECTIVE /ˌju.nəˈvɜr.səl/
1) containing everything. Example: universal set.
2) applying to everyone. Example: universal time.

universal set NOUN /ˌju.nəˈvɜr.səl sɛt/ a set containing all members that exist. The universal set is drawn as a box which contains all other drawings of sets.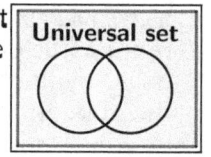

universal time NOUN /ˌju.nəˈvɜr.səl taɪm/ see *Greenwich Mean Time* (p 55).

unknown NOUN /ʌnˈnoʊn/ a quantity that has not been identified. Antonym: *known* (p 66). Synonym: *variable* (p 120).

unknown value NOUN /ʌnˈnoʊn ˈvæl.ju/ see *unknown* (p 119).

unlike ADJECTIVE /ʌnˈlaɪk/ not similar to; having differences that are important. Example: unlike terms. Antonym: *like* (p 68).

unlike fractions NOUN /ʌnˈlaɪk ˈfræk.ʃənz/ fractions that, when reduced, do not have the same denominator. Example: $\frac{3}{4}$ and $\frac{2}{3}$ are unlike fractions. Antonym: *like fractions* (p 68).

unlikely ADJECTIVE /ʌnˈlaɪk.li/ has a low probability of happening. Example: You are unlikely to get away with that. Antonym: *likely* (p 68).

unlike terms NOUN /ʌnˈlaɪk tɜrmz/ terms of an expression that have different variables or different exponents on the variables. Example: $2x$ and $3x^2$ are unlike terms. Synonym: *dissimilar terms*. Antonym: *like terms* (p 68).

unreasonable ADJECTIVE /ʌnˈriz.nə.bəl/
1) showing a lack of reason.
2) not justified.
Antonym: *reasonable* (p 96).

unsigned ADJECTIVE /ʌnˈsaɪnd/
1) not having a positive or negative sign. An unsigned number is assumed to be positive. Antonym: *signed* (p 105).
2) can take only zero or positive values. Example: unsigned integer (computers).

unsigned integer NOUN /ʌnˈsaɪnd ˈɪn.tɪ.dʒər/
1) (arithmetic) an integer without a '+' or '−' in front of it. Unsigned integers are assumed to be positive or zero.
2) (computers) an integer, variable or constant that can only take positive whole numbers or zero.

unsigned number NOUN /ʌnˈsaɪnd ˈnʌm.bər/
1) a number that does not have a plus or minus sign (+ or −) in front of it. Example: 5. Antonym: *signed number* (p 105).
2) (computers) a number that cannot be negative, only zero or positive.

unspecified ADJECTIVE /ʌnˈspɛs.ɪˌfaɪd/ not stated explicitly.

unspecified domain NOUN /ʌnˈspɛs.ɪˌfaɪd doʊˈmeɪn/ the domain of a function is not stated, so the domain is taken to be all points for which the function is defined.

up ADVERB /ʌp/
1) in a vertical direction moving away from the surface of the earth.
2) increasing. Keyword for addition.
Antonym: *down* (p 42).

3rd Dyslexic's Edition

upper ADJECTIVE /'ʌp.ər/ larger or higher. Example: upper extreme. Antonym: lower (p 71).

Upper and Lower Bounds Theorem NOUN /'ʌp.ər ænd 'loʊ.ər baʊndz 'θɪ.ə.rəm/ Let $P(x)$ be a polynomial with real coefficients. 1) If we divide $P(x)$ by $x - b$, $b > 0$, using synthetic division and if the row that contains the quotient and remainder has no negative entry, then b is an upper bound for the real zeros of $P(x)$. 2) If we divide $P(x)$ by $x - a$, $a < 0$, using synthetic division and if the row that contains the quotient and remainder has entries that are alternately non positive and nonnegative, then a is a lower bound for the real zeros of $P(x)$.

upper bound NOUN /'ʌp.ər baʊnd/ value which is greater than or equal to all other values in a set. Antonym: lower bound (p 71). See also least upper bound (p 68).

upper extreme NOUN /'ʌp.ər ɪk'strim/ see least upper bound (p 68).

upper quartile NOUN /'ʌp.ər 'kwɔr.taɪl/ the 3rd quartile of a dataset. See quartile (p 94).

upper triangular matrix NOUN /'ʌp.ər traɪ'æŋ.gjə.lər 'meɪ.trɪks/ a square matrix, possibly augmented, having all zeros above and to the right of the main diagonal. Plural: upper triangular matrices /'ʌp.ər traɪ'æŋ.gjə.lər 'meɪ.trɪˌsiz/

$$\begin{bmatrix} 3 & 0 & 0 \\ 2 & 1 & 0 \\ 4 & 3 & 1 \end{bmatrix}$$
Upper triangular matrix

US Customary Unit NOUN /ju əs 'kʌst.ə.mər.i 'ju.nɪt/ one of the units of measure customarily used in the United States. Examples: foot, mile, gallon.

US Standard Unit NOUN /ju əs 'stæn.dərd 'ju.nɪt/ see US Customary Unit (p 120).

V

V SYMBOL 5 in Roman numerals.

valid ADJECTIVE /'væl.ɪd/
1) well founded. Example: a valid reason.
2) justifiable. Example: a valid argument.
Antonym: invalid (p 64).

valid argument NOUN /'væl.ɪd 'ɑr.gjə.mənt/ an argument that is correctly justified based on axioms, definitions, constraints and previously proved theorems.

validate VERB /'væl.ɪ.deɪt/
1) to find out if something is correctly inferred, deduced or calculated. Example: validate a claim.
2) to show that something is correctly inferred, deduced or calculated. Example: validate a solution.
3) to check one's work.
Synonyms: check (p 21), verify (p 121).

validity NOUN /və'lɪd.ɪ.ti/ whether or not something is correctly inferred or deduced.

value NOUN /'væl.ju/
1) a number associated with a mathematical object. Example: the value of $3 + 5$ is 8.
2) (function) the output associated with a particular input. Example: "the value of $f(x)$ when x is 2."
3) how much something is worth.

valued ADJECTIVE /'væl.jud/ having variables with a particular property. Example: real-valued equation.

vanish VERB /'væn.ɪʃ/ to disappear. Example: vanishing point.

vanishing point NOUN /'væ.nɪʃ.ɪŋ pɔɪnt/ a point in a perspective view where a figure appears to vanish in the distance.

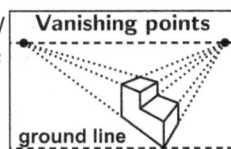
Vanishing points / ground line

variable NOUN /'vɛər.i.ə.bəl/
1) something that can accept any of a set of values.
2) a symbol representing a variable.
3) a characteristic of a population being studied. Examples: age, gender.
4) something that is subject to change.
Synonym: unknown (p 119).

variable expression NOUN /'vɛər.i.ə.bəl ɪk'sprɛ.ʃən/ an expression that contains at least one variable. Example: $3x - 2$.

variable of interest NOUN /'vɛər.i.ə.bəl ʌv 'ɪn.trɪst/ (statistics) a characteristic of a population that is being studied.

variance NOUN /'vɛər.i.əns/ a measure of the spread of a dataset; the average of the squares of the deviations of the members of a dataset. Standard deviation is the square root of the variance. Formula:
$$\text{Var}(X) = \frac{(x_n - \overline{X})^2 + (x_{n-1} - \overline{X})^2 + \ldots + (x_1 - \overline{X})^2}{n-1}$$
where x_n is the nth value of the dataset, $\overline{X}$ is the mean of the values of the dataset. Notation: $\text{Var}(X)$, $\mathbb{V}(X)$, $V(X)$. Synonym: mean square deviation.

variation NOUN /ˌvɛər.i'eɪ.ʃən/ one of several types of functions with a constant of variation. Formulas: $y = ax$ is direct variation; $y = \frac{a}{x}$ is inverse variation, and $z = axy$ is joint variation. In all of the formulas, a is the constant of variation.

vary VERB /'vɛər.i/
1) to change together. Examples: varies indirectly, varies inversely, varies jointly.
2) to differ one from another.

vector NOUN /'vɛk.tər/ a value having a magnitude and a direction, but not a location. Notation: $\overrightarrow{ab}$ (vector from point a to point b); $\langle 3, -4 \rangle$ (a vector with a horizontal component of 3 and a vertical component of -4); $\langle 2, 0, 1 \rangle$ (a vector with an x-component of 2, a y-component of 0 and a z-component of 1). See also Properties of Vectors (p 130).

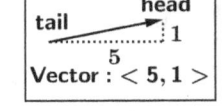
tail / head / 5 / 1 / Vector: $\langle 5, 1 \rangle$

vector decomposition NOUN /'vɛk.tər ˌdi.kɒm.pə'zɪ.ʃən/ the process of creating two vectors that are perpendicular to each other. The two vectors are components of the original vector, and add together to make the original vector. Formulas: $v_1 = \frac{v \cdot w}{|w|^2} w$, $v_2 = v - v_1$, where v is the original vector, v_1 and v_2 are the resulting vectors, and w is a vector to which v_1 is parallel.

vector field NOUN /'vɛk.tər fild/ a function that defines vectors over a plane or over a space. Example: $F(x, y) = \sin(y) i + \sin(x)$.

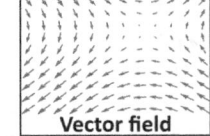
Vector field

vector product NOUN /'vɛk.tər 'prɒ.dʌkt/ see cross product (p 32).

vector projection NOUN /ˈvɛk.tər prouˈdʒɛk.ʃən/ the projection of vector **a** on vector **b** is a vector with the same direction as **b**, and a magnitude determined by a line segment passing through the head of **a** that is perpendicular to **b**. Notation: $\text{proj}_v u$. Math definition: $\text{proj}_v u = \left(\frac{u \cdot v}{|v|^2}\right) v$. Formula: $v_1 = \frac{v \cdot w}{|w|^2} w$.

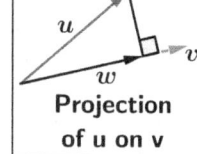
Projection of u on v

velocity NOUN /vəˈlɒ.sɪ.ti/ see speed (p 107).

Venn diagram NOUN /vɛn ˈdaɪ.əˌɡræm/ a drawing used to represent operations on sets. The box represents the universal set and each circle represents a set.

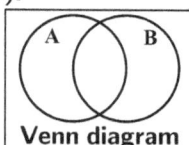
Venn diagram

Venn, John PERSON /vɛn dʒɒn/ (1834—1923) an English mathematician known for his work in logic.

verbally ADVERB /ˈvɜr.bə.li/ using words rather than a formula or a graph.

verbal phrase NOUN /ˈvɜr.bəl freɪs/ a set of words giving a math problem. Example: the quotient of a number divided by 3 plus 6.

verify VERB /ˈvɛr.ɪ.faɪ/ to check for validity or correctness. Synonyms: check (p 21), validate (p 120).

vertex NOUN /ˈvɜr.tɛks/
1) a point that is the endpoint of two or more line segments or rays. Synonym: common endpoint (p 23).
2) a turning point of a polynomial or conic section.
3) a point where the sides of a polygon meet.
4) a point where edges of a polyhedron intersect.
5) (graph) a point where two or more lines intersect. Synonyms: node (p 79), corner point (p 30).

vertex angle NOUN /ˈvɜr.tɛks ˈæŋ.ɡəl/ an interior angle at a vertex of a polygon.

vertex form NOUN /ˈvɜr.tɛks fɔrm/ (quadratic equation) $f(x) = a(x - x_0)^2 + y_0$ where (x_0, y_0) is the coordinate of the vertex.

vertical /ˈvɜr.tɪ.kəl/
1) ADJECTIVE perpendicular to the horizon; straight up and down.
2) ADJECTIVE away from a center of gravity.
3) NOUN a line, line segment or ray that is vertical.
4) ADJECTIVE opposite each other. Example: vertical angles.
Antonym: horizontal (p 57).

vertical angles NOUN /ˈvɜr.tɪ.kəl ˈæŋ.ɡəlz/ angles formed by two intersecting lines that are opposite each other.

Vertical Angles Congruence Theorem NOUN /ˈvɜr.tɪ.kəl ˈæŋ.ɡəlz kɒnˈɡru.əns ˈθɪ.ə.rəm/ vertical angles are congruent.

vertical asymptote NOUN /ˈvɜr.tɪ.kəl ˈæ.sɪmˌtoʊt/ a type of essential discontinuity where y goes to positive or negative infinity on both sides of the point of discontinuity. Antonyms: horizontal asymptote (p 57), oblique asymptote (p 81). See also essential discontinuity (p 45).

vertical axis NOUN /ˈvɜr.tɪ.kəl ˈæk.sɪs/ in a rectangular coordinate system, the axis that goes up and down. Synonyms: y-axis (p 123), imaginary axis (p 59). Antonym: horizontal axis (p 57).

vertical bar graph NOUN /ˈvɜr.tɪ.kəl bɑr ɡræf/ a bar graph whose bars extend up and down.

vertical component NOUN /ˈvɜr.tɪ.kəl kəmˈpoʊ.nənt/ the part of a vector in the vertical direction. Antonym: horizontal component (p 57).

vertical compression NOUN /ˈvɜr.tɪ.kəl kəmˈprɛ.ʃən/ a transformation of a function that shrinks the function vertically. Example: $f'(x) = 2f(x)$.

vertical dilation NOUN /ˈvɜr.tɪ.kəl daɪˈleɪ.ʃən/ see vertical enlargement (p 121).

vertical enlargement NOUN /ˈvɜr.tɪ.kəl ɛnˈlɑrdʒ.mənt/ a transformation of a function that stretches the function vertically. Example: $y = \frac{1}{2}x^2$. Synonym: vertical dilation.

vertical intercept NOUN /ˈvɜr.tɪ.kəl ˈɪn.tərˌsɛpt/ see y-intercept (p 123).

vertical line NOUN /ˈvɜr.tɪ.kəl laɪn/
1) a line that is perpendicular to the horizon.
2) a line that is parallel with the y-axis. Equation: $x = a$. Example: $x = 1.5$.

vertical line test NOUN /ˈvɜr.tɪ.kəl laɪn tɛst/ a way to see if a relation is a function: If all vertical lines in the domain of a relation cross the graph of the relation no more than once, then the relation is a function.

vertical reflection NOUN /ˈvɜr.tɪ.kəl rɪˈflɛk.ʃən/ a reflection of a function across the x-axis. Formula: $f'(x) = -f(x)$.

vertical shift NOUN /ˈvɜr.tɪ.kəl ʃɪft/ a shift of a function either up or down. Formula: $f'(x) = f(x) + b$. Synonym: vertical translation.

vertical shrink NOUN /ˈvɜr.tɪ.kəl ʃrɪŋk/ see vertical compression (p 121).

vertical translation NOUN /ˈvɜr.tɪ.kəl trænzˈleɪ.ʃən/ see vertical shift (p 121).

vibration NOUN /vaɪˈbreɪ.ʃən/ a periodic movement in some object. Example: vibration of a violin string.

Viète, François PERSON /ˈvi.ɛt frɑnˈswɑ/ (1540—1603) a French mathematician credited with introducing letters as parameters in equations.

view NOUN /vju/ the direction from which a 3-dimensional object is drawn. Examples: front view, side view.

viewing rectangle NOUN /ˈvju.ɪŋ ˈrɛk.tæn.ɡəl/ on graphing calculators, the portion of the graph that can be seen on the screen. Synonym: viewing

3rd Dyslexic's Edition 121

window, display window.

viewing window NOUN /ˈvju.ŋg ˈwɪn.doʊ/ see viewing rectangle (p 121).

vinculum NOUN /ˈvɪŋ.kjə.ləm/ a line segment or brace drawn over a mathematical expression showing that they are to be considered together. Example: $\overline{a+b}$. Synonyms: bar (p 15), overbar (p 122).

visual fraction model NOUN /ˈvɪʒ.u.əl ˈfræk.ʃən ˈmɒ.dl/ a way to show fractions using objects split into parts.

visualize VERB /ˈvɪʒ.u.ə.laɪz/ to form a mental image of. Example: visualize the problem.

vol ABBREVIATION volume.

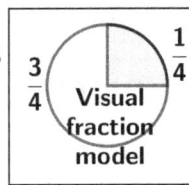

volume NOUN /ˈvɒl.jʌm/ the amount of space enclosed in a solid. Abbreviation: vol.

volume by cylindrical shells NOUN /ˈvɒl.jʌm baɪ sɪlˈɪn.drɪ.kəl ʃɛlz/ a method of approximating the volume of a solid of revolution by taking multiple cylindrical slices of the solid, then adding the volumes of the slices.

volume by slices NOUN /ˈvɒl.jʌm baɪ ˈslaɪ.səs/ a method of approximating a volume by taking the volume of slices of the object, then adding the volumes of the slices together.

voluntary response sample NOUN /ˈvɒl.ən.tɛr.i rɪˈspɒns ˈsæm.pəl/ see self-selected sample (p 103).

vulgar fraction NOUN /ˈvʌl.gər ˈfræk.ʃən/ see common fraction (p 23).

W

wave NOUN /weɪv/ a periodic motion.

wavelength NOUN /ˈweɪv.lɛŋkθ/ the distance from the crest to crest of a wave. See period (p 87).

week NOUN /wik/ a period of time equaling seven days.

weight NOUN /weɪt/ a measure of the pull of gravity on an object. Example: an object on the moon weighs about $\frac{1}{6}$ of what the same object weighs on Earth.

whole /hoʊl/
1) ADJECTIVE all of something. Example: the whole apple.
2) ADJECTIVE, NOUN something that is not divided into parts. Example: a whole number.

whole number NOUN /hoʊl ˈnʌm.bər/ the natural numbers and zero. Notation: $\mathbb{Z}^+$. Math definition: $\{0, 1, 2, \cdots\}$, $\{x \in \mathbb{Z}, x \geq 0\}$.

whole part NOUN /hoʊl pɑrt/ the digits to the left of the decimal separator. Example: in 52.627, the whole part is 52.

whole-part ratio NOUN /hoʊl.pɑrt ˈreɪ.ʃoʊ/ a ratio between a whole and a part of that whole.

wholesale price NOUN /ˈhoʊl.seɪl praɪs/ a price a retailer pays for something.

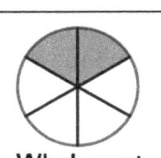

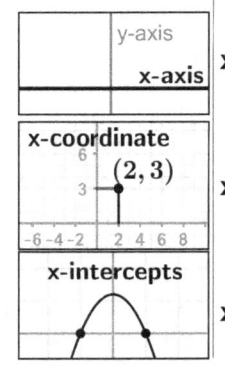

Formula: wholesale price + markup = retail price. Synonym: cost (p 31).

width NOUN /wɪdθ/
1) a measurement of distance at right angles to length.
2) the distance from the front to the back of something.

withholding tax NOUN /wɪθˈhoʊl.dɪŋ tæks/ a tax that is deducted from every paycheck.

with respect to IDIOM /wɪθ rɪˈspɛkt tu/
1) when compared to.
2) when considered with.
Example: distance with respect to time.

word phrase NOUN /wɜrd freɪz/ a math problem given in regular words. Example: Fred has three pencils. Alice has two pencils. How many pencils do they have all together?

work /wɜrk/
1) VERB to perform one or more tasks.
2) NOUN (physics) the amount of effort required to do a task. Formula: the work $\mathbf{W}$ done by force $\mathbf{F}$ along vector $\mathbf{D}$ is $\mathbf{W} = \mathbf{F} \cdot \mathbf{D}$.

work backwards VERB /wɜrk bæk.wərdz/ to start at the end of a problem in order to solve it.

written form NOUN /ˈrɪt.ən fɔrm/ a number written out using letters. Example: 21 in written form is twenty-one.

X

X SYMBOL 10 in Roman numerals.

x-axis NOUN /ɛks ˈæk.sɪs/ the horizontal axis in a 2-dimensional rectangular coordinate system. Plural: **x-axes** /ˈɛks.æk.siz/. Synonym: axis of abscissas.

x-coordinate NOUN /ɛks koʊˈɔr.də.nɪt/ the coordinate corresponding to the x-axis. Synonym: abscissa (p 6).

x-intercept NOUN /ɛks ˈɪn.tər.sɛpt/
1) a point where a graph crosses the x-axis.

2) the value of x where a graph crosses the x-axis. Synonym: horizontal intercept.

x-y axial plane NOUN /ɛks waɪ ˈæk.si.əl pleɪn/ in a 3-dimensional coordinate system, the plane that contains the x-axis and the y-axis.

x-z axial plane NOUN /ɛks zi ˈæk.si.əl pleɪn/ in a 3-dimensional coordinate system, the plane that contains the x-axis and the z-axis.

xor NOUN /ˈɛks.ɔr/ see exclusive disjunction (p 46).

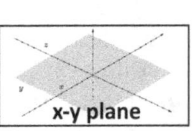

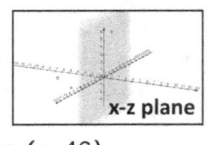

Y

y ABBREVIATION yocto- 10^{-24}. Example: 4.7 ys = 4.7×10^{-24} s. Synonym: septillionth.

Y ABBREVIATION yotta- 10^{24}.

yard NOUN /yɑrd/ a unit of measure of distance. Formulas: **3 feet = 1 yard. 1760 yards = 1 mile. 1.08 yards ≈ 1 meter.** Abbreviation: **yd**.

y-axis NOUN /waɪ ˈæk.sɪs/ the vertical axis of a 2-dimensional rectangular coordinate system. Plural: **y-axes** /ˈwaɪˌæk.siz/. Synonym: **axis of ordinates**.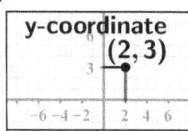

y-coordinate NOUN /waɪ koʊˈɔr.də.nɪt/ a coordinate corresponding to the y-axis. Synonym: **ordinate** (p 84).

yd ABBREVIATION **yard**.

year NOUN /jɪər/ a unit of measure of time equal to the time it takes for the Earth to rotate once around the sun. Formulas: **100 years = 1 century.** $365\frac{1}{4}$ **days ≈ 1 year.** Abbreviation: **yr**.

yield VERB, NOUN /yild/ income received from an investment, often written as a percentage of the amount invested. Example: a bond yielding 5%.

y-intercept NOUN /waɪ ˈɪn.tərˌsɛpt/ 1) a point where a graph crosses the y-axis.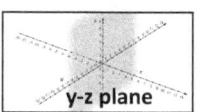
2) the value of **y** at a point at which a graph crosses the y-axis. Synonym: **vertical intercept**.

yocto- PREFIX /ˈyɑk.toʊ/ 10^{-24}. Abbreviation: **y**. Example: **2.2 yoctometer = 2.2×10^{-24} meters.** Synonym: **septillionth**.

yotta- PREFIX /ˈyoʊt.ə/ 10^{24}. Abbreviation: **Y**. Example: **5 yottameter = 5×10^{24} meters.** Synonym: **septillion**.

yr ABBREVIATION **year**.

y-z axial plane NOUN /waɪ zi ˈæk.si.əl pleɪn/ in a 3-dimensional coordinate system, the plane that contains the y-axis and the z-axis.

Z

z ABBREVIATION **zepto-** (p 123). 10^{-21}. Example: **4.2 zm = 4.2×10^{-21} m.** Synonym: **sextillionth**.

Z ABBREVIATION **zetta-** (p 123). 10^{21}. Example: **9.8 Zm = 9.8×10^{21} m.** Synonym: **sextillion**.

Z_n SYMBOL an $n \times n$ zero matrix; an $n \times n$ matrix where all elements are zeroes. Example: $Z_2 = \begin{bmatrix} 0 & 0 \\ 0 & 0 \end{bmatrix}$.

z-axis NOUN /zi ˈæk.sɪs/ the vertical axis of a 3-dimensional rectangular coordinate system. Plural: **z-axes** /zi ˈæk.siz/

z-coordinate NOUN /zi koʊˈɔr.də.nɪt/ a coordinate corresponding to the z-axis.

zenith NOUN /ˈzin.ɪθ/ the angle above the horizon of an object in the sky. Antonym: **azimuth** (p 15).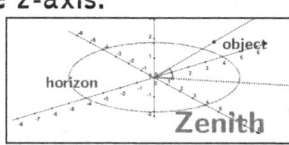

zepto- PREFIX /ˈzɛp.toʊ/ 10^{-21}. Abbreviation: **z**. Example: **9 zeptometer = 9×10^{-21} meters.** Synonym: **sextillionth**.

Zermelo's axiom of choice NOUN /zɜrˈmɛl.oʊz ˈæk.si.əm ʌv tʃɔɪs/ an infinite set can be created from a collection of other infinite sets. Example: The set of all even integers can be created from set of all integers.

zero /ˈzɪə.roʊ/
1) NOUN the number that represents nothing. Synonym: **null**. Antonym: **nonzero** (p 80).
2) NOUN the place-holder digit.
3) NOUN (functions) any point where the function equals zero, where $f(x) = 0$.
4) ADJECTIVE (matrix) contains all zeros.
5) ADJECTIVE equaling 0.

zero exponent NOUN /ˈzɪə.roʊ ˈɛks.poʊ.nənt/ anything to the zero power except zero equals one. Formula: $a^0 = 1, a \neq 0$. Example: $5^0 = 1$.

zero matrix NOUN /ˈzɪə.roʊ ˈmæ.trɪks/ a matrix containing all zeros. Notation: Z_n. Example: $Z_2 = \begin{bmatrix} 0 & 0 \\ 0 & 0 \end{bmatrix}$.

zero pair NOUN /ˈzɪə.roʊ pɛər/ two numbers that, when added together, make zero. Examples: 5 and -5, a and -a.

zero power NOUN /ˈzɪə.roʊ ˈpaʊ.ər/ see **zero exponent** (p 123).

Zero Product Property NOUN /ˈzɪə.roʊ ˈprɒ.dʌkt ˈprɒ.pər.ti/ see **0, Property of Multiplication by** (p 6).

zero sum NOUN /ˈzɪə.roʊ sʌm/ a value plus its additive inverse equals 0: $a + (-a) = 0$.

zero to the zero power NOUN /ˈzɪə.roʊ tu ðə ˈzɪə.roʊ ˈpaʊ.ər/ 0^0 is undefined.

zero vector NOUN /ˈzɪə.roʊ ˈvɛk.tər/ a vector containing all zeros. Example: $\langle 0, 0 \rangle$. Synonym: **null vector**.

zetta- PREFIX /ˈzɛt.ə/ 10^{21}. Abbreviation: **Z**. Example: **5 zettameter = 5×10^{21} meters.** Synonym: **sextillion**.

z-intercept NOUN /zi ˈɪn.tərˌsɛpt/ 1) the point where a graph crosses the z-axis.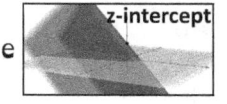
2) the value of **z** where a graph crosses the z-axis.

zone NOUN /zoʊn/
1) part of a geometric solid between two parallel planes.
2) an unbroken connected portion of the surface of a geometric solid.

zoom /zum/
1) VERB to make larger by 'zooming in'. Synonyms: **enlarge**, **dilate**.
2) NOUN the act of zooming.

Zulu time NOUN /ˈzu.lu taɪm/ see **Coordinated Universal Time** (p 30).

Appendix
Algebra

Addition Facts

+	0	1	2	3	4	5	6	7	8	9	10
0	0	1	2	3	4	5	6	7	8	9	10
1	1	2	3	4	5	6	7	8	9	10	11
2	2	3	4	5	6	7	8	9	10	11	12
3	3	4	5	6	7	8	9	10	11	12	13
4	4	5	6	7	8	9	10	11	12	13	14
5	5	6	7	8	9	10	11	12	13	14	15
6	6	7	8	9	10	11	12	13	14	15	16
7	7	8	9	10	11	12	13	14	15	16	17
8	8	9	10	11	12	13	14	15	16	17	18
9	9	10	11	12	13	14	15	16	17	18	19
10	10	11	12	13	14	15	16	17	18	19	20

Multiplication Facts

×	0	1	2	3	4	5	6	7	8	9	10
0	0	0	0	0	0	0	0	0	0	0	0
1	0	1	2	3	4	5	6	7	8	9	10
2	0	2	4	6	8	10	12	14	16	18	20
3	0	3	6	9	12	15	18	21	24	27	30
4	0	4	8	12	16	20	24	28	32	36	40
5	0	5	10	15	20	25	30	35	40	45	50
6	0	6	12	18	24	30	36	42	48	54	60
7	0	7	14	21	28	35	42	49	56	63	70
8	0	8	16	24	32	40	48	56	64	72	80
9	0	9	18	27	36	45	54	63	72	81	90
10	0	10	20	30	40	50	60	70	80	90	100

Keywords

Keywords for Addition

Add	Both	Increased by	Raised
Added to	Combined	Increase of	Sum
Additional	Gain	Join	Together
Altogether	In all	More than	Total
And	Increase	Plus	

Keywords for Subtraction

Change	Farther	Left	Nearer
Decrease	Fell	Less	Reduce
Decreased by	Fewer	Less than	Remain
Difference	Grow down	Lost	
Diminished	How much less	Minus	
Dropped	How much more	More than	

Keywords for Multiplication

Area	Of	Times	Volume
As much	Multiplied	Total	
By	Per	Tripled	
Doubled	Product	Twice	

Keywords for Division

Average	Equal pieces	Part	Shared
Cut	Every	Per	Shared equally
Divided	How many times	Quotient	Split
Each	Out of	Ratio	

Keywords for Equals

Are	Equals	Result, the same as	Equals
Equal to	Is	Equal to	Is

Result, the same as

Properties of Real Numbers

Properties of Addition		
Property	Description	Statement/Example
Additive identity; Property of adding zero	Zero added to any number does not change the number.	$a + 0 = 0 + a = a$
		$3 + 0 = 0 + 3 = 3$
Additive inverse	Any number plus its negative equals zero.	$a + (-a) = 0$
		$2 + (-2) = 0$
Associative property of addition	It does not matter how addition is grouped.	$a + (b + c) = (a + b) + c$
		$2 + (3 + 5) = 2 + 8 = 10$ $(2 + 3) + 5 = 5 + 5 = 10$
Commutative property of addition	It does not matter in which order addition is performed.	$a + b = b + a$
		$2 + 3 = 5 = 3 + 2$
Addition property of equality	Any number can be added to both sides of an equation without changing the truth value of the equation.	If $a = b$ then $a + c = b + c$ If $a \neq b$ then $a + c \neq b + c$.
		If $2 = 2$ then $2 + 4 = 2 + 4 \rightarrow 6 = 6$. If $2 \neq 3$ then $2 + 4 \neq 3 + 4 \rightarrow 6 \neq 7$
Addition property of inequality	Any number can be added to both sides of an inequality without changing the true value of the inequality.	If $a > b$ then $a + c > b + c$. If $a < b$ then $a + c < b + c$.
		If $3 > 2$ then $3 + 4 > 2 + 4 \rightarrow 7 > 6$ If $2 < 3$ then $2 + 4 < 3 + 4 \rightarrow 6 < 7$

Properties of Multiplication		
Property	Description	Statement/Example
Definition	Multiplication is repeated addition	$a \cdot b = \underbrace{a + a + \ldots + a}_{b \text{ times}}$
		$2 \cdot 3 = \underbrace{2 + 2 + 2}_{3 \text{ times}} = 6$
Property of multiplying by one	Anything times one equals itself.	$a \cdot 1 = 1 \cdot a = a$
		$3 \cdot 1 = 1 \cdot 3 = 3$
Property of multiplying by zero	Anything times zero equals zero.	$a \cdot 0 = 0 \cdot a = 0$
		$2 \cdot 0 = 0 \cdot 2 = 0$
Multiplicative inverse	Any number except zero times its reciprocal equals one.	$a \cdot \frac{1}{a} = \frac{a}{1} \cdot \frac{1}{a} = \frac{a \cdot 1}{1 \cdot a} = \frac{a}{a} = 1, a \neq 0$
		$3 \cdot \frac{1}{3} = 1$
Associative property of multiplication	It does not matter how multiplication is grouped.	$a \cdot (b \cdot c) = (a \cdot b) \cdot c$
		$2 \cdot (3 \cdot 5) = 2 \cdot 15 = 30$ $(2 \cdot 3) \cdot 5 = 6 \cdot 5 = 30$
Commutative property of multiplication	It does not matter in which order multiplication is performed.	$a \cdot b = b \cdot a$
		$2 \cdot 3 = 3 \cdot 2 = 6$
Multiplication property of equality	Any number except zero can be multiplied by both sides of an equation without changing the truth value of the equation.	If $a = b$ then $a \cdot c = b \cdot c$ If $a \neq b$ then $a \cdot c \neq b \cdot c, c \neq 0$
		If $2 = 2$ then $2 \cdot 3 = 2 \cdot 3 \rightarrow 6 = 6$ If $2 \neq 3$ then $2 \cdot 4 \neq 3 \cdot 4 \rightarrow 8 \neq 12$

Properties of Multiplication

Property	Description	Statement/Example
Multiplication property of inequality	Any positive number can be multiplied by both sides of an inequality without changing the true value of the inequality. If a negative number is multiplied by both sides of an inequality, the inequality 'flips'.	If $a > b$ and $c > 0$ then $a \cdot c > b \cdot c$ If $a < b$ and $c > 0$ then $a \cdot c < b \cdot c$ If $a > b$ and $c < 0$ then $a \cdot c < b \cdot c$ If $a < b$ and $c < 0$ then $a \cdot c > b \cdot c$
Distributive property of multiplication over addition and subtraction	Multiplying a number by a sum is the same as multiplying each number in the sum, then adding.	$a(b+c) = ab + ac$ $a(b-c) = ab - ac$ $2(1+3) = 2 \cdot 1 + 2 \cdot 3 = 2 + 6 = 8$

Properties of Negation
All variables in this section represent positive numbers.

Property	Description	Statement/Example
Multiply by negative one.	A positive number times negative one equals the negative of the number.	$(-1)a = -a$ $(-1) \cdot 3 = -3$
Double negation	The negative of a negative number is positive.	$-(-a) = a$ $-(-4) = 4$
Positive times positive	A positive number times a positive number is a positive number.	$a \cdot b = ab$ $3 \cdot 4 = 12$
Positive times negative	A positive number times a negative number is a negative number.	$-a \cdot b = -ab$ $a \cdot -b = -ab$ $-2 \cdot 7 = -14$ $5 \cdot -2 = -10$
Negative times negative	A negative number times a negative number equals a positive number.	$-a \cdot -b = ab$ $-2 \cdot -3 = 6$
Distributive property of negation over multiplication and subtraction	A negative outside parentheses is applied to each term inside the parentheses.	$-(a+b) = -a - b$ $-(a-b) = -a + b$ $-(3+2) = -3 - 2 = -5$ $-(3-2) = -3 + 2 = -1$

Properties of Fractions

Property	Description	Statement/Example
Definition	The definition of a fraction	$\frac{a}{b}$ means $a \div b$ $\frac{3}{2}$ means $3 \div 2 = 1.5$
Addition	To add fractions, make the fractions into like fractions, then add the numerators.	$\frac{a}{b} + \frac{c}{d} = \frac{ad}{bd} + \frac{bc}{bd} = \frac{ad+bc}{bd}$ $\frac{a}{b} + c = \frac{a}{b} + \frac{bc}{b} = \frac{a+bc}{b}$ $\frac{2}{3} + \frac{3}{4} = \frac{2 \cdot 4 + 3 \cdot 3}{12} =$ $\frac{8+9}{12} = \frac{17}{12} = 1\frac{5}{12}$
Subtraction	To subtract fractions, make the fractions into like fractions, then subtract the numerators.	$\frac{a}{b} - \frac{c}{d} = \frac{ad}{bd} - \frac{bc}{bc} = \frac{ad-bc}{bd}$ $\frac{a}{b} - c = \frac{a}{b} - \frac{bc}{b} = \frac{a-bc}{b}$ $c - \frac{a}{b} = \frac{c}{b} - \frac{a}{b} = \frac{bc-a}{b}$ $\frac{3}{4} - \frac{2}{3} = \frac{3 \cdot 3 - 2 \cdot 4}{3 \cdot 4} = \frac{9-8}{12} = \frac{1}{12}$ $\frac{5}{2} - 2 = \frac{5}{2} - \frac{2 \cdot 2}{2} = \frac{5-4}{2} = \frac{1}{2}$
Multiplication	To multiply fractions, multiply the numerators and multiply the denominators.	$\frac{a}{b} \cdot \frac{c}{d} = \frac{ac}{bd}$, $c \cdot \frac{a}{b} = \frac{ac}{b}$ $\frac{1}{3} \cdot \frac{4}{5} = \frac{4}{15}$

Properties of Fractions

Property	Description	Statement/Example
Division	To divide fractions, multiply the dividend by the reciprocal of the divisor.	$\frac{a}{b} \div \frac{c}{d} = \frac{a}{b} \cdot \frac{d}{c} = \frac{ad}{bc}$ $\frac{a}{b} \div c = \frac{a}{b} \cdot \frac{1}{c} = \frac{a}{bc}$ $\frac{2}{3} \div \frac{1}{4} = \frac{2}{3} \cdot \frac{4}{1} = \frac{2 \cdot 4}{3 \cdot 1} = \frac{8}{3}$
Exponents	A fraction raised to a power is equal to the numerator raised to a power divided by the denominator raised to a power.	$\left(\frac{a}{b}\right)^n = \frac{a^n}{b^n}$ $\left(\frac{2}{3}\right)^2 = \frac{2^2}{3^2} = \frac{4}{9}$
Convert between mixed number and improper fraction	To covert a mixed fraction to an improper fraction, convert the whole part to a unit fraction and add.	$C\frac{a}{b} = \frac{C \cdot b + a}{b}$ $2\frac{2}{3} = \frac{2 \cdot 3 + 2}{3} = \frac{6+2}{3} = \frac{8}{3}$
Zero numerator	Any fraction with a zero numerator equals zero.	$\frac{0}{a} = 0, a \neq 0$ $\frac{0}{5} = 0$
Self division	Any fraction with the same nonzero numerator and denominator equals one.	$\frac{a}{a} = 1, a \neq 0$ $\frac{6}{6} = 1$
Zero denominator	A fraction with a zero denominator is undefined.	$\frac{a}{0}$ is undefined $\frac{8}{0}$ is undefined
One denominator	A fraction with a denominator of 1 equals the numerator.	$\frac{a}{1} = a$ $\frac{3}{1} = 3$
Negatives	Two negatives make a positive. One negative and one positive make a negative.	$\frac{-a}{b} = -\frac{a}{b}, \frac{a}{-b} = -\frac{a}{b}, \frac{-a}{-b} = \frac{a}{b}$ $\frac{-2}{3} = -\frac{2}{3}, \frac{3}{-2} = -\frac{3}{2}, \frac{-4}{-5} = \frac{4}{5}$

Properties of Exponents

Property	Description	Statement/Example
Definition	Exponent means repeated multiplication	$a^b = \underbrace{a \cdot a \cdot \ldots \cdot a}_{b \text{ times}}$ $2^3 = 2 \cdot 2 \cdot 2 = 8$
Multiplication	If the same base is multiplied, add the exponents	$b^m b^n = b^{m+n}$ $2^2 2^3 = 2^{2+3} = 2^5 = 32$
Division	If the same base is divided, subtract the exponents.	$\frac{b^m}{b^n} = b^{m-n}$ $\frac{2^4}{2^2} = 2^{4-2} = 2^2 = 4$
Distributive property of exponents	Exponents can distribute through multiplication and division.	$(a \cdot b)^m = a^m b^m, \quad \left(\frac{a}{b}\right)^m = \frac{a^m}{b^m}$ $(2 \cdot 3)^2 = 2^2 3^2 = 36, \left(\frac{2}{3}\right)^2 = \frac{2^2}{3^2} = \frac{4}{9}$
Negative exponent	A negative exponent means reciprocal.	$a^{-m} = \frac{1}{a^m}$ $5^{-2} = \frac{1}{5^2} = \frac{1}{25}$
Equality of exponents.	If the same number raised to powers are equal, the powers are equal.	If $a^m = a^n$, then $m = n$. If $a^5 = a^n$, then $n = 5$.
Root of a root	The root of a root is equal to the double root.	$\sqrt[n]{x \sqrt[n]{x}} = \sqrt[n]{x^{\frac{n+1}{n}}} = x^{\frac{n+1}{n^2}}$ $\sqrt{x\sqrt{x}} = \sqrt{x^{\frac{3}{2}}} = x^{\frac{3}{4}}$
Exponent of an exponent	A base raised to a power which is raised to another power is equal to the base raised to the product of the powers.	$(b^m)^n = b^{m \cdot n}$. Important: $b^{(m^n)} \neq b^{m^n}$ $(2^3)^2 = 2^{3 \cdot 2} = 2^6 = 64$

Properties of Exponents

Property	Description	Statement/Example
Fractional exponent	The denominator of a fractional exponent means take a root.	$b^{\frac{m}{n}} = \left(\sqrt[n]{b}\right)^m = \sqrt[n]{b^m}$
		$4^{\frac{3}{2}} = \left(\sqrt[2]{4}\right)^3 = 2^3 = 8$
Exponent of one	Any number raised to the 1 power equals itself.	$b^1 = b$
		$3^1 = 3$
Base of zero	Zero to any power except zero equals zero.	$0^a = 0, a \neq 0$
		$0^7 = 0$
Exponent of zero	Any number except zero raised to the zero power equals one.	$b^0 = 1, b \neq 0$
		$5^0 = 1$
Zero to the zero power	Zero to the zero power is undefined.	0^0 is undefined
Rationalizing the denominator	To remove a radical from the denominator, multiply the numerator and denominator by the radical.	$\frac{1}{\sqrt[n]{a}} = \frac{\sqrt[n]{a^{n-1}}}{\sqrt[n]{a} \cdot \sqrt[n]{a^{n-1}}} = \frac{\sqrt[n]{a^{n-1}}}{a}$
		$\frac{1}{\sqrt{2}} = \frac{\sqrt{2}}{\sqrt{2} \cdot \sqrt{2}} = \frac{\sqrt{2}}{2}$

Properties of Logarithms

Property	Description	Statement/Example
Definition	A logarithmic function is the inverse of an exponential function.	$\log_b c = a$ if and only if $b^a = c$
		$\log_e 3 = a$ if and only if $e^a = 3$
Logarithm of 1	Any logarithm of 1 equals zero.	$\log_a 1 = 0$
		$\log_{10} 1 = 0$
Logarithm with the same base and argument.	Logarithm with the same base and argument equals 1.	$\log_a a = 1$
		$\log_5 5 = 1$
Logarithm with the same base and argument raised to the x	Logarithm with the same base and argument raised to the x equals x.	$\log_a a^x = x$
		$\log_7 7^5 = 5$
Logarithm as exponent	A base raised to a logarithm with the same base of x equals x.	$a^{\log_a x} = x$
		$14^{\log_{14} 6} = 6$
Product property	The logarithm of a product is equal to the sum of the logarithms.	$\log_b m \cdot n = \log_b m + \log_b n$
		$\log_{10} 3 \cdot 2 = \log_{10} 3 + \log_{10} 2 \approx 0.47712 + 0.30103 = 0.77815$
Quotient property	The logarithm of a fraction is equal to the logarithm of the numerator less the logarithm of the denominator.	$\log_b \frac{m}{n} = \log_b m - \log_b n$
		$\log_{10} \frac{3}{2} = \log_{10} 3 - \log_{10} 2 \approx 0.47712 - 0.30103 = 0.17609$
Exponent property	The logarithm of a number to a power is equal to the power times the logarithm of the number.	$\log_b m^n = n \log_b m$
		$\log_{10} 4^2 = 2 \log_{10} 4 \approx 2 \cdot 0.60206 = 1.20412$
Change of base	How to change the base of a logarithm.	$\log_b m = \frac{\log_c m}{\log_c b}$
		$\log_7 10 = \frac{\log_{10} 10}{\log_{10} 7} \approx \frac{1}{0.84510} \approx 1.1832$
Inverse property 1	The log of an exponential expression is equal to the exponent of the expression.	$\log_b b^x = x$
		$\log_5 5^2 = 2$
Inverse property 2	A logarithm in an exponent is equal to the exponent.	$b^{\log_b x} = x$
		$6^{\log_6 5} = 5$

Properties of Radicals

Description	Formula
The principal n^{th} root of a, $n \geq 2$	$\sqrt[n]{a} = b$ means $a = b^n$
The nth root of a product is equal to the product of the nth roots.	$\sqrt[n]{ab} = \sqrt[n]{a}\sqrt[n]{b}$
The nth root of a fraction is a fraction of the nth roots.	$\sqrt[n]{\frac{a}{b}} = \frac{\sqrt[n]{a}}{\sqrt[n]{b}}$
The nth root of a value to the mth power is the nth root of the value to the mth power.	$\sqrt[n]{a^m} = \left(\sqrt[n]{a}\right)^m$
The nth root of a value to the nth power is the value or the absolute value of the power.	if $n > 0$ is even $\sqrt[n]{a^n} = |a|$ if $n > 0$ is odd $\sqrt[n]{a^n} = a$
Rationalizing the denominator	$\frac{1}{\sqrt{a}} = \frac{\sqrt{a}}{\sqrt{a}\cdot\sqrt{a}} = \frac{\sqrt{a}}{a}$
Fractional exponents	$a^{\frac{1}{n}} = \sqrt[n]{a}, a^{\frac{m}{n}} = \sqrt[n]{a^m} = \left(\sqrt[n]{a}\right)^m$

Factoring Formulas

Name	Formula
Difference of squares	$a^2 - b^2 = (a-b)(a+b)$
Perfect square	$a^2 + 2ab + b^2 = (a+b)^2$
Perfect square	$a^2 - 2ab + b^2 = (a-b)^2$
Difference of cubes	$a^3 - b^3 = (a-b)(a^2+ab+b^2)$
Sum of cubes	$a^3 + b^3 = (a+b)(a^2-ab+b^2)$

Rules for Rounding

Operation	Rule
Multiplication and division	Round to the least number of significant digits of the operands.
Addition and subtraction	Round to the decimal place of the least decimal place of the operands.
Exponentiation and roots	Round so the result has the same number of significant digits as the operator.

Inverse Algebraic Operations

Operation	Inverse operation
Addition	Subtraction
Multiplication	Division
Exponent (power)	Logarithm

Complex Numbers

Operations on Complex Numbers

Operation	Formula/Example
Addition	$(a+bi)+(c+di) = a+c+(b+d)i$
	$(3+2i)+(-2-3i) = 3-2+(2-3)i = 1-i$
Subtraction	$(a+bi)-(c+di) = a-c+(b-d)i$
	$(2-i)-(3+2i) = 2-3+(-1-2)i = -1-3i$
Multiplication	$(a+bi)(c+di) = ac-bd+(ad+bc)i$
	$(1+2i)(2-3i) = 2+6+(-3+4)i = 8+i$
Division	$\frac{a+bi}{c+di} = \frac{ac+bd+(bc-ad)i}{c^2-d^2}$
	$\frac{2+i}{-1+3i} = \frac{2\cdot(-1)+1\cdot 3+(1\cdot(-1)-2\cdot 3)i}{(-1)^2-3^2} = \frac{-2+3+(-1-6)i}{1-9} = \frac{1-7i}{-8} = -\frac{1}{8}+\frac{7}{8}i$

Magnitude (absolute value)	$\|a+bi\| = \sqrt{a^2+b^2}$
	$\|1-2i\| = \sqrt{1^2+(-2)^2} = \sqrt{1+4} = \sqrt{5}$
Direction	direction of $a+bi$ is $\arctan\frac{b}{a}$.
	direction of $1-2i$ is $\arctan\frac{-2}{1} = \arctan(-2) \approx -1.10715$ rad.
Polar form	$a+bi = \left(\sqrt{a^2+b^2}, \arctan\frac{b}{a}\right)$
	$1-2i = \left(\sqrt{1^2+(-2)^2}, \arctan\frac{-2}{1}\right) \approx (\sqrt{5}, -1.10715)$

Properties of Complex Conjugates

Description	Formula
The product of a number and its conjugate is a positive real number.	$(a+bi)(a-bi) = a^2 - (bi)^2 = a^2 - b^2i^2 = a^2 + b^2$
The conjugate of a real number is the real number itself.	$a = (a+0i), \overline{(a+0i)} = (a-0i) = a$
The conjugate of a conjugate is the original number.	$\overline{\overline{z}} = z$
The conjugate of a sum of two numbers is the sum of the conjugates of the numbers.	$\overline{z_1 + z_2} = \overline{z_1} + \overline{z_2}$
The conjugate of a product of two numbers is the product of the conjugates of the numbers.	$\overline{z_1 \cdot z_2} = \overline{z_1} \cdot \overline{z_2}$

Properties of Vectors

Operation	Description	Example
Addition	Add the corresponding components.	$u + v = \langle u_1 + v_1, u_2 + v_2 \rangle$
Subtraction	Subtract the corresponding components.	$u - v = \langle u_1 - v_1, u_2 - v_2 \rangle$
Scalar Multiplication	Multiply the scalar by each component.	$a \cdot u = \langle a \cdot u_1, a \cdot u_2 \rangle$
Equality	For vectors $v_1 = \langle a_1, b_1 \rangle$, $v_2 = \langle a_2, b_2 \rangle$, $v_1 = v_2$ if and only if $a_1 = a_2$ and $b_1 = b_2$.	$v_1 = \langle 1, -1 \rangle, v_2 = \langle 1, -1 \rangle$. Since $1 = 1$ and $-1 = -1$, $v_1 = v_2$.
Magnitude	The length of a vector, ignoring direction.	For $v = \langle v_1, v_2 \rangle$, $\|v\| = \sqrt{v_1^2 + v_2^2}$ For $u = \langle u_1, u_2, u_3 \rangle$, $\|u\| = \sqrt{u_1^2 + u_2^2 + u_3^2}$.
Unit vector in the direction of v	This produces a vector of magnitude one that goes in the same direction as v.	$u = \frac{v}{\|v\|}$
Find a vector given a direction and magnitude	This produces a vector in the form $\langle a, b \rangle$ from a direction and magnitude.	$y = \|v\| < i\cos\alpha, j\cos\alpha >$ where i is the horizontal component of v, j is the vertical component of v, and α is the angle measured from the positive x-axis.
Dot product	This produces a scalar from a multiplication of two vectors.	Given $v = \langle a_1, b_1 \rangle, w = \langle a_2, b_2 \rangle$: $v \cdot w = a_1 a_2 + b_1 b_2$
Commutative property of dot product	Dot product can be done in any order.	$v \cdot w = w \cdot v$
Distributive property of dot product.	Dot product distributes over addition and subtraction.	$u \cdot (v + w) = u \cdot v + u \cdot w$
Dot product on the same vector	A vector dot product with itself is equal to the magnitude of the vector squared.	$v \cdot v = \|v\|^2$
Zero dot product of a vector is zero	Multiplying zero by a vector gives zero.	$0 \cdot v = v \cdot 0 = 0$
Angle between two vectors	The angle between two vectors is defined using the dot product.	$\cos\theta = \frac{u \cdot v}{\|u\|\|v\|}$
Orthogonal vectors	Two vectors are orthogonal if and only if their dot product is zero.	Vectors u and v are orthogonal if and only if $u \cdot v = 0$

Properties of Vectors

Operation	Description	Example
Vector projection	The projection of vector **a** on vector **b** is a vector with the direction of **b** and a magnitude determined by a line segment perpendicular to **b**.	$v_1 = \frac{v \cdot w}{|w|^2} w$
Vector decomposition	From vectors **v** and **w**, produces two vectors, one of which (v_1) is the projection of **v** on **w**, and the other (v_2) is perpendicular to v_1.	$v_1 = \frac{v \cdot w}{|w|^2} w,\ v_2 = v - v_1$

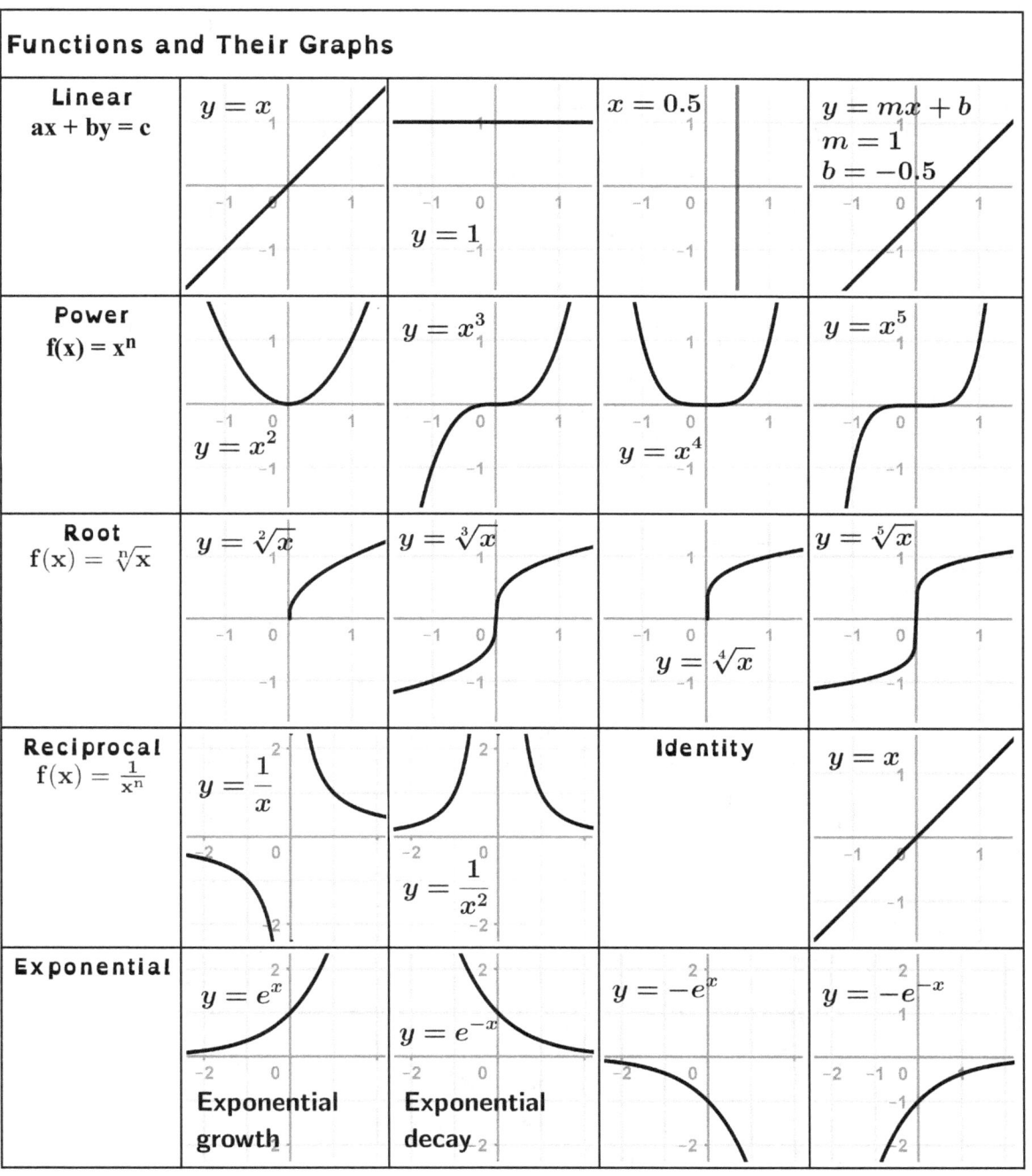

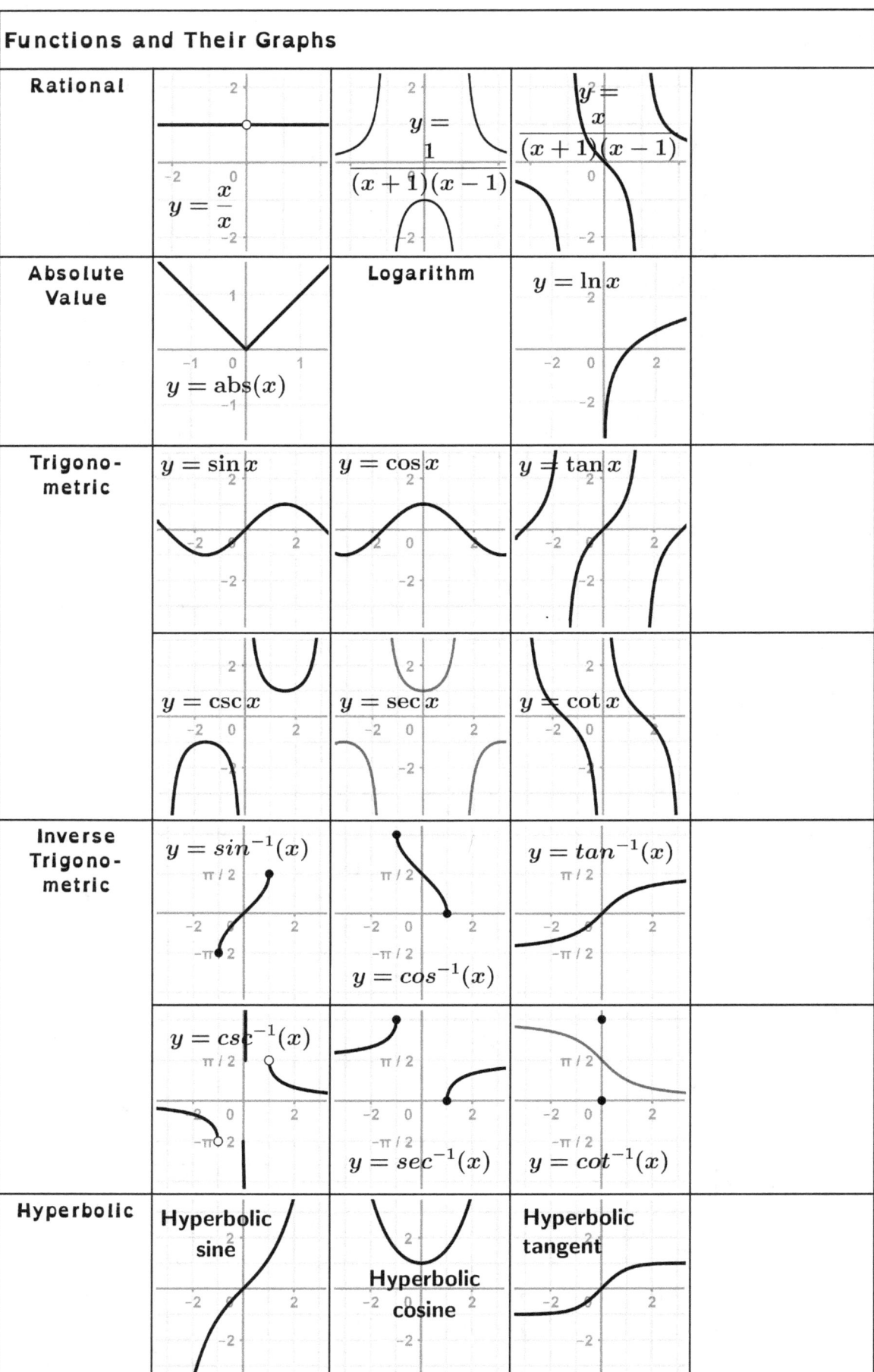

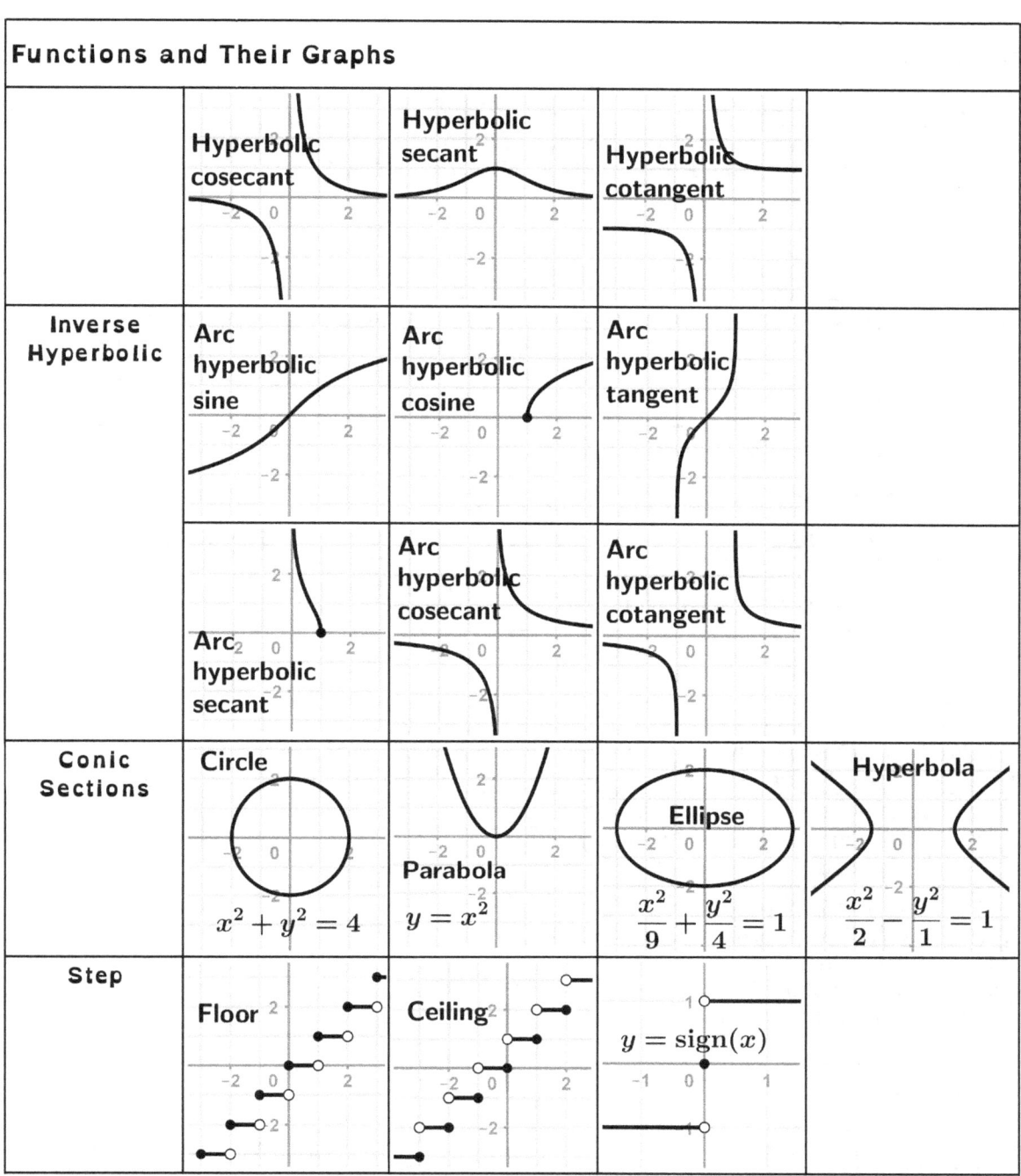

Graph Shifts

Shift	Explanation	Graph
Vertical – Up	The output value of the function is increased by a constant amount. Formula: $f'(x) = f(x) + 2$ (shift up by 2).	Shift up by 2
Vertical – Down	The output value of the function is decreased by a constant amount. Formula: $f'(x) = f(x) - 2$ (shift down by 2).	Shift down by 2

Graph Shifts

Shift	Explanation	Graph
Horizontal – Left	The input value of the function is decreased by a constant amount. Formula: $f'(x) = f(x+2)$ (shift left by 2).	Shift left by 2
Horizontal – Right	The input value of the function is increased by a constant amount. Formula: $f'(x) = f(x-2)$ (shift right by 2).	Shift right by 2

Properties of Determinants

Description	Example
The value of a determinant changes sign if any two rows or any two columns are exchanged.	$\begin{vmatrix} a & b \\ c & d \end{vmatrix} = - \begin{vmatrix} c & d \\ a & b \end{vmatrix}$
If all the entries in any row or any column equal 0, the value of the determinant is 0.	$\begin{vmatrix} a & b \\ 0 & 0 \end{vmatrix} = 0$
If any two rows, or any two columns of a determinant have corresponding entries that are equal, the value of the determinant is 0.	$\begin{vmatrix} a & b \\ a & b \end{vmatrix} = 0$
If any row or any column of a determinant is multiplied by a nonzero number k, the value of the determinant is also changed by a factor of k.	$\begin{vmatrix} 1 & 4 \\ 3 & 2 \end{vmatrix} = -10, \begin{vmatrix} 2 \cdot 1 & 4 \\ 2 \cdot 3 & 2 \end{vmatrix} = \begin{vmatrix} 2 & 4 \\ 6 & 2 \end{vmatrix} = -20$
If the entries of any row or any column of a determinant are multiplied by a nonzero number k and the result is added to the corresponding entries of another row (or column), the value of the determinant remains unchanged.	$A = \begin{bmatrix} 1 & 3 \\ 2 & 4 \end{bmatrix}, A' = \begin{bmatrix} 1 & 3+1 \cdot 2 \\ 2 & 4+2 \cdot 2 \end{bmatrix} = \begin{bmatrix} 1 & 5 \\ 2 & 8 \end{bmatrix}$ $|A| = 1 \cdot 4 - 3 \cdot 2 = 4 - 6 = -2$ $|A'| = 1 \cdot 8 - 5 \cdot 2 = 8 - 10 = -2, |A| = -2 = |A'|$

Properties of a Limit

Description	Math Statement
The limit of a constant is that constant.	Given $f(x) = b$, $\lim_{x \to c} f(x) = \lim_{x \to c} b = b$
The limit of the identity function $f(x) = x$ is the value of x.	Given $f(x) = x$, $\lim_{x \to c} f(x) = c$
The limit of a sum is the sum of the limits.	$\lim_{x \to c} [f(x) + g(x)] = \lim_{x \to c} f(x) + \lim_{x \to c} g(x)$
The limit of a difference is the difference of the limits.	$\lim_{x \to c} [f(x) - g(x)] = \lim_{x \to c} f(x) - \lim_{x \to c} g(x)$
The limit of a product is the product of the limits.	$\lim_{x \to c} [f(x) \cdot g(x)] = [\lim_{x \to c} f(x)] \cdot [\lim_{x \to c} g(x)]$
The limit of a polynomial is the value of the polynomial at the limit.	$\lim_{x \to c} P(x) = P(c)$
The limit of an exponential function is the limit of the function raised to the exponent.	$\lim_{x \to c} [f(x)^n] = [\lim_{x \to c} f(x)]^n$
The limit of a root of a function is the limit of the function to the root.	$\lim_{x \to c} \left[\sqrt[n]{f(x)} \right] = \sqrt[n]{\lim_{x \to c} f(x)}$
The limit of a quotient is the quotient of the limits.	$\lim_{x \to c} \left[\frac{f(x)}{g(x)} \right] = \frac{\lim_{x \to c} f(x)}{\lim_{x \to c} g(x)}, g(x) \neq 0, \lim_{x \to c} g(x) \neq 0$

Roots of Integers

All inexact values are rounded to 6 decimal digits.

n	$\sqrt{n}$	$\sqrt[3]{n}$	$\sqrt[4]{n}$	$\sqrt[5]{n}$
1	1	1	1	1
2	1.41421	1.25992	1.18921	1.14870
3	1.73205	1.44225	1.31607	1.24573
4	2	1.58740	1.41421	1.31951
5	2.23607	1.70998	1.49535	1.37973
6	2.44949	1.81712	1.56508	1.43097
7	2.64575	1.91293	1.62658	1.47577
8	2.82843	2	1.68179	1.51572
9	3	2.08008	1.73205	1.55185
10	3.16228	2.15443	1.77828	1.58489

Divisibility Rules

n A number is divisible by **n** if ...
2 the number ends in 0, 2, 4, 6, or 8; the number is even. *Example:* 738: the number ends in 8 so 738 is divisible by 2.
3 the sum of the digits is divisible by 3. *Example:* 168: 1 + 6 + 8 = 15; 1 + 5 = 6. 6 is divisible by 3, so 168 is divisible by 3.
4 the last two digits are divisible by 4. *Example:* 948: 48 is divisible by 4, so 948 is divisible by 4.
5 the last digit is 0 or 5. *Example:* 525: The last digit is 5, so 525 is divisible by 5.
6 the number is divisible by 2 and the number is divisible by 3.
7 double the last digit, then subtract the double from the rest of the number. If the result is divisible by 7, then the number is divisible by 7. Repeat for large numbers.
8 the last three digits are divisible by 8.
9 the sum of the digits is divisible by 9. *Example:* 414: 4 + 1 + 4 = 9; 9 is divisible by 9, so 414 is divisible by 9.
10 the last digit is 0.

Greek Letters

Name	Upper Case	Lower Case	Conventional Use
Alpha /ˈæl.fə/	**A**	α	Geometry: angle.
Beta /ˈbeɪ.tə/	**B**	β	Geometry: angle.
Gamma /ˈgæm.ə/	**Γ**	γ	gamma function, a generalization of factorial.
Delta /ˈdɛl.tə/	**Δ**	δ	Change. 'Δx' (read delta-x) means the change in x.
Epsilon /ˈɛp.sə.lɒn/	**E**	ϵ	An arbitrarily small quantity. Eccentricity of conic sections.
Zeta /ˈzeɪ.tə/	**Z**	ζ	Riemann zeta function
Eta /ˈeɪ.tə/	**H**	η	Dirichlet eta function
Theta /ˈθeɪ.tə/	**Θ**	θ	variable that represents the measure of an angle.
Iota /aɪˈoʊ.tə/	**I**	ι	
Kappa /ˈkæp.ə/	**K**	κ	Kappa curve.
Lambda /ˈlæm.də/	**Λ**	λ	
Mu /mju/	**M**	μ	Abbreviation for a micrometer, or micron.
Nu /nu/	**N**	ν	Nu function
Xi /ksi/	**Ξ**	ξ	Xi function
Omicron /ˈɒm.ɪˌkrɒn/	**O**	o	

Greek Letters

Name	Upper Case	Lower Case	Conventional Use
Pi /paɪ/	Π	π	The constant ratio of the circumference of a circle to the diameter. $\pi \approx 3.14159$.
Rho /roʊ/	P	ρ	
Sigma /ˈsɪɡ.mə/	Σ	σ	An operator used to indicate repeated addition.
Tau /taʊ/	T	τ	An alternate notation for the divisor function. The half-period ratio of an elliptic function.
Upsilon /ˈʌp.səˌlɒn/	Y	υ	Physics: one of a family of heavy, short-lived, neutral mesons.
Phi /faɪ/	Φ	φ	Golden section
Chi /kaɪ/	X	χ	
Psi /saɪ/	Ψ	ψ	
Omega /oʊˈmeɪ.ɡə/	Ω	ω	Omega constant.

Algebraic Identities

Operation	Identity	Equation(s)
Addition of numbers	0	$a + 0 = 0 + a = a$
Multiplication of numbers	1	$a \cdot 1 = 1 \cdot a = a$
Exponentiation	1	$a^1 = a$
Matrix addition	$\begin{bmatrix} 0 & 0 \\ 0 & 0 \end{bmatrix}$	$A_{m \times n} + Z_{m \times n} = A_{n \times m}$
Matrix multiplication (square matrices only)	$\begin{bmatrix} 1 & 0 & 0 \\ 0 & 1 & 0 \\ 0 & 0 & 1 \end{bmatrix}$	$A_{n \times n} \cdot I_{n \times n} = I_{n \times n} \cdot A_{n \times n} = A_{n \times n}$
Vector addition	$z = \langle 0, 0 \rangle$	$u + z = z + u = u$

Units of Measure of Area

Unit	Notation
square meter	m^2
square centimeter	cm^2
square foot	ft^2
square mile	mi^2
hectare	Ha
acre	acre

Geometry

Figurate Numbers

Name	Sequence Formula	Illustration
Triangular	1, 3, 6, 10, 15, ... $t(n) = \frac{n(n-1)}{2}$	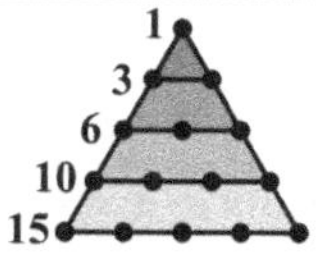 Triangular Number
Square	1, 4, 9, 16, 25, ... $s(n) = n^2$	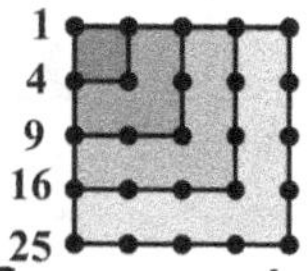 Square number
Pentagonal	1, 5, 12, 22, 35, ... $p(n) = \frac{n(3n-1)}{2}$	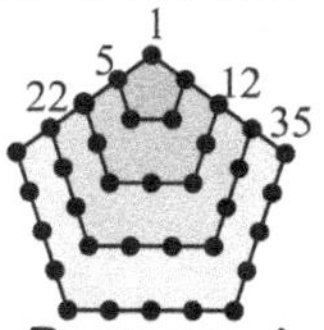 Pentagonal number
Others	$f(n, i) = \frac{n((i-2)n-1)}{2}$ where **i** is the number of sides in the figure and **n** is the index of the number.	

Properties of a Circle

Property	Description	Diagram
Arc	A portion of a circumference of a circle.	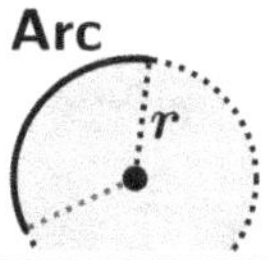 Arc
Area	The surface contained by a circle. Formula: $A = \pi r^2$.	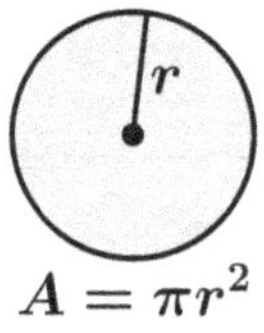 $A = \pi r^2$
Center	The point from which all points of the circle are equidistant.	 Center
Chord	A line segment from one edge of the circle to another.	 Chord
Circumference	1) The edge of a circle. 2) The length of the edge of a circle. Formula: $C = 2\pi r$.	 Circumference

3rd Dyslexic's Edition

Properties of a Circle

Property	Description	Diagram
Diameter	1) A line segment from one edge of a circle to the opposite edge passing through the center. 2) The length of a diameter. Formula: $D = 2r$.	
Radius	1) A line segment from the center of a circle to the edge. 2) The length of a radius.	
Secant	A line that crosses the edge of a circle exactly twice.	
Sector	The portion of the interior of a circle between two radii.	
Segment	The part of the interior of a circle between a chord and the edge of the circle.	
Tangent	A line that touches a circle exactly once.	
Unit circle	A circle with a radius of 1, usually centered at the origin. Formula: $x^2 + y^2 = 1$.	

Equations for an Ellipse

Description	Major axis parallel to the x-axis	Major axis parallel to the y-axis
Graphic		
Equation	$\frac{(x-h)^2}{a^2} + \frac{(y-k)^2}{b^2} = 1, a > b > 0$	$\frac{(x-h)^2}{b^2} + \frac{(y-k)^2}{a^2} = 1, a > b > 0$
Center	(h, k)	(h, k)
c	$c = \sqrt{a^2 + b^2}$	$c = \sqrt{a^2 + b^2}$
Foci	$(h \pm c, k)$	$(h, k \pm c)$
Vertices	$(h \pm a, k)$	$(h, k \pm a)$

Adjacent in Geometric Figures

Type	Example
Adjacent arcs share an endpoint.	arc AB is adjacent to arc BC
Adjacent angles on intersecting lines share a side and a vertex. Synonym: **consecutive angles**.	α is adjacent to β
Adjacent angles of a polygon share a side.	∠α is adjacent to ∠β
Adjacent faces of a polyhedron share a common edge.	Adjacent Common Edge Adjacent
Adjacent sides of a polygon share a vertex.	a is adjacent to b

Altitudes of Geometric Figures

Figure	Altitude
Cone apex / Altitude / base	The line segment from the vertex of the cone to the plane containing the base. The altitude is perpendicular to the base.
Cylinder base / Altitude / base	A line segment between the planes containing the bases of the cylinder. The altitude is perpendicular to the bases.
Parallelogram Altitude	A line segment between extended parallel sides. The altitude is perpendicular to the parallel sides.
Prism Altitude	A line segment between the base planes of the prism. An altitude is perpendicular to the base planes.

3rd Dyslexic's Edition

Altitudes of Geometric Figures

Figure	Altitude
Pyramid	A line segment between the base plane of the pyramid and the apex. The altitude is perpendicular to the base.
Triangle	The line segment from a vertex to the extended opposite side. The altitude is perpendicular to the opposite side. Each triangle has three altitudes.

Centers of Geometric Figures

Object	Center
area	The point upon which a 2-dimensional object will balance. Synonym: centroid (p 20).
circle	The point that is equidistant from all the points of a circle.
dataset	A value around which data in a dataset is clustered. See central tendency (p 20).
dilation	The point from which the dilation is measured.
ellipse	The midpoint of an ellipse's major axis.
hyperbola	The midpoint of a hyperbola's transverse axis.
gravity, mass	Of a 3-dimensional solid, the point that can be used to calculate gravitational attraction for the object. Synonym: centroid (p 20).
regular polygon	The point at the exact middle of a regular polygon. The center of a regular polygon is at the intersection of the perpendicular bisectors of any two sides of the regular polygon that are not opposite each other. The center of a regular polygon is also the incenter, the circumcenter and the center of area or centroid of the regular polygon.
rotation	A fixed point about which an object is rotated.
set	An element that has a symmetric relationship to a set.
sphere	A point from which all points on the sphere are equidistant

Properties of a Line

Property	Description	Diagram/Equation
slope	The slope of a line shows how steep it is.	$m = \frac{y_2 - y_2}{x_2 - x_1}$
x-intercept	Where the line crosses the x-axis. Horizontal lines do not have an x-intercept.	

Properties of a Line

Property	Description	Diagram/Equation
y-intercept	Where the line crosses the y-axis. Vertical lines do not have a y-intercept.	

Equations of a Line

Form	Equation	Diagram
Point-slope form	$y - y_0 = m(x - x_0)$	
Standard form	$ax + by = c$	
Horizontal line	$y = a$	
Vertical line	$x = a$	
Two point form	$y - y_1 = \frac{y_2 - y_1}{x_2 - x_1}(x - x_1)$	
Slope-intercept form	$y = mx + b$	
Intercept form	$y = \frac{b}{a}(a - x)$	
Normal form	$y = -\frac{\cos \beta}{\sin \beta}(x - l \cos \beta) + l \sin \beta$	

Equations for a Parabola

Graphic	∪	∩	⊂	⊃
Description	Axis of symmetry ∥ y-axis, opens up	Axis of symmetry ∥ y-axis, opens down	Axis of symmetry ∥ x-axis, opens right	Axis of symmetry ∥ x-axis, opens left
Vertex	(h, k)	(h, k)	(h, k)	(h, k)
Focus	$(h, k + a)$	$(h, k - a)$	$(h + a, k)$	$(h - a, k)$
Directrix	$y = k - a$	$y = k + a$	$x = h - a$	$x = h + a$
Equation	$(x - h)^2 = 4a(y - k)$	$(x - h)^2 = -4a(y - k)$	$(y - k)^2 = 4a(x - h)$	$(y - k)^2 = -4a(x - h)$

Equations for a Hyperbola

Description	Transverse axis parallel to the x-axis	Transverse axis parallel to the y-axis
Hyperbola	$\frac{(x-h)^2}{a} - \frac{(y-k)^2}{b} = 1$	$\frac{(y-k)^2}{a} - \frac{(x-h)^2}{b} = 1$
Center	(h, k)	(h, k)
c	$c = \sqrt{a^2 + b^2}$	$c = \sqrt{a^2 + b^2}$
Foci	$(h \pm c, k)$	$(h, k \pm c)$
Vertices	$(h \pm a, k)$	$(h, k \pm a)$
Asymptotes	$y - k = \pm \frac{b}{a}(x - h)$	$y - k = \pm \frac{a}{b}(x - h)$
Conjugate axis	$x = h$	$y = k$
Transverse axis	$y = k$	$x = h$
Directrix	$y = k \pm \frac{a^2}{c}$	$x = h \pm \frac{a^2}{c}$

Distance Formulas

Distance ...	Formula
between real numbers a and b.	$D = |a - b|$
between a point (x, y) and the origin.	$D = \sqrt{x^2 + y^2}$
between a complex number $a + bi$ and the origin.	$D = \sqrt{a^2 + b^2}$
between two points (x_1, y_1) and (x_2, y_2).	$D = \sqrt{(x_1 - x_2)^2 + (y_1 - y_2)^2}$
between two points (x_1, y_1, z_1) and (x_2, y_2, z_2) in a 3-dimensional coordinate system.	$D = \sqrt{(x_1 - x_2)^2 + (y_1 - y_2)^2 + (z_1 - z_2)^2}$
in polar coordinates, between two points (r_1, θ_1), (r_2, θ_2).	$D = \sqrt{r_1^2 + r_2^2 - 2r_1 r_2 \cos(\theta_2 - \theta_1)}$
between a point (x_1, y_1) and a non-vertical line $y = mx + b$.	$D = \frac{|y_1 - mx_1 - b|}{\sqrt{m^2 + 1}}$
between two parallel, non-vertical lines $y = mx + b_1$ and $y = mx + b_2$.	$D = \frac{|b_2 - b_1|}{\sqrt{m^2 + 1}}$

Trigonometry

Trigonometry Definitions

$\text{sine} = \frac{\text{opposite}}{\text{hypotenuse}}$

$\text{cosine} = \frac{\text{adjacent}}{\text{hypotenuse}}$

$\text{tangent} = \frac{\text{sine}}{\text{cosine}} = \frac{\text{opposite}}{\text{adjacent}}$

$\text{cosecant} = \frac{1}{\text{sine}} = \frac{\text{hypotenuse}}{\text{opposite}}$

$\text{secant} = \frac{1}{\text{cosine}} = \frac{\text{hypotenuse}}{\text{adjacent}}$

$\text{cotangent} = \frac{1}{\text{tangent}} = \frac{\text{cosine}}{\text{sine}} = \frac{\text{adjacent}}{\text{opposite}}$

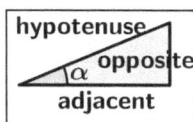

Trigonometric Identities

Pythagorean Identities
$\sin^2 u + \cos^2 u = 1$
$\tan^2 u + 1 = \sec^2 u$
$\cot^2 u + 1 = \csc^2 u$

Cofunction Identities
$\sin\left(\frac{\pi}{2} - u\right) = \cos(u)$
$\cos\left(\frac{\pi}{2} - u\right) = \sin(u)$
$\tan\left(\frac{\pi}{2} - u\right) = \cot(u)$
$\cot\left(\frac{\pi}{2} - u\right) = \tan(u)$
$\csc\left(\frac{\pi}{2} - u\right) = \sec(u)$
$\sec\left(\frac{\pi}{2} - u\right) = \csc(u)$

Even Odd Identities
$\sin(-u) = -\sin(u)$
$\cos(-u) = \cos(u)$
$\tan(-u) = -\tan(u)$
$\csc(-u) = -\csc(u)$
$\sec(-u) = -\sec(u)$
$\cot(-u) = -\cot(u)$

Sum and Difference Identities
$\sin(u \pm v) = \sin(u)\cos(v) \pm \cos(u)\sin(v)$
$\cos(u \pm v) = \cos(u)\cos(v) \mp \sin(u)\sin(v)$
$\tan(u \pm v) = \frac{\tan(u) \pm \tan(v)}{1 \mp \tan(u)\tan(v)}$

Double Angle Identities
$\sin(2u) = 2\sin(u)\cos(u)$
$\cos(2u) = \cos^2(u) - \sin^2(u)$
$\cos(2u) = 2\cos^2(u) - 1$
$\cos(2u) = 1 - 2\sin^2(u)$
$\tan(2u) = \frac{2\tan(u)}{1 - \tan^2(u)}$

Half Angle Identities
$\sin^2\left(\frac{u}{2}\right) = \frac{1}{2}(1 - \cos(u))$
$\cos^2\left(\frac{u}{2}\right) = \frac{1}{2}(1 + \cos(u))$
$\tan^2\left(\frac{u}{2}\right) = \frac{1 - \cos(u)}{1 + \cos(u)}$

Power Reduction Identities
$\sin^2(u) = \frac{1}{2}(1 - \cos(2u))$
$\cos^2(u) = \frac{1}{2}(1 + \cos(2u))$
$\tan^2(u) = \frac{1 - \cos(2u)}{1 + \cos(2u)}$

Sum to Product Identities
$\sin(u) + \sin(v) = 2\cos\left(\frac{u-v}{2}\right)\sin\left(\frac{u+v}{2}\right)$
$\sin(u) - \sin(v) = 2\sin\left(\frac{u-v}{2}\right)\cos\left(\frac{u+v}{2}\right)$
$\cos(u) + \cos(v) = 2\cos\left(\frac{u+v}{2}\right)\cos\left(\frac{u-v}{2}\right)$
$\cos(u) - \cos(v) = -2\sin\left(\frac{u+v}{2}\right)\sin\left(\frac{u-v}{2}\right)$

Product to Sum Identities
$\sin(u)\sin(v) = \frac{1}{2}(\cos(u-v) - \cos(u+v))$
$\cos(u)\cos(v) = \frac{1}{2}(\cos(u-v) + \cos(u+v))$
$\cos(u)\sin(v) = \frac{1}{2}(\sin(u+v) - \sin(u-v))$
$\sin(u)\cos(v) = \frac{1}{2}(\sin(u+v) + \sin(u-v))$

Rules for Converting to and From Polar Coordinates

$\theta = \arctan\left(\frac{y}{x}\right)$
$r = \sqrt{x^2 + y^2}$
$x = r\cos\theta$
$y = r\sin\theta$

Exact Values of Trigonometric Functions

Angle Degrees	Angle Radians	sin x	cos x	tan x
0°	0 rad.	0	1	0
30°	$\frac{\pi}{6}$ rad.	$\frac{1}{2}$	$\frac{\sqrt{3}}{2}$	$\frac{\sqrt{3}}{3}$
45°	$\frac{\pi}{4}$ rad.	$\frac{\sqrt{2}}{2}$	$\frac{\sqrt{2}}{2}$	1
60°	$\frac{\pi}{3}$ rad.	$\frac{\sqrt{3}}{2}$	$\frac{1}{2}$	$\sqrt{3}$
90°	$\frac{\pi}{2}$ rad.	1	0	Undefined
120°	$\frac{2\pi}{3}$ rad.	$\frac{\sqrt{3}}{2}$	$-\frac{1}{2}$	$-\sqrt{3}$
135°	$\frac{3\pi}{4}$ rad.	$\frac{\sqrt{2}}{2}$	$-\frac{\sqrt{2}}{2}$	-1
150°	$\frac{5\pi}{6}$ rad.	$\frac{1}{2}$	$-\frac{\sqrt{3}}{2}$	$-\frac{\sqrt{3}}{3}$
180°	π rad.	0	-1	0
210°	$\frac{7\pi}{6}$ rad.	$-\frac{1}{2}$	$-\frac{\sqrt{3}}{2}$	$\frac{\sqrt{3}}{3}$
225°	$\frac{5\pi}{4}$ rad.	$-\frac{\sqrt{2}}{2}$	$-\frac{\sqrt{2}}{2}$	1
240°	$\frac{4\pi}{3}$ rad.	$-\frac{\sqrt{3}}{2}$	$-\frac{1}{2}$	$\sqrt{3}$
270°	$\frac{3\pi}{2}$ rad.	-1	0	Undefined
300°	$\frac{5\pi}{3}$ rad.	$-\frac{\sqrt{3}}{2}$	$\frac{1}{2}$	$-\sqrt{3}$
315°	$\frac{7\pi}{4}$ rad.	$-\frac{\sqrt{2}}{2}$	$\frac{\sqrt{2}}{2}$	-1
330°	$\frac{11\pi}{6}$ rad.	$-\frac{1}{2}$	$\frac{\sqrt{3}}{2}$	$-\frac{\sqrt{3}}{3}$
360°	2π rad.	0	1	0

Calculus

Differentiation Formulas

General Derivation Formulas	
The derivative of a constant is zero.	$\frac{d}{dx}(c) = 0$
The derivative of a constant times a function is the constant times the derivative of the function.	$\frac{d}{dx}[cf(x)] = cf'(x)$
Sum rule: The derivative of the sum of two functions is the derivative of the first function plus the derivative of the second function.	$\frac{d}{dx}[f(x) + g(x)] = f'(x) + g'(x)$
Difference rule: The derivative of the difference of two functions is the derivative of the first function minus the derivative of the second function.	$\frac{d}{dx}[f(x) - g(x)] = f'(x) - g'(x)$
Product rule: The derivative of a product of functions is the first function times the derivative of the second function plus the second function times the derivative of the first.	$\frac{d}{dx}[f(x)g(x)] = f(x)g'(x) + g(x)f'(x)$
Quotient rule: The derivative of the quotient of functions is the denominator times the derivative of the numerator minus the numerator times the derivative of the denominator all divided by the denominator squared.	$\frac{d}{dx}\left[\frac{f(x)}{g(x)}\right] = \frac{g(x)f'(x) - f(x)g'(x)}{[g(x)]^2}$
Composition rule: The derivative of the composition of functions is the derivative of the outer function give then inner function as an argument times the derivative of the inner function.	$\frac{d}{dx}f(g(x)) = f'(g(x))g'(x)$
Power rule: The derivative of a power of x is equal to the power times x raised to the power minus 1.	$\frac{d}{dx}(x^n) = nx^{n-1}$

General Derivation Formulas	
Linearity rule: The derivative of a constant times a function plus a constant times a function is the first constant times the derivative of the first function plus the second constant times the derivative of the second constant.	$\frac{d}{dx}[au + bv] = au' + bv'$

Derivatives of Exponential and Logarithmic Functions	
$\frac{d}{dx}(e^x) = e^x$	$\frac{d}{dx}(a^x) = a^x \ln a$
$\frac{d}{dx}\ln|x| = \frac{1}{x}$	$\frac{d}{dx}(\log_a x) = \frac{1}{x \ln a}$

Derivatives of Inverse Trigonometric Functions	
$\frac{d}{dx}(\sin^{-1} x) = \frac{1}{\sqrt{1-x^2}}$	$\frac{d}{dx}(\cos^{-1} x) = -\frac{1}{\sqrt{1-x^2}}$
$\frac{d}{dx}(\tan^{-1} x) = -\frac{1}{\sqrt{1+x^2}}$	$\frac{d}{dx}(\csc^{-1} x) = -\frac{1}{x\sqrt{x^2-1}}$
$\frac{d}{dx}(\sec^{-1} x) = \frac{1}{x\sqrt{x^2-1}}$	$\frac{d}{dx}(\cot^{-1} x) = -\frac{1}{1+x^2}$

Measurement

(All inexact ratios are rounded to 7 significant digits)

International System of Units

Prefixes			
Value	Name (Short scale)	SI Prefix	Abbreviation
10^{24}	septillion	yotta-	Y
10^{21}	sextillion	zetta-	Z
10^{18}	quintillion	exa-	E
10^{15}	quadrillion	peta-	P
10^{12}	trillion	tera-	T
10^9	billion	giga-	G
10^6	million	mega-	M
10^3	thousand	kilo-	k
10^2	hundred	hecto-	h
10	ten	deka-	da
10^{-1}	tenth	deci-	d
10^{-2}	hundredth	centi-	c
10^{-3}	thousandth	milli-	m
10^{-6}	millionth	micro-	μ
10^{-9}	billionth	nano-	n
10^{-12}	trillionth	pico-	p
10^{-15}	quadrillionth	femto-	f
10^{-18}	quintillionth	atto-	a
10^{-21}	sextillionth	zepto-	z
10^{-24}	septillionth	yocto-	Y

SI Base Units		
Symbol	Name	Quantity
s	second	time
m	meter (British English: metre)	distance
kg	kilogram	mass
A	ampere	electric current
K	kelvin	thermodynamic temperature
mol	mole	amount of a substance
cd	candela	luminous intensity (the brightness of a light)

SI Defining Constants		
Symbol	Name	Exact Value
Δv_{Cs}	hyperfine transition frequency of Cs	9 192 631 770 Hz
c	speed of light	299 792 458 m/s
h	Plank constant	$6.626\ 070\ 15 \times 10^{-34}$ J·s
e	elementary charge	$1.602\ 176\ 634 \times 10^{-19}$ C
k	Boltzmann constant	$1.380\ 649 \times 10^{-23}$ J/K
N_A	Avogadro constant	$6.022\ 140\ 76 \times 10^{23}$ mol^{-1}
K_{cd}	luminous efficacy of 540 THz radiation	683 lm/W

SI Derived Units				
Name	Symbol	Quantity	Equivalents	SI Base Units Equivalents
hertz	Hz	frequency	1/s	s^{-1}
radian	rad	angle	m/m	1
steradian	sr	solid angle	m^2/m^2	1
newton	N	force, weight	$kg \cdot m/s^2$	$kg \cdot m \cdot s^{-2}$
pascal	Pa	pressure, stress	N/m^2	$kg \cdot m^{-1} \cdot s^{-2}$
joule	J	energy, work, heat	$m \cdot N, C \cdot V, W \cdot s$	$kg \cdot m^2 \cdot s^{-2}$
watt	W	power, radiant flux	$J/s, V \cdot A$	$kg \cdot m^2 \cdot s^{-3}$
coulomb	C	electric charge or quantity of electricity	$s \cdot A, F \cdot V$	$s \cdot A$
volt	V	voltage, electrical potential difference, electromotive force	W/A, J/C	$kg \cdot m^2 \cdot s^{-3} \cdot A^{-1}$
farad	F	electrical capacitance	$C/V, s/\Omega$	$kg^{-1} \cdot m^{-2} \cdot s^4 \cdot A^2$
ohm	Ω	electrical resistance, impedance, reactance	1/S, V/A	$kg \cdot m^2 \cdot s^{-3} \cdot A^{-2}$
siemens	S	electrical conductance	$1/\Omega$, A/V	$kg^{-1} \cdot m^{-2} \cdot s^3 \cdot A^2$
weber	Wb	magnetic flux	$J/A, T \cdot m^2, V \cdot s$	$kg \cdot m^2 \cdot s^{-2} \cdot A^{-1}$
tesla	T	magnetic induction, magnetic flux density	$V \cdot s/m^2, Wb/m^2, N/(A \cdot m)$	$kg \cdot s^{-2} \cdot A^{-1}$
henry	H	electrical inductance	$V \cdot s/A, \Omega \cdot s, Wb/A$	$kg \cdot m^2 \cdot s^{-2} \cdot A^{-2}$

SI Derived Units				
Name	Symbol	Quantity	Equivalents	SI Base Units Equivalents
degree Celsius	°C	temperature relative to 273.15	K	K
lumen	lm	luminous flux	cd·sr	cd
lux	lx	illuminance	lm/m²	cd·m⁻²
becquerel	Bq	radioactivity (decays per unit time)	1/s	s⁻¹
gray	Gy	absorbed dose (of ionizing radiation)	J/kg	m²·s⁻²
sievert	Sv	equivalent dose (of ionizing radiation)	J/kg	m2·s⁻²
katal	kat	catalytic activity	mol/s	s⁻¹·mol

Comparative Length

The preferred unit of measure of length is the meter. A baseball bat is about 1 meter long. A regular doorway is about 2 meters tall.

1 meter ≈ 3.280840 feet
1 foot = 12 inches
1 yard = 3 feet
1 mile = 5280 feet

1 mile ≈ 1.609344 kilometers
1 nautical mile = 1852 meters
1 nautical mile ≈ 1.150780 miles

Comparative Mass

The preferred unit of measure of mass is the kilogram. A quart of milk and a quart of water mass about 1 kilogram each.
1 kilogram = 1000 grams.
1 kilogram ≈ 2.2046226 pounds on the Earth's surface.
1 tonne = 1000 kilograms.

Comparative Time

The passage of time is usually measured in seconds. It takes about a second to say, "one-one thousand" at a normal speed.

1 minute = 60 seconds.
1 hour = 3600 seconds.
1 day ≈ 86400 seconds.
1 week = 7 days.
1 month = 28, 29, 30 or 31 days.

1 year ≈ 365¼ days.
1 decade = 10 years.
1 century = 100 years.
1 millennium = 1000 years.

Comparative Temperature

In science, temperature is usually measured in kelvins or Celsius. At sea level, water freezes at 273.15 kelvins and water boils at 373.15 kelvins. 0 degrees kelvin is the theoretical temperature at which all atomic movement stops.

Event	degree Fahrenheit	degree Celsius	kelvin
Water freezes	32°F	0°C	273 k
Water boils	212°F	100°C	373 k

Formula for converting Celsius to kelvin: $k = 273.15 + c$
Formula for converting Fahrenheit to Celsius: $c = \frac{5}{9}(F - 32)$.
Formula for converting Celsius to Fahrenheit: $F = \frac{9}{5}c + 32$.

Comparative Angle

Angles are measured in portions of a full circle. The preferred unit of measure is radians. There are 2π radians in a full circle.
1 radian ≈ 57.295780°
π radians = 180 degrees
1 radian ≈ 51.566202 gradians

π radians = 200 gradians

Comparative Speed

The preferred unit of measure of speed is meters per second. A fast runner over medium distance runs about 6.7 meters per second.

1 meter per second = 3.6 kilometers per hour.
1 meter per second ≈ 3.2808399 feet per second.
1 meter per second ≈ 2.2369363 miles per hour.
1 kilometer per hour ≈ 0.62137119 miles per hour.

Comparative Acceleration

The preferred unit of measure of acceleration is meters per second squared (m/s^2).

1 meter per second squared ≈ 3.2808399 feet per second squared, 1 m/s^2 ≈ 3.2808399 ft/s^2.

Help Your Child Learn Math[1]

1) Talk with your child's math teacher. Find out how your child is performing in math class.
2) Know your child's assignments and when they are due.
3) Check your child's homework. Is your child completing their assignments? Does your child put in the effort necessary to do the assignments correctly?
4) Make sure your child understands the concepts of mathematics. Can they explain each concept to you? The most important question you can ask is, "Why is that?"
5) Encourage group study. In the interactions of a group, children learn things they may not grasp on their own. Children, especially teenagers have ways of teaching each other.
6) Set high achievement standards for your child in math. Children respond positively to high standards.
7) Help your children learn the vocabulary of mathematics. Mathematics has its own language and, with fluency in this language, many concepts will be acquired much more easily.[2]

Illustration credits

All illustrations are by David E. McAdams unless otherwise noted below. Most illustrations by David E. McAdams were created using GeoGebra dynamic geometry software (http://www.geogebra.org).
By entry:
Abacus. Pablo Eder. Licensed image. Do not copy.
Agnesi, Maria Gaetana. Longhi Giuseppe. Bossi Giuseppe. Public domain.
  https://commons.wikimedia.org/wiki/File:Maria_Gaetana_Agnesi_bulino.jpg.
al-Khwārizmī, Muhammad ibn Mūsā. from Russian postage stamp. Public domain.
  https://commons.wikimedia.org/wiki/File:Mu%E1%B8%A5ammad_ibn_M%C5%Abs%C4%81_al-Khw%C4%81rizm%C4%AB.png.
Ampère. André-Marie. Practical Physics. 1920. Millikan and Gale. Public Domain.
  https://commons.wikimedia.org/wiki/File:Andre-Marie_Ampere.jpg.
Analog clock, hour, half-hour. Franck Camhi. Licensed image. Do not copy.
Angle of repose. H.D. Connelly. Licensed image. Do not copy.
Archimedes of Syracuse. Domenico Fetti. Public domain.
Balance, beam balance. Maren Wischnewski. Licensed image. Do not copy.
Boole, George, Public domain.
Calculator. Cory O'Neill. Licensed image. Do not copy.
Cantor, Georg. Unknown. Public domain. https://repository.aip.org/islandora/object/nbla%3A295186.
Capacity, gallon. Michale Flippo. Licensed image. Do not copy.
Cavalieri. sculpture by Giovanni Antonio Labus, picture by Giovanni Dall'Orto 19-Jan_2007. Licensed (see
  http://en.wikipedia.org/wiki/File:IMG_4064_-_Milano,_Palazzo_di_Brera_-_Cavalieri,_Bonaventura_-_Foto_Giovanni_Dall%27Orto_19-jan_2007.jpg).
Celsius, Anders. Olof Arenius. Public domain.
Compass. First Steps in Geometry by G.A. Wentworth and G.A. Hill, 1902. Public domain
  http://www.archive.org/stream/firststepsingeom00wentrich#page/31/mode/1up.
Computer. Eduardo Segovia. Licensed image, do not copy.
Cuboctahedron. Svdmolen, Public domain. https://commons.wikimedia.org/wiki/File:Kubocta%C3%Abder.png.
Degree, thermometer. Unknown. Public domain. https://commons.wikimedia.org/wiki/File:Thermometer_CF-ca.svg.
de Moivre, Abraham. Unknown. Public domain.
Descartes, René. Unknown. Public domain.
Die. Stephen Silver. Public domain. https://commons.wikimedia.org/wiki/File:Two_red_dice_01.svg.

---

[1] *Helping Your Child Learn Mathematics*, US Department of Education.
[2] Peggy Gisler and Marge Eberts, *Top 10 Ways to Help Your Kids Do Well in Math*,
  http://school.familyeducation.com/math/parenting/38812.html.

Digital clock. Peak of Thailand. Licensed under the Creative Commons Attribution 3.0 Unported license. https://commons.wikimedia.org/wiki/File:Digital_clock_3.00_AM.jpg.
Dodecahedron. SvMolden. Public domain; http://commons.wikimedia.org/wiki/File:Regelmatig_twaalfvlak.png.
Dollar. Public domain.
Double cone. Théon de Smyrne. Public domain. https://commons.wikimedia.org/wiki/File:C%C3%B4ne_surface_r%C3%A9gl%C3%A9e.png.
Echelon. Airplane silhouette Royal Netherlands Navy. Adapted by David E. McAdams.
Ellipsoid. Thrawn562. Placed in public domain by artist. https://commons.wikimedia.org/wiki/File:Ellipsoid_321.png.
Euler, Leonhard. Emanuel Handmann. Public domain.
Fermat, Pierre de. Unknown. Public domain.
Flip a coin. Cara Purdy. Licensed image. Do not copy.
Gauss, Johann Carl Friedrich. Christian Albrecht Jensen. Public domain.
Geoboard. MaiAne. Placed in public domain by artist.
Geodesic. Ralf Roletschek, Licensed under the terms of the GNU Free Documentation License, Version 1.2 only as published by the Free Software Foundation.
Germain, Sophie. Unknown. Public domain.
Hilbert, David. Unknown. Public domain.
Horizon. Remco van der Kruis. Licensed image. Do not copy.
Icosahedron. Tom Ruen. Placed in public domain by author.
Jordan, Wilhelm, Schriftsteller und Politiker. Public domain.
Kelvin, William Thomson, 1st Barron. Unknown. Public domain.
Kovalevskaya, Sofia. Das Fotoalbum für Weierstraß. Public domain. https://commons.wikimedia.org/wiki/File:Sofia_Kovalevskaya.jpg.
Level curve. USGS. Public domain.
Log graph. Dow Jones. https://commons.wikimedia.org/wiki/File:DJIA_historical_graph_(log).svg.
Lovelace, Ada. Alfred Edward Chalon. Public domain. https://commons.wikimedia.org/wiki/File:Ada_Lovelace_portrait.jpg.
Möbius, August Ferdinand. Adolf Neumann. Public domain. https://commons.wikimedia.org/w/index.php?search=M%C3%B6bius%2C+August+Ferdinand&title=Special:MediaSearch&go=Go&type=image.
Möbius strip. Fropuff. Public domain. https://commons.wikimedia.org/wiki/File:MobiusStrip-01.png.
Newton, Sir Isaac. Godfrey Kneller. Public domain. https://commons.wikimedia.org/wiki/File:Sir_Isaac_Newton_(1643-1727).jpg.
Noether, Amalie Emmy. Artist unknown. Public domain. https://commons.wikimedia.org/wiki/File:Noether.jpg.
Odometer. Kellie Folkerts. Licensed image. Do not copy.
Paraboloid, Rectas, Placed in public domain by creator. https://commons.wikimedia.org/wiki/File:Elliptic_paraboloid_quadric.png.
Pascal, Blaise. Unknown. Public domain. https://commons.wikimedia.org/wiki/File:Blaise_pascal.jpg.
Pisano, Leonardo. Firenze, Ducci. Public domain. https://commons.wikimedia.org/wiki/File:Fibonacci.jpg.
Plato. Marie-Lan Nguyen. Public domain. https://commons.wikimedia.org/wiki/File:Plato_Pio-Clemetino_Inv305.jpg.
Prolate spheroid, Spheroid. J. Diemer. Public domain.
Protractor. Luigi Chiesa. This file is licensed under the Creative Commons Attribution 3.0 Unported license. https://creativecommons.org/licenses/by/3.0/deed.en.
Pythagorean triple. unknown. Public domain.
Rhind Papyrus. Unknown. Public domain.
Riemann, Georg Friedrich Bernhard. Unknown. Public domain. https://commons.wikimedia.org/wiki/File:Georg_Friedrich_Bernhard_Riemann.jpeg.
Robinson, Julia. Bancroft Library, UC Berkeley. Used with permission.
Ruler, straight edge. Lit Liu. Licensed image. Do not copy.
Saddle point. Nicoguaro. Licensed under Creative Commons Attribution 3.0 Unported license.https://commons.wikimedia.org/wiki/File:Saddle_point.svg.
Semielliptical. Dantia. Licensed under the terms of the GNU Free Documentation License, Version 1.2 or any later version.
Sierpiński, Waclaw. Author unknown. Public domain. https://commons.wikimedia.org/wiki/File:Wac%C5%82aw_Sierpi%C5%84ski.jpg.
Slide rule. Susan Montgomery. Licensed image. Do not copy.
Somerville, Mary. Thomas Phillips. Public domain. https://commons.wikimedia.org/wiki/File:Thomas_Phillips_-_Mary_Fairfax,_Mrs_William_Somerville,_1780_-_1872._Writer_on_science_-_Google_Art_Project.jpg.
Speedometer. Bluescan. Placed in public domain by artist. https://commons.wikimedia.org/wiki/User:Bluescan_sv.wiki.
Spherical triangle, Pbroks13. Public domain. https://commons.wikimedia.org/wiki/File:RechtwKugeldreieck-3.svg.
Tesseract. Lambiam. Placed in public domain by creator.

Torus. Pokipsy76. Placed in public domain by creator. https://commons.wikimedia.org/wiki/File:Torus1.png.
Truncated icosahedron. SvMolden. Placed in public domain by creator.
  https://commons.wikimedia.org/wiki/File:Afgeknot_regelmatig_twintigvlak.png.
Vector field, Jim Belk, Public domain. https://commons.wikimedia.org/wiki/File:VectorField.svg.
Venn, John. Maull & Fox. Studio. Public domain. https://commons.wikimedia.org/wiki/File:John_Venn_2.jpg.

www.ingramcontent.com/pod-product-compliance
Lightning Source LLC
Chambersburg PA
CBHW080444090526
44586CB00047B/2281